Goodbye Forever

volume two

Ngakpa Chögyam

Aro Books WORLDWIDE

2022

Aro Books WORLDWIDE, PO Box 111, 5 Court Close, Cardiff, Wales, CF14 1JR

© 2022 by Ngakpa Chögyam

First Edition 2022

ISBN: 978-1-898185-60-4 (paperback)
ISBN: 978-1-898185-61-1 (ePub)

For further information about Aro Books WORLDWIDE please see http://aro-books-worldwide.org/

To obtain copies of all our publications please visit https://www.lulu.com/spotlight/arobooksworldwide

Dedicated to Kyabjé Düd'jom Rinpoche Jig'drèl Yeshé Dorje—who asked me to establish the gö kar chang lo'i dé in the West—and to his twin incarnations Kyabjé Düd'jom Rinpoche Sang-gyé Pema and Kyabjé Düd'jom Rinpoche Ten'dzin Yeshé Dorje who have shown me great kindness in remembering me as the student of their previous incarnation.

'Kyabjé Düd'jom Rinpoche Jig'drèl Yeshé Dorje told me that he had dwelt upon the nature of the White Lady and that she also had the name Khyungchen Aro Lingma: Garuda who Tastes the Primordial A. She was a gTértön. She had taken rainbow body earlier in the century. I had been her son in my previous life. My name had been Aro Yeshé. That was what he knew at the present time – but when he knew more, he would tell me. He said that Aro Lingma was known to him —and had been known by Düd'jom Lingpa—but no Lama to whom he had spoken had heard of her apart from Kyabjé Dilgo Khyentsé Rinpoche, who had said that he had heard the name many years before as a yogini who had realised Ja'lü in Southern Tibet.'

Chapter 19, *demon destroyer.*

Acknowledgments

Firstly it gives me great pleasure to acknowledge my Sangyum, wife, and teaching partner: Khandro Déchen Tsédrüp Rolpa'i Yeshé. Her influence, encouragement, support, and unflagging enthusiasm for the lineage are incomparable. Kyabjé Düd'jom Rinpoche Jig'drèl Yeshé Dorje, Kyabjé Künzang Dorje Rinpoche and Jomo Sam'phel Déchen Rinpoche all stressed that it was vital that I found the right sangyum if I was to teach the Aro gTér in the West. They each gave instructions and predictions that proved accurate and immensely valuable.

I acknowledge all the Lamas with whom I have studied, met and conversed – but most of all: Kyabjé Düd'jom Rinpoche Jig'drèl Yeshé Dorje; Kyabjé Künzang Dorje Rinpoche and Jomo Sam'phel Déchen Rinpoche; and, 'Khordong gTérchen Tulku Chhi'mèd Rig'dzin Rinpoche.

Although I do not teach the Düd'jom gTér, it was the major part of my training as a Lama. I owe so much to the Düd'jom gTér and to the Lamas of that lineage I know and have known: Dung-sé Thrin-lé Norbu Rinpoche; Dung-sé Garab Dorje Rinpoche; Dung-sé Namgay Dawa Rinpoche; Chag'düd Tulku Rinpoche; and, Lama Tharchin Rinpoche.

It is not possible to function as a Nyingma Lama without being connected to the Nyingma Tradition through friendship, and for the kindest friendship I am grateful to Tulku Dakpa Rinpoche, and Wangchuk Rinzin Rinpoche and his son gTértön Drukdra Rinpoche.

I would like to thank all our students – without whom Khandro Déchen and I would not be teachers. Dung-sé Thrin-lé Norbu Rinpoche pointed out to us 'It is students who make people teachers. If Lamas have no students – they are not teachers.' Goodbye Forever has been edited and proofread by students. Rig'dzin Shérab checked the Tibetan spellings and it was finally brought to publication by the painstaking efforts of Ngakma Nor'dzin and Ngakpa 'ö-Dzin – the first two people to become my students in the early 1980s.

To those many people I have not acknowledged, I apologise – but to have acknowledged everyone would have taken another book.

PelDrukdraling Foundation

Brief Introduction to Goodbye Forever – Volume II

Ngakpa Chögyam—Ngak'chang Rinpoche—the incarnation of gTértön Aro Yeshé, meditation master, artist, musician, vocalist, poet, and author—was recognised as the lineage holder of Aro gTér Nyingma Vajrayana teaching, at the age of nineteen by Kyabjé Dud'jom Rinpoche, 'Jig'dral Yeshé Dorje. He underwent a period of intensive training in Vajrayana practice, meditation, philosophy, and ordination under the tutelage of many great Vajrayana masters of Nyingma Tradition.

Ngak'chang Rinpoche's fascinating book 'Goodbye Forever – Volume II' illuminates the numerous Dzogchen teachings and empowerments he received from Kyabjé Dud'jom Rinpoche, the 16th Gyalwa Karmapa, Kyabjé Kunzang Dorje Rinpoche — and many important great Dzogchen masters. This account is interwoven with the period of training in Illustration at Bristol Art school during his twenties.

Thus, we take this especial privilege to urge various levels of different readers to read this singularly unusual book which offers cogent indications which can be implemented throughout one's life.

Sönar-tsul Wangphuk Rig'dzin Rinpoche (PhD)   HH Trülku Ugyen Döndrul Dorjee Kuenchap Rinpoche

Executive Director - Pel Drukdraling Foundation, Bhutan   Incarnation of gTértön Drukdra Dorje Rinpoche

Resident Lama - Drala Jong Aro gTér Vajrayana Centre, Britain President - Pel Drukdraling Foundation, Bhutan

Fulbright Scholar - Wheaton College, USA

Introduction

Ngakpa Chögyam—Ngak'chang Rinpoche—the incarnation of gTérton Aro Yeshé: meditation master, artist, musician, vocalist, poet, and author – was recognised as the lineage holder of Aro gTér Nyingma Vajrayana teaching, at the age of nineteen by Kyabjé Düd'jom Rinpoche, Jig'drel Yeshé Dorje. He underwent a period of intensive training in Vajrayana practice, meditation, philosophy, and ordination under the tutelage of many great Vajrayana masters of Nyingma Tradition.

Ngak'chang Rinpoche's fascinating book 'Goodbye Forever – Volume II' illuminates the numerous Dzogchen teachings and empowerments he received from Kyabjé Düd'jom Rinpoche, the 16th Gyalwa Karmapa, Kyabjé Künzang Dorje Rinpoche – and many important great Dzogchen masters. This account is interwoven with the period of training in Illustration at Bristol Art School during his twenties.

Thus, we take this especial privilege to urge various levels of different readers to read this singularly unusual book which offers cogent indications which can be implemented throughout one's life.

Khar-trül Wangchuk Rig'dzin Rinpoche (PhD) Executive Director Pel Drukdraling Foundation, Bhutan Resident Lama – Drala Jong Aro gTér Vajrayana Centre, Britain Fullbright Scholar – Wheaton College, USA

HE Trulku Ugyen Drodrul Thinley Kuenchap Rinpoche Incarnation of gTértön Drukdra Dore Rinpoche President – Pel Drukdraling Foundation, Bhutan

Contents

Goodbye Forever

1

to stare directly

Past-mind no longer exists. Future-mind is not yet present. Whatever arises in the moment is indecipherable because it cannot be translated by thought without converting it into thought.
Kyabjé Düd'jom Rinpoche Jig'drèl Yeshé Dorje

Words known by heart. Dwelt upon four times a day; every day. These words were experientially true – because the past seemed to have nowhere to abide.

Memories were there—certainly—but variable, inconsistent, mutable, fluctuating according to whichever *transient identity* was remembering.

Memories change according to a person's state-of-mind, when a memory occurs. A dejected mind remembers an event in one way. An elated mind remembers the same event in another way. The permutations are infinite and directionless – unless one discovers an impetus which transcends compulsive self-referencing.

My future had no shape. It had no vector, other than the indications I had received from Kyabjé Düd'jom Rinpoche Jig'drèl Yeshé Dorje: the revelation of a cycle of visionary teachings and practices;[1] teaching; accepting students; and functioning as a Lama.

How was *an old Bluesman* to do that? I was not *an old Bluesman* because I was old. One cannot be old in one's twenties – but perhaps one can feel as if a great deal of time has passed. The *Bluesman I'd been* in my final two years of school seemed long distant – and the distance gave a sense of age. Five years may as well have been fifty years.

Düd'jom Rinpoche however, had re-awoken that old Bluesman at the most unlikely moment. Time had telescoped. He asked me to let him hear the music I'd sung when I was younger.

1   See Appendix One – *gTerma*.

I'd sung *Hoochie Coochie Man* – and he surprised me by being rather animated in his enjoyment of my rendition. He didn't tap his foot or clap in time – but he was evidently involved in the rhythm of the song. He made subtle movements with his hands which may have had some relation to Tibetan folk dance. I was preoccupied however. I was trying too hard to give the best performance I could, to take note of what else was happening in the room. I was also too much in awe of Düd'jom Rinpoche to watch *him* watching *me*.

Having heard me, he told me never to abandon Blues – or any of the Arts with which I'd engaged. He said *"Arts very much important for Vajrayana. Religion-Arts from nature of elements coming. Secular-Arts also from nature of elements coming. In essence – no difference coming."*

Kyabjé Düd'jom Rinpoche said that the Arts would be important to me as a Lama in terms of communicating with people of my own culture. This was because people would know that I knew my own culture sufficiently to demonstrate its value – and thus, its value in terms of Vajrayana. It was not enough merely to tell people that the Arts were important – one had to be able to demonstrate it. He made it clear that the pinnacle of every civilisation was its Art. The capital cities of every country had museums for the purpose of displaying the greatest Art of its people. It was Art that marked a people as being civilised. Because of this, Lamas in the West had to demonstrate—to whatever degree—the genius of their culture.

I pointed out, apologetically *"Blues Rinpoche… is Black American culture – and I'm… a White Englishman. Some people are of the opinion that one has to be a Black American to sing or play Blues. I'm not sure whether I can honestly disagree with that point of view – because it's important to me to honour the African American culture which created Blues."*

Düd'jom Rinpoche shook his head *"Both Western. Blues Western. Chögyam Western. Both in the world. Electric music not Tibet coming. Electric guitar not Africa coming. England language, not Africa coming.*

"England language, England coming. Western lands – all cultures everywhere going. Everything everyone belonging: all foods eating; all wines drinking; all clothes wearing. Black American music: all young people's music inside – no difference coming. Vajrayana not Tibetans belonging. Vajrayana all peoples belonging."

It was extraordinary to be talking with Düd'jom Rinpoche on this subject – and, to realise that he understood more about the West than I could have guessed. Blues was indeed the root of Rock Music. There were Western people who didn't know that – but somehow Düd'jom Rinpoche was aware of it. It was self-evident to Düd'jom Rinpoche even though he had never set foot in the West. The point he made about culture ricocheted round my head later in the day and I realised that the Willow pattern crockery from which I'd eaten for the greater part of my life – was Chinese in origin. Pasta is said to have been introduced to Italy from China by Marco Polo. The tea the English drank was Indian. The Axminster carpets in many hotels were Persian in design – and those who could afford it, like Ron Larkin's parents, had actual Persian carpets on their floors. Fish and Chips was originally Jewish.[2] These—and yet further foreign imports—are now regarded as typically English. The chili—which is ubiquitous in the East and seems so characteristic of Indian and Bhutanese cuisine —came from South America.

> *Past-mind no longer exists. Future-mind is not yet present. Whatever arises in the moment is indecipherable because it cannot be translated by thought without converting it into thought.*

So much for the past and future – but what of the present? The present was a *moving moment* in a series of largely irrelevant travel-events—on trucks, buses, and trains—and suddenly I was on a flight to London Heathrow.

---

2 The first *Fish-&-Chip Shop* was opened in London in 1860 by Joseph Malin, a Portuguese Jewish immigrant – who advertised '*Fried Fish and Potatoes in the Jewish Style*'.

As the aeroplane took off, I'd whispered whimsically *"Cry God for Harry, England, and St George"*[3] because I was a little glad to escape from Monsoon heat of India. The Western Buddhists in India and Nepal would have pilloried me for that. I relished being in the Vajrayana culture of India and Nepal – but I didn't love 'the East' as much as the other Western Buddhists.

I recited Yeshé Tsogyel mantra as the aeroplane lifted off – with no particular sense of disjuncture between that and the Shakespeare I'd whispered.

> *Let thoughts of past and future settle in the present moment – and, in that moment, simply experience what is naturally there.*
> Kyabjé Düd'jom Rinpoche Jig'drèl Yeshé Dorje

I recited Padmasambhava mantra on landing. It was naturally there. It was the sound of my mouth: pharynx, larynx, and oesophagus – as natural as respiration. Then, as I disembarked from the Afghani Airways aeroplane, I sighed *"O–yah*[4] *– Jolly Old Blighty."*[5] No one said 'Jolly Old Blighty' apart from my father and other old British Raj soldiers – and *'O–yah'* was an exclamation that Kyabjé Düd'jom Rinpoche often made. *O–yah* has many shades of meaning: surprise; astonishment; amazement; wonder; pleasure; hilarity; satisfaction; gratification; delight; regret; ennui concerning foolishness; dissatisfaction; doubt; suspicion; misgiving; curiosity; and many other permutations. The meaning is indicated mainly by tone of voice, facial expression, or gesticulation.

The incongruity of *tongue-in-cheek jingoism* and *mantra recitation* was as typical of me at the time, as it is now. It's not a deliberate affectation. It's merely a random unstudied appreciation – uninhibited by established conventions.

---

3   William Shakespeare—Henry V—spoken by King Henry, from the speech that commences *"Once more unto the breach, dear friends, once more; or close the wall up with our English dead."*
4   O-yah *('ong yag)*
5   'Blighty' is British slang term for Britain. It derives from several Indian languages where it is spelt various ways – the most common being 'bileti' meaning 'foreign land'.

I never rebelled against convention *on principle* – I enjoyed The Proms and many other time-honoured aspects of British culture. I merely diverged from *hippie convention* through an individuated delight in phenomena – and deviated from *mainstream convention* on the same impulse. I wore Levi 501 Strauss Serge de Nîmes trousers – but I ironed them. I also starched them when they became faded and floppy. I never considered myself to be unconventional – merely because I liked aspects of various different social mores, customs, and traditions.

I had a love of well phrased grammatically perfect English – and a love of Blues patois with its double negatives. I disliked swearing and vulgarity – but there was no obscene slang word that I would abjure entirely. I considered that *any* word—slang or otherwise *(that had a meaning)*—also had a use in the right time and place. Even clichés and hackneyed phraseology could be employed – if a useful or creative purpose was served.

I saw no problem with being an anarchist and monarchist. I was a *tactical Labour voter*[6] who enjoyed seeing Ted Heath[7] conducting a choir with his own melodic adaptation of *The Twelve Days of Christmas.*[8] The only problem with such societal deviations, was that it made people uneasy or wary – unless, of course, they were Art students or similar creatures.

> *Whatever is perceived is radiantly clear, like the changeless blue nature of the sky. Whatever arises in Mind is inseparable from primordial radiant clarity-awareness.*
> Kyabjé Düd'jom Rinpoche Jig'drèl Yeshé Dorje

6   Tactical voting does not require belief or agreement with the party for which one votes – but rather an antipathy to the opposition.
7   Ted Heath: Sir Edward Richard George Heath KG MBE (1916–2005) served as Prime Minister of the UK from 1970 to 1974 and Leader of the Conservative Party from 1965 to 1975. He was a Member of Parliament from 1950 to 2001.
8   The Twelve Days of Christmas is an English Christmas carol published in 1780 without music as a chant or rhyme. The melody dates to 1909 as an arrangement of a song by Frederic Austin, who introduced the 'five gold rings' line.

The Himalayas were far distant – yet Düd'jom Rinpoche remained vivid. I'd seen those mountains. The highest in the world and the subject of poetry and painting – and yet they didn't remain, as Düd'jom Rinpoche remained. The first impulse that arose therefore—when I'd unpacked—was to read one of the final teachings I'd received.

What is considered to be Mind, is not what it is imagined to be. It is purposeless to attempt to understand Mind with thought.
t is better simply to allow Mind to see itself – for there is no difference between Mind and seeing.
Past-mind no longer exists. Future-mind is not yet present. Whatever arises in the moment is indecipherable because it cannot be translated by thought without converting it into thought.
Let thoughts of past and future settle in the present moment – and, in that moment, simply experience what is naturally there.
Visual projections appear in meditation if one distracts oneself with 'here and there' or 'then and when'. If however, it is considered that Mind is nothing, it will become 'the prison of numb emptiness' – in which the richness of the nature of Mind will not self-emerge.
Mind can be investigated with the intellect for the entire duration of a life – but one would be no closer to realisation. The real meaning of Dzogchen is 'natural immediacy' in which the presence of awareness is without limit. Whatever is perceived, is radiant – like the changeless blue nature of the sky. Whatever arises in Mind, is inseparable from primordial radiant clarity-awareness. It is unborn and unceasing in splendour. It joyously manifests in every aspect of phenomenal reality. When namthogs arise: stare directly into their arising. When namthogs dissolve: stare directly into their dissolution. It is the same, in life. With each life-circumstance: whatever is enacted, stare directly into the enactment – with all the senses.
Considering this will make you happy. Be of great good cheer.
É: Ma: Ho:
Kyabjé Düd'jom Rinpoche Jig'drèl Yeshé Dorje

I could hear Düd'jom Rinpoche's voice through what I'd written –
even though the words came through a translator. It was merely
my handwriting – but I'd written the words in Düd'jom Rinpoche's
presence, so they carried a sense of wonder. That fact that I had
written the words in Düd'jom Rinpoche room, seemed miraculous.
I had no vocabulary or grammar however, through which I could
explain that to anyone.

Whenever Düd'jom Rinpoche gave me Dzogchen teachings, he
asked me to *re-present* them in my own language in order that they
could be translated back to him in Tibetan. He wanted to check
my understanding – and also to give me confidence in respect of
my teaching in the future. I was going to have to express Vajrayana
for Western people. That would require my not merely substituting
Tibetan words for English words – but conveying the meaning of
the words in a way that delivered their dynamic value. How I
taught, had to make cogent sense in Western ears.

'Making sense' is a bland lacklustre expression. If or when I ever
taught, I'd want it to have the *cathartic immediacy; invigorating
imminence;* and, *emancipating conviction* which rang in my ears when
Düd'jom Rinpoche taught. How was I—*ever*—to accomplish
anything remotely like that? I knew I didn't want to employ the
pietistic or academic linguistics I read. I'd made a start. When
explaining Vajrayana to Westerners, I'd commenced expressing
Vajrayana with less of that type of language in my representations
of what Kyabjé Düd'jom Rinpoche had taught – but what more
could I achieve? I did not know. I'd be at retirement age before
anything like *cathartic immediacy* was feasible – even if I used every
holiday for solitary retreat.

I'd been inspired by Chögyam Trungpa Rinpoche's books,[9] in
terms of expressing Vajrayana in contemporary English.

---

9   *Born in Tibet* (1966), autobiography; *Meditation in Action* (1969); *Mudra* (1972);
    Cutting Through Spiritual Materialism (1973); *The Dawn of Tantra* (1975); *Glimpses
    of Abhidharma* (1975); *The Tibetan Book of the Dead: The Great Liberation through
    Hearing in the Bardo*; and, (1975) *Visual Dharma: The Buddhist Art of Tibet* (1975).

I would not set out to emulate his personal stylistics however; much as I enjoyed and was inspired by them. It was his use of contemporary vernacular and psychological terms that presented me with the key – and for that alone I remain indebted to him. Kyabjé Düd'jom Rinpoche had said that there was some connection between me and Chögyam Trungpa Rinpoche – but that might only unravel itself in the future depending on circumstances. Kyabjé Düd'jom Rinpoche had made so many life-changing declarations in such a short period of time – that I felt as if it would take the rest of my life to unpack them all.

Sometimes I felt as if Düd'jom Rinpoche might simply appear in our front room – or emerge from a crowd in town. There were a few occasions when I caught fleeting impressions of him in the faces of passing people—in shops and in railway stations—as though he were keeping a spacious surveillance. Nonsense—of course—and I had no desire to spiritualise such fantasies. I'd always been given to seeing what wasn't there—according to my father—but, sometimes, these fantasies have proved to touch on reality.

> *With each life-circumstance: whatever is enacted, stare directly into the enactment – with all the senses.*

My mother had recounted her paranormal experiences – particularly around her brother Bernt dying on the Russian Front in WWII.[10] She had sustained bruises in the places where the bullets had hit Bernt. I never experienced anything that visceral – but sometimes *something genuine* washed through me. I'd been unusually close to Düd'jom Rinpoche for a short period of time – and it had changed my life. I was most bereft, baleful, and bemused – but also brilliant, bodacious, and beatific. Little wonder I kept seeing Düd'jom Rinpoche.

---

10 Bernt Schubert was involved with an attempt to assassinate Hitler. When the plot was discovered, he and the complicit section of the Brandenburg Company were pushed beyond the battle-front to be wiped out in seconds by Russian gunfire. They were awarded the Iron Cross for propaganda purposes by Heinrich Himmler (1900–1945) who had ordered and directed their deaths.

After a day or so recovering from jetlag – my father's quote came back to me: *'Home is the sailor, home from the sea, And the hunter home from the hill.'* This is what he said when he first saw me on the day of my arrival from India. I looked it up in his large book of English verse.

> *Under the wide and starry sky / Dig the grave and let me lie: / Glad did I live and gladly die, / And I laid me down with a will. / This be the verse you 'grave for me: / Here he lies where he long'd to be; / Home is the sailor, home from the sea, / And the hunter home from the hill.*

Glad did I live and gladly die… Well, *glad did I live*—certainly—but I was not *quite* ready to die: well, not *as* gladly. I didn't think that my father was trying to be profound. It wasn't his way. Those were simply words which could be used when someone returned from somewhere. I'd heard those words used before in that way before – and that was the style in which he'd quoted them. There was no reason however, why I shouldn't look at the meaning of the verse as it could apply to me.

In a sense, I'd already died. My National Health Insurance number was identical. My driving licence was the same – and, barring some exotic visa stamps, my passport was indistinguishable. These documents testified that *someone* lived on – but maybe only as *printed paper and cardboard*. My mother, father, and brother knew who I was – but, I was uncertain.

> *With each life-circumstance: whatever is enacted, stare directly into the enactment – with all the senses.*

I knew how to be *who I had been* – but it felt a little as if I were acting. Not in the sense of performing a rôle—*it wasn't possible to forget lines or let my accent slip*—but because *being me* seemed unreal. I concluded that it was merely the result of reverse culture shock. Yes – *that could be it*. The days went by however, and I knew that I'd died. The old version of *whoever I was*, was merely haunting my new life. I'd have to accept the sensation – and simply live it, without mawkish self-consciousness.

11

The idea of inhabiting different versions of myself took me back to an afternoon in Bodhanath, sitting with Düd'jom Rinpoche – and listening to his teaching on the Twelve Manifestations of Guru Rinpoche.[11] I went directly to my folder of notes and read what Kyabjé Düd'jom Rinpoche had said on that occasion.

"Times when Guru Rinpoche most important actions of life displaying" Düd'jom Rinpoche explained *"on the tenth days of lunar calendar*[12] *falling. Then you must—always—be practising."*

He then gave me a list of Guru Rinpoche's activities on each of the tenth-days in the year.[13]

Düd'jom Rinpoche then explained that in *The Sér Treng Instruction*[14] it is stated that:

> *On the tenth day in particular, I shall come to the Himalayan Lands – but shall be present everywhere, riding the rays of sun and moon and the mists of rainbows, to abolish obstacles of my sons and daughters. I shall then give all empowerments you wish. This is my pledge. If you practise every tenth day your community will enjoy happiness and well-being.*

Düd'jom Rinpoche smiled *"Guru Rinpoche this promise—many—times making; so completely trusting. Every tenth day practising."* PAUSE *"This instruction…"* Düd'jom Rinpoche laughed *"like a beautiful girl dress towards you flaunting. So must be welcoming – then she stepping forward. Then you must feasts of every kind of happiness offering."*

---

11 Also known as Padmasambhava – but mainly in the West due to Chogyam Trungpa Rinpoche using that name. Guru Rinpoche's primary form is known as Padmakara – and one of the Eight Manifestations of Padmakara is called Padmasambhava.

12 Each month of the lunar calendar is named after one of the 12 animals by which the years are also known: the first month is the hare; the second is the dragon; the third is the snake; fourth is the horse; the fifth is the sheep; the sixth is the monkey; the seventh is the bird; the eighth is the dog; the ninth is the pig; the tenth is the rat; the eleventh is the ox or yak; and, the twelfth is the tiger.

13 See Appendix Two – *tenth days*.

14 Ser Treng *(bKa' thang gSer phreng)* The Golden Garland Instructions of Dro'dül Sang-gyé Lingpa (1340–1396).

Kyabjé Düd'jom Rinpoche often teased me about my predisposition in respect of girlfriends. This was not in any sense of it being an error – but because it was part of my personality that he enjoyed. His *enjoyment* however, was mysterious – because it always burgeoned with a wealth of knowledge and foresight. On these occasions he would always emphasise the need to find the right consort – and I would feel the seriousness of that responsibility.

Thinking back to this occasion—as always—I felt it most appropriate to sit and practise the Four Naljors.[15] As soon as I sat —or no sooner than I had concluded my sitting—I was exactly where I was. Nothing felt alien after that. I simply felt fresh and refreshed. The old collection of personality traits seemed to be gone – but I could do whatever the old personality could do. I could still blow Blues harp. I could still play a barely adequate Blues on guitar. The person I'd been, had dissolved. 'I' had vanished with the dissolution of each context in the unlikely curriculum vitae that unrolled. That had been the pattern since I was cognisant of the world. *Goodbye forever* was the obvious atavistic aphorism.

The period of time before going to Art School looked inviting. It would be a bardo[16] – and I would have to inhabit it as such. It would be an indeterminate intermediary interregnum in which I'd have less coherent identity than I'd had in the Himalayas. In India and Nepal, I'd been clearly defined as a Nyingma practitioner— albeit an Inji[17]—but until mid-September I'd be wafting with the winds of alternating circumstances. Düd'jom Rinpoche had told me that I needed to *learn to live in the West as a ngakpa.*[18]

---

15 Naljor zhi *(rNal 'byor bZi)* the four modes of remaining in the natural state.
16 Bardo *(bar do / antarabhava /* intermediate state) – the intermediate state between any two identifiable points in time. Interval between death and rebirth.
17 *Inji* is a Tibetan word based on the sound of the word 'English' – but applied to anyone of European or Scandinavian descent.
18 Ngakpa *(sNgags pa / mantrin).* See glossary: *ngakpa / ngakma.*

He explained that this did not mean that I should dress in my robes or keep myself aloof from everyday life – quite the reverse. His advice was to *live as everyone lived* – or at least as Art students lived. I had to be an Art student. I had to experience the world as Art students experienced it. Unless I could be *part of the world in the West*, I could never teach Western people with real conviction. I had to belong to the Western world – whilst also living as a ngakpa. He said that it would not be easy. It would be easier to live in Nepal and India – but that would never serve to establish the tradition of ngakpas and ngakmas in the West – or to transmit the gTérma of Khyungchen Aro Lingma. This was going to be a strange adventure.

> *With each life-circumstance: whatever is enacted, stare directly into the enactment – with all the senses.*

After some weeks at home—having put on a little weight—I slotted back into the Art School scene: as a life model. It wasn't important to earn a great deal and so life-modelling suited me. I'd earn the serious money in the Summer holidays on building sites – but as long as I could, I wanted to take up John Morris' generous offer and avail myself of the Art School facilities. I'd be some-sort-of *Art student emeritus*. It worked well. As far as the other students were concerned, I was as much of an Art student as they were – apart from the fact that I was sometimes the life model. I mainly life-modelled at Guilford Art School – but I had some sessions in the old Art School building for portraiture. The portraiture paid less – but fortunately I always got more work in the posing-pouch. Strangely enough women could model entirely naked – but men had to wear posing pouches, due to the presence of those under eighteen years of age. I was lucky inasmuch as men were a rare commodity as life models – and so there was no lack of employment.

> *With each life-circumstance: whatever is enacted, stare directly into the enactment – with all the senses.*

It was strange – but then life was always strange. I couldn't help but reflect that a few months previously I'd been sitting with Kyabjé Düd'jom Rinpoche – and now I was sitting in a posing pouch with twenty-odd people observing me. They'd walk into the room with their pencils in their hands – but unlike Bob Dylan's song[19] they saw me *almost* naked but never asked '*Who is that man?*' I was simply *the life model*. There was nothing else to know. Life-modelling was useful employment for a Nyingma ngakpa.

> *With each life-circumstance: whatever is enacted, stare directly into the enactment – with all the senses. Considering this will make you happy. Be of great good cheer.* É: Ma: Ho:

---

19 Ballad of a Thin Man. *You walk into the room with your pencil in your hand / You see somebody naked and you say "Who is that man?" / You try so hard but you don't understand / Just what you will say when you get home / Because something is happening here but you don't know what it is / Do you, Mr. Jones?*

2

no difference coming

*"Electric music not Tibet coming. Electric guitar not Africa coming.
England language, not Africa coming. England language, England
coming. Western lands – all cultures everywhere going. Everything
everyone belonging: all foods eating; all wines drinking; all clothes
wearing. Black American music: all young people's music inside – no
difference coming. Vajrayana not Tibetans belonging. Vajrayana all
peoples belonging."*
Kyabjé Düd'jom Rinpoche Jig'drèl Yeshé Dorje

Farnham Art School. Lunch time. A day on which I was not
required as a life-model at Guildford or Farnham. I sat on the
steps of the new Farnham annexe of the Art School, having
concluded an intense life-drawing session. A hundred sketches of
figures in motion. The timing of these sessions varied from 10
seconds to 30 seconds. Discombobulating for a slow careful
draftsman. At first the drawings were appalling – but as the session
proceeded, I got a feel for the way lines could move in peripheral
vision tracing the movement of the model. By the end of the
session I could see the value of the process in terms of intuitive
hand-eye coordination – and in terms of meditation.

As advised – I stopped *thinking* about the end result. I kept focus
on describing movements in the visual field. In one way this was
easier for me than the others – as the instruction *not to think* was
not new. What was not easy, was abandoning the habitual attention
to precise detail. When I was 16, I'd copied a poster of Jimi
Hendrix, as an oil painting on architects' photographic linen.[1]
School friends were astonished by the accuracy of the painting.

---

1   The spent paper-backed photographic linen was given to me by my father
    who had obtained it from the Ministry of Works. He worked as a 'quantity
    surveyor' for the Army as a civilian – and the photographic linen was being
    scrapped. It made ideal material for both thangka paintings and photograph-
    realist imagery.

For me however, it was not particularly astonishing – because Photorealism merely requires patience and close attention. What *was* astonishing to me, was launching myself into the unknown with pencil and paper – drawing lines without judgement. This was where Buddhism and Art School coincided – where I could *be a practitioner* entirely within the bounds of the project at hand.

Maybe Düd'jom Rinpoche had known that this was how Art School would be. Maybe that is why Düd'jom Rinpoche instructed me to continue my Art education and obtain a degree. I decided that I would write about the experience of nonconceptual drawing in order to be able to explain it all to him when I next saw him. That would be the October of 1975.

I felt fortunate to be *more-or-less an Art Student* during my year out. I worked off-and-on as an Art School model – and, when I wasn't working, I took life drawing classes. John Morris had set that up – and I made full use of the opportunity. John Morris was the head of the Foundation Course and gave me a great deal of help. He'd thought it wise to take a year out from Art School – to decide what direction I'd take. It was seeming as if Fine Art[2] was not my best option – even though I saw myself as a Fine Artist. I was a confirmed figurative artist – and so a Fine Art degree would not have been what I wanted, as the emphasis in Art Schools was on Abstract Expressionism. It looked therefore, as if I was headed for Bristol – as it was the only full time Illustration degree in Britain. Illustration—John Morris had told me—would allow me to develop my passion for combining word and image – and the Bristol Illustration degree course was known to be liberal with regard to giving plenty of leeway to figurative Fine Artists – who opted for Illustration to avoid being channelled into Abstract Expressionism.

---

2   Fine Art is art developed primarily for aesthetics and beauty, distinguishing it from decorative art or applied art, which serve a practical function, such as ceramics. In the aesthetic theories of the Italian Renaissance, the highest Art allowed the artist's imagination to be unrestricted by practical considerations. The primary Fine Arts are painting, sculpture, music, poetry, literature, and performing Arts.

Anyhow—there I was—sitting in the unusual January sunshine. I decided I'd play some harp. A Black American third year Fine Art student called Frank Berger sauntered down the steps – and hailed me *"Man! You play that—thang—like a fuckin' nigger."*

"Thank you—very—much indeed Frank!" I beamed *"Can't tell you just how much I appreciate that."*

That's exactly how I wanted to sound. Frank grinned broadly and sat next to me with a can of beer – listening to me blow an extended 'Traintime'.

*"Yeah man, y'do that thang—real—well. If'n you was down in Miss'ssippi or Louis'ana someplace – you c'd play harp with **any**body."*

"That would be a fine thing – but that's pretty unlikely…"

"No man, no way… not unlikely 'tall. Maybe I'd hav't'be there y'know – else y'all might get ate. There's some—right fine—big-leg mammas down there."

"Heard that, Frank. Sounds like a good place." Then I gave a blast of the harp and sang *"Ah big leg mamma get your—big leg—over me / Said big leg mamma get your—big leg—over me / Well you know I ain't tired – but I'm as sleepy as any honky has a right to be."*

Frank laughed a fit at the word 'honky' and said *"Man you ain't no reg'lar honky—that's f'sure and f'certain —and I bet you ain't 'fraid-a no big-leg mammas neither. Even though…"* Frank laughed *"… they might just eat a White boy like you fo' breakfast."*

"I'm game for being eaten Frank" I grinned. *"To be honest… I'm a little —weary—of middle class white girls… well, their snooty parents, that is. They all died in the war to save Britain. And they've got me pegged as a deranged criminal who's ruining this green and pleasant land as badly as the Nazis would've done."*

"Yeah man… but not all Nazis are German! Whole slew-a-Nazis 'round Farnham y'know…" Frank drawled with a shake of his head.

"Too many folks folla orders – without un'erstandin' the nature of their 'bedience. Some ol' stiff said somethin' 'bout—Negros—in my hearin'—jus' last week – and I found ma-self havin' t'say 'You suh, can kiss ma EN-tire black ass!' Shoulda seen his face!"

"I bet." I laughed rather loudly. *"Love that expression though, Frank. Think I might need to try it out – mind if I run it past you?"*

"Go ahead."

"You sir, can kiss my entire ass!"

"Yeah, well, good start – but yer gotta get more—music—in it Vic. Like this." Frank struck a defiant posture and announced dramatically *"You—suh—can kiss ma EN-tire ass!"*

"Alright Frank." PAUSE for the adoption of a defiant posture *"You—sir—can kiss my en-tire ass!"*

"Better, bro – but ... you still got that slight Prince Charles sound with it."

"Prince Charles! Gimme a goddamn break!" I laughed.

"That's better! That's better! Now say it 'gain jus' like you did then."

*"You—**suh**—can kiss ma **EN**-tire ass!"*

"Righteous bro! That's mo' like it! Never thought I'd be givin' no English dude ela-cution lessons." PAUSE *"Y'know... I think... you'n'me—well ... we's hit out free, man. Free of—race—an'—place—an'—time—an' culture... and man, that's the—only—space to be."*

"That's about the shape of it Frank."

"Like... you can blow that Blues out here—and that's cool—but you oughta be able to play that down South where I come from – only there'd be a few people with tight asses 'bout it." PAUSE *"It ain't no good to have tight-ass ideas – that's why I'd have to show you round so people'd know it was awright and nobahdy'd turn their shooter on yer."*

"I'd really like that Frank. If we stay in touch, I'll do my best to make it over to America after my degree course is done. It would be ... a big thing for me to play down in the Delta ... but I'd have to go in the winter, otherwise I'd fry."

"Like Deep Fried Southern Chicken!" Frank laughed. *"I just—bet—you would."*

We sat for a while gazing into the distance – and after some minutes Frank said *"Yeah... y'know what you said this morning... I been a-thinkin' on it."*

"What was that Frank?"

"Why, that too many people got no sense – they's—not—free ind'vidjals. You said plen'y peoples 'came ind'vidjals in the '60s—and owe their ind'vidjal'ty to it—but then... they seemed to let it all go."

"Yes... I see that happening."

"Goddamn shame."

"Doesn't have to be that way though. I'd like to be able to tell people that – y'know write a song, or something."

"Yessir – gotta hang with it, gotta hang with it."

"Quite – you have to seize the day—carpe diem—you have to seize the essence of whatever allows you to become an individual."

"Man that's—so—true! Ind'vidjal'ty surely is the first step on that—road—to freedom."

"D'you ever read that Jean Paul Sartre trilogy?"

"Tried man... too damn... depressin'. There's only so much I can stand reading 'bout of the meanin'lessness of life – I mean—jeeeeez—gimme a goddamn break."

"Know what you mean" I laughed. *"I read them all. Maybe just because I'm addicted to finishing books once I start them – but I should've bailed out, as you did."*

"Yeah… well… I al'a's bail out. Ain't al'a's smart to bail out – but maybe that time I was right. That Sartre dude—or his character anyhow—wasn't no free ind'vidjal." PAUSE "You gotta get to be an ind'vidjal or you ain't worth doodly-squat." Frank noticed my expression "Doodly-squat—that mean 'insect shit'—like it ain't worth nothin'."

"I'll remember that one Frank – it's a good one… but, when I talk about individuality, I don't mean 'the—cult—of the individual'. That's as bad or worse than being a follower of fashion."

"Cult of the individual?"

"Yeah, individuality can turn into some kind of fetish or preoccupation – and that's just another trap."

"How's that then?"

"Well… what I mean by 'the cult of the individual' is the idea that individuality is a 'birth right' – and you don't have to work for it. You absolutely have to—work—for it. Then, there's another thing. I don't think you become an individual by wanting to be different, per se… You see, some people just get as quirky as possible. Then they feel they have the right to demand that they're either as important, or more important, than those who've worked hard – and are—genuinely—creative."

"Yeah… I seen—that—bro. Lotta—that—about: zero talent with a fuckin' big mouth. Shit-head dumb-ass celebrities jerking off on people. Ever'thin' gettin' 'terpreted on how it makes'em look."

"Absolutely. In a nutshell Frank. Pseudo-individuals demand recognition, whatever the deal. They need praise for what they tell you they are – rather than what they actually are."

"So… how would you—defarn—a free ind'vidjal?"

"Mmmm… that's a hard creature to define… I'd need to be sure I really was a free individual before I could be too precise about that."

"Oh hell man, just get-on-in."

"Well... a free individual is someone who appreciates the sense fields." PAUSE *"... and, if you appreciate the senses fields, you're free to appreciate others. I mean, if you—can't—appreciate others... if you can't be kind and open; you're not a free individual."*

"Amen to that bro."

Frank and I sauntered off after a while and found ourselves at the Hop Blossom. You could get a good lunch at that pub. It was small and had a 'snug' – a little side room. The Rover's Return—in the television soap *'Coronation Street'*—had a snug where Ena Sharples, Minnie Caldwell, and Martha Longhurst took their evening tipple of stout. The Hop Blossom was a pub that had imposed dress and hair restrictions – but as long as I was with Frank, there was no problem. It amused Frank enormously to observe racial prejudice in reverse. The only reason we were not thrown out was because Frank was Black. Frank was Black but he also had long hair – so, their hands were tied. They couldn't refuse him admittance, because he was Black – and thus they couldn't refuse me admittance because I had long hair – and... Frank also had long hair. Bon appetit! The homemade steak and kidney pies at the Hop Blossom were quite something. We tucked in. Two each —with—chips.

"That life drawin' sho gives a man an appetite" Frank grinned.

"Never a truer word was spoken, Frank."

"What got you into Blues then?"

"Long story... but... it was a gentleman called Mister Love..."

"That's quite some name bro – Mister Leurve!" Frank drawled.

"Never thought of his name like that before Frank – y'know... that's hysterical." PAUSE *"... but no, he was nothing at all like that. He was a charming elderly English gentleman... very kind... and well... I'd call him an individual."*

Then I told Frank the whole story.[3]

"Whoa man – that's quite some hist'ry you got there—quite some hist'ry— and that cycle ride to meet Papa Legba! That was far out man. You are one far out motherfucker."

That made me laugh.

"Guess you ain't never been called a far out motherfucker befo'… well – that's like a compliment y'know."

"I thought it was Frank… I'm catching on y'know." PAUSE *"Know anything about Papa Legba?"*

"No man… nothing. I reckon… maybe there ain't no Legba fella – no devil neither. Good story though and… I've seen some brothers play—sisters too— maybe they all met Legba some ways. Maybe meetin' Legba's just what it's called, y'know. Maybe it's when Blues bites yer ass, like it bit yo's."

"Yeah…" I drawled. I always found myself adopting something of Frank's Southern drawl when I was talking with him. I didn't do it on purpose – it just snuck up on me. *"It sho as hell bit—mah—ass Frank. The teeth marks are pretty much tattooed there… and them hell hounds sho got Steve and Ron."*

"Yeah man… Sonovabitch! They sho did – they sho did." PAUSE *"That's 'bout the worst bad luck I—ever—heard."*

"Yeah Frank…" Then I sang *"Born under a bad sign – I been down since I began to crawl,/ If it wasn't for bad luck – I wouldn't have no luck at all."*

"Man you's a—bad-ass—singer. But the voice ain't Black as yer harp – yet…" Frank looked a little embarrassed after making his comment on my voice – and continued *"Didn't quite mean that, man – well, not the way it came out… well… y'know…"*

---

3   See *an odd boy*—Doc Togden—Volume I—chapter 2—Mr Love—Aro Books WORLDWIDE—2011. The four volumes of *an odd boy* were published under the author name 'Doc Togden' rather than 'Ngakpa Chögyam'.

"Yeah Frank… I know, I know… it's true. You're only saying what I know already. If there was some goddamn operation, I'd have it. I think my voice works well enough over here – but I'm still a Limey… As you said… I sound like Prince Charles."

"No man—no way, no how—not like that! I was jus' jokin' on you."

"Frank… y'know… you—can—be honest with me – it's really alright." I laughed *"I have to know how it is and you might be the one person who can really tell me how it is."*

*"Well man… you could use some work on the vow'ls… but man! You's—in the groove—y'know, the—stone—groove. Wouldn't take much to geddit down 'cause you's 'ready mostways there. You got the—*Black soul*—man – and you got the voice rhythm. Tell you man, you come on down see me in Louisiana—just as soon as you get the bread together—and we'll do some things there man – we'll do some things. I'll take you 'roun' some places – y'know where you won't see no—*White*—face—nowheres. And ya'll be talkin' like* the *mojo-man by the time you's get through. Y'all will be The Pink Nigger! Yeah! That's how we'll bill yer man –* Vic Simmerson The One and—Only—*Pink Nigger!"*

That made me splutter *"The Pink Nigger! I like that! That's me – or … that's what I used to hope I'd be."* I thanked Frank for the offer. I had the sense that he really meant it. I could see myself down there in Louisiana with Frank—the solitary honky—and a Limey to boot – in the midst of a sea of Black folks I could hardly understand. Then I'd learn *that* language—*and that sound*—and then I'd be like Jo Ann Kelly – except… she'd somehow learnt it without ever having set foot in the USA, let alone the Delta. Exactly—*how*—had she done that? Anyhow… I had Frank's address and it was a done deal. I'd be heading South one day from whichever airport was closest. I'd find the crossroads on Highway 61 and absorb everything like a vacuum cleaner. I'd get a head full of sounds and imagery. I'd come back and paint it all – as well as singing it all. Maybe I'd make that six-album set of *Robert Johnson* songs… maybe… if I could find another Ron and another Steve – but there the dream came to an end. How likely was that?

That was the unlikeliest possibility in the world either this century or the next. Where would I find another child prodigy comparable to Bach and Mozart rolled into one – who was also hooked on Chicago Blues? Where would I find another world-class bass-player who played eerie slide-riffs on bass? I knew where. Exactly nowhere.

I always felt a little… guilty when such ideas crossed my mind – because Jack was never in the picture. Where would I find another Jack? Simple – I'd put an ad in the Melody Maker and I'd have a list of applicants willing to sell their whole family down river for the chance to play with Ron and Steve. But there was no Ron or Steve now – and I was nobody without them, unless… unless I had some major breakthrough.

"You's thinkin' too darn hard Vic" Frank grinned.

"Sorry Frank… got a little carried away there with dreams y'know." PAUSE *"It's a dream that keeps coming back to me… It's like you said Frank… Blues bit my ass – and there's no turning back is there."*

Of course, Vajrayana *bit my ass* first – and with far more of a vengeance. In spite of that however – Blues was still there and still had its distinct allure. Düd'jom Rinpoche had told me I should always sing Hoochie Coochie Man. He said that I should always play Blues. Back in November Düd'jom Rinpoche said he wanted to talk about Art. He knew I was interested in music and poetry as well as painting – and asked *"What music playing and singing?"*

"Blues, Rinpoche. It's from America – but it originally came from West Africa."

He asked me if I'd sing something so that he could hear it. I launched into 'Hoochie Coochie Man'.

> *"Gypsy woman told my mother before I was born/ Y'got a boy childs coming, gonna be a son-of-a-gun/ Gonna make pretty womens jump and shout/ Then the world wanna know – what's it all about?/*

"'cause I'm here – ever'body knows I'm here/ I'm the Hoochie Coochie Man – ever'body knows I am."

He asked me what the words meant. *"That's not easy, Rinpoche – because some words are untranslatable."*

Düd'jom Rinpoche smiled *"O—yah… but many words in Tibetan you must be English translating. Then much more difficulty. You poetry writing – so for you it is not too difficult. So now you poetry-system using – and meaning telling."*

I said I'd have to work out a form of English that would translate into Tibetan and—*after a minute of scribbling*—I had something that could be translated into Tibetan.

> *"Nomad khandro told my mother, before I was born/ You will have a boy child and he will be strong and charismatic/ He's going to cause beautiful women joyful fascination/ And everybody is going to be extremely curious about him/ Because I'm here – everybody knows I'm here/ I'm the man with siddhis – everybody knows I am."*

Düd'jom Rinpoche laughed appreciatively *"Good song! This song very much liking! Very strong! Very powerful! Always you must be singing like this in your country!"*

I explained that the words were sometimes a long way from the original – but Düd'jom Rinpoche chuckled *"Poetry writing since child. So natural coming, good translation making!"* He said this was an important part of the work that lay ahead of me as I would have to translate the meaning of the most profound Vajrayana teachings I received. *"No purpose word-for-word translation giving. This Sarma style. You must Nyingma style teaching."*

Düd'jom Rinpoche explained that the Arts were crucial to Vajrayana, and not simply the Vajrayana Arts – but the secular Arts —both Tibetan and Western—were important. It was through the secular Western Arts that I could reach out to people.

"Secular Arts by ngakpa practising, not secular coming. Secular Arts by ngakpa practising, Vajrayana coming! Ngakpa everything into dimension of Vajrayana transforming! You must—always—music playing. This I see. This important – very important. Always painting. Always poetry writing. Always Arts in every part of life. In this way, changchub sem [4] always manifesting. This prediction I am making. Always Arts making. Never difference in Vajrayana and Art coming! Always together manifesting. In this way people nature of Vajrayana understanding."

He said that it was crucial in terms of my potential for the benefit of others. Every human being had potential that must be realised. If I gave up playing Blues, how could those who loved Blues come to know about Vajrayana? I should never abandon Blues or any of the Arts with which I had been involved. I had to earn a living somehow – and being a Bluesman was as good a way as being an Art School lecturer. After all, George Harrison was a Krishna devotee and a Rock Musician. These possibilities were already out there in the world.

"No man – not if you's bit" Frank responded and I only just connected what he said with my previous statement *'... Blues bit my ass – and there's no turning back...'*

"I'll be biting back tonight though Frank." I laughed *"Down 'The William Cobbet'. The Folk and Poetry night – you coming along?"*

"You's bringin' that DEBIL *a-yo's?"*

"As always... Might be reading some poetry too."

"Oh man – that stuff of yo's is a bit deep for me. Beats me how you can write that and sing Blues like you do. It's like you's in two worlds man. That's —so—differ'nt, it's wild." PAUSE *"How the hell d'you come up with that stuff – you eat dictionaries or what?"*

---

4   Chang chub sem *(byang chub sems,* Skt. *bodhicitta)* – active compassion. The awakened heart of empathetic appreciation in which mind is directed towards total presence of awareness.

I laughed with a shake of my head *"No Frank... well maybe yes – I do browse the dictionary. I've got an etymological dictionary and that's a really interesting thing because you can find the roots of words. It's really good to know that Legba comes from 'Alegbara'..."*

"Right..." Frank mused *"... so... what's the history there?"*

"Well... Papa Legba's an intercessor between the L'wha—the spirit world—and people. He stands at any intermediate juncture ..."

"Like the crossroads – y'mean?"

"Exactly – or the eves of a wood. Or like the shore line—the margin that's neither land nor sea—because it's keeps being either." PAUSE *"So anyhow... Legba gives—or denies—permission to speak to the djinns* [5] *– and they're the ones who can turn you into Robert Johnson."*

"That cool – nice work if you can get it."

"Exactly... and the idea is that djinns speak all human languages. Alegbara is an elocutor who enables speech, communication, interpretation, elucidation, and understanding. He's from the Yoruba culture – and still held in esteem in Nigeria, Cuba, and Brazil. He's also a trickster. He usually appears like an old man with a cane, wearing a broad-brimmed straw hat and smoking a pipe. Dogs are scared of him – so if your dog runs away, you know it's Legba."

"Hell man, all that stuff's in the dictionary!?"

"No... I had to research to find that out."

"So, how's it end up you have to sell your soul to this dude? I mean would—you—sell your soul?"

"Sure Frank—no question—but then... maybe I'm trickier than the trickster, y'know." PAUSE *"I'm a Buddhist you see..."*

"Buddhist eh... Alright... but how does that save yo' goddamn ass?"

---

5   Djinn (Arabic: جِنّ jinn)

"Buddhist don't have souls…" I laughed *"… so I'd be selling the fella a big goddamn nothing. Y'know… I could sell you my 'fame' if you wanted it. I'd say 'Here's my 'fame' Frank – seven hundred million and it's—all—yours.' And then, what would you have…? Nothing. Because I have no fame."*

"That's one fancy trick you got there!" Frank laughed. *"You's one tricky motherfucker. But what's with this 'no soul'? What does that mean?"*

"Well Frank—I'm partially joking—but… 'no soul'… dag'mèd[6] is … difficult to explain. Difficult to explain properly, I mean. It's not that there's —nothing—there… but there's no 'soul' that's a fixed—thing—like an object. There's energy, and it's in flux – but you can't ever say what it is. It can't be named or described outside the moment. We'd say it was 'empty'. You see… it moves through time but the 'it' has no shape or colour – or anything." PAUSE *"If you think of a sand dune… and the way it moves. You could track that dune – and, after some time, there'd not be a single grain of sand that remained—in the shape of that dune—after an hour. The 'shape' would be there—and it would* look like *the same dune—but:* that *would be an illusion."*

"Hot Damn!" Frank whooped *"That's just—too—cool!"* PAUSE *"And— that's—Buddhism?"*

"As… as I understand it, Frank. Yes."

"Well I hope you find ol' Legba then!" Frank said shaking with laughter *"so as you can sell that sonovabitch what you ain't got."* PAUSE *"Y'know… I might have to look into this Buddhism – I like the thinkin' of it."*

Frank suddenly looked at me quizzically *"So… how did you get to be a Buddhist – being an English Dude?"*

After a brief moment of complete blankness, I replied *"That's a long story Frank – are you up for hearing something the length of Tolstoy's War and Peace?"*

Frank grinned *"I got all the time in the world bro."*

---

6 Dag'mèd *(bDag 'med / anatman)* absence of self-identity or self-referencing.

War and Peace was something of an overestimate and I managed it in a quarter of an hour or so – concluding with the time that I spent with Kyabjé Düd'jom Rinpoche Jig'drèl Yeshé Dorje.

"That some mutha-ov-a-story you got there bro—some mutha-ov-a-story—and looks-as-if I needs to come back to it sometime and ask you some questions 'bout what you tol' me."

"Any time Frank. Just as long as I don't bore you."

Frank smiled and shook his head to say that it was unlikely he'd be bored. *"The question—right now—is: Blues' called 'the Devil's music' by Christ'ans – so I'm wond'rin' how that Tibetan Lama would look at it… like did-y'ever tell him you was a Bluesman?"*

That caused me to smile so broadly it hurt my ears. *"Sure did Frank. Sang him 'Hoochie Coochie Man' too."*

Frank chuckled *"You's joshin' me."*

"No Frank. Düd'jom Rinpoche asked me questions about my life and I told him I'd been a Blues vocalist – and he asked 'What does that sound like?' because he'd never heard it. So I just launched in."

"An' what did he make-a-that? Must have thought it was crazy? Right?"

"Not all Frank. He seemed to like it. In fact, he seemed to like it a great deal – and said I should always sing that song. He said I should never stop being a Bluesman."

"You really—are—one far out motherfucker – ain't—never—heard no story like that anywhere ever befo' .. I bet you'd sing that to the Pope if he asked you."

"If he asked me – although… the Pope might not be so keen on the Hoodoo references."

"How was the Lama with that? Wasn't that baaad juju in his book too?"

"Not at all – you see… Vajrayana Buddhism has a category of beings like Papa Legba – and so it was nothing outlandish to Düd'jom Rinpoche."

Frank adopted something of a contemplative look *"This Buddhism's got me thinkin'… We really gotta talk mo' 'bout this. I like what I's hearin'…"*

And so, this was 'Ngakpa Chögyam' – being a ngakpa in the West. Ngakpa Chögyam in a Western cultural situation talking about a Western Art form – and Buddhism emerging from it in a way that wasn't forced or artificial. I hadn't planned to bring Buddhism into the conversation – it had simply happened. Maybe it would always be like this. Maybe I wasn't doomed to have a dual identity. Maybe I would discover the experiential sense in which I was the incarnation of Aro Yeshé. Maybe it would just dawn on me as if I'd recovered from amnesia. Maybe somehow the visions of my childhood and the pastiche of my teenage dreams would become a unified thread. Maybe it didn't matter – because I had Kyabjé Düd'jom Rinpoche's pronouncement and that was all that was needed. Everything else would simply happen as it happened.

3

mojo hand

1972

We paid for our meals at the *Hop Blossom* and went back to the Art School for the afternoon session of life drawing. This time it was *short poses*. One minute and the pose would change. I could see how the morning session had set me up for that – and I kept the same focus on getting the dynamics of the form down in a series of marks, made without hesitation or uncertainty. At first, I worked too quickly – but when I got the measure of the minute, I learnt to use the sixty seconds at a pace that created a well-formed representation. Then came five-minute poses and ten-minute poses – and, as the time increased, the earlier experiences proved their worth. That day improved my drawing skills more than I would have imagined possible. We worked through 'til 5 o'clock and then everyone headed off to the William Cobbet. I sat on the steps of the Art School looking out at the evening sky. I'd felt an inclination to stare into the colour of it before socialising and performing.

The colour of the sky was every imaginable shade of pink, orange, red, and maroon together with mauve, lilac, lavender, amethyst, purple, violet, and indigo. There were also seams of azure, cobalt, caerulean blue and impossible hints of green. Suddenly I saw something I'd seen as in my infancy. I'd often seen beings in the clouds as a young child: people, animals, and hybrid entities. I thought they were real before the age of eight – but learnt to apprehend them as imagination, as sanctioned by my parents, when I grew older. Here however, there was something somewhat more than an imaginary creature from the bestiary of beatific bemusement. A goat and rider. They were well defined – if only for a few seconds. The wind gusted through them. Them…? Maybe 'them' is not accurate. A horse and rider in the conventional world would be 'them' in relation to their being two entities.

The *goat-and-rider* I perceived was in some way singular – but not like a centaur in which human and horse are combined. Was what I saw simply a paranormal perplexity which defied scrutiny. The entirety of Dorje Legpa[1] was never visible – only swiftly alternating facets of his being which built an impression in time. Seeing him was more like reading a paragraph in which he was described – and in which the sense of the paragraph is only available in the final few words. The paragraph was made of cloud – erratically riven by cloud. The clouds continually coagulated, coalesced, and vaporised. I tried to get what I saw into focus – and that is probably what dispelled the apparition. The name was there – but was I certain? Dorje Legpa was 'the sound' I'd apprehended. I'd not had to search for the name – it self-enunciated. I don't know how long I sat there on the steps – but darkness had fallen by the time I made my way to the William Cobbet.

Everyone was there when I arrived. Frank greeted me and I was suddenly back in the recognisable human dimension. The place was buzzing. Frank raised an eyebrow. Then—with a motion of his head—he indicated that he was moving across to talk to Cynthia Grantham. Frank had had his eye on her. *"She's 'bout as white as any human being c'n be—without being albino—but she gotta Black ass an' that's f'sho"* he confided. *"So I'm gonna see what kind of conv'sation I can git goin' with her."*

"Good luck Frank. Jes make sho she don't eatcher fo' breakfast" I replied attempting an imitation of Frank's accent.

"You's getting' it down, bro" Frank replied with a huge grin.

"Why, thank you, kind sir" I replied in mock upper-class English. *"I'm heading upstairs now to get tuned and so forth."*

Frank laughed *"See y'up there, bro – an' if'n I gets lucky, I might have me some comp'ny."*

---

1 Dorje Legpa *(rDo rJe legs pa* / རྡོ་རྗེ་ལེགས་པ་ / *Vajrasadhu).* Nyingma protector. See glossary: *Dorje Legpa.*

There was something strange about being in this context. It was 'me'—there was no doubt about that—but what of *the 'me' who'd sat with Düd'jom Rinpoche* in Bodhanath? Where was 'he'? He's just been on the steps of the Art School witnessing a fleeting glimpse of Dorje Legpa. He was here in the William Cobbett—sure enough—but only I knew he was here. Well, Frank knew something of my time in Nepal – but nothing that was too 'otherworldly'.

I sometimes felt that it would be good to go and see Lama Chime at Kham House in Essex – in order that I could spend a short time being who I was in Bodha. I missed being *that version of myself* – even though *that version* was sitting right here. It occurred to me that there was something missing in how I *felt*. I experienced no difference in terms of my orientation toward Kyabjé Düd'jom Rinpoche – but I felt different in relation to myself. It was as if I was unaccountably ten years younger in terms of maturity. It was a loss of confidence in what *the Aro Tulku*[2] was supposed to be. It's not that I really felt like a tulku in Nepal and India—because I had no idea how a tulku might feel—but the idea did not seem alien. It was like being half-German – but not really knowing what the German part was. I couldn't speak German beyond a rudimentary level – and I knew even less Tibetan. It was like being a chameleon. In Nepal with Kyabjé Düd'jom Rinpoche I could feel like *the Aro Tulku*. In the William Cobbet, I simply had no idea who I was – other than a Blues performer who had once belonged to the Savage Cabbage Blues Band.

With this ambivalent conjecture I ascended the stairs to the room where I would perform. Sure enough, half an hour later Frank walked in. He had a grin as large as a crocodile. He was arm in arm with Cynthia Grantham. She was also grinning like all the Cheshire cats there'd ever been.

---

2   Tulku *(sPruk sKu / nirmanakaya)* the incarnation of a previous Lama—in this case Aro Yeshé—the son and heir of Khyungchen Aro Lingma.

"Hey Frank" I called out *"Y'know Muddy Water's song about the Hoochie Coochie Man?"* Frank nodded. He knew that song *"Well you —are—that–man Frank. No doubt about it."*

Goddamn…! Frank had *all* the luck. He was Black. He had that fabulous accent. The ladies swooped down on him from every direction. Not that I'd want the attention Frank got from ladies – I just wanted a relationship with a lady whose father didn't want to have me hung by the neck 'til dead. But then… I had *some* luck. Frank was no musician. Well, I was no musician either – not in real world-stage terms. At *The William Cobbet* however, I was all I needed to be – and perhaps a little more. Frank laughed and interrupted my brief reverie *"Well ain't—that—a goddamn coincidence! – I just said the self-same thing to Cynthia here just 'fo' we came up. I said 'You gotta come upstairs and hear the Hoochie Coochie Man – The One and Only Pink Nigger!'…"*

"That's what he said" Cynthia grinned.

"And now we's here—Mister Hoochie Coochie Man—what y'gonna play?"

It was almost time to kick off the evening so I said *"You called it, Frank"* and proceeded to run my introduction. *"Good Evening people. Thank you for showing up equipped with: porcupine quill quilted coiffure, garrulous Gabonese gibbons, macerated marsupial metacarpals – and—all— those good things. My first number's a song f'my friend Frank Berner here— and for his charming lady—Cynthia. It's a song Muddy Waters sang 'bout djinn and tonic – but that's 'gin' spelt D–J–I–N–N 'cause this song's called Hoochie Coochie Man."*

I got a boom of laughter and applause for that – and that set me up to give it hell.

> *Gypsy woman told my mother – befo' I was born, Y'gotta boy child coming – gonna be a sonovagun, / Gonna make pretty womens – jump and shout, / And th'world wanna know, what's—it—all—about / Because I'm here – hever'body knows I'm here, / I'm the Hoochie Coochie Man – ever'body know I am.*

I played that song as an alternation of guitar and harp. I had a loop on my guitar strap where I could slide the harp when I wanted to go back to guitar. It worked well and made up for my modest guitar skills. Then I threw a change on the words:

On the 'leventh hour – day befo' the seventh day / On the sixth month – nurse and midwife say: "He was born for something – we just cannot see." / I got seventeen shillings and sixpence - -you can mess all you want with me / 'cause I ain't he-ere – lord knows I ain't even near / Well I'm the Hoochie Coochie Man—yeah—ev'ral people know I am.

I got a black fox stole – kimono too / I'm John the Kangaroo – I al'ays jump the queue / Gonna ask some nice lady – take me by the hand / But I hope she don't say – you ain't no hoochie coochie man / Because I'm weird – ever'body knows I'm weird, / I'm the spooky lookin' man – ever'body knows I am.

I'd usually break my set with a piece of poetry – and this time I was keen to try out something new. Adrian Henry and Roger McGough had visited the Foundation year to give a talk on poetry. Those who were keen adjourned to *The Seven Stars* pub with them afterwards; to talk and tipple. It was an illuminating evening for me because I was able to put a problem to them. I'd found that I'd reached some kind of impasse with poetry. I seem to be stuck with having to be poetic. My poetry was too baroque and congested with the metaphor. What I wanted to do was to bring something different into my writing. I wanted to be able to introduce a mundane element but had no idea how to do that without it seeming contrived.

Adrian Henri could understand the problem and made a brilliant suggestion *"Why not just write a list of as many different places as you can imagine where poetry could be performed?"*

So that is exactly what I did – and tonight was its first outing.

"I've got a thing for you now, good people… It's a thing… a thing I've never tried before. If you like it, you can thank Adrian Henri for giving me the idea – and if you don't… I suppose I'll have to re-think it. It's called 'List of Settings for Poetry' and it's dedicated to Adrian Henri and Roger McGough."

The day will come when poetry will be recited on: trains; buses; trams; ski-lifts; escalators; elite escargot bistros;

In dishevelled Nessun Dorma refreshment interludes; dormant Dorniers and Dormobiles; duo-diablo dormitories;

Double entendre dovecotes; Victorian dormer windowed attics with bijou miniature fireplaces; fried-out combies;

Sections of rusted aircraft fuselage left in fields awaiting rape-seed oil-paint conflagrations of Vincent Van Gogh;

Cross channel ferries; Rubenesque rigmarole riots; inviolate brassière conventions; the Albert & Victoria Museum;

The Albert Hall replete with holes; Stately Home garden parties, replete with salmon and cucumber sandwiches;

In plum patisserie potting sheds; atavistic abattoirs of abstract Art; ghostly glens under grimoires of moonlight;

Crab-apple orchards; gallows-tree arboretums; covert culvert confectionery congresses; airport waiting lounges;

Simone De Beauvoir re-enactment soirées; sultry skylark meadows; fundamentalist ski resorts; and, bicycle sheds.

The day will come when poetry will be recited in: Hay-on-Wye bookshops; gentleman's outfitters; railway sidings;

The White House; street cafés in Paris; the Department of Promontories; agricultural shows; yachting clubs;

Baudelaire's pied-à-terre; Byzantine ballerina boudoirs; late-night octogenarian banquets; Siberian florist shops;

Elizabethan choir stalls; bathroom display suites; Merchant Ivory film sets; coal mines; Sodom and Gomorrah;

Nautical newsagents; seditious saddleries; Royal Weddings; metallurgical laboratories; public swimming pools;

Pubic depilation parlours amongst potted palms; St Paul's Cathedral;
Vicarage tea parties; the Chrysler Building;
Church fêtes; La Grotte de Lascaux; equestrian centres; inventive
inventory symposia; weight watchers' meetings;
Lord Montague's Motor Museum; abandoned airfields; shopping
precincts; legendary pissoires; old olive groves;
Honourable Society of Charles De Gaul Impersonator Reunion
Dinners; and dainty daguerreotype departments.
The day will come when poetry will be recited in: sinister Hairdressers;
Anonymous meetings in Cornish tin mines;
Disused railway sidings; piers where pole-vaulting demonstrations are
presented by gargoyle-fancier fellowships;
Promenade Concerts; Formula 1 Race tracks; subterfuge prismatic-
incantation-league rallies; Sheepdog trials;
Tupperware parties at dude ranches, rainbow trout farms, and doctors'
surgeries; parent-teacher associations;
Amongst shoals of green turtles navigating the mercurially mazed
Sargasso Sea; Burlesque Brigadoon bar-rooms;
Belligerent bugle consultation rooms; budgerigar bursary appointment
bureaux; ballroom dancing competitions;
Darts championships; West Kennet Long Barrow; vegetable markets;
madcap mosaic sites; antique antic attics;
Blood-donor clinics; Madame Tussaud's Waxworks; French Châteaux
lawns; greyhound tracks; Greyhound buses;
Greystoke Castle Estate; the Orient Express; trailer park mortuaries;
and, patent leather indebtedness cliques.
The day will come when poetry will be recited in: tepees during the
Olympic Games; derelict wayside wickiups;
Wigwams whilst highly skilled Great Masters copyists reproduce the
works of Bruegel and Hieronymus Bosch;
Marquees once owned by Le Marquis de Sade; igloos frequented by
Frank Zappa's Esquimaux Euphoniums;

Huts; lodges; gatehouses; motile motels; harbours; chalets; cottages; villas;
palaces; porticos; porches; entrances;
Doorways; balconies; verandas; terraces; Ragnarök roustabout rostrums;
egregiously engrossed ego ingresses;
Grievous egresses with gregarious egrets; suburban sunburn sitting-rooms
replete with sautéed settees, sans Suttee;
Grizzled garden allotments; natural amphitheatres open to raging
torrents of wind despatched by wings of cloud
Once seen delving the boiling heart of the ocean, where boarding kennel
anterooms eat the Houses of Parliament
And leave its ministers–both with and without portfolio–suspended in
mid-air as pinstriped bowler-hatted gossamer.

There were another eight nine-line stanzas—making thirteen in all
—but this should suffice as an example. When I concluded the
audience were silent. They sat staring at me and I felt that I'd just
ruined the evening for everyone. Then—as if released form a spell
—they launched into a gale of applause that was lengthy in
duration. I had to agree to recite it again the following week.

Then I finished my set with a Son House number *Don't You Mind*
People Grinning in Your Face – but again I sang two extemporaneous
verses.

Don'cher mind people grinning at your plaice / Don'cher mind people
grinning at your plaice / Please bear this in mind – good fish is hard to
find / Don'cher mind people grinning at your plaice.
Don'cher mind people grinning at your plaice / Don'cher mind people
grinning at your plaice / They all got halibut and sturgeon, while you's in
the water searchin' / Don'cher mind people grinning at your plaice.

At the end of my set, Frank came up and asked in a discreet tone
"Hey Vic – d'you just make some-a-that up—I mean, right there on the spot
— or's that from befo'?"

"Just made that up as I went along Frank" I laughed. *"I do that from time*
to time."

"That was real funny Vic – what you did to Hoochie Coochie Man. But y'know… that self-deprecatin' number… it works real well here. But… when I take you 'roun' them juke joints back home – you gotta make up differ'nt lines: lines about how you's eve'ry woman's heart's desire. That's what they wanna hear down there."

"Mmmm… that'll be the challenge, Frank…" I mused *"… but maybe that'll just come to me. It'll be a very different audience…"*

"Sho' will."

"Don't you think it would sound pretentious—even for The One and Only Pink Nigger—to be making out he's a heaven-sent hot-shot and answer to every woman's dreams? Like… aren't they going to say 'Who's he think he's kidding?' and have a good laugh before they whupp my goddamn ass and throw me out the door?"

"No man–no way–no way!" he laughed *"… anyways, I'll be there. My friends be there too – so nobody gonna mess with you."*

"So I could just sing…" I thought for a moment.

"Lawd I got a mamba – ever' gal here gonna r'member,/ Honey chile—I, got a mamba—ever' gal here gonna r'member,/ An' when they samba with my mamba/ Hooooo! They's all be screamin' hey caramba!"

Frank laughed. Cynthia laughed too – but I saw that she was somewhat taken aback. I wasn't known for being lewd. The most depraved I got was singing *'If You See Kay – tell her to hurry home…'*

"That'll do the trick" Frank chuckled.

"Really Frank?" I was genuinely surprised. *"I mean… I could just stand up and sing stuff like that – and they wouldn't throw scraps of fœtid offal at me?"*

That made Cynthia laugh – but Frank had a serious expression *"Not if you sing it like—you—sing it, man."* PAUSE *"Gotta mean it though."* Then Frank narrowed his eyes. *"Did you just make that up on the spot too?"*

41

"Errr... yeah."

"That's too much man! You are one—far out—motherfucker."

The way Frank talked it was a done deal. I was going to hit the Chitlin' Circuit. I told Frank that I'd probably have to change my stage name because 'Frank Schubert' probably wouldn't do the trick in Mississippi.

"Yeah... maybe... But hell, Frank's a cool name! Hey! I should know!!" he laughed *"and that 'Schubert'! That's got real class, man. Where-in-hell d'yer git a handle like that?"*

I told Frank about being the great grandnephew of Franz Schubert.

"Hell man, that's a mind-bender. You straight up? This fo' real, right?"

"It's for real Frank – but y'know... it doesn't make me anything. There must be a whole slew of people who're distant relatives of Franz Schubert."

"Yeah man—but they ain't in Mississippi—and, they won't be The One and Only Pink Nigger."

The conversation flowed with a lot of laughter and Cynthia asked *"So... what's the German connection Vic?"*

"My mother. Her maiden name was Schubert. Her mother's name was Clara Schubert." I saw amazement on Cynthia's face and hurried to correct her misimpression. *"No, not—that—Clara: wrong generation and you may be thinking of Clara Schuman."* Understanding dawned on Cynthia's face *"My grandmother—Clara Schubert—was a niece of Franz Schubert."*

"You speak English quite fluently" Cynthia commented and Frank laughed.

"That 'cause the dude—is—English."

"My father's English you see... and I was brought up in Farnham. My German's really rather poor."

"That's no loss" Cynthia smiled *"and anyway – your Black American accent when you sing Blues is really convincing."*

Frank smiled and winked at me *"Yeah ol' Frank… One and Only Pink Nigger! What did I tell yer! He'll kill'em all dead when he lets rip on that Chitlin' Circuit."*

"When he sings, Frank…" Cynthia commented with raised eyebrows *"… but not when he talks. You'll have to work on your speaking accent Vic."*

"No…" Frank mused *"I think… singin' like Muddy Waters and talkin' like Prince Charles is just the right angle. That's what's gonna give him the edge – 'mer'cans jus love that shit."*

Cynthia almost choked on her gin and tonic when she heard my accent being described as 'Prince Charles'. *"He may sound like Prince Charles to you Frank – but…"*

"Cynthia's right" I cut in immediately. *"My accent is decidedly plebeian and I probably imitate Prince Charles about as well as I imitate Muddy Waters."*

"Let's hear Prince Charles then" Frank chuckled. I gave it my best shot with *'Oh lawd won't you buy me a Mercedes Benz'* and both laughed till they had tears in their eyes.

"Well that was a hoot" Cynthia cackled. *"Maybe you—will—pick up Frank's accent."*

"Well it's fine when I sing… but I couldn't—speak—like Prince Charles. Anyway, what I just did was a caricature. You can get away with a caricature of an accent when you sing – but to keep it up in ordinary conversation would be difficult."

"Oh man" Frank laughed *"you just sing like you sing and talk like you talk and them big-leg mammas gonna be round you like bees 'round a honey pot."*

"One big-leg mamma do me jus' fine bro – I ain't lookin' t'have no harem" I said in as close as I could make it to Frank's accent.

"I thought you were with that girl, Hell?" Cynthia queried.

"Was once – but she done quit me."

"Oh… I thought you seemed to be quite close."

"That's what I thought too – but it turned out that she didn't want to be with someone for whom Fine Art wasn't 'The One True Way'. She didn't seem to like me being a Jack-of-all-trades… y'know… painting, poetry, and Blues…"

"That's plain dumb man – 'specially from her, like she wasn't no—oil— painting. Never could see what you saw in her."

I paused for a moment *"Well… no… maybe not… I can't either, from this distance. And… it's a while back now… I've been to India and Nepal since then – so it's all part of another life."* PAUSE *"She had a wicked sense of humour… at least at first."*

"What happened?" asked Cynthia.

"She… got a bad case of 'Fine Art Puritanism' y'know…" PAUSE *"And then… well – I don't want to say too much. I suppose I wasn't such a great prospect… not in the painting world she's gone into. I'm always ready, at the drop of a hat, to give it all up for Blues – or taking off to the Himalayas."*

"Not befo' we git you down in Louisiana, bro" Frank affectionately demanded.

"Y'know… maybe I should just do that… Maybe I should forget about applying to Bristol and go to Louisiana – get me a mojo hand."

"No man – you take yo' time. Shame to give up on Art School. Never know what's gonna happen next and havin' that Illustration experience might be what you need some time. Them Juke Joints ain't going' away nowheres – they still be there when you come over."

Cynthia had picked up on my Blues vernacular and asked *"What's this mojo hand?"*

Frank nodded to me to speak and so I gave forth *"… 'Well the night I was born, lord I swear the moon turned a fire red. Well I'm a voodoo chile, lord I'm a voodoo chile.' So… Jimi Hendrix was singing about having powers because he's a 'voodoo child'. The word 'voodoo' comes from the African word hoodoo which was a type of herbal magic. One of the magical objects that a Bluesman likes to carry is a mojo hand. As I was singing up there a while back 'I Got a black cat bone, and a mojo too, I got Johnny Conqueroo, I'm gonna mess with you.' So… a mojo hand is a pouch–usually red–and it contains some special things."*

"Like five finger grass" Frank offered.

"Yes, digitaria. It's native to hot countries. It's also called crabgrass, finger-grass, and fonio."

"Digitus is Latin for 'finger'" Cynthia commented as if Frank and I wouldn't have known that – but neither of us commented.

"Yeah… then… there's a mercury dime. That's 10 cents."

"I know a dime is 10 cents Frank…" smiled Cynthia *"… but what's a mercury dime?"*

"D'you know Vic?" Frank shrugged *"All I know, is got Mercury on it – like this feller with wings on his hat."*

"That's right. It was a coin struck by the US Mint from… somewhere early this century—can't remember the exact date—but, around the end of WWII. Designed by Adolph Weinman. It was properly known as the Winged Liberty dime. Liberty wears a winged Phrygian cap – and people got her confused with the Roman god Mercury."

"Well don't that beat all. This here Vic's a goddamn Blues scholar! So, what else in that bag, mojo man?"

"Lodestone – which is a naturally occurring magnet. It's either black or brownish-black with a metallic lustre. Then, van-van oil. Van-van is a mispronunciation of the French word Verveine. In the Creole French dialect of Louisiana, Vervain is pronounced 'vaah-vahn'. I don't know what that would be over here."

45

"Verveine's 'Verbena' in English" commented Cynthia.

"Excellent – thank you, I'll remember that." Cynthia looked happy she's been able to contribute and so I gave her a big grin.

"Anything else on the list?" she asked.

"Yes… there's a cat's eye shell – a mollusc's operculum. That's a plate, usually round, smooth and thick, which allows the mollusc to close its shell. The cat's eye shell is the operculum of a group of molluscs known as Turbos. Then…"

"There's more?" Cynthia asked with slight amazement.

"Yeah – there's John the Conqueror Root" said Frank. *"In Blues that sound like 'Johnny Conqueroo' like 'I got Johnny Conqueroo, I'm gonna—mess— with you!'"*

"John the Conqueror's a folk hero associated with hoodoo. He was an African prince who was sold as a slave – but his spirit was never broken. He survived in folklore as a trickster figure – because of the tricks he played to evade capture when he escaped from slavery. John the Conquer Root is St John's wort. Then… the last thing on the list—or the only other thing I know—is a $2 dollar bill.

"They's rare now" added Frank. *"It got Jefferson on the one side and a picture of the Decl'ration of In'ependence on the other."*

"It was discontinued in 1966."

"That's a lot of information…" Cynthia grinned *"D'you plan to make one of these things Vic?"*

"Well… I had it in mind once… but… I'd need to find the hoodoo man or woman to do whatever they do – or it would just be a bag with things in it."

"D'you really—believe—all that stuff?" asked Frank.

"I don't know… I don't think it's a question of believing it or not believing it. It's part of Blues culture… and it's… it's the poetry of it I believe. Well 'believe' isn't the right word really. It's more a question of it being a symbol. You'd have to put some work into collecting all those things."

"Well you already put in the work of all that research man. I think I'm gonna help you get all that stuff."

And so the evening wound to a close with Cynthia having found herself in some kind of Blues coven in the heart of middle-class England. Frank announced that I was '*... some kinda Ti-betan Buddhist wizard...*' as well as being a Bluesman and poet – and so I had a deal of explaining to run through. Cynthia was not quite as interested as Frank had been – and so I kept my explanations brief. She was more interested in asking me about the poetry I'd recited.

"That piece you read – that was a tour de force, I must say. How long have you been writing poetry?"

"Since I was five years old."

"You have quite a way with words – I'm surprised you chose Art School."

"Well... I did think of taking an English degree – but I didn't really want to study other people's writing and have to: analyse it, scrutinise it, dissect it, investigate it, compare it, contrast it, or evaluate it. I found that—so—utterly tedious when I was at school. Having to regurgitate what the literary authorities gave as the meaning of the metaphors and allegories in the books and poetry on the syllabus, would have been terminally mind numbing. I love reading – but I wouldn't want my reading governed by the erudite rules and regulations of rigor mortis. And... there didn't seem to be a creative writing degree on offer anywhere – so where I am suits me perfectly because I also love painting..."

"And Blues" Cynthia chuckled. *"Quite the polymath."*

"Maybe Poly the Parrot" I dissembled, wishing to deflect the praise. I never knew what to do with compliments. Compliments were not unpleasant – but they left me at a loss for an appropriate response. Not wishing to sound gauche I continued *"I've always loved the whole spectrum of the Arts – and so trying to specialise has always gone against the grain. The main problem with that is that unless you're Leonardo Da Vinci, you stand the chance of merely being mediocre in all fields."*

"So all thy words comes back to thee in shades of mediocrity?" Cynthia quipped – but followed immediately *"Sorry – I didn't mean that in the way it sounds."*

"Homeward bound, I wish I was" I burst out laughing. *"Sounded brilliant to me – I love word play."*

Cynthia looked relieved—and so did Frank, as it was clear he was aware that offence could have been taken—so I sang

> *Tonight I'll sing my Blues again, I'll play the harp, the notes'll bend*
> *And the lyrics all come back to me in shades of immortality*
> *Like emptiness in harmony, won't someone stand a drink for me*
> *Homeward bound I wish I was, homeward bound*
> *Home, where my thoughts escaping, there'll be Muddy Waters playing*
> *Home, where my guitar's waiting silently for me, silently for me."*[3]

They both cracked up laughing at that – and I was glad I'd managed to make everything feel light again. Cynthia seemed to enjoy the evening, and she and Frank remained an item.

Frank was always glad to see me and often showed up for my sets at the William Cobbet. He always reminded me about coming to Louisiana. He always gave me that big smile to make it obvious that he meant every word. He also asked me questions about Buddhism. I always answered – but, at first, tried to keep my answers brief. I had no wish to proselytise. Frank, however, was persistent and gradually coaxed more detailed information out of me. I never asked him what he wanted to do with the information – but just assumed that he, like all Art students, was fascinated with the nature of reality.

We had some excellent conversations back and forth between Buddhism and Blues – almost my twin religions. I'd written Frank Berner's home address in Louisiana in my address book: we'd become good friends. Although he was no Blues performer –

---

3   Parody of *Homeward Bound* by Simon and Garfunkel.

Blues ran through him like the words in a stick of Brighton rock.[4] Absurd expression – but then, that's apparently what he liked about me. I was a quaint old-fashioned Englishman who played Blues. The anomaly appealed to his sense of poetry – as did the fact that I was an ordained ngakpa. Frank always returned to the subject of Vajrayana – and I got the sense that he had an authentic desire to learn more. He was particularly interested in the nature of personality – and how emptiness manifested individual personality as a reflex of natural compassion. The idea of compassion and wisdom being nondual intrigued him – and the fact that this nonduality was the underpinning of Art was a subject to which he kept returning. By the time the end of the Summer term was nearing, Frank told me that he was starting to think that Vajrayana might just be his direction. It fitted with how he saw things as a Fine Artist, in a way that Christianity didn't. I pointed out that Christianity had a wealth of painting sculpture and music – but he shook his head. *"Man… that was all way back with Leonardo Da Vinci when 'ligious paintin' was everywhere and it was the main culture. Dudes like that could express themselves through 'ligion – and it was a serious thing. Today it's Jesus Christ Superstar*[5]*"* Frank rolled his eyes *"and ain't gonna be painting no goddamn sets for that – not for Godspell*[6] *or Joseph and his goddamn hippie slicker*[7] *neither. Anyhow, I can't see no serious Christian—Art—nowheres."*

4   An outmoded British expression for someone who is thoroughly conversant with, or enthusiastic about, something. Brighton Rock is a hard rod-shape boiled-sugar British confectionery flavoured with peppermint or spearmint sold at seaside resorts such as Brighton, Southend-on-Sea, or Blackpool. The Rock has embedded words which run the full length often the resort where the rock is sold, so that the name remains legible when sections are eaten.

5   *Jesus Christ Superstar* was a 1970s rock opera by Andrew Lloyd Webber and Tim Rice. The story is loosely based on the last week of Christ's life, and portrays a political contretemps between Judas Iscariot and Christ to which there are no Biblical references.

6   *Godspell* was a musical by Stephen Schwartz based on the book by John-Michael Tebelak. The show opened Off-Broadway on the 17th of May, 1971. It was built on a series of parables from the Gospel of Matthew.

7   *Joseph and the Amazing Technicolor Dreamcoat* is a musical by Tim Rice and Andrew Lloyd Webber. The story is based on the 'coat of many colours' story of Joseph from Genesis. It was first staged as a 15-minute 'pop cantata' at Colet Court School in London in 1968.

"Right…" I pondered *"Well, it's not my job to put you off looking into Vajrayana – but I'm not a proselytiser. I'd hate to come across like a Vajrayana missionary or anything, so I feel slightly obliged to mention the alternative."*

Frank nodded *"… 'preciate it. Never saw you as no 'vangelist. That's why I's al'as askin' questions. It's 'cause there ain't no goddamn* preacher-number *you's tryin' t'sell."*

"True enough Frank – although there are plenty of Western Buddhists out there who think it's alright to proselytise."

"So… why is that?"

"Well… from what I've seen, they don't seem to understand that Buddhism isn't a religion of Truth – it's a religion of Method. It doesn't require faith – it simply requires personal experience."

"Yeah, God's fine if'n you's got the faith, man – but I got no faith in no uncreated creator. I can't go that way – so if'n it wasn't for this here Vajrayana, I'd have no interest in no religion." PAUSE *"But—that—wouldn't settle right with me; havin' no religion don't really suit me either – so I's gotta folla this through and see where this Vajrayana takes me."*

That was somehow startling – because I'd had no sense of *anything I'd said* being *that* convincing. I'd certainly made no attempt to convince Frank of anything. I'd merely answered his questions. I'd merely explained. I cast my mind back and it occurred to me that Frank had asked me a lot of questions over the time we'd known each other – but that he'd left it right until the end of his time at Farnham Art School to tell me that he was on the cusp of thinking of himself as a Buddhist.

Frank always gave me valuable guidance on just the right way to pronounce words in order that I'd sound as if I'd been born in the Mississippi Delta. I never did get to be as good as Jo Ann Kelly – but Frank enabled me to be streets ahead of a fair few other English Blues exponents.

I offered him my address but he said *"I'll get it when you write me man. If yer give it me now, I'll prob'bly lose it when I's packin' up t'go home."* And that's how we left it – but sometime later, the idea took an unexpected nose-dive. It was in September – just before I set out for Bristol. I'd gone on some wild goose chase to meet *a man who knew a man* or something of that nature. He was supposed to be in the know and well equipped with the wherewithal to get me better known as a Bluesman. It turned out to be a wasted journey. *Blues* was history.

Sid—Sidney Arthur—the *man who knew the man*, expressed great interest in seeing the DEBIL. I took it along and we talked. The DEBIL proved fascinating – but Sid wasn't hopeful. *"No album mate… Problem there… ain't it. Y'know what I mean, Sonny Jim?"*

I shook my head. I had no idea what he meant.

"Well y'see mate… no—proverbial album—no large gigs. An' wiv-owtcher large gigs… ain't a snowball's chance in 'ell of an album. Definitive closed loop d'y'see?" PAUSE *"Keep you in mind though… like as when I'm talkin' to people… mention yer t'Georgie Kaminski* [8] *when I'm up Town.* [9] *Y'never know."*

Sid meant 'Giorgio Gomelsky'—the proprietor of the Crawdaddy Club—so I had some inkling that he didn't really know Giorgio Gomelsky that well. I knew the name because Ron had chatted with him about Savage Cabbage playing a gig at the Crawdaddy. Giorgio Gomelsky had been interested as Ron had sent him a tape. We'd been due to play the Crawdaddy the Summer after Ron and Steve died.

---

8   Giorgio Gomelsky was a Georgian émigré who in 1963 decided he needed a venue. He knew the landlord of the Station Hotel in Richmond, and took the back room as 'The Crawdaddy Club'. The name derived from Bo Diddley's 1960 song 'Doing the Craw-Daddy'. The Rolling Stones and Kinks regularly performed there amongst others.

9   'Town' meant London in the vernacular of those who looked to London as the prime place.

Sid listened to a tape I'd made of my performance at the Farnham Folk and Blues Festival. He liked my voice – but no. *"Five years back – and we'd be talkin' mate – but now… it's—Rock, mate—fast'n'furious. Mind you… I love the Blues! Always did! Always will! Best you can get… but, there yer go… that's the way-a-the-world mate – ain't it. Way-a-the-world."*

"You're probably right."

"Don't play any—other—material do yer?"

I shook my head. *"No… I only play Blues. Got no heart for anything else."*

It wasn't strictly true because I wrote psychedelic ballads and Acid Rock numbers – but I wasn't going to go down that road. I'd sell my non-existent soul to Papa Legba – but I wasn't about to sell it just to be on stage again.

The road I took that evening however, led me to lose the DEBIL. The elasticated cord gave way and the DEBIL fell off the sissy bars of my motorcycle. I stopped as quickly as I could to save it – but it was too late. The DEBIL was crushed. The eight double wheels of an articulated lorry pummelled it into the tarmac. I sat and stared for a minute or two at the remains that I'd dragged out of the road. A blank thoughtlessness. It was what Düd'jom Rinpoche called the 'prison of numb emptiness[10] – in which *the richness of the nature of Mind could not self-emerge.* When I recognised this, some sense of time and place asserted itself. I remembered the words of Düd'jom Rinpoche *'With each life-circumstance: whatever is enacted, stare directly into the enactment – with all the senses.'*

It had become dark. Stars had appeared. A pattern had appeared – a pattern of stars. I wondered what constellation it was – because I did not recognise it. I observed without cogitating – because there was nothing on which I could make a comparison.

---

10 Prison of numb emptiness: 'ö-gyu'i namtog *('og gyu'i rNam rTog)* the undercurrent of ideational wandering.

It was in the wrong part of the sky for Orion, Taurus, Gemini or Canis Major – they were all in the South and I was looking North. It was however nothing I would have recognised in the Northern sky: Ursa Major, Draco, or Cygnus. I had been fascinated by the stars as a child and it gave me great pleasure to be able to identify stars and constellations. I knew how to find the Northern Star—the Pole Star—by tracing a line from the two stars that formed the rear leg of the Great Bear. I had no interest in astrology – as it had always seemed a little too arbitrary and impossibly generalised to be taken seriously. The stars in themselves were a subject of sufficient wonder – and on this evening the wonder suddenly transmogrified into the wildest wonderment as Dorje Legpa glittered into my perception out of what should have been Ursa Major, Ursa Minor, and Draco. As before on the steps of Farnham Art School. The visual impression did not last long enough to form a focus on which I could dwell for more than a few minutes – at the outside.

I thought about my vain attempt to meet Legba at the crossroads when I was 12. I thought about my hoodoo conversations with Frank. I noticed the fine layer of dust that lay on the ruins of the case that housed the DEBIL. I felt moved to write a few words with my finger tip. I almost wrote Dorje Legpa རྡོ་རྗེ་ལེགས་པ་ in Tibetan U-Chen script. I decided against it almost immediately—it would have been to treat religion flippantly—and wrote 'Bye-bye Papa Legba.' That was always the danger with whimsy. The similarity between the names Legpa and Legba however, was intriguing. I knew that there were many of these 'false friends' in linguistics – and that merely because there was a similarity between two words did not prove a connection between them. Be that as it may, the DEBIL was gone. Building another was not feasible.[11]

11 Another DEBIL was made—a 12 string DEBIL—in 2016. Düd'dül Dorje—Robert Togden, my son—heard the story of the DEBIL when Khandro Déchen read *an odd boy on* retreats and was passionate about having it remade. It was remade by Miles Henderson Smith, the Cornish Luthier who was enthused by Düd'dül Dorje's passionate wish to re-create the DEBIL. See *an odd boy*—Volume I—chapter 10—Aro Books WORLDWIDE—2011; and *Goodbye Forever*—Volume I—chapter 9—Aro Books WORLDWIDE—2020.

Then I straddled the Pixie Chariot—its swept-up ape-hanger handlebars seeming vaguely like the horns of a goat—and thrust my foot down on the kick-start. I twisted the throttle—lovely deep throated roar—and let fly the clutch. There's a section of road where you can hit the ton[12] if you accelerate fast enough – and slow down immediately the needle tips 100 mph.

The next day I realised I'd made a rather serious mistake. When I'd ridden off to see Sid I'd popped my address book in the DEBIL's case. It had occurred to me that Sid might give me a slew of useful music business contacts. I was wrong – but I was further in error than I guessed. I'd forgotten all about the address book in my distress about the DEBIL. As soon as that fact hit me, I rode off immediately to find the wreckage of the DEBIL to retrieve my address book. After searching the roadside for an hour I gave up. The address book was lost. Goodbye forever.

Many of the addresses were replaceable – but not Frank's. I tried the Fine Art department – but the secretary told me that she couldn't give people personal addresses. *"What if I just gave you the letter—postage paid for the USA—and you wrote the address and posted it?"*

She was not keen on the idea—even when I told her how I'd lost my address book—but she finally agreed, with ill humour – and told me *"This is the first and last time."*

Time passed. No reply ever came – and I have always wondered whether she really posted that letter or not. I tried sending others to Frank Berner C/O Farnham Art School but in the end I gave up. Those good people in Louisiana and Mississippi weren't gonna hear no Blues from no Frank Schubert – the almost 'One and Only Pink Nigger.'

---

12 'The ton' is British slang for 100 mph and 'hitting the ton' therefore meant 'reaching 100 mph. Rockers, young bikers who wore black leather motorcycle jackets, were—by extension—known as 'ton-up boys'.

Sad? Yes – but Düd'jom Rinpoche didn't say that I had to play the Chitlin' Circuit. Düd'jom Rinpoche had simply told me to maintain my connection with Blues and the Arts – so Art School would have to stand in for Blues and the other Arts for the next three years.

Then, suddenly—life always seemed to happen suddenly—I was in Bristol. I was an Art student again – and mighty glad to be so. At least this was real. Chasing the Djinn for another moment of glory on the Blues stage was terminally finished. All that *chasing* accomplished, was to convert me into a wraith. With Frank Berner on the scene I felt I was real as a Bluesman. However, at the point the DEBIL died—and Frank Berner's address vanished—Frank Schubert became a big pink nothing: a Blues Blancmange. In Bodhanath with Kyabjé Düd'jom Rinpoche I'd also felt I was real – but the reality of that was not ephemeral. To be a Bluesman I had to have a context – but to be a ngakpa, all I really required were the practices that I had been given. Those practises were indestructible. Those practises would not change with the changing of fashion. There was no *Sid-arthur* to tell me that nondual realisation had had its day. No Sid. No stage. No album. No gigs. There was no fame or shame either – and no applause other than the self-existent applause of natural co-emergent appreciation.

Chögyam—the Art student—however, was alive and well and looking toward three years of pure creativity. I was a real person again. I was engaged upon an adventure into the realm of word and image. The Head of Illustration was a marvellous man – open-minded, friendly, and enthusiastic. He even had an interest in Buddhism – and was reasonably knowledgeable. I felt at home.

4

them that weave the wind

The first term was entirely engaging. I worked at Illustration projects with enthusiasm – even though they concerned subjects which were only of oblique interest. It occurred to me that I was not the same Art student who went to the Himalayas. I had a greater degree of acceptance. I had far less need to put spins and twists into my work. I could simply be creative without the compulsion to personalise everything according to any penchant for weirdness. Weirdness had been part of the hippy gestalt – but that gestalt was fading. Although I still enjoyed sartorialism as Art, it was no longer *de rigueur* to be outrageous – and I was never really outré, per se. Most people on the Foundation Year at Farnham were gaudier by far. I enjoyed their appearance – but I was never drawn to *vivid velvet and floral flamboyance.*

As an illustrator, I simply rejoiced in the use of the facilities and being supplied with materials. I was happy simply to develop old skills and learn new skills. I was engaged upon an adventure into the realm of word and image. Derek Crowe, the head of Illustration, was a marvellous man: open-minded, friendly, and enthusiastic.

By the later part of the first term I'd met 'dette—Claudette Gascoigne—and was in a romantic relationship again. It transpired as an accident of circumstances. I'd had no intention of taking up with anyone, but… 'dette was a good conversationalist – and one thing had simply led to another. If I'd have had the intention – I would have been looking for a young lady who was at least interested in Eastern religions. As it was, I simply allowed life to happen. In someone with realisation that could have been perfect – but with me, it was merely the roulette wheel of random destinies.

'dette was a highly cultured lady. She loved attending the three Bristol theatres. Her plan was to become a theatre wardrobe-designer – and thus had chosen the Fashion and Textiles degree course at Bower Aston. With everyday contact, our relationship blossomed rapidly. 'dette was intelligent: highly witty—in Dorothy Parker mode—and, *a walking, sitting and otherwise lounging*, book of classical quotations. She sometimes made me feel so entirely plebeian that I wondered what the attraction was, for her. I had my own native wit – and knowledge of the Arts. I had a smattering of quotations—mainly Shakespeare and Blues—but beyond that, it was evident that I was a card-carrying primitive-autodidact. I'd not attended a private school. I'd never learned Latin, toured museums, art galleries, or theatres. I hadn't sat in prestigious seats at the opera houses of Europe: Amsterdam, Athens, Avignon, Bruges, Florence, Geneva, Graz, Lille, Madrid, Marseille, Paris, Rotterdam, Venice, and Vienna. There were others too – but I lost count. Well I'd been to a few places in Germany – and, of course, India and Nepal.

The East was probably my saving grace, but for the fact that I'd not seen the Taj Mahal – or anything else with which she had a passing familiarity. She thought that Kyabjé Düd'jom Rinpoche—the Head of the Nyingma Tradition—must be 'equivalent to the Pope'. I'd had no desire to impress her on that basis – but neither could I take issue with her assumption.

"Is he more important than the Dalai Lama?" 'dette asked.

"To me, yes…" I found myself struggling for words *"… and to an unquantifiable percentage of Nyingmas."* PAUSE *"Y'know… this is not really a question I can answer easily – not briefly, anyway."*

"Well – you begin and I'll tell you when I know enough for general purposes."

"Right…" I almost sighed. *"The Dalai Lama… is like the King of Tibet – although not in a secular monarchic sense. You see… because Tibet was a theocracy, he was also the emblematic spiritual head of Tibet. He's now the political head of 'Tibet in Exile'. The heads of the four schools are, however, not subordinate to him in a definitive hierarchic sense.*

"Each Lineage head is supreme in each lineage – and the Dalai Lama doesn't interfere in the separate lineages."

I noticed 'dette glaze over a little and so I curtailed what could have been a three hours lecture at that point – and 'dette—slightly grateful I'd concluded—said *"I can see you're an expert on this subject – but I think that is all I can take in at the moment."*

"I think that's all you really need to know" I smiled. *"I'm far from being an expert, however. In fact – the more I learn the more I realise there is to learn."*

I had some notion that she *might* become interested in Vajrayana – so I thought I should probably be careful with my answers to her questions. My answers needed only serve to allow her interest to grow – as it has grown with Frank Berner. I'd simply answered Frank's questions– and he'd found himself moving inexorably towards the point at which he felt that he could embrace Buddhism. There was no obvious reason why the same could not happen in the case of 'dette.

I was trying to be careful. I'd been advised, in terms of ladies – that I should find someone who would be a practitioner. Well… practitioners were not exactly common in Britain – so all I could hope is that a lady might become interested, if I appeared to be *a sufficiently interesting result of practice*. I could not simply wait for a female Western Nyingma Vajrayana practitioner to appear – as the chances of that were extremely slim.

I spent the first term in a bedsit—in Chesterfield Road, St Andrews—but before the second term commenced, three friends of 'dette's were looking for a 'third girl' to share a rented house in Hotwells. I was—*at 'dette's suggestion*—a postulate as the third girl. 'dette was keen on the idea for various reasons. The first was that she hated my bedsit.

She described it as 'something from *Down and Out in Paris and London*.[1] The second reason was that parking her Rolls Royce Silver Cloud[2] in St Andrews was asking to have it stolen or vandalised. The third was that she'd rather visit me in elegant surroundings. The final reason was that it would be cheaper and more spacious for me.

The renting agency would only accept female applicants – and 'dette's three friends—attending the College of Music and Drama —were unable to find a fourth. Without a fourth, they'd lose the house – and so, I was their last hope. I'd met the ladies briefly in my bedsit and they'd observed my living situation. Their verdict was that I was odourless, hygienic, orderly, and pleasant. I passed the test. They apparently found me 'a little shy' which was a point in my favour. They had no wish to live with someone 'brash, boisterous, bombastic, and bumptious'.

Well… I wasn't too *brash, boisterous, blustering, bombastic, boastful, or bumptious* – but neither was I *shy*. I was simply a little old fashioned. Politeness and courtesy had been schooled into me by my parents. I could have rebelled against that training – but decided that it was something I valued; especially as it was not the standard mode with young people.

I was therefore registered at the agency as Miss Victoria Hillary Simmerson – the part being played by 'dette. My chequebook was inscribed with the name VH Simmerson. I was Victor Howard Simmerson – but saw no reason to use my first names on a cheque book when it was not required.

1   *Down and Out in Paris and London* by George Orwell, published in 1933, is a memoir in two parts on the theme of poverty in the two cities. The first part is an account of Paris and casual labour in restaurant kitchens. The second is a travelogue of life on the road in and around London from the vagrant's perspective, with descriptions of the accommodation of those living in the margins.
2   The Rolls Royce Silver Cloud was produced between 1955 and 1966. Claudette Gascoigne's car was one that had been acquired and refurbished by her father – who was an engineering executive with Rolls Royce.

And so yet another fictional entity came into existence: Chögyam —in addition to being Frank and Victor—was now also Victoria. I was to live in the attic rooms where I was least likely to draw attention should the renting agent come to check the house. Within days I'd moved my clothing and appurtenances into the attic rooms in Hotwells – and was soon to come and sit with my new housemates.

So there I was—sitting in the drawing room of an exquisite house —with three young ladies I hardly knew. They were good long standing friends of 'dette. Penelope had rather an intimidating surname – Cholmondeley, pronounced *Chumley*. She didn't like being contracted to Penny – and as I had no desire to contract her, there was no barrier to our friendship. Rebecca and Meryl had names less intimidating – but equally as impressive: Rebecca Albemarle and Meryl Stanhope. They were evidently top-drawer, upper-circle, or whatever, and I wondered if they'd be anything like Todd – because if they were, I was not destined for a fabulously pleasant time in Hotwells.

Todd Whelcombe and Veranda Nugent were two *middle* to *upper-middle class* persons on the Illustration course – and they'd taken an almost instant dislike to me on the basis that I was a working-class upstart with pretensions above my station. Pretensions as to what, was not clear. My clothing clearly upset them – but for reasons I was unable to fathom. I was later to discover that only Rock celebrities were supposed to affect the sort of attire I wore: *dark blue ankle-length Civil Defence greatcoat; emerald green leather jacket and waistcoat; high-collared indigo moss-crepe shirt; dark brown Cuban-heel Chelsea boots; and, the standard Levi 501 Serge de Nîmes shrink-to-fit button-fly trousers which went with everything.* That was an average costume for me at the time – in fact, from 1966 to the present day. The wardrobe has expanded but it has remained stylistically similar. Be that as it may – how was I to know what Rock celebrities were supposed to wear? Still… 'dette liked me – and she was obviously some sort of débutante.

And I say "Aw come on now, you know about my debutante." / And she says "Your debutante just knows what you need – but I know what you want." / Oh, Mama, can this really be the end / To be stuck inside of Mobile – With the Memphis blues again.
Bob Dylan—Stuck Inside of Mobile with the Memphis Blues Again—Blonde on Blonde—1966

What was a débutante anyway? I had no exact idea. All I knew was that Hotwells was a long way from Bodhanath in Nepal, where I'd studied with Düd'jom Rinpoche. I'd have to research the word *débutante*. I didn't like knowing words by their sound – but having no clear concept of what they meant. I realised it was probably some young lady with a wealthy background – but I was sure it must have some more precise meaning. I checked my dictionary and there it was. I was none the wiser. A débutante is a person making a début.[3] From that description, the members of the Savage Cabbage Blues Band were all débutantes – on the first gig at Weyflood Village Hall.

'Oh mamma can this really be the end – to be stuck inside of Hotwells with Burk's Peerage[4] *Blues again?'* The three ladies sat on the couch looking at me. They'd provided tea. We sat politely drinking it. I remarked upon the weather. They agreed that it was pleasant *"Unusually mild for the time of year."* Meryl added with what appeared to be a well-hidden grin.

"Quite so" I nodded. *"I wouldn't be surprised if there were not a few croci to be seen."*

Meryl's grin then became slightly more visible *"You have an impeccable sense of the Latin plural."*

---

3   *Débutante*—from the French 'female beginner'—is a young lady—either from an aristocratic or upper-middle class family—who attains adulthood and is formally introduced to 'society' for the first time. Débuts vary according to culture and are referenced as debutante balls or cotillions.

4   *Burke's Peerage* – historical guide to the royal and titled families of Britain. Founded in 1826 by John Burke, an Irish genealogist, and continued by his son, Bernard Burke.

Then they all burst out laughing and Rebecca said *"We're all sitting here sounding like something out of Jane Austen."*

"And I'm sure she would be proud of us – as would King Richard II.*"*
Then I quoted:

> *This royal throne of kings, this sceptred isle, / This earth of majesty, this bar of Mars, / This other Ealing, demi-paradise, / This fortress built by nature for herself / Against infection and the hand of war, / This hippy breed, this samovar, / This precious tea set in a silver urn, / Which serves its office to us all / Or as a cake delicious to a mouse, / Against the envy of less grand demands, / This blessed tea pot, this hearth, this tiffin, this England.*[5]

"I didn't expect a literary soirée" Meryl giggled.

"No one expects the literary soirée!" I replied à la Monty Python, with mock drama.[6]

"Oh, that's too funny – especially 'this hippy breed, this samovar'…" Penelope laughed *"I can see we shall be quite jolly here."*

"I hope so" I replied – but thought *'… when I can have a cup of coffee?'* I hadn't got 'round to telling them that I didn't really drink tea that often. I was a useless Englishman. I drank coffee, black and strong with no sugar. It was a custom I'd developed staying with relatives in Germany. Tea was fine—in fact preferable—with a big fried English breakfast, Cornish pasties, or Christmas cake – but for all other purposes: *give me coffee or give me death.* The English drank tea all day long it seemed. A pot of tea is brewed almost every hour of the day – but after my morning pint of coffee I go over to fruit juice, half-and-half with carbonated water.

The ladies had been in residence for a week before I moved in – and now, we were having a 'get acquainted' soiree.

5 Partial parody of Act 2—scene I—King Richard II—William Shakespeare.
6 Parody of Monty Python *'No one expects the Spanish Inquisition.'*

It *had* felt a little like an interview with the three of them facing me – 'til I used the unnecessary Latin plural of crocus. Things eased out at that point – but there was still a slight feeling of wariness. I decided to launch forth again *"I'm glad to be here…"* I commenced *"… it's a lovely house – so thank you very much indeed for being willing to take me in. My bedsit was somewhat grim… so it's nice to have a room that's not multipurpose. I'm glad to see the last of the wretched* OSOKOOL[7] *and the evil* BABY BELLING[8] *too."*

"An 'Oh—so—cool'?" Meryl laughed. *"What's that?"*

"Where ignorance is bliss 'tis folly to be wise…" I laughed. *"It's some sort of attempt at refrigeration. It's a nasty plaster box lined with zinc. It has an aluminium door—lined with polystyrene—which is supposed to keep the heat out. The vile object has a depression—apt word—in the top into which you pour a little water every day. That's supposed to lower the temperature of the inside of the box."*

"Does it work?" asked Rebecca.

"Not as far as I could ever tell – but then I never tested the inside and against the outside with a thermometer, so I suppose I'll never know … I'd say that if it was cooler inside the box it could only have been a degree at the most." PAUSE *"Get thee behind me Satan, I say."*

That made Penelope laugh – and I was delighted to have broken the ice again. *"Welcome to the wonderful world of real refrigerators"* she laughed.

"I'm both privileged and delighted" I replied. *"I shall install a few choice cheeses later, if I may."*

---

7   An OSOKOOL was an un-powered refrigerator. The casing was made of plaster with an indentation into which cold water had to be poured periodically. The natural evaporative effect of the wet plaster meant that the warmer it was outside the box, the more the water on top evaporated leaving the internal temperature the same. They became popular in the 1950s and 1960s because they were far cheaper than refrigerators.

8   BABY BELLING was the name of a combined oven and hot plate with which most British bedsits were equipped. They were cubic in shape and measured roughly a foot in all directions.

"You surely may. We all love cheese – the stinkier the better!" Meryl grinned. *"Can I ask though… do you—always—speak like this…? I mean, sort of old fashioned… or have you taken part in amateur dramatics – sorry I didn't mean to be rude."*

"Not at all… and yes, I've always tried to… speak with some kind of …" words failed me.

"Je ne c'est quoi…?" Meryl offered.

"I don't know what either – commes les femmes françaises perhaps? But yes, that's exactly what I want of my speech."

"You're a hoot!" Rebecca laughed. *"I think we're going to have fun together."* PAUSE *"… I… must say… that I was… a bit—not exactly anxious—but… 'cautious' about how it would work out – but it seems that if we go on the way we've started, it'll all be great fun."*

And so, we talked 'til it was time to go shopping for the evening meal. The ladies decided they'd cook the first meal together to welcome me to the house. They ascertained whether I could cook – and were pleased to hear that I enjoyed cooking and that I was reasonably proficient with the culinary art.

I retired to my room and lay back on the bed. I'd bought a rather fine woven Moroccan bedspread that was almost thick enough to be a carpet. It was full of vivid reds, yellows, and blues – and turned the bed into some kind of settee if I arranged a few large floor cushions up against the wall. The bed was a simple baseboard and mattress – which was ideal for the room. It could easily double as a living room and felt like some kind of palace. I'd survived the introduction and the ladies seemed both friendly and lively. It occurred to me that they'd had as much trepidation as I'd had in respect of our first meeting. I knew that 'dette had assured them that I was house-trained – and lacking in whatever the major obnoxious male proclivities might be. This had been assured on the basis of my bedsit in St Andrews having been constantly as immaculate as a bedsit could be. Male bedsits—as I knew only too well—often stank of fœtid underwear and rank socks.

They were congested with unwashed crockery – and bore little trace of civilization. I'd had the misfortune to enter a few such pits of hell and had almost succumbed to the fumes.

So, this was where I would live for the next three years. What a delight. I picked up a book that was on the bookshelf in the drawing room: Ulysses.[9] I'd read it when I was at school and wanted to find a certain passage I remembered '*… the void awaits surely all them that weave the wind…*' What a phrase… I could base a piece of poetry on that line. I jotted it down in my poetry notebook. Poets often quoted each other – and it was too good a line to pass by. My sense of poetic grammar, however, would have had to have changed the line somewhat. Maybe '*… the void awaits surely, all those who weave the wind…*' or '*… the void surely awaits whosoever weaves the wind…*' or I could play with the idea of 'the void' being a waiter in a deserted restaurant '*… voidness waits on those who weave the wind…*' juggling ideas of the Marie Celeste[10] with a bain-marie.[11]

I read on. A 'stately plump' fellow called Buck Mulligan is found wandering about in his dressing gown. He's shaving – and mocking the Roman Catholic mass, by using his shaving bowl as a chalice. He calls down to Stephen Dædalus. '*Ah… the fellow from 'Portrait of the Artist as a Young Man'…*' I mused.

---

9   *Ulysses* by James Joyce chronicles an ordinary day in Dublin—on the 16th of June 1904—in the life of Leopold Bloom. The title refers to Odysseus *(Latinised as Ulysses)* from Homer's *Odyssey,* and provides parallels between Homer's *Odyssey* and James Joyce's novel: correspondences between Leopold Bloom with Odysseus, Molly Bloom with Penelope, and Stephen Dedalus with Telemachus. James Joyce's stream-of-consciousness style and experimental prose made *Ulysses* a highly regarded Modernist novel.

10 *The Marie Celeste* was an American brigantine discovered—deserted—in the Atlantic off the Azores on December 4, 1872 in seaworthy condition under partial sail and with no lifeboat missing. The last entry in the log was dated ten days previous to discovery. *The Marie Celeste* left New York for Genoa on the 7th of November and was well provisioned when discovered. The cargo of denatured alcohol was unspoiled. The captain and crew's belongings were untouched. No one on board was ever traced.

11 *A bain-marie*—also known as double porringer—is a cooking device used to heat food gently. A bain-marie is also used to melt ingredients for cooking.

I'd studied that book for my English 'A' Level at Virginia Water school… I read on… Stephen Dædalus listens to Mulligan's mock of the Catholic mass, and Mulligan notes the absurdity of Dædalus' surname. Dædalus built the Labyrinth and then the wax wings which allow him and his son Icarus, to escape from Crete. He warns Icarus not to fly too close to the sun or to the sea – but Icarus gets carried away with himself and flies too close to the sun. His wax wings melt and he falls into the sea and drowns. This stuff was just so incredibly rich and vivid! I read on and eventually had to laugh.

> *'Buck Mulligan sat down to unlace his boots. An elderly man shot up near the spur of rock a blowing red face. He scrambled up by the stones, water glistening on his pate and on its garland of grey hair, water rilling over his chest and paunch and spilling jets out of his black sagging loincloth. Buck Mulligan made way for him to scramble past and, glancing at Haines and Stephen, crossed himself piously with his thumbnail at brow and lips and breastbone. 'Seymour's back in town,' the young man said, grasping again his spur of rock. 'Chucked medicine and going in for the army.''*[12]

Some strange old man erupts out of nothing—evidently from the sea—scrambles by without saying a word – and the conversation continues as if nothing had happened. This stuff was Pythonesque – I loved it. A picture formed itself in my mind of the rag-clad ancient who appears at the start of each episode. After taking some while to get close enough to speak, he says *'It's…'* Then they cut to *'Monty Python's Flying Circus'*. Was there influence? Probably not – but it was intriguing to find this parallel.

Time to sit. It took a while to settle into a state undisturbed by thought – which was unusual. The decision not to let that concern me, made itself without my having to make any conscious choice or consideration.

12 From Episode I—Telemachus—Ulysses—James Joyce—1922

The room was new to me – and so the ambience was empty of history; empty of plans. I only recognised it later when recalling the atmosphere of the room – but the colour had intensified as I sat. After some moments of this intensification I found myself in the presence of Khyungchen Aro Lingma. I had no idea how long the vision lasted or when it ceased. I suddenly found myself feeling as if I'd been motionless—*and comfortable in having been motionless*—for an unquantifiable period. As was sometimes the case – I found that there was *something* I knew: a sense of *knowingness without subject*. This room was going to be my home for a few years. The three ladies would become extremely good friends – but I knew nothing about 'dette. I'd had no sense of her being involved in my life at all. It was not easy, at first, to recollect her face – whereas the faces of Penelope, Rebecca, and Meryl seemed as clear as if I had known them for years. What was there to make to such an impression? Nothing – or nothing that I could explore with a quotidian rationale.

I heard the front door open – and slam closed in the wind. A burst of laughter – probably in reaction to the loudness of the door slamming. My name being called. That was probably just as well. I would otherwise have spent useless time pondering something that would not avail itself to pondering. Nothing ever did avail itself to pondering – and yet I *would* persist in the futile pursuit. If the sense of the *vision* revealed itself – it would do so without my conceptual meanderings being involved.

I descended the stairs to greet the ladies. They were in the kitchen when I reached the ground floor, depositing shopping bags. They'd evidentially *gone to town* when they went to town – and I was amazed to see the array of delights they'd procured. *"Tea?"* I asked and they nodded appreciatively. *"Go sit down and I'll be through with the teapot directly."*

Penelope threw herself down in one of the large armchairs *"Blimey…"* she groaned kicking off her shoes *"… my feet are killing me!"*

No sooner were the words out of her mouth than Rebecca pointed a finger at her in mock accusatory indignation *"And did those—**feet**—in ancient times walk upon England's mountains green!?"*

"No!" Penelope laughed in mock consternation *"That's the third time this week!"*

Rebecca and Meryl were cackling almost violently with glee – and I stood there watching them in confusion. Once they'd calmed down, I grinned at them and made my usual curl-of-the-hand to suggest an explanation might be welcome.

"Rebecca just 'laid a william' on Penelope" Meryl explained. *"You see ... well, actually, no, you won't see at all – because you've no idea what I'm talking about."*

"True enough…" I smiled *"so what does 'laying a william' mean – nothing like 'laying a Henry', I trust?"*

"Henry…?" Rebecca enquired.

"Cockney rhyming slang… 'Henry' as in 'Henry the Third'… or 'Richard' as in 'Richard the Third'." Meryl obviously had no idea what I was talking about – so I proceeded *"With Cockney rhyming slang, you leave off the rhyming word – and it's the rhyming word which gives the clue as to the other word… which rhymes with it. It's a code language. It's designed to be incomprehensible if you're not a Cockney."* Meryl still had no idea what I was talking about – so I concluded *"Well… 'third' would have to be described as having fæcal implications…"*

"Oh—right—turd! I see. Oh, that's very funny. I never did get it with Cockney rhyming slang – so you're from London then?"

"No… but where I went to school was close enough to London that stray Cockneyisms drifted – words like 'butchers' which is 'butcher's hook' for 'look'; as in 'take a butchers at this me old china' – china being 'china plate' for 'mate'. Then there's 'plates' – which is 'plates of meat' and means 'feet'…"

A howl of laughter went up and Meryl levelled her finger at me in an accusatory manner *"And did those* feet *in ancient times walk upon England's mountains green!?"*

I was naturally baffled. *"Sorry about this Vic…"* Penelope laughed *"It's silly really – but we have this game that's been going on since… well for years."*

"I think it started when we were in the 3ʳᵈ year at school" Meryl offered *"maybe earlier – I couldn't say…"*

"None of us really remember how it started…" Penelope mused *"but I suppose you know 'Jerusalem'?"*

"William Blake – yes. I've always found 'Jerusalem' quite moving – in fact it's the only hymn I ever liked. Even though it's not really a hymn we used to sing it from time to time in the school assemblies."

"Right…" Penelope continued *"so we have this silly thing where we avoid using the plural of 'foot' – and if any of us ever make the hideous error of pluralising 'foot' then someone can say 'And did those—* **feet** *—in ancient times walk upon England's mountains green!?' and that's called 'laying a william'… William Blake you see… so if we absolutely have to pluralise 'foot' we call them… 'blakes'…"*

The three ladies looked at me apprehensively, as if awaiting sardonic sneer. After a moment I laughed *"Blakes eh… now—that's —extremely funny."* PAUSE *"I love the Surrealism of it."* PAUSE *"Can I join in?"*

"You don't think it's stupid?" Rebecca asked.

"Not at all. I think it's completely loony. I love that kind of thing." PAUSE *"… and it greatly puts me in mind of… Admiral Lord Nelson."*

"Pardon?" queried Meryl *"Why Nelson?"*

"Well…" I replied *"he had a ship called the 'Victory' didn't he – and… I was just wondering… whether he ever renamed his ship when he lost a battle…"*

"What…?" Meryl laughed *"… the Defeat?"*

And—*there*—I had her *"And did those—**feet**—in ancient times walk upon England's mountains green!?"*

"Oh! Terrible! Terrrible! Terrrrible!" Meryl shrieked and flopped back in her chair crying with laughter.

"That's too funny Vic! That's paid you back for 'laying a william' on me, Rebecca!" PAUSE *"We're going to have to watch this one – he's a card!"*

"It—was—a little unfair…" I ventured *"it was a homonym after all …"*

"Homonyms are allowed…" Penelope smiled *"or 'laying a william' would be a little limited."*

"… and—of course—you hadn't actually agreed to my joining in."

"I think we had, Vic… Meryl 'laid a william' on you – and you couldn't get more of an invitation than that" grinned Penelope. *"I think you're one of the girls now."*

"Most happy to be accepted as such" I smiled. *"I think I'll take the weight off my blakes, now I've made the tea – but d'you mind terribly if I—don't —join you…? I'm not much of a 'tea-drinker' you see. Coffee's my preferred hot beverage – and I only drink that in the morning. The rest of the time I drink fruit juice."*

That was fine with the girls, and so I brought through a pint of apple juice – half-and-half with sparkling water.

So this was the world—*the world of the West*—that I was supposed to plumb. That is what Düd'jom Rinpoche had advised. I was supposed to feel at home here – and, that's what I'd done. I felt completely at home – but I was supposed to be a ngakpa as well. Well… it wasn't that I wasn't – but I wasn't sure that I was. I knew it whilst I practised. I'd wind my ngakpa shawl around my shoulders and either sit silently or chant liturgy. That however, was little different to being in the Himalayas. Where was the ngakpa however: when shopping in Clifton; when eating lunch in the Art School canteen; or, when being 'one of the girls' in Hotwells?

71

There was something missing – but I could not name it. I thought about it. I tried to penetrate the conundrum, enigma, paradox, or oxymoron. Maybe there was nothing missing. If what was missing was so intangible that I couldn't identify it – maybe the situation was perfect as it was. Be that as it may, I could not shake the vague idea that I'd lost *what I was in Nepal.* That idea seemed to haunt me. The only thing that dissolved that mind state was Vajrayana practice. That was not entirely due to *the nature of the practice* – but because that was how ngakpas would occupy their time. When I was practising, I knew who I was – but viscerally, rather than conceptually.

"You must 'what is mind?' asking" Düd'jom Rinpoche had commented when I was with him in Nepal. Unless he asked me to do otherwise, I always wrote down what the translator said – word for word. This was for two reasons. The first reason was that trying to convert Tibetan syntax into fluent English whilst it was being spoken seemed to get in the way of trying to understand. Half my mind would be on making grammatical sense of what I was hearing. The other reason was that I simply enjoyed hearing Tibetan syntax because it took me back to being with Düd'jom Rinpoche. Sometimes he would ask me to convert a passage of writing into my own English in order that it could be translated back to him. He did this in order to check my understanding. I ended up however valuing both versions of what he had said equally. Both the Tibetan syntax version and my own reconstructions seemed advantageous to practice.

Düd'jom Rinpoche asked me where the identity was located, that attaches to itself? What was it that identifies 'other' as being other? *"This, Mind – but where Mind finding? Mind must in body finding. When Mind not there finding – there only corpse finding. If mind is in body – where in body? What size? What shape? What colour? Pain and pleasure, all over body feeling – so mind and body interrelated. Mind and body indivisible seeming – but when dying where Mind going?"* I was to question how mind entered or vacated 'body' – and whence? When examining mind, I would discover a web of unquestioned notions.

Düd'jom Rinpoche had said that we cling to phenomena as though they were permanent. That was the style of human derangement. The artificial mental self-identity we create enslaves us. When arriving at a genuine comprehension of mind, one sees that present thoughts are like waves on water or clouds in the sky. They arise. They dissolve. *"When no empty Mind seeing – then Mind only thoughts showing."* It was all there in my notes – and I read sections of these notes every day.

> *"Empty mind: from this, thoughts coming – but thoughts also empty. Mind itself 'khorwa* [13] *fabricating—then Mind's own nature not recognising—and element essences never seeing. When this knowing: then under control bringing – and mastering."*

In order to do this, Düd'jom Rinpoche said that that one must keep one's body in equanimous stasis in order that the spatial nerves[14] would be in natural alignment – and the spatial winds[15] unobstructed. If the spatial winds were unobstructed, then mind would abide in its natural dimension where the spatial essences[16] manifest as primal creativity. Düd'jom Rinpoche's practice instruction often involved me in a great deal of study to 'unpack' what he had said – and I was often entirely out of my depth. I tried asking a number of English-speaking Lamas if they could either elaborate or simplify what Düd'jom Rinpoche had taught – but no one felt able to tackle the subject. It therefore took a long time to understand that he had been describing the perceptual correlate of particle physics.

> *"Namthogs into appearance flashing – like lightning, or like waves on ocean swelling. There is constant movement. We must this arising, immediately recognising.*

---

13 *'Khorwa ('khor ba / samsara)* the experience of cyclic entrapment.
14 Spatial nerves: Tsa *(rTsa / nadi)* the subtle energetic channels of the visionary dimension.
15 Spatial winds: Lung *(rLung / prana)* the subtle energetic winds of the visionary dimension.
16 Spatial essences: Thig-lé *(thig le / bindu)* the quintessential elemental potential of the visionary dimension.

"If failing, then movement unnoticed below surface continuing. This is useless."

If dark thoughtless blankness, experiencing – immediately you must be clearing. Over and over clearing – otherwise meditation will be sinking. If many namthogs arising, not discouraged becoming – not meditation 'failure' thinking. This sign that awareness having. If namthogs unnoticed – this failure. Noticing – not 'failure' thinking. Namthogs not suppressing or eliminating."

Whatever happening – always without hoping or fearing. No uncertainty or anticipation coming. This essential, instruction in heart keeping – then everything fine coming."

Whenever I read these words, I felt confident. I always kept Düd'jom Rinpoche's instruction in my heart. It was impossible to do otherwise – because their value was beyond question. When I read the words, he was always there with me – and I never felt there would ever be any problem with anything. There would certainly be difficulties—and my practice might not evolve as swiftly as could be wished—but there would be no disjunction or falling away from the primary intention to be what Kyabjé Düd'jom Rinpoche intimated I could be.

5

if it's a matter of religion

I packed ngakpa robes.[1] I'd had them since Nepal, 1971. Kyabjé
Düd'jom Rinpoche Jig'drèl Yeshé Dorje instructed me to have
them made and had dictated instructions[2] for the tailor. Wearing
the gö kar chang lo robes therefore, always made me feel closeness
of connection with him.

Robes notwithstanding, I hadn't become stereotypical. That
proved problematic on occasion, when I met Western-born
Tibetan Buddhists who turned out to be stereotypical. This was a
phenomenon I recognised almost immediately. To be fair, they
probably recognised me just as quickly – as someone who didn't
fit. It must be similar to the way in which one can tell if someone
is not of one's own nationality. No matter how linguistically fluent
such a person might be – there are always tell-tale signs of
otherness. I must have come across like Eliza Doolittle.[3] I knew the
technical vocabulary – but I never adopted the mien. Mine was a
peculiar mien – neither culturally Tibetan nor English. It was
something else – but whatever it was, it was not the *mien of the
convert*. I obviously was a convert—I'd converted at Junior School
—but maybe I'd been a convert so long that I no longer acted like
one. I didn't wear a teng'ar like a necklace.

---

1   Ngakpa *(sNgags pa)* robes are the clothing of the gö kar chang lo'i dé *(gos dKar
    lCang lo'i sDe)* the non-celibate wing of the Tibetan Buddhist Nyingma
    Tradition.
2   The precise specification of the robes – is exactly what is worn by the
    ordained sangha of the Aro gTér Tradition in the West. Kyabjé Düd'jom
    Rinpoche Jig'drèl Yeshé Dorje stated that these robes should be worn on all
    occasions associated with Vajrayana.
3   *Eliza Doolittle* is character in George Bernard Shaw's play *Pygmalion*. She is a
    Cockney flower girl, who comes to Professor Henry Higgins asking for
    elocution lessons, after a chance encounter. Professor Higgins agrees, for the
    purposes of a wager, that he can make her entirely acceptable to elite London
    society. At a social function she enunciates perfectly but her vocabulary
    remains unchanged. Professor Higgins passes her Cockney patois off as 'the
    new small talk' – but, when she is leaving, and asked if she is going to walk
    across the park, she replies *"Walk? Not bloody likely!"*

I didn't wear a Nehru jacket, Manali hat, or Kulu shawl. I hadn't taken to saying 'A-cha' for OK. I never said OK in any case – as: alright, fine, certainly, surely, indubitably, positively, absolutely, definitely, or completely, seemed to cover all eventualities. Be that as it may, I just had no desire to judge or be judged. I certainly *made* judgements – but I kept them to myself.

Being a Buddhist occasionally proved problematic with people who were antithetical to Eastern religions. *"Why would you want to follow an Eastern religion rather than that of your own country?"* To which I'd reply *"I thought Christianity came from the Middle East? If I wanted to follow the indigenous religion, it would be difficult because it's more or less lost."* That response invariably roused people's ire – so I decided it was better to say *"I have great respect for Christ – but I never found as good an exemplar of his religion as I found in Düd'jom Rinpoche. I found an exemplar – and so I follow my exemplar's religion. Had I found a Christian exemplar; I would probably be a Christian."* That reply seemed, mostly, to work in terminating argument – but there were always some people who had *something else to say*. Then I'd have to explain that I didn't enjoy discussing religion. It sometimes felt a trifle isolated to be viewed with suspicion from two quarters. I was neither one thing nor another.

I'd naturally told 'dette about being a *non-celibate Tantric priest;* not long after we began our relationship. I'd had to endure her being faintly amused by the idea. She'd wanted me to *dress up for her inspection.* I'd almost refused. Fortunately, I caught myself being the kind of person I don't appreciate – and changed into the maroon waistcoat, white ankle-length widely-pleated skirt, and red shawl with a white panel down the middle.

To 'dette's credit, she didn't titter or make one of her customary Dorothy Parker style remarks *"Well… I can see that you know how to wear these garments… and… I can see that they're not at all the run-of-the-mill Hari Krishna get up…"* PAUSE *"But… it's as if I'm no longer looking at Vic… you look so… removed from… my world. It's as if I don't really know how to talk to you."*

I removed them – and suddenly we were in the usual situation in which clothes are absent. Sometime later I felt I needed to normalise the situation and said *"I hope this isn't going to develop into a fetish with you 'dette."*

"Good god no. I've seen you wear your vestments once and—once—is enough. You can tuck them away now and bring them out when you go to that place in Scotland. You know that religion's not really my thing… unless it's Norse or Celtic."

"Yes. That's why I don't often say anything."

"Oh… I don't mind from time to time – when it's… pertinent to our conversation and not too concerned with my loving everyone one more than I'm inclined."

"Fine with me 'dette" I laughed. *"You're making a fine job of being more like Dorothy Parker than Dorothy Parker – but I don't think you're actually as cynical as you like to appear."*

That caused 'dette to harrumph slightly. I knew that harrumph and knew that she felt unmasked whenever she made that sound. *"Maybe…"* she responded *"… but that will have to remain a subject of mystery if you don't mind."*

"Not a bit – mystery is one of your charming characteristics."

And there we left the subject. It merged with the dusk as the sun dipped far enough below the horizon of houses to flood our eyes with night.

The robes were never mentioned again with 'dette. Nor were the Vajrayana vows that went with them mentioned – apart from the *hair vows* and the vows concerning *other-gender appreciation and respect.* This gender-vow concerns never deriding women. The same applies to women in respect of men. The natural extrapolations of this vow open out into the possibility of romance as a Vajrayana practice; in which men and women in relationship commit to this view.

I explained this to 'dette later in the year—because she had enquired—but she told me she didn't feel any need to bind herself to artificial religious constraints. *"If a person is worthy of respect then I'll give respect—and if a person proves worthy of trust I'll be trusting—but I'll never offer either just to obey a rule. That just sounds like those awful wedding vows to love, honour, and obey."*

"I don't think those vows are so bad – if both partners love, honour, and obey. In terms of Vajrayana however, it's simply the pragmatic extrapolation of a natural phenomenon. When two people are in love – it's quite natural to be open and kind, trusting and respectful… without any artificiality being involved. All a couple has to do, is to continue in courtship mode."

"But what if you have ideas I don't respect? Why should I feel obliged to respect that?"

"Well… you might feel regretful about the lack of respect?"

"Maybe – but what would be the point?"

"… the point…" I really had no idea how to answer that without saying that I wouldn't feel happy in relationship where mutual trust and respect were not the basis. *"The point… is that I prefer the 'atmosphere of romance' to the 'atmosphere where romance appears to be in decline' – and lack of respect seems in decline."*

"You could see it like that – or you could see it as a more mature form of relationship in which respect had to be earned."

"Yes… I'm not saying that respect shouldn't be earned – but… respect is there in the romance when it first appears."

"Alright then—but that's all a bit unreal isn't it—and after a while you just have to be realistic."

"Well 'dette… I suppose that you're naturally more cynical than I am – and… I respect your cynicism in many cases – especially in respect of what I might term 'the air-headedness' of much of the counter-culture."

"So, you see, respect—can—be earned."

"Indeed, it can…" I replied – but 'dette never volunteered a comment on what she respected in relation to me… and, I didn't ask.

Maybe it simply slipped her mind – or maybe she found my penchant for *the reciprocation of respect* a little twee… It was strange to find that I could be regarded as 'cutesy'. It wasn't how I saw myself. I thought I was reasonably lacking in mawkishness. Maybe I was wrong – but I saw nothing excessively saccharine in romance, as I saw it. It sometimes struck me that 'dette and I operated somewhat in reverse in terms of *customary gender orientation*. In certain respects, a feisty lady was exactly what I wanted – but maybe without the tendency to lose tenderness after romantic conquest. That is what seemed to have happened. 'dette seemed to have hardened in some way that was not fabulously endearing. At this point, I realised that I had been uneasy for a while – in terms of what a ngakpa was doing in such a situation. Nepal and Düd'jom Rinpoche seemed somehow more distant when I was with 'dette. At first, I thought it was entirely my fault – and that I should be able to integrate my sense of Düd'jom Rinpoche with every situation. As time passed however, I realised that it was entirely my fault for being in relationship with someone who was entirely closed in terms of Vajrayana.

I would have liked to have talked with 'dette about how wonderful I found these Vajrayana ideas – in terms of what it could mean to society. This was an idea, that—although fundamentally esoteric— was brilliantly pragmatic. Why did men and women seek each other out as romantic partners whilst disrespecting each other? It was ludicrous. It was set up to create dissatisfaction, if not misery. I often wondered what society would be like if men and women genuinely admired and respected each other.

The subject had come up with Penelope, Meryl, and Rebecca. They thought it a remarkable aspect of Vajrayana.

"It's interesting y'know… that you've had this idea in your mind for the year you've lived with us – without our knowing about it…" Penelope mused *"… because it's now… kind of obvious that we've all been influenced by it."*

Meryl nodded *"I supposed we must have taken it on board subconsciously… I mean… maybe it's the way you've never made tedious 'women driver' remarks – or anything else like that."* PAUSE *"I did think at first that it might have been because you were outnumbered or something – but it was so obviously not like that."*

"I think…" Meryl smiled *"… that the fact that you—never—speak like that, has… sort of inhibited me—at least—from making the typical comments that women make about men."* PAUSE *"I mean… I have made that kind of comment from time to time – but mainly in retaliation. I can see what a bore that is – because it's just so unnecessary."*

"Yeah really. I'd say the same" Rebecca enthused. *"It's so strange though… isn't it? I mean – how that works"* PAUSE *"but then… you're hardly the average kind of man anyway."*

"No… I'm not" I sighed. *"That's certainly true… I'm not the average kind of anything – which can often be irritating to other people. It irritates the hell out of Todd and Veranda that I'm neither fish nor fowl nor good red herring."*[4] PAUSE *"But… I wouldn't be any—other—way, unless it would be: being better at what I try to do."* PAUSE *"Y'know… I have to say this… I feel normal here in this house. Most other places… I tend to feel like the geek* [5] *or something…"*

"Geek?" enquired Penelope.

"Yeah—you know—from 'Ballad of a Thin Man'… the Dylan song." [6]

---

4 *'Neither fish nor flesh nor good red herring'* is a 16th century definition of society according to diet. The clergy ate fish, the well-to-do laity ate fowl or other meats, and the peasantry ate red herring. Herrings cured in saltpeter turned red.

5 *Geek* derives from geck which is found in middle English, and from Low and Middle Low German. It means 'fool'. The root word 'geck' still survives in Dutch and Afrikaans as 'gek', meaning 'stupid'. In the Alsatian dialect the word gickeleshut is a fool's hat worn for fun in carnivals.

6 Ballad of a Thin Man—Bob Dylan—Highway 61 Revisited—1965

Then I sang *"... 'You hand in yo' ticket / to go see the geek, / Who walks up to you / when he hears you speak, / And he says 'How does it feel, to be such a freak? / And you say "Impossible!" / as he hands—you—the bone. / And something's happening—but yer don't know what it is—do you —mister Jones'... something like that."*

"And it really feels like that?" Meryl asked with a slightly sad variant of a frown.

"No... not quite like that." PAUSE *"I'm neither at the circus as one of the crowd – nor in the cage... the only thing I can say is that I'm where I put myself – and it ain't nobody's fault but mine."* Then I sang *"I got a bottle in a hole / I got a bottle in a ho–o–o–ole / If I die and my soul belong, / ain't nobody's fault but mine. / Nobody's fault but mine, / Nobody's fault but mine, / If I die and my soul belong, / ain't nobody's fault but mine."* [7]

"You've got a song for every occasion Vic" Rebecca laughed.

"Yes... more-or-less... I see it as a Bluesman's rôle somehow. Blues is some sort of running social commentary that makes emotional sense of the circus of existence."

"Speaking of circus – I still haven't got a clear idea of what the geek is?" asked Penelope.

"Ah... the geek is..." I pause to consider what I was going to say *"The geek's a tragic character – an alcoholic in some advanced state of physical deterioration upon whom the circus seizes. They make a deal whereby they supply all the whiskey the geek can drink in return for his or her being in a cage every night wearing a scrap of rag as a loincloth. The geek would simply have to roar and bellow occasionally – and they'd advertise 'The Missing Link' – y'know the stage of evolution between anthropoids and homo-sapiens."* PAUSE *"They'd sometimes be encouraged to bite the heads off chickens or snakes... They usually didn't live long as they'd die of alcoholic poisoning... and that... was supposed to be their own responsibility. It's a sad story. People were fairly brutal back in the earlier part of the century and before."*

7   Author's mishearing. The original song runs *'I've got a bible in my home, If I die and my soul be lost ain't nobody's fault but mine.'*

"I think they still are really…" Penelope sighed *"I don't think it takes much for people to degenerate to that level."*

"Yes…" I sighed *"I think you're right… you only have to think of Nazi Germany."*

"Exactly" said Rebecca.

"Sorry about that…" I offered. *"I didn't mean to put a crimp in the evening."*

"No—not at all—we have to be able to look at these things… a lot of people don't though… and I think that's what makes them… as hard-hearted and narrow-minded as they are."

"That's true" Penelope sighed. *"You have to pay the price for an awareness of reality… and… part of that is the way so many relationships seem to go – y'know, where men and women live as connubial enemies."*

"Yes… that is horrible to see – and horrible to be around." PAUSE *"The idea with Vajrayana is that men and women have to maintain what occurs in courtship – that is to say, they have to be open minded and kindly before all else. The problem is that although this happens at the start of a romance – it tends to dilute over time. Eventually of course, the romance degenerates and finally disappears. The idea with Vajrayana is that this needn't happen. If you maintain courtship behaviour the romance never has to end."*

"It takes two though…"

The statement had slipped from Rebecca's mouth before she realised it and the room went silent. I knew exactly what she was thinking. The girls knew what Rebecca was thinking. They knew that I knew, as well. The girls had observed how 'dette could be with me from time to time. I sat there not knowing what to say. Rebecca was right – of course. It did take two. 'dette had decided the Vajrayana approach was artificial. She'd told me that she'd rather not take on artificial modes of being – whether they were good for Buddhists or otherwise. So – that left me on my own with my approach to what romance ought to be.

Eventually I replied *"Yes… it does. It takes two."*

The ladies looked highly embarrassed and Rebecca said *"I apologise Vic… I'm so sorry… I shouldn't have said what I said."*

"I'm not such a delicate flower…" I laughed – but the laugh was forced. I laughed merely to put them all at their ease *"… and there's nothing for which you need to apologise. I wouldn't like to think you had to pussy-foot around me or anything. There are plenty of times in life when things aren't exactly… straightforward – and it would be a shame if friends couldn't be open and discuss whatever presented itself."*

"Absolutely Vic—now—how about opening a bottle of wine and drinking a toast to the best outcome for us all? A bottle of rather nice Claret presented itself to me last week and we haven't touched a drop yet."

"Fine notion! I have a bottle of Barolo tucked away—allow me the hoik it out—and we can move from one to the other. The Barolo's quite heavy."

I felt relieved that the subject could be changed and that I wouldn't feel obliged to explain that my relationship with 'dette *was* in question with respect to my religious views on how relationship should be. There was so much *avoidance* with 'dette. I'd felt no pressing need to be too specific about my time in India and Nepal back in '71. That was something I kept hidden from most people – mainly because I preferred to avoid questions. I didn't mind questions if they arose from serious interest – but I revolted against casual curiosity. I also wasn't keen on questions that turned into arguments or discussions in which I was edged into the position of 'apologist'. Someone once asked *'What's Tibetan Buddhism got to offer the world anyway?'* and I replied *'Your guess is as good as mine.'* I purloined that response from Chögyam Trungpa Rinpoche. He gave it in answer to an impertinent question – and I liked the mild humour of it. Anyone one who tags 'anyway' to the end of a question is unlikely to be asking a serious question. It's more of a challenge – and my preference, when challenged in such a way, is to cause the question to evaporate into its own vapidity.

To another impertinent question, Chögyam Trungpa Rinpoche replied *'Quite frankly – fuck you sir.'* I never purloined *that* answer. Not because I felt any disapproval for the response; it was simply that it wasn't my style. Beside which it's not wise to ape one's betters. I'd discovered that the subject of religion makes some people quite belligerent. It makes others pretentious, self-righteous, querulous, sanctimonious, hypercritical, censorious, supercilious, condescending, contemptuous, and self-obsessed. Not that I entirely lack those propensities – but I prefer to live and let live. I tend to feel that my opinions are merely opinions. Opinions are subjective – and therefore I see no reason to make bludgeons out of them. Why would I wish to demand conformity of others?

'dette once took me to task for saying I preferred Bach to Mozart. She explained to me *"World-opinion would not be on your side."*

I responded *"I don't doubt you. I'm quite prepared to accept that world opinion's not on my side."*

"Then why do you persist in holding a contrary view?"

"I don't quite see it as a contrary view. It's merely my preference. I enjoy Mozart a great deal, but were I to be cast away on Roy Plumley's Island – I'd take Bach rather than Mozart."

'dette shook her head – as she did when I exasperated her. So I continued *"I'm not trying to influence the world with my subjective opinion. The world's free to believe whatever it wishes, I suppose."* PAUSE *"I'm not even saying that world opinion is wrong – I'm just voicing a subjective personal opinion."*

"Yes, but opinions have to be backed by fact."

"Yes…" I sighed *"they do… if, you wish to challenge someone else's opinion – but… I have no desire to challenge anyone else's opinion—or, have them demand that that their 'subjective opinion' is objective—and therefore invalidates my non-objective opinion."*

"But—some—things are objective."

*"Yes 'dette – I'm not saying that there are—*no*—objective facts. I accept that terminal velocity is roughly* 120 *miles an hour, depending on buoyancy, texture, and air-pressure. So, an accordion, ukulele, or xylophone—that could, or should, be ejected from an aircraft—are likely to hit the earth at more or less the same time.*[8] *I accept that gravity is a fact and that objects— on this planet—fall at 22 feet 'per second–per second' – even though I have no idea what that mathematical formulation means. I don't have any subjective opinion as to whether it would be more æsthetically pleasing to fall at the rate of* 21 *feet or* 23 *feet per second – because that would be silly. Art —and ideas of beauty—however, are almost entirely subjective."*

"Well – you won't find any intelligent person who would agree to such a proposition."

"You may well be right 'dette… but… I'm not looking for anyone to agree with me." PAUSE *"You see… I don't need approval – I never have done."*

"So, you don't care what I think?"

"Yes… just not terribly much, on this *subject."* 'dette looked at me rather severely at that point. *"I do care what you think of–*me*–'dette… and that isn't* always *unproblematic. I do* care *what* you *think, or I would not be able to be with you. I—*can*—see that there is value in criticality. I— can—see that everything that's called Art can't have the same value. Some works of Art are staggeringly wonderful and others I might not even describe as Art."*

"So, what's the problem then?"

"The problem is that I wouldn't demand that other people agreed with my definition of what constituted Art."

"Maybe not – but there are well accepted criteria."

"Yes 'dette…" I sighed *"… there are – and, sometimes I find myself in agreement with them, and… sometimes I don't. I'm obviously open to guidance – but I won't be ruled… because, in the end it's all subjective."*

"And so we're back to the same thing again – no matter what I say?"

8   I later discovered that my understanding of this 'fact' was inaccurate.

85

"It would seem so 'dette... but... you also have to bear in mind that we're back to the same place – no matter what I say." PAUSE *"We would both seem guilty of the same offence."*

"A neat evasion..."

"I think... 'dette, that I'll not reply to that."

"So, you'll just ignore me."

"No... I just do not choose to respond to caustic accusations." PAUSE *"Y'know... the world would be a far friendlier place if people allowed each other to have subjective opinions without challenging them on the basis of consensus-reality. Blue is—not—a better colour than green or vice versa. Blue and green should—always—be seen, if someone likes that combination – and not, if they don't. It's fairly simple. Human beings are, or should be, free to enjoy whatever subjective criteria they please in their own lives."*

"But there are objective criteria that govern whether value or beauty can be ascribed or not."

"Yes, there are 'dette – and, whilst I have no problem with you holding that view, it does not suit me to hold it."

"But then everything is arbitrary."

"From my point of view—yes—that is often the case – but I'm not demanding that you accept my subjective criteria..." PAUSE *"I've said that I see the value of the criteria you've mentioned – and I'm certainly always open to bearing it in mind. I'm just not open to being ruled by it."* PAUSE *"Just as you are not open to being ruled by a religious framework."*

And so it went on. I was always mild and well-mannered about it – but always obdurate in my conviction. *Consensus-realists* could eat cake as far as I was concerned *(lovely rich fruit cake encased in delicious home-made marzipan)*.

Reaching this impasse with 'dette however always left me feeling ill-at-ease with myself. We'd reached this impasse before – and I could never find a way out of the situation.

I was content for 'dette to hold whatever view she wanted – but she always *had* to launch assaults on my *freedom of perception*. The reason these impasses left me feeling ill-at-ease was that they spotlighted the fact that mutual respect was lacking. I didn't want to lay the blame at 'dette's door for starting it – even though I knew quite well that it was 'dette who'd first found me wanting in terms of impeccability vis-à-vis *my Artistic standpoint*.

I'd tried to take on as much of her view of Art as I could – but she refused to find any value in the view of reality that I was presenting. I knew that this was a major problem in terms of relationship: as it was presented from the point of view of Vajrayana. Couples were supposed to suffuse their relationship with openness and kindness. They were supposed to trust and respect each other with equal enthusiasm. They were supposed to appreciate each other with gleeful delight. I felt that mutual appreciation *had* been there at the beginning of my relationship with 'dette – but that as time passed, she'd wanted to coach me increasingly vis-à-vis what was 'culturally superior'. Bob Dylan and Shakespeare could not be spoken of as being on equal terms – even though I'd never expressed that idea. I would never attribute exact equivalences. I would only speak of equal enjoyment. I enjoyed Bob Dylan. I enjoyed Shakespeare. Ideas of 'higher' of 'lower' were alien. The style of enjoyment was different perhaps – but that was far as I was ever prepared to take it.

Whenever I reflected on this impasse a sense of gloom stole over me. I knew that the dynamics of our relationship were awry from the point of view of Vajrayana. We *should* respect each other – but… we'd failed to do so. There were many things we liked about each other – but 'dette mainly enjoyed me as a sexual amanuensis. That seemed peculiar to me – as that was mainly women's complaint about men. A fundamental sense of respect was lacking. I tried in vain to share the blame for the lack of respect between us, but I knew that I had not been the first to launch offensives – nor had I been the one to continue onslaughts. I actually never criticised 'dette on a subjective basis.

I listened to Fred Astaire songs with her – and even had some idea of what she liked about them. That openness however, was almost never reciprocated.

I merely continued to be *more-or-less as I was* when I met 'dette. At first, she'd found me intriguing – but that intrigue seemed to be moving incrementally in the direction of irritation. My conviction concerning subjective opinions being equal in their subjectivity was not open to be assailed. More to the point, I had no interest in defending my view. I avoided the subject whenever I could – and changed the subject as quickly as possible if it ever looked as if it was going to emerge. One day 'dette rebuked me for being unwilling to see reason.

"Would you just like me to agree with you?" I enquired with a sense of perplexity.

"But you wouldn't mean it."

"Quite" I sighed. *"That – would be the problem, wouldn't it."* PAUSE *"Y'know 'dette… what you—actually—want of me… is religious conversion."* There was a splutter of objection from 'dette at that point but I raised my hand and continued *"No 'dette."* I snapped my fingers and pointed directly at her.[9] *"For—once—I would like you to hear me out – because I have something to say that you might find helpful in terms of understanding where I'm coming from. You want me to embrace the Artistic cultural equivalent of 'the One True God' – because it's your religion. There's no problem with that in one way – but I've never tried to convert you to Buddhism. I mean – how would you feel if I tried to do that? How would you feel if I used the battering ram of Buddhist logic on you – and brought Buddhist logic to bear whenever we disagreed on the subject of the Arts?"*

For once 'dette thought for a moment before replying *"That would be a valid point – all but for the fact that we are both at Art School and not at a Buddhist seminary.*

9   This was a gesture that indicated that I'd reached a point I regarded as terminal. This is a gesture I have not used more than half a dozen times in my life.

"You chose to apply to Art School and—that—is what we have in common. We don't have Buddhism in common – and I've never trespassed on your field of expertise. I've never talked to you about Buddhism and rearranged all the rules of the game in ways that are not concordant with it."

That was something of a shock. The comment 'dette had made was entirely valid. I had no choice but to acknowledge it. *"You're entirely right 'dette. That's… an irrefutable position."* PAUSE *"I'm going to have to dwell on what that means – in terms of… well… Anyhow, I must say I admire your logical acuity – I'll always bow to superior logic."*

'dette sat and stared at me as if I'd just agreed that the earth was not flat. *"So, you're saying that what I just said was right and you have no argument with it."*

"Correct. I cannot contest what you've said."

"So?"

"So… now… I need to dwell on what the implications are."

I sat in silence for a while and 'dette eventually asked *"So… where–are–you in your ruminations?"*

"Well 'dette… it seems that I may well have made an error – and one for which I owe you an apology. It seems that I should not have wasted your time…"

"What—do—you mean?"

"I simply mean that I've been a waste of your time – and I'm sorry for that."

"I still don't know what you mean."

"I mean that I'm not a suitable partner for you – and you'd probably best be rid of me."

"Now you're just being dramatic to shock me – why would you say a thing like that?"

"Well 'dette... you're not interested in Buddhism – and as Buddhism informs the way I see the world. It conflicts with your perspective on Art. As far as Buddhism is concerned the entire realm of phenomenal reality is subjective–or illusory–and so it's not likely that I can ever change my view on that. Because of that I'm going to be a ceaseless cause of irritation to you..."

"Ah!" several moments of silence followed. 'dette was obviously shocked. She recognised the possible termination of our relationship – and, for reasons I never understood, decided to pull back. She knew me well enough to know that I could suddenly become absolutely serious – and capable of making life-changing decisions in which I'd not vacillate.

"Well... if it's a matter of religion..." 'dette harrumphed *"I suppose I will have to... let you have your own ideas on the subject of Art. Far be it from be from—me—to get between a man and his religion."*

"... and... that's—really—alright with you?"

"Well of course it is – I just never realised that this subjectivity thing was of such enormous doctrinal importance."

And that was it. I'd been on the edge of bidding 'dette adieu, with the real sense in which my departure would be welcomed – but it hadn't been welcomed at all. I think that 'dette had no idea at all of how frustrated I'd become – and it seemed that it might be possible that we needn't have any more of these hideously turgid arguments about Art. I took my leave of 'dette and we parted as amicably as if we'd never been conceptually embattled. These contretemps never seemed to cause 'dette long term disquiet. She could act—and really seem—as if they'd never occurred. It was certainly a more pleasant way to be than hanging onto the ambiance of strife – but it also seemed unreal. I knew that Lamas could manifest fleeting displays of something that looked like anger – but 'dette's capacity for the *sudden onset of equanimity* was more likely a question of repression rather than nondual nonchalance. Of course, I'd reciprocate her change of mood as a matter of course – and then... go sit with how that felt.

I remembered the words of Düd'jom Rinpoche *'With each life-circumstance: whatever is enacted, stare directly into the enactment – with all the senses.'*

What would Kyabjé Düd'jom Rinpoche make of my situation? I tried to imagine explaining it to him and the result was that I felt like a complete idiot. The scenario felt like explaining theft to a policeman *"You see officer, it just happened – I put these things in my bag because they looked as if they were the right size…"* Appalling analogy because Düd'jom Rinpoche was as unlike a policeman as I could imagine – but my mindset felt criminal in terms of how I was supposed to be living my life. I was supposed to be learning how to live in British culture rather than merely acquiescing to it. I was merely learning what a mess I was making of life. There was little or no choice involved in my relationship with 'dette – she'd simply made overtures and I'd accepted them. I'd done that before with Helen McGilvray – and had obviously learned nothing from the mistake. Helen McGilvray had corrected the mistake by leaving me – but I had the feeling that 'dette was not going to take the same initiative. I was going to have to be the one to say *Goodbye Forever…*

On the night before I left for Samŷe Ling I started packing. I got out the splendid leather panniers and Meryl chuckled *"You're taking several changes of wardrobe I see."*

"Well yes… but only because I need to take my robes…"

"Robes?" Meryl asked – and then I explained. The ladies all wanted to see them. Then they wanted to see me dressed in them – so I obliged. They were surprised – but not distanced. They were intrigued and asked endless questions. I enjoyed answering them and felt entirely at ease being who I was. I was an art student but I was also a ngakpa. I'd probably always led some sort of double life. After all I planned on a career as an Art School lecturer. I'd planned to return to the Himalayas for longer sojourns when I retired. I could make visits to India and Nepal in the winter recess from Art School every year. It was also possible to take year-long sabbaticals. I'd just see how it all fell out.

It was impossible to plan the rest of my life that minutely – but the general theme of it seemed workable.

"You don't seem..." commented Rebecca *"... like the usual sort of Buddhist—not that I have any idea what a Buddhist should be like—but I'd imagined someone... less... fun to be around."*

"Thank you – glad to hear it. I think you're right though, inasmuch as I'm possibly not the usual sort of Buddhist. I was never the usual sort of hippie, and... I'm probably not really the usual sort of anything. That's always been something of a problem... not for me – but for other people."

"It's never been a problem for us three – it's what makes you interesting to talk to." Rebecca laughed *"I think us three girls would have bored each other to death if you hadn't moved in."*

And so it was resolved. I could just be what I was and life could flow on as it would. Sometimes one of the three ladies would come up to my room when I was wrapped in my shawl and staring into space and simply leave me to it. It became a normal part of *what Vic was* in the house. Sometimes Buddhism would become part of the conversation – but it would arise naturally and dissolve naturally.

I wasn't entirely sure whether I would wear my robes at the 'Kagyu Samŷe Ling Buddhist Centre' or not. I supposed that would depend on what things fell out on my arrival. I supposed I would enquire what the etiquette was and act appropriately. I'd never been to a Buddhist centre in the West before and—whilst it seemed entirely natural to wear robes in the Himalayas—I had no idea what it would feel like in Britain. I put the issue to the ladies.

"I'm curious..." said Meryl *"... you're entirely blasé about unconventional dress and don't seem self-conscious in your white suit – but when it comes to your robes, it all changes."* PAUSE *"That's not a criticism Vic – it's just... an observation. I mean – I find it actually... nice that you have this side of you."*

"Mmm…" I mused, rubbing leather preservative into one of my leather motorcycle panniers. *"I think I just have the terrors of being a holy roller [10] or some sort of creep. I've met a fair few 'alternative-religion' types – and I'd hate to be seen to be anything like that. You see… and I think you understand – that I'm not doing this to be superior or whatever."* PAUSE *"That's what makes me a little tentative."*

"Well just to let you know…" smiled Meryl *"… you don't need to be tentative with us."*

"I shall remove every shred of unsightly canvas immediately." I chuckled – then, in response to Meryl's evident bewilderment I continued *"Did you hear of the fellow who went to his doctor because he thought he was schizophrenic? His doctor asked him why he'd come to that conclusion – and the man replied 'Well doctor, sometimes I think I'm a wigwam and sometimes I think I'm a tepee.' 'Ah' said the doctor 'I see your problem – you're not schizophrenic, you're just too tense.' So be gone all yurts, marquees, bivouacs, and tents of every kind."*

"That's better!" laughed Rebecca. *"That's the Vic we know and love! Pass over the other pannier and I'll give it a rub. I think you should wear your robes in Scotland. After all, it's a Buddhist Centre and if you can't wear them there – where else in Britain could you wear them?"*

I nodded in agreement.

"They were given to you to be worn, so wear them" added Penelope.

"I'd say the same" Meryl smiled. *"Anything we can do?"*

"There are the leather straps… if you like – and then there'll be a little work with BRASSO[11] *on the buckles."*

---

10 *Holy Roller* is 19th century term referring to some Free Methodists and Wesleyans. It describes shaking and boisterous movements under the influence of the Holy Spirit. Holy Rolling is sometimes used derisively by those of other denominations. The term as applied here, is as it was used colloquially in the 1960s and 1970s to mean a 'mindless devotee'.
11 BRASSO—originating in 1905—is a metal polish that removes tarnish from copper, bronze, brass, chrome. It is available either as a liquid or impregnated pad.

And so, we chatted through the evening – sipping wine and working at a leisurely pace on the panniers. It was hard to imagine a better life than this – I felt twinges of regret that being with 'dette was nowhere near as delightful as being with her three friends. I also felt twinges of regret that my time in Hotwells would have to end. Of course, life had to end as well – so who was I to whine?

6
Samŷe Ling

The next morning, I enjoyed a marvellous English fried breakfast[1] cooked by the ladies. An hour later, straddling my 500 BSA chopper, I headed up the Gloucester Road – and thence north on the M5. The M5 turned into the M6. I smiled at a sign that read 'The North' and took it up to 90mph for a short spell. The road was almost empty and so I felt easy about the speed. The M6 finally vanished into the 'A road' that led into Dumfriesshire. I reached Lockerbie by the early evening and hooked off to Eskdalemuir. Then suddenly I saw the sign for Samŷe Ling. I turned into the drive—parked my motorcycle—and entered the lobby of the lovely old building.

There was no one around. I went and sat in the library. The door had been ajar – so it had revealed itself as a place to sit. After a while a head poked round the door *"Are you…"* she looked at a sheet of paper *"Nah-gak-pa Chog-yam or Victor Simmerson?"*

"Both…" I grinned.

"Which would you prefer?"

"Which would be more appropriate here?"

"Either… but I wouldn't know."

"Well Vic Simmerson dresses like this – and… Ngakpa Chögyam wears… ngakpa robes."

"I choose… how do you pronounce your Tibetan name?"

"Ngakpa Chögyam."

"I choose Ngakpa Chögyam then" she smiled. *"My name's Jan—Jan McCulloch—and I'm filling in for the secretary who's… somewhere else."*

---

1   A traditional English fried breakfast used to be: fried, poached, or scrambled egg; with fried mushrooms and tomatoes; with bacon and toast. Baked beans and hash browns are foreign additions.

95

"Nice to meet you Jan."

"Nice to be met" she responded raising her eyebrows in an unexpected manner. She showed me to my room and—as we ascended the stairs—Jan said *"You'll have to tell me what you name means later and how it goes with the robes."*

"My pleasure."

"There aren't many people here at the moment so I'll give you the double room at the end there – it has a nice view of the garden."

"Most kind of you." A room to myself with a double bed. This was major comfort. I was delighted. Jan told me that dinner was available in half an hour *"It's just vegetable soup with toast – but it's good soup unless you're one of these people who can't exist without meat."*

"No, I'm not one of those. I'm happy with most things. Vegetable soup sounds lovely – but… is there butter or margarine for the toast."

"Butter if you're on—my—table – I bring my own. I can't bear margarine." PAUSE *"I think we're going to get on"* she said over her shoulder as she disappeared down the hall.

That was a good start – a friendly person. With any luck they'd all be like this and I'd have a splendid week. I went down to unload my roll-bag that was strapped to the sissy-bars, unpacked, and settled into my room. It was a sparse room – but clean and airy. The last haze of the day was simmering on the window ledge and suffusing the room with hues—I recall—of ripe banana. Most people think that bananas are ripe when they're yellow – but by the time they're entirely yellow they are actually starting to rot. They are perfect when there's still a green tinge on them and they are ever-so-slightly crisp.

I changed into my ngakpa robes and descended into the dining room – and suddenly all eyes were on me. I smiled and wished the gathering good evening and took a seat at what looked like Jan's table. Her knitted shawl was draped over the back of one of the chairs.

96

Jan came and sat next to me after a few minutes, joined by a tall lady of about my age. Jan introduced her *"This is Kate—Kate Partridger—she's from Liverpool."*

Kate smiled *"And I live in a pear tree."*

"Hello Kate, I'm... Vic or Chögyam – whichever you prefer..." PAUSE *"... the 'pear tree' was funny – I enjoy word play."*

"Can't say I'm very good at it..." Kate replied *"... but I was teased so much when I was young that I had to find something to say before the next idiot would ask me if I lived in a pear tree. Now I seem to say it out of habit."*

"Wise choice – but... what d'you say when you—are—wearing a habit?" I replied with a grin.

Jan and Kate both laughed – and Kate said *"I wasn't expecting much laughter here."*

"No one expects the Spanish Inquisition" I replied and felt as if I'd landed in a splendid situation.

Kate had long hair parted in the middle. She wore a collection of layered vests and long-sleeved T-shirts. Jan McCulloch, I judged to be somewhat older – probably somewhere in her mid-30s. She wore what seemed to be a shoulder to floor garment made of thick jersey-cotton. She had an assortment of them—as I was to discover—and wore a different colour almost every day. They all bore a placket down the front like a grandad vest. Wrapped around her torso she wore something vaguely reminiscent of a corset – but it was evidently only modelled on a corset, as it was made of satinised-cotton. These she also had in various colours. They laced up as an old-fashioned corset would have laced – but the laces were decorative rather than functional. It had the effect of turning her dress into an empire-line garment. Kate was from Liverpool and came across rather like a female John Lennon. Jan—despite the Scots surname, McCulloch—appeared to be from somewhere amongst the Home Counties.

"You're wearing your hair differently from the earlier Chögyam" Jan commented. *"Is that how it's worn with robes?"*

I usually had my hair hanging loose. *"Yes—mostly—although if I was going to be a little more formal about it – I'd tie it into a topknot ..."* PAUSE *"... but I thought I looked conspicuous enough as it was... I didn't want to make too much of an exhibition of myself for those who haven't seen ngakpa robes before."*

As we were introducing ourselves to each other—having acquired toast and soup—a man sauntered over and demanded – albeit blandly *"Why are you dressed like that?"* The voice was not one of friendly enquiry. What to answer? *'Your guess is as good as mine? Quite frankly, fuck you sir?'* No ... neither. What about *'It's a socially acceptable alternative to nudity?'* No... not really an occasion for wit – so I went for *"I'd be most happy to explain – but... first... would you be so kind as to tell me why you are asking?"*

He stared at me slightly shocked at being held accountable for his intentions—not knowing what to say—and was about to reply when Jan shot him a severe glance. He turned on his heel—with the look of one who has been reprimanded by a superior—and returned to his seat. *'Not a good start'* I thought. *'Maybe I shouldn't have put the robes on after all...'*

"That's Jarvis" Jan commented with a smile. *"Don't mind him – he's a puppy."* PAUSE *"He wants to get me into bed – but he's—such—a little boy, I couldn't even think of it."*

That was a revelation. I'd never really met a woman with such a force of personality before... apart from Anelie.[2] Certainly 'dette had force of personality – but somehow it was... held in place to cover what I'd discovered to be a vulnerable persona. Jan was clearly entirely self-confident. She was also kindly and didn't have to exert her evident personal authority unless she found it necessary.

2 Anelie Mandelbaum – my Swiss girlfriend in 1966. See *an odd boy*—Volume I— Doc Togden Aro Books WORLDWIDE—2011; and *Goodbye Forever*—Volume I —Chapter 7—euphoria—Aro Books WORLDWIDE—2020.

"Are there… many people like Jarvis here?"

"Yes… a few – but don't let it worry you. It's often like this with converts of a new religion – they're always more ardent than those born to it. They'll get used to you in a day or two – once they've got over 'the shock of the new' as it were." PAUSE *"By the way – that was an admirable response you gave Jarvis. You managed to put him in his place without any aggression – it almost sounds as if you've had experience of making replies like that."*

"Yes…" I sighed. *"I have…"* PAUSE *"I really don't like having to account for myself to a perfect stranger – and I don't like having to defend myself either. It would be easy to bark – but I refuse to be forced into counter-aggression."* PAUSE *"So… the approach I take with such people, is to be warm and smile, but at the same time, call their number – that is to say, ask them why they're saying or asking or whatever. That seems—mainly—to put an end to it."*

"And if it doesn't?" asked Kate.

"Then I address their anger – by… asking them why they're angry. Then they deny being angry. Then I apologise for thinking they were angry and bid them good day."

"Too funny!" hooted Jan. *"Good for you."* PAUSE *"Can I ask where you've come across this kind of reaction before?"*

"I met it in 1971 *when I first went to India… and… I tend to meet it whenever I meet Tibetan Buddhists. It's… not wonderful, I must admit."*

Jan laughed *"They'll soon change their tune when they hear you've got your* BTI.*"*

"… BTI … is?" I enquired.

*"**B**een **T**o **I**ndia. It's like a qualification here – like a BA or Bsc."*

"Ah… Will they be even more impressed that I have my BTN *as well –* **B**een **T**o **N**epal.*"*

"Ooooh yes—that—would have to count as an MA *at least"* Jan laughed. *"They all think I have the edge on everything because I've spent a year in India – but it's silly because it actually means very little."*

"Yes… I've seen that. Some people just smoke themselves into oblivion there – but you must tell me about your time in India. I'd be most interested to hear about it." PAUSE *"I must tell you however that my* BTI *and* BTN *make your time in India look like a* PhD. *I was only there for 3 months – so it's not so much to brag about."*

"I've been to Wigan Pier" Kate added with a mischievous expression.

"I've never been there Kate – but in spite of that some people think I have a Wigan address[3] – but only when I'm wearing robes" I countered and the gathering erupted into a gale of laughter.

"I'm very glad you're not stiff and pompous" Kate remarked. *"The nun here is… well… she's probably alright when you get to know her – but she's not a person I can talk to in this kind of way."*

"Yes… Attila the Nun… and Jarvis is alright too – once you get to know him…" Jan added. *"He's… rather proud of his knowledge."* PAUSE *"It just doesn't reach as far as he thinks. He's read a lot and knows far more than I do about the Kagyüd School. Most of what I know is Theravadin Buddhism and the Mahayana studies from the Soto and Rinzai Zen. I've not been exploring Tibetan Buddhism for more than a year or so …"* PAUSE *"… and—speaking of which—your name and robes…"* PAUSE *"My reason for asking is that I'm interested."*

"I wouldn't have asked you for your reason, Jan – I'd be delighted to tell you as much as you'd like to know."

"Am I included in this conversation?" asked Kate. *"I mean – it's not secret or something. It seems that you can't ask anything here without running into secrecy."*

"Certainly. There's nothing that's secret about me – or if there is… I don't advertise it, only to refuse further disclosure. I hate that kind of posturing."

---

3   A Wigan address – a wig and a dress.

"Good to know" Kate replied. *"I've had about enough of people being superior with me here."*

"And me…?" asked another tall lady with amazingly frizzy hair – hair that reminded me of Steve Bruce. She wore one of those Levi-skirts made by opening up the inside seams of the legs and adding large triangular panels.

"Et tu Brute"[4] I grinned and welcomed her to sit down. She was introduced to me by Jan as Dot—Dorothy Jenkins—and I got the impression that Jan knew everyone there – *and* most things about them. I'd mistakenly assumed that Jan was part of the establishment – but she wasn't. She was a guest – as I was. It seemed that helping out in some way was the order of the day – and I'd been assigned the duty of feeding the yak and dri in the morning. I then had to explain to her what *Et tu Brute meant* – as well as the fact that it meant nothing at all in connection with her. I was merely being surreal. She found that funny and laughed *"Glad we're such a jolly crew."*

Once Dot had taken a seat I explained as much as they wanted to know. I explained the gö kar chang lo'i dé[5] of which I was an ordained member. *"It's a non-celibate ordination…"* I explained *"… it's based on the Tantras rather than the Sutras. The monastic vows come from the Sutras. They're the renunciate vows – whereas the Tantric vows are based on the principle of transformation."*

"Transformation?" queried Dot.

4 *'Et tu, Brute'* is a Latin phrase meaning 'and you, Brutus.' or 'also you, Brutus?'. The quote appears in Act 3, Scene I, of William Shakespeare's play Julius Caesar – uttered by Julius Caesar, at the moment of his assassination by his friend Marcus Junius Brutus.

5 See *Wisdom Eccentrics*—Ngakpa Chögyam—Aro Books inc.—2011. *Wisdom Eccentrics* continues where Volume IV of *an odd boy* finishes and follows Ngakpa Chögyam's life as he proceeds to explore Vajrayana Buddhism in depth under the guidance of Kyabjé Künzang Dorje Rinpoche. The four volumes of *an odd boy* were published with the author name 'Doc Togden' rather than 'Ngakpa Chögyam', by Aro Books WORLDWIDE, 2011–2018.

"Transformation is the principle of Tantra. It's based on the experience of emptiness." PAUSE *"With Sutra the principle is renunciation – because you're renouncing attachment to form in order to discover emptiness. Tantra, then, begins with emptiness and moves toward the nondual experience of emptiness and form."* PAUSE *"So… form—in terms of the dualistic rational—is seen as something that can be transformed rather than renounced."* PAUSE *"Errrm… is this all a bit abstract?"*

"Well…" replied Dot *"… it's a bit deep… but maybe you can give an example of what that would look like?"*

"Well… the basic premise is that we're beginninglessly nondual."

"Enlightened?" asked Kate.

"Yes – I'll explain why I prefer the word nondual later…" PAUSE *"… and so —being beginninglessly nondual—all our neuroses are simply distortions of the nondual state. Because that's the case: all our neuroses partake of the energy of the nondual state – and, therefore, can be transformed through tantric practices."* PAUSE *"So… as to what that would look like… Greed would be liberated into generosity – equanimity and self-realised wealth. Anger would be liberated into clarity – the mirror-like state of undistorted presence. Desire would be liberated into compassion – the 'passion beyond passion' as Chögyam Trungpa Rinpoche described it. Paranoia would be liberated into the unconstrained facility for self-accomplished action… and… wilful-stupidity would be liberated into ubiquitous intelligence in all-encompassing space."*

"And you know all that?" asked Jan.

"No… not in the sense of—knowing it—like knowing my date of birth or anything like that…" PAUSE *"… but… I know it to the extent that I have a —sense—of its reality…"* PAUSE *"… I don't really know what to say beyond that. I know it intellectually – and I'm… working toward knowing it experientially… but that might take the rest of my life."*

"I'm glad you're not one of these people who try to put on a show of what they know" Jan grinned. *"I find that horribly boring."*

"Yes..." I replied. *"I don't even really like explaining it that much—unless someone asks—and then ... I never know how much or how little to say."*

"I'd say you pitched it perfectly" replied Jan. *"Who gave you your ngakpa vows?"*

"Kyabjé Düd'jom Rinpoche [6] *in 1971."*

"I've heard of him – he's the head of the Nyingma School, isn't he?"

I nodded *"Yes—Düd'jom Jig'drèl Yeshé Dorje—he's the incarnation of the great gTértön, Düd'jom Lingpa and really the most amazing Lama."*

"The Nyingma School?" asked Kate. *"Is that different from what happens here?"*

"Yes – this is a centre of the Karma Kagyüd School. It's quite close to the Nyingma Tradition in a lot of ways and many of the Lamas take teachings from each other. The Nyingma Tradition—I'd call it a tradition rather than a school—is the oldest in Tibet. Nyingma means 'Ancient'. I call it a tradition because it's heterodox – it contains many different lineages. There are six major lineages and many minor lineages. The Kagyüd School is one of the three new translation schools. They came roughly a hundred years later..." PAUSE *"... please tell me when I start boring you – because I could blather on all night and all tomorrow about this."*

"People are only boring when they're trying to impress you with their knowledge" Jan smiled *"so if you're happy to go on answering questions, I'll keep asking them – until the evening practice that is."* PAUSE *"Then—as you've got the big double room—we can join you and talk the night away. It's not always easy to get straightforward answers to questions – so I'd like to take the opportunity; if it's on offer?"*

"It's on offer. I'd be delighted" I replied – but it was time then for the evening practice session in the shrine room. We adjourned – and I was delighted to feel as if I was back in Nepal. It was a pleasure to know that such a place existed in Britain.

---

6   Kyabjé Düd'jom Rinpoche Jig'drèl Yeshé Dorje (1904–1987). See glossary *Düd'jom Rinpoche Jig'drèl Yeshé Dorje.*

103

The perfectly organised bands of colour that wrapped the room and a thousand years of meaning, shimmered in the dim light. The chanting commenced – but as I had no text, I simply sat and allowed my awareness to be suffused by the sound.

After the session of chanting the three ladies accompanied me to the double room – which for the rest of my stay became some kind of private club with a gradually increasing membership. And so the evening wove itself on a loom of loquacious fascination.

I told Jan of my own Zen and Theravadin background – in terms of the books I'd read before I went to India.[7] She was intrigued that we had similar backgrounds in terms of our approach to Vajrayana. My approach was different inasmuch as I knew I was headed in the direction of Vajrayana whilst I was gaining what I could from my Zen and Theravadin readings.

"So… there was nothing available on silent sitting in the Tibetan tradition when you started out?" asked Jan.

"No, nothing at all." PAUSE *"Chögyam Trungpa Rinpoche was the first to write about it but it was only slightly touched upon in 'Born in Tibet'… which… came out in '66. That was an autobiographical account of his life in Tibet and his subsequent escape to India."*

"I read that – I really enjoyed it" Dot commented. *"I'd really like to go to Tibet and it would be amazing to meet Trungpa Rinpoche."*

"Yes…" said Jan with a grin *"… he was quite remarkable, in a lot of ways, by all accounts. I just missed him when I came here – but the rumours were quite astonishing."* PAUSE *"Samyé Ling is quite quiet now in comparison."*

"Yes…" I commented. *"I met a lady called Emily on the way back from Edinburgh in '71 and she'd just come from Samyé Ling and she told me about the way he'd shout suddenly as a means of transmission. Like an idiot I didn't change my plans and go straight back up north.*

---

7   See chapter 1 of *Wisdom Eccentrics* by Ngakpa Chögyam – published by Aro Books Inc. 2011.

"I would have met Chögyam Trungpa Rinpoche if I'd done that – but... it was a chance lost. I thought he was going to be staying here indefinitely – and then, suddenly, he was gone."

"That..." said Jan in a slightly wistful tone *"... seems to be a lesson that everyone has to keep learning over and over again."*

"Too right..." I concurred *"... that's happened to me a good few times. I wish I could see the full potentiality of the present moment."*

"Yes..." Jan mused *"... that's the object of meditation – but what would be more difficult—if not impossible—is to know that moment everywhere simultaneously."* PAUSE *"I don't think you can blame yourself for not being omniscient – I mean... how could you have known that Trungpa Rinpoche was about to leave for the USA?"*

That made me reflect a moment *"Well... it's not that I'm blaming myself for lack of omniscience... I think I'm blaming myself for lack of... spontaneity. As it was... I went down to Devon and spent a few days there ... just because I'd been invited."*

"And that didn't turn out well?" asked Dot.

"It turned out very well indeed. I played some Blues at the Art School Folk and Blues Club and had some rather fine conversations." I didn't mention Rose and Valerie. In some ways I hardly believed Rose and Valerie had happened. It's not every day one is coaxed into bed by two young ladies. Casting my mind back it seemed as if it could almost have happened to someone else.

"For me..." I continued *"... it's more a matter of... having a greater sense of spark – or abandonment to the possible."*

"That's important" said Kate. *"I feel that it's good to allow ourselves to be increasingly spontaneous."*

Jan roared with laughter at that idea. *"Yes... well... I think that's a wonderful idea – but sometimes it plays out very badly indeed."* PAUSE *"I've been 'spontaneous' a few times when I've regretted it badly. So I'm not so sure it's wise as a general policy – not unless you really don't mind what happens."*

"Yes… I think you're right, Jan…" I replied. *"I think that would require realisation – or something very close."* PAUSE *"You'd need the 'Three Terrible Oaths' as your experiential framework to carry that off."*

"The 'Three Terrible Oaths?" asked Jan.

"They're connected with Dorje Tröllö – the most wrathful manifestation of Guru Rinpoche: 'Whatever happens – may it happen. Whichever way it goes – may it go that way. There is no purpose.'"

"Wow!" Dot almost yelled. *"That is really—far—out! But I can't imagine living like that."*

"No…" I replied *"Neither can I – but… it helps to bear it in mind when I'm trying to manipulate my circumstances too much just in order to be comfortable."*

"Being uncomfortable is a luxury of people under 30…*"* Jan laughed *"… there's enough discomfort without looking for it."*

"Yeah…" I sighed *"… that's true. Finding an appropriate… equation, is probably what I'd prefer."*

"A balance?" asked Dot.

"Not quite… that would be… wanting things to be equitable in some way … No – what I'd like is to be able to know when to take risks and when a risk is a step too far."

"Wouldn't we all?" Jan grinned. *"That would make for a perfect life."*

"Well…" I grinned *"I don't think I'd object too much to that."*

This was turning into a lively evening and I was most glad I'd come to Samŷe Ling.

"Are there any other books by Trungpa Rinpoche?" asked Dot.

"Yes… Meditation in Action … *that came out in '69 so I got my first real introduction to silent sitting in the Tibetan tradition then."* PAUSE *"Then…* Mudra *came out '72 – excellent poetry book with brilliant insights into the 'view' of meditation.*

"The big blast came just recently with Cutting Through Spiritual Materialism. *That book… nailed my ears to the sky."*

"Fabulous – s'cuse me while I kiss your ears" Dot squeaked and fell back laughing.

"I can see you have a way with words" commented Jan. *"You don't write poetry by any chance?"*

"Yes…" PAUSE *"I have written poetry since I was… at junior school."*

"D'you have anything here?"

"Not really… although I have my notebook with me and there are some examples of work in progress…"

There was a general eager agreement about seeing them so I hooked my notebook out of my bag.

"This is the last verse of a piece I've been working on for a while. It's far from finished so – don't be too harsh in your… well – here it is."

> *Husky feast of topsy-turvy fiasco limitations quivering against the splintered stockades of imperious pluripotential pliancy;*
>
> *In pre-emptive reflection, predestined meanderings reveal well-cooked applications to summon significant verve or vital vivacity;*
>
> *Raucously embroidered moments; catapulted into entrancing impulsiveness of pendulous profanity – bulging with capriciousness.*
>
> *Water-resistant stimuli trounce camouflage of flippant dismay – ingeniously malleable in multifarious surreptitious peculiarity.*
>
> *Burgeoning brazen gleaming smokescreen insinuations – inaudible shrewdness: jumbled adjacency of wreckages at anchor*
>
> *The density of improbability—cavernous with insatiably amiable metaphors—provoke reckless symposia in Chesterfield Road.'*

My audience sat in silence for about a minute.

"Yes…" commented Dot.

"I'd say the same" Kate added.

Jan grinned *"That was… unexpected. I wouldn't have thought you would have been given to write anything quite so… intricate. It's both delicate and dense – and… you obviously have no interest in linear meaning."* PAUSE *"I like that though."* PAUSE *"Could you read it again? I'd like to try – not trying to understand as I'm listening."*

I read the piece again.

"It's weird…" Kate commented. *"It's as if I'm understanding something in words… that vanish as soon as the words move on."* PAUSE *"It seems to be more about the sounds of the words than the meanings."*

"Yes—that's right—although 'fragments of meaning' are intended to emerge from the chaos; as the piece moves on. There are five stanzas in the piece and they all follow the same form."

"The same form?" asked Jan.

"Yes… the word order is maintained with changes to the words. Each stanza in the canto conveys almost the same message – apart from changes that arise out of the juxtaposition of the words themselves."

"Yikes!" exclaimed Dot. *"You're like some sort of psychedelic Einstein or something!"*

"That is far too kind Dot. I think I'd—like—to be something like that – but I think I have a long way to go before I find a voice that really works. My material is still far too… cerebral… and I need to weave it with more ordinariness."

"Such as?" asked Jan.

"Fish and chip papers, fire extinguishers, sewing machines, moles, Victorian paving-slabs, railway compartments, fire engines, roller skates, harpoons, assortments of mismatched cutlery, cuttlefish, box cameras, plimsolls, tailcoats, bagpipes, blowpipes, organ pipes, rotisseries, and… well anything that summons up a contrast to abstractions." PAUSE

"I really love Chögyam Trungpa Rinpoche's poetry – but I daren't allow myself to be influenced too much or I'd just write imitations of what he wrote."

"What d'you think of him driving his car into a joke shop – that was kind of wild" said Kate. *"I mean, it seems that he deliberately set out to crash his whole situation and derail people from their dependence on him. I really like the way he wasn't part of the institution."*

"Mmmm…" I pondered. *"I'm not sure there's any future in trying to understand fragments of Chögyam Trungpa Rinpoche's life."* PAUSE *"For me, the most important thing is his emphasis on silent sitting."*

"Yes – I'd say the same" Jan opined.

"I understand the rest in the same way I'd read Ted Hughes' poetry" I added.

Turning to Kate, Jan asked *"But… what do you understand by 'institution' – I mean, in terms of his not being part of it."*

"Wasn't he against organised religion?" Kate asked.

"No…" Jan came back fairly quickly *"He was against making a big difference between Tibetans and Western people – and he was against his being enshrined as a holy object. He never said anything anti-establishmentarian. He established Samÿe Ling with Akong Rinpoche – so he must have had some idea that it was useful to have an institution that would provide a focus for the study and practise of Dharma."*

I pondered Jan…. She was obviously a serious person. She had a sense of respect that seemed in line with mine. She was a lively good-natured person who wasn't afraid of expressing herself – but neither was she obnoxiously outspoken.

"You like institutions then?" asked Kate.

Jan laughed at the question *"Yes – I eat them for breakfast."* PAUSE *"Why would you jump to that conclusion Kate? I only said what I said because I see no reason to pigeon-hole Trungpa Rinpoche as some kind of anti-establishment rebel."*

"I prefer rebels, I suppose."

"Nothing wrong with that" Jan returned. *"I think 'the other Chögyam' here, might be a bit of a rebel?"* Jan turned to me a little sheepishly *"Sorry about that – I haven't embarrassed you have I?"*

"No, Jan, not in the least. I'm not exactly 'embarrasable'." PAUSE *"In terms of rebelliousness, I think I'm merely a rebel without a clause; or perhaps without a sub-clause. I'm an un-rebellious quasi-Rabelaisian, yet recidivistically recondite, type rebel – riotous yet reserved, if y'know what I mean."* I was doing my best to dissemble with this volley of verbiage.

"Oh—very witty—very witty—but" laughed Dot *"... you're saying you're —not—embarrasable?"*

My dissembling was in vain *"No... although, I can't give any cast-iron guarantees about it."*

"Mmm..." chuckled Dot *"... that sounds like a challenge to me!"*

"I'm... probably... not absolutely averse to that" I laughed *"... but... what do you have in mind?"*

"Let's see..." laughed Dot *"... would you wear a pair of my knickers all day tomorrow?"*

That caused me laughter. *"Certainly—that's no problem—go fetch a pair, the prettier and frillier the better."*

The room convulsed at that and Dot went off to get a pair of knickers. She came back after a few minutes and handed them over. I took charge of them and perused them momentarily *"Yes I think they'll fit."*

Dot then asked Jan and Kate what it was like not wearing a bra – and I realised she was trying another angle on me. *"I've tried it but it's a little painful towards the end of the day."*

"Doesn't seem to make any difference to me – but then my breasts aren't that large. What about you, Jan?"

"That's why I wear this bodice – it gives me some support without restricting me like a brassiere would. I used to wear those ghastly underwired things – and, in the end, I just couldn't stand it anymore."

"As for me…" I opined *"I've never quite understood the need for them – especially the cone shaped things that some ladies wore in the '50s. A lad I used to know at school had a sister who wore those and she looked as if she was concealing weapons."*

"Alright Chögyam—I believe you—you're—not—embarrasable…" Dot laughed *"… you're a complete hoot—you really are—but you're also the unlikeliest man in robes I ever met."*

7

a tributary to the esk

July 1974

I awoke. I sat up immediately. I sang the syllable **A**. I sat for twenty minutes. There was morning practice to attend – or I would usually have sat for an hour. I'd felt extremely clear and alive on waking. The air in Scotland was good – and there was plenty of it in the bedroom as I'd left the window wide open. It had been cold – but there'd been blankets aplenty, so I'd slept well. No dream however. I'd rather hoped that there would have been some dream – and new revelations. *Hope* and *fear* were two of the mundane concerns that I was supposed to reject, and although I was not given to fear to any unseemly degree – I was a devil for hoping; or rather, I was bedevilled by hopes. I had more *hopes* than a hedgehog has quills. I could recognise my mundane hope and not fall prey to giving them undue weight – but the religious hopes were governed by the sense of what was expected of me. I was supposed to be a tulku—the incarnation of Aro Yeshé—but beyond a wealth of infant visions and a smattering of childhood and teenage dreams, there was scant evidence of my being anything other than an average eccentric. I was an artist, a poet, and musician. Such people were commonly inspired by the muse – but if there was more than that, only Düd'jom Rinpoche had confidence concerning it. Of course, I had complete confidence in Kyabjé Düd'jom Rinpoche – and so, by extension, I had confidence in what he declared. That is why I felt frustrated – and why I hoped. I simply wanted to be in alignment with Düd'jom Rinpoche's insight.

That was all in the few minutes it took me to get dressed. Dot's knickers were part of the ensemble – not that anyone would be the wiser. I'd taken the challenge however, such as it was – and descended to the shrine room for the morning practice and thence breakfast.

The morning practice was magnificent. It was not magnificent in any normal sense because these were the early days of Samye Ling. It was simply a room with coloured stripes around the walls – and a small shrine. It was magnificent in placing me exactly where I felt natural. I felt as if I'd come home. I'd left Britain. I was in Bodhanath again – even though Kyabjé Düd'jom Rinpoche was not there. I'd requested a copy of the chanting text in advance and it was duly provided. The text was large and easy to follow. The chant melodies were not familiar – but they became familiar quite rapidly. The residents seemed to like the fact that I had quite a loud voice – and afterwards they said that they'd appreciated my vocal encouragement. Apparently Akong Rinpoche had been pleased by the increase in decibels. I failed to tell them that I'd only chanted at level two on my amplifier.

The practice concluded and we left the shrineroom in silence.

"So… how d'they fit, then?" asked Dot at the breakfast table.

"A teensy low on the hip – I prefer the 'Superhero' style" I laughed. *"Y'now like Superman and Batman. Otherwise, they fit admirably."*

Dot laughed *"He was broad at the shoulder and narrow at the hip – and everyone knew you didn't give no lip to Big John.'* [1]

"Splendid" I smiled broadly. *"I've always enjoyed quotation. It's a good song too."*

This was almost like being back in Hotwells with Penelope, Meryl, and Rebecca – but slightly more riotous.

"You're a new species to us" remarked Jan *"so please don't blame us too much for sporting with you. None of us are used to men who lack characteristic male… inhibitions."*

---

1 *'Big Bad John'* is a Country and Western song in the American folklore idiom, reminiscent of John Henry. Written and performed in 1961 by Jimmy Dean – composed in collaboration with Roy Acuff.

And so our conversations continued. Breakfast being over, I set out on the task assigned – and went into the meadow on the other side of the road. I was to feed the yak and 'dri[2] who lived in a field up a slight incline overlooking Samŷe Ling. That yak and 'dri—son and mother—were not on good terms. They tended to smack their foreheads together in unaccountable rage. The romance of being a solitary yak herder became somewhat lessened after that spectacle. gTértön Rang-rig Togden[3] was said to have been able to wrestle one of those creatures to the ground with his bare hands – but I wasn't that kind of ngakpa.

After feeding the yak and dri, I spent some hours in the candle-making shed where I was taught how to make candles – and then left on my own to make them. I had to use sections of plastic drain-pipe. The insides of the pipe had to be oiled – and then I'd pour in the coloured wax with any perfume I chose. The idea was to tilt the tube to build up shapes that looked like landscapes. I'd then have to weigh the candles I'd made, wrap them – and price them for the shop. I talked with Nigel Reading off and on when he came in to see how I was getting on and he proved to be a friendly person.

"I see you've become friends with Jan" Nigel commented with a certain tone in his voice.

"Yes – she's a most cordial and intelligent lady."

"Probably..." Nigel mused *"underneath that prickly exterior..."* PAUSE *"we're probably all nice people really."* PAUSE *"She seems to need to put men in their place for some reason though – and... I find it difficult to have a conversation with her without running into trouble with her views on gender."*

---

2 Yak (*g.Yag* / གཡག / *male*) and 'dri (*'bri* / འབྲི / *female*) are long-haired bovids (*bos grunniens*) who range across the Himalayas, Tibetan Plateau, Mongolia, and Siberia. They descend from the 'drong (*'brong* / འབྲོང / *bos mutus* or *bos grunniens Linnaeus* / *undomesticated bovid*) which still roam wild.
3 gTér sTon Rang rig rTogs lDan – a Lama in the Aro gTér Lineage of Khyungchen Aro Lingma. Rang-rig Togden was a Body Incarnation of Thangtong Gyalpo, one of the great Nyingma gTértöns or discoverers of spiritual treasure.

"Yes… I think I know what you mean" I obfuscated. I'd run into no such trouble. *"Maybe it's my skirt?"* PAUSE *"Maybe that's given me an easy time conversationally."*

"Perhaps…" Nigel laughed slightly mirthlessly *"… hadn't looked at it like that."*

I was trying to avoid saying that Jan probably just didn't like being objectified and that I found women in general easier to get on with than men. Fortunately, Nigel moved onto other subjects and we talked about the different Tibetan Schools and what made them particular.

As time went by the people there learnt that I wasn't a threat or some kind of imposter in drag. Even Jarvis came round in the end. I never encountered the nun—who seemed to be more-or-less in retreat—but I never sought her out either. She was supposed to be around at certain times – but that never seemed to be when I was around.

I came to learn that Jan—although a guest—was more-or-less a resident. *"I'm staying here to see whether I would like to make my home here. I've been here since January… but, haven't quite decided yet. I'm almost sure I'll stay now because I have a lot of respect for Akong Rinpoche."* [4] PAUSE *"We had Leonard Cohen here not long after I arrived. He was thinking about becoming a monk – but Akong Rinpoche advised him to remain a musician and think about becoming a monk later in life. That's what I like about Akong Rinpoche. He's not out to convert people."*

"I would have liked to have met Leonard Cohen" I commented regretfully.

"To get his autograph…?"

---

4   Chö-je Akong Rinpoche was an incarnate Lama of the Kagyüd School and—
    together with Chögyam Trungpa Rinpoche—founder of Samýe Ling. See
    glossary *Akong Rinpoche*.

This comment caused me to narrow my eyes a little. Jan apologised immediately, asking me—almost deferentially—what my interest would have been. I explained that I admired his lyrics – and that I had tried in the past to write lyrics that worked as marvellously well as those of Leonard Cohen and Bob Dylan.

"My lyrics are always too much like poetry – too complex and stuffed with unnecessary adjectives." Then of course I had to say something about Savage Cabbage[5] and the whole history – and before I knew what was happening interest in my robes was forgotten and a whole discussion on Blues commenced.

"A man with a history—I am impressed—it seems we're sitting here with someone famous" Jan commented addressing her remark to Kate.

"Yeah..." I sighed *"... if you could get famous on history, I'd be famous – but no. I think Savage Cabbage was famous to a small number of people around the London end of Surrey – but that's the extent of it."* PAUSE *"I was never interested in 'fame' per se... but with what was possible through it. I was interested in getting into a recording studio and being able to chat with people like Leonard Cohen – to..."* PAUSE *"... to exchange ideas. To be part of a creative culture..."* PAUSE *"Of course, the money that goes along with fame is always useful. It gives you time and space to be creative."*

"Like the Beatles" Kate commented.

"Yes" I beamed. *"I'm a big fan of the Beatles – from Revolver onward. I would have loved to have been involved with all that. I used to have so many ideas – and... well... that's all in the past now. It was completely wonderful while it lasted – but..."*

The history of the tragic deaths of the lads seemed to touch them quite deeply and Kate commented *"So you've already had your share of teachings on impermanence and death."*

5   Savage Cabbage Blues Band. Doc Togden was the vocalist, harp and 2nd bass player from 1966 to 1970. See *an odd boy*—Doc Togden—volumes I and II—Aro Books WORLDWIDE—2011 and 2012.

"Yes…" I sighed *"… I have, and I'm about as convinced as I need to be."*

Kate smiled wanly and asked *"Is that what made you look at Buddhism?"*

"No—not at all—I've been more-or-less Buddhist from… from about the age of 8."

Then of course I had to explain the whole context with regard to trying to find the religion of the Vikings and finding colour picture books on Tibetan Art at my Junior School and thinking the wrathful awareness-beings were something the Vikings would have liked.

"That is as far from the average story as I ever heard" Jan commented with some surprise. *"You're really quite an oddity – in the nicest possible way, of course"* she chuckled. *"So… with you, it's all about excitement and fascination?"*

"Yes…"

"Nothing to do with compassion or…?"

"No… compassion was never my major interest…" Then I noticed slight shock on Jan's face *"… but not because I have no inclination toward compassion. It's just that there's nothing that interesting about it other than being it. It delights me when I see it in others – but it's not otherwise fascinating as 'a subject'."*

"True…" mused Jan. *"I'd not thought of it like that before."*

"You see…" I continued *"… I take compassion as a 'given'. I'd be motivated to be kind whatever my religious, philosophical, or psychological interest was. I don't see that you can call yourself a human being if you're not motivated by compassion."*

"Fascinating!" Jan exclaimed. *"I can see we'll all be up talking tonight."*

"I'm in…" I grinned *"… but… you may have to excuse me at some point – it's been a long day and I may just fall unconscious. I'm not used to getting up quite as early as they get up here."*

"We'll be merciful" Kate condoled and turned to Jan *"Can I ask how you're going to live here – are you going to find a job locally or…?"*

"No… I have an inheritance. It's not large – but the interest would support me here and I'm thinking it might be a good place to settle if I can get a few wrinkles worked out."

"That's a good situation…" I commented *"and… I think you're good for the place."*

"Do you indeed…" Jan chuckled *"and why might that be?"*

"Well… I was mightily impressed by the way you handled Jarvis the night I arrived. I think that people sometimes need someone like you around in order to get a sense of… realism."

"Realism?"

"Yes… y'know, learning to be real with other people – and… learning how to live with others with some degree of common courtesy."

"I see… yes… Tibetan Buddhism does seem to give—some—people the impression that they have the right to be rude and obnoxious. There's a lot of rivalry and one-upmanship sometimes – but I just laugh at them."

"And—that's—exactly why they need you here."

"Maybe they need you too?" Jan smiled in a strange far-off way – as if she'd had some distant memory of something filter through.

"That would be a nice idea in a lot of ways – but… I'm taking a slightly different direction. I need a job that will take me out to India and Nepal once a year to see Kyabjé Düd'jom Rinpoche. So, I need to find myself a job as an Art School lecturer."

"That makes sense" Jan nodded. *"But now… it's time for a swim! Want to join us? Kate, Dot, and Georgina are going for a dip in the Esk. We like to do that around this time of day if it's good weather."*

"Certainly, I enjoy swimming – but is the Esk deep enough? It seemed quite shallow from the bank down there."

"We go up that little tributary stream. There's a twist in it where there's a deep pool and it's ideal for a swim unless the local farmer is on the prowl. We have to keep a look out for him as he doesn't approve of skinny dipping – and Akong Rinpoche has asked us to be careful not to offend him. That's just so you know – and so you can keep your eye on the horizon. It's been a long time since we saw him, so maybe he's decided to back off."

I sloped off to grab a towel and went to join the party outside. We waded across the Esk and headed up the little tributary. The place where the pool was to be found was not far off and was actually fairly sheltered. There was no real chance of being observed at a distance.

On removing my shamthab Dot shrieked with laughter *"He really —is—wearing my knickers!"*

"What did you imagine?" I asked as I took them off. *"I wouldn't say I'd wear them and then—pretend—to wear them. I don't do things like that."*

"Is everyone in the non-monastic thing like this?" Dot asked.

"I couldn't really comment." PAUSE *"There is no vow against wearing lady's underwear, as far as I know."*

"Woo—hoo!" Dot shrieked as I gained both feet again from having removed the undergarment in question. Dot seemed to be quite a one for shrieking *"I never saw a man who—shaved—before!"*

"Right…" I responded. *"It… goes back to Anelie… my Swiss lady friend… of a long time ago…"* PAUSE *"She told me she thought pubic hair was unhygienic – so… I obliged her by removing it."*

"My–my…" Jan said, accompanied by the familiar movement of her eyebrows *"… you certainly are an obliging man."*

"I do my best… and then… even though we're no longer together—she had to go back to Switzerland—and… well, it's a long story – but anyway… I found it cooler in the Summer and so I continued to depilate."

"I think… Dot…" said Georgina *"… that as Chögyam accepted—your —challenge by wearing—your— knickers – you could respond by shaving."*

"Right on!" Kate called out. *"I think that's only fair Dot – especially after drawing attention to Chögyam."*

Dot looked a little befuddled and turned to Jan *"What d'you think Jan? D'you think that's fair?"*

"Well... I don't think it's fair to make a challenge on Chögyam's behalf. He didn't ask for a return challenge..." and then turning to me *"What do you say, Chögyam – are you going to back this challenge?"*

"No." PAUSE *"My acceptance was my own choice – and, it's not really in my personality to issue challenges."*

"So, it's up to you Dot..." Jan grinned *"... whether you do the honourable thing or not."* PAUSE *"Tell you what – if you do, I'll join you."*

Dot looked cornered. I felt sorry for her. *"Y'know... far be it from me to comment – but this is starting to look a little like how men are with each other..."*

"And who says we can't be like that?" Jan enquired.

"Certainly not me. I was simply commenting – but I would also comment that this is an aspect of male interactions that never appealed to me. I may accept a challenge for the hell of it – but I'd never be inclined to issue one. I hated sport at school and have never understood what's supposed to be so exciting about competition."

"You're an interesting bloke, Chögyam..." Jan mused *"... rather... unpredictable... in a kind of... almost... old fashioned way."* PAUSE *"So you really—don't—like jousting?"*

"No... unless I used a quintain.[6] *I am not enamoured of making anyone feel uncomfortable. I do appreciate challenge – but... I'd really only want to challenge myself."* PAUSE *"That—for me—is the... essential challenge... the challenge of existence – especially when no one knows about it.*

6   The quintain (Latin. meaning 5th), also known as pavo (Latin, Meaning 'peacock') used as training for jousting, where the one would attempt to strike an object with his lance. Even up to the 19th century jousting at the quintain survived in Britain. One variation used water-filled quintain, which drenched the jouster if the blow was inadequate.

"Then… there's nothing to be proved… no one to prove anything, and no one to whom it could be proven."

Jan nodded with a smile *"I can't argue with that… the last part sounds almost like the Heart Sutra."*

"Well…" I laughed *"thank you for such a great compliment – I didn't mean to wax profound or anything."*

"Speaking of waxing…" stated Kate *"… I'll join Jan in the shaving thing – what about you Georgina?"*

"I'm in" Georgina laughed *"but only if we can find a decent razor."*

"Well, there I can oblige you" I offered. *"I have enough fresh blades for you all—some rather fine shaving soap—and a beautiful old badger-hair shaving brush that's soft enough for the most delicate requirements."*

Dot burst out laughing *"Well that's settled—that—then! Looks as if we'll have an interesting… parade tomorrow."*

Jan shook her head with a mixture of mirth and incredulity.

"It's a shame Trungpa isn't here" Kate chuckled. *"I think he would have been at home with all this."*

Jan frowned slightly at that statement – but said nothing. I decided it was time to clamber down the bank into the water. There was a deal of shrieking as the ladies entered the stream – but finally we all submersed. Dot then called attention to the fact that breasts float in the water and asked whether I'd ever noticed the fact. *"Not personally …"* I replied *"… and my experience of skinny dipping has usually been at night – so I've never encountered the phenomenon before."*

"And what do you think of it now you have encountered it?"

"I'd say…." What would an English gentleman say? I pondered for a second *"I'd say… it's one of the wonders of the universe. I'm glad to have improved my education in the witnessing of it."*

This caused great hilarity – and I decided that speaking in archaic mode was by far the safer option in such circumstances.

We then decided that we needed to warm up on the bank of the river. The sun was quite warm and so the water—although cold— was refreshing up to a point – at which it needed relieving.

"I'm not keen on the sun" I commented *"but after chilling out in the river the warmth is quite welcome."*

We sat chatting about all manner of subjects that wove themselves through: Buddhism, Blues, Bach, Buxtehude, Boccherini, and Botticelli. I noticed the succession of B names with unaccountable delight. I also noticed with delight how a group of naked people could sit and discuss the Arts and Buddhism with no evident discomfort. Just before we headed back to Samŷe Ling, Jan gave me a curious look and said *"I'd like to thank you for saying nothing about my breasts."*

That was a little surprising and I was not sure how to respond *"Glad not to have been inappropriate – but... what would there be to say?"*

"You're not one of these men who's frightened of large breasts, are you?"

"Frightened? No, far from it."

"You don't dislike large breasts, then?"

"What's there not to like?"

"Or have a thing about them?"

"What kind of thing do you mean?" I asked, somewhat perplexed. This was a slightly awkward situation for me – even though I considered myself unembarrassable. I had to admit to myself that I was feeling ever-so-slightly tentative. If we'd been clothed, I could have discussed attitudes toward breasts the livelong day – but with Jan right there in front of me, her opulently ample bosom brushing her navel, I felt somehow slightly gauche.

"Well... men of both persuasions seem always to have to—say—something about it." PAUSE *"Bernard—you know, the one with the grey Aran sweater and enormous moleskin trousers—came along one day and decided he had to say something."*

123

That comment came as a relief because a response was simple *"I'd consider any such comment to be crass, and… invasive. Appreciative remarks are only proper within a relationship and unappreciative remarks are vulgar and ungallant to say the least."*

"Bravo!" she gave a small round of applause. *"Listen to this!"* she called out – and then regaled the other ladies with what I'd said.

"How refreshing!" Dot grinned. *"We were—wondering—what it would turn out like when Jan suggested inviting you on our lunch-time swim – we've only ever had a few men along before—and as Jan said—one was very silly."* PAUSE *"Terribly tedious actually…"*

"Well… it ought to be possible for human beings to take a swim without having to behave like junior school children" I observed.

"That's what I've always thought" Jan replied. I nodded in her direction and went to take another dip in the river.

This had definitely been an unusual situation. The main difficulty I was having, was the uncomfortable idea that I was nowhere near as blasé as I thought I was in this sort of situation. I would have thought I was up for almost anything, but… I clearly wasn't – internally at least.

I remembered the words of Düd'jom Rinpoche *'With each life-circumstance: whatever is enacted, stare directly into the enactment – with all the senses.'*

I walked back to Samŷe Ling with Kate. I felt she'd somehow excused herself from the group to atone for her inappropriate remark concerning Chögyam Trungpa Rinpoche. I thought it would be useful to put her at her ease, as I was the one—if anyone —who represented what he represented. As soon as Jan was a safe distance away Kate said *"Jan's quite a powerhouse isn't she – I think you coped very well with being put on the spot like that. And Dot last night with all that thing of hers about her knickers and discussion of breasts and bras."*

"I coped less well than you think." PAUSE *"I was feeling… a little on edge to be honest – but I don't object—too—much to being put on the spot."* PAUSE

"It makes life interesting... and makes me feel as if the '60s haven't entirely disappeared."

"Interesting point of view... but – what would you have said if you were being dishonest?"

"I'd have said 'This kind of thing happens to me quite often, It's not just Naked Lunch.[7] *Where I live, it's naked breakfast, elevenses, high tea, and dinner to boot."*

Kate laughed at that *"Have you ever read Naked Lunch?"*.

"Took a look at it a few years back, but didn't warm to his style – or the subject matter. Maybe I'm some kind of recidivistic Victorian prude – but I don't find the subject of heroin addiction that interesting. Wandering around America in a psychologically debilitated state, is... well... maybe it was novel in the '50s – but now it's vaguely moronic." PAUSE *"Errrm... sorry about that – I should have asked you if you enjoyed the book before I burdened you with my opinion of it."*

"No, I didn't enjoy it that much either – it's just that there are some books that you feel almost compelled to read because it's the done-thing."

"Know what you mean" said Dot who'd just caught up with us *"and that's more-or-less why I took a look at it. It didn't take long though, to arrive at the conclusion that the title is the most interesting thing about the book."*

"That's a little bit like I felt about 'Fear and Loathing in Las Vegas'." [8]

7   *Naked Lunch* by William Burroughs—published in 1959—is a series of loosely connected vignettes. The chapters were intended to be read in any order – the reader following the narrative of a heroin addict called William Lee, who moves through various aliases from the USA to Mexico, and the hallucinatory Interzone. The vignettes are based on William Burroughs' experience of the places he describes and to his ingestion of narcotics.

8   *Fear and Loathing in Las Vegas: A Savage Journey to the Heart of the American Dream* is a roman à clef autobiographical novel by Hunter S Thompson, Illustrated by Ralph Steadman. The narrative follows Raoul Duke, and his attorney Dr Gonzo, as they travel to Las Vegas to explore the American Dream through a drug-promoted alternation of dream and nightmare. It first appeared as a two-part serialisation in Rolling Stone Magazine in 1971, and was published as a book in 1972.

Kate continued *"… apart from the fact that it was more fun to read. Did either of you read that?"*

We both had and agreed that *Fear and Loathing in Las Vegas* was more fun – but not a book we'd be inspired to read a second time.

I really was feeling as if I'd time travelled. I was back somewhere between 1966 and 1969. I had the feeling that I was living inside a play that had been scripted for all characters apart from me – and I was having to ad lib as best I could in order that the play could go on. I'd come to Samŷe Ling for Buddhism – but, apart from the formal sessions in the shrine room, I was getting a hearty draft of the Summer of '67.

I wondered what I was going to say about my sojourn here when I got back to Bristol? I could imagine—somehow—telling Penelope, Rebecca, and Meryl about it… but 'dette…. What *would* I say to 'dette? Then it occurred to me that I didn't like being a person who couldn't be frank about everything in my life. I should not feel constrained in this way – and realised that I'd accidentally allowed myself to be governed by 'dette's sensitivities. After all skinny dipping wasn't a crime and—all things considered—I'd not planned to be the only male in the group. I decided that I'd publish and be damned.

It was no way to live, to be compulsorily clandestine. I hated deceit. I'd hated it as a child.

I hated it as a young adolescent – but it had been forced on me by an overbearing father. Well… maybe that's an odd way to look at it. My honesty or lack of it was my responsibility, but there seemed to be no choice if I was to be as I wanted to be – rather than how my father wanted me to be. And now… my father was no longer a problem. We got on just fine. It had even ceased to be surprising. He was even proud of my success at Art School. Derek had been lavish in his praise of my work and attitude, when my parents had visited the Art School – and… apart from the fact that it was Art —rather than mathematics, physics, or engineering—I'd turned out to be *almost* normal.

He seemed to have developed a blind spot as far as my hair was concerned and my clothes—although weird—were always clean: and ironed where ironing was required. I probably caused the average hippie more consternation than I caused my father – and that was all to the good. I'd never meant to cause him vexation – and now that I no longer provided fuel for his ire, no one was more pleased about it than I found myself to be. Of course, this was good news for my mother – and had been good news since the Summer of '68.

My mind flitted back to that time and, as usual, I remembered Steve and Ron – and Savage Cabbage. I remembered being so glad when I could come out into the open with being a Buddhist.It was so good not to be deceptive. It was such a massive freedom – that the memory of it made me uneasy about where I was with 'dette. I didn't blame her for being as she was. I had no real grievances. One day we'd separate. We'd made no promises or life-long vows – but although we still had fun, we were a little too different from each other. Maybe we should face the mismatches? Were we both taking up each other's time when we could both be available for someone more suitable? Maybe she'd find someone to replace me, who'd be what she *actually* wanted. It even caused me to smile, when I thought of her telling some new beau what a dreadful madman I was. I could even hear her voice '... *and he'd go off on these long and tedious expositions of things that even—he—didn't understand. He was continually philosophising about everything when he hadn't the slightest idea about philosophy...*'

There was a question at the back of my mind whilst I was at Samyé Ling. I'd somehow expected that it would precipitate dreams or visions of Khyungchen Aro Lingma. But so far nothing had occurred. There was no accounting for it. Dreams and visions functioned according to factors that were entirely arbitrary – so there seemed to be nothing I could do to encourage them. If a Tibetan Buddhist Centre could not act as a secondary case – what would?

The secondary causes were mainly those associated with the later 1960s and the Hippie Epoch – but I would have thought that the Tibetan centre would have provided *something that prompted something*. Nothing.

I was disappointed. I was a disappointment to myself. Where was this tulku—this incarnation—of Aro Yeshé? I always had a sense of waiting—of anticipation and expectancy—but continued to feel more-or-less as any relatively typical Englishman might feel, having the experience of an adolescent in the late 1960s. Fortunately I was not having to live up to anything in particular apart from being a decent human being. There was no gompa[9] or ngakpa dratsang[10] over which I was to preside – and no reverential assembly or practitioners looking to me to provide inspired guidance. Himalayan Buddhist tulkus would have had contemporaries with whom they could discuss such matters – but *"I'm on my Todd"*[11] I whispered, feeling the need to speak the words. Still, Kyabjé Düd'jom Rinpoche wanted me to live as a ngakpa in the West – in the Art School environment and whatever followed. At least I was following his instructions. Maybe I was expecting something to happen too soon? I was practising consistently every day. I was studying. I'd come to Samŷe Ling. Then I burst out laughing *"I even jumped at the chance of being a part-time yak herder."*

9   Monastery *(dGon pa)*.
10 Ngakpa college *(sNgags pa grwa tshang)*
11 *Todd*—as in *Todd Sloan*– is Cockney rhyming slang for *alone*.

8

Akong Rinpoche

I had requested a consultation[1] with Akong Rinpoche – as public teachings were not his œuvre. He preferred to offer consultations, as-and-when requested. I wasn't quite sure how I was going to *consult with* Akong Rinpoche. I'd never had a *consultation* with a Lama before – at least not designated as such. I had not thought of it as *a consultation* when I'd met Düd'jom Rinpoche. I'd simply asked for an *audience* – and suddenly, there I was sitting in front of him. Looking back, I cannot quite conceive why the word 'consultation' caused me apprehension. I'd had them with doctors – and Akong Rinpoche was a doctor of Tibetan medicine. Maybe it was the sense of formality I projected onto the meeting – having been told that I should prepare my questions in order not to waste Akong Rinpoche's time.

I'd written down my questions – but the list had become ridiculous. There were too many questions to ask, so I decided to wait until I met Akong Rinpoche. Then I'd just ask the first things that occurred to me from the list. The list wasn't hard to remember because the questions had been in my mind for months.

I knocked on the door indicated—at the appointed time—and a voice requested *"Come in."* I entered. Akong Rinpoche motioned me to sit – after waving away my attempt at prostration. I sat— slightly awkwardly—after having the expected formalities laid aside. He offered me a slight smile and sat gazing at me – obviously waiting for me to ask something. I'd expected to see him in the black chuba he'd worn for the *Observer* Sunday newspaper colour-supplement photograph I'd seen. I could not ask why he was not wearing his elegant black chuba, for two reasons. The first was that it would be discourteous. The second was that it was a stupid question.

---

1   That is what Akong Rinpoche termed *audiences* at that time.

I decided to ask what he thought of my plan to become an Art School lecturer and see my Lama in the winter recesses. He seemed a little distant and noncommittal at first – and replied that he couldn't really say… but… that it sounded as if it would work. I remembered the words of Düd'jom Rinpoche *'With each life-circumstance: whatever is enacted, stare directly into the enactment – with all the senses.'* I told him that I was grateful for his opinion on the matter – as it was important to me that I was able to combine my career with serious practice of Vajrayana.

"Who—is—your Lama?" Akong Rinpoche asked with the very slightest edge of *something* in his voice.

"Kyabjé Düd'jom Rinpoche."

"Düd'jom Rinpoche…" Akong Rinpoche repeated as if he was pondering the plausibility of my statement. I could understand why he might ponder – because Western people would often say they were the student of a Lama merely on the basis that they'd taken an empowerment. This prompted me to follow up with *"… but I also studied for a short time with Ngakpa Yeshé Dorje."*

Akong Rinpoche shook his head slightly as if to say he didn't know the Lama. *"It was Ngakpa Yeshé Dorje who suggested I should go to Nepal and meet Kyabjé Düd'jom Rinpoche and request empowerment."* Akong Rinpoche nodded and looked as if what I was saying was starting to make a little more sense.

"Ngakpa Dorje? Where living?"

"Ngakpa Yeshé Dorje is a Nyingma Lama who lives in McLeod Ganj. He's sometimes known as Khamtrül Yeshé Dorje – and… also, as the weathermaker[2] *of the Dalai Lama."*

"Oh yah! This one I am knowing. Yeshé Dorje – yes. Never meeting – but knowing. And he is sending for study with Düd'jom Rinpoche?"

---

2 Nam-çun *(gNam bCun)* weather manipulation or decupling. Nam-gÇod *(gNam gCod)* weather cutting.

"Yes – because I had been practising Tröma Nakmo with him—alongside Düd'jom gTérsar Ngöndro—and he said I should receive instruction directly from Kyabjé Düd'jom Rinpoche."

"Oh yah! Düd'jom Rinpoche meeting—much respecting—much respecting!" Akong Rinpoche gave me a broad smile. *"He same like His Holiness 16th Gyalwa Karmapa."* PAUSE *"It is good. It is—very—good that Düd'jom Rinpoche is your Root Lama."*

Suddenly everything seemed to slot into place for Akong Rinpoche and his view of me took a much brighter turn. I had become a comprehensible person rather than *a wandering weirdo out to waste his time.*

Akong Rinpoche then asked how much time I'd spent with Kyabjé Düd'jom Rinpoche – and I explained that for four weeks I saw him almost every day for an hour or sometimes more. At this point Akong Rinpoche changed in his demeanour quite radically – and the 'consultation' became relaxed and cordial. The initial sense of suspicion—albeit slight—evaporated and we conversed as if we had known each other for… however long it takes to feel relaxed. Then Akong Rinpoche grinned at me – and made a complete non sequitur.

"You, not 'previous life' asking?"

I could not work out whether he had asked me a question or simply made a statement.

"No, Rinpoche" I answered, understanding him to have stated that I'd not asked him about my previous life.

Akong Rinpoche smiled very slightly *"Oh yah… all Western peoples Tibetan past life wanting – so always asking… but you; you not asking?"*

"No, Rinpoche." My second *'No, Rinpoche'* felt a little stilted and I fumbled round mentally trying to find something more intelligent to say – or something that didn't sound as if I didn't want to have a proper conversation.

Akong Rinpoche smiled again – but a little more visibly. *"Maybe 'past life' already knowing?"*

This was a step too far. Answering *'Yes, Rinpoche'* would have sounded evasive and silly – so I replied *"Kyabjé Düd'jom Rinpoche told me that he knew my previous incarnation…"* As soon as I'd said it, I realised I should have said 'previous life' rather than 'previous incarnation'. I hate the idea of giving my airs by using that word *"but, he told me that I should not speak about it to anyone until a minimum of twelve years had passed. Although…"* I continued suddenly flustered *"I can obviously tell—you—anything – I don't think Düd'jom Rinpoche meant I could not tell a Lama such as yourself."*

Akong Rinpoche smiled broadly and told me that he would not ask me to break my vows with Düd'jom Rinpoche. I'd told him all he needed to know. He required no further details. It was enough for *me* to know whatever Düd'jom Rinpoche had told me – and enough for him as well. This was a huge relief to me because Düd'jom Rinpoche had advised that I need not mention it to Ngakpa Yeshé Dorje. He'd said that such matters were best kept secret until the right time. If such matters were revealed prematurely it could cause obstacles and impede progress with the Vajrayana activities that I needed to fulfil.

Akong Rinpoche returned to the subject of my career plan and told me that it was important for me to address such a question. He told me that he had worked as a hospital orderly in Radcliffe Infirmary to support himself at Oxford University – and that this had obviously been easier than hodding bricks on a building site. He said that it must have been hard for me to engage in such manual work and practise in the evenings. I assured him that it had been no problem for me – as I had been living at home with my parents and so all I had to do was work, eat, and sleep. The rest of the time had been at my disposal for practice. It had also been during the Summer months and so there was no particular hardship.

Akong Rinpoche then said *"Earning money necessary for living – and practice into everyday life incorporating. This important. Balance needing. High-pay work too much time demanding. Low pay work less time demanding – but then not yearly Nepal visits making or time in presence of Düd'jom Rinpoche. Art lecturer – very good idea, then good money and time also having."*

He pointed out that I'd need to find time for solitary retreats. I told him that I'd be able to use the long Summer holiday period for those. I wondered if retreats would be possible at Samŷe Ling – and Akong Rinpoche was pleased to tell me that he would welcome it.

"So, when Düd'jom Rinpoche next seeing – more instructions receiving?"

"After I finish Art School, I will stay a year or so in India and Nepal – or as long as I can, on the money I earn. I'd like to engage in study and retreat… and… in the meantime – I have the practices he gave me."

"These practices every-day doing?"

"Every day, Rinpoche."

"Good. What practices already completing?"

"The Shorter and the Longer Düd'jom gTér Ngöndros – and now I am practising Khandro Thugthig Ngöndro.[3] Once I've completed that, I'll begin Tröma Ngöndro.[4] That is what Kyabjé Düd'jom Rinpoche set down for me to complete before we meet again in 1975."

"Then much success in practice, I am wishing. This very much work…"

3   Khandro Thug-thig *(mKha' 'gro'i thugs thig)* Dakini Heart Essence or 'Treasury of Accomplishments: The Practice of the Profound Path of Khandro Yeshé Tsogyel' is a practice of Dud'jom Rinpoche, revealed as a gong gTér in 1928. This is the main Khandro practice of the Dud'jom gTérsar lineage, and one of the four main gTérma cycles of Kyabjé Düd'jom Rinpoche Jig'drèl Yeshé Dorje.
4   The Tröma Nakmo Ngöndro is otherwise known as Chö-nyid namkha'i long-dzöd lé: Khandro Tröma Nagmo'i yang-sang drüp-pa dorje nying-gi drübpa dorje nyingpo zhag so *(chos nyid nam mKha'i kLong mDzod las: Kha' 'gro khro ma nag mo'i yang gSang gi sGrub pa rDo rJe sNying gi sGrub pa rDo rJe'i sNying po bZhags so)*.

133

PAUSE *"And all at Art School completing?"*

"I hope so. It's not so difficult because there are fairly long holidays and although I work quite hard at the Illustration degree – there's still time every day for practice. I don't have any social life really – not that takes me away from where I live. I don't like pubs because of the cigarette smoke, and so—apart from conversation with the three young ladies with whom I share the house—the evenings are more-or-less free for at least an hour's practice."

At this Akong Rinpoche laughed *"Oh yah 'khordu khandro mangpo 'khor* [5] *"* which I recognised as a line from the Seven Line Song of Padmasambhava[6] and continued *"Khyé kyi jé-su dag drüb kyi: Chin gyi lob chir shè su sol: Guru Pema Siddhi Hung:"*

Akong Rinpoche smiled *"Ha! This well knowing! But khandros practice not disturbing? Not too much khandros always thinking?"*

"Well, I have a lady-friend – and she is a friend of the three young ladies… and that is how I came to be living with them. My lady-friend lives at home with her father."

"Then no problem." PAUSE *"I think maybe Düd'jom Rinpoche robes giving?"*

"Yes Rinpoche – Düd'jom Rinpoche specified these robes—just as you see them—and I had them made according to his instructions in Bodhanath. He then gave me ngakpa ordination." [7]

"Then it is good—this is good—and all well for you. Maybe good you also Gyalwa Karmapa [8] *seeing. He next year coming. London first staying – then teachings and empowerments giving. You must transmission of Vajra Crown receiving."* PAUSE *"This also very important for you."*

I asked Akong Rinpoche if he would be so kind as to tell me

---

5   *Khordu khandro mang-pö khor* means *'Surrounded by kyil'khors of many khandros.'* Khandros are female manifestations of realisation. See glossary: *Dorje Tsig Dün.*

6   See glossary: *Dorje Tsig Dün.*

7   Ngak'chang dompa *(sNgags 'chang sDom pa)*

8   The 16th Gyalwa Karmapa, Rangjung Rigpa'i Dorje (1924–1981) head of the Karma Kagyüd branch of the Kagyüd School. See glossary: *Rangjung Rigpa'i Dorje.*

something about his life as I felt it was important to know about the Lamas I met. I explained that Kyabjé Düd'jom Rinpoche had told me about his life and I had found that to be a great inspiration.

"I was born in Dharak. This village in Riwoche, Kham. You know where Kham?"

"Eastern Tibet, Rinpoche."

"Yah – much natural beauty there. Anyway, at age two they discover as incarnation of previous Akong – Tri-gèn [9] of 'Lho Tsawagang Drölma Lhakang' in Pa-shu, in Chamdo, by monks following instructions of 16th *Karmapa. 1st Akong was Karma Mi-gYö – tulku of ngakpa, founder of Drölma Lhakang."* Akong Rinpoche chuckled at the point and said *"First ngakpa like you—then one monk—then me."*

At four he was taken to Dolma Lhakang to receive an education that included traditional Tibetan medicine. As a teenager he travelled, performing religious ceremonies, and treating the sick. Later he went to the Shéchen where he received transmission of the Kagyüd lineage from Shéchen Kongtrül, one of two incarnations of the first Jamgön Kongtrül. He also received instruction from the 16th Karmapa. In 1959 he fled to India at age twenty. Of the three hundred in his party only thirteen arrived in India. They were so hungry after running out of food on the journey that they had to boil leather shoes and bags to make soup. After some time in Tibetan refugee camps he was asked to teach at the Young Lamas Home School in Dalhousie, Himachal Pradesh, India. In 1963, a sponsor funded Akong Rinpoche and Chögyam Trungpa Rinpoche to travel to Britain where he went to Oxford University to learn English. Chögyam Trungpa Rinpoche had a bursary, but he did not, so Akong Rinpoche worked to support himself – as he had explained previously.

9   The title tri-gè *(khri rGan)* roughly equates to abbot.

"Lama Chime Yönten Rinpoche joined us at Oxford University – you should meet him one day, you would like him. He will establish Kham House in South England and that is closer for you for retreat. It will be…" Akong Rinpoche stood up and went over to his desk where there were some papers. After a moment or two he articulated with only the slightest difficulty *"It is village Ashdon near Saffron Walden, on border of Essex and Cambridgeshire"* and then added *"is near your home where parents living?"*

"It is not—near—exactly, Rinpoche – but it is much nearer than Scotland. My parents live in Farnham in Surrey – and Surrey is one of the 'Home Counties' as is Essex." Akong Rinpoche looked quizzical on the mention of the 'Home Counties' and so I explained *"They're the counties contiguous with London."*

Akong Rinpoche shook his head at the word 'contiguous' so I explained *"They're the counties that have a border in common with London: Surrey, Essex, Berkshire, Buckinghamshire, Hertfordshire, Kent, and Sussex. Sometimes Bedfordshire, Cambridgeshire, Hampshire, and Oxfordshire are included – because they are also quite close to London. Travel is easy between these counties – so it is much easier to hitchhike around them than it is to get to Eskdalemuir.*[10] *However, Rinpoche, I should tell you I have already met Lama Chime Yönten Rinpoche at the Buddhist Society before I went out to the Himalayas."*

Akong Rinpoche beamed at me *"You are liking?"*

I almost replied *'Oh yah very much liking'* because I tended to find Tibetan syntax slightly infectious. *"Yes Rinpoche – he was very kind to me. He was the first Tibetan Lama I ever met. I asked him if he would be my teacher – but he told me that I should go to India and Nepal first. He said that it was too early for me to make such a choice. He said I should meet other Lamas first, and that if I met no one to whom I could relate as a Lama by the time I came home again – he would be accept me as a student."*

---

10 Eskdalemuir where Samŷe Ling is situated is located in Dumfries is a small
    village near the White Esk river in Dumfries and Galloway, Scotland, It is 10
    miles northwest of Langholm and 10 miles northeast of Lockerbie. The area
    comprises high wet moorlands, used for sheep grazing and forestry plantation.

We talked for a little while about my discussions with Lama Chime Rinpoche, and Akong Rinpoche seemed happy with what I told him. He told me that there was always a good relationship between the Nyingma and Kagyüd Schools – and that it was advantageous for both Nyingmas and Kagyüds to take teachings form each other. He spoke about some of the important historical meetings between important Lamas of both schools and how they had exchanged lineages. He emphasised that there had never been a sectarian dispute between the Nyingmas and Kagyüds.

That was to be the one time I spoke with Akong Rinpoche[11] on that visit – but he arranged for me to spend time with Shérab Palden Beru[12] the artist and thangka painter at Samŷe Ling. Shérab Palden Beru gave me instructions in drawing the elements and I spent hours copying the shapes of clouds and water. There were similarities between the cloud and water shapes – but also highly specific and subtle differences. There were difficult angles to be formed in the wave shapes – angles that were almost 90° but came to a minute sharpening. The shapes had to be produced in two swift strong strokes in order to work perfectly and it took me some days before I could produce them to Shérab Palden Beru's satisfaction.

Shérab Palden Beru was born in 1911. This was the year that Aro Yeshé was born – and that was a strange thought. I would be meeting a man, born in the same year my predecessor was born. That idea created a strange conceptual ripple in my sense of time. This was how old I would have been had Aro Yeshé not died in an avalanche – and Ngakpa Chögyam would not have existed. Savage Cabbage would not have existed. Maybe many aspects of life would have changed for people I knew and people I'd never met. Ngakpa Chögyam was the result of an avalanche who seemed to be beset with emotional avalanches almost annually.

---

11 Ngakpa Chögyam did see Akong Rinpoche again the following year when the 16th Gyalwa Karmapa was visiting Samŷe Ling – and again several times in the 1980s when the 16th Gyalwa Karmapa visited.
12 *Shes rab dPal lDan be ru* (1911–2012). See glossary: *Shérab Palden Beru.*

Shérab Palden Beru was born to a nomad family in Eastern Kham and entered Namgyal Ling Gompa at the age of nine. His aptitude for drawing was quickly recognised – and his formal art training in the Karma Gadri[13] style began when he was thirteen.

Shérab Palden Beru said *"Karma Gadri origin is Namkha Tashi from Upper Yarlung. Eighth Karmapa Mi-kyö Dorje prophecy making – Namkha Tashi his emanation and influence extending. Namkha Tashi with Könchog Phendé—emanation of Gyalmo Konjo—studying. From Könchog Phendé, Sharli [14] proportions learning. Namkha Tashi also from fifth Shamarpa Könchog Yanlag and fourth Gyaltsap Rinpoche Drakpa Döndrüp instructions receiving. They are distinctive style advising from many examples: Chinese scroll painting offered to fifth Karmapa Dézhin Shegpa by Chinese Emperor Yong Lo and Da Shelma masks. Da Shelma 'face in moon' meaning. This drawn by many artist who see miracle of third Karmapa Rangjung Dorje showing face in the full moon to Chinese Emperor. Then Chinese scroll painting called Yerwa Rawama, showing kyé-chog."* [15]

Shérab Palden Beru paused for a moment—gazing into space— and then continued *"Karmapa Dézhin Shegpa saying this style must three countries together blending. Forms must be India according. Colour and shading must be China conforming. Composition must be Tibetan conforming. So… thangka tradition Namkha Tashi establishing is Karma Gadri – 'encampment style' of Kagyüd. Gar means encampment – because early Karmapas custom having—and importantly seventh Karmapa Chödrak Gyamtso—of retinues many hundreds people travelling different places with provisions and baggage on yak. At different places encampments of large felt tents making. Very famous and 'huge encampment adorning world' as name calling. So custom and traditions from this 'camp culture' calling – and painting known as 'encampment style' or Gardri."*

Listening to Shérab Palden Beru speak of the encampments was strange. It was strange because it felt as if I'd been immersed in wide screen film at a cinema where the scene had unfolded with enormous richness of colour and sound.

13 *Kar ma sGar bris*
14 Eastern casting method from India.
15 *sKyes mChog* – Arhats.

I'd seen the film Genghis Khan[16] and remembered being spellbound by it. The sense of being there had been visceral – and that same sense arose as Shérab Palden Beru spoke. I'd asked questions about these tent encampments and he told me that some Lamas lived in encampments for months or years – and some lived in permanent encampments. I had no clear idea why I found this encampment style to be ideal. The major romantic association in the West was with the large gompas like the Potala[17] – but whilst I found these building beautiful, they were not as *viscerally intuitive*. There was a sense that I should live in an encampment or that I'd lived in an encampment. The intensity of this sensation didn't arouse any fantasies or even trains of thought. The sensation was entirely sufficient in itself. It didn't fade with time exactly – it simply merged with my experience of being alive. I rarely thought about it afterwards – but only in the same way in which I rarely thought about having been born in 1952. It was simply there as something that I knew – only I did not know exactly what it was that I knew. It was like having once seen the film Genghis Khan – the atmosphere returns whenever I think of the film.

Shérab Palden Beru continued to relate his life story. At Namgyal Ling Shérab Palden Beru attained a high level of skill, not simply in thangka painting, but also Vajrayana music and gar'cham. In 1956, after over thirty years of living at Namgyal Ling, he left for Lhasa, where he stayed for three years, until his escape to India. Once in India, he commenced to paint thangkas in Dalhousie where he was commissioned by Lokesh Chandra to produce a series of drawings of kyil'khor for publication.

16 *Genghis Khan* is a 1965 film directed by Henry Levin and starring Omar Sharif, depicting the life and of the Mongol emperor Genghis Khan. The film also features James Mason, Stephen Boyd, Eli Wallach, Françoise Dorléac and Telly Savalas.
17 *The Potala* is a dzong fortress in Lhasa, Tibet. It was the winter palace of the Dalai Lamas from 1649 to 1959. It is named after Mount Potalaka, the dimension of Chenrézigs. The 5th Dalai Lama inaugurated its construction in 1645 after one of his Lamas—Könchog Chö'phel—died in 1646. Könchog Chö'phel had indicated the site as an ideal seat – situated as it was between Drepung and Sera monasteries and the old city of Lhasa. It was built over the remains the White Palace built by Songtsen Gampo in 637.

He was then instructed by the 16th Gyalwa Karmapa, Rangjung Rigpa'i Dorje,[18] to go to Samŷe Ling, His greatest work can be seen at Samŷe Ling. There, he designed and painted the shrine room and several cycles of thangkas, depicting the Kagyüd Lineage holders, the Mahasiddhas, and the Kagyüd cycles of awareness-beings.[19] The paintings in the temple at Samŷe Ling are large and exquisite in their detail. These paintings took as long as three years to complete. He also helped retrieve, restore, and preserve thangkas from Tibet.

18 The 16th Gyalwa Karmapa, (1924–1981). He was head of the Karma Kagyüd branch of the Kagyüd School. He was born in Denkhok, Der-gé in Kham. In 1931, at the age of seven, he performed his first Black Vajra-Crown ceremony which was witnessed by thousands. The sky filled with rainbows and he took his attendant's sword and tied it in a knot. 'Gyalwa' *(rGyal ba / jina / victorious one)* means a buddha – one who has conquered the four bDud *(devils of duality / maras).*

19 *Awareness being* – see *Wearing the Body of Visions* by Ngakpa Chögyam—Aro Books Inc.—1995.

9

crashing into joke shops

Still no dreams of Khyungchen Aro Lingma or Aro Yeshé – or anything that would illuminate anything. I was conscientiously not disappointed – but I had to keep remembered that I was not disappointed. It was obvious that I was disappointed – but at least I could avoid indulging in it. It was not possible not to care whether I had dreams or not – because Düd'jom Rinpoche had told me I'd have dreams. I was therefore wishing that I was more as I should be – more as the namthars described tulkus. I was an ordinary person in spite of the Arts and in spite of the wonderful experiences I'd had. It's not that I wanted to be special or be seen as special – I just wanted to live up to Düd'jom Rinpoche's vision of what I was. It was as if he saw me as a millionaire – but when I checked my bank account, it looked like that of the typical strapped-for-cash Art student. By extension of the analogy – there had to be some savings account somewhere. The problem there was that I had no details in terms of where to look for it.

I sat for some time in the Samŷe garden pondering the vagaries of existence. I wondered exactly what I would say to 'dette about my time at Samŷe Ling—*interspersed between interludes of silent sitting meditation*—before concluding that it would be better to go to the library and read. There were many books there and some were out-of-print, so I needed to absorb whatever I could from them.

Jan came upon me later—sat alone reading—and stood for a while before interrupting me. *"I want to apologise for how I was earlier…"*

"Not at all…" I interrupted.

"No. Let me finish, I have something that I need to express." PAUSE *"I'm afraid that I got a little carried away with my own sense of freedom. I'm so used to having to fight men—just to be heard or to express an opinion—that I always grab the bull by the horns and make sure they know exactly who I am right from the beginning.*

141

"Then I feel I have to spar with them and put them in their place in order that they don't even think of trying to get the upper hand with me. So… anyway…" PAUSE *"I shouldn't think that just because I can say anything I like, that—that—gives me the right to say whatever I like."*

"Good of you to say so."

"It must have made you feel quite awkward."

"Yes… it did make me feel a little… I can't say I wasn't… a—little— awkward – but… I'm glad it happened… in retrospect that is. I'm glad that I was able to…"

"Respond with such poise and—dare I say it—dignity."

"Well… I don't know about that – I was just trying to make sure that it all remained light-hearted and…"

"Exactly – and that's exactly what you did" Jan interrupted me with some gravity *"… and… there's something else too… I keep forgetting you're ordained – and… that I shouldn't treat you like everyone else. The problem is that you don't act in… I don't know how to say this – but I expect ordained people to be more… aloof and distant – and so… I forgot to be appropriate."*

"Well now, I certainly—am—glad you that you—did—forget. I wouldn't have had it any other way."

We both laughed and whole episode dissolved into the texture of… something almost unfathomable.

"Y'know… what I can't quite work out about you… is that you seem— mainly—to be… not quite an innocent abroad – but… you seem almost shy and innocuous – and then you suddenly come out of nowhere with a kind of complete conviction and determination that's… almost a shock – because it's so unexpected…" PAUSE *"… like what you said about not wanting to prove yourself or challenge anyone but yourself… It's as if you shift between a slightly gauche twenty-year-old to being an early-middle-aged man-of-the-world."*

I was silent for a moment – not really knowing what I thought of what Jan had said *"Thank you for… what feels like a compliment."* PAUSE *"I've never really looked at myself in that way – but I understand what you're saying."* PAUSE *"I think what you're describing as 'middle-aged' is just me when I have something—real—to say. I don't give my subjective opinions any weight – and, don't like arguing. So I mainly come across as… innocuous – although I'd rather call it inoffensive. If I've got something—real–to say I don't like to be offensive about it either – but I won't be talked down by anyone… well… not counting Düd'jom Rinpoche of course. So… if it came to an argument I'd simply welcome any gainsayer to their own point of view… and retire from the discussion on the basis that I have no need to be right by making someone else wrong."*

"That's what I mean" Jan laughed. *"You just whipped into your Mr Hyde mode – not that I mean anything…"* Jan ran out of words.

"I understand…" I laughed *"… and I think that the Dr Jekyll and Mr Hyde analogy—can—be understood in a… benign light."*

"Thank you." Jan grinned and departed for the secretarial duties she had to perform.

The days went by. They went by, in a way in which everything merged. Daily swims occurred – but sans any attempts to make the ngakpa blush. Dot came and sought me out one afternoon after a swim. There was a knock on my door. *"Come in"* I called and Dot entered. *"Can I… have a word?"*

"Absolutely" I replied.

Dot sat down looking quite serious and said *"I'd like to apologise for all that stuff with the knickers and bosoms… and everything else. Jan's already talked with you about it… she told me… but we both felt bad about it afterwards."*

"That's kind of you – but there really is no need to apologise – I said the same to Jan."

"Yes… she told me… but there is…" PAUSE *"I do feel I need to say something personally…"* PAUSE

143

"We both felt that we should have remembered that you wear robes and all that – and that it's not good to act in that way with an ordained person."

"I wouldn't have had you act in any other way. It was an experience I've never had before – and it didn't exactly kill me, did it?"

"No... but... still..."

"It's more likely to be my fault..." I stated matter-of-factly *"or... being as I am."* PAUSE *"I mean... I'm just—not—very 'spiritual' in the way that word is usually understood. It's not that I'm not—serious—about what I'm doing – but I don't like being stereotypical. I like to be... normal. I used to be a Bluesman you see... and... I still am – even though I'm not on stage. The Bluesman is still there in me. He's not gone away or taken some vow never to boogie again. In fact, Düd'jom Rinpoche told me I must always sing and play Blues. So, as far as I see it you were just responding to me as I am – and that is perfectly fine with me."*

Dot nodded *"... and... there's something else too..."* PAUSE *"it's not just that I forgot you were ordained – it was also... a reaction I have to ordained people. I've met quite a few that I haven't liked – because they were pretentious, inconsiderate, high-and-mighty, or condescending. So... I tend to avoid ordained people – because if I don't avoid them... I tend to take them on – and... with you I got caught off my guard... Not that that's your fault at all – but I found myself being able to have a normal fun sort of conversation with you and so... I got caught in wanting to see if you were really what you appeared to be. I've found the robed people I've met, put on a show. They hide behind a façade of correct statements and never say anything real."* PAUSE *"So... anyway—as I said—sorry for acting like that."*

"That's kind – but apologies really aren't necessary" I smiled. *"I've met people like that in India and Nepal too – and not even ordained people. I generally avoided Western people when I was out there – because of just what you're saying... so I understand entirely."* PAUSE *"By the way..."* I said standing and going over to the window ledge *"Here is your nether-garment—freshly laundered and aired—but, alas, not ironed."*

Dot laughed and took charge of her underwear *"Now—I—feel embarrassed"* she grinned.

"You know… I just caught myself in time when you gave my knickers back."

"Yes…?" I enquired.

"I almost told you that, if you liked – you could keep them as a souvenir."

We both laughed and Dot departed—laundered knickers in hand —to attend to her kitchen duties. There was the vegetable soup to prepare.

I sat thinking about these apologies. They had seemed entirely unnecessary – but charming and kindly. I was touched by their heart-warming genuineness – but felt awkward about the deference. I didn't feel comfortable with deference. And then, the *Dr Jekyll and Mr Hyde* description. In one way, I recognised that I could appear like that—*where both characters were kindly*—but, what did it mean about what I was – or what I was becoming. I was definitely leading a split life in all areas apart from the house in Hotwells – where I could be the ngakpa, artist, and fellow who played sitar. Penelope, Rebecca, and Meryl didn't defer to me. We could discuss Vajrayana, painting, music, literature, poetry, or anything within the field of the Arts.

Hotwells was the only place in the West where I felt I was not a covertly heterodox anomaly. There was nothing to hide or to play down. My Vajrayana practice was an occasional part of the domestic soundscape. Vajrayana emerged in conversation quite naturally from time to time – but that was not typical of the world I inhabited. I decided that part of my practise would have to be relaxing with the fact that I would always be an anomaly. I would never fit – and yet, I could always fit, simply by being cordial with everyone. Todd and Veranda were not typical of the kind of human beings I met – and so they were simply a creative challenge. I was going to have to learn to be *the creature I was* in as many situations as life threw at me. That was one meaning of Vajrayana.

Düd'jom Rinpoche's advice to live in the West—*as a ngakpa*—was a colossal amorphous challenge. Colossal is probably an overstatement – but 24 hours a day, 365 days a year, felt colossal.

It was, of course, feasible in retreat in the Himalayas—or in some quite rural location in Britain—but living as part of Western culture threw up an array of bizarre situations. Even coming to a Tibetan Buddhist Centre in Scotland was replete with bizarre situations. Admittedly nothing had occurred that caused me to break precepts[1] or damtsig[2] – but certain situations simply felt anomalous.

I could be a ngakpa on the open road on my motorcycle and in the bathroom engaged in ablutions; conversing with the three ladies in Hotwells; and, shopping in Broadmead – but what was I, when dispiritedly debating with 'dette; or, here at Samŷe Ling in whatever unlikely scenario unfolded next? What would Düd'jom Rinpoche make of these passing scenes – and how would I explain them all to him? Maybe he would not ask – but if he did… what would I say? I would mainly have to say that I fell in with situations and then experienced the outcome of that default pattern. At least I knew it was a default pattern. The problem was that the default always occurred when I felt as if I was merely being relaxed. The word *chatral*[3] came to mind – along with the idea of *chatral 'dré bu'i theg pa*.[4] Being a duty-free yogi was both path and result – but I was a long way from actualising that; even as 'path'. Yes, I could float around the world participating in this-and-that without employing *too many of my critical faculties* – but that was not *chatral*. That much was clear to me – but the opposite was no better. To forge ahead with preconceived conditions that had to be perfunctorily met in terms of precisely how each situation had to be… What use was *that* in terms of any kind of approach or pretension to Dzogchen?

1   Labpa-nga *(bsLab pa lNga)* the five precepts. See glossary: *precepts*.
2   Damtsig çu-zhi *(dam tshig bCu bZhi)* the 14 Root Vows of Vajrayana.
3   Chatral *(bya bral)* free of occupations; free of any deliberated actions; transcending obligations; free of duties; effortlessness.
4   Chatral 'dré-bu'i thegpa *(bya bral 'bras bu'i theg pa)* the vehicle of fruition in which nothing needs to be done – the vehicle of effortless fruition, free from both activity and inactivity; action and nonaction; effort and effortlessness.

There was no use in drifting with the tides of circumstances – or in attempting to steer where there was no evident road. Whilst at Bristol Art School, of course, there *was* a road – and that made life simple. Outside that context however, anything could happen. To come to an understanding of my culture and my epoch – I had to be *open to anything happening*. If I sheltered myself from the wilder side of existence – I would never be able to teach anyone how to live as a tantrika in the West… when, eventually, the time came to teach.

Chögyam Trungpa Rinpoche had plunged into the Western cultural milieu and emerged with a mode of expression which was unsurpassed. Chögyam Trungpa Rinpoche had crashed his car into a joke shop[5] during his engagement with Western culture – so maybe I wasn't proceeding as badly as I thought. Maybe I was *crashing into joke shops* in my own way? Chögyam Trungpa Rinpoche took the joke shop crash as a symbol emanated by Mamo Ékajati[6] – but what could I say? I saw no symbolism in my life that would equate with that – other than appearances of Aro Lingma. She had appeared after my failed assignation with Papa Legba at the Runfold / Badshot Lea crossroads – but not at Samŷe Ling. She had appeared once in Germany when I fell asleep on my motor cycle at 70mph[7] – but the appearance was so brief that I was left uncertain as to whether she was simply the lights of a fast car on the other side of the carriageway. If it had been her, she saved my life – but I could never be entirely sure. I was wary of attributing meaning where there might be no meaning.

---

5 Before leaving Samŷe Ling, Chögyam Trungpa Rinpoche crashed into a joke shop in Dumfries having blacked out at the wheel. He sustained injuries that left him partially paralysed on the left side of his body for the rest of his life. He described this event as a pivotal moment which inspired the direction of his teachings – and the need to open up completely and directly to Western students.
6 *ma mo e ka dza ti* or Ral gÇig ma *(ral gÇig ma)* one of the major triad of Nyingma protectors – the ma gZa rDo gSum or Ma gZa Dam gSum: Mamo Ékajati, gZa Rahula, and Dorje Legpa.
7 See *Goodbye Forever*—Volume I—Chapter 11–*Ich Bin Ein Dichter*—Aro Books WORLDWIDE—2020

Would Düd'jom Rinpoche see my life in the West as analogous to Chögyam Trungpa Rinpoche's joke shop crash – or would he be disappointed that I lacked common sense? The joke shop crash had left Chögyam Trungpa Rinpoche partially crippled – and, I wondered, *'Was that the price one had to pay?'* I had not been crippled by any of my *joke shop crashes* – or at least, it didn't seem so. I had no way of knowing, however, what damage I might have sustained in terms of subtle obstacles to practice. I would only know that when I next had the chance to speak with Kyabjé Düd'jom Rinpoche. With that thought I opened my satchel and pulled out my book of the teachings I'd received from Düd'jom Rinpoche.

> *The qualifications of disciples with respect to whether they can authentically follow a Lama.*

> *Disciples need impartiality and intelligence. They must be straightforward. They must abandon any tendency to decisive partiality – such as being friendly to those in their own sangha and unfriendly to those in other sanghas.*

Well… I was impartial and relatively straight forward – but my intelligence was not exactly pronounced. Derek Crowe told me that he expected me to obtain a 1st in my Illustration degree – but that was down to hard work rather than intelligence. I might be intelligent for Chögyam Trungpa Rinpoche to crash into a joke shop – but I could not say the same about my multiple fiascos. They were merely dim wittedness.

> *Disciples need to be able to distinguish between Vajrayana and Tibetan culture without rejecting what is cultural when that culture is supportive of Vajrayana.*

I had a deep love of Tibetan culture – but I was confident that I was clear about what was Vajrayana and what was Tibetan culture. I was also confident that I appreciated the aspects of Tibetan culture that were supportive to Vajrayana. I'd applied myself with diligence to making texts covers, drum tails, and so forth. I did not consider these things unimportant or unnecessary.

Some people I'd met took the view in which externals had no value. This seemed to be a form of ultimatism that I decided was bogus. To deify objects was an error – but not to appreciate their value was also an error. It was spiritual materialism to collect spiritual appurtenances as if owning them was concomitant with meditative experience. To reject spiritual appurtenances however, was to sever one's relationship with phenomena. Materialism concerned existential-perceptual territorialism – but the mere rejection of objects was no substitute for abandoning the materialism of the 'ME Project'.

> *Disciples need to be powerfully inspired by the tradition and feel respect (method) and trust (wisdom) for Lamas who teach the tradition they seek to follow.*

I felt assured that this was the case in terms of where I found myself to be.

> *These are the fundamental qualifications that are necessary. When practice leads to the development of meditative experience however, there will be further qualifications that will be naturally arising. With experience of rang-jung rigpa strong confidence and natural diligence will arise. From this, greater intelligence will arise – that is free of referentiality.*

That all sounded plausible in my case apart from *the greater intelligence, free of referentiality.* I could not say that this was the case. To all intents and purposes I still felt like the kind of dolt who crashed into the joke shops of life without any transformative result.

> *Disciples have great respect, and practice the secret mantras. Their minds free of discursive thoughts, they are undistracted.*

Great respect, yes – but my mind was not free of discursive thoughts and I was frequently distracted.

> *Disciples keep damtsig, are diligent in the practice, and act concordantly with the Lama's speech.*

In that I passed muster on all counts – apart from diligence. It's not that I wasn't diligent – but that I was aware that my use of time was possibly open to question.

> *Good disciples have vivid certainty and conviction – great joy and keen interest with regard to the Lama and instructions. They have an eager yearning for the result of practice. They have confident consummate trust that entertains no doubts and is unaffected by petty circumstances. They are thus completely ready to receive transmission.*

> *Disciples are firmly committed in their determination to realise nonduality – they are constant in their practice and never postpone it.*

What I lacked in this itemisation of qualities was *eager yearning for the result of practice*. Somehow the only eagerness I possessed was the eagerness not to disappoint Düd'jom Rinpoche. Most people seemed to want 'enlightenment' in the next hour – or the next day, week, month, or year. I didn't quite understand how one could want what one could only understand intellectually. If the idea of enlightenment was merely intellectual one couldn't know what one was wanting

Certainly, I'd rather be free of pain under all circumstances. Certainly, I'd rather be happy under all circumstances. In general, I was about as happy as I needed to be. I did want to be a good practitioner – but whatever accomplishment there might be, I only really wanted it in order that Düd'jom Rinpoche would feel that his time had not been wasted. I was, however, constant in my practice and almost never postponed it.

> *As they have the intelligence and clarity to investigate the profound meaning of reality, experiences and realisation come to them easily. They have little attachment and clinging to mundane happiness or possessions such as food and clothes.*

Intelligence again. I had a low IQ – so I fell at that hurdle. I had a high level of interest in investigating reality – but experiences and realisation did not come to me easily. Nothing came to me easily. Learning to play guitar—even to a modest standard—had not come to me easily. I had not reached the lowest professional standard. On Blues harp, I was reasonable but I'd never be a Little Walter. I had to work hard at everything – and anything I learned took me at least twice as long as anyone else. As to having little attachment to mundane happiness or possessions such as food and clothes – I was not sure where I was on the scale. I liked happiness well enough – but I was generally content with whatever life threw my way. I enjoyed my food and I enjoyed my clothes – but… it didn't feel excessive. I'd have to talk about that with Düd'jom Rinpoche – because I had no idea whether I was taking an extreme point of view in respect of 'little attachment'.

> *Since they have great respect for the Lama and the yidam, they are open doors through which transmission enters. They have cleared all doubt and hesitation regarding the path of the secret mantras and are therefore able to engage in profound practices. Since their minds are not prey to mundane conceptualisation in terms of obsession, aggression, or indifference, they are not distracted.*

Great respect for Kyabjé Düd'jom Rinpoche the Düd'jom gTér yidams was unquestionable. I had no doubt or hesitation – but my mind… that was prey to fascinations and whimsies. Probably not aggression or indifference – but, a healthy dose of obsession. The standard terminology for obsession, aggression, and indifference were lust, hatred, and ignorance – but these terms never sounded quite right to me. They were somehow redolent of the seven deadly sins. I could also use the terms attraction, aversion, and indifference – but ignorance seemed out of place in the list. Ignorance was simply lack of information – and being laden with information was not actually guaranteed to make a person kinder or more open minded. Being highly knowledgeable could often make people less charitable and benevolent – more intolerant and prejudiced.

I'd witnessed that in those who fancied themselves as scholars. For me the word ignorance only worked if re-cast as *ignore-ance*. One could not necessarily be blamed for one's lack of education – but one could be culpable of indifference to learning or indifference to reality. To be indifferent is to shut down and close off to the world – and that was entirely anathema to me. So, my main problem was the spectrum of attraction, lust, passion, and obsession. I was like a moth to the flame.

> *Disciples keep their promises and do not contravene the root and branch damtsig that they have taken. They do not tire of practising the profound path and never go against the Lamas' instructions. It is disciples with just such qualifications as these that one should accept to teach. Their opposites are bad disciples.*

To the best of my ability, I could feel at ease with that. I kept my promises to Düd'jom Rinpoche. I maintained damtsig. I always followed his instructions – but… only as far as I was able with my level of capacity. That was always the problem. Of course, at school in the mathematics class, I'd always say *"I tried my best"* and the response would be *"Your best is not good enough, Simmerson."* Of course, the mathematics teacher was not unreasonable – because 'my best' was based on a severe lack of interest in mathematics. What I called 'my best' was merely the best I was prepared to offer to mathematics. With regard to Kyabjé Düd'jom Rinpoche however – I really was trying my hardest. It occurred to me that, as a tulku, I should have greater capacity than I evidently had. It did not occur to me to doubt my recognition as 'the incarnation of Aro Yeshé' because I had no doubts concerning Düd'jom Rinpoche. His pronouncements were not in question – it was merely 'me'. Maybe 'I' was merely the result of Aro Yeshé having died in an avalanche. Maybe that was why I was so limited in my capacity – and so easily seduced by the shine on the passing moment. I was also far too easily seduced by ladies. All ladies had to do was smile at me. I had no sense of appropriateness.

My answer was always 'Yes' unless I was already in a relationship – and so here I was again with a relationship I should either have avoided or left. There was nothing so terribly 'wrong' with Claudette Gascoigne – she was simply not suited to someone whose life looked like mine. She would never be interested in Vajrayana – and I should have made a polite exit when I discovered that. Of course, Claudette was also deluding herself. I was not her ideal by a long stretch. The man to have suited her would have been a modern-day George Bernard Shaw, William Walton, Noël Coward, or Oscar Wilde – or anyone radically witty, intellectual, and massively culturally well informed. I was not that person. I was not *that person* – but was I *that disciple*? I certainly wanted to be – and I certainly was to the extent that Düd'jom Rinpoche had accepted me as such. I decided, at this point, that I'd contemplated Düd'jom Rinpoche's teaching thoroughly. I let out a deep sigh of… some nameless mixture of feelings. I concluded that although I was not a good disciple –I was not the opposite of all the qualities enumerated, therefore I might not be such a bad disciple; despite my propensity to crash into joke shops.

10
Ocean of Space

The initial training in iconographic drawing continued. Shérab Palden Beru began gave me a great deal of information and I wrote it all down in my note book. Before beginning to draw the first necessity was to determine the vertical axis. This is followed by the horizontal line and the four outer lines for defining the edges of the painting area. There were eight major lines two diagonals, the vertical, the horizontal, and four bordering lines. The first two of the eight major lines were the diagonals lines drawn from one corner of the canvas to its diagonal opposite. These two lines facilitated the placing of the vertical and horizontal. To draw these lines one needed a chalked marking string.[1] A simple chalk line could be obtained by rubbing a length of string with chalk powder between the hands. The chalk line mostly used was a string passed through a powder bag.[2] This bag would be made of leather or cloth – and the marking powder was often a mixture of ochre and charcoal. Lines were made by positioning and snapping the string against the canvas. These lines were called dry lines.[3]

When using a chalk line with a stick one could use both hands to hold the string – and twang it to create the line. One fastened the string to the end of the stick – so a notch needed to be incised at the end of the stick and a groove around the circumference of the stick. To fasten the string to the stick the string should be pulled through the notched end, and then wrapped and tied around the shaft within the groove.

1 *thig rKud*
2 *thig rKyat*
3 *sKarn thig* as distinct from the 'wet lines' produced with a wet marking string. Wet lines were only used in mural painting.

There is much more information I could give here – but it would be better placed in a book about thangka painting.[4] Suffice it to say that I took copious notes.

I continued candle-making, yak feeding, and engaging with the morning and evening meditation sessions in the shrine room.

There was plentiful conversation. I provided a great deal of information about Vajrayana in the Nyingma Tradition. People had almost endless questions. The books available at the time were mainly academic and incomprehensible to anyone apart from scholars – and it was by no means certain what benefit scholars derived from them. The atmosphere at that time was characterised by an enormous hunger for useful knowledge concerning Vajrayana.

After my meeting with Akong Rinpoche even the slightly remote Jarvis became friendly and asked a few questions in a cordial manner. I acted as if he'd never been obnoxious and he—on his part—acted accordingly. He'd joined us in my room on my last night and I'd welcomed him to pull up a cushion. *"Chögyam"* he opened *"I was wondering whether they have ngakpas in the Kagyüd School?"*

"Yes, they do—especially in the Drukpa Kagyüd and Drigung Kagyüd Schools—but they have them in all branches of the Kagyüd." PAUSE *"After all, Milarépa [5] and his disciple Réchungpa, were not monastics. There were other non-monastic disciples of Milarépa too – Ngèndzong Tong Répa,[6] Répa Zhiwa 'ö Sé-ban Répa, Kyi-ra Répa, Dri-gom Répa and, Répa Sang-gyé Khyab. There were other too – but those are the only ones I can recall."*

---

4   Khandro Déchen plans to produce a book of iconographic line drawings which represent the Aro Dri-ku *(A ro bris sKu)* style of representation which was originally instigated by 'Khordong gTérchen Tulku Chhi'mèd Rig'dzin Rinpoche in 1983.

5   Jétsun Milarépa *(rJe bTsun mi la ras pa* 1052–1135) the famous poet and yogic master. He was the heart son of Lhodak Marpa Chö-kyi Lodrö and a major figure in the history of the Kagyüd *(bKa' brGyud)*.

6   *ngan rDzong sTon ras pa*

"Of course…" Jarvis nodded *"I was forgetting about the répas – can you still find répas in India?"*

"Yes – there are a wonderful gathering of them at Tashi Jong who are associated with Khamtrül Rinpoche. There they're called the togdens – and they practise incredibly rigorous psycho-physical yogas."

Jarvis wanted to know more and so I commenced to tell him what I knew. *"It was the 8th Khamtrül Rinpoche[7] who established a community for the preservation of Vajrayana for the Drukpa Kagyüd togdens, monastics, and laypeople who had followed him into exile from Kham. They all worked together to build Khampagar Gompa to replicate what they had left behind in Tibet. Every Spring they perform gar'cham to celebrate the birth of Padmasambhava. This Vajrayana dance was first performed in Tibet 300 hundred years ago. The Khamtrül Rinpoche is a master of gar'cham."*

"What do these dances look like?" asked Jan.

"Well the dancers are dressed in brocade robes and, they move according to an intricate – yet dramatically dauntless choreography. It's alternately wild and stately. Hard to describe really – but the dancers swirl, often spinning around on one leg – with the other raised. It is Mahayoga meditation in movement – manifesting visualisation as dance."

"Are these dances ever performed by women?" asked Jan.

"Yes, although it would be rather more rarely seen. Khandro Ten'dzin Drölkar was skilled in gar'cham."

Jan enquired, so I gave her some detail.

---

7   The incarnation line of Khamtrül Rinpoche: Khampa Karma Tenphel (1569–1637); Kunga Ten'phel (1639–1678); Ngawang Kunga Ten'dzin (1680–1728); Ten'dzin Chökyi Nyima (1730–1780); Drupgyüd Nyima (1781–1847); Ten-pé Nyima (1849–1907); Sang-gyé Ten'dzin (1909–1929); Dongyüd Nyima (1930–1979). There are two incarnations of Khamtrül Dongyüd Nyima Rinpoche: The 9th Khamtrül Dokham Shedrüp Nyima Rinpoche (1982–) of Khampagar Monastery in Tashi Jong, India, and the 9th Khamtrül Jig'mèd Pema Nying-jèd Rinpoche (1981–) in Bhutan.

"Khandro Ten'dzin Drölkar had spent some time at Tashi Jong before she married Ngakpa Yeshé Dorje and she had learned gar'cham from one of the togdens there. There were a group of amazing togdens: Togden Chö-legs, Togden Zopa, Togden rTa-mChog, Togden A-jam, and Togden A-trin. Later, Togden Sem-dor and Togden Achos were able to escape and join Khamtrül Rinpoche. Togden Chö-legs was known as Togden Rinpoche, as he is the main meditation teacher in Tashi Jong.

Khandro Ten'dzin Drölkar studied with Togden A-trin [8] for a time – because although he was ostensibly Drukpa Kagyüd he was mainly Nyingma Dzogchen in terms of practice. She told me that—in Tibet—he'd been in solitary retreat for six years – but, at that point, he'd felt that his practice had become slow and turgid. He told Khandro Ten'dzin Drölkar that he felt his practice had turned him into a 'serene vegetable'."

"That's very funny…" laughed Kate *"… it sounds almost… un-Tibetan."*

"Oh, Togden A-trin had a fine sense of humour according to Khandro Ten'dzin Drölkar – and a way of expressing himself that was quite individual." PAUSE *"Anyhow, Togden A-trin asked Khamtrül Rinpoche, whether it might help him to practice in a more rugged, inhospitable place – perhaps even a frightening place. Khamtrül Rinpoche had agreed and given directions to a specific location. Having arrived, Togden A-trin found a large cave into which the sun never shone. In the evening, a flock of noisy pigeons flapped 'round inside defæcating – so he'd get splattered with pigeon excrement."*

Wild laughter ensued at this point – and I had to wait for the gathering to calm down. I wondered what it was about people that made defæcation such an amusing topic.

"Anyhow…" I continued *"Togden A-trin placed a container to collect the water trickling down the rock face – but when he drank the water it tasted vile. He then realised the water was partly pigeons' urine."*

8 Togden Atrin Thrin-lé Lodrö (1922–2005) was born in Lhatok, Kham. He was named Trinlé Lodrö by the 7th Khamtrul Rinpoche of Khampagar. Under the guidance of Tulku Sônam Ten'dzin Rinpoche, Togden A-trin meditated alone in caves from the age of 24 – where he practised Dorje Shin-jé shèd, rTsa rLung, the Six Yogas of Naropa, and Dzogchen.

Again the gathering found this highly amusing – and I began to feel awkward about the account. I had not meant to amuse people – and although I enjoyed being entertaining and telling jokes, I found myself feeling that I would rather not be seen as someone who made these stories comical.

"So..." I resumed "... *the cave was wet and noisy. It was frightening at night – because of the strange sounds that seemed to erupt out of nowhere. These sounds were not sounds made by pigeons – but by other creatures he could not see. He found that his former tranquillity had vanished entirely – and was perplexed as to how he should proceed. He concluded that whatever he'd practised in the past was of little use. So, he tried to cultivate greater calm by not surrendering to distraction within any of the sense fields. He took all phenomena as equal – and in this mode, he remained in that cave for a further six years. After that, nothing affected him – and whatever occurred he never left the state of rigpa.*"

"*So there really are yogis just like Milarépa today*" Jarvis beamed.

"*Certainly... and others with the same realisation who've endured fewer austerities – such as Khandro Ten'dzin Drölkar. She's very much a Dzogchen yogini.*"

Jarvis then asked "*Did Khandro Ten'dzin Drölkar practise the Six Yogas of Naropa?*"

"*Yes – and especially the physical yogas belonging to the trül'khor system.*"

"*So, Togden A-trin was her Tsawa'i Lama?*" asked Jarvis.

"*No. Her Tsawa'i Lama is Karma Gyalpo Rinpoche.[9] He's one of the greatest living rTsa rLung Karmamudra masters – but I've not met him.*"

9   Karma Gyalpo Rinpoche *(kar ma rGyal po)* was another name of Kyabjé Künzang Dorje Rinpoche *(sKyabs rJe kun bZang rDo rJe)*. See *Wisdom Eccentrics* —Ngakpa Chögyam—Aro Books Inc—2011. At this time I did not know that Karma Gyalpo Rinpoche and Kyabjé Künzang Dorje Rinpoche were the same person – and that Khandro Ten'dzin Drölkar and I had the same Tsawa'i Lama.

Jarvis proceeded to get highly technical at that point and ask all manner of questions. Although fascinating... I started feeling concerned that the others were being left out of the conversation. I therefore excused myself on the pretext that I needed to pay a visit to the toilet. I remained away just long enough to allow another stream of conversation to take over and strolled back to my room. By the time I returned they were talking about Chögyam Trungpa Rinpoche.

"We were talking about the fact that you both have the name Chögyam – is there some connection?" asked Kate.

"No... not apart from the fact that I have a great deal of respect for Chögyam Trungpa Rinpoche. He's really the first Lama to communicate in contemporary English – and I find that an enormous inspiration." PAUSE *"Our names however are not exactly the same. Trungpa Rinpoche's name is a contraction of chö-kyi gyamtso and mine is a contraction of chö-ying gyamtso.*[10] *Chö-kyi Gyamtso means 'Ocean of Dharma', and Cho-ying Gyamtso means 'Ocean of Space' – or... 'Oceanic Chö-ying'."*

"Chö-ying?" queried Jan.

"That's dharmadhatu in Sanskrit."

"You speak Tibetan then?"

"No... I wish I did. I know the technical language of Vajrayana to a certain degree – but I can't string it into a sentence. I can only say 'Thank you very much indeed'; 'I'm going to town'; or wish people 'Sit in comfort' when I'm leaving – and... other social pleasantries."

And so, we moved through ideas until they all drifted off to bed. It had been an extremely pleasant last evening and I was happy that Jarvis had been there. It fulfilled something important in my mind. It was possible for human beings to be friends and to accept each other as equally valuable. The warm glow of such comradeship was the ideal mood in which to go to sleep on the final night at Samyé Ling so I packed my robes away.

10 *Chos kyi rGya mTsho* and *chos dBying rGya mTsho*.

Tomorrow I'd be back in my civvies again – ready to hit the road.

I'd got into bed and just turned out the light when Jan appeared in my room, slipped out of her dress, and climbed into bed.

In as relaxed a manner as I was capable, I said *"Jan… I'd be extremely happy about this under other circumstances – but… I'm—not— single, you know."*

"That's a shame… but I'm only looking for a cuddle – a woman needs that from time to time. Nothing else has to happen. It's not a—life or death— decision you know."

What was I going to say to that? It took a moment or two – but finally I said *"This is… completely outside my sense of what's possible… but… I'll take your word for it – and… I wouldn't like to be ungentlemanly."* Nothing more was said. She spooned up behind me and went to sleep almost immediately as far as I could tell by her rate of breathing.

I—on the other hand—lay awake for something close to eternity. It may have been 20 minutes – but it was 20 minutes crammed with concept. I had a range of ideas and sensations that were difficult to reconcile. I knew that in some way I could have found myself teetering—for a microsecond—on a pivotal molecule of precariousness. I was a 16th of an inch from a torrid departure from my understandable continuum. *That* thought was highly unwelcome in my mind. It left me wondering about my relationship to 'dette. I knew—in some way—that I should have asked Jan to return to her room. My failure to do so reflected the nature of my relationship with 'dette. I *was* loyal to 'dette. That much was obvious by my pointing out I was not single. It was also obvious by my stated intention of going to sleep. However… I did not feel innocent… and it was evident to me that any sense of my being '*in love*' with 'dette had ceased to be viable – and had not been viable for some time.

How would I have acted if I was with Lindie Dale?[11] I knew immediately. Jan would have had to have returned to her room. That could have been a ghastly revelation for anyone in relationship – but somehow it was merely a stark fact of my existence. I'd already offered to spare 'dette my irritating association – and she'd performed a backwards flip. I wouldn't have been bereft by any means if we parted on that day. I was fond of 'dette – but love? No… that had gone. That had been squashed out me. I remembered the words of Düd'jom Rinpoche *'With each life-circumstance: whatever is enacted, stare directly into the enactment – with all the senses.'*

When I woke, Jan was gone. I breathed a sigh of relief, as waking up next to Jan would have been somewhat awkward.

At breakfast, Jan was as cheery and bright as ever – and it was as if I'd dreamed the whole thing. Then she said *"You know, you really— are—the perfect old-fashioned gentleman. You and Jarvis have back-to-front ages. He's 42 and you're 22. But he's a teenager – and you're an adult… and, I'm nearly old enough to be your mother."*

I raised my eyebrows and made a movement with my right hand that requested her age.

"A few years or so older than Jarvis."

"You surprise me" I said in genuine surprise. *"I thought you were in your early-30s."*

"There's no end to your gallantry is there…" Jan laughed *"… but hush now – we have the others joining us."*

Kate, Dot, and Georgina joined us and we plunged back into the stream of conversation that had continued almost unabated since I arrived.

11 Lindie Dale was my beau in 1968. See *an odd boy*—Volume II—Doc Togden—Aro Books WORLDWIDE—2012; and also *Goodbye Forever*—Volume I –Ngakpa Chögyam—Aro Books WORLDWIDE—2020.

"I was just telling Kate…" grinned Georgina *"… that Chögyam reminds me of Adam Adamant."*

"Adam Adamant?" Jan queried.

"He was a character on television back in… about '66–'67 … on the BBC*"* Kate responded.

"He was some kind of adventurous hero who was supposed to have been born in 1867 *but got put into some kind of hibernation and got revived in* 1966. *It was a fun show – a sort of comedy thriller."* PAUSE *"It was a satire about the '60s because the '60s are seen through the eyes of an honourable Victorian gentleman."*

"He had an imposing name too…" added Kate *"… something like… Adam Llewellyn DeVere Adamant."*

I sat faintly bewildered as I'd never seen the series. In those years I'd been fairly free of television and most of my time had been absorbed with Savage Cabbage. *"What's the story with Adam Llewellyn DeVere Adamant – it seems I missed something on television after all?"*

"He's a swashbuckling Victorian hero…" said Georgina *"who, I think… oh yes, he was this officer in the Army listed 'missing, presumed killed' in* 1902.*"*

"Year my father was born" I added.

"Whoa, he was—old—then, when you were born I mean – so maybe that accounts for it." PAUSE *"Anyhow he has to rescue his kidnapped fiancé…"* PAUSE *"What's her name?"*

"Louise" answered Kate.

"Yeah Louise – so he's lured into a trap, captured and frozen in a block of ice by his arch-enemy—who's called 'The Face'—'cause he wears a leather mask all the time and speaks in this eerie whisper. The Face gives Adam Adamant a last request – and so he asks to see Louise."

"Yeah, then he makes this really nasty discovery" Kate chipped in. *"In his last moment before he's frozen he discovers that Louise was never really kidnapped – she's been working for The Face all the time."*

"So Adam Adamant gets found in 1966, *when a building's being demolished. He's revived and gets out of hospital but collapses somewhere in London where he gets rescued by this girl Georgina – I was about* 13 *then and always liked that she was called Georgina."*

"Sounds like a ripping yarn—I enjoy that kind of thing—and... I can almost see myself being like this gentleman—not that I think I'm a hero or anything—but... maybe I like that archaic style of being honourable. Maybe I got that from my father... now there's a thought... I never thought I'd find myself saying something like that." PAUSE *"So—sorry—I interrupted your flow."*

"No – that just makes it more interesting that we were talking about it... and so... anyway... although Georgina's a typical '60s hippie, Adam Adamant was her childhood hero and she read all about his late 1800s *adventures. So when Adam Adamant starts in on crime detection she gets in on all his cases. He tries to stop her—for her own protection—but she always sails in at the last moment to help."*

"Better and better – a hippie heroine!" I laughed. *"I love this story."*

"So—right—Adam Adamant's this brilliant swordsman with this sword that comes out of a walking stick – and he's also a boxer and expert in Judo and Karate. So he can just about do anything. So anyhow, Georgina's threatened after seeing her grandfather being murdered by the Mafia and they're after her, and Adam Adamant saves her." PAUSE *"There's also this mystery because no one knows where his money comes from or how he rebuilds his old home on top of this multi-storey car park in London. The wild part is how he gets into his house in this secret lift that's hidden by a sliding wall."*

"So... apart from my being somehow quaint... what the similarity?"

"Well… when The Face captures him, Louise—who betrayed him—tells him 'You're so clever, but oh so vulnerable.' He has this Victorian naïveté, you see… and that reminds us of you. I mean… I can't imagine any other man being coaxed into wearing Dot's knickers."

"Yes – you've got me there…" PAUSE *"Maybe that's just because I don't enjoy having limitations"* PAUSE *"although… I wouldn't argue about my naïveté – I think that's probably accurate."*

Jan said nothing during the Adam Adamant exchange – but smiled occasionally and eventually said to me, almost in a whisper *"You'll even own up to naïveté then… that's impressive."*

Jan evidently didn't expect an answer – so I simply smiled and gave a slight shrug of the shoulders. Once breakfast was over, I discovered that Kate was headed back to Liverpool that day and so I offered her a lift. She was to have hitched from Samŷe Ling and I knew that would be difficult until she got to Lockerbie. Kate was evidently pleased with the prospect because more often than not people ended up walking most of the way to Lockerbie. The locals weren't that enthusiastic about picking up hitchhikers.

"Do you have to leave soon?" she asked.

"Yes… well… I don't have to head out immediately – but I need to get back to Bristol before it gets too late. I don't like driving when I'm overtired. Almost ended up dead doing that in Germany when I was 16."

"Right—of course—but… I was wondering… if you don't need to be back in Bristol for a day or so – I'd like to introduce you to my friends Amy and Atlas in Liverpool?"

"Atlas…?" I queried *"… as in Charles?"*

"No – but I can fill you in on that later. They're really interesting people and I think you'd really like them. They're really different and outside the establishment thing. I've known them for about five years and they've been really good friends. They don't lay any conventional conservative trips on you and they live life like Art."

"They sound like my friends in Bristol—the world needs more people like that—and I'm always happy to meet open minded people."

"Right! They're completely open minded and free! You'll really get on with them well – and they'll really like you too."

What could I say? *"Well… I—could—go back to Bristol a day or two later… but, I'd have to make a few telephone calls."*

"Then we don't need to head out until just before lunch?" Kate smiled. *"I'd like to say goodbye to a few people and see the yaks one last time – sorry, I forgot, I mean the yak and the dri."*

And so it was arranged. A leisurely departure seemed most welcome to me. I went upstairs and knocked on Jan's door. She opened the door and beckoned me to come in. *"Just come to say goodbye"* I said *"… and to give you my address."*

Jan smiled—a little sadly I thought—and said *"I think… I'd better not take your address…"* PAUSE *"I don't think it would be… sensible."*

"I wasn't meaning…" I started – but Jan interrupted.

"No of course not…" Jan demurred – but I interrupted.

"It's just that I've come to regard you as a good friend."

"Yes" Jan replied. *"And that's just what we are – but… I'm not sure I trust myself as much as–you—trust—your—self, if you understand…"*

"Yes… I do." PAUSE *"You really are a most remarkable person"* I answered in some kind of strange daze or purple haze. *"Well… maybe we'll meet again…"*

"… don't know where, don't know when…" Jan broke in, in the words of the song.[12]

"… but I'm sure we'll meet again one sunny day" I completed the line.

---

12 Vera Lynn—*We'll Meet Again*—recorded in 1936. *We'll meet again, don't know where, don't know when, But I know we'll meet again some sunny day. Keep smiling through, just like you always do, Till the blue skies drive the dark clouds far away.*

"Yes… maybe we will" PAUSE *"… but, before you leave, I'd like to give you a little advice… if you will hear it?"*

"Keep smiling through?"

"I'm sure you will…" laughed Jan *"…but seriously…"*

"Certainly" I smiled. *"One can't get enough advice if it's kindly and intelligently given – as I'm certain it is."*

"Yes, it is…" PAUSE *"You're going to be taking Kate back to Liverpool, I hear."* I nodded in the affirmative and Jan continued. *"Kate has… spoken to me about her two friends—Amy and Atlas—they share a house with her in Liverpool…"* PAUSE *"I don't know exactly how to put this – but I'm not sure they're your kind of people exactly. I've got no more to say than that—because I may be entirely wrong—but take care, keep your eyes wide open, and remember to leave as soon as you want to leave."*

I thanked Jan for her advice. I told her that I'd not forget what she'd said – and suddenly wished she'd given her advice before I'd agreed to go to Liverpool. But what could happen beyond my finding these Amy and Atlas people uninteresting? They could turn out to be like the hippie cannibals in Jean-Luc Godard's *Weekend*.[13]

That was the last time I ever saw Jan. 'Goodbye Forever'…

---

13 *Weekend* – a black comedy film. See glossary: *weekend*.

11

Sergeant Pepper

Strangely enough, people came out to wave us goodbye. There'd been a deal of discussion concerning the 'Hells Angel' motorcycle that had stood dormant on the grounds of Samŷe Ling. Jan had told me about it. *'Why would a Buddhist be riding a Hells Angel motorcycle?'* some people had wondered *'Is he an ex-Hells Angel or what?'* Jan had explained to them that I had no connection with the Hells Angels. Jan said *"Hells Angels aren't the only ones who like to ride choppers. There's no law to say what a Buddhist should ride is there?"* She'd shaken her head in disbelief when she told me. *"Some people are so trammelled in their thinking. I'm sure if you'd come here on a racing bike they'd have thought you were in training for the Tour de France."*

That made me smile. *"Yes… that seems to be the way people work. They tend to perceive in pigeon holes—y'know, this looks like that— so it must be one of those. It was like that at school. If you were one of the clan who liked Blues you weren't supposed to like the Beatles. The girls like Motown and the Beatles. The boys like Blues and Rock music. It was almost as if I'd broken the rules of the club and was in danger of being expelled."*

"Yes…" Jan sighed. *"I've heard them called pashus:*[1] *which—I think— means 'sheep mentality'. They think in strict categories and it makes them uncomfortable if anyone crosses those categories."*

I had a wealth of excellent conversations at Samŷe Ling – but now it lay somewhere behind us. I'd found a fairly simple means of lashing our two roll-bags together. Kate also had a US army rocket bag – they were standard hippie issue at the time. They were sometimes decorated or embroidered – but mine was plain and dyed dark blue. I had a parka coat too, that was dyed peacock blue. I'd had to bleach it before dying it. I never enjoyed khaki.

---

1   'Pashu' is neither Tibetan nor Sanskrit. It may be from one of the Indian Languages. In Hindi it has a range of meanings covering fauna, animal, livestock, beast, brute, and budgerigar. It would therefore relate to herd behaviour.

The thing I liked most about the rocket bag was the huge brass press-stud closure which I kept polished.

And there we were – heading South to Liverpool. I'd never been to Liverpool and asked Kate if we could make a pilgrimage to the Cavern – the place the Beatles used to play. She told me there was nothing there to see. I'd be disappointed. We passed Carlisle and I flashed back to my notion of the inadvisability of calling in on Emily. It seemed I'd launched into a sequence of inadvisabilities in spite of my caution. A sign for Blackburn appeared and I asked *"Are there really 4,000 holes in Blackburn Lancashire?"*

"If your name is Sgt Pepper, there are." I liked the way that Kate was always quick with repartee.

"Well, it was 20 years ago today…"

> *I read the news today—oh boy—4,000 holes in Blackburn Lancashire / And though the holes are rather small / they had to count them all / Now they know how many holes it takes to fill the Albert Hall.*
> Day in The Life—Lennon McCartney—Sgt Pepper Lonely Hearts Club Band—1967

We passed Preston and Wigan and Kate said *"Here's the town for your wig and a dress."* I was surprised she'd remembered my joke. Then, almost unexpectedly we arrived.

Kate lived with Amy and Atlas in a three-storey Victorian warehouse in Wood Street. The ground floor was still a warehouse of some sort and there was an entrance beside the main entrance that led up a flight of wooden stairs to their two-storey flat. The upper floors had obviously been part of the warehouse at one time and the rooms were all quite large. The top floor was divided into three bedrooms – the third of which was a guestroom-cum-storage room.

Amy and Atlas were still out at work when we arrived. Amy worked as an assistant curator in the Liverpool Museum and Atlas was a PE teacher[2] at one of the local schools. I wondered what age this would make them? Older than me I supposed. People who'd entered the regular working world were in another category – and one with which I was not familiar. I wondered how it would be with them. I'd been expecting that they'd be students sharing a house—as I was—but no, they were beings from the work-a-day world. That was somehow mysterious to me. Amy was Amy Pilgraughan – pronounced Pilgroon and Atlas was Atleigh Lascelles. Atleigh Lascelles could—by some mathematical formula which made no sense to me at all—be recalculated as Atlas. Each letter apparently had its number in the alphabet and if you made them into an equation where Atleigh = Lascelles—or some such thing—the end result was Atlas. Kate explained in great detail – but I had no idea what she was talking about. *"Did I mention that I was not allowed to take 'O' Level Maths on the basis that it would have been a waste of the school's money? I don't know equations from equestrianism and antiquarian aquatics."*

"I'll get Atlas to explain – he's better at that kind of thing than I am."

"Thank you Kate – but… I don't think I'd want to punish Atlas with my numerical illiteracy." PAUSE *"It sounds highly ingenious…"* I grinned *"… and—y'know—it also works if you take the first syllable of each name: Atleigh Las-celles… At… Las… that's how my name works. It's actually* **Chö**ying **Gya**mtso *– Chö… gyam."*

"What does that mean then?" asked Kate

"Chö-ying is dharmadhatu in Sanskrit – and means 'spatial dimension'. Gyamtso means 'ocean'. So… Chögyam means 'ocean of space' or 'oceanic spaciousness'…"

2   Physical Education.

"Ah... right... you said something about that at Samȳe Ling – but I think I was drifting off to sleep and didn't quite catch what you said. That's an interesting name" Kate replied. *"Amy will like that – she likes spiritual names. She says her name is like Amen – 'let the will of God be'."*

Now... this 'God' business bugged me – but I realised that I had no right to be bolshie about it. Chacun à son goût...[3] It wasn't my business to express my subjective opinions like some verbally incontinent cretin. Kate set about telling me about Amy and Atlas. They were both unusual people, Amy more so than Atlas. They were somehow free of all normal societal constraints – like some sort of witch and warlock of way-out wonderfulness, but without the usual *eye of toad and tongue of newt* connotations.

"They're 'real hippies'—as hippies should've been—if everything had been different."

"Alright..." I said, wondering quite how that worked with an assistant museum curator and a school teacher. *"I enjoy meeting people... and I like it when people are not wallowing in pedestrianism."*

"Then you'll be glad to have met them. We've been friends since I was 16. Amy and Atlas don't have the usual kind of relationship – they have an open relationship... but they've never really found anyone else to..." Kate found herself lost for words – so I volunteered *"... to participate?"*

"Something like that."

"I'm... a little old fashioned in that way—not that I'm moralistic about it— but I'm monogamous and..."

"You have a girlfriend?"

"Yes in Bristol – I think I mentioned that...?"

"Maybe... I forget. Things went by so fast up there. What's her name?"

"Claudette Gascoigne – but friends call her 'dette."

---

3   *Chacun à son goût* is an English corruption of the French *à chacun son goût*— meaning 'each to his own taste'—and stems from Louisiana regional patois.

"She sounds as if she's one of these people whose family can be traced back to Norman aristocracy."

"Yes... she may be – but 'dette's never said anything about that."

"And you've never enquired?"

"No... it never seemed a vital subject. Everyone's family goes back to somewhere or other."

"I'm not asking too many questions, am I?"

"Not yet... no... but it's... not something I'm used to – I mean, telling someone about 'dette when they've never met her."

"I suppose not." PAUSE *"What about you then? Do you have interesting ancestry?"*

"My only claim to fame is on my mother's side. Her mother was Clara Schubert – she was the niece of Franz Schubert... so... I'm his great grandnephew."

"Ah... that's where the music comes from then – does..." but then there were footsteps on the stairs and the approach of Amy and Atlas interrupted our conversation.

They smiled broadly at me as they walked in and Atlas—in a big brawny voice—said *"Well there – who are—you—then?"*

"I'm someone you haven't met yet" I replied with a broad smile, responding to the style of his question. Then I regretted it, in case I'd come across as hostile. I hastily rephrased myself *"I'm Vic – I meant to say."*

"No—the first thing was good—if everyone just spoke expectedly it would be a drag."

"I see we think alike."

"I doubt it!" he replied and burst out laughing.

"This is Atlas and that's Amy, I met Vic—or Chögyam—up at Samÿe Ling. I thought you'd all like to meet each other."

"Really…" Amy responded with a huge smile *"Chögyam… that's a Tibetan name isn't it?"*

"Yes." Then there had to be a whole story about everything I'd explained at Samÿe Ling.

"Why do you want to belong to a religion?" Atlas asked. *"We're spiritual seekers—so we're very interested in all religions—but why tie yourself down to a religion when there's so much to be found by looking at everything."*

I sat in silence for a moment. Atlas looked at little ill at ease in respect of my silence – but that was not my aim so I began to respond *"Well… it wasn't a choice – I just fell in love."*

Amy nodded as if she understood – but Atlas wore a frown of consternation, so I continued.

"Put it this way… I didn't choose Blues either – but Blues is like a religion to me. I fell in love with Blues when I was 8 – and… I'm still in love with Blues. So… as you see, I simply do what I love to do…" PAUSE *"There's not much more to say than that."*

"You believe Tibetan Buddhism has the Truth?" Amy asked in a mild dreamy kind of way.

"Mmm… I've never thought about it in those terms…" PAUSE *"Truth isn't a word that I use – apart from the ordinary sense of 'truth' and 'lie'."* PAUSE *"I looked it up once. Truth comes from the Saxon word triewð, and used to mean faithfulness, loyalty, veracity – or being solid and steadfast. By the mid 14th Century it meant accuracy, or correctness."*

Atlas had adopted an expression that resembled something one might find at the fishmongers *"What's that got to do with anything?"*

"The history of language…?" I smiled. *"I'm sorry – I thought you might find it interesting."*

"We do" smiled Amy. *"Knowledge is valuable."*

Atlas looked slightly irked – so I continued hoping to ameliorate the tense atmosphere I'd created by being unnecessarily erudite. *"The word that equates to truth—for me—would probably be 'reality'. I don't think any religion—owns—that or could ever own that exclusively."*

Amy smiled a vague attenuated smile that could have betokened anything *"Yes… no system can own the Truth."* PAUSE *"You have to seek the Truth in everything."*

"Yes… I think I could say that I seek reality in every aspect of the phenomenal world."

"But Truth is spiritual – not material" Atlas countered with an expression that betrayed his being accustomed to being authoritative.

"Well in terms of 'truth'… maybe… I don't know. I wouldn't know what to say about that. You see – I'm not looking for 'truth'. 'Truth' is—according to my understanding—more connected with the Judæo-Christian world view."

"That's just semantics though isn't it" countered Atlas. *"Truth and reality – what's the difference?"*

"Well… I don't see spiritual and material as polarised."

"Again that's just semantics" retorted Atlas. *"Reality and spirituality – what's the difference?"*

"The difference lies in the connotations and implications of the words." PAUSE *"Perhaps…"* I continued in another vain attempt to ameliorate *"… it's due to my writing poetry that makes me feel that semantics are not just semantics. Language is Art to me and so the differences between words is artistic as well as logical."*

"But we all know what we mean – so we can ignore the connotations and implications."

"Yes… we—could—do that… but I choose not to ignore them. I am not saying that you shouldn't ignore them – that's your choice. My choice isn't right or wrong – it's just my choice."

"So, you're saying it's all arbitrary – and you're a nihilist."

"No…" I enunciated with slow deliberation. *"It's not all arbitrary – I'm simply saying that we are both free to have our own opinions without right or wrong being involved. As to nihilism – that is one of the four denials in terms of Buddhism and so I do not subscribe to that view."*

"I don't know what these four denials are but we all know what nihilism means – and you sound nihilistic."

"Well yes… I imagine that is how it might seem. From a theistic point of view an atheist might seem nihilistic. As to knowing what 'we' mean—I can't say that I could concur with that as a fundamental premise—and that still leaves the question of spiritual and material not being polarised from my point of view." My speech always became somewhat academic when I was put on the spot in this kind of way. *"As I said… the poetry of language is central to the way I see things."*

"Poetry—is—important…" offered Amy. *"I see poetry as Truth."*

"Yes! I can go along with that!" I almost whooped with glee, turning to Amy – to distance myself from the offensive Atlas. *"That makes entire sense to me. It has a veracity that lies outside the ordinary structure of communication."* I was hedging my bets whilst wishing to acknowledge Amy's conciliatory comment.

"So, you can see that Truth and reality are the same" Atlas stated matter-of-factly.

"Reality, as I experience it…" I responded slightly wearily *"… is more akin to geography and meteorology. The Northern Lights for example – or with the way caves in limestone escarpments gives rise to the stalagmites and stalactites in caves."*

"But that's just science. Truth is knowing God" Atlas announced.

The 'God-word'– what was I to say now? This Atlas fellow was really quite some ape. I was wondering if it wasn't time to pack my bags and leave.

"I imagine…" I replied with extended languor *"that… that is—one way—to describe it, for those for whom God is a concept."* I'd become slightly exasperated with Atlas at this point and decided to be humorous. *"I tend to take a Liverpudlian line on this."* Atlas looked confused – so I continued *"As John Lennon said 'God is a concept by which we measure our pain.'"*

"John Lennon's first solo album…" Kate added. *"We've always loved the Beatles."*

Atlas looked highly irked by the discussion having been spun in another direction and commenced *"Ah but…"*

But I chimed in before he could continue *"As an atheist, the word—God—does not translate. I'm not saying I take issue with your way of seeing, or with monotheism—I'm sure the formulation is fine for you—I'm just trying to answer the question Amy asked."* I turned to Amy at that point and said *"You asked me whether I believed Buddhism had the Truth."* Amy nodded – so I continued *"Which is why I made the distinction between Truth and reality. I don't see Buddhism as owning 'truth' – because Buddhism isn't a religion of 'truth'. It's a religion of 'method' – and, its methods are ways of discovering the nature of reality."*

"But…" Atlas began again – but I broke in on him again. I'd settled on the fact that he was a cosmic gorilla. Amy—whatever she thought—was courteous. I could respect that – but Atlas needed keeping in a cage somewhere.

"Atlas… I think I'd really prefer—not—to have to defend myself—quite—so much… I'm not out to prove—I'm right—and—you're wrong. I'm not a proselytiser. I'm not an evangelist and I'm not a philosophical debater with a point to prove – so there's no need to think I'm trying to get one over on you."

"But you're taking a contrary stance."

"No…" I smiled wearily *"… although saying 'no' at this point is obviously a 'contrary stance'. All I've done… is answered your questions. You decided to challenge* me. *I did not set out to challenge* you.

177

"This discussion only came up because you *questioned why I'd want to 'tie myself down to a religion'. I didn't set out to challenge your position – it was* you *who challenged mine."*

"You don't like open discussion then?" Atlas asked.

"I do if it's open ended – but I don't enjoy the kind of discussion where I find myself in an artificially embattled position." PAUSE *"So… if you don't mind, I'd rather—not—justify myself all evening. I'll talk by all means – but I do not wish to argue. I am not attacking your point of view and I have no desire to defend mine."*

"Yes" said Amy. *"Argument isn't what we want. It's not good to argue."*

"Thank you. I agree with you entirely" I said ignoring Atlas. *"So, tell me about your approach. I'd like to hear about—your—approach."*

"I don't really put things into words…" said Amy *"but I like to do whatever takes me to the Truth."*

"So… can you give me an idea of what that looks like?"

"It looks like whatever it is at the time." PAUSE *"I meditate—and that is all I need—but I don't believe in meditation that accords to any system because the system just makes a prison – and then you only find what the system sets you up to find."*

"That's a wise observation" I pondered. *"I think that—is—one problem with following systems blindly. I—have—seen that, so I know what you're saying."* I thought, momentarily, of concluding my reply by saying *'That's the problem of seeing method as Truth'* but decided that would be an aggressive statement in view of their view of 'Truth'.

"Are you free then?" Amy asked *"… in terms of that problem of following a system?"*

"I can't answer that immediately" I replied. *"You'll have to let me dwell on that."* We sat in silence for about a minute before I continued *"… as far as I can see… the problems are addressed by the methods themselves… and… as far as I've taken the methods… they've opened up my ability to see more directly."* PAUSE

"The direction of the methods is towards structurelessness – so... that would be more like breaking down the walls of the prison."

"Yes... I can see that..." murmured Amy. *"We all look for God in our own ways."*

I had no idea what to say to that without treating her in exactly the way in which I'd objected to being treated. *"Exactly"* I replied. *"I always feel that people have to find what suits them best..."* and that was the best I could manage in terms of giving a response that was not a direct challenge.

"You're not critical of that?" Amy asked in a reasonably inoffensive way. *"I'd have thought you'd see problems with that."*

"No..." I replied slowly and deliberately. *"I... prefer to live and let live. I don't look for problems in other people's approaches unless their approaches affect me in some way... that I find irksome or... offensive."*

"But aren't you being offensive quoting John Lennon about God?" Atlas blurted.

"I don't think it would serve any purpose if I answered your question as you've asked it Atlas..." PAUSE *"... I was actually just trying to lighten the atmosphere a bit... and I'm sorry that it was offensive. It wasn't my intention"* PAUSE *"but... I think that discussing entirely different—or diametrically opposite—points of view... is... unnecessary."* PAUSE *"I mean, I may be—entirely—wrong... and you maybe be—entirely—right... but I'd rather be wrong than embrace ideas that don't move me. I think we could look at it as being like music. I prefer Blues to Rock&Roll, I prefer Bach to Mozart. I..."*

"You'd be satisfied with being wrong?" Atlas interrupted.

"Yes. As Amy said earlier 'Argument isn't what we want. It's not good to argue.' And—that—is my preference."

"That's an easy way out" Atlas snapped.

"Atlas… do you—mind—terribly—if we dropped this subject? I've just arrived here – and… I really don't feel welcome. I know you didn't invite me – but Kate—did—and she lives here too… but, if you would rather I left, I'll leave."

Kate interrupted us that that point *"I invited Chögyam. He's my guest."*

"Thank you, Kate, but if Atlas would prefer me to leave – I'll leave. I can pack up and ride on out, with no hard feelings. Just let me know. I don't want to impose on anyone, or anything, anywhere."

"No need to get angry –it's just a discussion" Atlas interjected with some degree of nervousness. Atlas had the air of one who expected physical assault. As if I might take a swing at him. His anxious expression struck me as out of character for a PE teacher – as I would have imagined such a person to have a sense of physical confidence when it came to a bar brawl or any such thing.

"Atlas…" I sighed with a wan smile *"do I—look—angry?"* and, before there was time for an answer, I continued *"I'm not raising my voice, am I? I'm just trying to make what I feel to be a reasonable request. I know my views may be entirely alien to you – but I have no desire to push them on you. I have no desire to prove you wrong and prove myself right. All I want is—not—to argue about religion."*

"Yes, you're right Chögyam" said Amy. *"Argument—isn't—what we want. It's not good to argue – especially about spiritual things."*

"Thank you, Amy. Splendid. Exactly, just my point of view – so let's just leave it there and talk about music or almost anything else you enjoy."

I remembered the words of Düd'jom Rinpoche *'With each life-circumstance: whatever is enacted, stare directly into the enactment – with all the senses.'*

Atlas rose suddenly and disappeared into his bedroom in an evident huff. Amy excused herself—smiled at me—and followed Atlas. *"We need to change out of our working clothes."*

I smiled and nodded in answer – and she joined Atlas in his bedroom.

"Kate…?" I enquired when they'd left *"I don't mean to be critical… but you kind of left me on my own there."*

"I wanted you to get to know each other – so… I thought it best not to interfere."

"Do you—think—we got to know each other?"

"Yes – you know each other's ideas now."

"Do we?" I sighed in slightly puzzled disbelief. *"I don't think they have a—clue—where I'm coming from – and, all I know of them is what I could glean from Atlas' aggressive oppositional stance…"* PAUSE *"I'm really —not—quite certain what I'm doing here."*

"Why?"

"Well… I don't think your friends… are exactly warming to me… especially Atlas… and I think the feeling's mutual… I really don't enjoy being lambasted with 'God'…"

"You seemed to do fine with Jan when she challenged you."

"Yes… but I had the sense that Jan respected me. She wasn't out to attack me on the basis of what's meaningful to me. What I do with my life is my own concern unless it impinges on anyone else – and it was obvious that she respected that."

"Ah… yes – but that's because she fancied you. I'm surprised you didn't end up in bed with her."

What was I to say to that? Kate was obviously quite perceptive. I *had* ended up in bed with Jan – but we'd slept together in the literal sense rather than the figurative. That however was not up for discussion. I didn't want to be dishonest about it – but I also felt it was none of Kate's concern.

"I don't know about that Kate… and as you know, I have a lady friend in Bristol – so I won't be ending up in bed with anyone" I commenced.

181

Then, taking a logical tack *"It doesn't necessarily follow that just because Jan wasn't out to attack me – that she therefore fancied me."*

"It seemed obvious to me."

"Well, maybe… I'm not saying you're wrong – but I can't agree you're right either." PAUSE *"I'm just making a logical point."*

"Life isn't always logical though, is it?"

"No… it's not. I'd agree with that entirely… but I try to understand situations—-and logic is a useful tool—-'til it proves inadequate, that is." I reflected for a moment on what Jan had said about leaving as soon as I found I wanted to leave. *"Y'know… Kate… Thanks for inviting me here—I appreciate it—but I think I'd better leave at this point."*

"I thought you said you didn't want to drive when you're tired."

"True…" PAUSE *"Maybe – I'm overreacting."* Damn – why couldn't I just follow my impulse and have done with it? I knew why. I was committedly flexible in situations where I should be obdurate. *"I did mean what I said though. I really do—not—want to argue about anything. I don't like arguing – and if Atlas starts again I really—will—have to leave. I'll just ride out 'til I can find a comfy field somewhere. I've got a ground sheet so it's really not a big deal."* PAUSE *"The whole attack and defence thing is—not—what I enjoy – and I have—no—desire to be right by making someone else wrong."*

"Yeah… I can see that… and I think Amy understands that." PAUSE *"She's on your side you know."*

"Yes…" I sighed. *"I think she seems to be… but Atlas… I don't think he…"* I deliberately stopped short of saying '*knows his arsenal from his wheelbarrow.*'

"No…" Kate agreed. *"Amy is a wise women. She's experienced enlightenment… but Atlas… well… Atlas has a good heart and he's really very much reliant on her wisdom. He knows that and really respects her a lot, but sometimes he forgets that he can't be like Amy – not yet at any rate.*

"He just thinks that anyone who doesn't think exactly like Amy has to be wrong and needs putting right."

"A faithful student then…"

Kate frowned slightly at that. *"Don't… mock him. He's a good friend"* she replied – but not in a scolding fashion. *"Atlas is passionate… and when you get to know him better – he could become a good friend of yours too. He just needs to find out that you're… understood by Amy."* PAUSE *"I think I'll go and have a word with them."*

Kate put a Pink Floyd album on and disappeared into the room that Amy and Atlas had entered. When one side of the album was finished, I turned it over and played the other side – but there was still no sign of my hosts. After some ten minutes I got up and looked through the albums. I found a cluster of Tangerine Dream albums.[4] I'd heard of the band—vaguely—but had never listened to an album. I set it on the turntable – sat back and listened. It was electronic music – and although pleasantly intricate, it wasn't really the kind of music I enjoyed. If I wanted intricacy I'd opt for Bach – but there was nothing Baroque and nothing Classical either.

Eventually Kate remerged *"We've talked about it and we think we've been misunderstanding each other. I explained that you were not antagonistic to them and that you just want to be allowed to be yourself. Amy and Atlas are all for people being individuals – but they think people would be happier away from institutions."*

"I'd agree entirely. I'm not keen on institutions either."

"Right – so we won't be talking about it anymore."

"Excellent."

Then Amy and Atlas reappeared. Amy heard Tangerine Dream playing and asked *"Do you like Tangerine Dream? Kate said you'd put it on."*

"Yes—fascinating sounds—I'd never heard Tangerine Dream before."

4   Electronic Meditation, Alpha Centauri, Zeit, and Atem.

This was not the time to express my subjective opinion. I *could* express an enthusiasm for Tangerine Dream that was *partially* insincere, in order to be affable. After all – they'd decided to quit their assault on my personal religious choices. It seemed the least I could do.

"They're our favourite band. What music do you like?"

"All kinds… I love Blues—maybe first and foremost—but I also like Avant Garde Jazz. Then I like Baroque music especially Bach. I like also Early music [5] *and music of the Classical period."* Amy and Atlas just nodded – so I continued *"… and all kinds of modern composers, Eric Satie, and the minimalists."*

"Minimalists?" Amy queried.

"Minimalist music was originated by American composers like La Monte Young, Terry Riley, Steve Reich, and Philip Glass."

"Ah yes… We know Terry Riley – but I didn't know that was called Minimalism…" Atlas commented but without great interest.

"Yes!" Amy beamed. *"We have 'Rainbow in Curved Air' and 'Descending Moonshine Dervishes'. We listen to them a lot. I'd like to get more of his albums – do you know of others?"*

"Yes… let me think… there's… 'Music for The Gift'… 'Reed Streams'… 'In C', 'Church of Anthrax', and 'Persian Surgery Dervishes' – I'll write them down if you like."

"Thank you" Amy replied with evident pleasure. *"Can you say anything more about Minimalism – I'd really like to know more about it."*

The evening seemed to have taken a much better turn and I relaxed *"It originated in the New York Downtown scene in the '60s."*

Amy's face lit up at the mention of the '60s *"Ah… that's the kind of music we like."* Then she turned to Atlas *"This is great isn't it! There's suddenly all this new music – I'm really happy to find out about this."*

---

5   Early music – Mediæval music from around 500 to 1400 AD.

Atlas shrugged *minimally* and nodded. He added a smile seemingly to cover what could have been an underlying sullenness. I decided he may simply have been tired. Amy turned to me with a face that beckoned me to say more.

"It started as a form of experimental music called the New York Hypnotic School and features the consonant harmony or pulse of drone instruments. It spread to Europe and the style was adopted by Michael Nyman, Henryk Górecki, Arvo Pärt, and others." PAUSE *"I'll write the names I can remember down for you if you like."*

"Thank you" responded Amy. I took Amy to be the more culturally au fait of the two and certainly the more easy-going. Atlas yawned and I wondered whether he resented the fact that Amy and I were conversing with no apparent problem. *"I think you'd like Michæl Nyman. There are two albums I can think of: 'Divertimento for Flute, Oboe and Clarinet' and 'Canzona for Flute'. I was introduced to them by Meryl – she's one of the ladies with whom I share a house in Bristol."*

"One of the ladies? How many are there?" asked Atlas with awakened interest.

"Three" I replied *"Meryl, Rebecca, and Penelope – they're students at the College of Music and Drama and we rent a house together. They know a lot of modern music and I've learned a lot from them about the history of music. We have some fascinating conversations."*

"I bet" said Atlas with a lewd kind of grin.

"They're not his—girl—friends…" Kate interjected with a slight hint of exasperation.

Ah… the picture crystallized. The reason Atlas had suddenly re-entered the conversation was because he'd detected something salacious. Atlas really was an asinine ape. The words *'Atlas – go sit in the corner and eat a banana like a good lower-primate'* ran through my mind but I said nothing to that effect. It always troubled me when jibes of this nature sprang to mind. I wished I could simply not have such thoughts arise.

185

"No…" I concurred. *"They're friends of my ladyfriend, 'dette – Claudette. They went to school together. She introduced them to me because they needed a fourth person to be able to rent the house."*

"So…" Atlas asked *"why doesn't she live with—you—then?"*

"Well… she lives at home with her father. Her father's a widower, you see – and… she lives close enough to the Art School that it wouldn't be worth paying rent just to live a little closer… and… she has a rather splendid home. She has her own living room and sewing room. She stays over with me whenever it suits – and life is fairly perfect for all concerned."

"Wouldn't suit me" Atlas sneered.

"I suppose there are many different situations – and they probably suit many different kinds of people."

"Maybe" Atlas started *"but…"*

Then Amy interrupted *"Chögyam's right about that. There are many different situations and that's really good because people are all so different. Not everyone wants to live like a couple – I mean, we don't live the usual way couples live either."* PAUSE *"Tell us what you like about your situation Chögyam?"*

"I like living with three very good female friends with whom I have no sexual relationship."

"Yes—I can see that—really. That's really very spiritual."

I could see that Amy was doing her best. Prior to my time with Düd'jom Rinpoche I would have rolled my eyes at such a comment – but now, at least, I could smile in return for her kind intention.

"And then… 'dette and I see each other at Art School and usually on a few afternoons in the week and on most Friday and Saturday nights." PAUSE *"Sometimes we all spend time together and sometimes it's 'dette and myself on our own – just how it feels at the time… Sometimes 'dette sits and reads while we play music. I play sitar and Penelope, Meryl, and Rebecca play double bass, 'cello, and oboe. We improvise quite often and I really enjoy that."*

"We're having Latihan [6] tomorrow night" Atlas announced as a non sequitur rejoinder.

"Never tried that before – but I'm sure it'll be delicious" I replied.

"It's not food…" Atlas laughed with unmasked derision *"… it's a spiritual practice."*

I found my mistake genuinely amusing and laughed as well, adding *"Right, someone once asked me if I liked Brahms and I said I'd never tried one."*

Atlas' face froze slightly – as if he hadn't enjoyed the fact that I'd appeared entirely un-humiliated by the exposure of my error. Of course, I'd known Brahms was not the plural of Brahm. Of course, I'd never said such a thing, but my joke was a vain attempt to appear harmless – and put Atlas at his ease. But Atlas, like the fabled Atlas of Greek legend,[7] was carrying a world of hubris on his shoulders.

"It's a formless meditation from Subud" Amy expanded. *"Latihan kejiwaan is guidance from the power of God – the great life force."*

"Tell me about it" I asked. *"I've never heard of Latihan or Subud."*

"Not many people have. Muhammad Subuh said that the present age is one that demands personal evidence and proof of religious or spiritual Truth and that people shouldn't just believe in words."

"I'd agree with that entirely." PAUSE *"With the name Muhammad… is this part of Islam?"*

6   *Latihan kejiwaan* belongs to an off-shoot of Islam called Subud a religious movement from Indonesia, founded in the 1920s by Muhammad Subuh Sumohadiwidjojo (1901–1987). The practice of Latihan involves acting according to unpremeditated intuitional impulses — in order to 'surrender to the Divine or the will of God'. During Latihan participants involuntarily move, make sounds, walk around, dance, jump, skip, laugh, cry or whatever comes into their minds.
7   In Greek mythology, the Titan Atlas was responsible for bearing the world on his shoulders, as a punishment from Zeus. Atlas was the founder of astronomy. Atlas' name has been given to a mountain range in northern Africa, the Atlantic Ocean, and any large collection of maps.

"No – or at least it doesn't have to be. You can practice it in any religion or none. We find it very harmonious with Indian spirituality."

"That's interesting" I replied with a smile *"I have a lot of respect for the American Indians. They seem to have a way of living that respects the world as a living entity. I don't know that much about it but – I saw 'Little Big Man' a year or two back and really liked what I saw of their life-style."*

Amy shook her head *"I meant India… I should have said Hinduism – but that word's an English invention that doesn't mean very much. The English colonialists coined it to describe the religion of the people who lived around the River Indus. There are many different spiritual traditions in India and they give people the opportunity to find their way to God by many different paths. Our path is Agora Yoga and the Shaktipat of the Chillum Babas."* [8]

"Right… well… I know nothing at all about that…" I lied. I *knew* about Chillum Babas… and whilst I had no desire to decry them, I had no interest in religious practises that required hashish. In fact, the Chillum Babas in Kathmandu had moved on from hashish to opium and some were mainlining heroin. They were not well respected, as it was evident to many that they were merely drug addicts. Fortunately, Amy decided to leave the subject alone and continue with her explanation of Latihan.

"That's rather a lot to go into now – but Latihan is the proof of God we're all looking for. It's an exercise that's not thought about. You don't learn it or train in it. It's different for everyone who practises it – and it's passed on by contact with another person who practises Latihan. In the East, men and women practise separately – but that's just because of the culture in the East. We don't have to follow that here. Latihan usually happens in a large hall – but it can happen anywhere where there's the space to move. Everyone sits quietly for a while – and then the guru or helper says 'Let the Latihan begin'.

8   The chillum originated in India and predates the introduction of tobacco to India. It was used for smoking opium and other narcotics. But chillum smoking was an exclusively male practice, limited to the northern and predominantly rural areas of India. The Chillum Babas—sadhus—hold that use of hashish brings them closer to God, and thus closer to salvation. Hashish in the worship of Lord Shiva is not uncommon.

"Then the sanyasins surrender to the Divine. They follow what arises from within – without expecting anything. You don't focus on images or recite mantras or use any kind of ritual. You simply surrender to the divine – which is the ultimate practise as there're no organised religious ideas to get in the way. You don't pay any attention to the others in the room – because everyone is into their own Latihan and you don't allow yourself to be influenced by them."

"That sounds interesting" I said trying to look interested. *"What kind of thing happens then?"*

"It's impossible to say. If I could tell you it would be predictable and that wouldn't be Latihan… but… sanyasins discover new dimensions… physically, emotionally, and spiritually. They make completely spontaneous movements and sounds. They move or dance, laugh or cry or… anything at all. This develops in each person – and gives them the guidance they need in life."

"Right…" I replied, thinking 'this is what used to be a called a happening or a freak-out…' It seemed rather lame to spiritualise the modus operandi of the average hippie party. I'd attended a few of those and they really weren't that interesting. *"I see what you mean now about your meditation not being structured according to a method."* What else could I say without sounding offensive?

Amy smiled extremely widely at me and I got the sense that she assumed I was on the brink of conversion.

"What happens first" she continued *"is the opening. That's your first Latihan. It passes the contact – like a candle flame that lights another candle. The flame is the same flame even though the people are different."* PAUSE *"In the opening you're helped by helpers—that'll be us—and we'll ask you to stand and relax."*

I nodded in token of comprehension – but felt entirely peculiar about the fact that I'd never agreed to attending a Latihan. What to say? Was this time to say *'… errrm – I think I'll go and see a film while you have your Latihan. This isn't really my thing…'*

Somehow Amy's pleasant manner and evident benevolence toward me won me over—entirely against my better judgement—not to mention Jan's wise advice…

"Then we'll say 'We're helpers of the Latihan and we're here to be witnesses to your wish to worship the Creator of the whole universe – the all-knowing and all-powerful."

"That's just like emptiness in your terms" Kate translated as I sat there feeling vaguely like a potential human sacrifice.

"Then…" Amy continued as if Kate had said nothing *"… so that your feelings can become calm, we'll ask you to close your eyes, and to stand quite relaxed and to pay no attention to other people exercising. Then when movement arises in your body, don't resist it. Don't feel anxious. Just freely follow whatever arises within you."*

This whole thing was getting to feel increasingly creepy by the minute; not because the details of the Latihan were problematic in any way—I could ignore the monotheism—but because it was presupposed that I was some kind of willing victim. I decided to ask a question *"So… how did you come across this method?"*

"The first time I was tested by God… I was dancing at a party" Amy explained with a seraphic expression. *"I suddenly found myself… drowning in light. I looked up… to see… where the light was coming from. It was coming from everywhere and everyone… I wondered if I was dying and if this was the light you see when you die – so I lay down on the floor. I didn't want to fight it. I just wanted to surrender to God. Then I felt extremely energetic and stood up again. I started moving… but had no control of the movement. Then I knew that I wasn't moving by my own will – but by the power of God."* PAUSE *"After that… it took over a year to find out who knew about what had happened to me. I wanted to find my way back to God but I couldn't. I tried meditation in every religion I could find and went to every teacher I could find – but they all wanted me to learn their system. I knew that these systems weren't God and had nothing to do with God…"* PAUSE *"… and that's how eventually I found out about Latihan."* PAUSE *"Subud's spread all over the world now – and it's wonderful that now people can be free of all organised religion.*

"If they want to stay with their religion they can – but they don't have to be prisoners of their religions."

"Yes…" I replied—nodding slowly and perfunctorily—with whatever degree of cautious circumspection I had at my disposal. *"I can see… how that would work."* Certainly, I could see how that would work. It was the usual method of becoming the supreme religion. It was like saying 'all religions are one'. It sounds fine and highly accepting – but it undermines all religions. If you believe that all religions are one – you join the religion that states 'all religions are one' and then you lose your own religion. It is fundamentally an insidious ploy. I do not believe that I will go to Hell for not believing in God – but I defend the right of theists to believe I will go to Hell.

"We play music at our Latihan" Kate commented.

"Yes" continued Amy. *"We find it helps with the movements – but it can only be instrumental music. Words are distracting."* Amy got up and selected another album to play. Amy smiled at me and we all sat together without speaking… listening to Terry Riley's 'Rainbow in Curved Air'.

So… I seemed doomed to experience this Latihan – but… that wouldn't be terrible. It would just be an evening spent in a room with three other people moving around aimlessly for a couple of hours to Minimalist music. Fine by me. I used to dance when I was 14 or 15 years old – and I could probably still move around in a free-form manner. With any luck they'd all think I'd been moved by God and live happily ever after. *'Hallelujah'* I thought *'I'm saved!'* Then I reflected on my proclivity for cynical witticisms and wondered if I'd ever be free of them. There were—after all— these whirling dervishes… and they seemed to be onto something or other.

When 'Rainbow in Curved Air' finished, it was time to retire for the night. I lay there in the dark and wondered why I had let myself be talked into coming to Liverpool. This Latihan thing was probably going to be peculiar – but… life was not to be avoided.

Experiences like this could be interesting. At some remote point in time, I was supposed to teach Vajrayana and to accept students. It was stressed, by Düd'jom Rinpoche, to be important that I understood the West and what went on in the West in order to teach in the West. Maybe I'd have to address people who'd practised Latihan – and if so, it would be useful to have experienced it first-hand.

The day after the *ordeal* was over, I'd ride off back to Bristol where I'd be able to have conversations with people who weren't vaguely deranged. It wasn't that my conversation with Amy and Atlas had been *that* unpleasant. Well the first session had been vexing – but the second, even though… amiable… was… simply… tedious.

On that note, I went to bed. I wondered whether I might dream. Dreams of consequence had eluded me at Samŷe Ling: a place that I would have expected dreams – so maybe after such an unlikely evening, dreams might occur. That was a lunatic hope, to put it mildly.

12

fear and loathing in Liverpool

Dreams of consequence had not occurred. I'd slept extremely deeply and had no recollection of dreaming. Whatever the secondary causes were for consequential dreams – they'd not been in Eskdalemuir or Liverpool. Kyabjé Düd'jom Rinpoche had told me I would remember more of my previous life in dreams – but I was decidedly short of dreams. I had no idea what I could do about that. I practised mi-lam and I practised silent sitting. I practised the Tantric preliminaries with the necessary mantra recitations – so I did not know what else I could do to have the dreams I was supposed to be having. All I knew was that indulging in feelings of frustration would not help.

Amy and Atlas had left for work by the time I descended the staircase after my morning session of silent sitting. Kate was there in the kitchen.

"I hope you didn't mind me not joining you – but I had enough of silent sitting in Samÿe Ling to last a month or two."

I smiled to show I was not discommoded by her absence – but said nothing. I had nothing positive to say about Kate's lack of interest in silent sitting.

"I'm glad you're getting on well with Amy and Atlas after all."

What was I to say to that? Peace *had* erupted—it was true—but as to 'getting on well'? I could have had a better time with a crowd of ardent football enthusiasts. Still far be it from me to say something that might sound peevish or grouchy.

"I mainly listened…" PAUSE *"… I don't know exactly what's going to happen… you know… at this Latihan tonight – but… I guess… I'm up for anything."*

"It's much more interesting than all that silent sitting I can tell you" she opined. *"People just sit for hours and what's supposed to happen? I've never heard anyone say that something interesting happened."*

"Mmmm…" I hummed *"… I don't know how to answer that without talking for a couple of hours… I suppose I could make a parallel… and say… people just live for years and years and what's supposed to happen? I've never heard anyone say that something interesting happened… at least not something that anyone else couldn't say."*

"I don't get that…?"

"Bad ngakpa!" I said slapping my wrist *"Poor analogy!"* PAUSE *"Let's start again… I think it might be better to say that it only becomes interesting when 'nothing' happens – when there's nothing with no one watching nothing. That's what it takes to allow awareness to be what it is. Our natural awareness only becomes evident when we let the structure of conceptual mind drop – and… it's a long process because the habit of conceptual mind is well entrenched."*

"Yes… I can see that… but, as you say, it's a long process – and Latihan short-cuts all that."

"Well… I'm open to seeing what happens." I replied, feeling that I'd just talked to the wall. Then I noticed the electric guitar propped up against the wall. *"Who plays?"*

"No one. It belongs to Atlas." PAUSE *"He started learning to play once – but gave up because he felt it wasn't his way to God. Now we keep it so that anyone can play who comes here."*

Right. Not '… *his way to God'*… Well… PE wasn't mine – but I could at least admit to having no competence with kicking a ball 'round a muddy field with a lummox of sweating boys.

"Would he…" I almost said God but censored my own sarcasm *"… mind if I put a different tuning on it?"*

"I'm sure that would be fine. As I said he gave up trying to learn and he hasn't picked it up for two years at least."

I took a look at the guitar. It was some unrecognisable make that looked like a Stratocaster. Luckily it had an appallingly high action and surprising heavy-gauge strings.

"I'm not surprised that Atlas gave up playing this thing. You'd need to be— Charles—Atlas to hold a chord down."

"Atlas bought it like that from an ad in the papers I think."

"Ah... that would account for it. Guitars are sold with medium gauge strings – so someone must have fancied these hawsers. They're good for Blues if you have the finger strength and calluses for the job – but you wouldn't want to learn with strings like these." PAUSE *"Did Atlas take any lessons?"*

"I don't know... why d'you ask?"

"Well... a guitar teacher would have advised him to change the strings and probably would have adjusted the truss-rod for him to take the action down." PAUSE *"For me—however—it's perfect! I can play lap-slide on this thing!"*

I set about tuning it in 'open **A**'. The amplifier was only a 25-watt model but it had a reverb control. This was better! I was going to have some fun at last!

I started off into a slow swamp-Blues slide and Kate came over grinning *"That's amazing! Amy and Atlas will be really excited about this! You'll be able to play this in the Latihan!"*

"Errrm... I thought... latihan was supposed to be... spontaneous?"

"Yes—and it will be—I mean, just because you know the guitar's there doesn't mean you can't pick it up spontaneously does it?"

"No. I suppose not..." I wasn't going to get logical at this point. If I could sit playing guitar rather than goof around like a zombie urged by the will of a putative *omniscient omnipotent omnipresent omnivorous un-created creator deity* – then... all the better.

I decided I'd like to see the Cavern—in spite of the fact that there was nothing much to be seen—and because I felt in need of stretching my limbs.

Kate was right—there was nothing much to be seen—but I felt as if I'd fulfilled some sort of sacred duty. It was also good to experience the reality of Liverpool after the unreality of the previous evening.

It was a pleasant day in Liverpool and I settled into a sense of nominative normality. Kate was pleasant company and said nothing gozzy about God to make me wince. I only ever winced internally on the subject in any case – but I just never knew how to respond when people talked about surrendering to the divine, apart from *'Well… good for you – keep it up.'* I never said that out loud – but the words always ran through my mind.

"So…" I ventured after a while *"Latihan… and Amy's take on organised religion… Can I ask how that fits with your having been at Samˆye Ling?"*

"Yeah… well… Amy thinks I should be free to try things out like she did. There's no point in accepting Latihan as the path if I've never looked at anything else. Amy's read books on—all—religions for years – since right back to when she was a child. She's read everything there is to read about every religion – so she knows she doesn't have to do anything else. You see… she didn't find God through religion—it just happened—and so now she has Latihan, any kind of religion is just a side track to her."

"So… if that's her experience… and you believe it… why wouldn't you just follow her example?"

"Ah… yes… I can see how you'd think that – but Amy doesn't want people to follow her. She doesn't believe in that. She believes that gurus teach by example and through Shaktipat – that's like a Tibetan Buddhist initiation but without any of the ritual."

I didn't point out that Vajrayana had formless transmission[1] as well – because I didn't want to enter into any kind of 'mine's as good as yours' number.

---

1   Dzogchen contains direct, oral, and symbolic modes of transmission – none of which are ritual in their performance.

"Right... well..." I ruminated aloud *"that sounds good – but... if you travel around trying things when you have the idea in your head already that they're not going to match up to Latihan – then...?"*

"Ah... yes... I see..." Kate replied *"that is a problem—or could be—but I am really open to the possibility that I might make my own discovery."*

"I'm glad to hear that." PAUSE *"So... I'm still wondering exactly—why— you wanted me to meet Amy and Atlas?"*

"Well... it's good to try everything and I thought you were the kind of person who'd be open to anything. You seemed like that to me – especially after all that larking around in the river with Jan and Dot. You seemed a free spirit – and that's what Amy and Atlas are."

"Yeah" I laughed. *"I'm just the kind of lunatic who'd try anything – apart from hallucinogenics or walking on hot coals that is."*

"Oh..." Kate responded – evidently slightly troubled *"I didn't know that you don't... I mean not even dope?"*

"Not even dope."

"You seem very rigid about that."

"Like a steel transom, yes."

"Amy says it's not good to be rigid."

"She may well say that... but... Amy's not my teacher is she?"

"There's no reason why she shouldn't be – she's enlightened."

"That's as may be. I don't know that from my own experience. There is every reason why she shouldn't be my teacher however – but the reasons have nothing to do with whether she's enlightened or not." PAUSE *"From my point of view... you have to actually have experience of the nondual state to make an evaluation as to whether someone else has that experience... otherwise... how would you judge?"*

"Oh... I'd never thought of that..."

"So… I'm not saying that Amy isn't 'enlightened' – but I can't accept that she is, simply because you tell me she is. That's your experience. It's not my experience." PAUSE *"As to being rigid concerning hallucinogenics… Düd'jom Rinpoche wrote a text concerning why smoking tobacco and ingesting any kind of narcotic or hallucinogenic is contraindicated as far as Vajrayana practice is concerned. So, as Düd'jom Rinpoche is my teacher… and as I choose to view him as being—or dwelling—in the nondual state… I find my rigidity… to be entirely… fluid."*

"I see… so you really are very much in this system." PAUSE *"I suppose I should have known that from the robes and all that."*

"Yes… I never tried to give the impression that I was some kind of wild card ready to jump in any new direction. My direction was fixed back in 1971 – and I'm really happy with my choice… so maybe I'll skip the Latihan."

"Ah… I see… well… We always use something at the Latihan. As it's the Summer we have pixie-caps—psilocybin—and when those run out we use ganja. We don't smoke the ganja—because Amy says the same as Düd'jom Rinpoche about that – that smoking's really bad for you— unless you're a sadhu – because they can transform it… but we have hash-cakes you know."

"Well—sorry about that—but I have to draw the line there." PAUSE *"As I said, I can always take the evening out and see a film or something. I wouldn't expect Amy to change the rules of the game for me. I'm quite happy to skip Latihan."*

"Mmmm… I think it would put Amy in an uncomfortable position if you went out to see a film… I think she'd definitely prefer to make an exception for you. She wouldn't want you to do something that was against your principles" PAUSE *"… but then…"*

"There'd be Atlas…?"

"Yes" Kate responded with some surprise. *"How… did you work that out?"*

"Well… don't take this amiss… I like Amy well enough." PAUSE *"Atlas…"* PAUSE *"I'm sorry to have to say this… but Atlas isn't a person I…"* PAUSE *"Sorry… is it alright just to say that I don't like him?"*

"I don't think you've given him a chance."

"Kate... what I observed of him last night is really quite enough for me to have come to a conclusion."

"You sound very 'superior' you know – you only met him yesterday."

"Yes... I don't mean to sound superior – and I know that sounds entirely false because... in a way... I suppose I—am—being superior." PAUSE *"It's just that there's obviously a great difference between him and Amy – or... don't you see it that way?"*

"Yes..." Kate sighed. *"I see it that way too... sorry for accusing you of being 'superior'... I—do—see what you mean... and... it's not that I don't —know—that Atlas is... a little selfish in some ways"* PAUSE *"... and... he—was—rude to you last night – I did see that. So did Amy – and she told him he was rude..."* PAUSE *"but then he did stop being like that didn't he? I mean when he came out of his room again?"*

"Yes... he did – but he was quite sullen for the rest of the evening. He didn't exactly become the bon vivant or whatever."

"So, you hold that against him."

"No... I don't like to hold anything against anyone... I just like to be with people whose company I enjoy to the same degree they enjoy mine. It's alright by me if Atlas doesn't like—me—you know. I quite accept that he may find me quite... obnoxious. I think that being an atheist causes offence in-and-of-itself to theists. I'd not usually make a thing of it... but when people bring 'God' into the picture—and build an argument around it—then an atheist has no alternative but to lay that card on the table."

"It depends what people mean by God though. Amy and Atlas don't mean God the way that Christians mean God. They mean the one force of the universe that's in everything and in us – like we're all part of God and everything is one."

"Well... I don't accept that idea either."

"Why?"

"Because that would be described as monism according to Buddhism."

"So you don't accept God just because that's the Buddhist law?"

"No…" I laughed *"… not 'just because it's the Buddhist law'. There is no law about it – and I don't accept anything on blind faith. I simply have no faith in monism – because monism is a narrow vision of reality. I don't believe in dualism either—nor nihilism— nor eternalism…"* PAUSE *"… and… I don't think I ought to go any further – or I'll have to give a whole discourse on it and that might be horribly boring. I'm not trying to convince you of anything either. If the idea of 'God' is helpful to you then that's fine by me. I think the idea can be helpful – especially if it helps people to be kinder, more tolerant and generous."*

"Right… I see… well you sound like you've got it all worked out then."

"Not all… but enough to be going on with… and I'm not shut off—as you can see—I'm here and more-or-less open to what happens this evening – but getting back to Atlas… I mean, it's his place as well—as yours and Amy's —and it can't be too much fun for him having me there when I'm not… his idea of the perfect guest."

"Yeah…" Kate sighed *"I can see that – it's not unreasonable."* PAUSE *"Anyhow – I'll tip your psilocybin tea away when no one's looking – if that's alright with you."*

What could I say? *"Yes… that'll be fine with me."* PAUSE *"So… what's it like? The three of you living together, I mean."*

"It's good. I've known them since I was 16—when I left home—and we've just continued in this way."

"Right… and so now… you're… how old?"

"18 – 19 in July."

"… and… Amy and Atlas… I guess as he's a PE teacher he must be… somewhere over 25?"

"They're both 32-ish."

"Right…" PAUSE *"Well… I'm not exactly the ancient of days or anything —I'm 22—but your being 18 makes me feel… well… almost parental."*

"Age is irrelevant" Kate retorted rather crisply.

"Yes… I didn't—mean—anything condescending by that… I know that age is arbitrary when it comes to how mature a person is. Atlas—for example— seems younger than you, in terms of maturity – I'd put his emotional age…" I stopped myself before saying 12 *"… well… I'm no expert on such things."*

"Sorry… Didn't mean to snap."

"No problem. I can understand your reaction. I'd be the same if someone brought my age into a discussion – but… I'm just a little concerned that those two are as influential with you as they are. They're a decade older than you."

"14 years… to be precise."

"Alright" I laughed. *"Arithmetic never was my strong point – but… I was meaning that more in terms of a significant measure of time."*

"And so?"

"And so, having been alive for that much longer, especially at around—our— age, makes a big difference. I mean – look at how I related to Jan. She's more than a decade older than me…" I deliberately failed to be accurate *"… and she obviously had some clout by virtue of that. I know I held my own in relation to her – but I was always aware that she had some sort of… edge on me. She didn't use it against me in any way—apart for giving me a good run for my money with teasing—but a person—that—much older does have… some power you know. I think you might do well to be aware of that – especially with Atlas. Amy seems quite gentle and caring – but Atlas… I'm just not sure about him. He worries me – in relation to you."*

"They've been very good to me, you know. They took me in when my step- father started trying it on with me. My mother said it was alright for me to go and live with Amy and Atlas because it was causing a problem at home – and… she's continued to support me financially… so it all worked out well for everyone."

"They've been like parents then… in a way."

"In a way… yes. I left school and went to Tech [2] instead to get some A levels and Amy and Atlas helped me with all that. Then they helped me with my application to Teacher Training College. So, I'm as certain as I can be, that they both have my best interests at heart."

"Right… well… that's unusual – but it seems to have worked out well so far…"

Kate sighed a somewhat resentful sigh *"You still sound as if you're suspicious of Atlas?"*

"Yes… I'd be lying if I said I wasn't." PAUSE *"I can't just tell you I think Atlas is a stalwart and gallant gentleman just to please you, can I?"*

"No" PAUSE *"… but it seems you're suspicious after having known him for one evening. I think that's a little much – actually."*

"Sorry. Maybe you're right. I just have an uneasy feeling, that's all." PAUSE *"I don't usually sum people up—that—quickly… but… people aren't usually as easy to read as Atlas. He just seems immature and… well… manipulative. All I can say is—*look after yourself*—and don't be drawn into anything against your will."*

"I think I'm perfectly capable of looking after myself!" she snapped.

"Sorry again… I can see you can give as good as you get – with me at least. Maybe I'm just an interfering busybody – but I mean well."

"Yes… sorry – I know that…" PAUSE *"Before you came down here… I thought I… well… I thought – I don't know…"* PAUSE *"it seemed that I knew what was going on. Now I feel a bit confused. Life has just rolled on since I started living with Amy and Atlas."* PAUSE *"I've never really thought much about the future. Thinking about the future… well… that seems like a conventional materialistic approach – and, I want to avoid that."*

---

2   Technical College was an alternative in terms of taking A Levels at Secondary school. Technical Colleges also offer vocational trainings and business studies.

"Yes... I can see that... but I'm hardly mister normal – and I take account of the future." PAUSE *"What'll happen when a gentleman appears in your life?"*

"Right... I do wonder about that..." something passed across Kate's face at that point. *"That's a difficult question really... you see... Atlas has always hoped I'd fancy him and we'd all live together y'know – but... it's just never happened. I mean... you can't just fancy someone because it would make things work out... well... can you?"*

"No. Well... I couldn't anyway." PAUSE *"That's maybe what I was worrying about – with Atlas I mean."*

"Right..." PAUSE *"I have to say this... but it unnerved me a bit when you warned me about Atlas. That's why I snapped at you. I'm sorry about that. It was like you were reading my mind or something. That's not some sort of ngakpa thing is it?"*

"No" I laughed. *"Or rather, yes – but I can't read anyone's mind. My observation of Atlas is merely based on what I saw. I can't tell you exactly what I saw apart from the fact that he'll bully people if he can get away with it. He attempted to bully me—as you must have seen—but I don't exactly allow myself to be bullied, even though I don't respond angrily."*

"Yeah... Atlas—did—think you were angry, didn't he...? I wonder why...?"

"Because I wasn't intimidated by him. He expected me to be intimidated – and it threw him when I didn't respond as he expected. In a dog-eat-dog world you're either top-dog or under-dog. If you can't intimidate you feel intimidated. That's my reading of why he projected anger onto me." PAUSE *"I'm not saying I had—no—reaction to Atlas' rudeness – but it wasn't anger. I'm afraid to say it was merely... ennui..."*

"Ennui?"

"Sorry... it's French, it's what you say when you don't want to be so impolite as to use the word 'boredom'. Ennui is a little like: tedium, listlessness, lassitude, languor, weariness, enervation; or malaise..."

"Right… well… Amy and I—didn't—think you'd replied to him in an angry way."

"I think he just read anger into a firm non-emotional position – maybe because he's not used to being resisted."

"Yeah… I can see that…" PAUSE *"… y'know… Atlas does try-it-on sometimes. I wish he wouldn't. He says I'm not being open to the will of God. He says that if I was open to the will of God it would all be natural and easy and the three of us would live in perfect harmony."*

"Do you—want—me to respond to that? I'm not sure my opinions are…"

"Yes. Tell me what you think."

"Well… what I think is that the 'will of God' seems to coincide with 'the will of Atlas'… and, whether you believe in 'God' or not, that—has—to be a little suspicious."

"Yeah…" Kate let out a really long sigh… *"I can't say that hasn't occurred to me – but I think he'll eventually give up the idea."* PAUSE *"I've talked to Amy about it and she's told him that he mustn't put any pressure on me. It'll either happen or it won't and he has to be happy either way."*

"Good. I'm glad to hear it… Just make sure you let Amy know if he ever does it again; so that you have her on—your—side when you need her" PAUSE *"… but what does—she—feel about Atlas wanting a ménage a trois?"*

"She'd be fine with it—completely happy—because she's… kind of… asexual. Don't get me wrong… she does have sex with Atlas… but only because he needs it – and… so… she goes along with it in order to help him be closer to God."

The words *'A bullet through the brain would put Atlas closer to God'* were immediately in my mind – but I didn't give voice to them. Why did such heavy-handed witticisms continue to arise so readily?

"Well… there's a thing and no mistake" was my alternative reply. *"I wasn't expecting to feel sorry for Atlas – but that isn't a situation that would suit me. Why does he accept that? I mean, it must be… somewhat… humiliating… I mean, having my partner make love as a favour… on the basis that I had… an earthly need."* PAUSE *"I'd rather be celibate."*

"Right… I see… I 'spose it does sound humiliating, put like that. I hadn't really thought of it that way before. I don't think I'd want that."

"I don't think any—healthy—person would."

"Atlas doesn't seem to mind though – not as long as sex happens whenever he wants it to happen."

The picture was becoming clearer as we spoke. I felt sorry for Kate – and concerned. It turned out that Kate thought I'd be open to intimate dalliance when she invited me down – but I'd turned out to be disappointingly conventional on that score. I'd had to say that even if I had been single, I wouldn't have been up for a casual temporary liaison – and neither would I have been open to moving in with Amy and Atlas. I told her that as far as I was concerned the whole 'God' number was cuckoo – and that saying it was the same as emptiness in Buddhism was like saying Hitler's vegetarianism was the same as Gandhi's. Those kinds of comparisons were odious. My father had always said 'Comparisons are odious' but only when it meant comparing my lack of liberty with the freedom of other children.

"You're such a weird mixture of freak-freedom and… conservatism…"

"Yes. I'd agree to that."

"How d'you—deal—with that though? I mean… isn't that extremely confusing for people?"

"Yes… sometimes… but not with everyone. Not with the three ladies with whom I share a house in Bristol. We're good friends – and, they seem to understand me."

"And your girlfriend doesn't mind you living with them?"

"No. She suggested it. They're—her—friends. Maybe I'm not as conservative as you think? I'm just monogamous. But I'm not monogamous because of any kind of morality or anything like that. I'm monogamous because it's my preference. It always has been and always will be. What other people do is up to them."

"Yeah… that sounds as if you've settled on something that works for you."

"Yes… and, if you don't mind my saying, I think you—could—sometimes think about what would work best for you." PAUSE "I can't really see you three living this way for ever."

"No…" Kate said somewhat gloomily "… not forever… no… but I don't want to break it all up either… not just now – or not 'til I get through Teacher Training College at least."

"I'm not trying to encourage you to leave, Kate. I'm just concerned you'll do what's best for yourself… y'know… when the time comes."

On that note we left the subject and talked about a whole array of things. We eventually arrived back at the house to find Amy and Atlas moving furniture in order to make a clearer space. Atlas was busy stuffing it all into the room where I slept – and I wondered whether there was going to be room for me to get to the bed. *"Chögyam plays guitar"* Kate announced. *"He played some amazing stuff for me this morning."*

"D'you want to play something now? Why not" Atlas chimed in with a smile. I was glad he'd dropped his sullenness of the night before.

"Most kind of you – I love playing and haven't had the chance to play electric since 1970."

"Go ahead then – let's hear how good you are" replied Atlas as if he was throwing down the gauntlet – and so I did. I plugged in and set the guitar across my knees.

> *"Death ain't got no—mercy—in this land. Oh death ain't got no mercy —in—this land. By the time this song is sung – another friend has gone. Oh death ain't got no mercy – in this land."*

"*D'you know anything with more of a beat?*" Atlas interrupted. I stopped immediately.

"*Rolling and Tumbling?*" I enquired, ignoring the boorish way he'd curtailed my song. Atlas nodded.

> "*Well I was rolling and tumbling—god the whole night long. Yes I was rolling and tumbling—god the whole night long. And when I woke up this morning – all I had was gone.*"

Atlas clearly liked the faster tempo and start lurching around in some form of dance. He resembled—not that I'd ever seen one— a wounded bear.

> "*If the river was whiskey—and I was a diving duck / If the river was whiskey—and I was a diving duck / I would swim to the bottom – lawd, I would drink my way up.*"

I was just launching into the next verse when Atlas took over the vocals. He had a surprisingly loud voice that was also surprisingly out of tune.

> "*Divin' duck—yeah—divin' duck Blues! Oh—oh—oh divin', divin', divin' – I'm divin' with the ducks, Yeah ducks divin' – muff-divin' yeah muff-divin' with fifty ducks—Ahhh sixty ducks'll suck my duck— Ahhh-Ahhh-Ahh seventy ducks—Ahhh—fuck a duck—yeah fuck a duck—I'm gonna fuck all those ducks, Ahhh I'm gonna fuck every duck – I'll fuck all those sixty ducks*"

Atlas was on a roll. He continued to yell about puerile adolescent obscenities about ducks as long as I kept playing. I played for what I considered to be a length of time that wouldn't make it look as if I was cutting him short and then concluded. Amy and Kate were laughing as if it was the funniest thing in the world – and maybe it was. Maybe I was peevish about it – but I didn't quite enjoy him busting in on the song *he* had asked me to sing.

Atlas didn't notice immediately that I'd stopped playing *"Oh yeah, yeah I'm gonna fuck all those ducks – Ahhh I'm gonna fuck every duck! Fucky ducky—fucky ducky—fucky ducky fuckin' muff-divin' Blues—oh—yeah."*

Atlas finally desisted from the horrible noise he was making and asked *"How was—that—then!?"*

"Impressive, Atlas – I liked the way you hit all the blue notes…" I was safe in my sarcasm in relation to that fact that Atlas sang horribly—horribly—off key most of the time – but was dismayed with myself. I could have just let it go – rather than make a sarcastic remark. I had to unlearn that form of patterning. There was no need for sarcasm – whether it was perceived as such or not.

"I liked the 'fucky ducky' reference to Philip Whalen [3] *too."*

"Philip Whalen? Who's he when he's at home" Atlas asked as if to say that Philip Whalen was someone obscure.

"One of the Beat poets and a friend of Allen Ginsberg and Lawrence Ferlinghetti."

"Ah yeah Lawrence Fairly Yeti…" I like his stuff.

"Lawrence who?" asked Kate.

I waited for Atlas to have another stab at pronouncing the name of the poet he claimed to know – but after a second or two I decided to let him off the hook *"Lawrence Fer—lin—ghetti."*

"Who's that?" asked Amy.

Again Atlas stood mute and evidently uneasy – so I said *"An American Beat Poet. He wrote 'A Coney Island of the Mind'.* [4]

---

3   Philip Glenn Whalen (1923–2002) was an American poet, Zen Buddhist, and a key figure in the San Francisco Renaissance and close to the Beat generation. His poem 'Cynical Song' contains the repeated phrase 'fucky ducky'.

4   *A Coney Island of the Mind*—published in 1958—contains some of Lawrence Ferlinghetti's best-loved poetry – such as *'I Am Waiting'* and *'Junkman's Obbligato'*, written for Jazz accompaniment.

"You've probably heard of Allen Ginsberg." Kate and Amy nodded. *"He was one of that group."*

"Right…" said Amy *"… they were connected with Jack Kerouac weren't they?"*

"That's right."

"And he's the one who wrote 'On the Road'… and other books" said Kate. *"I only read 'On the Road' but that was great. Have you read any of the others?"*

"Yes… Visions of Cody, Book of Dreams, Maggie Cassidy, The Subterraneans, Visions of Gerard, Desolation Angels, Dharma Bums, Big Sur, Satori in Paris, and… Vanity of Duluoz."

"I read Dharma Bums" said Amy. *"I think that book really showed a picture of a free spiritual life. I've wanted Atlas to read that – but he's not really big reader. He always says he prefers direct experience."*

Yes indeed. Atlas, evidently, was barely literate – but I said nothing. I just smiled. By this time Atlas has somehow turned his back to us all and was looking through the albums as if he wanted to check what they were going to play that evening.

"You seem to have read a lot apart from Tibetan Buddhism" said Amy.

"Yes—I've always read—I think it's important to be well read and to have some kind of grasp of how people think in the world." I noticed that Atlas was making it obvious that he was not part of the conversation by ordering and re-ordering the albums (to no particular end as far as I could see). *"Literature is full of philosophy and it gives you a picture of how people interpret the world. Literature is also a history lesson – and I think it's valuable to know what the past was like in terms of ideas rather than successions of kings and queens."*

"Exactly" replied Amy. *"That's why I wanted to work in a museum – it's full of images of our past and visions of what brought us to this point. It's also very peaceful there and I like to be in a peaceful place away from the noise and confusion of materialist life."*

I nodded – but before I could venture a comment Kate spoke *"I told Chögyam that if he was moved to play during the Latihan – you'd probably like that."*

"Yes – we would…" Amy smiled *"… but it couldn't be Blues… I mean —not that I don't like it—but it can't be anything you've played before. It would have to be something that came from within."*

"I think I can go with that" I replied. *"You've got some effects pedals here and I've never used those before. I have no idea what will happen when those kick in."*

And so it was settled. I'd spontaneously play guitar at some point. I had to check the batteries in the pedals and they were flat. Fortunately, there was a chemist shop open that sold batteries and I was able to get the pedals working. The old batteries had leaked and corrupted the terminals but – that was no great problem to fix. Atlas watched me working on the pedals – but said nothing. Amy thanked me for the hard work I was putting into restoring the pedals to working order.

We ate a light dinner of vegetable stew and once we'd cleared up, Kate went down to answer the door bell. She turned back before disappearing from view and said *"Oh by the way – we all take our clothes off for Latihan. I didn't think you'd mind because you're used to skinny dipping."*

"Right…" I replied – and, when I turned, I was faced with a naked Amy and Atlas – who seemed to be waiting for some sign of my compliance. Atlas would have made a fine Geek in any travelling circus. He was somewhat surprisingly hirsute – almost like a walking beard. I kept finding myself thinking thoughts I'd rather not have been thinking. I began to feel irritated with my own reactions. It was not worthy to indulge in the dislike of another person. I knew I'd be better off letting those ideas slip into oblivion – but… Atlas just kept doing and saying things that encouraged my worsening opinion of him.

Well… *'in for a penny in for a pound…'* I thought and went to my room to remove my clothes. I navigated the morass of armchairs that Atlas had randomly dumped in the guest room and removed my clothing. There was no big issue in it for me. I went and sat in the living area which was now quite expansive – the armchairs all being rammed up next to my bed so I'd have to climb over them to get to bed. Atlas seemed quite childish in the way he evidently wanted to cause me problems in terms of using the room as a bedroom. Fine by me… The bed was still *just-about-accessible* so I wasn't majorly put out.

Several people of all shapes and sizes had arrived and were absorbed with removing their clothes. After a while there were around twenty people there and we all sat down for a period of silence.

At a certain moment Atlas stood up and set the stereo system going with Tangerine Dream.[5] That surprised me because it didn't seem as if a practice that originated in the East—and which was supposed to be spontaneous—should include prearranged music. Never mind – but I could see where guitar would fit with this. Whilst these thoughts were meandering, a sign was given and we all stood up. Amy and Atlas came over and stood on either side of me – taking my arms in theirs in a fairly gentle manner and said *"We are helpers of the Latihan. We are here to be witnesses to your wish to worship the Creator of the Universe – the All-knowing All-powerful."* PAUSE *"So that your feelings become calm, close your eyes, and relax. Pay no attention to other people. When movement begins to happen in your body, don't resist—don't try to control it—just follow whatever freely arises within you."*

I remembered the words of Düd'jom Rinpoche *'With each life-circumstance: whatever is enacted, stare directly into the enactment – with all the senses.'*

---

5   Tangerine Dream is a German electronic band founded in 1967 by Edgar Froese. They were considered pioneers of electronica and produced albums which explored synthesisers and sequencers.

Then they let go of my arms and brought rounds cups of tea for everyone. *'How frightfully English'* I thought with amusement – but Kate came over and said *"Don't drink it – it's the psilocybin I told you about. Just pretend to sip it and I'll take it from you and tip it into the plant pot when no one's looking."*

I nodded in comprehension. It was kind of Kate to remember our earlier conversation about my antipathy to drugs. I felt slightly cheesy about having to pussy-foot 'round the spiritual sensibilities of Amy and Atlas. My only excuse was that I felt obliged somehow not to create a bad scene for Kate. She'd invited me here and been perfectly pleasant to me. She'd insisted on paying for the petrol from Samŷe Ling to Liverpool and—like an idiot—I'd let myself be cajoled into accepting her fuel donation. This whole thing was one false step after another. There'd have been no problem if I didn't give a damn about anyone but myself – but I was supposed to be a tulku… I was supposed to be compassionate… but all I could manage was a slightly wearied acceptance. I remembered the words of Düd'jom Rinpoche *'With each life-circumstance: whatever is enacted, stare directly into the enactment – with all the senses.'*

Once the psilocybin tea had been consumed people began to glide around the room swaying from side to side to the music in what looked a fairly choreographic manner. Amy was noticeably better at it than Atlas – because she had a natural grace. Atlas was innately clumsy and highly self-conscious about his efforts to be fluid. After Atlas had worked hard for a while at the flowing business he lay on the ground and started howling. As ladies floated around the room, he appeared to be employing his supine position to gain a view of the undercarriages of the ladies who drifted near enough. Within a minute or two Atlas was sporting an erection. I found myself puzzled as to what ladies liked about male genitalia. Just as well they did of course… but just as this random conjecture was occupying my peripheral attention, I was distracted by a sudden movement. Atlas was now jumping around in an ungainly manner slapping the offending member on whichever lady was closest at hand.

This was gross. I was not puritanically shocked – but I found I was not enjoying this display of asinine prurient indulgence. If Atlas wanted an orgy – why not just stage an orgy? Not that I would have wished to be part of an orgy – but this was just plain stupid. Atlas was a grotesque combination of the five fiends in Shakespeare's King Lear – particularly Obidicut and Hobbididance.

> *Poor Tom hath been scared out of his good wits: bless thee, good man's son, from the foul fiend! Five fiends have been in poor Tom at once; of lust, as Obidicut; Hobbididance, prince of dumbness; Mahu, of stealing; Modo, of murder; and Flibbertigibbet, of mopping and mowing; who since possesses chambermaids and waiting-women. So, bless thee, master!*
> Shakespeare—King Lear—Act IV—Scene I

I looked around – mainly to see something other than Atlas and noticed that Kate and Amy were actually doing something that *seemed* internalised. It seemed like a trance of some kind. They were gyrating very slowly with the modulations of Tangerine Dream. Well – at least they seemed to be practising what was described. As my thoughts were thus occupied, a burlesque bathycolpian belle decided to lollop lubriciously over me. I remembered the words of Düd'jom Rinpoche '*With each life-circumstance: whatever is enacted, stare directly into the enactment – with all the senses.*' Fortunately, the Tangerine Dream album finished and so I slid out—at a speed that evidently surprised her—and went for the guitar.

I flipped on the amp and turned on the pedals and proceeded to experiment. This was a useful moment – because masturbation seemed to have become the order of the day for Atlas. He was grinning like a fiend and jumping around to make sure everyone got a good view of his preoccupation. This was the most banal excuse for acting out – but no one seemed to find his dishonesty ludicrous. Kate and Amy seemed sincere – but why were they not suspicious of Atlas' primary motivation? One was not supposed to think about what anyone else is doing at the Latihan.

One was not supposed to conceptualise about anything one saw. On that basis Atlas was free to be as bestially banal as he wished.

Be that as it may I was glad to have the guitar. I proceeded to experiment and surprisingly I managed to improvise for about ten minutes. Kate and Amy seemed to respond well to the sounds I was producing and began to move into my vicinity. Atlas observed from a distance with an aggrieved expression. He suddenly jumped up—went over to the stereo—and put Tangerine Dream back on the turntable and turned up the volume. I stopped playing immediately. That was clearly what Atlas wanted. I could have improvised for longer – but I had no investment in it. A few people looked disappointed – but were not discommoded for long.

The movements in the room changed with the change of music, and Atlas started making lewd moves in front of Kate and Amy – who appeared to keep turning away from him. He'd made no headway with the other ladies in the room and so he'd obviously concluded that Kate and Amy were his last hope. Amy and Kate showed no evident recognition that Atlas existed – and, finally, Atlas slunk away and sat in a corner weeping. Eventually someone came over to tell Amy that Atlas was weeping. He was indeed weeping violently enough to cause everyone to notice him. Amy went over to him and wrapped her arms around him. Eventually Kate went over as well and they both proceeded to envelope him. The crying subsided gradually – but before his lachrymosity abated, I made my way to bed.

Once I'd clambered over the armchairs in my room, I decided—in a moment of clear headedness—to wedge the armchairs against the door and hard up against my bed. If Atlas decided to do anything moronic in the night – he'd find the door impassable. Not that I had any fear of him – but I wanted to make sure I got a decent night's sleep before the morning's ride back to Bristol. Good night – and goodbye forever. I'd be off at first light.

Was this the kind of scenario that Düd'jom Rinpoche wanted me to experience? Or had I just subjected myself to something entirely useless? I realised that I should have run through some of the possible scenarios that were available in the West and asked Kyabjé Düd'jom Rinpoche for some guidelines. The idea had simply failed to occur to me. I'd requisitioned some cotton-wool from the bathroom for earplugs and so I was able to sleep without being disturbed by the relentless Tangerine Dream. I did not expect to dream – and was proved correct in my expectation.

13

the menu at 'Restaurant Reality'

Morning arrived. I had not dreamed – but I had not expected to have dreams of any significance after the lamentably ludicrous Latihan. It deserved a chapter in *The Joy of Suffering* by Carly Juga.[1]

I disappeared, as planned the night before. I had no wish to meet my hosts. I heard no noises of stirring as I carried my panniers—one at a time—down the stairs. I made the separate journeys in stocking-feet in order to be silent. I noticed no movements at any window, as I removed the groundsheet covering from my motorcycle and fixed the panniers. I finally brought down my rocket bag and strapped it to the sissy bars. I pushed my motorcycle a hundred yards—and down a side street—before I sat astride and kick-started. The 500cc engine booming into life brought a smile to my face. I was back in control of my life again. In five seconds, I was out of sight. In half an hour, I was out on the open road in the spacious embrace of the horizon.

It felt slightly like 'Escape from Colditz'[2]. Not that I had any idea of my departure being prevented. It would have taken more than Atlas to do that; PE teacher though he was. Even aided and abetted by Amy and Kate – he would not have detained me. The idea of their attempting to circumvent my departure actually caused me slight amusement – but then the humour of the idea was chilled by the idea that Kate had incarcerated herself there.

---

1   Carly Juga—a play on Kali Yuga—the age of degeneration *(tsöden gyi dü / rTsod lDan gyi dus /* རྩོད་ལྡན་གྱི་དུས་*)*, the aeon in which five aspects of existence worsen: life span; misinformation; neurotic emotions; ability to help others; and. strife amongst people and nations.
2   Göring declared Colditz—one of the most famous German Army prisoner-of-war camps for officers in WWII—to be escape-proof, yet over 30 Allied prisoners escaped. Colditz was a high-security prison camp *(Sonderlager)* and the only one of its type in Germany. Colditz Castle was situated on a cliff overlooking the town of Colditz in Saxony.

She'd made herself a conceptual prisoner of Amy and Atlas – and although I didn't believe that Amy had any ill intentions, I was now far less certain of Atlas than I'd been the previous afternoon. Still… Amy did seem entirely good-natured. I felt—in the end—that she'd probably not see Kate ill-treated. For my part… I'd said what I could to leave Kate with the idea that she might want to leave at some point. That was the same advice that Jan had given me at Samŷe Ling – and so… the rest would have to be up to her.

As I rode South, I concluded that Atlas was, to some degree, psychopathic. He wanted sexual attention. He got it, for what it was worth. He feared I'd stolen his limelight with my guitar playing so he curtailed me with Tangerine Dream. Good luck to him. He wanted to be the centre of attention. He succeeded. More power to his elbow.[3] I had no interest in being the centre of attention, so I didn't mind. I didn't care that he curtailed my guitar number. Ten minutes of strange sounds was quite enough for me. To have gone on longer would not have been interesting. I was not seeking attention – so I wasn't put out when the attention was taken away. I was relieved. It gave me the opportunity to slide off unnoticed by Kate, Amy, and the rest of the mushroom-befuddled company.

I had no desire to see any of them again. Kate was fine—or had been at Samŷe Ling—but Amy was vaguely vapid. Atlas…? Atlas was banal, boorish, and bestial. Amy and Atlas seemed to be caught in a massive self-created illusion – but what was new about that? That's how Buddhism viewed everyone who hadn't realised the nondual state. Maybe there was *normal illusion* and *socially-dysfunctional illusion*? They did however, hold down conventional careers – so… they obviously had to relate with the ordinary world in *some* way. Maybe there were other denizens of delirium out there of whom I was unaware? But did local butchers, bakers, and greengrocers attend luridly loathsome Latihans and spend evenings in tiresomely turbid trance states?

---

3   *More power to his or her elbow* is a British expression which carries an ambiguous meaning. It ostensibly wishes a person success – but in certain circumstances it can be an ironic or sarcastic dismissal of a person.

Of course, I researched Latihan later. I discovered that what I'd experienced in Liverpool was about as far removed from Latihan as bear-baiting.

Much as I repeatedly acquitted myself of responsibility for Kate – I kept returning in my mind to whether I could have acted differently or said more to put Kate on her guard. I felt worried about leaving her in that scene from Breughel. She *was* adult however – and I really had said enough to make her think. She *could* always write to me if she needed help. What could I do anyway? Kidnap her? No… I had no alternative but to make my last statement by departing without a word. I'd done that before in my life. Sometimes it seemed the best option – but was it the ngakpa's option? Would Düd'jom Rinpoche have thought I'd done my best?

I could have felt aggrieved at having my time wasted. I could have felt aggrieved with myself for not having left on the first evening – or for having gone to Liverpool in the first place. In the end, I decided that these occasional bizarre experiences were part of my education. Düd'jom Rinpoche had instructed me to *go and be a ngakpa in the Western world* to *experience what was experienced* by *those whom I would eventually teach.* I supposed that, in some sense, the Liverpool Latihan had been a part of that. At least I knew how deranged it was possible to be in the West – and at least I knew that I'd passed though the experience without having acted badly in any way.

My Vajrayana training in the Himalayas was by far the most important training – but I was not going to *live* there: I was going to *live* in the West. I had to learn how to *be* in the West. I had to learn how to be surrounded by people who had no idea what I was doing. I had to learn how to relate with different kinds of people with widely different points of view – and widely different viewpoints, philosophies, beliefs, and ethics. I had to learn how to navigate the vertiginous vicissitudes of the 1970s without succumbing to their shabbiness, seediness, sleaziness, sordidness, or squalor.

Vajrayana had to work in my own culture, and I could not teach Vajrayana here without living here – exactly as 'here' was. I couldn't immure myself in a Tibetan centre – attractive though that prospect might be. That would be no different from remaining in the Himalayas – and Düd'jom Rinpoche had advised against that, quite decisively.

I had much to learn. There was no curriculum however, other than whatever presented itself next on the menu at 'Restaurant Reality'. What was to be learnt then – was *how* I could *be* in every situation that presented itself. What was Vajrayana at a Latihan?

What was Vajrayana in: supermarkets; cocktail parties; theatres; swimming pools; greengrocer's shops; race courses; pubs and clubs; military tattoos; holidays camps; church graveyards; seaside esplanades; public parks; police stations; seaside resorts; Morris Dancing events; Napoleonic War Enactments; or walking down the typical quotidian Highstreet in the average small English town?

What was Vajrayana at an Art School? That was the most easily answered – because *that* involved appreciation. That was as far as my thoughts took me—interspersed with empty gazing—and eventually I was back in Bristol.

I was welcomed home by Penelope, Meryl, and Rebecca. It was heart-warming. It was refreshing and wholesome to experience their naturalness and—without any tedious implications—their carefree normality. They had a great love of *the weird* when it came to the Arts – but somehow, they were not demented, distorted, or degraded by it.

After an outrageously righteous ragout prepared by Meryl – Rebecca asked *"So… how was it at Samyé Ling?"*

"It was good" I smiled. *"I fed the yak and dri. I made candles. I met some charming people and had a deal of good conversation… and I was able to spend a lot of time in meditation."*

"… and the Lama? You were going to talk to him?"

"Akong Rinpoche? Yes. I had a wonderful conversation with Akong Rinpoche."

"So, what did he say?"

"He asked me about my practice. He asked me who gave me robes — and then... he told me that all would be well for me. He obviously had a great deal of respect for Düd'jom Rinpoche — and. well... that was it, without going into technical detail. I did tell him about my plan in terms of becoming an Art School lecturer and going out to the Himalayas as often as I could over the winter and spring holidays. He seemed to think that was good as long as I could also find time for solitary retreats." PAUSE *"So... really... yes — I got all that I could reasonably use in terms of my meeting. I'm happy with it all, or... almost happy with it all."*

"Almost?" enquired Meryl with a mischievous grin.

"Yes... almost. I wasn't quite so pleased, with..." I chuckled *"the Fear and Loathing in Liverpool..."*

"Fear and Loathing in Liverpool!" Rebecca shrieked with laugher.

"Right—yes—we were wondering what you did in Liverpool after you phoned — it sounded quite mysterious!" Meryl shrilled. *"What happened?"*

"You'll never guess..."

I gave them the unabridged account and there was more laughter that night than there'd been for a long time. *"You're a danger to yourself you know..."* Rebecca laughed *"you just fall in with situations — and one day... it might be more than you bargained for."*

"Yes... I think you're right." I shook my head in perplexed bemusement at my own gauche naiveté and gullibility.

"I think I'm going to have to avoid spiritual types in the future."

"Especially acrobatic masturbators!" Rebecca cackled. *"That's such an utter hoot—well, to hear about anyway—I imagine it must have been rather gross."*

"Yes… it was… gross, as you say. Any 'grocer' and he'd have been running a vegetable stall." The three ladies shrieked with laughter at that – so I gave it another twist *"The only grosser experience in my life was a toilet I had the discomfort to encounter in Lucknow.*[4]*"*

"That's really too funny" said Penelope. *"What were you doing in Lucknow?"*

"I was on my way to Nepal by train from Delhi and it was one of the stops… I wouldn't do that again – I'd fly from Delhi and avoid that if I could afford it. It's a nine-day journey from McLeod Ganj to Kathmandu – and I wouldn't even subject Atlas to that."

"I would!" stated Meryl quite firmly. *"Once a month for the rest of his life – or as long as it took to make him act like a human being. The man's an ape – an utter gibbon!"*

"Yes… true… gibbon-inch and he'll take a mile" I laughed. *"Although I feel that might impugn the character of gibbons in general."* PAUSE *"I wish there was another way of describing people like Atlas without having to abuse the names of animals."*

"Yes… I see what you mean – to call Atlas a gibbon would be a compliment."

"Quite!" Penelope chuckled. *"High praise indeed!"*

"Although…" remarked Meryl *"it's a little disturbing to think of him as a PE teacher… I mean with responsibility for children."*

"Yes…" I groaned *"I'm sorry to say that… that fact escaped me."* PAUSE *"Do you think… I need to do something?"*

"No…" Penelope sighed *"what good would it do… you have no proof of anything… and… what would you say anyway without describing the events? And who'd even believe a story like that? I mean we believe you—because we know you—but it's really too loony for most people to think believable."*

---

4   Lucknow—located in Oudh—is the capital of Uttar Pradesh. It lies on both sides of the Gomti river and is popularly known as the City of Nawabs. In 1971 the railway station toilet left much to be desired.

"I'd imagine..." suggested Rebecca *"he leads a double life. I mean, Amy works in a museum and so both of them probably have to keep their private lives quiet. They're probably used to lying low with what they get up to at home."*

"Yes—sorry I mentioned it—I don't think there's really anything to worry about" Meryl added with an enormous smile that looked as if it was designed to put me at my ease about the issue.

"No..." I groaned *"there definitely—is—something to worry about – and... I'm glad you—did—mention it. I'm just disappointed in myself... it should have occurred to me—before—your having to mention it."*

"I think you're being unnecessarily severe with yourself Vic – you can't be responsible for things that are outside your control" Meryl almost pleaded.

"Thing is Meryl... it—is—within my possible influence. If the school ignores me... then that's the end of my responsibility – but I just can't stand to think of young girls being subjected to PE *with that loathsome... loathsome... loathsome... words fail me."*

The three ladies burst out laughing at that point and Penelope exclaimed *"If that's what troubling you – you've got nothing to worry about! It might have escaped your attention – but they don't allow* men *to teach* PE *to girls!"*

Then it was my turn to laugh *"I've never been happier to look stupid in my life."*

"It's not stupid to care about other people Vic..." commented Meryl *"and besides which; we're not laughing—at—you."*

"I know that..." I laughed *"but... it—is—rather funny."*

"Yes... and I was laughing at myself too..." Meryl smiled *"because that fact had also slipped me – that he wouldn't be teaching girls."*

"Y'know... I just can't say what a profound relief that is. It would have cut across the grain with me to have to be some sort of 'informer'... there's always been something so disgustingly self-righteous about it – even though I know that wouldn't have been my motivation.

"There are some other things that are funny about it too."

The three ladies all motioned me to continue – with hands and eyebrow movements, according to their custom. *"Well… for a start… it's bizarre to find myself being like my father. I mean – how did I suddenly get to be the bastion of moral propriety? I mean my father was the one who was morally outraged that Alice's* [5] *parents gave me and three five-year-old girls a naked shower with the garden sprinkler hose one hot Summer's day. And here I am almost 20 years later being morally outraged by Atlas; when what he did had nothing to do—as far as I know—with how he is as a school teacher."* Rebecca was about to butt in – but I raised my hand to indicate that I had more to say. *"The other thing is a question of the adjectivally—thin—dividing line between skinny dipping in the Esk and the naked Latihan – I mean, who am I to be so goddamn censorious anyway?"*

"You're the one who thought Atlas would be teaching PE *to young girls"* Meryl stated quite seriously *"so I really don't think your court-case against yourself holds up very well. Beside which, you're planning to be a Foundation lecturer not a school teacher – so you can skinny dip to your heart's content without having to have any dark-night-of-the-soul about it."*

"Got me there…" I grinned. *"So now I think I can sleep in peace without having to gnaw a hole through the mattress or whatever."*

"So… now it's all shipshape and Bristol fashion. [6] *"* Penelope laughed.

"Nicely expressed" I laughed.

5   Alice Rosalind Trevelyan was my childhood girlfriend. See *and odd boy*—Volume I—Doc Togden—Aro Books WORLDWIDE—2011; and *Goodbye Forever*—Volume I—Ngakpa Chögyam— Aro Books WORLDWIDE—2020.
6   '*Shipshape and Bristol fashion*' was recorded as a phrase as early as 1840 – although 'shipshape' on its own is around 200 years older. The saying developed as a result of Bristol having a remarkably high tidal range of 43 feet – the 2nd highest in the world. Moored ships would thus be aground at low tide and—due to their keels—would rest on one side. If everything was not stowed away tidily, or battened down, chaos would ensue with the possibility of cargos being spoiled. So 'shipshape and Bristol fashion' meant that all eventualities were taken into consideration.

"Yes…" Rebecca almost choked on her own laugher *"and it sounds from what you told us that Bristols [7]were very much in fashion up there in the river Esk!"*

"So it would seem…" I laughed.

We all went off to bed in merry frames of mind. I lay awake for a while thinking back on the bizarre scenario in Liverpool. In terms of being a ngakpa – was it a mistake to have gone there? Or was it simply an experience which showed me more of what the world contained? I kept coming back to this question. I hoped it would eventually become too tedious to contemplate.

Did I *need* to know everything the world contained? Certainly not… but… what or where was the boundary line? I remember the Australian Hells Angel[8] who worked for a while on Sir Lindsay Parkinson's Scaffolding Yard. He'd been gaunt, taciturn, and forbidding – but not inimical. He'd experienced three *tours of duty* in Vietnam—as a volunteer—and was awaiting the confirmation of a fourth tour. I'd asked him why he went – and he'd replied that it paid well and gave him licence to kill. I remember being stunned by that. It was icy, the way he was so matter of fact about it. I asked him if he wasn't afraid of dying and he replied *"We all die."* Yes… we all die. The only thing he lived for was his immaculate motorcycle. His life and death were otherwise an irrelevance to him. His Levi's had never been washed—nor had any of his clothing—but his chopped hog[9] gleamed as if it has just been taken out of a showroom. I've always been grateful that I met him – if only to realise that there are people who are frightening, simply by virtue of whom they are. He was obviously a psychopath – but… an honest psychopath.

---

7 Cockney rhyming slang: Bristol City pertains to the word which rhymes with 'city', pertaining to breasts.
8 *Hells Angel* is spelt without an apostrophe – i.e. *Hells Angels* do not spell it *Hell's Angels*.
9 Harley Davidson motor cycle with extended forks, ape hangers, and *Frisco pegs*. See the movie Easy Rider.

He made no boast of the fact that he was a mercenary and enjoyed his work – but he gave no sense of 'glee' in his licence to kill. His enjoyment seemed sterile. There was no sense of ghoulishness about it – just... something spine-chillingly inhuman. It was as if he'd arrived from some extra-terrestrial culture where normal human feelings were genetically absent. The bizarre thing about remembering this man *(whose name I cannot remember)* was that—in comparing him with Atlas—Atlas came off worse. As soon as this thought emerged – I felt uneasy about it. How could I prefer a psychopathic mercenary to a bumbling sexually deranged poltroon like Atlas? Maybe it was simply because I'd never been on a battlefield. Maybe it was because it was just too strange—too far off and too abstract—to understand. Maybe *The Tale of the Hells Angel* had been a fabrication. If it had been fictional, however, there was no sense of the braggadocio that usually accompanies tall stories. On that outré observation I fell asleep.

I dreamt that night. It was not a dream of clarity – but it was a dream of the Aro Gar in Tibet. The valley high in the mountains – ringed by mountains. An isolated valley, the only entrance to which was a cavern through which a river ran. The was a greenness to the environment – and a kind of green that I could almost taste. It was a green I had never seen in my waking life and I had no way of comparing it with any shade of paint either in oil paint or gouache. I made a point of not mixing colours if I could help it – so I had quite an array of paints. Iron oxide green was the colour that come closest – but speckled with viridian and emerald. Somehow—in the dream—I was aware of wanting words to describe the colours I saw.

The valley was entirely cut off to the outside world in the winter months. I saw a sea of tents that were fabricated from felt—a few that were white—and one large tent made of tiger hides. I knew the tiger-tent was where I lived – or where I had lived. The strange aspect to the dream was that I was not entirely myself. I was partly Aro Yeshé. There was some strange oscillation in terms of being a stranger in the Gar and a person who was entirely familiar with it.

There must have been some moments of lucid dreaming – because at a few junctures I was able to question my identity in the dream. The frustrating aspect of the lucidity, was I that I kept losing it halfway through attempting to reconcile anything with anything else. Two names became evident. Jomo A-yé Khandro and Jomo A-shé Khandro. They were sitting in the sun just beyond the tent. I wanted to speak to them – but the dream dissolved before I was able to do so.

When I awoke, I forgot the dream. It only returned to me some hours later. The first thing that had occurred to me on waking, was the thought with which I'd fallen asleep. I wondered *'Would Kate's friends think I'd been frightened by the Latihan. Did they think I'd run off in a state of terror – because 'God was too much for me' or of some-such-thing?'* This distanced me from the dream – but I did not realise that until the dream re-emerged. I was surprised by the force of clarity with which the dream returned – but could not be sure whether I had remembered it all. I spent some time reconstructing the details of the dream memory and gradually more aspects fell into place. Remembering the dream was almost like dreaming – and I seemed to enter a state that was somewhat removed from conventional reality. It became a day dream – but a lucid day dream in which I was engaged in developing what the dream had been. In the end of lost track of what had been a day dream and what had occurred during the night. In the end it merged in terms of a sense of memory that seemed little different from memories of my current life.

The ladies entered and sat across the room peering at me in a half-amused manner. I opened the conversation *"I just got a letter from Kate. It confirms our notion – and, of course, Jan was entirely correct. I'm ever-so-slightly irked that I wasn't able to take her advice. I should have left the first night. I should have slept rough in the nearest stretch of countryside."* I sighed. *"I had my roll bag and blanket. I had the waterproof cover for my motorcycle that I could have thrown over. It had been warm and dry in any case – and I could've enjoyed gazing up at the stars."*

227

The ladies nodded matter-of-factly – and I concluded *"I wonder whether I should reply to Kate or not."*

I decided to show Kate's letter to the ladies and ask them what they thought

"Well…" Penelope offered when they'd all perused the letter *"you —could—just thank her for her letter and her concern… tell her you hope she won't be offended by your reply… and then just be direct about why you left."*

"Yes… I think I need to tell Kate that it wasn't 'fear' that drove me away – it was my motorcycle." I grinned. *"Y'know like Hotspur says to Kate when she asks 'What takes you away?' and he replies 'My horse—my love—my horse.'…"*

"Very funny – maybe you should" Rebecca laughed.

"I think some things are better savoured – unspoken or unwritten. The reason I went to bed early was because I'd had enough of being in a room with Atlas masturbating—trying to get women to fellate him—and laying on a monstrous crying jag because no one would oblige him. I may be squeamish— I have to admit—but I found it banal and terminally tedious."

"Yes…" commented Meryl *"I can't see what was supposed to be 'spiritual' about any of that that. Mind you, I thought it was very funny what Kate related about the opinion of the bestial Atlas."*

"Oh yes!" Rebecca laughed. *"You were frightened because religious conservatives are terrified of coming anywhere close to the experience of 'God'! That's a complete and utter hoot!"*

"Yes… it's a hoot alright…" I sighed *"but it makes me uncomfortable that Kate's so caught up in all that, that she's not able to challenge that point of view. I did—try—to warn her about Atlas."*

"It strikes me…" Penelope ventured *"… that whatever you said to Kate in Liverpool will have been blown away by now by what they've said. You're not there anymore to provide an alternative point of view – and… you—did —leave without saying a word."*

"You think that was a mistake?" I asked – perfectly prepared to admit I'd been in error.

"Hard to say…" Penelope replied with a frown of introspection *"what would your staying have achieved?"*

"Opportunity for an extremely unpleasant argument."

"Exactly. I'd have left, just as you did" Penelope shrugged. *"I wouldn't have seen any point in staying on, just to have an ugly argument with that asinine ape, Atlas."*

"For me… leaving as I did was…" PAUSE *"Well… I had two options. One was to have been frank – and the other to have been diplomatic. Being frank would have been quite explosive and would have been painful for both Kate and Amy. I don't think Kate deserved my frankness quite so directly – and I don't think Amy deserved it either. She had been reasonably friendly to me – and had given Atlas a private ticking off for being rude to me. So… that option wasn't workable. The other option was to have been diplomatic… but —even if I could have kept it up—it would have been quite an ordeal."* PAUSE *"No… I think I did the right thing by leaving as I did."*

"I think…" said Meryl *"that your best approach with answering Kate's letter… is to say exactly what you just said. Tell her your two options and why you couldn't take either. That way you don't have to comment in detail— on what you thought about it all—and you… may even give her something to think about."*

"All's well that ends well, then?"

"I'd say… just chalk it up to a cheesy experience" Rebecca grinned. *"It'll probably make a funny story one day."*

"Yes… it'll probably make 'dette laugh and give her complete validation in her opinion that religion is for the brain-dead." I said with a slightly wearied shake of my head. I decided to be slightly economical with the account I gave 'dette. There'd be no need to mention Jan's… slight indiscretion… or… the knickers or… the discussion of breasts on the bank of the Esk… or… maybe I'd simply not say anything.

No… that wouldn't work. I hated being secretive or having to edit my life in that way. I'd just have to deal with whatever 'dette's reaction might be.

"So, how did 'dette enjoy the story of you trip?" Meryl grinned rather too gleefully when I returned from the first day back at Art School.

"She didn't" I smiled and shrugged. *"She said: 'Spare me the details – I'm sure it was all very esoteric.'… and… so I spared her the details."*

"I think…" Meryl nodded thoughtfully *"… that's just as well."*

And that was the final outcome. The subject never arose again – and it was if as I'd never made the journey. It simply evaporated into space. The problem was however, that it remained with me as a reminder that 'dette and I were definitely not a long-term liaison. I couldn't settle to the idea of a relationship in which part of my life existed in a secret compartment. I couldn't imagine Lindie Dale wishing to live in ignorance of any part of my life – or of my being grateful that it should be so. I would not have kept anything hidden from Lindie – but then… she'd have come to Samŷe Ling with me… and then… the story would have been entirely different. I wouldn't have found myself travelling as a pseudo-single man. Thoughts of this kind were leading to a logical outcome. I'd approached an adieu with 'dette before[10] – and she'd retracted from the possibility in such a way as to turn the tables on me.

'… if it's a matter of religion, I suppose I will have to let you have your own ideas on the subject of Art. Far be it from be from—me—to get between a man and his religion.'

Once she'd said that, it took the wind out of my sails. I accepted that we'd either continue our cruise, become becalmed, flounder, sink, or… whatever. It wasn't that we didn't still have enjoyable times – but I missed the sense of lively romance there once was.

---

10 See chapter 5 – *if it's a matter of religion.*

It didn't feel... healthy to me – to be engaged in what felt like a marriage-of-convenience. Afternoon teas every Sunday at the Pump Rooms in Bath were fine by me. The string quartet was wonderful as always. So was the American Museum at Claverton[11] – and every other place. There was nothing wrong with anything— in one way—but there was nothing fabulously right with it either. There was always some sense in which I'd been co-opted into her father's vision of how life should be lived. I would really have to take a deep breath and say what had to be said.

'dette would not be—and could not be—the sangyum[12] I was supposed to find. I was wasting her time. I was wasting my time – and wasting the opportunity that Düd'jom Rinpoche had provided.

11 The American Museum is based at Claverton Manor, near Bath. The manor was designed for John Vivian by Jeffry Wyatville and built in 1820. The museum was founded by Dallas Pratt and John Judkyn. The collection includes cultural artefacts, decorative Arts and antiques – and Period Rooms 1690 to 1860. These rooms are reconstructions of historic American interiors, including a late seventeenth-century Puritan home, an eighteenth-century tavern, and a New Orleans bedroom.
12 Sangyum *(gSang yum)* – literally 'secret mother'. This term refers of a religious consort or spiritual wife. The male counterpart is Sangyab *(gSang yab)* literally 'secret father'. The word 'secret' here does not mean clandestine – but refers to person whose realised potential is not obvious to those who lack insight.

14

naked breakfast

I hadn't got to know anyone on my Illustration year particularly well. This was, of course, because my social life was located in Hotwells with Penelope, Rebecca, and Meryl. I was naturally cordial – but frequenting pubs was not possible if I wished to avoid inhaling cigarette smoke. The other factor was the somewhat irksome presence of Todd Whelcombe and Veranda Nugent. I was —to them—an interloper from the deranged demimonde of the '60s. I was a working-class upstart with irritating literary pretentions. The most vexing aspect of our interactions—for them —was that they tended to *twit themselves* through their attempts to *twit* me. I never set out to upstage them or make them look stupid – but, by one means or another, they seemed to arrange it by themselves. This infuriated them and predisposed them to passive aggressive hostility – and to making sure the other students on my year were cautioned as to my being partially deranged.

It was the time of the annual etching course, that occurred outside the Art School. So, there we were, in *Nettlemere Court* in the depths of Dorset. It could have been utterly delightful—and in most ways it was—but Todd and Veranda were basking in the vague sense that Roderick Peters was there as their advocate. Roderick Peters— second in command of the Illustration Department—was a good, conscientious, ethical man. He was a fine draftsman and meticulous lecturer – but he viewed me with the very faintest degree of derision and slight amusement. He had no time for alternative life-styles. He saw the hippie ethos—even though it didn't really apply to me *that* much—as something that needed to disappear. He viewed Todd and Veranda as a worthy young English couple who were professionally attuned and bound for successful careers in the world of illustration. Todd and Veranda were not weird – even though they were peculiar as Art students in being hostile to weirdness. That however seemed to endear them to Roderick Peters.

Todd and Veranda did not follow an Eastern religion. That was true of many Art students, of course – but they were overtly Anglican.[1] They also seemed offended by my Atheism, even though I never referred to it unless asked a direct question. Todd and Veranda dressed conservatively: camel cashmere sweaters; olive-green corduroy trousers; and, other such modestly hued raiment. This actually made oddities of them at Art school – but they affected not to be aware of being unconventional in that sense. No one noticed my clothing – but their 'Conservative Club' clothing made some people assume they were officials visiting the Art School on some bureaucratic errand.

Nettlemere Court was the venue for our first residential week. An entire week of etching lay ahead of me; so—even with a tiresome social setting—I would have a marvellous time. I would simply work. I was used to social isolation; so speaking when spoken to—and writing poetry in the evenings—would keep me from irritating Todd and Veranda. *"You're unusually quiet, Vic"* Roderick commented with a warm smile after dinner on the second evening.

"Sorry" I replied *"I'm rather absorbed with poetry – and, I've reached something of an impasse. I usually have recourse to a thesaurus at home. That usually provides inspiration at times like this."* PAUSE *"I should have brought it with me."*

I could see Todd in my peripheral vision and he was evidently having to hold himself back from some snide remark concerning my poetry. It wouldn't do for Todd to give any sign of his usual playground behaviour in front of Roderick.

"They may have one here in the house that you could borrow. I'll ask Geoffrey – when I see him. I'm just off to see him about the arrangements for tomorrow."

"Thank you, Roderick – that's most kind of you."

---

1   Anglican seems to be synonymous with Church of England – but there is a sense in which it is the word used to describe a higher degree of ritual practice. The definitions are too complex to give in a footnote.

Roderick gave me a warm smile and I almost got the impression that he was reassessing me. Maybe I was sane after all. I wondered what Todd and Veranda had told him about me. It didn't worry me what anyone thought about me apart from Derek Crowe and my friends. The ladies in the Illustration year[2] were all cordial enough and would exchange words with me from time to time – but I was evidently something of an outsider, even to them.

I'd arrived early and explored the meadows and woods a little around Nettlemere Court. There was a fabulous diminutive wooded ravine with a small river, that ran—almost like a torrent in parts—through the ravine and out through the undulating meadows. It was too good not to explore and so I walked up the river until I found myself on the banks of a deep pool with a stony bottom. I grinned at it. Suddenly I knew where I was going before breakfast in the morning. A plunge into cold water first thing in the morning is an ideal way to start the day and gives a person a keen desire for breakfast. It was thus that I set out for my early morning plunge and returned just as the others were seating themselves at the breakfast table.

"I didn't expect you to be an early riser Vic…" smiled Roderick *"… have you been out exploring the countryside?"* Roderick evidently heartily approved of early rising and country walking – so I was treated to the pleasant sensation of his unwithheld approval. Maybe he was coming to understand that I was fairly normal in many ways.

"I explored a little yesterday and found a lovely little pool up the river in the culvert of trees at the end of the meadow behind the house. So… I've just been for a pre-breakfast plunge – and jolly nice it was too."

"Good for you! Good for you!" Roderick exclaimed with genuine enthusiasm. *"I may take a dip myself before I leave here."*

---

2   Angela Grey, Janet Coleridge, Silvia Winstaunleigh-Greaves, Stephanie Lytton-Chatfield, Normanda Riley, Gloria Mytholmroyd, Pamela Beauchamp and Linda Essex.

I noticed Todd and Veranda looking aghast as Roderick and I exchanged pleasantries about the joys of nature and the pleasure of a cold plunge. They said nothing – but looked as if they'd found themselves in an unexpected hallucination: Victor Simmerson and Roderick Peters engaged in conversation on a subject of mutual interest. This was obviously not a pleasing turn of events for them. There was some general discussion of the horrors of a cold plunge – but Roderick and I assured the gathering that although it was a shock, one warmed up very quickly once clothed and that it gave a sense of wellness of being that was remarkable. That being said, I set to – and consumed a hearty breakfast.

The day went well. I found myself in the etching studio which had not been chosen by Todd and Veranda. Roderick was also mainly located in the other studio – but came to see what we were doing from time to time. I'd decided to investigate mezzotint[3] and began work on a large copper plate. I had to pay extra for that because it wasn't part of the package – but I was gleeful to explore a new process. I loved etching but it played hell with my skin vis-à-vis the turpentine for cleaning off the 'straw hat,[4]' and white spirit for cleaning off the ink. I'd spent a week down in Fine Art in the print making studio the week before and my hands had been rather the worse for wear by the end of the time. Mezzotint requires a device like a chisel—roughly 3 or 4 inches wide—with a curved blade. The flat of the 'chisel' is engraved with lines which create a serrated edge on the 'chisel'. The idea is to rock this 'chisel' across the surface of the copper plate in a pattern roughly corresponding to the Union Jack in order to roughen the copper plate.

3　Mezzotint *(manière noire / black manner)* is a method of engraving a copper plate by covering its entire surface with thousands of pin-prick holes which carry ink and, when printed, produces areas of tone. The pricking of the plate is carried out either with a roulette (a small wheel of sharp points), or an implement known as a rocker which resembles a chisel with a curved blade with 300 points per inch. This creates a burred surface – which is then smoothed in areas to allow tones of deep grey to white.
4　Straw-hat varnish is shellac mixed with black pigment used as stop-out in etching. Straw-hat varnish was originally made to waterproof hats.

The plate is then inked and printed – and, if it prints a uniform black, the plate is ready to be worked upon. The idea is to burnish away any area that you wish to print in shades of grey – or whatever colour ink is chosen. If you burnished too much away – you could simply use the chisel to roughen the area a little more and then burnish back to the desired level of grey. Areas to be left white, were simply burnished to a reflective shine.

My subject was the culvert of trees and the flowing line of meadows bounded by dry-stone walling and stunted bushes. Roderick was evidently pleased with my choice of subject and rejoiced in its lack of Surrealism. I wondered just how crazy Todd and Veranda had made me out to be. I said nothing about the nature of my observations and worked through the day – alternating in burnishing the copper plate and taking more detailed studies of the hedgerows. I'd decided that I would produce a collection of supportive studies that would accompany the mezzotint and use elements of these studies within the mezzotint.

It was a good first day followed by a good night's sleep – and in the morning I went for my second plunge. As I gained the surface of the pool however, I caught sight of Todd escaping from the scene with my clothes and towel. That was a surprise. What to do? It was an irritating situation – and I wondered just how infantile Todd was likely to become. I waited on the bank for a while but Todd showed no sign of reappearing. Nothing for it… I decided to walk back to the house. There was no point in standing under the trees cold and wet. At least the sun was shining out in the meadows and the exertion of the walk would probably warm me up somewhat. I remembered the words of Düd'jom Rinpoche *'With each life-circumstance: whatever is enacted, stare directly into the enactment – with all the senses.'*

As I proceeded across the meadow, I caught sight of Roderick who was evidently on his way to intercept me. *"Vic… I have no objection to naturism – but you really can't expect to walk into the house like that. What gave you the idea that this is acceptable?"*

237

"It wasn't my choice Roderick… I'm afraid Todd went off with my clothes while I was in the pool – and, by the time I got out of the water, he was nowhere to be seen."

"Dear me – school-boy pranks… but why didn't you just wait for him to come back? He surely intended to come back."

"Well… I did wait for a while – and, I did call out a few times… but… in the end I started feeling too cold to stand there like an idiot."

"So, you just decided to walk back and… how did you think to make your way into the house without being seen?"

"To be honest Roderick – I didn't really think too much about it… I was cold and wanted to get some clothes on and eat breakfast – and… I didn't think anyone was likely to die of shock or whatever."

"So you would have just walked into the house naked?"

"What other choice would I have had?"

"Well…" Roderick mumbled – unable to find an immediate answer *"I suppose you could have called for help from behind one of the bushes outside the house."*

I grinned very slightly – and said *"Help."*

"Oh yes—I see—do take my sweater… it's quite long and should cover… all eventualities. I should have offered it immediately – but I was somewhat taken aback by…"

"Thank you Roderick—I appreciate that—I am rather cold, as you can imagine."

And with that we walked back to the house. Roderick was a little silent at first – as if he were ruminating *"I'm sorry if… I seemed critical and unsympathetic Vic… I was simply rather surprised – and… your unusual degree of composure—striding naked across the field—led me to… imagine… well – I thought you were doing something to shock…"*

"I can understand that Roderick. I suppose most people would have grabbed a piece of hedgerow or something – but I think... I would have felt more humiliated by that *than by being blasé about my situation."*

"Yes—of course—I can see that there is... more dignity in... well, yes. Less said the better, I think."

"Absolutely. I'm looking forward to breakfast, the bacon here is marvellous – as are the fried eggs and granary toast."

"You will have done more than your share to earn it this morning, I feel." And with that we entered the house and I ascended the stair case to equip myself with clothing more to my taste than Roderick's massive ungainly fisherman's sweater.

Soon after I'd come down to breakfast and taken my seat Todd approached me and apologised. I accepted his apology with what I hoped would seem *supreme magnanimity*. I was keen that Roderick should have no reason to reverse his new good opinion of me – and, of course, it appealed to my sense of humour to act as if... I'd enjoyed the prank. Then Todd added *"... of course... when I came back you'd already gone."*

"I must have been a little too keen to savour this fine bacon" I replied and continued to savour it. Todd had obviously hoped to insinuate that I departed too hurriedly from the scene – but I could see by Roderick's expression that such a ploy would not be appreciated. Todd wore the look of one who'd received a thorough dressing down – or who, at least, had suffered a grievous loss of face. He'd been judged to have been childish by the lecturer who'd been something of an ally and I started to feel a little sorry for him. Todd was a fool. I had no doubt about that – but a fool also has his feelings. It makes me wince to see people humiliated. Although I considered Todd to be a royal pain in the rectum, I didn't wish him ill. I just wished him away. I wished him to be in Scunthorpe, or Little Wilting Under Marsh, or anywhere other than where I was. Todd handed me my clothes and boots. I nodded, smiled, and placed them on a wooden chest behind me.

"You'd really have walked in here naked?" asked Linda.

"Yes… I suppose my desire for breakfast would have overcome any trepidation I may have felt."

"I suppose we would have cheered you if you had" Silvia laughed.

"Maybe I'll give you the opportunity before we leave" I grinned and we fell to discussing etching and mezzotint. Just before taking my clothes up to my bedroom however – I noticed that the little subsidiary pocket in my Levi's was empty. I looked around on the floor but there was no sign of my keys. I always kept them in that pocket. *"Todd…"* I ventured *"… I think you may have lost my keys…"* PAUSE *"I always keep them in this pocket here… and… they were there when I left my clothes under that tree where you found them. I always check on them – so… you must have dropped them somewhere."*

Todd began to splutter some kind of attempt to rescind responsibility when Roderick interrupted *"Well Todd here's a fine adventure for you. You'll just have to retrace your steps and find Vic's keys. Maybe this will serve to dampen your enthusiasm for pranks?"*

Todd agreed to look for the keys and asked what they looked like. *"One's a house key—a brass Yale key—and the other is a steel key: that's the ignition key for my motorbike. The Yale key's no problem—I can always get another one made—but the ignition key's going to be necessary to get home from here unless the local garage can manage to do something…"* PAUSE *"… the two keys are linked with an iron military clasp that belonged to my father – so… I'd not like to lose that."*

On hearing this Todd underwent some kind of internal eruption. I've never seen such a glare of undiluted loathing on anyone's face before. All Todd could say was *"Yes"* and with that stalked out into the fields to find the accursed keys. It turned out that Todd made his search every day for an hour or more – but the keys never appeared. I never said anything about it – but decided that I'd have to go and look myself on the last day if Todd proved unable to locate them.

The days passed without incident and as Todd had blotted his copybook with Roderick, he did his best to treat me affably. I responded, as if Todd was the finest fellow I'd ever met – and hoped that the experience would mellow him a little. I had nothing to gain from entrenching Todd in his revulsion for me – and, if anything, I thought it might do Todd some good to realise that I was a fairly agreeable human being. I might be weird – but I wasn't politically aggressive in that stance as some people were. I didn't hate Todd for being a 'straight' and neither did I look down upon him as if I was one of the *psychedelic elite*. I was simply an Art student who enjoyed being an Art student.

On the morning of the last day Todd approached me—having searched every day for my keys—and said *"I'd think you—could— help me find these keys of yours. I've spent hours every day trying to find them for you."*

"Certainly Todd. I'd have looked before but I was busy with my mezzotint. Let's go and take a look now."

Todd looked vaguely surprised – but off we went. We were soon at the place where I took a plunge every morning and after scanning the area for I moment I said *"You... went off in that direction through those willows over there... just before the oak trees."*

"Really?" Todd queried. *"I don't remember going that way."*

"Well" I replied *"let's take a look down there anyway."*

"You can if you like but I'm sure I didn't go that way."

I shrugged and headed off along the line I remembered Todd to have taken. I scanned the area at every pace I took and after a while found myself amongst the willows. Then I saw them. I could easily have missed them. It was only the glint of the brass that caught my eye. *"Here they are Todd. Search over."*

There was no answer from Todd. As soon as he heard I'd found them he stalked off back to the house without waiting.

That was no problem to me – but as soon as I got back to the house I discovered why Todd had been so eager to return on his own.

"I think he's just kept them hidden all week so that I'd have to search for it every day and miss out on time for etching."

"No, Todd…" I answered as I walked through the door *"… I would —not—have done that."*

"And how do I know that! It would be typical of you to do something like that!"

"No, Todd…" I sighed. *"Typical's the one thing it would—not—have been."*

"Really!?" he jeered tossing his head like a petulant child.

"Well Todd… I suppose you'll never know, will you. But, whatever – I'm getting back to my mezzotint now."

"You deliberately hid those keys!" Todd threw back at me – but at that moment Roderick walked in. *"Todd…"* Roderick stated in a measured and rather serious tone *"you do yourself nothing but disservice by acting like this – I suggest you drop the subject and do something sensible with your time."*

There was some further discussion – but I heard none of it as I'd already left for the etching studio.

"He would have deserved it if you had only pretended to have lost your keys" Janet commented – then *"… did you pretend to lose them?"*

"No Janet… that would make me as much of an idiot as Todd." PAUSE *"It would have been fun—I must admit—but some kinds of fun are only worth imagining. Even then, I've got better ways of passing my time than dreaming up new ways for Todd to humiliate himself."*

Janet nodded in a solemn kind of way and replied *"Yes… he really does seem to do that doesn't he."*

Roderick wanted our work displayed at the end of the week – so that we could all get some sense of how we'd individually evolved. It was interesting to see everyone's work – and Roderick commented on each etching. He admired the strong points in each piece and gave critical appraisal of flaws he detected. I found his criticism interesting. I didn't always find myself in agreement with him – but decided that maybe my view was not as educated as his. I liked all the work – even the work of Todd and Veranda. Todd and Veranda's etchings received only faint praise from Roderick *"I think…"* he mused *"… that you could have been a little more adventurous; both of you."* PAUSE *"If you look at these other pieces—Stephanie's and Janet's in particular—where multiple etching plates have been used – you will see that much more is possible in this oeuvre. I especially like the way Janet ate a line through the plate at the surface of the pool of water. That made it possible to use two colours quite distinctly – and the result is quite dramatic. It's also important to thoroughly clean the bloom from the etching plate or the result tends to be somewhat… smeary."*

True. I thought Janet's piece was brilliant – and I thought Todd and Veranda's pieces looked… smeary. I commented how much I liked Janet's piece and how I was definitely going to experiment on multiple plates and split plates. Everyone was in agreement with that – and there was a distinct sense of inspiration in the air for what would follow back in Bristol when we could get some more time in the print-making studio. I wonder how my mezzotint would be evaluated. It was the last in the line. *"And this…"* Roderick hummed almost as if he were about to pour scorn upon my mezzotint. *"This really is something of which you can be proud Vic. Have you ever seen the mezzotints of John Martin?* [5]*"*

"Yes. I saw them in London when I was at school and can still almost see them. They're utterly remarkable – I was quite strongly moved by them. They seem to haunt me, somehow."

---

5   John Martin (1789–1854) was an English Romantic painter and mezzotint engraver. In 1823, he was commissioned by Samuel Prowett to illustrate John Milton's Paradise Lost. The notable prints include Pandæmonium and Satan Presiding at the Infernal Council.

243

"I can see that" Roderick smiled. *"I think you found your metier here."*

All the while Todd and Veranda sat to the side – somewhat subdued. I felt like saying something positive about their work – but felt that it would probably be taken amiss. And then it was over. The evening dinner. The farewell breakfast – and off on the road again. Todd and Veranda vanished from my mind. I purred through the countryside admiring the greenery – wondering what Düd'jom Rinpoche would make of the strange vignettes of human experience that constituted the story of my three years in the West as a ngakpa. Would he wish me to recount such events? I suspected that he would not be that keen to hear of every peculiar incident that formed the pastiche of my attempt to live as a ngakpa. I was accumulating a portfolio of peculiarly puzzling... what were they? peccadillos, imbroglios, predicaments, contretemps... There seemed to be no word that suited these curious cameos—but whatever word it might be—were these the situations in which I was supposed to be engaged in terms of learning about the culture of my generation? I was certainly in Britain. I was interacting with British people in a setting that was not too far out of the ordinary—at least at Art School—but having someone run off with one's clothes had been an intriguing situation. Casting my mind back – I felt that I'd acted as well as I could have acted. Todd had come out of it with egg on his face – but I'd not set it up to work out like that. Was it an accident that I met with what seemed an unusual degree of hostility – or was it something about me that invoked it? Was this simply life?

The Foundation year had been entirely free of interpersonal antagonism – but times seemed to have changed. The Foundation year had been so innocent in terms of personal interactions. It had been cordial, stimulating, and pleasurable. In Bristol however, normalcy had kicked in. The atmosphere amongst the students tended to resemble Secondary School rather than what I had experienced at Farnham. No one spontaneously quoted from books. No one stayed on late working. There was no Folk and Poetry Club.

I had no real complaints however, because Derek Crowe was a marvellous head of department – who became a personal friend. In the end I came to have a cordial relationship with Roderick Peters – but only after he had adjusted his initial impressions of me... and of Todd Whelcombe and Veranda Nugent. I was never aware which way their relationship with him went after Todd's immature behaviour. Whether their dinner assignations with Roderick Peters continued as mine did with Derek Crowe, I never knew. I did not pry. I simply continued to be as innocuous as I could with Todd. There was nothing that caused me shame in terms of my behaviour in that respect, other than occasional lapses into wit, when Todd became too outrageously obnoxious. The ladies of my year became far more cordial and conversational with me after the Etching Course at Nettlemere Court. I learnt from this, that I had no need to assert anything to anyone in respect of who or what I was. I would eventually be seen as a decent, reasonable, friendly person – by any other decent, reasonable, friendly person. Maybe *that* was an aspect of what Düd'jom Rinpoche intended me to discover.

15

the rat who came back

A year had passed in which I'd been the artist I enjoyed to be –
and tried to be the ngakpa I strove to be. The conclusion of the
Düd'jom gTér Tröma Ngöndro was in sight and I knew that I
could return to Kyabjé Düd'jom Rinpoche having fulfilled what I
had been entrusted to fulfil. It had taken some work beyond the
practice – as I'd had to get the texts translated in Nepal. That took
a deal of time – especially when the translations came back in
Tibetan U-chen script and English. There'd been no phonetic
version in Roman script to chant and so I had to laboriously
produce it myself. It was laborious because although transliterating
Tibetan text to Roman text wasn't difficult—working out that
sPrul sKu was *tulku* and brKyangs phyag[1] was *kyang chag*—it took a
great deal of time. I had books on Tibetan grammar – but they
were diabolically difficult to understand. There's nothing like
perseverance however – and with the application of sheer jaw-
grinding will-power I accomplished it.

We were to go to spend a week at Windlecombe Hall—
Windlecombe—Devonshire. It was to be a print-making course
and I was—of course—thoroughly delighted by the prospect. I'd
enjoyed the print-making course at Nettlemere Court at the end of
the first year and so this next weeklong foray – was going to be
equally as delightful.

Etching is a magical art – and the thought of devoting a week to it
was a cause of great happiness to me. Using hydrochloric acid to
eat into a zinc plate is somehow primæval. The etched-out
channels and pit marks in the zinc plate hold ink which is then
transferred to watercolour paper by being pressed under several
tons of roller operated by long wooden arms – like a huge ship's
wheel. The result is intriguing – both delicate and dramatic.

---

1   *brKyangs phyag* means 'full length prostration'.

Etching produces strong images that can nevertheless be highly intricate and subtle.

Todd Whelcombe and Veranda Nugent were somewhat less than enthusiastic at the prospect because it seemed to them like the *intrusion of Fine Art*. They'd not enjoyed the excursion to Nettlemere Court at the end of the first year because their draughtsmanship and aptitude with etching had not exactly caused wonder in anyone. Janet Coleridge and Stephanie Lytton-Chatfield had been the heroines of *that* event – and, I suppose, my efforts with mezzotint had also been applauded. To me the *intrusion of Fine Art* was always welcome – so I was eager to set out.

The first signs of Todd and Veranda seeking to skip the event came when Roderick Peters found he was unable to accompany us. This was due to personal circumstances which required him to remain in Bristol. It was decided that Derek Crowe would replace him as our accompanying lecturer. That didn't seem to suit Todd and Veranda – but they were discreet enough not to pass comment on Derek Crowe. They were probably aware that Derek was well loved by all of us and any adverse reflection on him would not be warmly received by the others in our year. They seemed to see Derek as 'an old fogie' – even though they never used that term. They found his *Somerset Maugham* [2] / *Evelyn Waugh* [3] style of clothing, outré – even though they tried to disguise their ridicule. I found Derek's clothing rather dapper and stylish – but my appreciative sentiments vis-à-vis Derek's sartorial sense were greeted with *"Yes you—would—say that wouldn't you – anything to be quirky."*

There was some rolling of eyes in the room at that remark – and I replied *"Well yes… almost anything – within the bounds of English decency, of course."*

---

2 William Somerset Maugham (1874–1965) was an English playwright and novelist. See glossary: *Maugham, William Somerset*.
3 Arthur Evelyn St John Waugh (1903–1966) was a novelist, biographer, journalist, and reviewer. See glossary: *Waugh, Arthur Evelyn St John*.

That caused mirth in the room and Todd returned to his work looking as if he was trying to crochet a mudguard with his eyebrows.

Todd had lived down his childish prank in Nettlemere Court – and there was no reason why he and Veranda could *not* have got on well with Derek Crowe. Derek Crowe was after all, uniformly cordial and genial with all. The problem was, that I had a social connection with Derek and Susan Crowe. We had dinner together a few times every term and 'dette mostly accompanied me. Derek obviously found me a pleasant hardworking student – and he took no objection at all to my surrealistic projects. After all – I was to become an Art School lecturer on a Foundation course somewhere. There was no need for me to produce a mainstream Illustration folder and Derek understood that quite well. In point of fact – my folder was developing in an ideal manner for someone who would have to guide students in a multi-disciplinary environment.

Roderick Peters no longer sided with Todd and Veranda in their dislike of me. Even before, he'd not been the kind of man who would fuel disharmony. Roderick Peters—although he'd warmed to me at Nettlemere Court—still found me... a little too weird for his taste. He had no taste for Monty Python. He had no great love of Surrealism either – if Surrealism left the canvas and entered conversation or sartorial expression. He disliked Salvador Dalí for that reason. It may have been that I wasn't an Illustrator. I was a multi-media creator of pictorial mayhem who'd landed in the Illustration department when I'd have been better suited to another three years on a Foundation course. I did once admit to him that this would have been my preference, had it been possible to take a degree structured in that way. It also may have been that I was a product of the '60s, or that I enjoyed puns – as did Derek Crowe. Roderick Peters was one of those people who groan when a pun is made – and act as if the pun were some kind of intellectual blasphemy.

Roderick thought nothing of groaning at Derek's puns even though Derek was the head of the Illustration department. Derek never took it amiss when Roderick groaned; and if I was there, it simply caused us both further jocularity – at a point directly subsequent to Roderick's escape from the scene of the crime.

The next incident was Todd and Veranda's cancellation vis-à-vis Windlecombe Hall. The decision that had to be made as to whether the cuisine on the menu was to be vegetarian or not. Windlecombe Hall could either provide standard fare or vegetarian fare – but not both. We had to vote on the choice of menu. This proved a far more unpleasant experience than I would have expected – even knowing Todd and Veranda to be as they were.

To say that Todd and Veranda were decidedly carnivorous would not quite describe their position. They were however, curiously 'religious' about their diet. They seemed to see vegetarianism as some sort of rebellion against the Church of England. They were coy about expressing the exact nature of their grievance – but it seemed that God had provided animals for us to eat and that not eating them was akin to blasphemy. Naturally they raised their hands for the meat menu. They were joined in this by Silvia Winstaunleigh-Greaves, Angela Grey, and Linda Essex. That made five votes for the meat menu. Janet Coleridge, Stephanie Lytton-Chatfield, Normanda Riley, Gloria Mytholmroyd, Pamela Beauchamp were vegetarian. That made five votes for the vegetarian menu.

Now… I wasn't vegetarian – but… *wouldn't you know it*… found myself with the casting vote.

"I'll opt for the vegetarian menu."

"But you're not vegetarian!" Todd stated with evident righteous zeal *"I've seen you eating bacon—and—steak and kidney pie in the canteen!"*

"And jolly nice they were too." PAUSE *"I never said I—was—vegetarian, Todd."*

"*Then why did you vote for the vegetarian menu?*"

"*The vote, Todd—unless I'm entirely mistaken—was not to indicate who was vegetarian – but who wanted to opt for the vegetarian menu or for the meat menu.*"

"*Oh—very—convenient!*" Todd snapped. "*Always the—plausible— reply!*"

"*I'll try my best to be implausible next time Todd.*"

Todd didn't seem to understand my reply and simply continued his harangue. "*Just so you can be contrary and make arbitrary decisions that will ruin our time at Windlecombe Hall.*"

"*Y'know Todd… I don't think I'm as complicated as you are – and… besides which… Derek is coming… and—as you probably know—he's vegetarian.*"

Veranda tried to speak but merely spluttered – probably due to that fact that I'd unexpectedly undermined Todd's position. Ridiculous as it was, it was now terminally deflated.

"*Oh right, I was forgetting!*" Linda gasped. "*I'll happily change to the vegetarian menu too—I don't mind what I eat really—but it would be insensitive to Derek to go for the meat menu.*"

Stephanie and Angela concurred without another thought – leaving Todd and Veranda outnumbered 9 to 2.

"*You're probably—very—pleased with yourself now* " Todd sneered.

"*No more than usual Todd* " I sighed – giving in to sarcastic humour. Why did I *have* to do that?

"*You think you're so—very—clever don't you!*" Todd vituperated.

"*Don't be so obnoxious Todd – you're acting like a child!*" Linda responded.

"*I won't have you speaking to Todd in that way!*" Veranda snapped.

It was surprising to hear her speak because she usually remained silent when things became heated.

"That'll be difficult for you then Veranda…" Linda laughed *"… but if you don't like it, you'd better advise Todd not to act like a child."*

This was unprecedented. The unpleasantries had previously only involved Todd and myself. I wondered how it would turn out. I decided that it might be better if I were not seen to observe the scene too closely for fear of carnage occurring.

"So you're hiding behind the girls now—typical—typical…" Todd jeered noting the fact that I had returned to my work.

I smiled. I shook my head from side to side without looking up from my work *"Todd—if you don't mind, I'm working—so… would you please be so very kind as to accept that I can no longer listen."*

I remembered the words of Düd'jom Rinpoche *'With each life-circumstance: whatever is enacted, stare directly into the enactment – with all the senses.'*

Laughter erupted in the room. Veranda fumed almost silently – apart from a few attempts to speak that stifled themselves in inarticulacy. They both stalked out of the room in high dudgeon and were not seen again that day.

"Oh dear…" sighed Gloria *"we've really upset them now haven't we?"*

"No Gloria…" I sighed *"… they've upset themselves… and if anyone's upset them – it would have been me."* PAUSE *"After all – I was the casting vote wasn't I?"*

"Yes – but I slapped Veranda down for being a cretin in defending Todd when he was acting like a four-year-old" Linda countered.

"Yes… you did—and well said too—but they'll probably overlook that on the basis that I inflamed you or some such thing… and… it's true… I— could—have voted for the meat menu."

"Yes… you—could—have done…" commented Janet *"… but you were thinking of Derek Crowe. So why should they be upset about that? You were just being considerate."*

"Yes… I was… but consideration of others is not their strong suit – or they'd try harder to be averagely sociable. I know I must be a monstrous irritation to them – but it doesn't seem to occur to them that they're not my favourite specimens of humanity either." PAUSE *"I'm not… one of these proletarian radicals who hate the upper classes or anything—two of my best friends were middle / upper-middle—but in general I don't really warm to people who imagine themselves superior."*

"But surely… if you've got that kind of class background you'd understand something about considering others – so why wouldn't they see your consideration of Derek as… well – as just that?" Linda asked.

"Because…" I sighed with a shake of my head *"… because they will have seen my being considerate to Derek… as a devious manœuvre deliberately designed to make them look bad whilst making myself look… whatever."*

"Oh… Jeee-sus… that is just—too—stupid…" Stephanie groaned. *"Not what—you—said Vic – but I can just* see *that that's the way they must have seen it… and… I know you really piss them off for reasons that are too mysterious to understand."*

"My understanding is that I annoy them because I'm working class – and have the audacity—not—to tug my forelock to them. I also have the audacity to… be eccentric and that upsets them."

"So…" Linda observed *"that – must have seemed like some kind of coup d'état."*

"Yeah… that's about the shape of it." PAUSE *"Anyhow I wouldn't worry about it. They'll lay all the blame on me – and I'm fine with that."*

"But we all voted for the vegetarian menu too…" Normanda volunteered *"not just you – it wouldn't be fair to blame you!"*

"That's still fine with me 'manda. I don't need it to be fair."

The Slogans of Chekhawa[4] came to mind: 'Drive all blames into one.' *"In fact…"* I smiled *"I think it's better that I—do—get all the blame as it'll make for a better atmosphere. I've got used to Todd and Veranda despising me – so it's nothing that wasn't already there. And y'know…"* I misquoted *"… as I ain't got nothing I got nothing to lose— I'm invisible now—I got no secrets to conceal."*

"Bob Dylan?"

"The very same – he's got so many lines that come to mind… just like Blues" PAUSE *"and folk songs too…*

> *Rod'rick Peters, Rod'rick Peters lend me your grey mare—All along, down along, out along lee—For I want to go down to Windlecombe Fair, with Janet Coleridge, Silvia Winstaunleigh-Greaves, 'manda Riley, Gloria Mytholmroyd, Pamela Beauchamp, Stephanie Lytton-Chatfield, Angela Grey, Linda Essex, Old Uncle Derek and all – Good Old Uncle Derek and all.[5]"*

That caused laughter from all – which eased the tension in the room, as I hoped it would.

"A song for every occasion!" laughed Janet. *"You're so much more out-going when Todd's not around – he must really put a crimp on you."*

"Mmm…" I pondered *"I suppose I do—let—him do that… but then I think it might be unpleasant for everyone else in the room if I got lively. We'd be exchanging sarcastic invective the livelong day – and I wouldn't wish that on anyone."*

"Yeah…" Janet sighed *"yeah… I see that… but you will be lively next week at Windlecombe."*

"That's a promise" I grinned and bid them all farewell.

---

4   The Slogans of Chekhawa Yeshe Dorje are a synthesis of *Lojong, (bLo sByong)* – a mind training practice based on the 11th century aphorisms of Atisha. See glossary: *lojong*.
5   Parody of 'Widecombe Fair'. The phrase 'Old Uncle Tom Cobley and all' is a humorous form of 'et al' (and others), originating from the Devonshire folk song 'Widecombe Fair'. See glossary: *Widecombe Fair*.

Todd and Veranda opted out of the trip on the basis that they preferred to take on a packaging design project with the Graphic Designers. They deemed it more necessary for their professional folders than etching. *"No design studio is going to be interested in etchings"* Todd sneered when he and Veranda announced their alternative plans – but no one commented. That left Todd standing—at the closure of his announcement—with an audience who appeared to be busy with their work. He mooched around for a while – seemingly in order to show he was in no way embarrassed by the silence which had met his speech. I was almost tempted to say *'I think you're right Todd'* but felt that such a remark would not serve any useful purpose. I had no need to crow – and certainly no desire to fuel some diatribe from Todd.

And so it was, that I went to Windlecombe Hall in Windlecombe, Devonshire; not by grey mare – but on my motorcycle with Silvia Winstaunleigh-Greaves riding pillion. She fancied the ride on the *Easy Rider machine* and our combined luggage was fairly easy to accommodate strapped on either side of the sissy bars and in the leather panniers. With the padding of the backrest removed, the large paperclip-shaped chromium bars provided ample support to a surprising amount of luggage – as long as that luggage was vaguely tubular.

The journey was pleasant and I took a picnic of bacon, brie, tomato, and scallion sandwiches. *"I thought I'd make up to some extent for your lack of meat this week."*

"Your quite the humourist" Silvia laughed as she devoured her sandwich.

"I do my best… it just seemed… fitting, somehow."

"Interesting what you said the other day about Todd and Veranda not liking the fact that you're working class." PAUSE *"It seems to me that what they don't like is that you're always witty – and always unaffected by their remarks. I think they're used to being the ones who come out on top… and it infuriates them that they never get the better of you – and never manage to make you angry."*

"Well… I don't like anger – and… although they do irritate me, it would really upset me if I allowed myself to become angry."

"How d'you stop yourself being angry though? Because, sometimes they're completely insufferable and rude."

"Well… I remember that they're not adults. They… probably have the emotional age of…" PAUSE *"… I couldn't say exactly – but I'd place it somewhere in junior school."*

"That's an interesting perspective… I think I see what you mean…" PAUSE *"Yes… that really—does—seem to fit…"* PAUSE *"… I suppose, if you always remember they're children… then that really could work."* PAUSE *"But what happens when other people treat them as adults – or when they have an effect on you in the adult world?"*

"Yes… that can happen… and it has happened – but only in the past."

"How d'you mean?"

"Well… in the first year they did tend to influence the way I was viewed – but now you all seem to have come round to thinking that I'm not quite the self-indulgent deranged lunatic they portrayed me as being."

"Jesus!" Silvia gasped. *"That's really true! I'm sorry about that… I suppose I really did think that to some degree."* PAUSE *"And… you don't hold that against any of us?"*

"No" I chuckled *"you're all nice people and… I'm looking forward to getting to know you all better without Todd and Veranda being around."*

"Yes – that'll be fun. And—didn't—that—work out perfectly! It would have been pretty intense to have been with those two all day long—everyday— and in the evening for a week. Jesus—just think of it—that would have been hell!"

"It would have been something or other" I laughed. *"But I think that Derek would have ameliorated… as it were."*

"Yeah – Todd and Veranda are always more wary of being too obviously antagonistic to you when Derek's around. It's pretty creepy really the way they can turn it on and off."

Before long we were back on the road again and soon, we were in Windlecombe.

Windlecombe Hall was not too hard to find, and—having arriven—we stood staring at it. It was beautiful. It was a rustic sprawl of buildings. It looked to have been the home of some 18ᵗʰ century gentleman-farmer. The house was quite large – but not of the stately home style. It looked as if generations of family had added extensions – and the roof line was somehow hard to fathom. There were two large barn structures that had been converted into two-story studio spaces, and a multitude of out-buildings surrounded a cobbled courtyard. That was where we ate most meals.

I parked my motorcycle with a group of cars and covered it with the tarpaulin that I'd tied behind the rear of the saddle. We were the first to arrive so we got the pick of the rooms. We both chose attic rooms facing the courtyard. The rooms were small but comfortable. The ubiquitous stripped wood and white wall were an ideal environment for me and I sat on the bed for a while just smiling at the décor.

Whilst I sat in my room, I heard a car arrive and then another – and another. The familiar voices rose after a while from the cobbled courtyard and soon they were joined by the ever-mirthful Derek. Time to go down and join the others. The atmosphere, when I descended the stairs, was ebullient – and I was quite moved by the greeting I received. There's nothing quite like radiant smiles to enhance a situation – and when the smiles emanate from eight delightful young ladies the effect can be almost overpowering. Then there was Derek—chuckling as usual—but what the subject was never became apparent. The laughter brought out the proprietors John and Karin Weatherby. *"I see we're going to be a lively gathering this week"* John Weatherby exclaimed.

"Too true!" Karin added *"and… almost all gels* [6] *I see. That makes a change."*

"I was almost a gel, once" I launched in and almost wished I hadn't. I was not used to spontaneous speech in terms of the Illustration room. Karin and John looked quizzical and so I told them about my attempt to obtain a place at Farnham Girls' Grammar School. Neither Derek Crowe nor the ladies in my year had heard that story – so I regaled them with it. This caused much laughter and questions which were answered in such a way as to cause yet more laughter.

"Quite the raconteur" John smiled. *"We like a good story here, of an evening. Maybe you will oblige us with more as the week goes on?"*

"It would be a pleasure, good sir."

These people were intriguing. They seemed to have a flare for *old-world English* that matched my own – and that of Derek. Dinner was brought out without much further ado and we seated ourselves round a massive oak table festooned with vast brass candlesticks that looked as if they had once graced a church. Dinner turned out to be three gargantuan tureens of Swiss fondue with a mountain of bread. There was also a truncated wooden bucket brimming with home-grown tomatoes – and another of radishes. I'd never considered radish with cheese – but it was surprisingly pleasant.

At a discreet point Derek confided *"I would like to thank you for your choice of the vegetarian menu. Gloria travelled down with me and she told me about the trouble it caused you."*

"No need for thanks Derek – it was my pleasure and I'm used to Todd and Veranda being… as they are."

"Yes… we have never had a situation like this before – and it is really rather upsetting. I'm sorry at how this is affecting your time in the Illustration department."

6   *Gels* – 'girls' in a British upper-class accent.

"It might…" I ventured somewhat hesitantly *"be less upsetting for me than you think. I'm very happy to be here—for example—and I don't really actually have to see that much of Todd and Veranda back in Bristol."* PAUSE *"They mainly ignore me."*

"I'm happy that you can be so forbearing – and thank you once again for your kind and considerate thought with the menu."

"You know Derek… over the last year… I've been thinking about vegetarianism anyway. I think… I may well stop eating meat when I leave the house in Hotwells—in fact—I've more-or-less made up my mind to make the change. It would be unfair to my friends in the house to make that change now – but… especially after this amazing fondue." PAUSE *"So – anyway, I was actually happy to cast my vote as I did."*

Derek nodded to indicate that he understood my reluctance to be thanked and we re-entered the general conversation.

The next day I took a walk before breakfast to scout out the oak trees I'd seen in the near distance, and when I got to them, I wasn't disappointed. I suddenly had a flashback from my outings with Helen McGillivray in search of roots and branches. I remembered Janet's staggering marvellous split plate etching and decided that the roots of a particularly gnarled old oak tree were the perfect subject. I worked out how there could be five sections below and one above. The section above would be the low-hanging branch – and that would be a double printing. One would be an aquatint – that would be the green printing. Then there'd be a brown printing plate for the branch and twigs. The five segments below would be various shades of grey and brown. It would end up as a large piece of work – and I decided I'd have to find out just how large I could go with the etching bed available.

After breakfast I explained my idea to Derek. He thought the idea was workable although he wondered if I'd be able to undertake so much work in the time. *"If you don't think it's a good idea – I could… leave out the aquatint plate for the leaves and handle the image on one plate."*

259

Derek thought for a while and replied *"No, I would say go with your original idea – I think you have the stamina to take it on."*

And so I did. I made a series of drawings of the roots and low-hanging branch of the oak tree and set about preparing the plate for the initial carve-up. Rather than use hydrochloric acid to cut the plate into five sections however I went with Derek's advice to limit it to three and to cut the plate with a hack saw. It was less taxing on the acid and far quicker. Using hydrochloric acid to cut the plate was an accident on Janet's part *(I discovered)* and so the idea to take the same approach wasn't deemed an economical use of the acid. The more the acid has to work the weaker the acid becomes. That seemed a good idea – and using a hacksaw also reduced the time considerably. It was soon lunch time. An entire round of Cheddar appeared and we helped ourselves to wedges of it. It was delicious and I commented *"Y'know… I've always thought of cheddar as being a little low in flavour – but this is so good it makes my ears ache."*

Derek almost choked on his food at that remark and, in fact, the whole company convulsed. Karin Weatherby said that the sense of *pain at the base of the ears* had something to do with the secretion of acid from somewhere to somewhere else – and that this also happened with certain other foods. I replied that I'd make that my test of a good cheese in future *"If it fails to make my ears ache, I won't consider a cheese to be worth the candle.[7]"*

"Suffer not the brie to be thus cast aside" laughed Karin.

"Ah… I was forgetting – and nor the Cambozola.[8]"

---

7   'Not worth the candle' relates to games that were so lacking in merit that they were not worth the expense of the candle that provided the light by which to engage in them. Candles were a claim on a household economy that would equal an electricity bill.

8   Cambozola (combining the names Camembert and Gorgonzola) was invented in 1980. It is made from a combination of Penicillium camemberti and the same blue Penicillium roqueforti mould used for Gorgonzola and Roquefort. Extra cream is added, giving it a consistency characteristic of triple crèmes with an edible bloomy rind similar to Camembert.

"We use up inferior cheese on the mousetraps" commented John Weatherby. I smiled a faint smile – but concern crossed my mind. *"Beastly business I know…"* he continued *"… poor little blighters – but we have the health regulations to consider. They'd close us down if there were signs of rodents in the kitchen."*

Lunch continued in a jovial manner – but I started thinking about the mice and the way that spring came down and broke their necks. It was not a happy thought – and by the end of the afternoon I decided that although mice were meeting their ends by that method everywhere – it didn't have to happen whilst I was in the house.

And so it was that I waited 'til I thought everyone was asleep and crept down into the kitchen to spring the traps. I was just in the process of exploring the likely cupboards when Veronica the cook appeared. She looked a little startled *"Vic – can I help you?"* She was a young woman probably in her late 20s' with curly hair and an impish grin. She appeared to be wearing a nightdress.

"Ah… yeah…" I mumbled thinking quickly what probable excuse I could find. *"I was… getting myself a glass of water."*

"The glasses are all in the top there – didn't you see them?"

"No…" PAUSE *"We… ah… keep them in the bottom cupboards where I live and… well—yes—there they are."*

I got a pint beer glass and went to the refrigerator.

"There's no water in there."

"No – I'd be wanting some fruit juice or something to mix with it. I never drink water on its own."

"Oh… it's just that you said you came for a glass of water."

"Yes – well it's late and I don't know what I'm talking about. I hate water without flavour. It's like drinking something that tastes like my mouth – and… well, I'm sure you wouldn't want to drink anything that tasted like my mouth."

261

Veronica laughed at that and that did the trick as far as obfuscating my suspicious speech and suspicious behaviour. So, armed with watered-down orange juice I retired to bed. I was unable to sleep however and decided to steal down to the kitchen again. The kitchen was dark but for a figure holding a torch. It was Veronica and she appeared to be involved in some mysterious activity inside one of the cupboards. I heard a sharp crack and then she detected my presence. She flashed the torch on my face and I blurted out the first thing that came into my head *"I drank it all—very thirsty— just came back for some more."* Then I thought to ask her what she was doing in the cupboard *"Are you after a midnight snack?"* I enquired.

"I'm... ah... I couldn't sleep and I remembered this cupboard had a loose hinge – so..." she raised the screwdriver *"... I thought I may as well fix it."*

I poured myself another glass of orange juice and water and went to bed. Veronica didn't ask me why I helped myself to a fresh glass – and I felt grateful not to have had to have made some lame excuse about having forgotten to bring the old one with me.

I went to bed again. I still couldn't sleep. It was partially the mice and partially that I wasn't enjoying being thwarted. After a discreet period of time I stole down to the kitchen and I was just about to open one of the cupboards when Veronica appeared. I remembered the words of Düd'jom Rinpoche '*With each life-circumstance: whatever is enacted, stare directly into the enactment – with all the senses.*'

"Look..." I sighed. *"I may as well own up – even I can't drink three pints of fluid in one night. I know this is bad of me... but I came down to spring the mousetraps."*

Veronica clapped her hand over her mouth to stifle her laughter *"That's what I've been trying to do – but you kept appearing. It's been like some kind of nightmare – but isn't that just such a complete hoot."*

Veronica proceeded to open all the cupboards with mousetraps and spring them with her screwdriver.

Once having completed her task she said *"Would you like to see my rat?"*

"Of all things in the world—I'd like nothing better—lead on."

And so, we mounted the stairs to her room which lay to the rear of the kitchen on some kind of lower version of the first floor that had been tagged onto the back of the house. Veronica had a rat in a large and commodious cage. She closed her door and released the rat which climbed up her arm and sat on her shoulder. It looked quite tame and looked at me with highly inquisitive eyes. *"He'll sit on your shoulder if you like – some people find a rat's tail off-putting…"*

"Not me." Veronica leant over and the rat—Albert—hopped over onto my shoulder vanished under my hair and came out on my other shoulder. *"Nice little fellow – but larger… somehow than I imagined a rat would be."*

Albert had a red patch on his back. It turned out that Veronica stained all the mice she caught in the humane traps her brother made in order that she could make sure they wouldn't return to the house. *"I have to release them at least ten miles away in case they end up coming back again – but Albert even came back from that distance. He came back three times and then I felt bad about it. It was like he didn't want to leave me – so… so… now I look after him."* PAUSE *"You… won't… tell anyone… will you…?"*

"Of course not. I'll tell Derek—but only when we get back to Bristol—he's vegetarian and he'd love the story."

I excused myself and went to bed with a sizeable smile on my face. Life was nothing if not interesting.

The days passed quite delightfully – and the evenings too. Karin was a music teacher and had two grand pianos in a large room dedicated to teaching.

One was a Bösendorfer[9] and the other a Steinway. Karin was kind enough to let me tinkle on it. I couldn't play piano but I had a method of rambling around on the white keys in mixed C and A minor scales in a manner remotely reminiscent of Keith Jarret[10] *(unless you'd happened to hear Keith Jarret)*. The music room had various guitars and violins hanging on the walls – and a cluster of timpani instruments including a brace of tambourines.

"That's lovely for someone who doesn't play piano" Karin commented. *"I think you must play some other instrument because your phrasing is… not piano phrasing."*

"I play guitar and harp" I replied.

"Harp?" she queried.

"Sorry, I meant harmonica. It's just that Blues players call them harps."

"Ah yes…" Karin smiled. *"I remember John saying something along those lines – that would be a diatonic harmonica rather than chromatic?"*

"Exactly."

"Well that's very interesting because John is a great fan of Boogie Woogie." She pronounced the vowels as an assonant rhyme with 'booby'[11] and I had to resist the urge to smile. *"John would like to have you accompany him if you have your instrument with you."*

9   The Bösendorfer is an Austrian piano, unusual in that it comes in 97 and 92 key models. Bösendorfer was established by Ignaz Bösendorfer in 1828. In 1830, it was granted the status of official piano maker to the Emperor of Austria.
10   Keith Jarrett—born in 1945, in Allentown, Pennsylvania—is a pianist and composer who performs both jazz and baroque music. He is of Hungarian, Scottish, and Puerto Rican descent and had significant early exposure to music. He was a child prodigy who possessed absolute pitch. He began piano lessons before his fourth year, and gave his first formal piano recital at the age of seven, playing works by composers including Mozart, Bach, Beethoven, and Saint-Saëns – ending with two of his own compositions.
11   The double 'o' in Boogie Woogie should make an assonant rhyme with 'book' rather that 'boot'.

"That would be a great pleasure. It's been about four years since I played harp with another musician."

Karin enquired why that was – and… I had to tell the old tale of death and the demise of Savage Cabbage.

"Oh dear—oh dear, oh dear, oh dear—that is so very sad. I am so very sorry."

Karin seemed physically moved by my account and I had to tell her that although it was sad – I'd appreciated the time I had with my friends… and now it was over.

"Most stalwart…" she responded. *"One could carry such sadness all one's life."*

"Yes… I think I will…" I sighed *"but… I think I'll carry the joy of it at the same time – so maybe… well…"* I ran out of words.

Karin changed the subject *"Do any of your fellow students play?"*

"I'm sorry to say… that I don't know…" PAUSE *"We've not been a close group up until recently… for… reasons a little too complex to go into. I can always ask though…"*

"Please do – it would be lovely to have some musical evenings. I do so love them – but so few people learn to play music these days…"

"I live in a house with three ladies who play. They go to the College of Music and Drama."

"What are their instruments?"

"Double bass, 'cello, bassoon, and oboe – and I often improvise with them on sitar."

"Really! How marvellous! How good to know that there is still culture in the world amongst the young. It's a shame you couldn't have brought your sitar with you – I would have loved to have heard that instrument played."

"I'm… errrm about as skilled on that as I am on a piano—because I've never had lessons—but I love the way it sounds and it seems to work very well with strings and woodwinds." PAUSE *"I used to play guitar – and in Savage Cabbage I played electric bass."*

"Really… well—as you can see—there are some guitars here. Why not take a look at them?"

"Certainly. I would be delighted."

I walked over to the wall where they hung. There were three of them – but they were all nylon strung. *"They look very fine"* I said *"but I'm no judge of Spanish and Classical guitars – I've only ever played steel strung guitars."*

"Are they so very different?"

"Yes and no… They're tuned the same and… you can play anything on anything – it's just how it sounds. Spanish and Classical sound best with that style of music – but Blues needs steel strings, especially for strumming." PAUSE *"I bought a cheap-and-nasty Spanish guitar when I was 15 and converted it into some-sort-of* RESOPHONIC *guitar…"*

*"*RESOPHONIC*?"*

"Yes… it's a system of mechanical or acoustic amplification that was invented by John Dopyera[12] back in the 1920s in America. If John knows about Blues – he'll probably have heard of them."

"How intriguing… so how did you accomplish the conversion?"

"Well… at the time I knew nothing of the RESOPHONIC *cone—which is like an aluminium speaker cone—and so I just filled it with ferrotype diaphragms from WWII field telephones. Of course… it sounded nothing like a* NATIONAL RESOPHONIC *guitar – but it worked well enough for me.*

12 John Dopyera (Ján Dopjera 1893–1988) was a Slovak-American inventor and a maker of stringed instruments. He invented a guitar with three aluminium cones mounted beneath the bridge, which was three times louder than a normal acoustic guitar and had a vibrant metallic sound rich with overtones. See glossary: *Dopyera, John.*

"I played it lap-slide style – which worked well because the neck was so bowed that it was unplayable any other way."

"Was it the steel strings that bowed the neck?"

"No... it was badly bowed when I got it – and I screwed a brass brace from the heel of the neck—up to about halfway down the neck—to stop it getting worse. The steel strings weren't too much of a problem anyway because I started with a 5th string gauge and used a banjo string for the first string. Then I played it tuned in open **E** *or open* **A** *tuning and tuned it lower than standard to suit my voice."*

"An inventor I see!" Karin exclaimed. I loved the way she was so enthusiastic about everything. I could see her as being an excellent music teacher.

"Well... maybe—it does interest me a great deal—and... I like to work on ideas like this." PAUSE *"My other guitar—that I played in regular tuning— was a 12-string."*

"Ah... I see... so these guitars will not hold much interest for you."

"Oh..." I replied a little sheepishly *"I don't know about that. I'd certainly have a try – just don't expect much of me."*

"No—no—no, please, you mustn't dissemble. A musician is fully entitled to his preferred instrument. There are some pianists who would abjure my Bösendorfer – but to me it is magnificent and I prefer it by far to a Steinway."

"That is... most understanding of you."

"Not at all – and, if you think it will not bow the neck, you're most welcome to re-string that one... there..." she pointed to the guitar at the end *"... with light gauge metal strings for the time you are here."* PAUSE *"On the condition that you give us a performance of... lap..."*

"Delta Blues lap-slide."

"Ah yes. That will be of great interest to John."

I took the guitar down from the wall and looked at it more closely *"This is actually a steel-string guitar..."*

"That's interesting – how can you tell?"

"Well… the neck is narrower than a Spanish or Classical – and it has a truss-rod. You see this little cover plate here just above the nut? Well, that covers an adjustment for the truss-rod that goes down the centre of the neck. That's to stop the neck bowing and also to adjust the action. I can see that someone has taken the action up quite high – but that's understandable if you wanted to put nylon strings on it."

"You could adjust it back to steel strings if you like."

"I wouldn't need to do that Karin" I grinned. *"It's perfect for me as it is – because I need a high action for lap-slide… and… I see someone's inserted a higher nut too… even better."*

"You obviously know a lot about guitars."

"Not as much as my old friends Steve and Ron – especially Ron. Ron could look at any guitar and tell you whether it was good or not or whether it needed adjustment. He could also tell if it had been played a lot or not. He said that instruments have to learn how to be instruments by being played – that the more they vibrated the more the molecules of the wood aligned in a way that made it more natural for them to produce the sounds they made. He said it was even true of electric guitars."

"That's obviously why a Stradivarius is so valuable."

"Yes… it would seem that—within reason—the older the better. I suppose that warping will spoil an instrument – but unless something like that happens an instrument will just keep improving – like these pianos."

"Yes indeed. They have a beautiful sound don't they – although I can't remember what they sounded like years ago. They were not new when we bought them and they must date back to the 1930s." PAUSE *"Can I ask you —going back to the guitars—why do you would you need the strings to be set higher from the fret-board for nylon strings?"* Karin asked with delighted curiosity.

"Because nylon strings have a different vibration pattern. They oscillate far more than steel strings and if the action is too low the strings buzz on the frets. This means that—with steel strings—this guitar will be absolutely ideal for what I play." PAUSE *"All I need now is a slide…"* I was grinning like a fiend.

I then described the slide and said I'd made my last one from a length of towel rail. Karin told me she'd enquire of John as he had a whole workshop full of odds and ends. Sure enough, there was a length of old towel rail. It was rusty in parts – but cleaned up well enough.

And so, it was that I enquired of the Illustration ladies as to whether any of them played. I was delighted to find two pianists, Janet Coleridge, and Silvia Winstaunleigh-Greaves. There were two guitarists, Amanda Riley, and Gloria Mytholmroyd. There was a violinist, Pamela Beauchamp; and a flautist, Stephanie Lytton-Chatfield. Fortunately, the violinist and the flautist had brought their instruments. All the ladies were quite capable of improvising in Blues scale.[13] The final evening was thus an eruption of New Orleans in the heart of Dorset. The Blues numbers seemed to be enjoyed by all and the ladies—my Illustration confederates—seemed astonished that they had never known I was a musician of sorts.

"It was not that I've kept it a secret – but… I've never really felt that offering autobiographical anecdotes would be enjoyable to anyone."

"Yes…" Pamela sighed *"I can understand that. Todd and Veranda told us all that you were a 'show off' – and that's not an atmosphere where you'd feel like saying anything about anything. I don't blame you for not saying anything. You must have picked up on what they were saying, I suppose."*

---

13 Blues scale is often incorrectly termed pentatonic or minor pentatonic with an extra note. Blues scale is neither. It is a 6-note scale that can either sound major or minor depending on how the notes are sequenced. It is similar with the **C** major and **A** minor scales – in as much as they contain the same notes. The scale is West African in origin and there is no major or minor differentiation in that musical system. The example in a scale equated with **C** would be: **C—D—Eb—E—G—A**.

"Yes… I overheard that comment—and others like it—quite often – when they thought I was out of earshot."

"We can understand now why you were so quiet" commented Stephanie.

"Yes… it seemed best to say as little as possible" I replied.

"The problem was though…" said Sylvia *"with your being almost withdrawn – was that it made you seem aloof and that… well, it had the effect of, well…"*

"I can well understand that." I smiled ever-so-slightly. *"I wish I'd found some other way of dealing with it."*

When the ladies realised what had happened—and how they'd been set up —they expressed a great deal of resentment about it.

"I'm astonished you were never angry with them" opined Pamela *"apart from your occasional witty come-backs, that is."*

"It was actually those come-backs that I regret. I don't like to use wit as a weapon." They all wanted to know why. *"It's too easy – it gives me an unfair advantage… and, I don't like to use anything as a weapon. I don't like to combat people or engage in verbal duels. I don't like the whole winning and losing business. The problem is that I tend to resort to wit at times of frustration – and mainly as a means of terminating a pointless exchange."*

"But it was always very funny when you did that – and would have been much funnier if we'd all known you better. We'd have been completely on your side."

I thought about it for a moment before replying *"That would be most welcome in so many ways – I have no enthusiasm for being embattled and no enthusiasm for defending myself. I'm not angry with Todd and Veranda because they simply are as they are – and have the attitudes they have. It's merely part of their upbringing and they have attitudes they've never questioned. I think there's something that's simply threatening about me being evidently working class and evidently fairly literate."*

"You've obviously thought about this quite a lot – or has this come up before?" asked Janet.

"Well... I have had other experiences in my life where the combination of a working-class origin and an uncommonly extensive vocabulary have caused people irritation. I've found, that my vocabulary tended to either intimidate or humiliate those who felt inadequate in response to it. That happened with Jack Hackman's parents. They really disliked me. I never tried to impress people with my vocabulary. I never deliberately use polysyllabic, unusual, or partially archaic words. It's not easy to know which words are not in common usage – when those words seem normal enough in my own mind. I'd been used to my father's extensive vocabulary – and that has probably created an unrealistic sense in me of how it was possible to communicate. When you're reared by a father who makes a deliberate practice of learning as many words as feasible – it's not possible not to be influenced by it."

"Why did your father do that?" asked Janet.

"Well... he never explained – and I just assumed that this was one of the efforts one made if one wished to evolve into a worthwhile human being. He was a self-made man – so it made sense in that context. He started out working in the docks and decided to join the Army to better himself. He then launched himself into the educational opportunities the Army offered and eventually gained engineering and building qualifications. He then rose to be a major – where he discovered he was socially out of his depth." PAUSE *"So... I suppose he set about educating himself in terms of culture – and part of his method was to learn a word a week and use it in conversation as many times as seemed practical. It was a habit he maintained – and still maintains even though he's retired."*

"That explains a lot about you!" laughed Pamela. *"It sounds almost like something out of a Charles Dickens novel."*

"That would fit. My father loved Charles Dickens. He read everything he ever wrote to my mother to help her with her English. My mother's German, you see. Her vocabulary wasn't extensive – but she was a treasury of knowledge in terms of the Arts, especially music. She used to sing Schubert songs with her mother accompanying on piano."

"That explains even more about you..." said Pamela *"and, I suppose you must have enjoyed all that – and loved language."*

"Yes, I've always enjoyed words and linguistics – maybe all the more because I'm hopeless at anything connected with numbers. Arithmetic—let alone mathematics—was entirely beyond me. I can only just count my change in a shop – so I'm more or less doomed to be regarded as either pretentious, ostentatious, conceited, overconfident, pompous, affected, supercilious, patronising, vain, self-important, self-enamoured, narcissistic, arrogant, bumptious, grandiose, or grandiloquent."

That had them all in hysterics laughing.

"You can just roll synonyms off as if you were reading them from the page!" laughed Sylvia.

"Yes… but that's often annoyed people – so now I only do it to be amusing, with… people I think might enjoy it."

"Don't worry about us on that score – we enjoy it even if it irritates Todd and Veranda. No need to bother about them."

"Thank you… but I wouldn't like to bother, peeve, irk, gall, annoy, vex, rile, aggravate, exasperate, incense, enrage, or infuriate Todd and Veranda – albeit with your kindly support. That would be mean-spirited of me – dare I say unpleasant, resentful, implacable, spiteful, malicious, vindictive, malevolent, vicious, vengeful, and rancorous?"

The ladies were now in tears of laughter *"Where d'you get all these words?"* Janet enquired when she found herself able to speak.

"When I was young, I used to browse the thesaurus just for fun." My *'when I was young'* phrase brought Lewis Carroll to mind and I launched into a parody

> *"In my youth" Vic Simmerson replied to Janet "I feared it might injure the brain—But now that I'm perfectly sure I have none—Why, I do it again and again."*

Gales of laughter ensued after which Pamela said *"I've always enjoyed 'You are Old Father William.' Lewis Carroll's a big favourite with me – but it's like you should be on stage or something."*

"I was once…"

"As a comedian?" Pamela enquired in astonishment.

"Maybe in part – but no. I was the vocalist of the Savage Cabbage Blues Band – and I used to enjoy throwing out manic lines at the audience when I was introducing the members of the band. It became some sort of signature rôle and people came to expect it of me."

"But browsing a thesaurus for fun is wild" Janet remarked.

"Well… one thing leads to another, as it were. I had an etymological dictionary too – and used to enjoy finding out the origin of words. The fact that the word 'scorned' was derived from the Nordic term for 'lack of horns' was something I found fascinating – but word derivations seemed irritating to some people. It was unnecessary extraneous information."

The ladies said they were both saddened and annoyed that I had not had any actual company for two years—due to Todd and Veranda—because, according to them, I was 'highly entertaining and interesting'. I thanked them kindly for their good opinion and said that I'd try to be more myself—within bounds—back in Bristol.

We all were enjoying each other's company – and they were free to ask me whatever they liked about the Savage Cabbage Blues Band and anything else about which they cared to enquire. The end of the evening turned into some kind of interview peppered with a great deal of laughter. I even spoke a little of my time in the Himalayas as Todd and Veranda had told them I belonged to an Eastern Religious cult. I had to start by defining the word cult.

"Todd and Veranda are correct according to the original meaning of the word 'cult'. It means 'a system of religious practice connected with a deity or deities.' The modern meaning of 'quasi-religious organization which uses devious psychological techniques to gain control of adherents' doesn't apply to world religions such as Buddhism, Sikhism, Judæism, Christianity, or Islam." PAUSE

"*Although… it might apply if individuals within a world religion set up their own insular organisations. That can happen in any religion – however, Todd and Veranda know nothing at all about Himalayan Buddhism or the Nyingma Tradition. Books are quite rare… and they haven't enquired – with me at least. The only person in the Art School who knows anything about me in that sense is Derek – and I doubt whether they have asked him. All they know therefore it that I'm a Buddhist – and that is as vague as saying I'm a Christian. A Christian could be Roman Catholic or a member of one of a wide range of Protestant Churches: Anglican, Methodist, Wesleyan, Baptist, Pentecostal, Quaker, Lutheran, Calvinist, Seventh Day Adventist, Jehovah's Witness, Mormon… the list is vast – and even from the little I know, there are substantial differences between them.*"

We talked 'til quite late. I tried to keep my explanations as simple as possible – but they pressed me for ever-deepening levels of information. I obliged and they all thanked me for answering their questions.

On retiring to bed, I reflected on what had occurred. It seemed that it was possible to rely on the fact that people would eventually come to their own conclusions about me. It seemed that I had taken more-or-less the right approach in terms of simply not defending myself. It only seemed a pity that I'd inadvertently colluded with Todd and Veranda in depriving the ladies on the Illustration year of my company. I felt that this was something I could tell Kyabjé Düd'jom Rinpoche in terms of having had *some* success—albeit mixed—at living as a ngakpa in the West.

16

the chance won't come again

And this our life, exempt from public haunt, finds books in the running brooks, tongues in trees, sermons in stones, and good in everything.
William Shakespeare—As You Like It—Act II—Scene *i*

"Y'know... I find it a little weird the way 'dette teases you about being a hippie..." commented Rebecca *"... when... you're not typecast in that way at all... or, not as far as I can see... you're not that different from me – and I was never really a hippie even though I took on parts of what was going on."*

"That's how I see it... but y'know... It's just her way" I smiled. *"I don't think she means anything by it – more than having some fun."* PAUSE *"I think she knows that I'm too... peculiar in my likes and dislikes to be designated like that. She enjoys teasing me – and I don't mind her doing it."*

"But... you don't usually look as if you're experiencing it as a tease – I mean, you don't bridle about it."

"Well no... I'm not tease-able" I grinned. *"I'm not actually tease-able about anything – as far as I know. To be tease-able... you have to have something you're sensitive about... or something you're trying to reject. So... as I'm not trying to reject the idea of being 'something like a hippie' teasing me about it doesn't achieve much."*

"But..." Rebecca pondered *"but... 'dette seems to think that she's teasing you."*

"Yes... she does..." I responded *"and I never say anything to make her think otherwise."*

"Can I ask why?"

"Well if I told her she wasn't succeeding in teasing me... it would sound as if I felt myself to have been teased. As it is – the whole excahnge is quite brief. To say anything about it, would be to extend it."

275

"Mmmm… that's… really unusually circumspect of you" Rebecca almost chuckled. *"I'm not sure I could have worked that out—it's quite psychologically subtle—but I can see it's a good approach. I think I'll remember that with my father next time I'm home."*

"I think the only way it works is if you really—aren't—tease-able… I don't know how far it would get you if you were just pretending not to be tease-able – I mean… as you noticed, it doesn't exactly deter 'dette, does it?"

"Right… you have a point – there…" Rebecca considered *"but anyway – it sounds as if it's worth a try. I think that whether it works or not – it puts the power back into your hands."*

"Yes… it could do that" I replied *"but it also creates a little distance…"* PAUSE *"I think… in the long run… the distance it creates might not be the best thing for a relationship…"* PAUSE *"so… I might have to mention the teasing at some point – maybe… in some situation where it hasn't just happened."*

"That would be a useful idea too. You get the best of both worlds that way – and it would be less… confrontational." PAUSE *"Can I ask you something, Vic?"* I nodded assent and Rebecca continued *"Have you studied psychology?"*

"No."

"Then…?"

"I've always tried to understand the way people work… I suppose… having had an angry overbearing father probably set me up for it…" PAUSE *"Then, Buddhism's highly psychological and I must have a fair amount of grounding from that – but… if I can get back to this question of 'hippie', a few ideas have occurred to me as we've been talking."* Rebecca made a movement of her head that indicated the change of subject was in order and I launched in *"There were good things about the whole hippie genre that I liked – that still like. It's just that I'm not tightly locked into back-to-the earth anti-establishment alternativism.*

"I've nothing against people singing '… we are stardust we are golden and we've got to get ourselves back to the garden…'[1] but it was never the direction I took from the clues I had found etched into the '60s."

Rebecca nodded *"Yes… I'd say very much the same – and… I think there are a lot of people who were never really hippies in the stereotypical sense…"* PAUSE *"Trouble is… most of them are effected self-conscious non-conventionalists of one sort or another."*

"True…" I replied. *"I feel a sense of faint bewilderment as to what motivates people. What has meaning for people beyond hidebound conventionality and hidebound unconventionality. I look 'round and wonder who else there might be out there—apart from you three ladies—who's free of that. I find damn few."* Then I laughed remembering the Scots toast *" Wha's like us? Damn few—and they're a' deid!'… That how it feels sometimes."*

Rebecca sighed *"D'you remember that Dylan song…?"* then she sang *"… 'Come writers and critics who prophesise with your pen, and keep your eyes wide, the chance won't come again… and don't speak too soon, for the wheel's still in spin, and there's no telling who that it's naming.'[2]"* PAUSE *"I used to love that song because of what I felt lay in the future… and now — what is left of that hope?"*

"Not a lot as far as I can see" I replied. *"But y'know… I'd wager that there are a few people in most towns with Art Schools and Music Colleges who might be having this self-same conversation."*

"That's a heartening thought." PAUSE *"Y'know, this morning…"* Rebecca intoned dreamily *"I remembered the Beatles… their final live performance on the roof of the Apple building in Savile Row in…"*

"That would've been '69 – I remember it well. The police arrived at one point due to complaints about noise and they were asked to end the performance."

1 *Woodstock* by Joni Mitchell on *Ladies of the Canyon* and the B-side of the single Big Yellow Taxi. The lyrics refer to the Woodstock Festival of 1969 – and a pilgrim on the road to the festival. The song is anthemic and symbolic of the 1960s' counterculture.
2 Bob Dylan—The Times They Are a'Changing—1961

"Right…" Rebecca mused *"and the Beatles said later that they were disappointed they weren't arrested – because a scene with the police hauling the band members off in handcuffs would have been an appropriate conclusion for the film."*

"Yes… I can see that…" I commented with a wry expression that formed itself a little too evidently *"but… I can also see that this was a part of that time that was problematic…"*

"Problematic?" Rebecca cut in.

"Yes, in terms of Art and the ethos that supported the Art of the time. The problem with the Beatles' response was that it was reactive. *Hell, I was reactive too – but I realised early on that reactivism has a short life. The whole idea of 'counterculture' is doomed – because it relies on a conservative culture against which it can rebel."*

"Oh, yes… I can see that." PAUSE *"That's why that time was as it was—to a certain extent—and why that time has been lost…"* Rebecca commented.

"The '60s existed because of many factors: post war pacifism and new affluence. I'm no social historian – and don't like theorising without some real research."

"I don't think research would add anything to the picture" Rebecca remarked. *"I know something of the social history of the first half of the 20ᵗʰ Century — but I have no idea why things looked as they did. All I can do is portray what an innocent eye saw – and how I reacted to what was around me. There was a great deal of humour involved with belonging to the counter culture – and that is perhaps more important than looking at why it existed."*

"Yes…" I pondered *"… in terms of counterculture… I probably still find myself in a counterculture position – it's simply that the culture to which I ran counter is changing. I suppose that I always tend to run counter to unthinking conformity—the herd mentality—the work force who keep the fashion industry affluent."*

"*Right!*" agreed Rebecca. "*The legacy of the '60s is found in a sector of what has now been accepted – and it seems to be turning slowly into the new conformism. There are now wholefood shops everywhere – where the 'rights and wrongs', 'goods and bads', are as inflexible as those to which my father adheres.*"

"*As time goes on, I shall probably relate more to being a hippie than I did at the time*" I laughed. "*Maybe I'll parody Robert Burns when I'm an old man – 'Ye see yon birkie ca'd a straight, wha struts an' stares an' a' that, / Tho' hundreds worship at his word, he's but a coof for a' that, / For a' that, an' a' that – his company pension and a' that, / The freak o' independent mind – he looks an' laughs at a' that. Ayee f'a' that an' a' that a freak's a freak f'a' that.*[3] *... or something like that.*"

"*That's hysterical Vic! You should have taken to the stage as an actor.*"

"*Maybe there's time for that yet – who knows… maybe I am the coof* [4] *f'a' that.*"

"*Yeah… maybe that accounts for the four of us here in Hotwells…*" Rebecca nodded "*… but, I'd say the whole world is three drinks behind.*"

"*You've got me there Rebecca… that must be a quote from something…?*"

"*It's from 'Three Drinks Ahead', a Humphrey Bogart movie made in* 1950. *He said something like 'If everyone in the world would take three drinks, we would have no trouble. If Stalin, Truman, and everybody else in the world had three drinks right now, they'd all loosen up and wouldn't need the United Nations.'*"

"*I think he's got something there…*" I smiled "*or if they'd remember—a little more often—that they're all going to die at some point… and all their schemes will then be over.*" PAUSE "*We've really only got a small pool of time to do what we set out to do – and so we may as well leave everyone else as free to get on with it as they see fit. So many people however, are mad keen on controlling others – and bludgeoning them with their wretched opinions.*"

3   Robert Burns—A Man's a Man for All That—1795
4   Fool or idle worthless fellow.

279

"Yes… You'd think we could all be free of having to take notice of people's opinions as to how we dress and what we happen to enjoy." Rebecca sighed. *"We could all just decide to be free of the duties imposed by fashions and by the latest conservatism – however liberal it happens to look."*

"Right… and even though we all have duties to those around us – we owe nobody a bean when it comes to appreciation. We're all essentially free to appreciate what we appreciate without having to answer to anyone."

"Yes… Or maybe they'd all get fighting mad and every nuclear silo everywhere will open up and let rip – and we'll hear Vera Lynn singing: 'We'll Meet Again'… y'know… from the 'mushroom cloud scene' at the end of Doctor Strangelove.[5]*"*

"That's a sobering thought isn't it…" I said with slightly widening eyes. *"It was* 1964 *when that came out… I grew up with the view that* Doctor Strangelove *was closer to reality than comic fantasy – y'know I can still imagine that someone could really say 'There will be no fighting in the war room' and see no irony at all in the words."*

"That's true… I think if people had more sense of the irony of many situations they would act differently or stop talking such rubbish all the time." PAUSE *"Just look at Trophy-head*[6] *– he really has no idea at all does he… I mean he just acts as if it was his natural position to rule the roost and he has no sense that he's blown his cover and the others in the Illustration studio see him for what he is."* PAUSE *"I mean…"* Rebecca laughed *"… that whole scene where he ran off with your clothes and lost your keys and all that – and had to search for them every afternoon in the baking sun."*

"That was quite amusing… I must admit – and yes, he did make himself look like an idiot." PAUSE *"The sad thing for me about Todd—and Veranda —is that I'd be friends with them tomorrow if they'd simply let go of it all."*

"You would?"

"Yes… I would." PAUSE *"I might not ever get to be that close—because we*

5   *Dr Strangelove, Or How I Learned to Stop Worrying and Love the Bomb* is a 1964 film, starring Peter Sellers. See glossary: *Dr Strangelove.*
6   *Trophy-head* was the nick name that the three ladies had for Todd Whelcombe – with reference to his large protuberant ears.

don't have that much in common—but we could be sociable, even cordial – *and… who knows."*

"Really—you'd just forget everything—all the snide remarks and all the *stupid aggressive slurs?"* Rebecca asked with a look of perplexity.

"Well… I've never really enjoyed recrimination that *much – and… anyone* can *change… or I have to allow that anyone can change."*

"You think Trophy-head *could change?"*

"Not really… no – but it cannot be impossible." PAUSE *"I think… that if* *Todd was cast away on a desert island with me and we had to survive… that* *we'd get some kind of friendship going – if only for our survival. I think that* *kind of thing happens."*

"Yes… I can see that…" Rebecca laughed *"but I hope you don't have to* *endure the desert island with Trophy-head – that would be an ordeal I* *wouldn't wish on anyone."*

*"Yes… I don't think I'd relish it—*too*—much – but… 'He shall not grow* *old as we who are left grow old – age shall not weary him nor the years* *condemn'*[7]*…"* I laughed *"I have no idea why I said that…"* and I really didn't.

---

7   Parody of a line from *For the Fallen* by Robert Laurence Binyon (1869–1943).

17

the bathyscaph

A sad portrait – but it must be provided if 'dette is to be understood. Mr Gascoigne—I was never privy to his first name— was a grey emotionally-ailing lizard somewhere in his early 50s. Encountering him was vaguely like walking onto the set of a 1940s' movie – sans glamour. His pale-grey suits—he had many of them —had lapels so thin I suspected them of anorexia. A narrow dark-grey tie barely covered his shirt buttons. He wore an anæmic dove-grey shirt, the collar of which had died of malnutrition in 1951. The mother-of-pearl buttons on his shirt however, were superb – when one caught sight of them.

My mother had a vast array of mother-of-pearl buttons. She'd inherited them from her grandmother and I stitched them onto every shirt I had. Mr Gascoigne wore a pair of those spivey shoes[1] worn by businessmen on the lounge-lizard circuit. Mr Gascoigne however, only wore them as 'house-shoes'. He was a pallid man of slightly less than average height. His languid expressionless eyes revealed nothing of what lay behind them. His mind was indecipherable – as his range of facial expressions could only be detected with the aid of an electron microscope.

I met him only once toward the end of the degree course. An interview was deemed obligatory. I attended – punctually. Subsequent to the interview, he gave his report to 'dette. I was better than imagined – but outré in appearance; abject in social background; quirky in speech; and, gauche in manner. I was a working-class hippie with amateur-cultivated airs.

No wonder 'dette had been so keen to have me espouse all the correct views regarding the Arts – but she'd never made it plain that it would be necessary in terms of impressing her father. It was transparent however, that I'd failed – as soon as my first sentence made its unwelcome début in his hearing.

---

1   They used to bear the name *'Top Gallants'* in the Grenson shoe range.

"So you are Victor Simmerson" he opened – but whether it was a statement or a question, I could not ascertain. *"It would appear so"* I replied with a smile – but could tell immediately from his frozen expression, that I was not expected to treat with him on equal terms as an adult. I remembered the words of Düd'jom Rinpoche *'With each life-circumstance: whatever is enacted, stare directly into the enactment – with all the senses.'*

Having met Mr Gascoigne however, I understood a great deal about 'dette – and her view of life and the Arts. She'd absorbed her father's philosophy on the subject entirely – probably as a way of getting any semblance of love from the man. I could imagine 'dette coming home in the school holidays desperate for affection from her father – and learning by heart, the Cultural Creed according to Sepulchrave Gascoigne. His name wasn't actually Sepulchrave. I always thought of him by that name however – because the ladies called him the Earl of Groan.[2] They'd met him on several occasions and had not relished the experience. He'd not been hostile to them – merely sterile and aloof. He reminded Penelope—the gentlest of the three ladies—of Lady Catherine De Bourgh.[3] *"I can just hear him saying '… and—if I'd ever learned—I too, should have been a true proficient…' It would have been just like him."*

Mr Gascoigne had been bereaved when 'dette was 12 years old – and he had never recovered. As a result, 'dette was packed off to board at Badminton: a prestigious public girls' school in the North of Bristol. It was there that she made friends with Penelope, Rebecca, and Meryl. 'dette only saw her father on school holidays – although from as close as Bath, she could have been a day student. Mr Gascoigne however, felt he was not well equipped for parental duties beyond what was absolutely necessary.

---

2   Lord Sepulchrave, the Earl of Groan is a melancholic character in the *Gormenghast Trilogy* by Mervyn Peak. He is burdened by his endless duties as Earl and his only relief lies in reading. When he loses his library to a fire he loses his already insecure sanity and goes to live with the death-owls in the Tower of Flints. They eat him alive.

3   Lady Catherine de Bourgh is a character form *Pride and Prejudice* by Jane Austen (1813). She is haughty, pompous, domineering, and condescending.

I found that incomprehensible. What duties? A 12 year old girl hardly required much in the way of physical care – and she would have made any normal father a wonderful companion. 'dette showed me a photograph of her mother *"You take after her far more than your father…"* I observed *"she was a beautiful woman."*

"Naturally – but I think I probably take after my father more in temperament."

I made no response to that – as saying *'that is unfortunate'* would have been churlish. Her father's temperament was something she needed to avulse as if it were a tumour – but it was not my place to say that. 'dette had a high opinion of her father – as a father. *"I have to say 'dette… that I could never quite see why you had to board at Badminton. I know you said that your father couldn't cope – but you were 12 years old and I think he did himself a disservice."*

"And how would that be?" 'dette replied in a flat tone that betokened it wasn't my business to comment.

"Well… I know it's not my business to comment – but wouldn't it have helped him with his bereavement?"

"Not really – I would have reminded him of her."

"Yes… well… I would have thought that would have been good – because he could have seen how he had not entirely lost his wife… because you'd be there to show him something… positive… and be a companion."

"I wouldn't imagine a 12-year-old girl could be much of a companion."

"I've never had a 12-year-old daughter, so I can't say – but there are references in literature—two at least in Anthony Trollope's 'Chronicles of Barsetshire'[4] —that depict wonderful relationships between fathers and daughters."

4   *The Chronicles of Barsetshire* is a series of six novels by Anthony Trollope, set in the fictional English county of Barsetshire and Barchester, its cathedral town. The series concern the dealings of the Victorian clergy and gentry, and the socio-political manœuvrings between them. The series includes: *The Warden* (1855); *Barchester Towers* (1857); *Doctor Thorne* (1858); *Framley Parsonage* (1861); *The Small House at Allington* (1864); and, *The Last Chronicle of Barset* (1867).

"Yes – but they were adult women."

"In the books—yes—but they didn't appear out of nowhere as adult daughters. I'm sure Doctor Thorne [5]wouldn't have come down one morning and said 'Goodness gracious – it appears I have a 21-year-old daughter[6] – who'd have thought it! Are you called Mary by any chance?'…"

"Very droll, I'm sure – but I suppose I see what you mean…"

"I think you survived because you met Penelope, Rebecca, and Meryl – but I think your father might have come through it all better if you'd been at home with him. My impression of him is that he once had emotions but now they're vacuum-sealed inside himself somewhere."

"Yes… there's some truth in that – but I think that being a boarder at Badminton was a highly valuable experience. As you say yourself, my relationship with Penelope, Rebecca, and Meryl was extremely important at that time – and that couldn't have happened if I'd lived at home."

"Yes… and I'd still be living in a bedsit in Chesterfield Road."

"So – as you see, it all worked out for the best."

Well yes… I thought '… *if only you could stop trying to be your father…*' Was it possible to cure her of that? Or was she doomed to become Lady Groan…?

My meeting with Mr Gascoigne had been brief and meaningless. It wasn't hideous—as my meeting with Lindie Dale's parents had been back in 1968—but it was equally inhuman. Mr Gascoigne was almost benign in comparison with Brigadier Dale and I hadn't had to fight for my life as I had done back then. I'd simply been *processed*. He'd accessed me swiftly and dismissed me *"I now have other concerns that require my attention. I wish you goodbye. Claudette will— no doubt—take you home directly."*

5   *Doctor Thorne* (1858) is Anthony Trollope's third novel in the *Chronicles of Barsetshire* series. It follows the problematic romance of Mary Thorne, niece of Dr Thomas Thorne, and Frank Gresham, the only son of the local squire.
6   Mary was actually Doctor Thorne's niece – but he brought her up as his own daughter.

I almost burst out laughing. I almost said *'I'm sorry I've taken up so much of your time'* but checked myself. I didn't approve of my unexpressed sarcasm – but I was glad, at least, that I hadn't felt compelled to express it. I stood for a while in the kitchen waiting for 'dette to appear and after five minutes I noticed 'dette waving at me from the Rolls Royce outside the front window, as if I should have known to look for her there. I left by the front door —rather than by the tradesmen's entrance through which we'd previously gained admittance—and within seconds I'd swung myself into the passenger seat. *"Right on cue with the bathyscaph 'dette."*

"Very droll... 'bath escape' indeed..." 'dette commented with affected solemnity – but then burst out laughing. It was a relief to hear 'dette laugh about the situation—because it normalised her—if such a word can be used. It wasn't that I needed her to be normal in the average sense – but it certainly felt better when I saw she was not entirely in tune with her father's point of view.

"He's a lovely gentleman, really" she said *"but as you'll never get to know him – you'll never find out."*

"I'm sure you're right. I'm sure... that I could say that about my father, now..." PAUSE *"Maybe they should meet..."*

"What!?" 'dette almost choked.

"My little joke 'dette... it would be like King Kong meets Godzilla.[7]*"*

"You may not respect your father – but I respect mine."

"I am jesting 'dette – just as you like to jest. I have no wish to detract from your respect for your father – but I don't think it's healthy not to see the things that are comical about parents... and, it's—not—that I have—no— respect for my father. In fact, now that we get on better, I have a growing appreciation of his... better qualities. It takes a lot for a dock worker to gain qualifications in mathematics, engineering, and surveying.

---

7 *King Kong Meets Godzilla* was a 1962 Japanese science fiction film directed by Ishirō Honda.

287

"He became a major; having entered the Army as a private soldier – and that is somewhat uncommon."

"But, you wouldn't like to be like him?"

"No 'dette… not in some respects at least – but, I would like to have his perseverance and tenacity. I'd like to have his massive application to work and ability to learn. All-in-all however, I'd like to be like my mother because…"

'dette cut me short *"I never had the—chance—to learn to be like my mother!"*

A silence ensued – after which I said *"I'm genuinely sorry about that, 'dette."* And I was – but it was an accidental double entendre. I hoped it had escaped her notice. It had – or seemed to, at least.

Then I wondered why I was immediately aware of what I'd said as a double entendre. Nonsense – of course I knew why. It was what I actually felt – but I felt both aspects of the double entendre: I was *genuinely sorry that 'dette's mother had died* and I was *genuinely sorry that 'dette had not learned to be like her mother rather than her father.* It was always impossible to speak as plainly to 'dette, as she did with me, without hurting her. Somehow, I could never quite bring myself to do that.

She could speak plainly and directly to me because she lacked awareness and sensitivity. She felt she had the right to speak her mind. I rarely spoke plainly and directly in terms of giving her feedback – unless it proved absolutely necessary. I'd done so once before – but it had signified the probable end of the relationship. Our relationship should have ended at that point – but 'dette, for reasons too mysterious to fathom, had not wanted that. I knew 'dette was highly vulnerable and brittle under her camouflage-carapace of sophistication. I knew that we could never have an equal exchange in terms of my being as direct with her as she was with me – but it was my obligation, as the stronger person, to be gentle. The problem with my being gentle in that fashion was that it put me in a parental position, of being loving to the child with a proclivity for spitefulness.

I only ever commented when she went too far and it would have been utterly unrealistic not to have reminded her of her manners. She was always aware of my shift in approach at those times – and became pleasant. The problem there, was that I never enjoyed relating to someone who was in need of periodic reprimands for haughty or acerbic speech. So, why did I not take my leave of 'dette? I often asked myself that question – and the answer was always the same. The Degree Show was approaching and it would have been damaging to 'dette to bid her adieux at such a critical time. Staying with 'dette until the end of the Art School year was not such an imposition. She had many fine qualities – and often amused me with her witty observations. We still laughed together and still enjoyed seeing plays together at one of the three theatres in Bristol – but the end was approaching. Sometimes I felt she had some sense of that – and was making the most of my companionship while it was still on offer.

18

the indestructible crown

I remembered what Akong Rinpoche had advised – and, as soon as I caught wind of the 16th Gyalwa Karmapa[1] coming to London, I booked a ticket for the event. I also booked a day return to London by train. It was a little expensive – but somehow, I didn't want to hitch or to wind up sleeping on someone's floor. Actually – what I really did not want, was to find myself in another stupid situation akin to what I'd experienced in Liverpool. In any case, the rain had set in, and I didn't like leaving a bunch of wet gear where I parked the pixie chariot – free for anyone who fancied it.

Maybe I was getting to be like 'dette? A seeker of comfort and ease? Maybe… but whatever, I wanted a simple experience – unadulterated by anyone too socially dysfunctional. The return-ticket to London was a self-protective move – and… I wasn't entirely sure whether I approved of myself. I wanted to attend the Vajra Crown Ceremony of Gyalwa Karmapa. Then after seeing Gyalwa Karmapa, I wanted to leave for the railway station, secure in the knowledge that I had a seat on a train that was bound for Bristol. I did not wish to have to converse with anyone 'spiritual'. With a seat booked, simplicity was guaranteed — unless, of course, the train was taken over by Ersatz Hindu Hippies from the locked broom cupboard in Hell.

I planned to be silent for the whole day. I'd leave early and simply show my ticket. I'd smile at the railway staff—naturally—but I'd utter not a word. Maybe I'd pretend I was dumb… That may sound cranky — but it was the early 1970s and I still remembered my trips to Samŷe Ling. I'd made three trips and, on each occasion, I'd encountered people who seemed incapable of normal human interaction. I'd begun to feel that the whole scene around Tibetan Buddhism was riddled with personality disorders.

---

1   The Vajra Crown *(dorje zha-nak / rDo rJe zhwa nag)* is an important symbol of the Karmapas – the heads of the Karma Kagyüd school of Tibetan Buddhism. See glossary: *Vajra Crown.*

Then I'd chide myself for this pusillanimous parsimonious view. Who was I to speak? Exactly. At least however—if I also had a personality disorder—I was never unfriendly or gratuitously obnoxious. I struggled with this idea. How did it sit with the altruism I was supposed to be developing? Compassion for all beings: wasn't that the main point? It was – but where was compassion in *my* outlook, *most* of the time. The best I could manage seemed to be self-control in respect of caustic wit. I could pride myself on my lack of *expressed anger* – but the aggression contained in my unspoken witty rejoinders was something that caused me shame. Well… maybe not 'shame' per se. Maybe the very mildest mortification? It *should* have been 'shame' – but there would have to be a few more years of practice before that was likely.

"Don't blame you, Vic" Penelope condoled – on hearing my plan for isolation. She was the most tender-hearted of the three ladies and so I was reassured that I wasn't becoming misanthropic. *"… there are some—total—screwballs out there."*

"I suppose I came to the wrong person for a severe reprimand" I laughed.

"D'you want one?"

"Probably not… but I deserve one."

"You take this too gravely." PAUSE *"You're about the kindest person I know – so I don't think you need to chastise yourself just because you want to spare yourself exposure to too many raving antisocial lunatics."*

"Right… well… if you say so." PAUSE *"No, sorry, that didn't sound as I meant it, I mean, I'm grateful for your opinion – and… it does put my mind at rest. I'll just relax about it and accept the fact that I'm not quite the sociable being I thought I was."*

"But you are perfectly sociable Vic – it's just that you're moving in circles where there are more loonies than average. I mean, I seem to be able to live without meeting them – but Eastern religions look as if they have more than their fair share.

"I walked into the 'shine-a-light' shop, or whatever it's called…"

"Divine Light Mission?" I suggested.

"That's right – well I went into their shop because they have some interesting second-hand clothes there—a lot of 1920s and 1930s things—but it wasn't possible to look around without being harassed by people asking me if I'd 'taken knowledge' or whatever. I just told them I hadn't taken anything and didn't want to take anything – I just wanted to buy the emerald green dress… They sold it to me in the end but not without a whole sales pitch about Guru Margarine."

"Guru Maharaj Ji" I smiled. *"He's a young Hindu teacher who's popular right now – but yes, I know what you mean. Buddhism's not really so very different in terms of the people – apart from the fact that Buddhism seems to draw a more intellectual clientele."* PAUSE *"They're not so very different in many ways – apart from the old-school brigade such as Christmas Humphries* [2] *at the Buddhist Society. They seem to think that Tibetan Buddhists are all more-or-less Satanists. Some are of course… I met some down in Tintagel—a South African couple—who were right out of one of Poe's Tales of Mystery and Imagination.* [3]*"*

"As in 'Man you shoulda seen them kicking Edgar Alan Poe'?" [4]

"You're getting quick at this Penelope – and yes something like that… apart from the fact that I'd rather have seen Mister Poe kicking them. They were from the other-side-of-creepy.

---

2   Christmas Humphreys (1901–1983) was an English barrister who prosecuted several controversial cases in the 1940s and 1950s, and later became a judge at the Old Bailey. He wrote a number of works on Buddhism. In 1924 he founded the Buddhist Society, which had a seminal influence on the growth of Buddhism in Britain. He was born in Ealing, Middlesex, the son of Travers Humphreys, a noted barrister and judge.

3   *Tales of Mystery and Imagination* is a posthumous compilation by the American, Edgar Allan Poe. The 1908 version was reproduced many times by several publishers. In 1919 George G Harrap and Co. published an edition illustrated by Harry Clarke in black and white. In 1923 an expanded edition was published with many more illustrations, including eight colour plates. In 1935 the artist Arthur Rackham produced another illustrated version which was popular with Illustration students.

4   Quote from Lennon McCartney—Beatles—I am the Walrus—1967

293

"They had this thing… If they suspected anyone of being a demon, they'd pull on their left ears whilst sticking out their tongues. Then if the person didn't react – that proved he or she was a demon. The husband—Gilbert Harris—was the worse of the two—as he was rather power-crazed and seemed to live to manipulate people's words in conversation—so they'd come to feel doltish. He'd then establish himself in an unassailable position of authority with anyone who fell for his logically aggressive posturing."

"Did he try that one on with you?"

"Yes. On several occasions – but I'm afraid I frustrated him by being impervious."

"How did that work – I mean, what did you say?"

"I just kept repeating that I didn't play word games."

"How did he respond to that?"

"He raised his level of aggression – and when he did that I told him that becoming increasingly aggressive would have no effect on me unless he became physically violent. He then told me I was acting hysterically – and I replied that I was not marvellously interested in his opinion. In the end he gave up. I think that the worst aspect of me—as far as he was concerned—was that he could not induce me to be aggressive in return. I can't say I felt happy about the situation – but I don't tend to be frightened by bullies…" PAUSE *"well… not unless they're armed to the teeth, or whatever."*

"So… if I can ask… why did you stay in the same vicinity as this creep for a minute longer than it took to put on your coat?"

"That's a long story. Ngakpa Yeshé Dorje—with whom he'd studied— suggested I might like to make his acquaintance. So… as I'd been invited by Gilbert and his wife Elzebe to stay with them for Lo-gSar—Tibetan new Year—I decided it would be too timid to leave. There was a Lo-gSar festival and ceremonies to attend – and it would have been vaguely lacking in seriousness to have missed that, just because of some personal awkwardness. I did ask whether they would rather I departed – but they replied that if I was not a serious practitioner, then—sure—I did not need to stay."

"Sorry to say this – but... I thought you said that you didn't let him manipulate you?"

"Yes... that was certainly manipulation – but the reason I stayed was that I wanted to get a complete impression of the situation. I wanted to see how he would perform the ceremonies. I wanted to check out his books too – he had an immense library of books on Tibet and Vajrayana Buddhism. They had a fairly nice shrineroom too – apart from the fairy lights, his gauche paintings, and the sickly-sweet Indian incense. The other thing was that I wanted to be able to tell Ngakpa Yeshé Dorje that I'd met Gilbert and Elzebe Harris. I didn't want to say that I'd gone to see them and left because I didn't get on with them that well." PAUSE *"In terms of manipulative behaviour – this might illiterate something. They gave a slide show – and in one photograph of the Ganges I noticed something that looked like a hippopotamus. I asked what it was—because I knew that the creatures weren't native to India—and they replied 'It's you.' Now, I didn't understand the answer – so I asked again. They replied 'It's you.' Again, I failed to understand and so one of the others told me it was a human corpse and that they bloated in the river and looked like hippopotami. Then Gilbert and Elzebe Harris opined that I knew quite well that it was a human corps – but that I was in denial because I was afraid of thinking about death."*

"How did you respond that?"

"I just smiled and said they were right – and that I wasn't frightfully keen on dying. Strange to say – that seemed to throw them."

"Well yes" Penelope laughed *"because you agreed without agreeing – by agreeing to a statement they'd not made. Most astute."*

"Maybe..." I grinned sheepishly *"but it's more of a 'typical reaction' of mine than anything astute. It's what I do more-or-less automatically if someone tries to be offensively clever with me. If they'd called my number on it – I'd have admitted my gambit and told them my semantic gymnastics were no better than theirs. They were expecting me to defend myself and give them just cause for lambasting me with how unenlightened I was."*

"Maybe Buddhism really—will—have to be a solitary pursuit for you."

"*Yes… but it was a mixed thing. There were other people there with whom I had a better rapport; although, they were all in awe of Gilbert — because he'd learnt Sanskrit and Tibetan.*"

"*That doesn't excuse him from being a sinister megalomaniac, though.*"

"*Well… I'll give him his due… he is highly knowledgeable about Vajrayana ritual, as far as I can judge. I don't trust everything he says – because he has a Western occultist angle that he insinuates where he can.*"

"*I'm glad you're cautious.*"

"*Well yes… I'm suspicious of his knowledge. I think that what he learnt form Ngakpa Yeshé Dorje is entirely valid – but he's something of an esoteric jack-of-all-trades. He seems to see Western astrology, Theosophy, and general occultism as being on par with Vajrayana. He had 12 volumes of 'The Golden Bough',⁵ 'The Grimoire of Armadel', 'The Golden Dawn', and a bunch of other stuff that I can't remember… Madam Blavatsky, and Alice Bailey – oh yes, and a few Alistair Crowley books—such as 'The Book of Thoth'—on his shelf and his wife read tarot with the Alastair Crowley deck.*"

"*That really—is—really creepy.*"

"*Yes… 'creepy' would probably be the operative word. They were also tediously bigoted about anything that wasn't 'alternative'. They wore things like knitted trousers – inventive, I must admit, but peculiar. They reminded me somewhat of baby clothes. In fact, they made all their own clothes – because 'buying clothes' was for bourgeois materialists. They made them from old blankets and sheets that they'd dyed maroon. They died everything maroon so that they would look like monastic robes. They were highly industrious and resourceful – but the clothes just weren't made that well.*"

---

5   *The Golden Bough – a Study in Magic and Religion* by James Frazer. *The Golden Bough* was first published in two volumes in 1890; in three volumes in 1900; and in twelve volumes in the third edition, published 1906–15.

Penelope, by this time, was almost crying with laughter at the description of their clothing… so I gave her some insights into their dietary preferences: endless dahl, rice, and porridge – with no evident distinction between breakfast, lunch, and dinner. *"I lost half a stone in weight in the days I spent there—because everything they ate was 'vague'—y'know, a step beyond bland. It's not as if I'm that fastidious – but I found it nauseating. I'm used to Indian food—and to extremely simple low budget Indian food—but what they ate was served with some sort of peevishly perverted puritanism. Everything they wore, ate, said, or read – seemed designed to show other people how others were regarded in comparison with Gilbert and Elzebe Harris."*

"Blimey!" Penelope almost squawked. *"All that—and—the South African accent."*

"Yes… that is not the most pleasant version of English I've ever heard. I guess the one good thing I could say about them, is that they don't' appear to be racist."

"Apartheid – might have been useful in respect of them however" Penelope laughed.

"Quite so" I smiled. *"The Tibetans I met in India and Nepal in* 1971 *weren't like that at all. Apart from being of another—and markedly different—culture, they were all quite normal and simple. They seemed genuinely happy – which was remarkable when you consider their hardships. The old chang lady in whose hut I stayed—I shared a bedroom with her son —was such a kind woman… she really was. They live in these ramshackle huts with roofs and doors built out of flattened-out oil cans."*

"Yes… that's impressive. Maybe you'll just have to be incognito over here."

"Yes… avoiding people in this quarter does seem to be the best option."

"And don't forget what Jan told you."

"Leave when you first think of leaving?"

"Yes."

Penelope nodded and I continued *"Jan was a nice person... I liked her... and that first trip to Samÿe Ling was a good one. There—were—a few neurotic types there – but even they became sociable before the end of my stay... and Kate—even though she introduced me to Atlas—was really alright. Her friend Amy was reasonable – even if she lived in fairyland..."* PAUSE *"... but since then... the number of genuinely uncomplicated sociable people have gone into severe decline."*

"Right... so just don't stay in places you don't want to be – and don't associate with people just because you feel obliged... or because you think you ought to be able to put up with anything." PAUSE *"Y'know... that was—very—good advice Jan gave you."*

"Yes..." I mused. *"I think it was. I should have taken that advice in Liverpool."*

Penelope gave me a sideways glance and said *"Yes... and maybe it could apply elsewhere too. Just take care and remember you don't have to accept everything that happens. It's not an act of cowardice to say 'sod this for a game of soldiers'* [6] *is it?"*

That made me laugh – and on that note I went to bed and slept well; but I did not dream anything significant.

The next morning, I was up early and sat in silence for an hour. I felt it was the perfect start to the day. The taxi arrived and I alighted. *"Temple Meads?"* the taxi driver enquired and I simply nodded with a friendly smile. It was true... I didn't necessarily have to speak. I didn't have to speak when showing my ticket either and somehow, I arrived in London without having uttered a word. The Vajra Crown ceremony was to be held at the Friends Meeting House in Euston, London. It's opposite Euston tube station – a ten-minute walk from King's Cross and St Pancras Stations. I decided I'd sit in Cartwright Gardens in between taking walks to a few places.

---

6   *'... for a game of soldiers'* is a British expression of no certain origin, which means that something is not worth the time spent.

It was cold – so my periods of sitting in Cartwright Gardens were relatively brief. I went to a few book shops. Arthur Probsthain's[7] was a marvellous shop near the British Museum and one of the places where I was sure to find books on Vajrayana Buddhism. I had my rocket bag which contained my robes *(I'd put those on later)* and there was room for a few books. I found too many to buy—let alone carry—and decided I'd have to make another trip at some point. I picked up a copy of the 'Chandra Das Tibetan English Dictionary' and 'Demons and Oracles of Tibet' by René De Nebesky-Wojkowitz.[8] I tried reading it when I was at school and had found it impenetrable. It was an important work, however, so I decided I needed to own a copy. I'd been told that René De Nebesky-Wojkowitz had met some terrible end due to his messing with matters beyond his ken and so – with his book in my bag I made my way to the British museum to see the Tibetan exhibits and to read in relative comfort.

As I walked the Four Tops song flitted through my mind and I sang—in memory of René De Nebesky-Wojkowitz's death by otherworldly misadventure— *"Just walk away Renée– You won't see me follow you back home."* [9] Now that was the kind of thing that Western Buddhists would find severely unamusing – and it would have been impossible to explain that it was merely whimsicality. I wasn't callous concerning René De Nebesky-Wojkowitz's tragic demise – nor was I blasé concerning the material his book contained.

---

7   Arthur Probsthain's bookshop was started in 1903 at Bury Place by Arthur Probsthain. It has been located on 41 Great Russell Street *(opposite the British Museum)* since 1905. The bookshop has been family owned for a century and is today managed by Arthur Probsthain's nephew Michael Sheringham. It is the oldest Oriental bookshop in London after Bernard Quaritch.

8   René de Nebesky-Wojkowitz (1923–1959) was an Austrian ethnologist and Tibetologist. See glossary: *Nebesky-Wojkowitz, René de.*

9   *Just walk away Renee, you won't see me follow you back home; The empty sidewalks on my block are not the same, you're not to blame.* The Left Banke—Walk Away Renée— 1966. The song was composed by the group's then 16-year-old keyboard player, Michael Brown, and Tony Sansone. The song became a hit for the Motown band *The Four Tops* in 1968.

It was simply word play or name play – and the fact that such humour was somehow irresistible to a dyed-in-the-wool punster such as myself would have been met with… some unpleasant reaction. People in this sphere of interest seemed terribly keen on judging each other.

I had an interesting day seeing a wealth of Tibetan Culture from Tibet House—a shop down near the World's End pub on the King's Road—to the Tibet Society in Finsbury Park. I took in the Lhasa and Kathmandu Trading Company in the Chelsea Antiques Market on the way. That was a remarkable place and it turned out that the proprietors knew someone called Karma Lama – a Newari Buddhist aficionado of Blues who might like to meet me when I went back to Nepal. I'd been calling in to the Lhasa and Kathmandu Trading Company since 1970 – and had made some splendid purchases there. They seemed to enjoy my approach to spending. I'd say *"Hello, I've come to buy whatever I can that's in my price range. I've got £123.00 to spend and I want to leave your shop without it."* They'd then manage the bargaining for me and usually gave me a good deal on a few items – the price limit was always exceeded. In the past I'd purchased some Vajrayana ritual appurtenances: a kangling, a nine-pronged grigug, and set of tingsha.[10] This time I obtained a reliquary box which contained a thumb-sized statue of Guru Rinpoche – the Tantric Buddha. They served me with tea and we talked a lot about Nepal. They advised me that I'd be better off going out there myself and buying the things I needed. They were making a living—naturally—but they saw no reason why I should pay their prices forever. I thought that was jolly decent of them and thanked them heartily for the good advice. They in turn gave me a list of places to visit – each different place being the best place to buy whatever.

---

10 Kangling *(rKang gLing)* – human femur trumpet. Grigug *(gri gug)* – flaying knife. Tingsha *(ting shags)* – small cast bronze cymbals—measuring 3 or 5 inches in diameter—which are used in tsog'khorlo *(tshogs kyi 'khor lo / ganachakra puja)* for making profferments to the yidags *(yi dwags / preta / insatiable spirits)*.

I was quite tired by the time I got to the Friends' Meeting House in Euston. There was already a throng of people waiting to enter the building and so I found a public convenience where I could change into my robes. The changing cubicle put me in mind of Superman's use of the telephone booth and that seemed suitably ridiculous to put me at my ease about appearing on the streets of London in a voluminous white pleated skirt.

I walked up the steps and stood with the others awaiting the opening to the double-doors. I hoped no one would speak to me. No one did. If someone had spoken, I would not have been taciturn – but I was not about to broach conversation uninvited. The doors opened before much time had elapsed and we all entered. Before long the place was full and the air of expectancy was tangible. I noticed Akong Rinpoche sitting up in front and another two Lamas – Lama Chime Yönten Rinpoche[11] from Essex and Lama Ato Rinpoche[12] from Cambridge. There was a short talk to which the three Lamas contributed and then we awaited the arrival of Gyalwa Karmapa. He arrived – but he did much more than that. What he did or what he was – was nothing I could describe.

I'm not really given to fanciful mystical experiences—or thinking that I have had them—but Gyalwa Karmapa was a vast presence in that hall. He simply entered and assumed his throne.

11 Lama Chime Yönten Rinpoche was born in Amdo in 1941 and recognised at the age of two as the 9th incarnation of Chime Yönten Dong of Benchen. There are three Lamas of Benchen: Sang-gyé Nyènpa, Tènga, and Chime. Chime Yönten is also called 'Rardha Chime' as he was born into the Rardha Pöntsong family, who originally gave the land on which Benchen was built to the 4th Sang-gyé Nyenpa. Lama Chime Yönten Rinpoche established Marpa House in 1973.

12 Ato Rinpoche—born in 1933—is a Kagyüd-Nyingma Lama. He is the nephew of the previous Kyabjé Dilgo Khyentsé Rinpoche and was recognised by the 11th Tai Situ Rinpoche as the 8th incarnation of Ten'dzin Rinpoche. In 1976 he moved to Cambridge, England and now lives there with his wife and daughter. He worked as a nurse at Fulbourn Psychiatric Hospital, Cambridge, until his retirement in 1981.

The Vajrayana orchestra commenced its familiar assault on ordinary reality. The long horns[13]—with their menacing combination of jangle-clatter and growling rumble—were the foundation of the sound. The shawms[14] were the high wailing vibrato descant. The drums and cymbals added another layer of bass and treble with a contrasting texture. This was punctuated by the bells and hand-held damaru drums.

After some moments a box was produced and Gyalwa Karmapa took out the vajra crown that he was to place on his head.

The entire ceremony was simply this.

He placed the crown on his head and held it in place for... how long? I have no idea. Minutes... hours... ? It was timeless. It was both entirely surprising and utterly natural.

What could I tell anyone about what happened? I went to London to watch the Head of the Karma Kagyüd[15] School of Tibetan Buddhism place a black crown on his head. It took a few minutes; or an hour—I cannot be sure—then he put the crown back in the box. Then it was over. He gave everyone a red cord in token of benediction. Then I caught the train back to Bristol.

Well... that's what *literally* happened... but what *actually* happened was inexplicable – and anomalous in the extreme. There was a great deal of colour. I had some sense that I could even have fallen asleep and dreamt it. The crown was black. It was decorated with symbols. It looked ancient and the black looked like... a hole in reality... or... a portal on space. There was some sort of *fear* evoked on looking at Gyalwa Karmapa wearing that hat – but not 'fear' as the word is usually understood.

---

13 Dung chen or rag dung – great horn. The size of an Alpine horn but – straight, without the upturned end.
14 Gya-ling *(rGya gLing)* – Tibetan shawm *(shawn* in the USA), is a reed instrument like an oboe or clarinet, but closer in sound and shape to the Indian shenai.
15 Karma Kagyüd *(kar ma bKa' brGyud)*

Fear is merely the closest word I can find. Maybe there is the fear
one would experience on seeing a lion snarling in the wild – six
foot away. Then there is the fear that might exist seeing the same
lion through a yard of glass. One feels safe – but fearful at the
same time. In this case however, it was not my life that was at risk
– but 'something' was at risk that I could not identify. There was
no word. There was no clue. Then—at the same time as the
'fear'—there was a great up-surging of elation. There was some
sense that Gyalwa Karmapa was a phenomenon like Khyungchen
Aro Lingma. He had the same *reality / non-reality / super-reality
/surrealistic tangibility* that I remembered from my childhood vision
of Aro Lingma. In that way he was similar to Kyabjé Düd'jom
Rinpoche – a force of nature. I had the wordless sense that I could
ask him about Aro Lingma – and that he would know immediately
who she was, just as Düd'jom Rinpoche had done. I felt extremely
light – almost as if I might have floated away or become invisible.

Then I knew that Aro Lingma was there. I cannot say either that I
saw her or simply felt her presence. Her felt-presence was visible –
but only, as if rippling in the air, as if she was an aspect of the
light in the room. It was as if she had been emanated by Gyalwa
Karmapa – but she was so intermittent in her appearance that I
could not identify her location. It seemed that I could either see
her or define her location – but when I tried to define her location
she vanished into the temperature of the hall.

I took the train home. It was simple. Nothing happened other than
falling asleep – but I woke up before the train arrived at Temple
Meads Station in Bristol. I decided to walk to Hotwells rather than
take a taxi. The ladies would have gone to bed by the time I got
back. I was not averse to speaking with them… but somehow, I
wanted to end the day as I had started it – in silence. I'd happily
tell Penelope, Rebecca, and Meryl what my experience had been –
over breakfast the next morning. I hadn't walked a mile before I
wished I'd taken a taxi. My rocket bag was heavy with books and
the walk felt a little too arduous after a long day in London.

When I finally got back to the house in Hotwells I was tired but content. The ladies had indeed gone to bed – but left me a note with a rather delicious ham, cheese, and mustard sandwich with thinly sliced onion and tomato. It was just what I needed before retiring for the night.

Strangely I did not fall asleep as soon as I turned out the light. That was not what I'd anticipated. I lay in the dark not feeling quite as exhausted as I'd expected. I've never had trouble sleeping so it didn't worry me. I simply enjoyed the thought-free state in the dark. Thought-free? Yes, thought-free. Nothing to think. Gyalwa Karmapa was not exactly within the realm of conceptuality – so images of the Vajra Crown were free to arise and dissolve without my intellectual interference. Then—after what felt like *momentary conscious oblivion*— I knew that Aro Lingma was present.

Aro Lingma was always present before I became aware of her. She was simply there – but this time she was wearing what appeared to be regal robes. A white shawl with panels of green, red, white, and yellow on the sides. It was emblazoned with lotus flowers around the border panels – each in one of the five colours. There were lotus flowers in each of the five colours that bordered each side – and vajras on the blue stripe down the middle of the shawl. She otherwise wore white. She wore a red lotus hat on her head like the one sometimes worn by Kyabjé Düd'jom Rinpoche – but with white lotus flaps between the outer red lotus flaps and the hat itself.

The detail of the shawl was absolutely clear. It was also clear that the pattern would be reversed for a male Lama: lotus flowers on the middle blue section – and vajras around the edge. The hat for a man would be white with red lotus flaps beneath the red. There was a banquet of detail – and the details continued to unfold and unfurl. Aro Lingma displayed many different costumes and many different hats or crowns. I could not tell how the costumes changed or when they changed because I was always aware of them fractionally after the change had occurred.

It was almost as if no change had occurred – and that there had been the same costume throughout her visionary appearance.

Aro Lingma emanated yidams who spiralled in and out of her as presences. The yellow aspects of the display dissolved into white. The white dissolved into red. The red dissolved into green. The green dissolved into blue. Finally, the blue became black and vision dissolved into the bedroom – but the bedroom was made of light. It was made of light for an indefinable period of time, after which it regained its normal solidity. The memory of light remained however, and a determination arose never to forget what I had witnessed.

I lay there absolutely still for some time longer before finally falling asleep in gradual increments.[16] The increments dissolved into each other just as the vision of Aro Lingma had dissolved. There was a sudden expansion of light. Then I was in the dream state with awareness that I was dreaming. My intention was immediate. I wanted to be in the Aro Gar. Then I was there. There were the tents that I had seen before. There was the tiger hide tent. I looked round for A-yé Khandro and A-shé Khandro. They were not there so I intended their presence. Suddenly they were there and I was talking with them – but I was no longer who I thought I was and I was not speaking a language I understood. I could not comprehend how I could be speaking whilst not understanding what I was saying or hearing in reply. I was aware that the situation was becoming—and had already became—vague and dreamlike. No sooner was I cognisant of the usual texture of dreaming than I woke up. The room was brilliant with light – but it was the light of the sun shining full onto me where I lay.

---

16 The dissolution was that of the psycho-physical elements—earth, water, fire, air, and space—sequentially disappearing into each other. See glossary: *dissolution*.

My immediate thought on waking, was that what I had experienced was not gTérma,[17] but something like a reflection of gTérma seen in a mirror – or a hall of mirrors. I knew it wasn't gTérma because there was nothing cohesive about it. A gTérma would be complete – and more important, there would be no doubt about what it was. Düd'jom Rinpoche had told me that a time would come when I would discover Aro Lingma's gTérma – but when that might occur was not yet evident. Maybe this was a precursor to that discovery. I made a record of every detail in order that I could relate it to Kyabjé Düd'jom Rinpoche – as he was the only one who would know what it meant or portended. It was important – but that was all. Many things can be or seem important – but they often mean very little. I willed myself not to be too excited about it or build anything on it. I'd annotated it and that was all that was required.

After my customary ablutions I went down to help with making breakfast – but it had already been made. As soon as they saw me the ladies chorused *"Tell us all about it, then!"*

None of it was easily communicable. I said nothing of the vision of Aro Lingma. I simply told them about the Vajra Crown Ceremony in London. The ladies really seemed to grasp something from what I said – but, later, 'dette understood nothing at all. *"Just as long as you enjoyed yourself – and you don't expect me to join you on one of these 'Mad Hatter[18]' events, I don't mind. Just don't expect me to want me to hear about it."*

"That's a deal 'dette" I smiled. *"I have no Expectations – Great[19] or otherwise."*

17 gTérma *(gter ma /* གཏེར་མ་ */ revealed treasure)* are hidden Vajrayana teachings, originally hidden by Padmasambhava and Yeshé Tsogyel during the 8th century. See glossary: *térma (gTérma)*.

18 *The Hatter* is a character in Lewis Carroll's book *Alice's Adventures in Wonderland* and its sequel *Through the Looking-Glass*. He is often referred to as the 'Mad Hatter' – but 'mad' was not used in Lewis Carroll's book. The phrase 'mad as a hatter' pre-dates Alice's Adventures in Wonderland. The Hatter and the March Hare are referred to as mad by the Cheshire Cat, in *Alice's Adventures in Wonderland i*n the seventh chapter titled *A Mad Tea-Party*.

19 Reference to *Great Expectations* by Charles Dickens, concerns the education of an orphan nicknamed Pip.

"Oh, very droll – am I to call you Pip now?"

"As in Pipistrelle? Yes, why not; I do—bat—for England after all." I grinned – but 'dette shook her head as if wearied. She enjoyed banter, badinage, and repartee – but seemed to resent it at the unlikeliest of times. Or maybe the times were *not* unlikely. Maybe they were the occasions on which she felt caught out. Maybe she recognised that she had been dismissive of me – and my repost had demonstrated that it did not matter to me. I never spoke of the Vajra Crown to her again. It no longer mattered – but it was consequential, that it no longer mattered. I wished that I'd not allowed 'dette to dissuade me from ending the relationship. It seemed that whenever she sensed she'd overstepped the mark with me – that she'd spin 180° and become the warm and charming lady she'd initially been. It just didn't last—and I was too naïve to understand I was being manipulated—on the basis that I was obviously incapable of responding unaffectionately, to affection.

One of the bizarre aspects of my life was the juxtaposition of visionary experience and responding to 'dette's 'Pip' jest with *"As in Pipistrelle? Yes, why not; I do—bat—for England after all."* It *was* a bizarre juxtaposition – but perhaps not as bizarre as the fact that it didn't seem bizarre. It was simply the texture of my life. I had nothing with which I could compare it. I had no peer group. I could not ask another English incarnation about what was normal. I could certainly ask Düd'jom Rinpoche – but when I spoke with Düd'jom Rinpoche, I was completely within his world. My English world was always too distant. It was distant with any elder Tibetan. In this respect was even distant with Tibetans of my own age. Considering this sometimes made me feel utterly lonely – but fortunately, I was able to avoid indulging in loneliness. There were many lonely people on the world other than Eleanor Rigby.[20] There was Queen Elizabeth. There were people like John Lennon, Bob Dylan, and other people who were—of necessity—alone in crowds. I was not alone in being alone.

20 Lennon–McCartney—The Beatles—Eleanor Rigby—Revolver— 1966. A song about loneliness written primarily by Paul McCartney.

Maybe everyone was alone to some degree.

Derek asked me about the Vajra Crown Ceremony, as I'd had to request a day away from Art School – and he was genuinely curious. *"Marvellous—simply marvellous—for something so remote to be available in London. It must have been like time travelling."*

"Yes… that… expresses it well" I replied. *"I wasn't even aware that it was the Friends Meeting House in Euston. That seemed to vanish and all I saw was Gyalwa Karmapa… I think the Vajrayana orchestra absorbed the setting in some way. It didn't seem possible to observe the event as I'd usually observe a performance. It was something like theatre… but… without the willing suspension of disbelief. It was more like the suspension of the observer. I just vanished and all that was left was the act of looking."*

"I see that you are going to have to make another trip to the East at some point" Derek grinned.

I answered in the affirmative – and returned to the Illustration studio. It struck me that 'dette had her own particular problem or difficulty with religious experience. She seemed to feel obliged to mock it. That she also mocked me was no massive inconvenience – but it meant that we had no real relationship. The Vajra Crown Ceremony was evidently something I could discuss with the ladies in Hotwells and also with Derek Crowe. The subject was therefore not as bizarre as 'dette deemed it to be – and… nor was I. I was fairly ordinary in many ways – as had been pointed out to me by Kate in Liverpool.

My life was going to be a strange mixture of worlds – the world of Art School and the Tibetan world. Both were essentially Art – but they seemed worlds apart to 'dette. Could I bring these two worlds together? There was thangka painting of course – but that was not really Art as I'd studied it. Thangka painting was certainly a field I'd explore – but it didn't cross the divide between Art School and Vajrayana. I didn't want to become one of those esoteric types who painted their own Tarot decks or whatever. I didn't want to create Western thangkas or weave Vajrayana symbolism into my paintings.

That seemed a waste of time and an insult to both traditions. It also seemed the surest route to manufacturing clichés and bazaar art. It occurred to me that there was something essential that would translate itself—of-itself—if I could only discover what made it all function. There was something about the nature of reality that would make sense of itself – almost as my experience of Gyalwa Karmapa had made sense of itself. That timeless sensation of experiencing Gyalwa Karmapa must surely be accessible in roots and branches, in rivers and streams, in clouds, in frost and snow – it must be accessible in everything.

19

thought can only resemble

Rebecca and I had been sitting – looking out over the river. We'd been waiting for the sun to set—without speaking—simply taking in the colour. We were unaware that Meryl and Penelope had joined us – because Arnold Schönberg[1] had masked their foot-tread on the stairs. Rebecca was mightily enamoured of Schönberg – and I grew to feel the same.

"So, Vic…" Penelope asked *"tell us about Surrealism, then."*

"The interviewer—hath—arriven!" My phraseology made Rebecca laugh. *"I'd forgotten we had our breakfast discussions to explore for the evening's entertainment – I've had various thoughts about this today…"*

"You don't mind, do you Vic?" Penelope enquired tentatively.

"Not at all. I'll blather on about this stuff for days and weeks together, if you encourage me… just let me know when it promotes ennui."

"Ennui is the last thing I expect" Penelope grinned. *"So… if I could ask what I was going to ask when we all had to disappear to College?"* I nodded and so Penelope launched in *"It seems… as if this is some sort of major driving force behind—everything—you do – and… it's not something anyone of us know that well."*

"I think you're right – that I'm fundamentally a Surrealist, I mean." PAUSE *"That's why I liked psychedelia while it lasted—or the best of it at any rate —because it's just another bubbling up of Surrealism. Surrealism has bubbled up throughout history."*

---

1 Arnold Schönberg (1874–1951) was an Austrian composer, associated with the 2nd Viennese School – and German expressionist poetry. His *developmental harmonic* approach was pivotal in 20th century composition. The Nazi Party labelled his music *(along with Jazz)* as degenerate – but his innovations in atonality became polemic. He developed the 12-tone technique, a mode of deploying a systematic arrangement of the chromatic scale. He coined the term 'developing variation' and was the first modern composer to develop motifs without defaulting to a predominant melodic theme.

"How far back do you think?"

"To the dawn of time I imagine – but I've only traced it back as far as Giuseppe Arcimboldo.[2]"

"Right… was he the one who painted people made up out of pieces of fruit and vegetable?"

"The very one!" I grinned. *"He was quite bizarre for a 16th Century artist. He painted composites—portraits amalgamated from objects—natural and fabricated. Most of these paintings were created for Rudolf the 2nd, who employed him as his court painter."*

"Shame there's no Rudolf now to set you up like that. I can see you as a court painter."

"Yes… although I can't quite see the Queen posing for a raven painting…" [3]

"Right!" cackled Rebecca *"… but that would be—really—surreal wouldn't it… maybe you could superimpose her face onto one of the Art School models?"*

"Intriguing idea… but…" I laughed *"it might be a treasonable offence."*

"So…" asked Meryl *"what about Surrealism other than psychedelia and Arcimboldo?"*

2   Giuseppe Arcimboldo (1527–1593). His father, Biagio Arcimboldo, was an artist. Giuseppe began his career as a designer of stained glasses and frescoes when he was 21 years old. In 1562 he became court portraitist to Ferdinand 1st at the Habsburg court in Wien, and later, to Maximilian 2nd and his son Rudolf 2nd at the court in Prague. He was also the court decorator and costume designer. King Augustus of Saxony, who visited Vienna in 1570 and 1573, saw his work and commissioned a copy of his *The Four Seasons* which incorporated his own monarchic symbols.

3   See *an odd boy*—Volume IV—chapter 12—Bower Ashton – Speaking With Ravens —Aro Books WORLDWIDE—2018. See glossary: *Speaking with Ravens.*

"Well… If I look at the creative work I most admire – I see it in the presence of dynamic incongruity. I see it in Allen Ginsberg's [4] 'hydrogen jukebox' – from 'Howl' [5] where he describes 'listening to the crack of doom on the hydrogen jukebox…' Just dwell on those words 'hydrogen jukebox'—I mean—what is that? I have no idea what that means—but it really conveys menace—and that's where you'd hear the 'cracks of doom'…"

"So… it doesn't really matter that Allen Ginsberg's a Beat Poet – his language can still be seen as Surrealism?"

"As far as I'm concerned… yes. Obviously, the Surrealism of his poetry is intermittent – but it's still surreal." PAUSE *"Like Bob Dylan – he's surreal too."*

"I wouldn't argue with that" said Rebecca *"especially Mister Tambourine Man – so what about literature?"*

"Well… I also see it in the linguistics of Mervyn Peak [6] … in his 'Gormenghast Trilogy'. He paints images of such utterly unbelievably believable strangeness…"

"Yes…" said Meryl *"… although… the books are crippled by the irredeemable psychopathology of the characters."*

---

4   Allen Ginsberg (1926–1997) was a 20th century American poet and leading figure of the 1950s' Beat movement. He opposed militarism, materialism, and sexual conformism.

5   *Howl* (1954–1955) written by Allen Ginsberg and published in his 1956 collection *Howl and Other Poems*. It is considered to be one of the great works of American literature. It was published by Lawrence Ferlinghetti, of City Lights Bookstore and the City Lights Press. He completed Part II and the Footnote after Lawrence Ferlinghetti promised to publish the poem. Howl was too short to make a book, so Lawrence Ferlinghetti requested other pieces and the final collection thus contained several works written at that time. He continued the experimentation with the 'long line' he had used in Howl – and these pieces constitute his most influential work.

6   Mervyn Peake (1911–1968) born in Kuling in the Jiangxi Province of central China, was an English writer, artist, poet, and illustrator best known for the *Gormenghast Trilogy*—an unfinished work, originally conceived of as a much longer work—the completion of which was prevented by his untimely demise. He also wrote poetry and literary nonsense verse, and short stories. He was educated at Croydon School of Art and the Royal Academy School of Art.

"Yes..." I groaned *"there is that... but I tend to screen that out... and... read it for the imagery."* I got up and pulled 'Titus Groan' off my bookshelf. *"Listen to this: 'A carpet filled the floor with blue pasture... the deep, unhurried purring was like the voice of an ocean in the throat of a shell... She tossed her long hair and it flopped down her back like a pirate's flag'.*[7] *It's that kind of imagery that makes these books worth reading."*

"Ah... I can see that... and the surrealism of it."

"Mervyn Peake's images remind me of Francis Bacon...[8]*"* I mused. *"They're beautiful in the... purity of their ugliness."* I got out my notebook. I always kept a notebook for writing down sentences or paragraphs that I knew I'd want to quote at some point. *"Ah... here it is... Francis Bacon's talking about how his paintings communicate: '... some paint comes across directly into the nervous system and other paint tells you the story in a long diatribe through the brain. If you can talk about it, why paint it?'"*

"That last sentence sounds just like you Vic" Rebecca announced – somewhat surprised. *"Is that where you got the idea?"*

"No – although I was glad to find the quote."

"I thought that you didn't really care that much about validating your work?" queried Rebecca. *"You're not taking 'dette too much to heart on this validation thing, are you?"*

"No... but also... yes. I'm not sure what to say about that. My disinterest in intellectual validation is... well, I don't like the idea of that hardening into some kind of arrogant position.

---

7   Mervyn Peake—Gormenghast Trilogy—Volume II—Titus Groan
8   Francis Bacon (1909–1992) was an Irish-born British figurative painter. His hybrids of figurative and abstract portraits were often presented in glass or steel geometrical cages set on neutral grounds. His career began in his early 20s – but he only came into his own with the 1944 triptych *Three Studies for Figures at the Base of a Crucifixion.* It was this piece—with his portraits of the 1940s and 1950s—that gained him the reputation as a chronicler of the bleaker aspects of the human condition.

"*So… if I happen to find out that Francis Bacon has the same idea – then I can find myself innocent of the kind of hippie anti-intellectualism that I hate.*"

"*Right…*" chuckled Meryl "*you mean the people who say 'it's all words man' as soon as you say anything that requires a little work or contains words that have more than two syllables.*"

"*The very same.*"

"*D'you have any more like that in your little book?*" asked Penelope.

"*Plenty… what about this… this is what he says about composition: 'I want a very ordered image, but I want it to come about by chance… I know that in my own work the best things are the things that just happened… images that were suddenly caught and that I hadn't anticipated… I believe in an ordered chaos and in the rules of chance.' You can imagine how exciting it was to read this in terms of what I have been trying to achieve with the Raven paintings.*"

"*That's totally clear Vic – what does 'dette have to say about that? That must put her mind at rest about your paintings not being outside the remit of Fine Art.*"

"*She's mentioned that idea, has she?*" I grinned in what I imagined would seem a sheepish manner.

"*Yes…*" Penelope offered tentatively "*but just in passing, you know.*"

Rebecca frowned in disagreement but said nothing.

"*Well… I think that 'dette tends to feel that I can't rely on the words of one artist to take the approach I've taken – that innovations have to be based on Art theory and on understanding what you're doing in an Art history context. I think she's right… in many ways… but… I don't think I want to immerse myself in too much of that kind of reading. It's not that I haven't studied Art history and the Art theory of different artists – but…*"

"*It's boring?*" laughed Meryl.

"Yes" I laughed. *"It*—can be—*fairly tedious… but mainly because it all seems to come out of a stew of Græco-Roman philosophy filtered through Judæo-Christian theology and 20*[th] *century political theorising."*

"And this from the man who's intellectually wanting!" laughed Meryl.

"Well…" I smiled *"it's a question of my knowledge having been acquired in a highly haphazard manner. I think 'dette has something of a point there, inasmuch as I tend to have a splattering of knowledge that looks more impressive than it actually is…"* Meryl was about to launch in – but I continued *"… from a Buddhist point of view – I find intellectualism ever-so-slightly futile… That's why I pick and choose what I read—and—why Francis Bacon is so refreshing"* I picked up my notebook again. *"This is what he says about realism… 'I've tried to make images that would unlock the values of feeling on different levels. For me, to be as realistic as possible has meant extreme deformations.' What I like about that is the way he's talking about something that really can't be communicated in words. He's talking about his paintings in poetry – and really… that's the only way I can talk about it."*

"Makes sense to me Vic" said Rebecca. *"I really don't see why 'dette has a problem with that—anyhow… that's none of my business really —can I go back to 'Easy Rider' as Surrealism? You made a passing comment about that this morning."*

"Oh yes the two epigrammatic protagonists of pipe-dream driving chopped hogs across America and spiralling into 'accelerated bizarre'…" PAUSE *"Somehow the Band's song 'The Weight' just had to be one of the songs used in that film."* I burst into song *" I picked up my bag, I went looking' for a place to hide / Then I saw Carmen and the devil, walking' side by side / I said "Hey Carmen, come on let's go downtown." / She said "I gotta go, but my friend can stick around.'…"* PAUSE *"It's hard to say what's so perfect about that song in that context… it's probably just the mystery of it. There's the way 'Carmen' and 'Come on' are more-or-less homonyms in American English. That had to be deliberate. And with Carmen and the devil… there's no direct meaning there – to their being together or why she has to go and why her friend can stick around."*

"You could read all kinds of things into that" offered Penelope *"such as Carmen is what he wants—and of course Carmen could represent anything —but in trying to get Carmen, he ends up with the devil. I think that happens in life—you want something good and end up somewhere bad because the two are inextricable—and somehow what you thought was good… was just the surface of something bad."*

"That's impressive Penelope… I would never have thought of that…"

"Well…" Penelope replied stretching her long Levi'd legs out across the floor *"… that's only because you're not overly analytical or hidebound by linear thinking."*

"Maybe – but then I always miss the obvious."

"Maybe the obvious is best missed when it comes to Art."

"Perhaps…" I nodded *"that would fit well with Salvador Dalí…*⁹*"* I opened my notebook again *"… let's see… here we are…"* PAUSE
"… he says: 'I believe that the moment is near when, by a procedure of active paranoiac thought, it will be possible to systematise confusion and contribute to the total discrediting of the world of reality.' And he talks about his painting as a '… spontaneous method of irrational knowledge based on the critical and systematic objectification of delirious associations and interpretations.' So… maybe I've got two painters to validate my Raven paintings."

"What did 'dette make of that?" Meryl asked.

"Oh well… that Salvador Dalí is not universally respected. He's apparently accused of squandering his talent on absurdity."

---

9   Salvador Domènec Felipe Jacinto Dalí i Domènech, Marquis de Púbol (1904–1989) was a Spanish Surrealist painter born in Figueres, Catalonia, Spain. His ancestors were descended from the Moors. He was a skilled draftsman, with skills influenced by the Renaissance masters. His artistic repertoire includes film, sculpture, and photography, in collaboration with a range of artists in a wide variety of media. He was highly imaginative with a penchant for eccentrically grandiose behaviour. His overt eccentricity in public media often drew more attention than his art. This caused irritation amongst his critics – but caused him no concern.

"But then there's probably no artist alive or dead who's never been accused of something or derided for something else" Meryl chided with a quick upturn of her eyes. *"At least this shows that there are painters out there who aren't hard-line about academic theory."*

"I suppose I should read a little deeper when it comes to Surrealism – but I seem to find myself learning what I need to learn from random references… and from looking at the paintings themselves." PAUSE *"I mean – you can read about Surrealist painting… or… you can simply look at the paintings…"* PAUSE *"… and anyway… I tend to move between looking at paintings and reading poetry… That quote from Dalí—for example—sparks thoughts about Ted Hughes'*[10] *Crow Anthology… where Crow—in being born— is…"* and this time I knew the quote by heart
"… 'Flogged lame with legs / Shot through the head with balled brains / Shot blind by eyes / Nailed down by his own ribs'."

"Have you ever seen 'Garden of Earthly Delights' by Hieronymus Bosch?[11]*"* asked Penelope. *"I love his work. His 'Earthly Pleasures' and painting of hell could have been painted by Dalí."*

"Yes absolutely" Meryl laughed *"… and—don't get me wrong, I'm not mocking—but Matthias Grünewald's* [12] *'Temptation of St Anthony' reminds me of the Stones album 'Their Satanic Majesties Request'."*

10 Ted Hughes (1930–1998) was British Poet Laureate from 1984 until his death and regarded as one of the best poets of his generation. He was born in West Yorkshire and attended Mexborough Grammar School, where teachers encouraged him to develop his interest in poetry. They introduced him to the poets Hopkins and Eliot and he was mentored by his sister Olwyn – herself an accomplished poet.

11 Hieronymus Bosch (1450–1516) was a Dutch painter known for the fantastic imagery he employed to illustrate moral and religious narratives. Nothing is known of his personality or thoughts on the meaning of art.

12 Matthias Grünewald (1470–1528) was a German Renaissance painter who rejected Renaissance classicism in favour of the intense expressive late medieval Central European style. Only ten paintings—several consisting of many panels—and thirty-five drawings survive. His reputation was obscured until the late 19th century – and many of his paintings were attributed to Albrecht Dürer.

"Right…" I exclaimed with a sense of delighted revelation. *"I'd never made that association – but you're both right… and you could see that in Bruegel's* [13] *'Tower of Babel'!"*

"Yes, really!" Penelope grinned. *"He has these crowded folk scenes where something singularly weird is—always—included."*

Rebecca—who'd been down to the kitchen to fetch a bottle of wine—asked *"So who d'you like most – when it comes down to it?"*

"I think… although I'm enthusiastic about Dalí's colour – I think Rene Magritte's [14] *approach to questioning the nature of reality is more subtle and more… part of the surrealism of everyday life."*

"The paintings of windows…" suggested Rebecca *"… with broken panes which still hold fragments of images of the mountain beyond?"*

"Yes" I replied. *"Dalí paints… in his words, 'systematic objectifications of delirious associations and interpretations' – and whilst I like that… I find I'm more intrigued by what's just beyond the edge of everyday vision. Dalí's images are from a world that maybe no one will ever see – but Magritte offers something that could be seen by almost anyone who was open to it."* This took me back to my notebooks again. *"These three quotes present some sense of René Magritte in terms of how he saw his painting: 'Thought can only resemble. It resembles by being what it sees, hears, or knows; it becomes what the world offers it.'… Now… I can relate to that directly from a Buddhist perspective – whereas Dalí's vision of Surrealism is a little too… sensational."*

13 Pieter Brueghel (1525–1569) was a Flemish renaissance painter and printmaker born in Breughel near Breda (now in Holland). He was an apprentice of Pieter Cœcke van Aelst, and married van Aelst's daughter Mayken. He lived for a time in France and Italy, and in 1551 he was accepted as a master in the painter's guild in Antwerp. He was nicknamed *Bruegel the Peasant* due to his practice of dressing in peasants' clothes in order to mingle at weddings and other festivities in order to collect authentic details for his paintings. He was the father of Pieter Brueghel the Younger and Jan Brueghel the Elder who both became painters.
14 René François Ghislain Magritte (1898–1967) was a Belgian artist famous for philosophically witty images, depicting ordinary objects in unusual contexts. He challenged preconditioned perceptions of reality – and his paintings were popular with those who majored in Psychedelia.

"I never took you to be a non-sensationalist Vic!" Meryl laughed – and my obvious puzzlement prompted her to continue *"I mean... making that giraffe hide greatcoat would have been sensational."*

"Yes... it would... in some respects – but... it would have been in the real world. It would have existed. If I'd painted a scene in Bristol where people were wearing exotic animals... then that would have been an idea that would never come into being... but—having said that—Magritte did say 'Art evokes the mystery without which the world would not exist...' so... maybe..." I laughed *"that completely undermines my argument."*

"No..." said Penelope *"I can see both ideas side by side. I think it's all extremely subtle and the differentiations probably can't help but evolve into each other – if you see what I mean?"*

"Absolutely – and that's why it's never that easy for me to make completely definitive statements when it comes to Art." PAUSE *"The next Magritte quote probably says it best 'Everything we see hides another thing; we always want to see what is hidden by what we see.'... and—that—is what I try to bring about with the raven paintings. The figure and the raven have to describe each other in some way and show what they are – behind what they appear to be."*

"Right... and we've all been—there—haven't we?" Rebecca announced. *"We're all in one of those paintings and so... us three must all have some sense of how we've been described by the raven and how the raven has been described by us..."*

"Yes..." I confirmed with some slight hesitation.

"I mean, you can't ask the Art School models about it... but we're all here and we can probably all tell you whether it makes sense or not – just on the basis of our own experience of seeing ourselves in the paintings."

"And...?" I asked looking at each of them briefly.

They didn't quite say it simultaneously – but they all said 'yes'. The effect was a little like having heard them through a phaser pedal.

The drum roll on 'Itchycoo Park'[15]came to mind so I sang
*"… 'Over bridge of sighs to rest my eyes, in shades of green, Under
dreaming spires to Itchycoo Park, that's where I've been…'"* I laughed at
their expressions of bewilderment and had to explain the
reference to the phaser effect on the song.

"You go off on the most unexpected tangents Vic!" Rebecca cackled
*"… but now you explain it, yes – it did sound like that, us all saying 'yes' at
almost the same time."*

Penelope and Meryl nodded assent and we sat for a moment or
two in silence. *"Well"* I said once the idea had settled on its own
"… 'yes'… and that, answers an enormous question…"

"But…" Penelope added somewhat seriously *"I don't think it's
evidence you could present to 'dette."* PAUSE *"Not that you need evidence, that
is."*

I wasn't sure how to respond to that so I let it pass and evaded
answering by reading to them again from my note book. *"Magritte
said 'My paintings are visible images which conceal nothing; they evoke
mystery and, indeed, when one sees my pictures, one asks oneself this simple
question 'What does that mean?' It does not mean anything, because mystery
means nothing either, it is unknowable.' I think… that's always my final
answer."*

"I wouldn't entirely agree with that though…" Rebecca stated. *"I'd say
that Magritte's work and the works of other Surrealists are unknowable to
the intellect – and intellect knows almost nothing in terms of experience. Art
in general is knowable through the senses and through intuitive
interpenetration of the senses."*

---

15 Written by Steve Marriott and Ronnie Lane – released in 1967 by The Small
    Faces. It was one of the first to use *flanging*, an effect heard on the drums in
    the bridge after each chorus. The effect was an electro-mechanical studio
    process in which two synchronised tapes were played simultaneously into a
    master recorder – and by manually retarding the rotation of one reel, the
    phase-difference between the two sources was manipulated, creating a
    whooshing phase effect.

"That's true" I conceded. *"What can I say… Thrown like a star in my vast sleep, I op'ed my eyes to take a peep, To find that I was by the sea gazing with tranquillity / 'twas then when the hurdy gurdy man…' "*

They all collapsed in hysterics at my suddenly launching into Donovan's 'Hurdy Gurdy Man' .

"You're nothing if not the master of creative non sequiturs in song!"

"Well… yes… my idea of Surrealism is that a Surrealist should live life like a surrealist." PAUSE *"I mean, without becoming some kind of irritating idiot who just lives to weird people out."* PAUSE *"So… '… if you can fasten on that moment and expand through the afterglow / You can reverse your mind in time and travel back to when / The earth was formed—the sky was born—and the universe began.*[16]*'…"*

Once the laughter had died down again Penelope ventured *"I suppose… it could have been a matter of development for the surrealist rock song—acid rock—but it never developed. It just died, or the bands died."*

"Yes…" I sighed. *"It was dependent on artificially altered states – and that had no future, from the outset."*

Rebecca stood up—stretched—and began one of her dance exercises. Maybe to assist her train of thought? *"It should have been possible to have taken the métier forward according to its apparent principles – all of which are obvious and evident."*

"Absolutely!" I cheered *"All that's lacking is the flair for that mode of expression – and that can arise out of the restructuring which naturally occurs as a result of silencing the conceptual chatter that gets in the way of the senses."*

"I was never inclined to listen to the grass growing…" chuckled Meryl *"but somehow, I'm happy that some people felt it possible…*

16 Paul Kantner, Grace Slick, and David Freiberg—Baron Von Tollbooth and the Chrome Nun—Your Mind Has Left Your Body—1973

" 'See the people all in line—I'm thinking they look at me / Can't imagine that their minds—are thinking the same as me / I can hear the grass grow— I can hear the grass grow—I see rainbows in the evening…[17]*'…"* Meryl sang. *"See – you've got me at it now!"*

"Songs like that were the background of my formative years too…" Penelope commented *"and, whether they're profound or trivial is less important to me than their effect on the gestalt of the time."*

"Exactly!" exclaimed Rebecca. *"I think they acted as a reminder that there was more to existence than met the heavily blinkered eye of semi-comatose suburbia."*

"And that's why…" I chimed in *"my interest has always revolved around the fact that there is a language of creativity which plays with incongruity, inconsistency, contradiction, improbability, irrationality, and illogicality…"* PAUSE *"also… strangeness, preposterousness, ludicrousness, eccentricity, idiosyncrasy, bizarreness, and just plain weirdness."* PAUSE *"Without these possibilities life would turn into a factory production-line stretching from birth to death."*

And so to bed, after an entire day of conversation and dining in the most pleasant company I knew. I could have lived the rest of my life this way – were it not for the fact that I was going back to the Himalayas. 'dette had been mentioned a few times – but only in comments to the effect that I need not take her academic artist appraisals seriously. That felt… not as awkward as it should have been – and that felt… How did that feel…? I felt supported and validated by friends who liked and respected me – just as I liked and respected them. That's who friends were: people who liked and respected each other. What 'dette liked about me – was anyone's guess. What she respected was… what? Nothing I could determine. I wished I could find a kind and gentle way to conclude the relationship. Every approach I considered seemed surreal – but not in any way that could be considered as Art. I was determined —as a ngakpa—to be a kindly gentle Artist, if at all possible.

17 The Move—I Can Hear the Grass Grow—1967

It occurred to me that the best outcome would be for 'dette to bid me adieu of her own volition and give me the opportunity to be entirely gentlemanly in my acceptance of her decision. That, of course, was cowardly – or could have been cowardly, if my motive had not been kindly. I was not afraid of facing 'dette – but she had been rejected once before and the affect had been catastrophic. It never occurred to me that the fellow who rejected her might have been a far more terrible loss than I could ever be. Sometimes there are simply no good choices.

20

as you like it

Just before the Easter recess, I heard that Gyalwa Karmapa would be giving teachings at Samŷe Ling – but that the spaces available were limited. He was also to give the vajra crown ceremony again with additional empowerments – so, naturally, I decided go. I sent my cheque – and there was space for me at Samŷe Ling. The ladies were going to their respective homes for Easter – and each had vaguely intimated that if I wanted a break… I could accompany them *"… with 'dette of course…"* they hurriedly added… but almost as an afterthought it seemed.

'dette had no inclination to visit the homes of her friends. The idea that it might be pleasant and interesting, met with a slight *frostiness* that I found slightly perplexing. I got the impression that there was something 'dette was not saying. I wasn't clairvoyant – but I knew that there was some reason why she wouldn't wish to visit her friends' homes. I decided not to pry. It would have been awkward for me to have made that journey—in any case—in view of my prior engagement at Samŷe Ling. I would have to have gone back to Bristol for my motorcycle – as that would have been my mode of transport for Scotland. 'dette's response did cause me to ponder, however. It was not simply lack of interest on 'dette's part. Had she met her friends' parents and disliked them? I asked the ladies but, no – 'dette had never met their parents. Then I picked up on what seemed to be reticence on the part of the ladies. I decided not to probe. There was a mystery here, that I was going to have to leave as a mystery. I decided that I did not need to know.

As the projected stay at Samŷe Ling lay in the middle of the three-week recess from Art School – I wondered how the cards would fall. An outing to see Shakespeare's *As You Like It* in Stratford contraindicated any idea of spending extended time with 'dette. The idea of living in the house in Hotwells on my own however – seemed ideal.

I had no idea what to say to 'dette anymore. The play *As You Like It*, had been *just as I liked it* – but seeing that play with 'dette had not. Having to sleep on the floor at the hotel—because 'dette couldn't share anything less than a king-sized bed—was the least of the inconveniences. I was happy to sleep on the floor. I'd brought a sleeping-bag and mat because I anticipated that eventuality. I would have appreciated a token of recognition for the sacrifice – but she seemed to take it for granted that I was *"… used to primitive conditions having spent time in India."* That was not the affront it could have been to some – it was 'dette's almost constant criticality of what she disapproved of in me. That wore me out. Not that I was in such need of approval – but it was enervating having to respond or attempt to converse.

I was ashamed of feeling worn out by 'dette – but at least all I felt was lassitude. There was no anger, or even irritation – merely depletion and ennui. When I looked at why I felt worn out – I realised that it was not just that every last vestige of romance was worn out. It was the fact that I was subject to connubial incarceration – a sentence to which I had been convicted by the judge and jury of my own rationale.

Being caustically bludgeoned by the opinion that I was a pseudo-philosopher because I'd never studied philosophy made conversation more-or-less impossible. Making any sort of observation on anything—other than the weather, or the time of day—was fraught with the possibility of irritable reactions.

My philosophy—where it wasn't Buddhist—was hand-knitted, home-made, and generally exploratory. I'd speculate at the drop of a hat on almost anything simply because life fascinated me. As far as 'dette was concerned I was out of my depth with all such theorising and needed to study Plato, Socrates, Aristotle, Agrippa the Sceptic, Heraclitus, Parmenides of Elea, Xenophanes of Colophon… 'dette sure could reel off names… I had no objection to that – in fact I found it most interesting. When I'd first met 'dette I was reading Aristophanes and she'd had to correct me for pronouncing him *A-rist-o-faines*.

At first 'dette seemed to like me – and my proletarian autodidactic concatenation of concepts culled from everywhere imaginable. As time went on however, she seemed to tire of my quaint plebeianisms.

I found this curious because Penelope, Meryl, and Rebecca were 'dette's old school friends. They'd attended Badminton Girls' School together. I therefore expected them to have similar modes of intellectual assessment – but no. There was no similarity. I'd shared a house with Penelope, Meryl, and Rebecca for over two years and we'd become close friends with a pronounced appreciation of each other's company. We had endless conversations – and they never seemed to tire of my oblique conjecture on Art, culture, and society. They'd plunge into any subject with gusto and talk the evening away, day-after-day, without remission – but 'dette, no. Conversation was bedevilled by her criticality. She could criticise – but she couldn't create. Meryl— having overheard 'dette berate me for ignorantly philosophising— said *"Y'know, 'dette's like a music critic who can read music – but can't compose."* There was a time when I would have defended 'dette and said that she'd had a point. I was an ignoramus in terms of philosophy. The time seemed long gone.

I wanted to bid 'dette adieu – but hadn't done so because I worried about her. I didn't want her thrown into despondency during the run-up to the degree shows. She'd been cruelly jilted during her Foundation year – and, according to the three ladies, it had almost ruined her life. They'd practically nursed her back to normality – and if it hadn't been for them, 'dette would not have applied for Fashion and Textiles at Bristol Art School. She would have immured herself in her palatial bedroom at home.

Penelope, Meryl, and Rebecca were delighted when 'dette took up with me. They'd grown to regard me as a valued friend – and, after a while, a closer friend than 'dette. They were now more concerned about *my* wellbeing – and made occasional enquiries and comments which betrayed the fact that they didn't approve of the way 'dette treated me.

I never complained to them about 'dette—or made any adverse comments about her—but they seemed to have extrasensory perception regarding our relationship. They seemed to know the lay of the land. I could see it in their faces – even when they said nothing.

I didn't want to have some kind of off-stage drama with 'dette – but, I didn't feel like pretending that nothing had happened. Something *had* happened – and there was no turning back. My entire physiognomy was against it now. I didn't dislike 'dette—and could probably still have amusing conversations with her—but, there was no amorous future. The thrill was gone. I was singing the song in my room one morning as the ladies were meandering around packing to go home.

> *The thrill is gone, it's gone away for good, / Oh, the thrill is gone baby – baby it's gone away for good.*[1]

Rebecca happened to catch the words *"Are you just—singing—that song, Vic—as a song—or… I mean… or are you singing what the words mean?"*

Caught in the act of *feeling what I felt—or not feeling what I was supposed to feel*—I froze. I stood still for a moment looking at Rebecca – and decided that I'd better answer honestly. *"Well Rebecca… it's not an easy subject for me to… well, you're friends of 'dette and…"*

"We're friends of yours—too—Vic. In fact, we're much closer to you than we have been to 'dette since, well… since quite a while." PAUSE *"So… anyway, just to let you know that we understand – and we're glad…"* PAUSE *"… you seem to have come to a decision… is that how it is?"*

"Yes…" I sighed. *"That is – how it is."* PAUSE *"But not 'til after the degree shows are over. I don't want to upset that for 'dette – but once they're over… I'm afraid—it—has to be over."*

---

1   The Thrill Is Gone—slow tempo Blues by Roy Hawkins and Rick Darnell—1951. BB King recorded the song in 1969.

As I was speaking first Meryl, then Penelope appeared in my room – each with a concerned expression. *"Welcome to the party…"* I sighed with a lame smile.

"I think it's for the best you know…" Penelope stated in a subdued voice. *"It really is."*

"I hardly know who 'dette is anymore" Meryl shrugged. *"She's become so crusty… and stiff. It really worries me – but your being trapped with her, that's worried us—all—a lot more."*

"I thought—at one time—that she could have gone back to being how she was before that vile sod John Willoughby dumped her for Little Miss Lift-and-Separate [2]" Rebecca almost sneered. *"All we can see, is that you've been incredibly nice to 'dette—really unbelievably nice—even though she's cantankerous and argumentative."*

"You'd think she was paying you back for John Willoughby, at times" Penelope added.

"Yes" Meryl agreed *"it's true… 'dette's moaned to us about your 'irritating philosophising'. Earlier on – we wondered if this was something you reserved for her, but then we asked her about it… and, all we could understand, was that it was the same kind of conversation the four of us have all the time."*

"Yeah… we told her as much, as gently as we could – and that…" Penelope said with a shake of her head *"was when she stopped coming round to see us as much. She just seemed to withdraw after that."* PAUSE *"I think she felt betrayed or something. It was as if we'd all colluded to make her 'the odd one out'. But… we really couldn't make any sense of what she thought the problem was – about having an interesting conversation. It seemed completely loony."*

"Yes, well, her father's a loony – and that's undebatable" Meryl pronounced.

2   The insinuation was that the girl in question was not generously endowed – but attempting to give the impression that she was. 'Lift and separate' was a catch phrase for the Gossard Wonderbra. The Canadian push-up Wonderbra was sold in Britain from 1964 under license by the Gossard division of Courtaulds Textiles.

"I think he turned into Mr Havisham [3] when he lost his wife – and then he seems to have done his best to turn 'dette into some version of Estella…"

"Oh… how very horrible…" Penelope groaned *"but how very true… it's uncanny. It—is—just like Dickens."*

"Maybe a little less ghoulish" I responded. *"I can't see him accidentally setting fire to himself in a bridal gown – even though he'd look better in a bridal gown that those grey lounge-lizard suits."*

That broke the tension and the three ladies burst out laughing. *"The main problem…"* I continued, after the mirth had abated *"is— as far as I can tell—that I'm working class. I went to a low-grade Secondary Modern School – and took care of my own cultural education in a weird and haphazard way. That… seems to be—in some way—intolerable."* PAUSE *"I'm some sort of suburban-cum-rural bumpkin with a folio of Shakespeare under one arm and a shoal of Blues and Rock quotations under the other."* PAUSE *"And, of course—according to 'dette—one cannot have a 'shoal' of quotations. One can only have a shoal of fish… as if I was not conversant with collective nouns and their usages. One cannot use collective nouns in any manner one chooses."*

"So" interjected Meryl with a upward roll of her eyes *"inventing one's own collective nouns is prohibited?"*

"It would appear so" I replied. *"A 'lummox of sweating boys' in the context of sport isn't plausible – and pointing out that Shakespeare coined several hundred neologisms.*[4]

3   Reference to 'Miss Havisham' in Charles Dickens' *Great Expectations*, published in 1861. She is a wealthy spinster living in a ruined mansion with her adopted daughter, Estella. Miss Havisham falls in love with a Mr Compeyson, a swindler. At 8.40 am on their wedding day, whilst dressing, Miss Havisham receives a letter from Mr Compeyson – she has been jilted. Wretched and humiliated Miss Havisham stops all the clocks in the house at 8.40 and remains in her decaying mansion in her wedding dress. She educates Estella to be the one who will take her revenge on men.

4   It has been estimated that Shakespeare may have coined in the region of 1,700 neologisms. A proportion of these words may have been in common use during the Elizabethan and Jacobean eras – simply not committed to writing prior to Shakespeare's use of them. One type of Shakespearean neologism was the conversion of nouns to verbs and adjectives.

"It simply led to my being informed that I was—not—Shakespeare."

"You don't have to be Shakespeare to coin neologisms: William Thackeray, Alexandre Dumas, and Charles Dickens coined neologisms. Most authors do. Lewis Carroll coined Chortle; John Milton coined Pandemonium…"

"Oh *clever!*" I laughed " *'place of all demons' fabulous!*"

"I thought you didn't take Latin at school…?"

"I didn't – but I know 'pan' form 'panchromatic' and 'ium' from 'Londinium', and demon is fairly obvious."

"I'm impressed nonetheless" laughed Penelope. "I suppose you can guess 'malapropism'…?"

"Yes – from Mrs Malaprop [5]—Sheridan—from 'mal à propos'…"

"Quite – but the reason I mention the word is that 'dette is sometimes guilty of them. She confused 'imply' and 'infer'; 'appraise' and 'apprise'; 'disinterested' and 'uninterested'; 'fortuitous' and 'fortunate'; 'meretricious' and 'meritorious'… I could go on. I imagine you've noticed that – and I would guess that you've never picked her up on it."

"Yes, on both counts… but only on the basilisk that I prolix gilded of the shame myself" I grinned. Penelope laughed and I continued "I've misunderstated too many words to juggle anemone Elsie. I'm sure I've heard many words that I think I understand because of their context – and discover my error later. I mean – of your list, I know I've confused 'appraised' and 'apprised' in the past."

Penelope suddenly looked rather serious and sighed "You were a constant trial to her."

"I believe I was—but that's 'past tense' now—or will be in a month."

Rebecca then shifted the topic "Are there any examples you know of Shakespeare's coinages?"

---

5   Mrs Malaprop is a character in *The Rivals*. She enjoys polysyllabic words but constantly misapplies them. Her name comes from the French 'mal à propos' which means inappropriately.

331

"*Yes…*" I paused. "*Let me think… admirable, bloodstained, bloodsucking, hint, consanguineous, blusterer, aerial, amazement, auspicious, barefaced, mortifying, baseless, fashionmonger, bedroom, characterless, oppugnancy, chimney-top, cold-blooded, cold-hearted, zany, courtship, dauntless, belongings, dewdrop, disgraceful, misgiving, distasteful, moonbeam, downstairs, dwindle, enrapt, fathomless, fretful, hobnail, howl, inducement, lacklustre, laughable, leapfrog, lustrous, foppish, madcap, malignancy, multitudinous, obscene, pageantry, pendulous, mimic, reclusive, refractory, besmirch, dexterously, castigate, grovel, unfrequented, unrivalled, vasty, yelping, expedience, flowery, rumination, and… fairyland…*" PAUSE "*That's it for how many I can remember… There's a list of them I once read. My English teacher—Mr Preece—showed it to me and I wrote many of them down – that's why I remember them. I could have given you a longer listing years ago.*"

"*It should have been obvious to 'dette that you weren't trying to tell her you were equal to Shakespeare*" demanded Rebecca. "*As Penelope said, there've been many authors who've coined words.*"

"*True. I pointed that out – but she reminded me that I wasn't an author.*"

"*But you write poetry*" Rebecca stated.

"*I do – but I'm not a published poet.*"

"*It's outrageous*" Meryl interjected "*in view of how—she was—in English at school, that she gets—that—picky. As I remember she only got passes in English Language and English Literature. I'm curious. What did you get?*"

"*An 'A' for each at 'O Level' and an 'A' at 'A Level'… but mind you, I only got two 'A Levels' – English and Art.*"

"*Did you ever tell her you'd got straight 'A' in English?*"

"*No*" I laughed. "*I'm not keen on defending myself. It seems silly…*" PAUSE "*but… in terms of her being picky—that's only escalated this year—and, especially of late…*" PAUSE "*but… sometimes it's deserved – and it's my mainly my fault…*"

"*Your fault!?*' the ladies chorused with mixed horror and hilarity.

"Yes—my fault—because I fail to compartmentalise. Mea culpa. Mea culpa. Mea maxima culpa. I somehow can't seem to understand that John Lennon and John Milton are not comparable – or that a whole herd of creative creatures can't co-exist as Art."

"Well!" snorted Meryl *"you know what we think of that!"*

"Yes… and that's really helped me come to my… sad conclusion."

"Is it sad?"

"Yes—it is sad—but not for me, not in that *way. I'm feeling sad, yes – but sad for 'dette…"* PAUSE *"Not that I think I'm any great loss or anything – but… I think she's going to be upset, for a while… and I don't like to… well, I sometimes wonder if I could have done anything differently."*

"Yes – you could have done something different Vic! You could have left her well over a year ago!"

I shrugged and remained silent for a moment or two. *"Yes… could've done… and maybe I should've done… but I didn't… and now – well…"* I quoted Bob Dylan *"I ain't saying she treated me unkind—she coulda done better but… I don't mind…"*

"She just kinda wasted your precious time" Rebecca finished the quotation.

"Well…" I grinned ever-so-slightly *"I won't think twice then."* PAUSE *"But I think we wasted each other's time. In that we're equal – but I feel that I am more to blame… because, with my Buddhist background… I have to take the responsibility."*

Penelope moved her head in a slow side-to-side motion that said 'no'. She was about to speak – but I held up my hand to continue and said *"I know you don't think that's fair—and that I shouldn't take the bulk of the blame—but it is extremely important to me that I do. It's a matter of honour, in terms of what I am supposed to represent. It's nobody's fault but mine."*

We talked a while longer and then the ladies betook themselves to leaving for their respective parental homes.

I sat gazing out of the little porthole window by the side of my bed. The river was acting quite normally and that, somehow, was a great comfort. Whatever else went on – there was the river winding its way toward the sea. The sea would receive the river and the river would simply vanish… but… there'd always be more river flowing. Life would go on 'til I arrived at some sort of sea somewhere. Then I'd die and be entirely forgotten. Everything that seemed so important would be a 'zero' that failed to register even as a cypher that betokened emptiness. Maybe Aro Yeshé would be recognised again by an incarnation of Kyabjé Düd'jom Rinpoche Jig'drèl Yeshé Dorje – and, maybe that future Aro Yeshé would make a better job of being who he was supposed to be. Maybe he'd avoid taking up with a series of improbable girlfriends – and do something sensible with his life. Maybe I was simply a necessary interim in the continuum. I knew that Pema Lingpa's[6] life was not without difficulties – so who was I to wallow in misgivings?

I was glad that the ladies had brought the situation with 'dette out into the open. It made everything so much less arduous. I wasn't locked into my decision as an isolated lump of lead. I had friends – and I had friends who knew 'dette, far better than I did.

'dette had reached some sort of peak of hostility on the way back from Stratford and—although I really didn't want to end our relationship before the degree shows—neither did I wish for an unrealistic rapprochement. If the ladies were to have remained in Hotwells I might not have taken off for quite a long as I did – but I thought I may as well absent myself for the entire holidays. Well… that's what I told 'dette – but I couldn't afford an entire three weeks at Samŷe Ling. I'd just stay in Hotwells and work during the time I was not at Samŷe Ling.

6   gTérchen Pema Lingpa (*gTer chen pad ma gLing pa*, 1450–1521) was a Bhutanese Mahasiddha of the Nyingma Tradition. He was a preëminent gTértön and the foremost of the Five gTértön Kings (*gTer sTon rGyal po lNga*). In the Nyingma history of Bhutan, Pema Lingpa is second in importance only to Guru Rinpoche.

No one would be any the wiser. I didn't like being devious – but my plan was set with the best intentions I could muster. It was unfair to bid farewell to 'dette on the eve of the degree shows. The last thing in the world I wanted was to damage her prospects in that way – but I did not want to spend any more time with her than I could help.

In many ways the plan worked extremely well. I had space on either side of Samŷe Ling – and I felt that this would enable me both to prepare for my time with Gyalwa Karmapa and… to spend time alone afterwards – in order to… absorb, digest, or whatever it was that would happen.

As it happened 'dette was not vastly put out by my absence *"I trust you will not get so transcendent that you'll transcend the ability to mount your degree show."*

"I've heard of mounting horses 'dette but I'd be hard put to, to swing my leg over an etching."

"You know what I mean perfectly well."

"Yes I do 'dette—yes… I do—and you know perfectly well… that making oblique references to Transcendental Meditation is not the best way to avoid my making-play with your language."

"Touché."

"So… anyway… sword-play apart, I'm glad it works out for you in terms of wanting to spend as much time as you have to complete your costumes. Good luck with that. I look forward to seeing them at the show. You've got some fabulous stuff there – the things I've seen so far that is."

"I'd be pleased to show you my 'stuff' – and to see your 'stuff' of course."

'dette was evidently vaguely affronted by my use of the word 'stuff'. *"We are such 'stuff' as dreams are made on, 'dette, and our little life is rounded with a sleep."*

'dette looked irked *"Shakespeare…"* she yawned.

"Indeed, Prospero—The Tempest—somewhere in Act 4 I believe."

"Touché une deuxième fois. However, I would have thought you'd have wanted to spend Easter working. You've worked every hour since the 1ˢᵗ year – so it's frankly bizarre that you now want to take off to see yaks in Bonny Scotland."

"Well… y'know 'dette… the yaks miss me… and… anyway… Derek says I have enough work for three degree shows as it is – so all I need to do is complete my prose-poetry piece for Related Studies. I can work on that at Samŷe Ling as there's always plenty of time between sessions on these events."

"Oh yes… your – Iliad. How's that going?"

"More-or-less finished… I just need to run through it a few more times to make sure it flows well."

"I'm surprised you can tell whether it flows or not. I can't understand a word of it."

"Well… there you go" I yawned. *"It's not the kind of writing that appeals to everyone."*

"Or anyone."

"As you say – or anyone." PAUSE *"You could always try Finnegan's Wake [7] as light relief?"* PAUSE *"Sorry… that was sarcasm."*

"I missed it. I've not read Finnegan's Wake."

I stood up and walked over to the bookshelf. I pulled down a copy of *Finnegan's Wake*. *"Try this…"* I said as the book fell open at chapter four:

---

7   *Finnegan's Wake* by James Joyce—renowned for its experimental style—is
    known as the most difficult English language novel. See glossary: *Finnegan's
    Wake.*

As the lion in our teargarten remembers the nenuphars of his Nile (shall Ariuz forget Arioun or Boghas the baregams of the Marmarazalles from Marmeniere?) it may be, tots wearsense full a naggin in twentyg have sigilposted what in our brievingbust, the besieged bedreamt him stil and solely of those lililiths un-deviled which had undone him, gone for age, and knew not the watchful treachers at his wake, and theirs to stay. Fooi, fooi, chamermissies! Zeepyzoepy, larcenlads! Zijnzijn Zijnzijn! It maybe, we moest ons hasten selves te declareer it, that he reglimmed? presaw? the fields of heat and yields of wheat where corngold Ysit? shamed and shone. It may be, we habben to upseek a bitty door our good township's courants want we knew't, that with his deepseeing insight (had not wishing oftebeen but good time wasted), within his patriarchal shamanah, broadsteyne 'bove citie (Twillby! Twillby!) he conscious of enemies, a kingbilly white-horsed in a Finglas mill, prayed, as he sat on anxious seat, (kunt ye neat gift mey toe bout a peer saft eyballds!) during that three and a hellof hours' agony of silence, ex profundis malorum, and bred with unfeigned charity that his wordwounder (an engles to the teeth who, nomened Nash of Girahash, would go anyold where in the weeping world on his mottled belly (the rab, the kreepons-kneed!) for milk, music or married missusses) might, mercy to providential benevolence's who hates prudencies' astuteness, un-fold into the first of a distinguished dynasty of his posteriors…' "

"*Enough… enough!*" 'dette laughed. "*That's diabolical!*"

"*That's English literature.*"

"*Irish literature to be precise – or Irish illiterate-ture.*"

"*Well it's all in a point of view I suppose – and pardon my insulting James Joyce with my ascription of his book as 'English' literature. It's a hang-over from 'A' level English Literature. We studied 'Portrait of the Artist as a Young Man' by James Joyce – and I would seem to have inadvertently retained that erroneous mis-categorisation of the author's nationality.*"

"Point taken – and also… I must say that Joyce makes your prose-poetry look eminently readable."

"Thank you 'dette – that's what I was hoping."

"Anyway… so you're off to see Fu Manchu put his hat on again."

"No 'dette I'm going to Clacton-on-Sea to have an illicit affair with an elderly octopus."

"Why do you always have to talk nonsense—I was just making a joke— have you lost your sense of humour?"

"Yes 'dette… I think… I—have—lost my sense of humour. I'm a dull, dreary, desultory, dolt… with arcane interests in literature as well as religion."

Having said this I gazed out of the window in silence and after a few minutes 'dette decided that it was time to leave. My statement was obviously loaded with the wish for her to leave – even though I'd not devised it deliberately. 'dette was capable of great subtlety of interpersonal perception and knew immediately whenever I reached a point of no return. It was as if she knew that one further acerbic aside would precipitate an irrevocable decision with regard to her. For all my peculiar perceptual opacity—vis-à-vis the thoughts of others—I could always read 'dette quite easily at these times. She'd have the look of someone who'd strayed onto a minefield and was taking tentative steps backwards. I always spared her the feared detonation— always—even though, from me, the explosion would have been innocuous in tone. I bade her goodnight. She wished me a wonderful time – almost as if she'd not endeavoured to goad me with indecorous facetiousness bare minutes before. I had no idea why 'dette felt compelled to do that. It was not as if I frequently bent her ear with Buddhism. In fact, I never mentioned the subject – or, not at least since the first year. The subject was taboo unless I wanted facile rejoinders or acerbic *faux Dorothy Parker* ripostes.

I breathed a sigh of relief after 'dette departed – and sat there somehow discombobulated by decisions. Why—I mean—*why?* Why was it that I'd decided to wait until after the degree show to end our relationship? Oh yes… I knew why… It was so that it wouldn't affect her at that vital juncture. I had to keep remembering the importance of that decision. I was only doing what I knew I was capable of doing. It wouldn't kill me. It wouldn't even affect me emotionally *that* much – unless I made an unseemly internal fuss about it.

I decided that as it was not the trenches of the Somme in WWI – I had nothing about which I could possibly complain. Three marvellous weeks lay ahead. They'd be three weeks where I could BE *whomsoever I turned out to be.* I'd be single—to all intents and purposes—although the idea of being romantically available was not on the cards. It wasn't even appealing. It was, in fact, so completely unappealing that I could almost have opted for monastic ordination. I remembered the words of Düd'jom Rinpoche *'With each life-circumstance: whatever is enacted, stare directly into the enactment – with all the senses.'*

I intended to remain single for the foreseeable future. I'd say goodbye to 'dette – and then I'd be extremely careful before I got romantically embroiled again. There was something about being single that seemed wonderfully alluring. I could go where I wanted. I could do whatever I pleased. I'd never have to see another Chekhov play. How many plays about a cherry orchard can one Russian write anyway? He did have the honesty to call one of them 'The Cherry Orchard' but then I had to see 'Uncle Vanya' and there was the cherry orchard again. Not that I have anything against cherry orchards – but I'd never given 'dette a hard time about plays that dip below my personal-enjoyment standards.

Maybe that's not entirely true – Eugene O'Neil's *Long Day's Journey into Night* [8] took the biscuit for *arduous evenings I have known*. That was not because it was poorly written – but three hours or so of watching human beings emotionally butcher each other, was not my idea of an edifying experience. I discovered later that Eugene O'Neil had never written with the idea of its ever being published. It was simply a *piece of personal process* that he never intended to see the light of day.

Just as I was thinking these thoughts, I stopped in my tracks. What was I doing ranting on in my mind about Chekhov and Eugene O'Neil? *This* would have to stop. I decided that freedom had to mean: freedom from time-wasting; freedom from internal dialogue; freedom from recriminations; freedom from resentment… What had I to resent anyhow? My situation had been all of my own making. My situation now—and in the future —would also be all of my own making. The only realistic mental state was openness to the future – and to whatever the future held. I was on the brink of a new adventure – and one that might change my life forever. I wrote a note to myself and placed it on my pillow so that I would see it on my return. It read *'Dear Vic, Goodbye forever – Yours Sincerely, Chögyam.'*

I spent the next five days working on various projects. I cooked meals. I went to bed early. I started getting up early so I'd be on the same time frame as Samŷe Ling by the time I arrived. The plan worked well. I noticed how much more I accomplished by getting up at 5:00 and being in bed by or before 10:00. Time flew and yet there was more time in the day than I'd known since being in the Himalayas in 1971.

---

8   *Long Day's Journey into Night* is a semi-autobiographical play in four acts written in 1941 – but published posthumously in 1956. Eugene O'Neill received the 1957 Pulitzer Prize for Drama for the play. He did not want it published. Soon after his death however, his widow Carlotta Monterey demanded that Random House contravene her husband's written wishes and publish his play. The publisher Bennett Cerf refused – but was '… *horrified to learn that legally all the cards were in her hands.'* He had no choice but to publish – even though he felt it wrong to do so.

21

yong-lé min'gyür dorje

Setting out for Samŷe Ling was not the adventure it had been the first time I took the road north to Scotland. I knew exactly where I was going. I knew what the place looked like – but the atmosphere would be different. It's people who make a place what it is.

I wondered if Jan would be there – or Dot… or Georgina? I doubted whether Kate would be there, after my hasty departure from Liverpool and my *'I regret to say this'* reply to her letter. She had no interest in 'organised religion'– so a return to Samŷe Ling would hold no attraction for her unless she'd freed herself from Amy and Atlas.

'On this occasion' I thought *'I'll not take 'challenges' vis-à-vis wearing lady's knickers or do anything at all that strays over the line…'* but what was that line? A conservative, conventional, orthodox, unadventurous, precautious, prudent, judicious safety-first line would be easy enough to draw – but was *that* what Düd'jom Rinpoche would have wanted? I'd crossed no moral ethical line as far as I was aware – but maybe I'd crossed a line in terms of… formality? dignity? decorum? Or maybe it was 'appropriateness' – but that was a vague term as I had no idea what was appropriate or not in my case. I knew of no other Inji ngakpas, Inji Lamas, or Inji trülkus – and so there was no yardstick. There was the idea of being *in the world but not of the world* – but how far *in the world* could one be without becoming *of the world*?

I knew that this would not be a question, had I not taken ngakpa vows. Everything I did now reflected on the robes I'd been given. It had all been so simple in the Himalayas. It had seemed impossible to put a foot out of line – but here in the West it was an entirely different story. The line had become a tightrope walk. I was grateful that there was always a net to catch me when I tripped over my own feet.

And so—with this somewhat turgid conjecture—I set out. The journey was as the previous one had been – but colder. I realised I'd passed Carlisle by some 20 miles without having thought about it – and somehow this gave me confidence that I could simply go to Samŷe Ling without finding myself involved in anything ridiculous. I'd give anyone a lift who wanted one – but I wouldn't be staying-over to meet—*anyone's*—interesting friends.

I arrived at Samŷe Ling sooner than I'd expected—unloaded my bags—and walked in. My name was on the list so there was no problem – apart from them having expected me to be Tibetan. *"Why are you using a Tibetan name."* I was asked by a thin woman with a florid complexion and almost absent nose.

"Because… I was ordained as a ngakpa and I use my ordained name when I'm in Buddhist places."

"But you have long hair and you're not wearing robes" she replied with the air of one who knows everything.

"Robes aren't easy to wear on a motorcycle…" I replied *"and, one of my vows is never to cut my hair. I was ordained as a ngakpa, you see—not a monk—I belong to the non-celibate wing of the Nyingma Tradition.*

"Oh… I see… well… I don't know what to do about your room now because all the ordained people are in the main house and the non-ordained are in the other one…"

"I don't mind where you put me."

"Well… as you're not celibate, it's probably best you go to the other house."

"Fine" I smiled. A stupid joke was instantly at the forefront of my mind *'It's just as well that I should be in the other house as a non-celibate like me would probably roger all the nuns.'* This was not a joke it took any effort to repress – but I wondered why it had even formed in my mind. *"Just tell me where – and I'll take my things over."* Would there ever come a time when such internal witticisms ceased to occur? They were harmless unless given voice – but it worried me that it might be some sort of *internal ploy* to make myself feel superior.

Meryl, Penelope, and Rebecca would have told me *'You're being unrealistically hard on yourself.'* It's what they always said. Maybe they were right. There was no point in doing anything other than noticing such quirks and letting them go. I let it go.

Thus it was that I was given my place in a large room with a number of beds over in another house just down-a-ways from the main house. I unpacked my things, changed into my robes, and sauntered back to the main house to sit in the library and await dinner. I was looking at a book by Helmut Hoffman in which I'd found two utterly remarkable photographs of a Lama who I later discovered to be Lingtsang Gyalpo Rinpoche.[1] How I loved looking at such photographs of ngakpas. As I was thus absorbed, a nun entered the library and looked somewhat perturbed to see me there. *"Who are you?"* she asked in a tone that betrayed a singular lack of human warmth. *"Are you a Hindu?"*

"I'm Ngakpa Chögyam…" I replied with a smile *"but I'm not a Hindu. What led you to believe I might be a Hindu…?"*

"You're wearing white. Hindus wear white."

"I don't doubt it – but I don't know anything about Hinduism… I'm a Nyingma ngakpa."

"A what?" she asked rather crisply.

"A ngakpa…" I turned the book round to show her the picture. *"One of these."*

"That's a picture of a Lama" she said – as if that meant I was wrong in what I'd said.

"Undoubtedly…" I replied *"but he is also a ngakpa. The word ngakpa applies to the style of ordination. You see… he is wearing a white shamthab and his robes—apart from the brocade—are more-or-less like the one you see me wearing."*

---

1   Lingtsang Gyalpo (*gLing tshang rGyal po dBang chen bsTan 'dzin*)—King of
     Lingtsang (1857–1942)— was a Nyingma gTértön and Phurba master
     recognised as an incarnation of Ling Gésar. See glossary: *Lingtsang Gyalpo*.

I remembered the words of Düd'jom Rinpoche *'With each life-circumstance: whatever is enacted, stare directly into the enactment – with all the senses.'*

The nun then did something quite peculiar. She turned round and left the room without another word. I returned to the Helmut Hoffman book and tried to find a textual reference for the Lama. Five minutes later the nun appeared again and said *"Akong Rinpoche says he's met you at Samŷe Ling before—and saw you at the Vajra Crown ceremony—so it's alright. Akong Rinpoche says you should be in this house with the ordained rather than over there in the other house – so if you can just go and move your things before dinner it will cause less of an accommodation problem. I don't know what made you go there when you should have been here."*

"Happy to oblige…" I replied *"… I went there because that's where I was told to go."*

"Didn't you explain that you're supposed to be like an ordained person?"

"Yes… I did explain that I was supposed to be something like that" I smiled *"but it was a question of my not being celibate that seemed to cause the difficulty."*

"Anyway—no need to go into such detail—could you just move your things as soon as possible."

"Without further delay" I smiled. *"I wouldn't like to be late for dinner."*

Then the nun turned on her heel again and vanished. What—*I mean, what*—was wrong with the woman? I wondered how many other 'friendly' persons were ensconced at Samŷe Ling – all eager to see Gyalwa Karmapa, the emanation of compassion. Still… it was no concern of mine. It would have to be my practice – simply to remain well-mannered and cheerful under all provocation. That was no great hardship. If I could endure Todd Whelcombe and Veranda Nugent in the Illustration studio—and 'dette on the return journey from Stratford—I could endure almost anything in the way of acerbity, acidity, or acrimony.

I moved my belongings to the room indicated by a pleasant fellow with a rather nice maroon Tibetan shirt and woollen waistcoat. I remarked on his rather fine colourful felt Tibetan boots. *"I use them as slippers when I'm here"* he replied *"… 'cause they'd wear out quickly, if I wore them outside."*

"They're really rather fine" I replied *"It would be a pity to get them dirty too – as it would spoil the colours."* They were red and green and had blue velvet shanks and they had a squared toe that I found intriguing. I'd seen boots like that when I was in India – but I'd had no money to buy a pair. *"I've seen leather Tibetan boots too – but they were all made of black leather."*

"You don't like black?"

"Not in leather… not so much, no. I find that it doesn't age as well as brown leather. When black leather scuffs it goes grey and then you have to use black polish on it. With brown leather boots and shoes, you just use neutral renovating cream and although they'll get blotchy – they always seem to look good; well… to me anyway."

"Never thought about it that way – but you're right. Thanks for the tip." PAUSE *"Nice to talk with you, maybe talk with you some more over dinner."*

"Yes – that'd be splendid." I was delighted to have met a human being at last *"I'll be down in a few minutes."*

I entered the room and placed my rocket bag and panniers down on the floor next to an unoccupied bed. There was a Western monk meditating in the corner and so I kept my actions as quiet as I could. As I was unpacking another monk entered and oblivious to the presence of someone practising, he asked in a rather loud voice *"You're not supposed to be in here – you're not a monk."*

I remembered the words of Düd'jom Rinpoche *'With each life-circumstance: whatever is enacted, stare directly into the enactment – with all the senses.'*

"True…" I replied somewhat wearily. *"I'm not a monk. I'm a ngakpa —but whichever—Akong Rinpoche instructed me to stay here – I originally moved into the other house but Akong Rinpoche said I should be here."* The monk stood gawping at me for a moment and then left the room. Why did ordained monastics not seem to be able to conclude conversations in a normal manner, I wondered? I passed the monk on the stairs—and like the nun—he told me that Akong Rinpoche had confirmed that my presence was to be tolerated. Was I to be checked at five-minute intervals throughout my stay? This was becoming a trifle bizarre – but I decided to find it amusing rather than annoying.

I entered the dining room and was served with a large bowl of rather excellent vegetable soup and looked around for the friendly young man – and there he was suddenly. His name was Geraint Williams. *"I'm Welsh"* he said with a grin. *"Some of the monks and nuns find my accent funny – but never wonder what I think of theirs."*

That made me laugh. *"Good to have a sense of humour about it – but hasn't everyone got an accent of one sort of another?"*

"Yes… I suppose they must have – never thought of it that way. Some people seem to think the Welsh are educationally sub-normal."

"Mmm… I would have thought that Buddhists—who'd actually studied and practised Buddhism—would have moved beyond relating to people as cultural stereotypes…" PAUSE *"Y'know… when I was at school I got beaten up a fair few times because my mother's German. Some of the them seemed to think my mother and I were personally responsible for WWII or some such thing."* PAUSE *"Everyone and his uncle seemed to have lost some relative in the war – and it was—my—fault"* I laughed.

"Good that you can laugh about that too" he said.

"Well… it's easy to laugh about being beaten up a decade or more later. It doesn't upset me personally in any way – but it does make me sad thinking about the mind-state of people who act like that… it's the irony of it. I have a German mother and am therefore a Nazi – so people feel the need to act like Nazis toward me.

"Now if anything can be described as educationally subnormal that must be a fairly good example – and that was in the heart of the Home Counties."

"Yes… see what you mean." PAUSE *"Y'know… one of the monks told me that wearing Tibetan clothes was spiritual materialism… d'you think that's true?"*

"Did you ask for his opinion?"

"No."

"Then he had no reason to give it." PAUSE *"Who's your teacher?"*

"Akong Rinpoche."

"Well… Akong Rinpoche is the only one who has the authority to give you his personal opinions… I'd ask him about it and settle with what he says… if you really—need—to be assured… but… as there's no law about what you should wear as a Buddhist, I don't see that it's anyone's concern but yours."

"Almost everyone's got some opinion here though…" Geraint replied with a certain tone of slight resentment.

"I wasn't here an hour before I met three considerable opinions" I laughed. *"Anyhow… as to spiritual materialism… that seems to be somewhat misunderstood. Spiritual materialism is the act of creating territory out of spirituality – of concretising spiritual ideas into personal territory. From that point of view the monk who told you that your clothes were 'spiritual materialism' – was a spiritual materialist in his motivation for telling you so."*

"Really?"

"That would be my opinion. Unless you're wearing those clothes in order to impress people that you are more spiritual than they are—merely because you're wearing them—they're simply clothes you like to wear." PAUSE *"I'd go so far as to say that I've met a few monks and nuns to whom robes are merely a status symbol. For example… my robes don't make me any better than you. Only my mind, speech, and behaviour can make me better or worse than another person. If I dress like a ngakpa and behave like a boor – then I'm a boor in ngakpa dress.*

347

"Dressing like a deep-sea diver wouldn't make me a deep-sea diver. Only children engage in make-believe. They dress like doctors and nurses, cowboys and cowgirls. They play at being as they appear. It's all great fun for children and there's little harm in it – but when adults dress up as ordainees and their minds, speech, and behaviour don't reflect their ordination… then… what makes them any different from children involved in make-believe except that they take themselves entirely seriously. At least children know when the game is over."

"Are you a teacher?"

"No." That was the simplest answer to give. The fact that I *was* to be a Lama in the future was a needless complication and would create a situation I would not want.

"Then… how did you get to know all this – you seem to know a lot."

"Well… I've been studying Buddhism for quite a long time. I could say, since I was 8 years old – but that would give a false impression. I first came across books on Tibetan Art at that age and then, of course, it took me a fair few years before I could actually read anything seriously. Then it took longer before I began to sit… but I've been silent sitting since I was… 14."

"That's young to start…"

"I suppose so – but I used to sit before I sat, as it were. I used to sit and look at colours when I was young – especially in an old yew tree in the woods and so… I suppose it came almost naturally to me."

"So… you don't teach anywhere?"

"No… what would I teach?"

"The meaning of spiritual materialism?"

"I just did…" PAUSE *"but only because someone used the term incorrectly and lambasted you with it. I wouldn't have mentioned it otherwise. You did ask me what I thought—so, I told you—but that's not teaching – that's just having a conversation."*

"Can I ask you some more questions?"

"Yes — but not if you're going to start looking at me as if I'm a teacher…" I smiled. *"I can't pretend to answer anything authoritatively anyway. I can only comment on what I know — or rather, I'll only tell you what makes sense to me in terms of my experience."*

"That was really interesting what you said about spiritual materialism—I couldn't help overhearing your conversation with Geraint—sorry to eavesdrop" remarked a lady who introduced herself as Lydia Evesham.

"No apology necessary… I'm happy to be able to say anything useful to anyone — and I like to meet people. I'm new here —so it's good to find anyone friendly." PAUSE *"I say I'm new here; I have been to Samye Ling twice before — but I can't see anyone here I ever saw before."*

"Right… a lot of people have come because Gyalwa Karmapa is here."

"That's why I'm here. Akong Rinpoche suggested—when I was here last— that I should see Gyalwa Karmapa and attend the vajra crown ceremony. So… I went to attend the vajra crown ceremony in London and that's when I found out he would be here."

"He'll be giving the vajra crown ceremony here too" said Geraint. *"That'll be the first thing that happens — over a series of evenings. The next evening he'll give the initiations of Amitabha, Avalokiteshvara, and Padmasambhava. Then there'll be Pakshi Tröllö."*

"Pakshi Tröllö?" I asked.

*"The wrathful manifestation of Guru Rinpoche—Dorje Tröllö—manifesting as the 2nd Karmapa, Karma Pakshi [2] "*Lydia explained.

"Now that is extremely interesting!" I exclaimed. *"I would like to know more about that…"*

---

2   The 2nd Karmapa (1203–1283) was a child prodigy fully conversant with all aspects of Buddhism by the age of 10. He assimilated the teachings effortlessly and required only one reading of a text to be familiar with it. He spent much of the first half of his life in meditation retreat. At the age of 47 he was invited to China by Kublai Khan—the grandson of Genghis Khan— and whilst there performed many miracles as a peacemaker. Various attempts to kill Karma Pakshi were thwarted by miracles.

"It's restricted though…" Geraint observed *"Like the Dorje Bernakchen[3] initiation on the following night – so neither Lydia or I will be attending those."*

"What's the restriction?" I enquired.

"Oh…" Lydia observed *"that you have to have completed ngöndro."*

"Ah… right… that would follow" I replied.

"What about you?" Geraint asked

"Me… well… I have completed ngöndro – but… there may well be other considerations. I think I will have to enquire what's appropriate in my case." PAUSE *"So, what can you tell me about Pakshi Tröllö?"*

"Well…" Lydia commenced *"we've had some teachings on this recently and so I can tell you a little. It's a practice that was revealed by Min-jour Dor-jay."*

"gTértön Yong-lé Min'gyür Dorje?[4]" I enquired.

"Yes—Min'gyür Dorje—I'd forgotten the full name and my pronunciation is terrible."

"No. It can be pronounced like that too. I have an Eastern Tibetan dialect from my Lamas – and they pronounce Tibetan closer to the written form. Anyhow please tell me what you know."

"He was a Nyingma gTértön you see – but although it's a Nyingma gTérma, Pakshi Tröllö is only practised by the Karma Kagyüds."

"How did that happen?"

"That's the interesting thing" Lydia replied. *"Min'gyür Dorje offered it to the 10th Karmapa – and then the 10th Karmapa became the lineage holder."*

---

3   *rDo rJe ber nag can* རྡོ་རྗེ་བེར་ནག་ཅན་ – *The Indestructible Great Black Cloaked One.*

4   gTértön Min'gyür Dorje (1645–1667)—revealer of the Namchö gTérmas cycle —was an emanation of Shu-bu Palgyi Seng-gé *(shud bu dPal gyi seng ge – Glorious Lion)* and the immediate incarnation of Trülshik Wangdrak Gyamtso. Shu-bu Palgyi Seng-gé was of one the ministers of Trisong Détsen.

"I like that. It shows how the lineages are wide open in terms of the authentic masters and how they relate to each other across the boundaries of schools."

"Min'gyür Dorje also discovered the Kagyüd Mahakala—Dorje Bernakchen —and gave that to the 10th Karmapa as well…" Geraint offered. *"So… that's probably why Gyalwa Karmapa is giving these two initiations. The collection revealed by Min'gyür Dorje also contains a cycle of teachings and practices of Dorje Tröllö, the wrathful manifestation – one of the eight manifestations of Guru Rinpoche."*

"I hope there will be some teachings on this during the week – I have really missed being able to hear teachings since I have been back in Britain." PAUSE *"Do you happen to know anything else?"*

Geraint shook his head – but Lydia knew a few more facts *"Well… Min'gyür Dorje lived during the times of the 10th and 11th Karmapas and contributed a lot to the Karma Kagyüd School. The gTérmas of Min'gyür Dorje are very important because they strengthened the Karma Kagyüd School in Kham. Through those practises practitioners in Kham were able to turn back enemies and bring about peace. That's why the practice didn't become lost."*

The nun loomed up suddenly. *"These teachings weren't given so that people could chat about them over dinner!"* she snapped.

"Probably not…" I replied *"but neither do I imagine they were given to encourage harsh speech."*

The nun stared at me in disbelief for a moment—turned on her heel—and walked away.

"Oh dear…" Lydia whispered *"I'm afraid you've made an enemy there."*

"Yes…" I sighed *"I think you might be right – but she can't kill me… and… she might get over it."* PAUSE *"I suppose I could have said something different… but I thought she was fairly unpleasant to you – and there was really no need for that. She can't wander about being nasty to people just because she's wearing nuns' robes."*

"*Exactly…*" said Geraint. "*I sometimes wish I could think of the right things to say quickly enough – but I get tongue tied when people say things like that… and… I tend to feel I'm probably in the wrong.*"

"*Well yes… you may be in the wrong – but right or wrong gives a person no excuse to be rude or aggressive.*" PAUSE "*Was any statement made about not talking about this material?*"

"*No*" they both replied together.

"*Then it's not restricted – and you were both free to tell me whatever you told me.*"

"*How come…*" Geraint laughed "*you always make the answer sound so easy? I mean… it seems as if I should have been able to have worked that out for myself.*"

"*Well… you probably could've done if you'd thought about it. It's always hard to think on your feet – and reply immediately to assaults like that. I've had a good teacher you see…*"

"*Who gave you a teaching like that?*" asked Lydia with a smile. "*That seems an amazing kind of teaching.*"

"*A—great—teacher… his name's Todd Whelcombe… and, he's on my year at Bristol Art School.*"

"*You're joking*" Lydia laughed.

"*Partially…*" I grinned. "*He's not a teacher – but he's certainly taught me how to respond to aggression without becoming aggressive. He's given me daily lessons. I'm afraid they've not always been delightful – but I realise that I owe him a great deal.*" PAUSE "*He doesn't know he's given me these lessons of course… it's just been my choice to see them that way.*"

Another nun appeared at this point "*I heard some of that…*" she said with a concerned voice – at which I inwardly groaned "*… and I just want to tell you that we're not—all—like that – some of us are… concerned with having a good atmosphere.*"

"*Thank you*" I smiled. "*I'm Chögyam – Ngakpa Chögyam.*"

"I'm Ani Chö-ying."

"What a splendid coincidence. Chö-ying is actually my first name – but it's contracted and joined with the 'gyam' [5] *from Gyamtso."*

"Like Chögyam Trungpa Rinpoche's name."

"Almost—his is Chö-kyi Gyamtso—but when you contract both names, they turn into Chögyam… and thank you again for coming over and being friendly – it was really kind of you."

"Well… we're supposed to try to be kind aren't we…?"

"Yes, we are" I grinned *"but thank you all the same – maybe we can find time to talk whilst I'm here."*

"That would be nice – because I'd like to ask you about your robes and… your hair. I had an audience—with a group of other monks and nuns—with Dilgo Khyentsé Rinpoche – and he had a white skirt and long hair… so I'm wondering if you are connected with him?"

"I have met Kyabjé Dilgo Khyentsé Rinpoche, yes… and received some advice from him on practise – but Kyabjé Düd'jom Rinpoche is my main teacher. He's also a ngakpa."

"I'll ask you about that when we get the chance to speak – it's almost time to go to the wang [6] *now – so I will look out for you tomorrow."*

Ani Chö-ying left the dining hall and Lydia, Geraint, and I talked for a short time about how good it was to find a friendly ordainee who was not sanctimonious or pietistic.

We entered the shrine room—made our prostrations—and I took my seat, as requested, amongst the ordained.

5   The syllable is not actually 'gyam'. I only discovered years later that Chögyam is the result of a quirk of Tibetan pronunciation. It should be chögya (*chos rGya*) as the name is a contraction of Chöying Gyamtso (*chos dByings rGya mTsho*). The 'm' in Chögyam belongs to the second syllable rather than the first – and is only added to rGya because it sounds better in Tibetan. Some Tibetans do not recognise Chögyam as a name unless one reminds them of Chögyam Trungpa Rinpoche.
6   *Wang (dBang / abhisheka)* empowerment.

353

Gyalwa Karmapa was—as always—not quite conceivable. Nothing happened at first, we simply sat and waited. The hostile nun glowered at me – but I decided to let her slip into peripheral vision. I wished her happiness in my mind and gazed at the coloured stripes on the wall. The colours were always radiant and soon my attention was lost in them. Settling into a thought-free state was easier than it had been years ago and it didn't take long to find the first flickering of *absence of thought with presence of awareness.* It was even quicker in that shrine room with Gyalwa Karmapa than it otherwise was. He was somehow slightly outside the normal three dimensions to which I was accustomed – and I found that it was not possible to be aware of him and of myself at the same time. If my attention was absorbed in him – my sense of myself simply vanished and I became some kind of 'merely-looking' without any sense of what was looking.

Then the Vajrayana orchestra commenced and the stages of the wang followed each other – then, seemingly seconds after it had commenced, it was over and I was on my way to bed. I was aware somehow, that something highly unusual had occurred – but it was impossible to say what it was. It had been powerful and vivid – mainly an experience of sound and colour and of something being conjured. I could describe every aspect of the wang and no one would be any the wiser by the end of the detailed description. I thus give no detailed description here – such descriptions can, in any case, be obtained elsewhere.[7] I could give a physiological description of what it's like to fall in love but it would bear no relation to the actual experience. That's why people write poetry – but here, even poetry would not suffice to describe any of the wangs or ceremonies given by the 16th Gyalwa Karmapa.

7   The stages of a wang *(dBang / abhisheka / empowerment)* can be found in *Wearing the Body of Visions* by Ngakpa Chögyam—Aro Books Inc.— 1995.

22

Begin the Beguine

Ani Chö-ying looked pleased to see me the next day. How I knew, I cannot say – it was something I sensed. There was no reason she should be displeased or indifferent – because we'd had the most pleasant and valuable conversations. So, what was I noticing? The question didn't linger long.

I felt cheered by her good nature. We talked about the differences and similarities between the Kagyüd and Nyingma Traditions. I was able to tell her something of the Drukpa Kagyüds and the Drigung Kagyüds – because they were in some respects closer to the Nyingma style than the Karma Kagyüd School. There tended to have more gö kar chang lo practitioners – more ngakpas and ngakmas. It was a great relief to find an ordained person who not only seemed normal – but embodied the good qualities one would expect to find in an ordainee.

"So, what I wanted to ask" Ani Chö-ying began *"was about your robes. They're lay tantrika robes aren't they?"*

"Yes and no… they're tantrika robes – but not 'lay'."

"Sorry, I mean 'lay' as in non-celibate."

I made an almost dulcet humming sound *"I am sorry to be pedantic – but 'lay' and 'non-celibate' are not the same. The word 'lay' does not mean 'non-celibate'."* PAUSE *"I know that Tibetans have latched onto the word 'lay' to mean 'non-celibate' – but that is entirely incorrect."*

"Really?" Ani Chö-ying asked – but with real interest.

"Yes… according to every English dictionary I've consulted.

"This includes the American Webster's – and also the Duden,[1] *and the Dictionnaire de l'Académie Française* [2]*… it means 'unprofessional' or 'not of the clergy'.*[3]*"* PAUSE *"I can see how 'layman' might apply to me – but how can it possibly apply to Kyabjé Düd'jom Rinpoche or Dilgo Khyentsé Rinpoche?"* PAUSE *"Düd'jom Rinpoche is the Head of the Nyingma Tradition and he is non-celibate. The head of an ancient Religious Tradition cannot be described as a layman. The term 'lay'– as an English, German or French word, cannot be used. The word in Tibetan that equates to 'lay' is kya-wo,*[4] *which means 'clothed in grey' or 'clothed in 'pale-homespun'. The gos dKar lCang lo'i sDe don't wear such colours* [5] *– so even in Tibetan, the word doesn't apply. 'Kya' can mean any sort of woollen colour. It could even be pale brown."*

"Quite… Maybe they got 'lay' from Roman Catholicism?"

"That's quite likely…" I mused *"because Tibetans do use Catholic ecclesiastic titles like 'His Holiness', 'His Eminence', 'His Serenity', and 'Venerable'. These titles don't equate with Tibetan titles. The main word in Tibetan is 'Kyabjé' – which means 'Lord of Refuge' or Kyab-gön* [6] *which means 'Protector of Refuge'.*

1 The Duden is a German dictionary first published by Konrad Duden in 1880. In 2017—in its 27th edition—it is printed as 12 volumes, each volume covering aspects of the German language such as loanwords, etymology, pronunciation, and synonyms.
2 The Dictionnaire de l'Académie française is the official dictionary of the French language. The Académie française is France's official authority on the usages, vocabulary, and grammar of the French language.
3 The definition of 'lay' as 'unprofessional or not of the clergy' is the same in Norwegian, Swedish, Danish, Finnish, Icelandic, Latvian, Estonian, Lithuanian, Dutch, Belgian, Spanish, Basque, Portuguese, Italian, Greek, Russian, Armenian, Georgian Moldovan, Polish, Slovakian, Croatian, Hungarian, Rumanian, Bulgarian, Maltese, Turkish, Welsh, and Gaelic.
4 *sKya bo* – layman.
5 From the early 21st Century the colour grey was adopted by Kyabjé Garab Dorje Rinpoche for non-ordained trainees practising Düd'jom gTér Tröma Nakmo. This was an initiative especially in Bhutan—but also many other countries—to encourage practice amongst the laity. Bhutanese and Tibetan refugee laity do not tend now to wear grey — so the word sKya bo no longer applies.
6 *sKyab rJe* and *sKyab mGon*

" 'Gyalwa'—as in Gyalwa Karmapa— means 'Victorious One'[7] which equates with Buddha." PAUSE *"To get back to lay – I should add that, to use 'lay' to mean 'non-celibate' is derogatory in respect of religions which don't have celibacy – such as… Judaism… and the Protestant Churches. There's also Zen… because not every Roshi is celibate.[8] Chögyam Trungpa Rinpoche's friend Shunryu Suzuki was married."*

"That's fascinating… I'd never thought of that… So… what—is—a ngakpa then… in terms of vows I mean?"

"Well… it's a little… involved – but basically with the gö kar chang lo'i dé —the long-haired white-skirted class—ordination is based within Vajrayana. The monastic ordination is based within Sutra."

"Right—the vinaya—but we also practise Vajrayana…"

"Yes – and we also practise Sutrayana. It's just that the ordination vows are based in different yanas – there's no exclusion in terms of practise… and, both practise Dzogchen."

"Is there a Dzogchen ordination then?"

"No… because Dzogchen is non-symbolic—non-ritual—so most Lamas who are primarily Dzogchen masters either wear gö kar chang lo dress – or whatever they choose. They sometimes wear lay clothes in Dharma colours or they wear white."

"This makes sense of a—lot—of things that were confusing, I'm really glad I asked you about this."

"Happy to oblige – but there's one more thing I should mention… the so-called 'married monks'…"

"Yes I've heard that term used and never understood it."

"That's because it's not actually understandable."

---

7   Gyalwa *(rGyal ba / jina / victorious one)* a buddha – one who has conquered over the four *bDud* (devils of duality / maras).
8   Marriage of monks in Japan existed as early as the Heian period (794–1185). See glossary: *marriage of monks in Japan.*

"But the Nyingma School has them… doesn't it?"

"No… but what it does have—and the Kagyüds and Sakyas have them too—is non-celibate Lamas who wear monastic robes and shave their heads. They only take the gé-nyèn level of vows – and gé-nyèn vows don't include celibacy. So… they look like monks – but they're not monks."

"So… why…?"

"Exactly…" PAUSE *"I have no clear idea… all I can think is that it must come out of the persecution of the gö kar chang lo'i dé that has existed since the inception of the 'Second Spread'*[9] *of Vajrayana. So, it might be a way of being an undercover ngakpa which has simply become accepted and institutionalised. Or, maybe, it's people who decided not to become monks after starting in that direction – or maybe it's for some other reason that… I just can't imagine."*

"I've heard that tantric vows are much harder to keep than the monastic vows" Ani Chö-ying commented. *"Do you find that's true?"*

"Well… I've never kept the vinaya – so I couldn't compare. What I imagine is meant is that there are vows of view. Vows of view are more difficult to keep because they involve how you see rather than what you do or don't do. The hair vow is easy for me to keep—and also the vow never to disparage women—but some of the others are almost impossible to keep… you have to keep restoring them when they're broken. Some really require you to be a realised being – and so, of course they're broken second by second."

"Of course, you can't tell me about those vows – but what of relationship? As a ngakpa, you have—or can have—a consort. I can't imagine what that could be like."

"Nor can I… at the moment." PAUSE *"I am in relationship… but my ladyfriend is not—and will never be—a consort. I had hoped that she might become interested in practice – but I obviously haven't inspired her sufficiently in terms of the result of practice."*

Ani Chö-ying formed a facial expression at that point.

---

9   Chi-dar *(phyi dar)* the second spread of Buddhism in Tibet.

It was easy enough to read. It read *'You're being self-deprecating – and there's no need for that.'*

"Alright" I replied to her facial appearance. *"No, I'm not guilty of self-deprecation... I just feel we're having an honest genuine conversation – and I feel it's important to be real."*

Ani Chö-ying's eyes widened *"Did you just read my mind!?"*

"No" I laughed *"I read your face. I'm an Art student – so I've been trained to look: to see. It's not that difficult."* PAUSE *"I chanced into the relationship by accident. It was happening before I had time to think about whether it was feasible or not – and early on she—seemed—rather open and curious about my life."*

"And then, within three months, it all changed."

"Did you just read—my—mind?"

"No." PAUSE *"It's fairly typical of romantic relationship – so there wasn't even guess-work involved. And that's simply what happened to me: too many times. That's what made me decide to become a nun. That was also a decision made quickly – but when the opportunity arose it just seemed so obvious. I didn't want to waste my life playing the relationship game – a game where someone always had to lose."*

This was not the time or place or circumstance to say *'It's shame for both of us that you never met me.'* So I didn't. Instead, I wore a studied placid expression—from which I imagined nothing could be read —and responded *"I can see that this could have been a viable decision for me too – given my current circumstances."*

"So—apart from your current circumstances—did you initially choose to become a ngakpa because of the possibility of finding a consort – I mean do you think it has advantages over celibacy?"

I smiled—almost laughed in some strange bittersweet way—and shook my head. *"Excuse me for saying this – but this is a most interesting conversation. I wouldn't otherwise get the chance to have a conversation like this... but to answer your question... no.*

"I didn't choose to become a ngakpa because of that possibility – it was more of a 'poetic choice'... and..." PAUSE *"I'd seen photographs of ngakpas. I'd read about Ajo Répa*[10] *in Anagarika Govinda's* 'Way of the White Clouds' *– and seen photographs of him in robes like these that I am wearing. Then, almost the first thing that happened to me in India was meeting a ngakpa. He was Ngakpa Yeshé Dorje – and he was wearing exactly what Ajo Répa was wearing. So, it all went on from there."* PAUSE *"As to advantages over celibacy..."* PAUSE *"at this point in time, I really think celibacy might actually suit me better."*

"I see..."

"Well... yes... finding someone who would be a real consort seems remote at this point. The chances of making mistakes seem all too likely. A consort would have to be a Vajrayana Buddhist with the same Tsawa'i Lamas. She would have to be a romantic partner who was prepared to live the vows..." I described the vows as I'd described them to the three ladies in Hotwells – but with more technical detail.[11] *"... so you see I've tried living those vows with someone who didn't – and it didn't work. It has to be equal."*

"Yes... I can see that."

"So... in some ways – it would have been better to have become a monk."

"But it's a higher calling to be a ngakpas – is it not?"

"I think..." PAUSE *"... there is no higher or lower calling—or higher or lower vows—just higher and lower capacities to make use of those vows – and monastics all practise Vajrayana anyway."*

"I think it admirable that you're so non-partisan in your view. That's a little rare."

---

10 *A jo ras pa rin po che* /ཨ་ཇོ་རས་པ་རིན་པོ་ཆེ was a great rTsa rLung yogi of Barom Kagyüd *('ba rom bKa' brGyud)* and Nyingma traditions who presided over Tsé Chö Ling in Chumbi valley *(tshe chos gLing gyi ri khröd).* He was an incarnation of Mahasiddha Dombi Heruka who lived to be over 100 years old. His incarnation was recognised by the 16th Gyalwa Karmapa – and his present reincarnation—born in Phari—resides at Tsé Chöling in Dromo, Tibet.

11 See *Entering the Heart of the Sun and Moon*—Ngakpa Chögyam and Khandro Déchen—Aro Books Inc—2009.

"It's not admirable..." I laughed *"it's more that I live in dread of being an ape."* PAUSE *"You see... I find competition, rivalry, enmity, dogmatism, and chauvinism unworthy even of lower primates."*

Ani Chö-ying laughed and replied *"Yes... I can't disagree with that... It's not been easy being a nun when I look round and see other nuns and monks behaving... well – just as you've seen here. It sometimes seems it would be preferable to be a devoted lay practitioner – to give the word 'lay' its correct meaning."* PAUSE *"However, there's no choice now – and all-in-all..."*

"Yes... the same applies to me. I've taken the vows and I shall keep them for the rest of my life" PAUSE *"I shall have to see what happens when I next go to the Himalayas."*

"You think you might marry a Tibetan?"

"That's not impossible, I suppose. I did have a relationship with a Swiss lady once. It was all rather perfect – but being from different countries didn't work." PAUSE *"Well... I should say that it was between the age of 14 and 16. Maybe at my age now it would be entirely different."* PAUSE *"Still, I'd learn Tibetan and make a cultural shift that kept me out of all kinds of typical Western trouble."*

"And land you up in all kinds of typical—Tibetan—trouble. There's plenty of that" she laughed. *"You still don't imagine that Tibet was Shangri-la do you? Or that most Tibetans are one step away from Buddhahood?"*

"No..." I grinned. *"I may be naïve in many respects – but I'm not the deaf, dumb, blind, kid. I can't play a mean pin ball either. I can however see what's in front of my nose – and, of course, I've read quite enough about Tibetan history not to have any romantic illusions."* PAUSE *"No, I don't have too many illusions about Tibetans – but I have found they're not as complicated or neurotic as many Western people tend to be. Of course, Buddhism is their natural religion – not their hobby. With Western people... you never know whether their Buddhism is real – or whether it's fashion. No matter how sincere people—think—they are; they sometimes come to think differently. It's not the same subject – but huge bellbottoms were once objects of desire and now they're starting to become objects of ridicule. So... all in all..."* I ran out of steam.

"Sorry" she apologised. *"I shouldn't have presumed…"*

"Nothing to be sorry about in the slightest. I've met a great many people who have just the illusion you describe – and there's' no reason, with my Arts approach, that you shouldn't naturally draw such a conclusion."

"Thank you." PAUSE *"You know what Paltrül Rinpoche said?"* I shook my head. I did not know. *"If you've got money"* she grinned *"you've got money-shaped problems. If you have a house, you've got a house-shaped problem. If you have goats, you've got goat-shaped problems. If you have yaks, you've got yak-shaped problems."* PAUSE *"There's a man I know who married a Tibetan woman – but she had no interest in Dharma in terms of practice. All she required was a portrait of the Dalai Lama on the wall and a set of offering bowls beneath it to fill every day. Her main interest in marrying a Canadian was to escape the refugee camp and live a life of domestic affluence in Canada – so you would have to be as careful in your choice of partner as you are here."*

"Thank you for the warning."

A few moments of comfortable silence passed.

"Are you going to take the Pakshi Tröllö and Mahakala initiations tonight and tomorrow night?" she asked.

"I hope to – but I shall have to enquire what is required."

"Yes – you have to put your name down in advance at the office… good luck."

We made our farewells and I walked off to the office. Good luck…? I wondered why I'd need good luck – but I soon found out. I asked the dowdy middle-aged woman wrapped in a felted maroon cardigan at the office. She wore her hair with a fringe[12] and bobbed just below the ears. It always struck me as peculiar when adults adopted the hairstyles of children – but… everyone was free to make their own choices.

---

12 Hair cut with a fringe over the forehead is termed 'bangs' in the USA.

"You will need to have completed the chariot ngöndro [13] *and be practising Chakrasamvara* [14] *– those…"* she almost sneered *"… are the only people allowed to take these empowerments. And if Akong Rinpoche is not your Lama you would need the permission of your Lama to take the Mahakala initiation in any case."*

I replied that I had completed ngöndro – but that it had been the shorter and longer Düd'jom gTér ngöndros. I explained that although I didn't practise Chakrasamvara – I did practice an equivalent Nyingma yidam. As to my Lama's permission… that was impossible to obtain at such short notice – as Kyabjé Düd'jom Rinpoche lived in Nepal.

"You won't be taking the empowerments then, will you" she replied in a ridiculously superior manner – as if she were a teacher addressing a school child.

"No… it would appear not" I smiled. *"Sorry to have troubled you."* The woman stared at me blankly for a moment as if I'd spoken in a foreign language – and then continued with something else that required her attention.

Ani Chö-ying passed me in the hall and asked how I'd got on. *"I'm not qualified…"* I replied. *"You have to have completed the 'Chariot for Travelling the Path to Freedom Ngöndro' to take Pakshi Tröllö – and I haven't."* PAUSE *"You have to have be practising 'khorlo Demchog as a yidam to take Dorje Bernakchen – and I'm not."* PAUSE *"You also have to have your Lama's permission for Dorje Bernakchen… and… I can't exactly ask Düd'jom Rinpoche for his permission without going to Nepal…"*

"Oh… I see… I had the idea that you'd have completed ngöndro…"

"I have – but not—that—ngöndro."

13 *The Chariot for Travelling the Path to Freedom*—composed by Karmapa Wangchuk Dorje *(dBang phyug rDo rJe* 1556–1603) the 9th Gyalwa Karmapa—is the principal Karma Kagyüd ngöndro. Chakrasamvara is Khorlo Demchog in Tibetan.
14 Khorlo Demchog *('khor lo bDe mChog – Cycle of Incomparable Ecstasy)* is a yidam and tantra of Anuttaratantra Yoga of the Sarma *(phyi 'gyur gSar ma)* New Translation Schools.

363

"Does it matter?"

"Apparently. Yes."

"Did you explain?"

"I did explain... yes... I told the lady that I'd completed the shorter and longer Düd'jom gTér ngöndros—and the Khandro Thug-thig and Tröma ngöndros—but that did not qualify me."

"Oh—that's complete nonsense—but... I suppose that's how they have it organised. I'm sorry."

"It's alright – I can't expect to walk in here—as a Nyingma—and presume I'd receive what people receive who committed themselves to the Karma Kagyüd School. I've attended the Vajra Crown ceremony twice now and I'm extremely happy about that. I've also received the 'ö-Pag'mèd, Chenrézigs, and Guru Rinpoche wangs – so I'm really delighted. I think it would be avaricious of me to be put out because there were two wangs I wasn't qualified to attend."

Ani Chöying smiled wanly and said *"I'm glad you don't find it disheartening."*

"Well... I'm not disheartened in any peevish sense – but I can't say I'm not disappointed, as I would have found it massively inspiring. The main thing, I suppose, is that I—probably—won't allow it to weigh me down – or not for long. I've found there's no purpose in regret and recrimination. When you're wallowing in—that morass—you miss the show – the magnificent display of reality that's constantly performing."

Ani Chöying smiled—nodded her appreciation of what I'd said— and left to attend to whatever it was to which she needed to attend. I went to sit in the library to see if I could find the book by Helmut Hoffman again. I found it and there was Lingtsang Gyalpo again. I wished I could photograph the pictures – as they were entirely wonderful. Maybe one day I'd find a copy of the book. I'd had standing search requests with George's Bookshop in Bristol and they occasionally found out-of-print books for me.

I'd not been gazing at Lingtsang Gyalpo[15] for long – when Ani Chö-ying appeared *"I asked Linneah—the woman you saw earlier about the initiations—and asked her why it had to be the Kagyüd ngöndro. I said 'ngöndro is ngöndro – they all contain the 100,000 practices and this is all that is required...' but she said it had been stipulated by Gyalwa Karmapa."*

"That's very kind of you—I must say—I'd offer to take you out to dinner with a fine bottle of wine – but I don't think that would be appropriate."

"No... not quite... but I appreciate the thought." PAUSE *"This sort of thing —this ridiculous exclusionary mentality—is all too common. It makes me quite weary – I sometimes wonder... but never mind..."*

"Quite so – never mind. As ngöndro means 'before beginning' – I guess I'll have to Begin the Begin *all over again."* And then I burst into song with a parody of *Begin the Beguine*.[16]

> *"When I begin the beguine / It'll bring back the sound of mosquitoes in Bodha, / It'll bring back the fright of the pain in my shoulders."*

Ani Chö-ying burst out laughing at that. When she regained her self-possession, she said *"Yogi, Bluesman, and stand-up comedian."*

"I don't think I can respond to that – apart from adding that I'm also a poet, artist, and biker" I laughed. *"No... I'm really just a jack-of-all-trades and master-of-none. I just follow my nose in terms of whatever I find inspiring. If I'm anything—or if I was to say I was anything—it would be that I was a Nyingma and a disciple of Kyabjé Düd'jom Rinpoche. All the rest is phantasmagoria."*

---

15 See glossary : *Lingtsang Gyalpo*.
16 *Begin the Beguine* by Cole Porter – who composed the song between Indonesia and Fiji on a 1935 Pacific cruise on the *Franconia*, a Cunard ocean liner. In 1935, June Knight introduced it in the Broadway musical *Jubilee*. The actual lyrics are: *When they begin the beguine / It brings back the sound of music so tender, / It brings back a night of tropical splendour.* The beguine is a dance and music form. It was a low rhumba popular in the 1930s, coming from the islands of Guadeloupe and Martinique. In Creole *Beke* or *Begue* means a White person – and Beguine is the female form. It is a combination of Latin folk dance and French ballroom dance. It is a spirited yet slow, close dance where one rolls the hips.

365

"Your humour will stand you in good stead though – because you need humour to deal with so many things in life. "

"Yes – that's certainly true."

"Humility too."

"No… certainly—not—humility. I don't believe in humility."

Ani Chö-ying looked a little taken aback by that *"So… what does that mean with regard to your earlier self-deprecation?"*

"It means, for me…" PAUSE *"… it means that I've seen so much false humility – that I wish no part of it. I feel, in some respects, that arrogance is more honest than most humility I've seen. At least arrogance is simple and direct."*

"That's an interesting point of view… I see what you mean – but you don't —sound—arrogant from what I have experienced of you."

I smiled at this. *"You've not doubted that I'll keep my word yet. Were you to doubt my word – you'd not just see arrogance, you'd see hubris and the most hideous hauteur."* I chuckled *"Be that as it may… I see arrogance as being as pretentious as humility. Both are postures. I'd rather—simply exist— without having to instruct people as to how they should view me. If people tell me I'm good at something or other, I thank them. I don't contradict them. If people tell me I'm bad at something or other, I say 'I try my best' and leave it at that."*

"So, you're not being humble when you say you're a jack-all-trades and master-of-none?"

"No. That's not humble. That's simply factual."

Ani Chö-ying laughed at that. *"I don't think, that I quite see the difference between humble and factual."*

"Humble, to me, would mean not accepting praise when it's offered. I see it as ungenerous to the person offering praise, to undermine it by denying its validity. It's like an accusation of flattery or sycophancy." PAUSE

"I wish there was a word that simply meant 'lacking in arrogance' – because I don't see 'absence of arrogance' as 'humility'—well, not in terms of what 'humility' has come to signify—all too often."

"What about unpretentiousness, modesty, meekness?"

"Yes – I could also go for decorum, restraint, discretion, propriety, appropriateness, politeness, gentility or simplicity – in fact I'd opt for 'simplicity' as the word I'd prefer. I don't see self-effacement as simple – unless one's making a joke or being factual."

"You've really given this some thought, haven't you?"

"Yes" I laughed. *"Now comes the arrogance. I give—everything—like this a great deal of thought. I feel that language is a powerful tool – and needs to be used with as much precision as possible. I've worked consistently over the years to develop a large vocabulary: one that allows me to be as subtle and meticulous as I'd wish to be – but I still have a long way to go."* PAUSE *"When I say I have a long way to go, I'm not being humble. English is three times the size of the next largest language – and I can't say that I know even a tenth of its vocabulary."*

Ani Chö-ying was now wearing a somewhat intrigued expression so I continued *"In spite of that – I would hazard the guess that I might have a substantially larger vocabulary than anyone at Samŷe Ling at this time."*

"Coming from you" Ani Chö-ying laughed *"I can understand that you're being factual rather than arrogant – but it's a narrowly defined position."* PAUSE *"I think I prefer the safety of… restraint… I can see that humility can be false – and that it can be ungenerous to anyone who offers praise…"* PAUSE *"… but the line you take requires a—very—high degree of attentive awareness…"* PAUSE *"Do you think that this is the difference between the monastic vows and the ngakpa vows? I mean… the monastic vows are there to keep you safe, in a way – so being humble or modest means you can't make mistakes as easily."*

I pondered my answer for some moments. *"I think you're entirely correct. I also think I'm a dolt for not having seen that this is a question of yanas – so thank you very much indeed for that. I thought it was just my personal angle – but of course it's simply an aspect of Vajrayana in terms of the commitment to awareness in the moment. It also links in with other aspects of the difference between Sutrayana and Vajrayana."*

"Can you elaborate?"

"I was thinking about the safeguards… in respect of Sutrayana – from my studies at the Tibetan Library of Archives and Works [17] with Geshé Ngawang Dhargyey.[18]"

"I'd like to ask you about those studies – but first, I want to ask you why calling yourself a 'dolt' isn't humble?"

Now I had a huge grin *"Because – it's simply a fact. However, I may not be a dolt in the same way again. I may not have been a dolt at other times – and I wouldn't let being a dolt on this occasion define me as a dolt on all other occasions. It is—in fact—important to be able to see myself as a dolt in order to cease being a dolt. It's only in the moment that I see myself as a dolt, that I know I've overcome doltishness – in respect of whatever area of field of experience it might be. Then, I can cease to be a dolt."*

Ani Chö-ying smiled through this explanation *"I must say that this is one of the most engaging conversations I've had for a long time – so, what would you say about Sutrayana and Vajrayana in this context?"*

"Well, what hit me immediately was remembering Geshé Ngawang Dhargyey's teaching on avoiding negative situations and negative people – in order not to provoke negative primary causes.

---

17 The Library of Tibetan Works and Archives is near Upper Dharamsala, Himachal Pradesh, India. It was founded in 1970 – and is one of the important libraries and institutions of Tibetan works in the world. The library contains sources which were relocated from Tibet in the 1959 escape, including important manuscripts related to Tibet's history, politics, culture, and art. It possesses more than 80,000 manuscripts, 700 thangkas, 10,000 photographs; books, documents, statues, and other artefacts. The 2nd floor is a museum that contains artifacts and items dating as far back as the 12th century.
18 See glossary: *Geshe Ngawang Dhargyey.*.

"*He emphasised that one should attempt to surround oneself with positive secondary causes in order to make the most of one's opportunities in terms of Dharma. The Vajrayana point of view—particularly in terms of Dzogchen —would be not to avoid anything. This would be in order that one could face all one's negative primary causes – and either transform them, or self-liberate them.*"

"*So you would deliberately seek out negative secondary causes, then?*"

"*No…*" I grinned shaking my head. "*I don't have to do that. Negative secondary causes come at me like heat-seeking missiles*" I laughed. "*As I said before… maybe I should have opted to be a monk. I know that being a monk or nun isn't easy – but it's—far—simpler. The engagement with everyday life—which is what Kyabjé Düd'jom Rinpoche encouraged—is a minefield of opportunities to make one blunder after another.*"

"*Not that I wish to pry – but could you give me an example of a blunder?*"

"*A blunder… well one blunder is the very aspect of me that you thought might be an advantage: my sense of humour. Witty rejoinders spring to mind all too easily – and although I don't always give voice to them, they're there. Sometimes the most sarcastic, acerbic, mordant, or caustic responses are there immediately. I never actually say anything nasty to anyone—I can control my speech—but sometimes I say things that are… needlessly clever. Sometimes these responses are not even understood – but I don't like the fact that badinage seems so instinctive. For example—Dick Taylor—the head of Graphics at Bristol Art School, is a rather unpleasant self-important man not well liked by most of the lecturers. In the first term of the degree course he gave a long speech in which he was dismissive of the 'Fine Art leanings' in Illustration. He saw Graphic Design—of which Illustration was a sub-set— as a 'communication science'. What upset me about this was that Derek Crowe—the principal lecturer of Illustration—was implicated in this derisory critique. Now Derek Crowe is a lovely man – warm, kind, enthusiastic and… closer to retirement age than Dick Taylor. So, toward the end of this lengthy speech – Dick Taylor must have realised that he'd been laying down the law a little too freely and said 'Still Graphic Design is a broad church — and I wouldn't want anyone to think this was a dictatorship.'…*" PAUSE

369

"So, without a pause, I said 'Sounds more like a Dick Taylorship'…" PAUSE *"What made matters worse, was that a fair few lecturers burst out laughing."*

"That—was—fast thinking" Ani Chö-ying chuckled. *"I don't think I could come up with something like that quite so… immediately; in fact, I don't think I could do that even given time – besides which I would not have been brave enough."*

"Thing is, it's not even bravery. It happens too quickly. I don't consider the consequences. He was undermining Derek Crowe – and I was simply impelled to come to his defence."

"But the main point for me is that you acted out of kindness in wishing to defend someone."

"I can accept that; apart from the fact that there was an insidious triumphal joy in the wit. That detracted from the honourable intention of coming to Derek Crowe's defence. Then… there's the question as to whether I would have come to his defence if there'd been no opportunity for an ever-so-clever witticism."

"I think you can live with that without—too much—self-recrimination. We're all—trying—to be perfect, aren't we. It's not likely that we're going to succeed—very—soon. And even when we do succeed our success will be sporadic or partial. It's a journey – we can't live the destination…" PAUSE *"But, I was forgetting – with Dzogchen the path is the same as the result…"*

"Yes…" PAUSE *"but that doesn't mean I actually practise Dzogchen. All I can say is that I practise the practice."*

We sat in silence for a few moments – after which Ani Chö-ying asked *"There's just another thing, if you don't mind?"*

"Ask away."

"You said that you'd studied with Geshé Ngawang Dhargyey. 'Geshé' – that's a Gélug title, isn't it." I nodded assent. *"Why… were you studying with a Gélug Lama when you went to India to search for ngakpas?"*

"*That's much simpler to answer than anything else you've asked. I went to India to study Buddhism – and I've never been sectarian. I didn't know when I might find a Ngakpa Lama – and so I went to study at the most obvious accessible place. It made no difference to me which school it was – so I began the course but never completed it. I was only a few weeks into it when I met Ngakpa Yeshé Dorje – and was plunged immediately into Düd'jom gTérsar ngöndro and the practice of Tröma Nakmo.*" PAUSE "*I learned a great deal from Geshé Ngawang Dhargyey— although it was less than a month of study—because I took the standard class and the advanced class at the same time.*"

"*That must have been taxing – good for you.*"

"*Actually, it wasn't—that—taxing really – other than the long periods of sitting cross legged on a hard floor with a minimal piece of padding. It was all fairly straightforward because of my previous autodidactic immersion. I knew a great deal of the technical language from Buddhist books and from reading* The Middle Way *– the quarterly journal of the Buddhist Society. Of course, the main thing that was taxing was that it seemed to irritate some people that I attended the advanced class. They considered I wasn't qualified to attend. Then, of course, they were indignant that I left to study with Ngakpa Yeshé Dorje.*"

Ani Chö-ying grinned somewhat impishly "*You certainly have a knack of upsetting people – I see that what has happened here isn't new to you.*"

"*No indeed – it's a familiar story.*" PAUSE "*Can I ask you if you have ever run into similar situations?*"

Ani Chö-ying pondered with a wrinkled brow for a few moments and replied "*Slightly similar – but I think my robes tend to protect me. It's considered very bad form to be hostile to the ordained – but expressions are easily read, as you read mine before. Still, I've had nothing close to the animosity that's been levelled at you.*"

"It's not bad" I smiled. *"And in any case, Kyabjé Düd'jom Rinpoche told me to expect it. He said that if I accepted his request to represent [19] the gö kar chang lo tradition in the West that people would attack me for it."*

"This is something of a series of revelations… I suppose there's no point in asking you how you feel about the idea of being attacked."

"No one gets out of here alive" I laughed. *"No, I'm not that courageous – I just don't dwell on the idea. Many wonderful things have happened too – and I have some extremely good friends. I feel extremely lucky – and the occasional person taking against me is nothing to get upset about. I imagine everyone has to deal with the slings and arrows of outrageous misfortune…"*

"Shakespeare…"

"Yes. Hamlet's soliloquy, although I delicately misquoted" and then I quoted:

> *"To be, or not to be, that is the question: whether 'tis nobler in the mind to suffer the slings and arrows of outrageous fortune, or to take arms against a sea of troubles, and by opposing end them: to die, to sleep. No more. And by a sleep – to say, we end the heart-ache, and the thousand natural shocks that flesh is heir to, 'tis a consummation devoutly to be wished! To die—to sleep—to sleep, perchance to Dream…"*

"Perchance… to dream…" Ani Chö-ying echoed in a voice that carried some meaning I couldn't fathom – so I jested *"Far be it from me to take arms against a sea of troubles – I'll just grab the nearest surf board."*

"Yes… I think you'll survive" Ani Chö-ying smiled *"but before I get side-tracked – I've been meaning to ask you what were you reading?"*

---

19 I chose not to say that Kyabjé Düd'jom Rinpoche had requested me to establish the gö kar chang lo'i dé in the West because to have done so would have led to questions that would have been awkward to answer vis-à-vis having been recognised at the tulku of Aro Yeshé. That would not be something that I was to mention for a decade.

"I'm not reading so much as looking at these two photographs of Lingtsang Gyalpo." I showed them to her. *"It was a photograph like this—of Ajo Répa Rinpoche—that first made me think of becoming a ngakpa."* PAUSE *"Well... no... that's not actually true – it's more that it made me want to meet ngakpas. I never had any idea that it was possible to become a ngakpa."*

"It really—is—a remarkable photograph" Ani Chö-ying commented with profound reverence in her voice. *"I can certainly see what would inspire you... this Lama just radiates such tremendous power."* PAUSE *"Are you drawn to power – and... the magical side of Vajrayana?"*

"No."

"Really?" PAUSE *"Then..."*

"It might seem so—from my fascination with these photographs—but no. My interest is largely... atmospheric."

Ani Chö-ying shook her head slightly in confusion.

"Perhaps it might be better to say 'artistic' – or..." PAUSE *"I mean, looking at this photograph, is like listening to Beethoven's 9th Choral Symphony. That is also powerful and magical – and—that—is what I see in these photographs. What draws me is Dzogchen. Silent or spacious sitting. The sky. The vast space of that view and practice. I'm not really much of a ritualist; even though I have practised Mahayoga ritual – and shall probably always practice it to a certain degree. I've met people who are drawn to power and magic – and, I don't really like what I see. Strangely I never saw that in Ngakpa Yeshé Dorje. Some of the Western people I've met however, are more akin with Alistair Crowley [20] than the ngakpas I've met. They seem to enjoy what—they—see as the similarities between Tantra and Satanism. I see no similarities. I've had the similarities pointed out to me – but all I see, is their desire to see similarity. I see no similarly between Armagnac and car battery acid. That's unfair however – because at least car battery acid has a useful purpose."*

---

20 Aleister Crowley (1875–1947) was an English occultist / black magician who founded the Thelema religion – having appointed himself as the prophet who would guide humanity into the Æon of Horus. See glossary: *Crowley, Aleister.*

This led Ani Chö-ying to asking me how I'd met such people – and that lead to telling her about Gilbert and Elzebe Harris,[21] and their sinister occultist approach to Vajrayana.

"This is something of an eye-opener." Ani Chö-ying was evidently quite shocked. *"I would never have imagined anyone would be interested in Dharma from—that—perspective…"* PAUSE *"but then, Milarépa* [22] *studied black magic to punish his uncle and aunt for disenfranchising his mother and her family."*

"Oh yes… I have heard about that – but only in passing. Do you know anything more about that?

"I don't know much in detail – but Milarépa [23] *was born to a prosperous family in Kya Ngatsa. When his father died, Milarepa's uncle and aunt appropriated the family wealth. So Milarépa's family was left homeless and destitute. Milarépa's mother—in desperation—urges him to go and study black magic with a sorcerer.* [24] *This he does and whilst his uncle and aunt are celebrating the marriage of their son, he takes revenge on them by summoning a giant scorpion to demolish their house. A score or more people are killed – although, by some fluke, his uncle and aunt survive. Milarépa then summoned a hailstorm that destroyed their barley crop. I heard teachings on this in much more detail. Like you, magic is not of primary interest to me – so I cannot recall more detail than that."*

I'd actually heard these details – but I thanked her for her explanation and made no allusion to being acquainted with them.

"Did you know" Ani Chö-ying enquired *"thinking of perverted occultism – that Hitler and many of the Nazi hierolatry were occultists?"*

"Right…" I pondered for a brief moment *"I find that both surprising and unsurprising… surprising at first but then it starts to make sense of itself – but I can't really say why."*

---

21 See chapter 18, *the indestructible crown.*
22 Jétsun Milarépa (1052–1135) was one of the most famous Naljorpas and poets – particularly revered in the Kagyüd Schools. Milarépa's birth name was Mila Thöpaga which means 'Joyful to Hear'.
23 Also known as Tsa in the Gungthang province of western Tibet.
24 Lhaje Nubchung *(lha rJe gNubs chung)*

"Yes. It seems to fit."

"I think" I ventured *"that the idea of black magic comes from a Christian origin. In terms of Vajrayana, there are simply processes of mantra and visualisation. There is no specific 'black magic' as a destructive or coercive art that is separate from other practices. From what I know, it's the motivation that gives the 'colour ascription' to the magic. There is no term 'black' magic in Tibetan as far as I know. There is ngèn-ngak…*[25] *That means… ngan means 'bad, unwholesome or mischievous' – and ngak means mantra. There's also mig'trul*[26] *which mean 'visual illusion' or 'conjuring tricks'. Then there's gam-chèd*[27] *– which means something like effectuating an interference. There are all sorts of words – but none of them include the word black unless it's a word I do not know.*[28] *All these words—as far as I know—deal with how to avert hindrances to practice."*

Ani Chö-ying shook her head with a slight chuckle *"I thought you knew—nothing—about this?"*

"I don't – or rather, I know nothing based on any kind of fascination with manipulating power or having control over others. I'd just like to be able to control myself and steer my life in a direction that was in line with what Kyabjé Düd'jom Rinpoche wishes."

"So why d'you think some people want power and the ability to control others?"

---

25 *ngan sNgags* – malevolent spell or subjugating mantra.
26 *mig 'khrul* – optical illusion; chimera, mirage, or figment.
27 *nGam byed* is often translated as 'black magic' but *'nGam'* has many meanings according to context that pertain to randomness, nebulousness, elusiveness, indistinctness, murkiness, darkness or being precipitate. *'byed'* means: effectuating, hindering, stoppage, interfering, or performing as in function. *nGam byed* therefore pertains to capriciousness impulsiveness or recklessness. This has more to do with motivation and intention rather than with the nature of the rites.
28 *mThu* – power, force, might, or authority / *mThu rGyas byed* – use of magical force / *mThu gTad* – power, strength, force to cast spells / *chad-phur bö-tong (byad phur rBod gTong)* malediction / *log-pa (zLog pa or bzLog pa)* to revert, reverse; contract, or extinguish.

"Well… I think… if one perceives a personal lack of power – one might want to acquire it. If one has power—or sufficient power to do what one needs to do however—then… why want power?"

"Yes…" Ani Chö-ying nodded.

"It seems to me" I continued *"that there are two ways to get something you haven't got – you can either work for it or you can steal it. It always strikes me that sorcery is some way of stealing it. If you steal it however, somebody has to go without it – and… what is the sense in that for a Buddhist, or anyone else for that matter."*

"Yes. That makes perfect sense to me."

"So—even in terms of debate—if I can't convince a person through logic, why should I wish to convince them through occult means? That's entirely vapid. If I have a point to make, I can make it. All that's required is a good understanding of the subject and a useful grasp of the English language."

"Quite."

"It reminds me of people who argued—almost as a sport—at School. It seemed to be a competition as to who could win the argument. People seemed happy to win arguments whether they were right or wrong. It seemed that if people were extremely clever, they could simply win arguments merely by cleverness – and I found that puerile. So, 'sorcery'—to me—is winning arguments through cleverness rather than through wholesome intelligence and authentic knowledge. It's also like ad hominem: the short cut to winning by humiliating another person on the basis of something that has nothing to do with the subject under discussion." PAUSE *"And so says the fatuous fat fellow…"* PAUSE *"… or my telling Dick Taylor that what he described sounded more like a 'Dick Taylorship' – that was also ad hominem."*

"Yes… but you weren't applying that as a shortcut to win an argument. It was just a comment – made to validate another person."

"Alright… I'll accept that. Most gracious of you."

"As to 'short cuts' however… isn't Tantra described as the short path?"

"Yes, it is – but it's also described as dangerous and I'm neither drawn to swiftness nor danger." PAUSE *"My interest in Vajrayana isn't connected to it being a short dangerous path. I walk coastal paths in Cornwall – but not because they're dangerous short cuts. It's because I enjoy the view of the sea."*

"And Dzogchen?"

"Dzogchen is, of course, the instantaneous path – but I have no interest in acting as if I've attained the nondual state." PAUSE *"I feel it has more to do with being an artist. I relate through the Arts. I'm not a scholar, mathematician, or scientist – so I relate with Tantra visually."*

"Visually?"

"Yes, in terms of the yidams – and to Dzogchen in terms of the sense fields. I seem to understand Sutrayana as more... scientific in its logic.

"Ah yes... I see what you mean – but what about compassion? Do you see that as scientific too?

"No – but there are extensive teachings on compassion. For me... compassion is something quite simple. It's simply having a good heart and caring about others. It's not putting my own interests first. It's taking joy in helping others. Beyond that I don't know what there is to explain. If there—is—more to explain, then it would seem to have to become a science rather than an art."

"That is the most unusual approach I have ever come across – but it makes complete sense to me, even though it leaves me with a host of questions that aren't quite formed yet. Can we talk more about this later?"

Yes, we could – and we did. Ani Chö-ying found me to be a continual series of surprising juxtapositions. I was never quite what she expected I might be – but then, nor was she. She had none of the monastic frostiness or somewhat morbid 'selflessness' of the Western monastics I'd met. She was a straightforward down-to-earth person who took her practice seriously. She had no axe to grind and no agenda. She could challenge me – but never with any sense of wanting to get the better of me. She had no interest in status.

She had no edge, angles, or hard-wired attitudes; no predisposition to anything that caused any sort of interpersonal awkwardness. Our conversations were always entirely natural and wholesome. She was entirely unlike any other western Buddhist I had ever met.

23

Pakshi Tröllö

Preamble: I have questioned whether to include the later part of this account in the body of this book, or place it as an appendix. This second and longer section of this chapter details my audience with Gyalwa Karmapa – and is extremely dense in terms of information, Himalayan Buddhist technical terms, and the names of Lamas and lineages. Not everyone would wish to attempt reading such an account – although there are others for whom it might be most welcome. The final choice was to leave it as a chapter – but convert sections of the account to footnotes in order to relieve the technical weight of the material. Some footnotes refer to recently acquired information – particularly concerning Wangchuk Rig'dzin Rinpoche and his son, HE Trulku Ugyen Drodrul Thinley Kuenchap Rinpoche, which will be of interest to those who wish a deeper understanding of the Nyingma Tradition.

The morning passed in pleasant reading – and then lunch. Ani Chö-ying was there – along with Geraint Williams and Lydia Evesham. We enjoyed a lively conversation. Geraint and Lydia were also unable to attend the empowerments – but said that they hoped they'd be given again in future when they'd managed to complete their ngöndros.

"I've been thinking" Ani Chö-ying mused *"about our earlier conversation – about why people are attracted to power and magic. There's something that I meant to mention – but we ran out of time. It's the association of Nazism with occultism. There are a few books and papers I read on the subject when I was at university. There are direct links between Ariosophy [1] and Nazi ideology. From what I've read, many of the Nazi Party leaders seem to have enjoined a form of quasi-scientific occultism. Hitler's Reich Chancellery, Goebbels's Propaganda Ministry, and Himmler's Gestapo espoused occultism, as many Nazis believed in its 'scientific value'."*

---

1   See glossary: *Ariosophy.*

"Scientific value!?" gasped Geraint.

"Exactly" replied Ani Chö-ying. *"The Nazis were fundamentally unscientific in their ideology. They merely chose whatever supported their worldview – so it suited them to vaunt a bogus 'scientific occultism; which they contrasted with popular occultism – in order to validate their higher form of occultism."*

"That's really creepy!" Lydia exclaimed – her eyes revealing a degree of disquiet.

"It is" I commented. *"Somehow, this doesn't surprise me. They were anti-Darwin. My German grandfather lost his career as the head of a prestigious school for refusing to teach Nazi propaganda. He said '… education concerns reality rather than make-believe…' and, of course, the Nazis weren't overly pleased by that response."* PAUSE *"Fortunately it was early enough in* WWII *that nothing worse happened to him."*

"So was the occultism there from the start?" asked Geraint.

"Yes, it seems so. The political group that eventually became the Nazi party was founded by individuals of the Thule Society – an esoteric group who believed the mythological origins of the Aryan race to be factual. Several prominent Nazis were active members of that society, including Rudolph Hess."

"Thule?" I queried.

"Thule is a mythological northern island. It has other names such as Hyperborea or Atlantis. Thule was supposed to be the origin of the Aryan race."

"Maybe I've got this wrong but I though Aryan [2] *referred to Asian peoples?"*

"Well yes – but Hitler had other ideas."

2   The term Aryan relates to the Indo-Iranian language root arya which Indo-Iranians adopted to describe Aryans. In Sanskrit arya means 'honourable or noble'. The term Indo-Aryan is still commonly used to describe the Indic half of the Indo-Iranian languages, i.e., the family that includes Sanskrit and modern languages such as Hindi, Urdu, Bengali, Nepali, Punjabi, Gujarati, Romani, Kashmiri, Sinhala and Marathi.

"So this was some sort of early 20th *century version of today's Tarot card culture"* I replied. *"It's somewhat disturbing that this can be adopted by fascism as easily as by the love-and-light back-to-the-earth movement."*

"The Nazis also espoused naturism – and they had many ideas about food that would sit well with hippie culture. Hitler was a vegetarian."

"That is quite illuminating in terms of some of the Western Buddhists I've met – the ones who are obsessed with magic. They seemed to have a sense of elitism, superiority, and exclusiveness – that is disturbingly similar to certain aspects of Nazi ideology."

"That's why I thought I'd mention it" responded Ani Chö-ying with a somewhat worried expression. *"It was what you told me about Gilbert Harris that made me think of this. It was the exploration of runes of the occultist Guido von List which led to the twin 'sig' runes of the* SS *insignia. The Thule society believed that the Aryan people were bred by electrical energy from intergalactic deities called Theozoa. They said that the other races were the result of interbreeding between humanity and apes which left the interbred Aryans bereft of their magical powers."*

"Although the subject matter is different – this all has the feel of Gilbert Harris and others I've met" I commented with a wearied shake of my head.

"What else do you know about this?" asked Geraint. *"Because I knew some people... and, well, this worries me."*

"I don't know that much more – because it was only a minor part of my studies. However, Himmler had a personal occultist, Karl Wiligut who developed a religion around worshipping the Germanic deity Irmin.[3] *According to Karl Wiligut, German culture dated back over* 200,000 *years, to when the Earth had three suns and was populated by giants, dwarfs, and other mythological beings. He claimed to be descended from a line of kings from this time and Himmler seems to have taken him at least partially seriously.*

---

3   Irmin is an Old Saxon adjective meaning great and strong – an epithet of Óðinn *(Odin)*. Irminism *(Irminenschaft)* was an invented religion based on a putative Germanic deity.

381

"On the basis of Karl Wiligut's prophecy, Himmler chose Wewelsburg castle [4] *as the base for the* SS *and adopted his design of the runic skull rings that Himmler awarded his favourites amongst his* SS *troops. Himmler was particularly attracted to paganism, as he detested the Jewish origins of Christianity. He believed that after Germany had won the war – the old Germanic gods would be restored. There are a number of stranger theories about the Nazis and occultism – but I have no interest in fanciful horror-story speculation. That's about all I can remember apart from Karl Wiligut having been diagnosed as schizophrenic."*

"Thank you very much indeed – that gives me much to consider." I paused. *"It seems to me that there's a danger of misinterpretation—deliberate or otherwise—with regard to the wrathful awareness beings and the protectors. Vajrayana is regarded as dangerous – but I don't think that I've ever really understood that in this respect. I think that unless a person is genuinely disinterested in power – it's best not to think about any form of wrathful practise."*

"But can't power be valuable?" asked Geraint.

I looked to Ani Chö-ying to answer – but she looked back at me to answer *"I'm interested to hear how you answer this."*

"Power is certainly valuable. For example – I'm quite strong. I'm strong because I've worked on building sites as a hoddie, carrying piles of bricks up ladders. I also have a strong back from prostrations. That means that if you need help lifting something heavy – I can cheerfully help you. If I can help a person, then I'm happy that I have the strength to do it – but otherwise I am not overly concerned with being strong. It rarely occurs to me that I'm probably stronger than most people I meet – because that idea has no function for me. I didn't work on building sites to develop muscles – I did that to earn money to take me out to the Himalayas. I didn't engage in prostrations to strengthen my back – I performed this practise as a necessary part of my training. The strength I gained in both cases was entirely adventitious." PAUSE

---

4   Wewelsburg is a Renaissance castle in Wewelsburg, Büren, Westphalia, Germany. The castle has a triangular layout, with three round towers connected by heavily built walls.

"Accidental, unplanned, unintentional, unintended, unpremeditated, inadvertent…" I added in reaction to Geraint's look of bafflement. *"I'm quite good with language too"* I laughed *"so I can give definitions or help someone who wants to write something. I'm an Art student – so I can produce informational material and letterheads of Buddhist centres. I was in a Blues Band so I can play Blues harp – and maybe sometimes some people still enjoy that. This all could be thought of as 'power' – but, if it is, I didn't arrive at it though wanting power. It doesn't make me superior to you or better than you."*

"Maybe – but it makes you much more interesting than me."

"How can you say that!?" I laughed *"when—you—have utterly fabulous multicoloured Tibetan felt boots – and I do not? You also have a far better head of hair. It's ginger too – whereas mine is merely thin meagre and mousy. To make matters worse – my hair's already starting to recede! I'll be as bald as a coot before I'm forty!"*

"Good point" laughed Geraint, with some degree of abandon.

Ani Chö-ying laughed too – but rather quietly. *"I think – what you said about wrathful practice is really pertinent. It's the—minds—of those who are attracted to magic, or wrathful practice, that make it either immensely valuable or immensely dangerous. Worshipping Odin is another question…"*

"Even that…" I interjected *"depends on the—mind—of the person. I was a card-carrying Viking as a child – and was terribly disappointed when I heard that the religions of the Vikings no longer existed. I was enormously keen on having a horned helmet, carrying a sword or axes, and sailing the sees in a longship."* That had them all in fits of laughter. *"But, my interest was more in line with Noggin the Nog [5] than Heinrich Luitpold Himmler [6] or the desire for rape and pillage on the coast of North Eastern Britain. Concepts of actual battle never crossed my mind.*

5   *Noggin the Nog* – a television series (1959–1965), and illustrated books (1965–1977), by Oliver Postgate and Peter Firmin. See glossary: *Noggin the Nog.*
6   Himmler believed the mission of the SS to be 'acting as the vanguard in overcoming Christianity and restoring a Germanic way of living' in preparation for the conflict between humans and 'subhumans'. See glossary: *Himmler, Heinrich Luitpold.*

"I didn't wish to die in battle after butchering as many people as possible so that I could feast in Valhalla – the Slaughter Hall. Feasting after a jolly longship journey in the North Atlantic was my idea of fun. I just loved the imagery – and, in the end, it led me to Vajrayana."

"Your joking!" Lydia almost squawked.

"Alas, no" I replied with mock solemnity. *"When I found two books on Tibet in the Junior School library I almost whooped 'This is a religion the Vikings would have liked!'…"*

I was interrupted by Lydia *"And how old were you then.?*

"About eight." PAUSE *"So, as you can see – my fascination was all in the realm of Art and creative imagination. The Vikings were theatre and sartorial exuberance to me when I was young – likewise Tibetan costume."* PAUSE *"Of course, the 'religious attraction' lay in the fact that Vajrayana was a religion that centred on kindness – but had no God, as an uncreated-creator. I'd been an atheist since the age of five – through the example of the parents of my first girlfriend. They were humanist atheists—extremely kind and open minded—and I was deeply impressed by them."*

At that moment a fellow came up and told me that Akong Rinpoche wished to see me. It seemed evident that it was more-or-less mandatory… so I apologised to Ani Chö-ying and the others – and left the table immediately and followed where the fellow led me. *'What could this portend?'* I wondered. Was my presence at Samŷe Ling causing too much consternation? Was I going to be asked to leave? That seemed quite possible – because various people had decided to dislike me.

I was led upstairs to a room. The fellow departed without a word. I knocked on the door with slight trepidation. Akong Rinpoche came to open the door himself, rather than calling for me to come in, as he had done when I had first met him. He told me—with a broad smile—that it was good to see me again – and that he was glad I had attended the Vajra Crown Ceremony in London. He'd seen me there. He'd watched me come forward and receive a protection cord. He noticed that I still wore it around my neck.

"Gyalwa Karmapa…" Akong Rinpoche began as soon as I'd taken my seat *"… asking 'why Pakshi Tröllö[7] and Dorje Bernakchen wangs not taking?'…"* He seemed to have a wry smile playing on his face.

"I was told I wasn't qualified" I replied — with perhaps—*also*—the slightest hint of wryness.

"No—ngöndro—completing?" he chuckled.

"Yes… Rinpoche… the shorter and longer Düd'jom gTér ngöndros; the Khandro Thug-thig,[8] and Tröma Nakmo[9] ngöndros." PAUSE *"I was told that I had to have completed the Chariot for Travelling the Path to Freedom Ngöndro[10] to take the Pakshi Tröllö wang. I was told that the ngöndros I'd completed didn't fit the requirements."*

Akong Rinpoche nodded, smiled, and said *"You, please, here waiting."*

Akong Rinpoche was gone for some few minutes. When he returned, he could not disguise the broadest of grins. He was known to be slightly dour and almost never to smile – but obviously something had happened that affected a striking change in his demeanour. He asked me to follow him. We left the room together and moved along the landing. I had some vague sense that I was in a play with an unknown script. It wasn't exactly surreal – but neither was it normal. We arrived at the door to another room. Akong Rinpoche paused for a moment. He tapped once on the door. Then we entered – or rather we exited from the fairly normal hallway, almost as if we were stepping out of a spacecraft onto the surface of the Moon.

---

7   *pa kShi gro lod /* པཀྵི་གྲོ་ལོད)

8   Khandro Thugthig *(mKha' 'gro'i thugs thig /* མཁའ་འགྲོའི་ཐུགས་ཐིག) *Khandro Heart Essence—Treasury of Accomplishments: Practice of the Profound Path of Yeshé Tsogyel* —revealed as Mind gTérma by Kyabjé Düd'jom Rinpoche Jig'drèl Yeshé Dorje in 1928. It is the main khandro practice of the Dud'jom gTérsar lineage, and one of the four major gTérma cycles of Düd'jom Jig'drèl Yeshé Dorje.

9   Tröma Nakmo *(khros ma nag mo /* ཁྲོས་མ་ནག་མོ */Krodhakali)* /he Black Wrathful Mother.

10 Phag-lam Drö-pa'i Shing-ta *('phags lam bGrod pa'i shing rTa)* the principal Karma Kagyüd ngöndro.

385

On the 20th of July, 1969 Apollo 11—with Neil Armstrong and Buzz Aldrin aboard— landed on the Moon. Neil Armstrong stepped onto the lunar surface first – and Buzz Aldrin joined him 19 minutes later. They spent about two hours together outside the spacecraft, and collected almost 50 lbs of lunar material to bring back to the Earth. What would I bring back to Earth from this sojourn on the immaculate Moon? Neil Armstrong's first step on the Moon was broadcast worldwide live on television. He said *"One small step for man; one giant leap for mankind."*

It had been like that when I met Kyabjé Düd'jom Rinpoche for the first time – although I would have said '*One brief quotidian interlude for Düd'jom Rinpoche – one giant aeon for Ngakpa Chögyam.*'

Be that as it may, I was suddenly aware that I was in the presence of Gyalwa Karmapa. I performed three prostrations. Gyalwa Karmapa indicated that I should be seated on a pile of cushions. I was glad of the height of the cushions as my legs have never been good for anything other than climbing hills. Sitting cross legged was never easy or comfortable for more than a few hours – and lotus posture[11] was more-or-less impossible.

Gyalwa Karmapa commenced with a mock frown – and Akong Rinpoche translated. *"His Holiness saying: I am Akong asking 'Inji ngakpa on wang list?' Akong 'no' saying. Then asking 'Why Inji ngakpa not wangs wanting?' Akong not knowing"* he laughed. *"Akong saying 'I don't know…' "* he repeated and laughed again. Akong Rinpoche was equally amused *"Then telling 'You quickly finding! You asking: why Inji ngakpa not wangs wanting!'"*

Gyalwa Karmapa obviously found the whole incident highly amusing. *"Too bad. Too bad. Düd'jom Rinpoche, my vajra brother. How his ngöndro not qualifying? How permission not giving when you are Düd'jom Rinpoche's disciple – and Düd'jom Rinpoche my vajra brother?"* PAUSE *"So. What yidam practising?"*

"The Düd'jom gTér Tröma Nakmo, Rinpoche."

---

11 Pema'i kyil-trung *(pad ma'i sKyil krung)*

Gyalwa Karmapa shook his head in consternation. *"O yah. Too bad. Too bad. Düd'jom Rinpoche vajra brother. How Düd'jom Rinpoche's yidam not qualifying?"* he laughed. *"Answering not necessary…"* PAUSE *"… anyway… sometimes people really too stupid becoming… Yong-lé Min'gyür Dorje is Nyingma Ngakpa. You also Nyingma ngakpa. No other qualification necessary."*

Gyalwa Karmapa then went on to tell me about gTértön Yong-lé Min'gyür Dorje – and as he spoke, I noticed the way he seemed to glow. It was as if he was super-saturated with colour to the extent that it spilled out into the room. I wondered if it was merely the effect of the sunlight – but it wasn't particularly bright and the light from the window was nothing out of the ordinary.

"Even though Nyingma gTérma; Yong-lé Min'gyür Dorje is Chö-ying Dorje [12] *offering – so this is how Lord of gTérma becoming."*

Yong-lé Min'gyür Dorje also gave Chö-ying Dorje the Dorje Bernakchen protector. At this time, he envisioned the kyil'khor of Karma Pakshi with Guru Rinpoche above Karma Pakshi as the central yidam with Tamdrin[13] and other yidams surrounding him. The Karma Pakshi practice is a Lama'i Naljor of various stages explained in accordance with Mahamudra in the Kagyüd Tradition – but the form of the Karma Pakshi Lama'i Naljor is explained according to Dzogchen. This is because Yong-lé Min'gyür Dorje revealed this practice as a Dzogchen master. Mahamudra and Dzogchen are not different in result – it is only the method that is different. Ultimately, they are the same.

"Now you must know there is only one Guru Rinpoche – but how many forms does he manifest?"

---

12 The 10th Karmapa *Chö-ying Dorje.*
13 Tamdrin *(rTa mGrin /* རྟ་མགྲིན་ */ Hayagriva)* is the wrathful manifestation of Chenrézigs *(sPyan ras gZigs / Avalokiteshvara)* who embodies nondual speech. He is mainly red in colour and with a horse head protruding from his crown. Hayagriva is one of the eight principal yidams of Kagyèd in which he is referred to as Lotus-Speech *(pad ma gSung /* པད་གསུང་ *).*

"Many..." I replied *"... but there are eight famous forms of Padmakara.*[14]*"*

"Can you name them?"

"Yes, Rinpoche. Pema Gyalpo, Pema Jung-né, Shakya Seng-gé, Nyima 'ö-Zér, Ögyen Tso-kye Dorje Chang, Seng-gé Dradog, Lo-den Chog-sré, and Dorje Tröllö."

"Yah—good—you are well knowing... and so... each form different name having. Düsum Khenpa [15] *manifested 16 times and each manifestation different name having – yet, all Karmapas same. Maybe—now—you, which aspect of Guru Rinpoche is Karma Pakshi, asking?"*

In this respect Karma Pakshi is Dorje Tröllö – because Dorje Tröllö's wrath is indivisible from Karma Pakshi. There are many gTértöns and many gTérmas – but the gTérma of Yong-lé Min'gyür Dorje is Karma Pakshi as Dorje Tröllö. So, you must understand that Karma Pakshi, Dorje Tröllö, and Yong-lé Min'gyür Dorje are not essentially different.

Yong-lé Min'gyür Dorje lived during the times of my 10th and 11th incarnations and contributed immensely to the Kagyüds. It happened—due to the evil of politics—that the Karma Kagyüd were split apart in the region of U-Tsang. This was because the central and northern provinces of Tibet were fighting with each other. In this troubled time the gTérma of Yong-lé Min'gyür Dorje was very important for the Kagyüds. Its practise strengthened the Kagyüd lineages in Kham, enabling practitioners to turn back enemies and bring peace. This is why this gTérma did not become extinct.

"gTértön Min'gyür Dorje, Namchö gTérmas cycle revealing" Gyalwa Karmapa commented. *"Did you know he emanation of Shu-bu Palgyi Seng-gé...?"*

---

14 See glossary: *eight manifestations.*
15 Düsum Khyenpa *(dus gSum mKhyen pa / དུས་གསུམ་མཁྱེན་པ་)* *Knower of the Three Times* – the 1st Karmapa, 1110–1193) disciple of Gampopa.

"Yes Rinpoche. Shu-bu Palgyi Seng-gé was of one of the ministers of Trisong Détsen and one of the 25 disciples of Guru Rinpoche."

"Good! Shud-bu Palgyi Seng-gé meaning: Glorious Lion form Shud-bu. Accomplishment attaining through Phurba and Mamo. Ha! He boulders splitting and river with phurba dividing!" PAUSE *"Maybe you are also with phurba similar performing!"* he laughed. *"Yong-lé Min'gyür Dorje's long-ku form is Chana Dorje* [16] *embodiment of Buddha's power, strength and ability."*

He incarnated as Shakyamuni Buddha's disciple Niruddha – and he had the most power of miracle among the disciples. In Tibet—as well as Shud-bu Palgyi Seng-gé—he was Mutri Tsenpo, the eldest son of King Trisong Détsen, the Dharma ruler prince, who was one of the twenty-five disciples. Then he was Rig'dzin Gö-kyi Dem Tru-çan,[17] who appeared as one of the regents of Padmasambhava. In the centre of Tibet—and four directions— there were gTértöns bearing the name Lingpa – and each had the nature of the five Buddha families. Rig'dzin Gö-kyi Dem Tru-çan was the central gTértön. As to those gTértöns in the four intermediate directions – he was gTérchen Dorje Lingpa[18] in the East, Pema Lingpa[19] in the West, and Zhigpo Lingpa,[20] lord of the intermediate directions. He was also Rinchen Phüntsog[21] and Rig'dzin Ja'tsön Nyingpo.[22]

---

16 Vajrapani – the Lord of Secrets.
17 Rig'dzin Gö-kyi Dem Tru-çan *(rig 'dzin rGod kyi lDem 'phru can, 1337–1408).*
18 gTérchen Dorje Lingpa *(gTer chen rDo rJe gLing pa, 1346–1405)*
19 Pema Lingpa *(Pad ma gLing pa, 1450–1521)*
20 Zhigpo Lingpa *(zhig po gLing pa, 1524–1583).* Zhigpo Lingpa is one of three names given to gTértön Cho'gyür Lingpa. The three names refer to Cho'gyür Lingpa's activities vis-à-vis base, path, and fruition. Zhigpo Lingpa relates to his fruitional activities. Cho'gyür Lingpa was a contemporary of Jamyang Khyentsé Wangpo and Jamgön Kongtrül and is regarded as one of the major gTértöns. In a previous incarnation he was Sang-gyé Lingpa, who revealed the Lama Gongdu.
21 Gyalwang Rinchen Phüntsog (1509–1557) was the son of Ten-pé Gyaltsen, the youngest brother of Gyalwang Kunga Rinchen (1475–1527), the 16th Drigung Kagyüd throne-holder. Before his birth, Kunga Rinchen announced Gyalwang Rinchen Phüntsog would be the reincarnation of Mahasiddha Hungkara.
22 Rig'dzin Ja'tsön Nyingpo (1585–1656) discoverer of the Könchok Chidu.

Of the incarnations of the 25 disciples of Guru Rinpoche there were 21 major gTértöns with the name Nuden – and the first incarnation of Yong-lé Min'gyür Dorje was among them because the 10th Karmapa, Chö-ying Dorje, gave him the name Rig'dzin Min'gyür Dorje Drakpo Nuden Tsal.

"25 disciples of Guru Rinpoche naming possible?"[23]

"I am not confident Rinpoche – but I can try... Yeshé Tsogyel, Mandarava... but maybe she was not one of the 25 because she never went to Tibet."

"Yes – but still disciple."

"Trisong Détsen, Dri'mèd Shényèn, Ba-gor Vairotsana [24] *... and of course Shu-bu Palgyi Seng-gé, Palgyi Yeshé, Palgyi Seng-gé, 'o-Drèn Palgyi Wangchuk..."* PAUSE *"... there are many more... but I must think for a moment."*

Gyalwa Karmapa smiled at me as I sat thinking. There were a few names that came to mind but I wanted to gather at least a dozen before I commenced. *"Ah... yes... Khyéchung Lotsa who communicated with the birds of the air..."*

"O yah!" Gyalwa Karmapa laughed. *"This one twice meeting. Already Düd'jom Rinpoche meeting. Kyabjé Düd'jom Rinpoche is incarnation of Khyéchung Lotsa – but later one other Lama meeting who also same line coming."* [25]

23 See glossary: 25 *disciples*.
24 Ba-gor Vairotsana *(ba gor bai ro tsa na)* was a translator whom Guru Rinpoche sent to Dhahena, India, to study with Shri Singha. He taught him in secret and entrusted Vairotsana with the task of propagating the Dzogchen sem-dé and Dzogchen long-dé in Tibet. He is one of the three main masters to bring the Dzogchen teachings to Tibet. The other two were Guru Rinpoche and Dri'mèd Shényèn. He was a major lineage holder of rTsa rLung trül'khor – the psycho-physical yogas of Anuyoga.
25 It became evident that Gyalwa Karmapa knew I would study later with 'Khordong gTérchen Tulku Chhi'mèd Rig'dzin Rinpoche.

This was extraordinary by nature of being ordinary – or by being delivered in such a matter-of-fact way. There were people who had existed for centuries, or for two thousand five hundred years – and they criss-crossed through time like a kaleidoscopic pageant of boundlessly beneficial beauty. Every moment—in every place on the Earth—was a possible intersection. Meeting Papa Legba at the Crossroads had come to nothing – but here I was, at a multidimensional crossroads that was vast and intricate. That Ngakpa Chögyam was part of this intricacy was almost intellectually incomprehensible. There was a sensation. There was a appearance of recognition – but it was entirely elusive. It seemed that it would be a serious error of judgement to build anything on such feelings of recognition. If anything was to shape itself into a comprehensible stream, it would happen of itself or not. To attempt to concretise anything in this area of experience would lead merely to fatuous fantasies.

"Nyag Yeshé Zhö-nu who drew water out of rock; Sogpo Lhapal who was a great blacksmith yogi; Ma Rinchen Chog was able to live by eating rock…" PAUSE *"Of course there was Nubchen Sang-gyé Yeshé who saved the gö kar chang lo'i dé by displaying the apparition of a scorpion 9 times the size of a yak above the head of King Langdarma."*

Gyalwa Karmapa laughed about this and nodded with evident pleasure.

"Then…" I continued *"Könchog Jung-né, Nub Namkha'i Nyingpo who flew in the sky and vanished into the sky on his death; Yudra Nyingpo who was a master of Dzogchen sem-dé; Na nam Zhang Yeshé De was a phurba master who had the siddhi of flight; and… and then… I think that is all I can remember Rinpoche."* PAUSE *"Ah yes! There was the brother—or father, some say—of Yeshé Tsogyel whose name was Kharchen Palgyi Wangchuk."*

"O yah!" Gyalwa Karmapa smiled. *"Maybe this one also meeting. Realisation through Dorje Phurba attaining. Very great Lama. Very powerful. Maybe in Bhutan finding. You must one day Bhutan travelling. Maybe there meeting possible."* PAUSE *"More siddhas coming?"*

"The last one who comes to mind is Lhalung Palgyi Dorje.[26] *It is strange that I thought of him last – because I know more about him than the others."*

"Lhalung Palgyi Dorje" Gyalwa Karmapa grinned *"born in Dromtö Gungmoche* [27] *north of River Kyichu* [28] *and Lhalung, was his clan name. Yab – some also 'born in Lhodrak, in Lhalung', saying."* Gyalwa Karmapa nodded, as if weighing up different ways of concerning the matter. *"Some 'family name Taknya Zang'* [29] *also saying. But anyway, he was a warrior and China fighting – but disillusioned becoming and religion needing. So what next knowing?"*

"Lhalhung Palgyi Dorje went to Samŷe [30]*"* I launched in again *"and was given monastic ordination by Dri'mèd Shényèn."* [31]

"Yah" Gyalwa Karmapa smiled *"but later ngakpa becoming – otherwise dröl* [32] *for Langdarma not possible performing. He accompanied by brother Rabjor Wangpo Tsunpa Pelyang.*[33] *Then many empowerments from Guru Rinpoche receiving."*

Gyalwa Karmapa observed me silently in a beneficent manner – but it seemed obvious that he wanted me to say more. *"He received the Dzogchen sem-dé and Dzogchen long-dé* [34] *from Dri'mèd Shényèn – and gave these transmissions to Nyag Yeshé Zhönnu."* PAUSE *"So... Lhalung Palgyi Dorje practised in Dribkyi Karmo* [35] *valley, where he attained the ability to pass freely through rocks, and fly from mountain to mountain."* PAUSE *"Of course... as you said—Rinpoche—he liberated Langdarma through the rite of dröl with a bow and arrow."*

---

26 Lhalung Palgyi Dorje *(lha lung dPal gyi rDo rJe /* ཕུ་ལུང་དཔལ་གྱི་རྡོ་རྗེ།*)* the Lama who rid Tibet of the apostate Langdarma in 842 AD.

27 *'brom sTod gung mo che*

28 *sKyid chu*

29 *sTag nya bZang*

30 *bSam yas*

31 Dri'mèd Shényèn *(dri 'med bShes gNyen)* was an Indian Buddhist Master. See glossary: *Dri'mèd Shényèn.*

32 *sGrol / sGrol bak* – to free, deliver, set free, liberate, through destroying, dispatching, or terminating existence.

33 *rab 'byor dBang po bTsun pa dPal dByangs*

34 *rDzogs chen sems dDe / rDzogs chen kLong sDe*

35 *grib kyi dKar mo*

"*O yah! Lhahung Palgyi Dorje—very—powerful.*" PAUSE "*Yah…*" he continued with a woeful shake of his head "*this Langdarma – this is Tri U-Dum Tsen* [36] *— very bad actions making.*" Suddenly I was aware of an aspect of Gyalwa Karmapa I had not witnessed before. It was as if night had fallen. It didn't become darker – so night falling didn't represent anything in the world of my ordinary senses. Those were merely words I used at the time to describe something that occurred. It was momentary however, so I had no time to make sense of the impression. Then suddenly the room seemed full of light again – even though nothing had changed. "*So… now, with Lhalung Palgyi Dorje explanation continuing.*"

"*Lhalung Palgyi Dorje was living in a cave called Drag Yèrpa* [37] *when he became aware, through clairvoyance, that Langdarma was persecuting Buddhism. He decided immediately that it absolutely necessary to save religion. So performed dröl for Langdarma – and Langdarma died.*"

Gyalwa Karmapa paused for a moment "*You know dröl meaning?*"

"*Yes Rinpoche – the rite of physical dispatchment for someone whose life is causing great harm to others and great harm also to themselves. It gives an opportunity for a more positive re-birth.*"

Gyalwa Karmapa nodded with a smile—when what I had answered had been translated—and asked "*Now more saying?*"

"*Yes Rinpoche. Through dispatchment by dröl, Langdarma was prevented from accumulating the terrible negative imprints in harming Buddhism. Lhalung Palgyi Dorje performed dröl for Langdarma whilst engaged in gar'cham – and this he accomplished with a bow and arrow that he'd concealed in the wide sleeves of his gar'cham costume. He then fled on a white horse… or rather, a white horse he stained black with charcoal. He wore a reversible costume too. It was white on one side and black on the other.*"

36 *khri u dum brTsan* – the brother of Tri Tsug Détsen *(khri gTsug lde brTsan)* better known as Ralpa-çan *(ral pa can)*. Ralpa-çan expanded the Tibetan Empire to its greatest extent and was a great patron of Buddhism. Langdarma banished monks and closed monasteries.
37 *brag yer pa*

"Then, crossing the river in the direction of his escape, his horse was washed clean of the charcoal – and Lhalung Palgyi Dorje reversed his costume to display the white side. By this means he escaped undetected as no one was looking for a white robed rider on a white horse. That is all I know, other than that he manifested rainbow body."

Gyalwa Karmapa beamed at me and added *"Ya-tsan! Very well remembering! Now more coming – so, many carefully notes writing."* PAUSE *"His incarnations were Pema Norbu,[38] Chakri Rig'dzin Nyima Drakpa,[39] and the Zurmang Trungpa Tulkus.[40] Important incarnation also in Bhutan coming."*

At this point Gyalwa Karmapa ceased speaking audibly. He did not whisper—and his lips did not move—but I was aware that he was continuing to communicate. I seemed to be experiencing transmission—almost as I had experienced it with Aro Lingma—when I understood but didn't understand what I had understood. That had also occurred with Kyabjé Düd'jom Rinpoche. There was a felt-sensation of knowingness – but no language with which to express it. Usually when silences occurred with Lamas, I took it as the sign that I should leave. Akong Rinpoche however, was also sitting, obviously in mediation – so I simply sat. To rest nonconceptually was extremely simple in that setting with Gyalwa Karmapa and Akong Rinpoche.

There was a sudden—yet peaceful—widening of Gyalwa Karmapa's eyes. There was a sense of intense joy in him as he recommenced his discourse. *"gTértön Drukdra Dorje,[41] incarnation of Lhalung Palgyi Dorje in Bhutan."* Then he conferred with Akong Rinpoche for a while and Akong Rinpoche explained *"His Holiness says: dates of birth and passing not knowing – but 18th Century living. Maybe you must ask and find out when you are Nepal again travelling. Then when possible – must Bhutan going. Much expense, so not soon.*

38 *pad ma nor bu* (1679–1757) of Palyul Gompa *(dPal yul dGon).*
39 *chags ri rig 'dzin nyi ma grags pa* (1647–1710)
40 *zur mang drung pa sPrul sku* – starting with Kunga Gyeltsen *(zur mang drung pa kun dGa' rGyal mTshan).*
41 *gTer sTon 'brug sGra rDo rJe*

"Maybe when my age coming." [42] He looked pensive and then revised his statement *"No. Maybe older… maybe after full cycle of years reaching – but not so long after."* [43]

gTértön Drukdra Dorje was a major gTértön who prophesied the birth and life of the Fourth King of Bhutan.[44] His prophecy was made when he was in retreat in the mountains between Bhutan and Tibet. Guru Rinpoche appeared to him in person and gave voice to the prophecy.

gTértön Drukdra Dorje—as prophesied by Guru Rinpoche—travelled through Chumo-phug, Paro, rTa-mGrin Nyé and Tsélung Nyé, Thimphu, Passang Ama'i Nyé, Chukha, and many miraculous places in Bhutan. He propagated Vajrayana by revealing many different gTérma and communicating opportune prophecies for the great benefit of Bhutan.

Gyalwa Karmapa said that he knew nothing of the incarnation of gTértön Drukdra Dorje – other than that he was a gTértön.[45] He then said that he had heard of no incarnation as yet of this gTértön – but that I might come to hear of him if I went to Bhutan. I might even meet him if I lived long enough. *"This you must remembering – and Bhutan going. Maybe not soon. Maybe when older. Maybe when students having. Then much value for Vajrayana lineage coming – so always remembering."* PAUSE *"Now… nothing more knowing and nothing more saying possible."* [46]

---

42 The 16th Gyalwa Karmapa was 51 years old in 1975.

43 A full cycle of years in the Tibetan calendar is 60 years. I was 60 in 2011 and went to Bhutan for the first time in 2019, so Gyalwa Karmapa's prediction proved correct. Khandro Déchen went to Bhutan in 2017 at a time when I was unable to travel to the East.

44 See glossary: *prophecy of gTértön Drukdra Dorje.*

45 gTértön Gé-chéla lived during the 19th and 20th Centuries. He was born in Tibet but left early in his life to settle at Gé-du with his sangyum, son, and daughter. He revealed some gTérma, established gompas, and propagated Vajrayana.

46 Kyabjé Trülku Ögyen Dro'dül Thrin-lé Künkyab—the 3rd incarnation of gTértön Drukdra Dorje. See glossary: *Ögyen Dro'dül Thrin-lé Künkyab.*

I'd been taking notes all the way through – but I had to work quite hard with what followed.

Gyalwa Karmapa began *"Then, Denma Tsémang fast writing – of all disciples most skilled."* Here Gyalwa Karmapa laughed heartily *"Like Ngakpa Chögyam must very fast writing!"*

Denma Tsémang's style of calligraphy has continued to the present day. Having received transmission from Padmasambhava, he achieved perfect recall of all teachings. He was the scribe who wrote down many gTérmas, including the Eight Great Drüpthabs of the Nyingma Tradition. Then Nanam Dorje Düd'jom, who was one of Trisong Détsen's ministers, was sent to Nepal to invite Padmasambhava to Tibet. He could fly with the speed of the wind and pass through solid rock. Rig'dzin Go'dem[47] and Lé-rab Lingpa were amongst his incarnations. This Lé-rab Lingpa is also called gTértön Sogyal. Gyalwa Karmapa shook his head at that point and said *"One very good tulku coming – in Tibet living. Jig'mèd Phüntsog Jung-né Rinpoche was great gTértön – many gTérmas discovering.[48] Also, one other gTértön Sogyal tulku in Bhutan coming [49] — name Gendün Rinchen Rinpoche. Great Lama – great meditator and scholar. There now one young one coming [50] – but not real incarnation of gTértön Sogyal. No study—no retreat—only name 'Sogyal' having. Only ordinary schools going. No need more speaking – maybe never Sogyal Lakar meeting.[51] Maybe better not meeting."*

---

47 See glossary: *Rig'dzin Godemchen Ngödrub Gyaltsen*
48 Jig'mèd Phüntsog Jung-né Rinpoche *(jigs 'med phun tshogs 'byung gNas* 1933–2004) from Sér-ta. His family were nomads. At the age of five he was recognised as an incarnation of Lérab Lingpa *(las rab gLing pa* 1856–1926). He was also known also as Nyala Sogyal *(nyag bLa bSod rGyal)* and gTértön Sogyal *(gTer sTon bSod rGyal)*. Jigme Phuntsok was one of the most influential Nyingma Lamas in contemporary Tibet. He was also an extraordinary gTértön who revealed many texts in Tibet, Bhutan, and China.
49 See glossary: *Gendün Rinchen.*
50 The 16th Gyalwa Karmapa was referring to Sogyal Lakar. See glossary: *Sogyal Lakar.*
51 See glossary: *Sogyal Lakar.*

Gyalwa Karmapa talked for a little about Jig'mèd Phüntsog Jungné Rinpoche and Gendün Rinchen Rinpoche – but told me I was not likely to meet them, unless I went to Tibet or Bhutan.

Lasum Gyalwa Changchub was one of the first seven Tibetans to receive full ordination as a monk by Shantarakshita. He visited India several times and translated many texts. He attained the siddhi of flight through the sky. Rig'dzin Künzang Shérab, the founder of Palyül in Kham, is one of his incarnations.

Nganlam Gyalwa Chöyang attained accomplishment through Tamdrin and later incarnated as the first Karmapa. He was born into the Ngan-lam clan. It is said that he kept his vows with perfect purity. He practised in solitude and reached realisation. As well as the Karmapa tulkus he has incarnations in the Nyingma Tradition – such as Chag'düd Tülku Rinpoche and Tülku Sang-ngak Rinpoche.

Dré Gyalwa'i Lödrö was an attendant of Trisong Détsen who also became one of the first Tibetans to take ordination. He became a great translator and attained accomplishment after receiving transmission from Hungkara[52] in India. He lived to a very great age.

Kawa Paltsèg made important contributions to the Nyingma Gyüdbum. He was also among the first seven Tibetan monks ordained by Shantarakshita.[53]

---

52 Hungkara (ཧཱུྃ་ཀ་ར / ཧཱུྃ་མཛད / *Hung ka ra* or *Hung mDzad*) – one of the Eight Rig'dzins of India. He received the Yangdak Trakthung *(yag dag khrag 'thung / Visuddha Héruka)* Tantra from the Kagyèd cycle. Hungkara's country of birth is Nga Thubchen *(nga thub chen).* He received empowerment into the Kagyèd from Guru Rinpoche and his consort Kalasiddhi.

53 Shyiwa Tsho *(zhi ba 'tsho* / ཞི་བ་འཚོ *Shantarakshita* / 720–791), was a great Indian Master and abbot of the Buddhist university of Nalanda. He was invited to Tibet by King Trisong Détsen where he founded Samyé. He worked extensively to establish Buddhism in Tibet – but malignant indigenous forces were hostile to Buddhism. Neither Trisong Détsen, nor Shyiwa Tsho could subdue them – so they implored Guru Rinpoche to come to Tibet.

Ba Yeshé Yang was a translator and scribe for transcribing the gTérmas of Guru Rinpoche. He was an accomplished yogi, able to fly like a bird in the sky.

Nyang Ting'dzin Zangpo attained the rainbow body of great transference. In the Vima Nyingthig lineage, it is written that he invited Dri'mèd Shényèn to teach in Tibet. He was a court Lama during the reigns of Trisong Dé-tsen, Tri-dé Songtsen, and Tri Ralpa-çan.

"So… anyway… Yong-lé Min'gyür Dorje, learned and highly accomplished master becoming – and then later life, Mahasiddha lifestyle following." Gyalwa Karmapa suddenly laughed *"Maybe Chögyam also Mahasiddha becoming!"* This was such a funny statement Akong Rinpoche and I also started laughing. The laughter was unusual however. It created a highly relaxed atmosphere. Maybe Gyalwa Karmapa had seen that I had grown somewhat tense from concentrated note-taking? Maybe he had knowledge of what had occurred the last time I had come to Samŷe Ling? That was a strange thought.

I had the strong sense in which Gyalwa Karmapa was similar to Kyabjé Düd'jom Rinpoche in being able to *see into me and know my history*. To say someone could become a Mahasiddha has various meanings. One is the epitome of praise. Another is derogatory. Lamas with no realisation—who acted in a wild, irregular, unconventional manner—were sometimes described as 'mahasiddhas' but no compliment is intended. Yet another meaning is 'the playful or teasing remark' which is merely intended to show kindliness on the part of the Lama toward a student. There was no severity in Gyalwa Karmapa's tone or expression – so I assumed the third meaning. He then continued teaching with no reference to my 'escapades'.

"Ba Yeshé Yang many to path of liberation bringing – many who before, vows are breaking."

He subjugated evil influences and obstructing forces that harm the teachings. He bound the Nine Demon Brothers under oath – as well as their retinues, the malignant forces that wreak disaster in the world. Yong-lé Min'gyür Dorje's other gTérma teachings included the Peaceful and Wrathful Pema Dorje and the longevity drüpthab known as Thab-shé Kha-jor.[54]

"gTérma of Yong-lé Min'gyür Dorje three volumes consisting – Karma Pakshi Drüpthab containing. Also cycle of Dorje Tröllö, and all manifestations of Guru Rinpoche containing." PAUSE *"Then… Dorje Bernakchen—black-cloaked one—dwarf [55] manifestation Mahakala. Dorje Bernakchen nine robes of black silk with black embroidery wearing. Copper crescent-shaped butcher's flaying knife in right hand holding. Skull-cup with oceans blood-brimming in left hand holding…"* PAUSE *"… and now you everything well knowing… for tonight and tomorrow."* PAUSE *"I am feeling… 7th incarnation of gTértön Min'gyür Dorje already incarnation taking. Maybe soon finding…"*

At this point I was somewhat exhausted from writing – but extremely glad about the time I had spent learning the rudiments of Tibetan spelling. I had not expected the equivalent of a university degree in Nyingma history. I was profoundly grateful and wonderfully tired. However, no matter how tired I was – I would have sat there for days taking notes if Gyalwa Karmapa had continued to supply me with information. His generosity was overwhelming.

Gyalwa Karmapa was silent for some moments – before continuing *"Chögyam Trungpa Rinpoche silent sitting at Samyé Ling teaching. What silent sitting practising?"*

"I practise the Four Naljors, Rinpoche."

"Oh yah… I will speak of this. Four Naljors like Formless Mahamudra.[56]"

54 The Coital Union of Method and Knowledge.
55 Zugpo té-po *(gZugs po gTe po).*
56 Tsé-çig *(rTse gCig)* – one pointed; Trö-dral *(sPros 'bral)* – freedom from conceptual elaboration; ro-çig *(ro gCig)* – one taste; and gom'mèd *(sGom 'med)* – non-meditation.

"Tsé-chig same shi-nè; trö-dral same lha-tong; ro-çig same nyi'mèd; and, gom-mèd same lhundrüp. Now meaning explaining. Tsé-chig 'one pointed' meaning —mind fixed—not with thought moving. Thoughts all let go—vanishing—no trace leaving. Trö-dral meaning freedom from conceptual elaboration. No distinctions—no observer—just what is there. Ro-çig meaning 'one taste' of emptiness and form – this is when tse-çig and trö-dral are one taste of same experience. Then gom'mèd meaning 'no meditation anymore'. Gom is meditation and 'mèd is 'not'. This is when meditation and life same." PAUSE *"Now we together sitting."*

We sat together for some unaccountable time – and finally Gyalwa Karmapa smiled at me and said *"Tsé-çig."* PAUSE *"Trö-dral."* PAUSE *"Ro-çig."* Then with a gesture of his hand that bade me stand up and leave he concluded *"Gom 'mèd"* and I stood, bowed, and left the room.

24

going beyond boundaries

I stepped backward slowly, from the room – keeping my face toward Gyalwa Karmapa. He gazed at me with a broad smile – as if intrigued by my reverse progress across the room toward the door. Akong Rinpoche was holding the door open for me. It was a wrench to pull myself away. I had spent an astonishing time with Gyalwa Karmapa. Suddenly—almost unexpectedly—I found myself walking with unaccustomed grace down the landing to the head of the stairs.

I descended the stairs as if every step brimmed with meaning – yet the *meaning* was simply *space*. I went to sit in the library – where eventually Ani Chö-ying found me. *"I hear you've been with Gyalwa Karmapa most of the afternoon…"* she asked excitedly *"what happened?"*

I explained in as much detail as she wished *"… and then, Gyalwa Karmapa ended with what must have been a transmission of Formless Mahamudra…"* [1]

"The pointing out instructions[2]?" Ani Chö-ying gasped.

A moment of silence *"Yes."* PAUSE *"However – please don't mention it to anyone else… because… well, I don't really feel I should have mentioned it at all – only I trust you… and wanted you to know — because you were so kind – y'know, trying to be helpful about what happened this morning."*

Ani Chö-ying was delighted on my behalf *"Well it looks as if your patience with things and your… acceptance, worked out well. A lot of people would have made a big fuss about it. Maybe that would have got you into the empowerments if you'd tried that – but it wouldn't have got you a whole afternoon with Gyalwa Karmapa and all that teaching on gTértön Min'gyür Dorje. That was amazing… and… maybe there's a lesson there… if some people around here can learn something from it."*

---

1 Tshan'mè chag-chen *(mTshan 'med phyag chen / formless mahamudra)*. See glossary: *mahamudra*.

2 Pointing-out instructions *(ngo-trö kyi dampa / ngo sProd kyi gDams pa)*.

"Errrm… about my patience and acceptance… it's all external I assure you. The only reason I didn't make a big fuss was because…"

"… you don't want to come across as a lower primate" Ani Chö-ying interrupted with a chuckle. *"I remember – but, whatever the reason, the end result is good. It's good to have self-control too."*

"Well… as I can't control anyone else – it'll have to do for the time being."

Ani Chö-ying laughed and shook her head *"You really do like to turn things into humour don't you."*

"Whenever I can – or rather, whenever I want to dissemble and divert attention from something, or… whenever a situation is bad." PAUSE *"I find humour… some sort of universal panacea."* PAUSE *"You could call humour the central Dharma message of Blues."*

"That's a novel idea – but you're going to have to explain that to me."

There was no one else in the library so I sang *"Got a handful of nickels, handful of dimes / Pocket full of nothing and no—body—seems to mind / Lawd you don't know, you don't know my mind / When you see me laughing – I'm laughing just to keep from crying."*

"You have quite a voice – have you ever sung in public? I mean – just to burst into song like that is quite unusual. But then you said earlier to Geraint that you'd been in a Blues band."

"Yes…" PAUSE *"I sang on stage… from* 1968 *to* 1972.*"* Then I told her a little about Savage Cabbage and my time as a solo Blues performer. Ani Chö-ying seemed intrigued that I'd had a whole other life apart from Art School and training as a ngakpa.

"It's interesting…" she mused *"to be able to see Dharma in Blues… and it makes me think that one could see Dharma anywhere if one was attuned to Dharma."*

"Yes… I tend to see everything as interconnected… and—although I don't place other things on a par with Dharma—I see no reason that the Dharma-value they can offer isn't also Dharma." PAUSE

"Maybe... like... Honi soit qui mal y pense [3] *... but reworded as 'Dharma is to whomsoever sees it as Dharma'."*

"I like that... it reminds me of 'pure vision' where you hear every sound as mantra and every form as the yidam."

"Yes... That sounds absolutely right – but I don't think I'd call my penchant of interconnectedness pure vision... it's just the way I've always seen things." PAUSE *"I think that pure vision is maybe the fruitional stage of that."*

Ani Chö-ying looked thoughtful for a moment as if she was struggling with a puzzle. *"Yes... pure vision and all the different styles of perception... I have always found it slightly... frightening, the way we see what we see – and take it to be real. It's not so difficult when I think of being reborn as a pig and eating pig swill. If I were a pig, pig swill would be acceptable food. That's not hard to understand – but the differences in the human realm are far more convoluted and contradictory."*

"Yes indeed" I replied. *"How does one understand a racist, a paedophile – or the Moors Murderers?"* [4]

"Yes... that is as alien as imagining oneself as a shark or crocodile."

"Yes... both are almost prehistoric..." I commented with a shake of my head *"and both seem to kill as a normal impulse."*

"I've been thinking back to our lunchtime discussion on Nazi occultism..."

"Yes, thank you very much indeed for that – it was illuminating, in a rather dark way."

Then, as if I'd not commented she continued *"It was your reference to Vikings being what led to your interest in Vajrayana – and I was wondering about that from a psychological perceptive."*

I obviously had a wary look on my face at that point – so she changed tack *"Don't worry, I'm not about to psychoanalyse you."*

---

3   *Honi soit qui mal y pense – evil is, to whom thinks it evil.*
4   The Moors Murderers: Ian Brady and Myra Hindley committed murders with sexual abuse between 1963 and 1965, in the Manchester area. The victims were five young people aged between 10 and 17.

"You're more than welcome. I'd be interested."

"In your case I would not find it that easy – and so I doubt if you'd find it interesting."

"Why… would you find it difficult?"

"That's what I wanted to mention. I've been thinking about the animosity you've experienced in relation to Western Buddhists – and I think I've started to understand why some people dislike you." PAUSE *"Your early interest in Vikings being what led to your interest in Vajrayana – that would be jarring to people."*

"It's not something I ever mention – as far as I remember. I only mentioned it here because it came up in conversation – and it's not a secret."

"That is just one example of what might be incongruent about you to some people. There's your Easy Rider motorcycle, your history on stage as a Blues vocalist, your sense of humour – and probably other things I've not seen as yet. The point is, that these things would not be what they'd expect – and most people, however alternative or bohemian they may think they are, are afraid of what goes outside their boundaries…"

"Isn't 'going beyond boundaries' *central to Buddhism?"* I interrupted.

"Yes" she laughed *"but it depends on how the boundaries are defined. If you go beyond the wrong boundaries—or boundaries that had not previously been identified as boundaries—then, people find themselves lacking references by which they can understand you – or whomever."*

"Ah… That's interesting… that hadn't occurred to me. So…?"

"So, what happens is: you present people with paradoxes. You don't fit into 'conventional frameworks' or 'unconventional frameworks'. That's by no means a criticism. If anything, it's a sign of good psychological health. You see, I don't fit into the customary Western Kagyüd nun framework. I come from quite a conventional background and was never really part of the counter-culture. I enjoyed the music and wore some of the clothes – but nothing too extraordinary. So, I wasn't a rebel, and taking nun's robes wasn't an act of rebellion.

"That is probably why the other monks and nuns here, see me as an outsider."

"Maybe they see you as an outsider because they can't understand why you would want to converse with me."

"That—could—very easily be the answer… but for the fact that I arrived here over a week ago – and I sensed the distance even then. It was evident before you got here."

"Yes?" I enquired.

"Yes… now they avoid talking to me – but even before, they didn't know how to talk to me."

I assumed a quizzical expression and so she concluded *"Because I don't use the same language or give the same style of responses."*

"So—let me get this right—you're saying that they don't know how to talk to you – because you don't have the same language or responses."

"Yes. It's a subtle thing. It is similar to knowing that someone is French or German – even if their English is perfect. There are clues in emphasis and in slightly misplaced colloquialisms. Every sub-group has its jargon and topics on which there is consensus agreement. A sub-group member can always tell an outsider simply through the lack of a smile or nod when some idea is expressed."

"I see… That is a valuable insight." PAUSE *"So… how does that work in reverse? I mean, how is it that you don't feel alienated from the other monks and nuns – or do you feel alienated?"*

"No – I don't feel alienated by their mode of expression. I don't expect everyone to have the same communication style. Also, I know something of tribalism – and so I don't indulge in seeing difference as problematic. The higher your level of psychological health the more you can tolerate difference without feeling threatened by it. I'm not saying I have a high level of psychological health – but it's not so low as to be threatened by differences. In terms of feeling alienated though – they take care of that by not engaging me in conversation."

405

"Can you give me an example of healthy psychological functioning?"

"One example would be that the psychosocially healthiest politicians would be those on the moderate left of centre and moderate right of centre, who are able to socialise. It's the ones that vilify each other who are less psychosocially healthy."

"Ah yes – and those who demonise each other belong in the locked ward."

"Perhaps" she laughed. "But, the more you dislike people, simply because they're different, the less healthy you're likely to be."

*"This is fascinating... You see... I was—expecting—Western Buddhists to be like Foundation Year Art students. The fact **that** other Art students in Farnham neither fitted conventional nor unconventional frameworks was the norm. We didn't—expect—each other to be understandable. I think we all came from situations where we'd been the weirdos. We were probably used to being 'the odd ones out' – and thus, were unusually accepting. Of course, that all seemed to change on the degree course."*

"That would stand to reason because a new normalcy had become established – then there'd be the consequent expectations in terms of conformity to that new normalcy."

I was ever-so-slightly stunned by this. *"That... is ghoulish, if I can use such a word."*

"It's karmic vision."

"Yes—of course—so... why am I surprised?" PAUSE *"That should have been obvious to me."*

"Well, you took Art and I took Psychology – so I'm more likely to make that association than you would be... even though you seem quite psychologically astute." PAUSE *"The thing I wanted to mention however was the similarity between you and the people you described as 'little more than Satanists' – the people in Tintagel."*

That made smile *"Please do give me the list."*

"Well in terms of Nazi occultism – you have a German mother and you were fascinated by the Viking and the Norse Gods. The Nazi High command wanted to replace Christianity with the old Germanic gods. You rejected Christianity and wanted to take the same direction. That doesn't make you a Nazi—or even a Nazi sympathiser—but it displays 'some' similarity. That seeming similarity can unnerve people. The people in Tintagel had no interest in the Norse gods as far as you've told me – but their fascination with occult power is what caused me to tell you about Nazi occultism. The similarity there is the desire for power and for covert access to power. You practice Tröma Nakmo and are drawn to Lamas of obvious power – and even magical power. So, in some ways, you are quite similar to the couple in Tintagel—apart from the fact that you're not manipulative— and it's clear to me that that you're not seduced by the idea of power. You have obvious charisma – but you don't seem to use it at anyone's expense. You have a great deal of knowledge in terms of Vajrayana – but you don't browbeat people with it. You have highly unusual status by virtue of your robes – but you don't appear to be interested in employing that status to get anything for yourself over and above what anyone else can have."

"Right…" PAUSE *"… and that makes me a paradox?"*

"Yes."

"It's going to take me a while to digest that." PAUSE *"No… I can't really disagree with any of that – apart from the charisma. I'm not aware of having any charisma. I sometimes get 'Charismas Presence' on the 25th of December – but beyond that, zero."*

Ani Chö-ying—after laughing at my jest—shook her head slightly in disbelief at that statement – so I continued *"Well – I may have had some charisma on stage with the Savage Cabbage Blues Band. That's possible. – but that was more due to Ron and Steve being world-class musicians. I used to call Steve 'the Beethoven of Blues' and Ron 'the Mozart of Mojo' – so there was plenty of reflected glory."* PAUSE *"I suppose I got some admiration at school—the final two years in Virginia Water, that is— because I certainly got none in the previous establishment. The previous quasi-educational intuition only went as far as 'O Levels' and for 'A Levels' one had to find another opportunity.*

"However, the difference in schools was more a matter of people being friendly. I had no sense of any adulation or deference."

"You're—honestly—not aware of having charisma?" she asked – obviously attempting to be as gentle as possible.

"No..." PAUSE *"If I—had—charisma, wouldn't people be less inclined to be aggressive with me?"*

"Aggression is based on fear."

"Yes. So it is." PAUSE *"That's another thing that I should have known – and in fact, I do know it. I know it well from the elements. Fear and aggression – the Water Element. They can be transformed into mirror wisdom – nondual clarity."* PAUSE *"I see that I am going to have to apply what I've learnt."* PAUSE *"The thing is – I thought I—was—applying it."*

"That's my problem too!" Ani Chö-ying laughed. *"I'm not that wide awake and aware. It's always far easier to see these things in others than it is to see it in oneself—and—it's one of the factors that makes you different from the people in Tintagel. I doubt that—the man—at least, is unaware that he's threatening. He's probably pleased to be threatening – whereas you seem to do your best to be unthreatening. You take trouble to put people at their ease in conversation."*

I was silent for a few moments.

"Apart from the times when you're silent" she grinned.

"Sorry, it's just that you've given me a great deal to consider."

"Now, if you—were—a manipulator, you would have asked me why I was afraid of silences in conversation."

"Ooooh—that's eerie—that sounds just like the kind of comment that Gilbert Harris would make. Y'know, I think I should have taken psychology instead of Art – but then, the academic side would probably have been too difficult."

"I think you made the right choice. There's a lot in psychology that really isn't that fascinating. There's a great deal of rather pedestrian information – and the degree I took wasn't geared to how one might apply it in life circumstances. I think Dharma is what helped me make sense of my psychology degree rather than the other way round." PAUSE *"Do you mind if I play devil's advocate?"*

"Is that a track on 'Their Satanic Majesties Request'?" [5] I jested. *"But seriously – certainly you may."*

"Why do you have Nazi symbols on your mala?"

"If I were answering a stranger, I'd simply reply that I didn't have Nazi symbols on my teng-ar. I'd answer in that way because it would have been an aggressive question – and I don't let people get away with aggression. I prefer them to admit to it. I don't return the aggression – but I do suggest that they own it." PAUSE *"As—you—ask however, I'd not put you in the position of having to explain yourself."* PAUSE *" So my answer would be – it's not a Hakenkreuz. That is what the Nazi symbol was called."*

"I thought it was a swastika?"

"No – that is what the Allied Forces called it. The German word was Hakenkreuz, which means 'hooked cross'."

"Isn't 'Swastika' German?"

"No... Most English speakers think that – but Swastika is a Sanskrit word. The clockwise version is Swastika and the counter clockwise is Sauwastika. In Tibetan the word is Yungdrung,[6] which means changelessness – but the same spelling is used for both directions."

"But it's the same as the Nazi symbol."

"Again, no. The Nazi Hakenkreuz sits diamond-wise; turned at 45°. The Yundrung, Swastika—and every other version in every other culture that it appears—sit square. *Only the Nazi Hakenkreuz sits diamond-wise.*

---

5 *Their Satanic Majesties Request* – an album by the Rolling Stones, released in 1967. The album title is a play on the text 'Her Britannic Majesty requests' that appears inside British passports.

6 *g.yung drung*

409

"This symbol exists in almost all Eastern cultures. It's also a Celtic symbol – and it's used by many of the North American Indian Tribes.[7] I can't go so far as to say that only the Nazi Hakenkreuz is black, in a white circle, on a red ground – but I have never seen that colour combination on anything other than the Nazi Hakenkreuz."

"And the direction?"

"The Nazis could never quite decide which way it should turn…" PAUSE *"But in Tibet it turned both ways – and each had a specific meaning. The right turning Yungdrung represented the earth, male, and Mahamudra. The left turning Yungdrung represented the sky, female, and Dzogchen."*

"This explanation is Buddhist…"

"Yes" I uninterrupted.

"… but, I thought the Yungdrung was a Bon symbol?"

"So it is. In Bön it is the major symbol – and there it is used as the dorje is used in Vajrayana Buddhism. In Buddhist Vajrayana the Yungdrung is often seen on the drapes at the front of throne tables – in each corner around a double dorje. In Bön it means changeless or unchanging – and that is also what it means in Vajrayana Buddhism."

"Does it also have the same left turning and right turning meanings?"

"There—I'm sorry to say—I run out of information."

"But Bön would have Mahamudra or Dzogchen would it?"

"More of less the same as Buddhism – yes, and nine yanas like the Nyingmas."

"The same nine yanas?"

"No, but at the level of Mahamudra and Dzogchen they're extremely similar. All I know is that the Bön replace the first yana—the vehicle of the listeners —with shamanic practices.

7   See glossary: *yungdrung.*

"In David Snellgrove's book The Nine ways of Bön [8] he describes the nine vehicles of Bon [9] as being a fairly accurate picture of Buddhism in Tibet – as their first vehicle contains the extracurricular activities in which most Lamas engage."

"Can I ask what caused you to read about Bön when you're a Vajrayana Buddhist?"

This question made me smile. *"When I started reading about Vajrayana, there were so few books that I'd read anything I could find — even whacky travelogues like 'In the Hidden Land' by Henry Savage Landor."* [10]

This made Ani Chö-ying laugh and clap her hands together *"You've more-or-less created you own degree course!"*

"Well…" I demurred *"I'm not good at half measures… If you're going to do a thing – you may as well do it."*

"Can't fault that." PAUSE *"So… as my final devil's advocate question – don't you think the Nazi association makes it contentious and that it shouldn't be displayed because of its horrific association with Hitler?"*

"No. I think that this is all the more reason *it should be displayed. Hitler wasn't powerful enough to corrupt a symbol that is 7,000 to 9,000 years old. People who feel that it should not be displayed make Hitler and the Nazi regime far too powerful. I am more in favour of disempowering Hitler and the Nazis – by showing the ancient and entirely positive use of the symbol. If I ever met with this argument, I'd have both a Yungdrung and the symbol of Yeshé Tsogyel on my gÇod damaru chö'phen."* PAUSE

---

8 *The Nine Ways of Bön: excerpts from gZi-brJid by David Snellgrove published by Oxford University Press* (1967).
9 See glossary: *Bön.*
10 Arnold Henry Savage Landor (1865–1924) was an English painter, explorer, and writer – occasionally of unfortunate witticisms.

"The symbol of Yeshé Tsogyel is the same as the Judaic 'Star of David'...[11] *so if people wanted to make an issue of it – I would draw this to their attention."*

Ani Chö-ying burst out laughing at that point *"And—that—utterly destroys my devil's advocacy. Thank you very much indeed."* Then she laughed again. *"However – this is just another reason why some people don't like you. You have such fully researched answers. People really don't like to be quite so—very wrong—as your line of argument would make them. It makes people feel stupid."*

"There's no winning, is there?"

"No."

"I have no intention of making people feel stupid."

"I'm fairly sure you don't – but you sometimes make a very good job of it nonetheless." PAUSE *"But of course—from what I have witnessed here—they bring it on themselves by making statements based on ignorance."*

"Yes... I suppose I prefer to have no opinion when I know I know too little to have an opinion."

"That's entirely rational. But many people are not rational – and are content to have opinions with no real factual basis."

"In terms of facts... I should say, that with regard to the Yungdrung, you hit on one of the few things that I have researched in detail. There are many subjects about which I know next to nothing."

"Knowing what you know—when you really do know it as well as this— makes people fearful, if they don't have a sufficient level of psychological health." PAUSE

---

11 The Star of David is not unique to Judaism. The hexagramatic form is a simple pattern used throughout human history – and not exclusively religious. It was also used in Christian churches as a decorative motif many centuries before its first known use in a Schule. The earliest Judaic use of the symbol was inherited from medieval Arabic literature by Kabbalists for use in talismanic protective amulets (segulot) where it was known as the Seal of Solomon in Islam.

"Subtlety—shades of grey—are disturbing to them. The fact that changing the angle of a Yungdrung turns it into a Hakenkreuz, or vice-versa, is too subtle for some people to grasp – and they'd be happier to abandon an ancient symbol rather than be faced with its 20th Century implications."

"That… is rather sad." PAUSE *"What percentage of the population have a level of psychological health that would be unable to cope with what I've explained."*

Ani Chö-ying was quiet for a while – and clearly trying to formulate an answer. *"That is impossible to say, for me at least. Low psychosocial health is only identifiable under certain circumstances. We all drop in psychological health when we're under pressure. There are some people who maintain a high level of social functioning when under pressure – and some people who are hypersensitive to any shift from average expectations. Bearing all that in mind – I could only say that more people than you might care to imagine have poor psychological health."*

I sat there staring at Ani Chö-ying – somewhat taken aback by what she'd said. Finally, I took a deep breath *"That… is a sobering thought."* PAUSE *"I shall try to remember that. It's a somewhat massive cause for compassion."*

The time for the evening meal was approaching – and Ani Chö-ying had various allotted duties to perform. She left with a warm smile saying she'd see me at dinner. As the door closed on the library – I detected a strange sense of *mystery* in terms of the conversation that had just concluded. There was nothing unfathomable about what had been said – it was the atmosphere in which we had conversed. I dwelt on the nature of the *mysteriousness*. It was visceral rather than conceptual – and, after a while, an idea appeared. The only experience of this kind with which I was familiar – was that of romance. It had occurred on enough occasions in my life to recognise it – but what had thrown me, was the fact that I'd been conversing with a nun. If she'd not been a nun, it would have occurred to me far earlier – and I would have known what was happening.

413

I questioned myself immediately I had this thought – and was quite prepared to believe I was entirely mistaken. I thought about my marvellous conversations with Penelope, Meryl, and Rebecca. We certainly talked for hours without my imagining romance was in the air – so this was obviously foolishness. Maybe it was simply a matter of the stark contrast between Ani Chö-ying and Claudette. The same could be said in relation to Penelope, Meryl, and Rebecca – but of course Ani Chö-ying was knowledgeable in terms of Vajrayana. She also had a good understanding of the technical vocabulary. I'd not had such a conversation before – and so, naturally, I'd be ebullient about it. That was all logical. That should have concluded the question of the mysteriousness – but it didn't. It remained. I detected the slight sense of looking forward to speaking with Ani Chö-ying again. Under normal circumstances I would probably have built something on that – but this was a situation on which nothing *could* or *should* be built. It was out of the question. I concluded that it had to be something else… simply another reminder that my relationship with 'dette was moribund – and had been so for far too long.

Word had got 'round that I'd had a private audience with Gyalwa Karmapa. Some seemed pleased for me. There were a handful of others however, who looked at me with renewed hostility – as if I'd perpetrated some despicable swindle. There were wealthy sponsors who irked people because of what they could buy with their sponsorship – but I'd never felt bad about that. Vajrayana needed sponsors – and it seemed ridiculous to blame people for being rich. The world had its rich and poor – and as long as people's wealth wasn't a direct result of exploitation, I had no problem with it. I'd certainly have had no objection to being wealthy. If someone were to bequeath me enough money to live on the proceeds of investing it – I'd have no qualms about it. I was working class but that was not a philosophical or political position. I did not see poverty as being a virtue.

I remembered what I'd studied at 'O level' in Religious Education – and the quote came back to me: *Then Jesus said to his disciples… it is easier for a camel to pass through the eye of a needle than for a rich man to enter the Kingdom of God. When the disciples heard this, they were greatly astonished and asked "Who then can be saved?"* [12] To which I would always whisper under my breath *'Why, camels, of course.'* Then I'd amuse myself with the idea that one simply had to construct a larger needle. It was not the wealth that was the issue – but desire of it and what that desire would allow in terms of bad behaviour.

As I sat there pondering such absurdities Geraint arrived and sat down next to me at the dinenr table. *"It's really quite nasty the way some people have reacted to you here. I'm really sorry about it – it seems so petty and ignorant"* he commented.

"Thank you for your concern Geraint." PAUSE *"Y'know… as far as I'm concerned… I'm actually thankful to those who had almost succeeded in denying me access to the empowerments… because… without them, I wouldn't have got to spend that amazing time with Gyalwa Karmapa."*

"It's very funny in a way…" Ani Chö-ying added *"because the whole thing just bounced back on Linneah and… her… friends."* PAUSE *"Ani Jinpa— the nun who first locked horns with you—is quite furious about it."*

"Jin-pa… that's… generosity isn't it?"

"Yes…" Ani Chö-ying sighed *"the first paramita: the practice of generosity."* [13]

"There are some lengthy teachings on that from what I've heard. Can you give an idea of what that's about?"

"A little…" Ani Chö-ying replied. *"It's about giving what is helpful and good without self-oriented motivation. There are three aspects to it: giving material things; giving loving protection; and giving loving understanding. The teachings on the first form of generosity, zang-zing gi jinpa, explain proper and improper charity.*

---

12 Matthew 19:23–26.
13 Zang-zing-gi jinpa *(zang zing gi sByin pa).*

"It is necessary to abandon improper giving and to know what's proper to give."

"That's most interesting" I remarked. *"My knowledge of Sutrayana is rather poor – as you know, I never completed the Sutrayana course with Geshé Ngawang Dargyay; so, could you expand on that for my benefit?"*

"Certainly—if you don't mind hearing it from me—I'd be happy to explain as best I can."

"I'd be delighted – can I take notes?"

"Yes – but please don't take this as if it was a teaching."

I smiled and gave a slight shrug to indicate that I'd do as she asked.

"Well… the first form of generosity concerns motivation. Motivation is very important in terms of being charitable – so… it's improper to give something to someone with the intention to harm, with the intention to become famous, or out of fear of your own imminent poverty. It's necessary to consider what you give. Ordained people should never give anything that can hurt others. They should never give anything that's helpful if they have harmful thoughts in mind – so it's important to reflect on the recipient of your generosity. It's not beneficial—for example—to pamper anyone who's obsessed or greedy. One should never be reluctant to be charitable and should never show antipathy, disrespect, or scorn in relation to it. Real generosity is giving whatever is possible – and doing so with good motivation and enthusiasm. There are inspiring stories about great beings who gave their own flesh to feed animals who were on the verge of starving to death – but not many can do that. So, you give what you can to those whose need you can supply.

The second form of generosity,[14] *is giving loving protection to those who're fearful of others, who fear sickness and death, and who are afraid of natural catastrophes.*

The third form of generosity [15] *is giving the gift of Dharma to others. This doesn't mean speaking about it with anyone. It means helping those who have respect and understand and appreciate its meaning.*

14 Mi'jigpa'i Jinpa *(mi 'jigs pa'i sByin pa).*
15 Chö-kyi Jin-pa'i Jin-pa *(chos kyi sByin pa'i sByin pa).*

416

"You should only pass on teachings you've received from authentic Lamas if you have actually understood those teachings. This is in order that distortions don't occur. So... it's important not to mix the teachings with personal opinion nor to pass them on out of self-aggrandisement.

Finally, the teachings should always be discussed in a pleasant environment and pleasant manner – which is why I'm sorry that Ani Jin-pa hasn't been reflecting that with you. It gives you a poor impression of monastics."

"Thank you for that... and, y'know... you needn't be concerned about the impression I'm receiving. You're also here – so I am also getting a favourable impression. I think that it's the same anywhere... I think there are ngakpas who would make me deeply ashamed... such as the South African couple in Tintagel."

"Yes... what a sad mess people can make of their lives" she sighed. *"I hope that they're never tempted to go too far with their emancipative behaviour – to the extent of causing any lasting harm."*

Ani Chö-ying, then—at my request—explained the other paramitas and I made copious notes. That process took up all the time before the Pakshi Tröllö empowerment – and at its conclusion I'd had more teaching that day than I'd had since I saw Kyabjé Düd'jom Rinpoche in 1971.

I realised that there was a great deal that I did not know concerning Sutrayana... but it was a vast field and I wondered whether I would ever have time to become as conversant with Sutrayana as I was with Vajrayana – when there was so much I needed to learn concerning the three inner tantras. This was a question that I would have to ask Düd'jom Rinpoche.

25

the great blackness

There were fewer people than previously, at the empowerment of Pakshi Tröllö. I noticed it as I entered the shrine room. I made my prostrations to Gyalwa Karmapa. I felt almost as if I were functioning in slow motion – as there was not the expected rate of fall. I made nothing of it. I was used to making nothing of strange sensations. I'd been told about strange sensations and experiences. They were termed nyams.[1] They were signs of practice – but nothing more. If one paid any attention to nyams it became a sidetrack and eventually an obstacle.[2]

The atmosphere was dense with something I could not define. There were no analogies. No similes. It wasn't the incense – even though I caught its earthy fragrance. It was as if the colours of the walls had permeated the room in such a way as to occupy the space. That could have been claustrophobic – but there was an immense lightness and spaciousness at the same time. It was as if I'd landed on some other planet in some other solar system in some other galaxy where the laws of nature were all different. There was a sound in the room. I define it as a *sound* but it could also have been described as an *absence of sound*. Neither definition would fit. It was not an echo. There was however, some echo-quality comparable to a high contrast photographic image – but without the commensurate loss of subtle detail. It was as in every sound had been polished. There was a sense of infinite reflection occurring – but without blur or distortion. I gave up after a few minutes of this futile attempt to define what was occurring.

The empowerment began and concluded. In its outer form it was not so different from the other empowerments – but the feeling in the room was entirely different.

1   *nyams* – temporary experiences, meditation-moods, experiential sign of the
    practice development.
2   Bar-chèd *(bar chad)* – obstacle, interruption, hindrance, obstruction,
    interference, accident, mishap, danger, problem.

I'd been a little concerned at first that there would be some strange atmosphere with Ani Jinpa and Linneah – but they did not seem to be there, nor the unpleasant monks I'd met on the first night. I wondered what had happened. Still it was none of my business even to be wondering about it. I was simply grateful to have been allowed to attend.

The next morning arrived and those who attended the empowerment were asked to relate their dreams. We'd all slept with kusha grass under our pillows – in order that we would remember our internal nocturnal events.

"I dreamed of Lamas…" I began *"It was an unusual dream. It was more of a sequence. Chögyam Trungpa Rinpoche was there in a landscape that looked like Scotland. He was dressed in a mixture of lay and monastic costume. It could have been a version of the gö kar chang lo I have never seen before. He carried a bow – and arrows in a quiver. A dog accompanied him. Then the landscape opened out and he was in a huge green valley in the arms of impressive mountains. It seemed that something was about to happen – and I was waiting to see what it would be. Then the scene changed completely. I saw Kyabjé Düd'jom Rinpoche speaking with you (Gyalwa Karmapa) – but you were too far away for me to hear what you were saying to each other. You seemed to be in a room in a very old house and there were two other Lamas there – but I could not make them out, as they had their backs to me. All I could see was that neither were monks – and that they were of quite different sizes. One short. The other was tall and well-built. Then the scene changed again — and I saw other Lamas. I didn't know who they were. Then I saw a Lady Lama who looked similar to White Tara.[3] She seemed to be slightly smiling. Then I woke up."*

Gyalwa Karmapa gazed intently into space as he listened to my dream. At the end he looked at me with a smile *"Oh yah… good dream. Many meanings. We private your dream talking."*

---

3   It was gTértön Khyungchen Aro Lingma *(gTer sTon khyung chen A ro gLing ma)* but I did not want to mention her publicly. I decided to tell Gyalwa Karmapa later if the chance presented itself.

Then followed a series of dream accounts – all entirely unlike mine. There were a few that sounded very much like the dreams of Tibetan Lamas I'd read in their namthars.[4] Gyalwa Karmapa made no comment on these. Some seemed to be anxiety dreams and some seemed like childhood memories – but Gyalwa Karmapa listened patiently to them all *"Yah… all may be coming to the Dorje Bernakchen wang – but you must all spend much time reciting Pakshi Tröllö today before the wang."*

I missed lunch that day and spent the entire day in recitation – but that afternoon I was called back to see Gyalwa Karmapa again.

"Ah! Mighty ngakpa!" he called as I entered the room with Akong Rinpoche. *"You—much—Pakshi Tröllö reciting! This very good!"*

I made my prostrations and sat down in the glow of the room that seemed to buzz with red and golden hues.

"Your dream of Chögyam Trungpa Rinpoche. This good dream. This very special dream – because this cannot be fabricated or imagined. Not many people knowing – Chögyam Trungpa Rinpoche: incarnation of Drukpa Künlegs.[5] How you saw with bow and arrow and dog is how Drukpa Künlegs showing. Also same with clothes wearing." PAUSE *"Anyway – how this name 'Chögyam' receiving?"*

"It was from Ngakpa Yeshé Dorje originally."

Akong Rinpoche explained who Ngakpa Yeshé Dorje was.

4 *rNam thar* – spiritual biography or autobiography; also life story, life example, liberating lifestyles and exploits; and accounts of those who attained liberation both for themselves and others,
5 Among the previous incarnations of Chögyam Trungpa Rinpoche formally acknowledged by the Trungpa lineage, were Mahasiddha Ḍombi Héruka and Drukpa Künlegs. Both were revered for their powerful unorthodox teaching styles. In Bhutan Chögyam Trungpa Rinpoche is known as The Dragon of Bumthang.

"He called me Chö-ying Gyamtso.[6] *Then when Kyabjé Düd'jom Rinpoche called me Ögyen Togden,*[7] *I asked him if I could join the two first names to make Chögyam Ögyen Togden – and he was happy to agree to it."*

"And these two names joining because Chögyam Trungpa Rinpoche liking?"

"Yes Rinpoche."

"Yah! Then this—very—good! Maybe something from this future coming. Gyalwa Karmapa is not knowing – but anyway good."

"This other dream. You are Düd'jom Rinpoche-with-me seeing. Other two Lamas: Dilgo Khyentsé Rinpoche and Chini Lama. We dinner together. Often happening after Tibet leaving and Bodha staying. Chini Lama dinner making every day. Very kind. Very much skill in cooking" he laughed. *"It is good you are this seeing! Great happiness coming. So…"* PAUSE *"what is this meaning? This meaning Tsawa'i Lama is Düd'jom Rinpoche. Chögyam Nepal returning. Again Düd'jom Rinpoche seeing… then studying and practice developing."* PAUSE *"Smiling Khandro Lama…"* Gyalwa Karmapa smiled at me in silence for what seemed a long time – but it was probably less than a minute *"This one…"* PAUSE *"This one name from Düd'jom Rinpoche you already knowing. Please you are now telling."*

"gTértön Khyungchen Aro Lingma" I replied—knowing exactly what was meant and what was required—but staggered by the fact that Gyalwa Karmapa could know what he knew of the revelation I had received from Düd'jom Rinpoche.

"This one your mother from previous incarnation. Düd'jom Rinpoche telling you will her gTérma in future time receiving." PAUSE *"Nothing for Gyalwa Karmapa to be saying necessary. All things Düd'jom Rinpoche will be telling and guiding."*

Then Gyalwa Karmapa asked me to give him whatever details I knew from Düd'jom Rinpoche and whatever I had seen in visions and dreams of clarity.

---

6   *chos dByings rGya mTsho.*
7   *O rGyan togs lDan.*

The fact that he knew I'd had visions and dreams of clarity was shocking – but in such a spacious sense that the shock was utterly absorbed in space. I simply knew that I was not within the normal flow of time. It was not dream-like – but it was as if the conversation were happening in another dimension. I was awake and in more-or-less my customary mind state – but I was unusually relaxed. I only realised later that my legs were a little painful from sitting. I never was any use at sitting on the floor. Because I understood many of the technical terms in Gyalwa Karmapa's speech – it was as if Akong Rinpoche's translation and Gyalwa Karmapa's Tibetan became a seamless communication.

He told me that he would not interfere in what Düd'jom Rinpoche had decided. He said that he could see that it was all good – but that I would have many difficulties because I was Western. I would also have difficulties because there were those who were antagonistic to the gö kar chang lo'i dé. There were those who believed that Western financial aid for the monasteries would be reduced if Western people became interested in the gö kar chang lo'i dé. He thought this was 'nonsense-thinking'. He said that there was 'ignorant fear' around the subject. He told me that I had already experienced this kind of 'ignorant fear' at Samŷe Ling from Western people.

"Anyway… there gTérma coming – but where and when I cannot be saying. Düd'jom Rinpoche is telling me last year 'There is one Injï tulku—one ngakpa—who gTérma revealing from past life mother. She also gTértön and her mother is gTértön. Also father is gTértön. All family gTérmas revealing. This is in Tibet coming – not unusual. Later you meaning knowing of everything that is inside gTérma coming. This must Düd'jom Rinpoche saying. O yah! Düd'jom Rinpoche is everything telling."

Gyalwa Karmapa then reached behind him and pulled out a deep-red lacquered box. He opened it and took out a bag of rilbu[8]
"These taking when serious illness having – then recovering possible."

8   Rilbu *(ril bu)* – medicinal pills made of herbs and minerals which can contain substances consecrated by Lamas.

423

Akong Rinpoche then informed me that these were rilbu that Gyalwa Karmapa had made personally and that they were extremely rare and precious. I was not to tell anyone at Samŷe Ling that I had received them or there would be jealousy.

Then Gyalwa Karmapa reached inside his waistcoat and brought out a tiny silver phurba wrapped in ancient emerald green silk. *"This always keeping. Always with you keeping – never showing. Only Düd'jom Rinpoche showing – otherwise not showing before one cycle of life completing—when my age becoming—and, 'signs' seeing. Then telling possible – but still private keeping. For 'signs' knowing, Düd'jom Rinpoche asking. Then if later showing – only disciples, never ordinary people showing."* PAUSE *"Yah… maybe now resting – then Pakshi Tröllö reciting."*

Then, as before, having backed out of the room I found myself again—almost as unexpectedly—walking with strange grace down the landing to the head of the stairs. I descended the stairs with some sort of effortlessness – as if I was walking on space.

I was somewhat rudely confronted with an alternative reality by Ani Jinpa *"Why aren't you practising as you were instructed?"*

"Trying my best… but as they always told me at school, my best was not good enough" I replied with a smile.

"Don't think talking nonsense will impress anyone" she almost spat.

"Last thing on my mind…" I commented—still faintly smiling—as I walked past her into the garden.

"You shouldn't walk away from people when they're talking to you" the unfriendly monk from the first evening called out in a fairly strident voice.

"I'm sure you're quite right" I replied and continued walking.

I went to sit in the garden and recite mantra – but was vaguely plagued by the idea that I should have been able to make better replies… something to have shown them they need not be unfriendly.

Should I go back inside and find them and tell them I just wanted to be friends with them? As I was turning this possibility over in my mind Ani Chö-ying approached me. *"I heard all that…"* she said with a sad expression *"… and… I find it really sad."*

"I'm sorry… I know I said the wrong things to them and made it all worse."

"No—not at **all**—*I wasn't saying anything about you. I was just going to tell you that I thought you were exemplary in how you replied – without any show of irritation or annoyance."*

"I was just wondering whether I should go back inside and try something different… I was thinking of telling them that I just wanted to be amiable – and that I had no feelings of rancour toward them."

"That…" PAUSE *"… although very well-motivated, would just create further animosity. I don't think there's anything you can do. There's just something…"* PAUSE *"I think they have a low level of psychological health – as I was saying earlier. They'd probably like nothing better than to have an on-going argument with you. If you did that, you might end up proving exactly what they want to prove about you."*

"So… what do they want to prove?"

"That you're an interloper—with bad intentions—who should be told to leave."

"Ah… well… I think they may be right in one way – that I'm an interloper… I mean, I'm not a Kagyüd practitioner – and, maybe, I should have known I'd cause resentment…"

"If that was the case, Samye Ling should have stipulated that this time with Gyalwa Karmapa was only for Kagyüd practitioners…" she smiled *"and, of course, if Gyalwa Karmapa doesn't object to your being here then I don't see what anyone else has to say about it."*

"Ah… yes… well – yes." I was aware that there was much I could not reveal to Ani Chö-ying – even though I knew her to be thoroughly trustworthy. I was feeling the *loneliness,* or *isolation*, of my situation.

It dawned on me that this could only increase over the years. There were secrets I had to hold… and the possibility of a growing number of antagonists – just as Kyabjé Düd'jom Rinpoche had indicated. Why did I imagine that I would not mind being vilified and subjected to animosity? I knew why… I'd been in Bodhanath with Düd'jom Rinpoche – and sitting with him in that wonderful room, everything seemed so utterly—utterly— possible. But now as an incognito tulku and lone ngakpa who had no real context – I was merely an anomalous apostle of aberrance.

"I suppose…" I grinned, sheepishly *"I'll just have to accept that some people have an existential-philosophical need to demonise me."* PAUSE *"It's a shame though – because I really would be friends with them at any point, and forget the past. It seems… that there ought to be a way to explain that I'm innocuous…"*

"That would just be to play into their hands. Chögyam Trungpa Rinpoche told me once that 'If you discuss a subject with a fool you become a fool. If you discuss a subject with a bigot you become a bigot. If you discuss anything at all with a debater you become a debater.' I've always found that extremely valuable."

"D'you mind if I write that down?"

She didn't—so I did—and then she left me to practise. I called after her however *"Thank you very much indeed Chö-ying – it would have been quite… difficult here without your friendship."*

I spent the afternoon in the garden reciting mantra and finally the time came for dinner. I walked back to the house with a fairly silent mind – but eventually fell to pondering. My time was running out at Samŷe Ling. My time at Bristol Art School was also running out. My twenties would be running out before too long.

There'd be some radical changes – and something about being at Samŷe Ling seemed to be pivotal. My mind turned to 'dette – and I knew that *the end was swift approaching.* I reflected on how easy conversation was with Ani Chö-ying and how difficult it was with 'dette.

It seemed strange that is was easier to converse with a nun than with my own lady friend. Ani Chö-ying could also challenge my view without being dismissive or disinterested in my opinion. I wondered what she'd look like with hair – and that wasn't too hard to imagine. Someone like Ani Chö-ying—who wasn't a nun— would make an ideal partner… That thought made me laugh – because it reminded me of the Peter Cook and Dudley Moore film *'Bedazzled'.*[9] It's a comedy version of Faust in which Peter Cook is the Devil and Dudley Moore is some kind of Faust. Dudley Moore is given seven wishes – and in each he tries to win the lady he admires. Peter Cook however grants each wish with a twist that undermines the wish. In the final wish Dudley Moore attempts to devise a plan that the Devil can't pervert. He requests that he and the lady he desires should be two genuinely good people who lived in isolation from the false glitter and glitz of big city life. They would always be together and they would always love each other. Unfortunately, Dudley Moore fails to specify the gender he desires to be in terms of his wish. The Devil turns him and the lady into nuns in The Order of Saint Beryl—*Leaping Beryllians*—who glorify their founder by springing into the air from trampolines.

My mind was a peculiar arena of possibility, where profundity and impulsiveness—sobriety and whimsicality—insight and delusion oscillated. I'd spent several hours in mantra recitation and minutes after heading for the house, I found myself involved with ludicrous conjecture based on a comedy called *Bedazzled*. Still… it was all part of my experience of existence in the West – and as long as I avoided taking the comings-and-goings of my conceptual mind seriously, I was not likely to get into too much trouble. Too much trouble… yes, too much trouble.

It dawned on me in imperceptible increments that there was a degree of romantic attraction in my appreciation of Ani Chö-ying.

---

9   *Bedazzled* (1967) – screenplay by Peter Cook—based on a narrative by Peter Cook and Dudley Moore—was a comedy version of the Faust legend, set in 1960's London.

We certainly enjoyed conversing and our conversations were both lively and mutually supportive. She told me that she felt somewhat alone as a nun. She'd never been a hippie – and had come to Vajrayana from a background in psychology. She initially wanted a conventional career in the conventional world. She wanted marriage and children. She'd wanted most things most normal people wanted – but then she'd read *Meditation in Action,* followed by *Mudra,* and *Cutting Through Spiritual Materialism.*[10] A friend at University had given the first of these books to her – and she'd been so absorbed by it that she searched for other books by Chögyam Trungpa Rinpoche.

"I'd had a series of relationships with young men who seemed entirely unsuited to relationship – and that's what made me take the step of becoming a nun" Ani Chö-ying had told me. *"I'd gone to see Gyalwa Karmapa at Rumtek, Sikkim – as he's the head of Chögyam Trungpa Rinpoche's School'. An ordination happened to be taking place – and at that time celibacy seemed a great relief. I had no desire to run the gauntlet of an ongoing series of worthless relationships in which I was objectified and treated as an adjunct."*

'What a shame' I'd thought. *'What a waste... when I was somewhere in the same country.'*

I wondered momentarily what would have happen if I'd said that? Not that I'd had any real impulsion to express such a sentiment. The only point on which I was certain, was that I would avoid doing or saying anything that was in any way capable of being interpreted as inappropriate.

I had no sense in which Ani Chö-ying might be having similar ideas – because she was evidently entirely committed to the vows she had taken. It was possible therefore, that I was entirely safe from impropriety – and I could make sure that she was entirely safe as well.

---

10 *Meditation in Action* (1969), *Mudra* (1972), *Cutting Through Spiritual Materialism* (1973).

After having been treated with such marvellous kindness by Gyalwa Karmapa the last thing I wanted to do, was conduct myself —as my father might phrase it—as *'a depraved lout'*. I remembered the words of Düd'jom Rinpoche *'With each life-circumstance: whatever is enacted, stare directly into the enactment – with all the senses.'*

Geraint and Lydia were sitting at their usual table when I entered the dining hall and so I joined them. *"I hear you've had—two—private interviews with Gyalwa Karmapa!"* Geraint exclaimed gleefully.

"Yes… I've been exceptionally fortunate."

"What happened today?"

"Oh… it was about my dreams. After the empowerment we were all asked to sleep with kusha grass under our pillows and to recount our dreams to Gyalwa Karmapa the next day. So there were a few things in my dreams that Gyalwa Karmapa wanted to discuss with me. He also wanted to explain a few things in relation to Bodhanath – because he knows that I am going back there to see Kyabjé Düd'jom Rinpoche." PAUSE *"He mentioned that he and Düd'jom Rinpoche used to have dinner with Dilgo Khyentsé Rinpoche and the Chini Lama – because I had a dream of him—with Düd'jom Rinpoche—in an old house. He said it was the house where they used to have dinner."* I said nothing of Chögyam Trungpa Rinpoche. It seemed to be something that I shouldn't mention to anyone else. I made no mention of Aro Lingma either.

"Wow! That's far out—I must say—you just had a dream about those Lamas…" beamed Lydia *"… and it turned out to be something that really happened!"*

"Well… it's not—quite—as amazing as all that. I've lived in Bodhanath and visited Düd'jom Rinpoche's house there – and, I saw Dilgo Khyentsé Rinpoche and the Chini Lama in 1971 … so, it's not so surprising that meeting Gyalwa Karmapa shouldn't spark something like that."

"Still – it must be amazing to have a dream like that and have Gyalwa Karmapa comment on it."

"Yes – that's certainly true. I'm massively lucky."

"It's certainly made up for those nasty comments you got from a few people."

"Yes, more—far more—than made up for it. I think it's pushing me to some sort of turning point in my life…"

"Are you…" Geraint asked *"staying for the rest of the time that Gyalwa Karmapa is here?"*

"No… sadly I have to leave tomorrow – I'm afraid my money won't stretch to staying longer. And… I have the Summer term at Art School about to start." PAUSE *"I suppose I can't have all the good luck – and some people here need a spell without me to cast a blight on their experience."*

"Never mind about them – they're responsible for their own karma."

"True enough… but… all the more reason I should wish them well."

"Good way to look at it…" Lydia commented with the faintest of smiles *"but they've still got their karma and they will have to experience the effect of those causes."*

"Well…" I commenced *"karma is how we see the world—it's our perception—and from the patterned perception we react according to what we see. If I see someone as an enemy then I have to attack. If I see someone as simply… troubled in some way – then I can wish them well."*

"But what about cause and effect?" Geraint asked.

"The cause is the perception – and the effect, is whatever action arises from the perception."

"Right… I've not heard it put that way before."

"I think I have…" Lydia mused. *"It was from a Theravadin monk who gave a talk on karma at the Buddhist Society in London. Have you studied Theravada then?"*

"No… well – I read a book once called 'Experiment in Mindfulness' by a man with the imposing name of Rear Admiral EH Shattock. It was the first book I ever read on meditation."

"So…" pondered Geraint *"… what happens about the results of actions in terms of everything being karma?"*

"Everything is karma, in the same way that everything **you** see, *is* as **you** see it. *That makes your experience of existence good, bad, or indifferent. It's not that stubbing your toe is karma – it's how you feel about stubbing your toe. It's not your wealth or lack of it – but what your wealth or lack of it means to you. One wealthy person can be miserable whereas another can be happy – and likewise with poorer people. Buddhism is primarily concerned with intention and—in terms of Sutrayana—developing more altruistic intentions."* PAUSE *"So, it's not your actions – but* why *you act and what you want to get out of your actions."*

At that point Ani Chö-ying came to sit with us. *"I've been thinking…"* she began tentatively *"that Vajrayana seems to attract people with… psychopathic tendencies…"*

"Really…?" Geraint said with some surprise.

"Yes… I've come to the conclusion that it's the only way I can understand people like Ani Jinpa."

"Could you define psychopathy?" I asked with some great interest *"I mean in terms of how they are. All I know is from Alfred Hitchcock's 'Psycho'* [11] *…"*

"That film has done a great deal to confuse the subject – and actually to make psychopaths harder to recognise" Ani Chö-ying sighed *"… maybe… I'll just run through aspects of the disorder…"* PAUSE *"They exhibit: glibness and superficial charm…"*

"That would count Ani Jinpa out" Lydia interrupted – but Ani Chö-ying continued without commenting.

"…they tend to have a grandiose sense of self-worth and proneness to boredom and need for stimulation." PAUSE

11 'Psycho'—directed by Alfred Hitchcock—was a 1960 American horror / thriller film. The screenplay—by Joseph Stefano—was based on the 1959 novel by Robert Bloch.

"They tend to pathological lying and manipulation… they're callous and lack empathy, feelings of remorse and guilt. They display shallow affect and have poor behavioural controls."

"That suddenly makes sense of a few people I've met…" I commented and both Geraint and Lydia agreed.

"There are approximately 8 per 1,000 in the population – so it's little wonder that you have run into a few." PAUSE *"I should have added that psychopaths tend to have parasitic lifestyles – but… who am I to say that, as a nun?"*

"I don't think…" I began *"that religious mendicancy counts—well not in the cultural context at least—and anyway, you're not living on hand-outs, are you?"*

"No – but one has to be careful not to sit in judgement…"

"True… but—that apart—what… turns someone into a psychopath?"

*"That's the big question… the 'bad or mad' argument. From what I've read… I tend to favour nature over nurture. As you know, I read psychology at university… and we looked—briefly—at the work of Robert Hare – a '60s prison psychologist in Vancouver who got psychopathic and non-psychopathic volunteers for tests. He monitored his volunteers on EEG, perspiration, and blood pressure gauges – and gave them electric shocks. He explained to the volunteers that he'd count backwards from **10** – and when he reached **1** they'd receive an electric shock."*

"So what happened…?" asked Geraint.

"Well… the non-psychopathic volunteers prepared themselves for the electric shock and were understandably anxious. Their anxiety registered on the EEG, perspiration, and blood pressure gauges."

"And the psychopaths…?" Lydia asked.

"They registered no anxiety at all. The test indicated that the amygdala—the part of the brain that anticipates the pain and sends fear signals to the central nervous system – didn't function as expected. Hare concluded that the brains of psychopaths were different from normal brains.

"He repeated the test with the psychopaths knowing exactly how much pain they would experience – but they still had no anxiety reactions. They had no memory of the pain of the electric shock – even when the shock occurred within a minute."

"What!" Lydia gasped *"that's really creepy stuff – what happened then?"*

"Robert Hare sent his findings to SCIENCE MAGAZINE *– but the editor wouldn't publish them on the basis that the* EEG *results couldn't have come from real people."*

"Did he find a cure for psychopathy?" I asked.

"No… and no one has. As far as psychiatry is concerned—to date—it's currently incurable."

"Psychopathy reminds me of… Matamrudra[12]…" I mused.

"Yes – and Devadatta [13]" Ani Chö-ying added.

"I'm wondering what Tibetan medicine has to say about it?"

"Nothing as far as I have found yet… which is a pity because psychopathy is probably responsible for most of the pain and suffering in the world."

And so we talked 'til it was time to prepare for the empowerment of Dorje Bernakchen. I felt I should recite a little more of the mantra of Pakshi Tröllö before entering the shrine room – so I went and sat in the garden to recite.

The empowerment externally was similar to the empowerments of Pakshi Tröllö – but the feeling in the room was entirely different again from that empowerment.

---

12 According to the Sangwa Nyingpo Gyü'trül Dra-wa *(gSang bas Nying po sGyu 'phrul drwa-ba,* Skt. *Guhyagarbha Mayajala)* Matamrudra was a demonic witch king, who threatened the existence of mankind who was subjugated—through violent humiliation—by Chenrézigs and 'ö-Pag'mèd.

13 Devadatta (देवदत्त) – a Buddhist monk who was the cousin of Shakyamuni Buddha, and parted from him with 500 monks to form their own Sangha. Devadatta—obsessed with his own worth—wished to supplant Shakyamuni. After failing in this he tried on various occasions to kill Shakyamuni – but always failed.

433

Gyalwa Karmapa looked different – but it wasn't possible to explain just how that was. It was as if he were both younger and older – fiercer and more benign. There seemed to be a sharpness of contradiction in his mien – but it may simply have been my imagination. I tried not to imagine anything or speculate about anything – but the dramatic quality of his presence remained awe-inspiring.

A protector practice is a means of protecting practice. The idea is that whatever gets in the way of practice is destroyed. You're not protected in the usual way – in terms of being nursed or cosseted. Instead – offending organs are avulsed, or you're inspired to avulse them. Dorje Bernakchen was a strange being: a maniacal black dwarf with a huge butcher's knife; a relentless fiend with a huge gaping mouth, carrying a skull bowl seething with oceans of blood. This was the doctor-cum-psychiatrist I was inviting to rearrange my reality.

Thinking about it afterwards, I wondered about my enthusiasm for such a practice. Did I really want to ruin my life – or my life as the person I still recognised? Did I really wish to destroy everything which had no strong link to practice? The answer—at this point—had to be 'yes'… but how would that play out in terms of becoming an Art School lecturer? I had to do something for a living – as I wasn't a freeloader or one of the independently wealthy types who spent time in India and Nepal. I decided I'd have to dive in—as I always dove—and see what happened. I felt sincere, if somewhat anxious – about the huge space that lay beyond the limits of my capacity. Anything could happen. With that thought I engaged in the practice. Sometime later I fell asleep.

The night became a blaze of colours. I experienced a long succession of dreams. Some were dreams in which there was no awareness. Some were lucid dreams – and some, appeared to be dreams of clarity.[14]

---

14 Ngö-nyam mi-lam *(dNgos nyams rMi lam)*.

There was a sequence of scenes that I perceived – sitting in a large white tent with Khyungchen Aro Lingma. She was dressed in a white sheepskin chuba over which was wound a shawl composed of many intricate stripes in red white and blue. It was not the usual bu-ré[15] gö kar chang lo shawl, made in Bhutan[16] – but vaguely similar. Suddenly—but entirely gracefully—she allowed her chuba and shawl to slip from her – and appeared naked to the hips. She immediately manifested holding a crystal sphere. She was gazing though it—but also gazing past it—at those who sat before her. Then she held a circular mirror at the level of her throat. Then she held a large natural crystal in front of her chest. Then all I saw was sky above mountains. I was sitting on a crag of rock overlooking the valley in which the large white tent was situated. Then I was leaving the tent. I turned and two girls of a similar age followed behind me – also leaving the tent. Then I was with the two girls in some other tent where a woman was playing a large stringed instrument and singing an intricate trilling song in a key that moved between major and minor modes.

There was—in the midst of a welter of such dreams—a period when I woke from sleep and became aware that Aro Lingma had emerged—in visionary form—within the room. She became the room. The vision did not last long. I went back to sleep, on an impulse which seemed informed by a nonconceptual communication. I then experienced a long series of dream vignettes in which I saw many aspects of the Aro Gar in Tibet. I saw a variety of people. Many seemed vaguely familiar. A few were people I knew as if they were part of my waking life. There were five women. They were all my mothers – or *were mothers to me*. There were sequences with music. Sequences with brightly coloured thread. Sequences in which arrows with streamers were moving gracefully as they might in a ballet. Sequences at night lying naked and staring into the stars. Several meteors streaked across the sky. They were far brighter than meteors I'd seen before. I could see the colour of the stars, white, yellow, and red.

15 Bu-ré *(bhu ras)* – Bhutanese raw silk.
16 *rGe po bKab ne*

435

Some even seemed green or blue. The sky was peppered with light to the extent that it was not so different from daylight. Then sequences followed in which I was staring toward the sun – seeing kaleidoscopic rainbows shimmering against a dark blue daytime sky. Sequences in a snow storm. Sequences where wind was causing tent flaps to rattle like the sails of an 18th Century ship. Sequences where a large stream was gushing between rocks. There were great white birds circling in the sky. A fire was burning. I was gazing at flames. I then became aware that I had woken up in Samŷe Ling.

In the morning I set out immediately after breakfast. I bade goodbye to the friendly people with whom I had talked – and made final prostrations in the shrine room that I dedicated to Gyalwa Karmapa. Ani Chö-ying was not to be found – and I decided that it was perhaps better that way, as there would be no temptation to exchange addresses. Maybe we'd meet again. That was not entirely unlikely as the Tibetan Buddhist world was surprisingly small.

Then I was out on the road – eating up the miles to Bristol.

There was one thing I knew with certainty: everything had changed. My relationship with 'dette was over. There was no more room for conjecture. I *had* made that decision before I set out to Samŷe Ling – but somehow the decision had been made in the abstract. It had been a decision that was to have played out on the other side of Samŷe Ling – but now, I was almost there. I was riding back to the fulfilment of that decision.

Her comment *"… so you're off to see Fu Manchu put his hat on again"* emerged out of past recollections – along with my reply *"No 'dette I'm going to Clacton-on-Sea to have an illicit affair with an elderly octopus."*

It wasn't even that 'dette's remark was offensive. She hadn't meant to be offensive – or if she had, there was little malice in it.

I know that some people would have been highly offended by such a remark – but she'd made it as a complete outsider. It wasn't her fault she was an outsider – it was my fault for maintaining a relationship with someone who was obviously so far removed from my main concern in life. It's not that 'dette was *the first to fall prey to Dorje Bernakchen's cleaver* – that would be to indulge in spurious spiritualised fantasy. The decision had been making itself for some time and I would have made my exit anyhow. The difference seemed to lie in the stark inevitability of the decision. Without this new sense of surety, I *could* have swayed for a period of time – and that would have been harmful to 'dette. It would have been problematic for me too – but the one who leaves needs to accept responsibility for… *the time and place that the axe has to fall.* As those words formed themselves, I understood something. Dorje Bernakchen was… *the time and place that the axe had to fall* – whenever it fell. The falling of the axe—*was*—Dorje Bernakchen.

I also realised that Dorje Bernakchen's axe was probably going to dismember more than my relationship. I wondered what else would have to go…

Maybe my life as a lecturer would also have to go? Anything was possible.

I remembered the words of Düd'jom Rinpoche *'With each life-circumstance: whatever is enacted, stare directly into the enactment – with all the senses.'*

437

26

passing strange

The long ride South from Samŷe Ling to Bristol. A windswept blur of *thinkingness and unthinkingness* under rain-sodden skies. It didn't rain – but I became increasingly moist from the 70–80 mph impact with damp air. Chilled to the bone arrival in Bristol.

I'd left Samŷe Ling without having exchanged addresses with Ani Chö-ying. I was not entirely comfortable with that. I was a fundamentally friendly, sociable individual. I would otherwise have naturally wished to stay in contact. Be that as it may, I'd remembered Jan McCulloch's advice from the first visit to Samŷe Ling. I'd remembered that she thought it wisest not to exchange addresses; on the basis that she did not trust herself – and, that she was almost old enough to have been my mother. This was an exaggeration on her part – but her choice was a matter of integrity. She did not wish to change the shape of my life in a manner that would run counter to my being young – and, she added *"… just at the beginning of the huge adventure of your life."*

By the end of my sojourn at Samŷe Ling I had started to feel that Ani Chö-ying and I had come to like each other a little too much. This was dramatically wrong. She was a nun. Not only was she a nun – but a nun ordained by the 16th Gyalwa Karmapa and he was a friend of Kyabjé Düd'jom Rinpoche Jig'drèl Yeshé Dorje. The consequences of impropriety were too horrible to contemplate. The words of Düd'jom Rinpoche had sprung to mind *With each life-circumstance: whatever is enacted, stare directly into the enactment – with all the senses.'* There was never a better way to deal with anything.

The other factor that predicated against dalliance of any kind was that I was still with 'dette. I had not left other than in my mind. I didn't hold myself guilty for having *warm feelings* – but I would have held myself culpable if I'd acted on them even to the slightest degree. In addition to this, I took a seriously dim view of anyone who began a new liaison before concluding their existing situation.

I deemed it dishonest and pusillanimous. One had to leave a relationship on the basis of its being inappropriate, in whatever way. One then had to spend time alone in order to be free for another romance. Morphing from one association to another was the proclivity of those who were afraid to be alone. I had no fear of being alone.

The other dysfunctional aspect of *seamless serial monogamy* in my view, was that if one leaves someone for someone else – one cannot be believed when one says *'I'm leaving you because you—in my experience—have appeared unkind, ungenerous, unsympathetic, and uncaring.'* If one has not made such a statement – the rejected partner is deprived of what could be valuable feedback. All that such rejected partners are likely to understand, is that they were deserted in favour of someone deemed more desirable.

Be that as it may – life was not always that neat and tidy. Or was that merely an excuse some people used? Still however other people ordered their lives – I was determined to order my life honourably. Life could be emotionally fraught – but didn't have to be an emotional mess. The idea that *one thing leads to another, however well plans are formulated* – was a slipshod slapdash slovenly view of existence. That was well deserving of Dorje Bernakchen's baleful butcher's blade.

The baleful blade appeared to start dispatching various aspects of my life not long after I hit the road from Eskdalemuir. Papa Legba never showed when I was twelve years old – but the 16th Gyalwa Karmapa had not been in Britain to force his hand. The motion of the scythe was subtle and subcutaneous however – and the assault occurred as if in a game of chess that operated simultaneously on multiple levels.[1]

---

1   Three-dimensional chess employs multiple boards allowing chess pieces to move in 3 physical dimensions. 3D variants have existed since the 19th century – the oldest being Raumschach *(Space chess)* invented in 1907 by Ferdinand Maack.

I bade 'dette farewell – in as kindly a way as I could. I didn't need to act the part of looking miserable – because that came quite naturally. I knew I'd be glad at some point – but delivering the information was something I found quite hideous. She accepted my decision however; without the high degree of emotional carnage I'd feared. There was a long and fraught discussion as to 'why?' and 'why now?' – and I answered dutifully on every point.

She then accused me of amorous interest in either Penelope, Rebecca, or Meryl. I denied it fairly calmly and matter-of-factly. That was simple. There was no reality in the accusation. Penelope, Rebecca, and Meryl were my friends. 'dette insisted for a while – but I ended the discussion by saying that the veracity of my denial would be self-evident to an increasing degree with every day, week, or month that followed. That was all I would say. Spending too long on denial is what one does if one is guilty. 'dette could see I was in my *intransigent mode* and so she did not prolong the discussion of my suspected interest in Penelope, Rebecca, or Meryl. It must have been clear to her from my demeanour that I found the suggestion as implausible as sudden conversion to Scientology.

"Even if I had been romantically inclined in that direction" I concluded with as well-crafted English as I could muster on the spur of the moment *"I imagine that their parents would have welcomed me as much as your father – and, I'd rather not submit myself to that kind of high-society censure. I'm a randomly self-educated, working-class, avantgarde eccentric, with outré clothing, a demode hair style, outrageous philosophical speculations, and untenable perspectives on Art."* PAUSE *"So, I would—not—be so gauche as to imagine I'd be well-received at their homes. I shall stay within my own class bracket in future."*

For once 'dette had nothing to say. She knew from the tone in my voice that I was *'speaking from the pinnacle of righteous certainty'* as she'd once phrased it.

441

"Beside which" I continued after a momentary PAUSE *"I have not been, nor will I ever be, guilty of disloyalty, betrayal, treachery, infidelity, adultery – or anything else as contemptibly perfidious."*

She accepted the rebuttal of my supposed impropriety without demurral – and at the same time accepted that we had no future. She accepted that her father would not be alone in his disapproval of me – and I'd seen it too many times before to doubt the outcome of a liaisons with debutantes. Such things happened in stories—such as *Lady Chatterley's Lover*—but I wasn't a character in a story. I lived in whatever the real world might be. The real world was open to question – but I knew the prejudices that it contained and they were as they were.

There'd been recriminations – but I'd simply allowed her to say whatever she needed to say. I'd decided not to justify myself – and didn't. I had decided to take the blame for everything. I did. The only perspective I volunteered was an enumeration of the aspects of my personality to which she most objected. I acknowledged that I was reprehensible in having entered into a relationship with someone who had no interest in Buddhism. I apologised for having wasted her time. I pointed out that her father had a fairly low opinion of me – and that, as she respected her father highly, she should maybe consider taking his evaluation seriously.

'dette was upset to lose me – but, in the end, only as upset as if one of her collection of Georgian boxwood eggcups had broken. I was entirely dispensable. There was nothing about me that she would seriously miss. Tears were shed… but the loss of Ngakpa Chögyam—alias Vic Simmerson—didn't occupy her mind for more than a few days – or at least, that was the intelligence I received from Penelope, Meryl, and Rebecca. I knew however that 'dette could feign a degree of stoicism that was convincing.

Strangely she distanced herself from the ladies. She practically cut them dead in the street. She declined a dinner invitation on the basis that her father had described partaking of fondue as being like 'pigs at the trough'.

"She always had a touch of that…" said Rebecca *"… but this time I felt there was an edge to her voice – as if she actually meant to be hurtful… I mean, rather than putting on her usual Dorothy 'dette Parker."* PAUSE *"I really don't know how you stood it for three years."*

"Well… let's say two…"

"Alright—two years—but she always had that hoity-toity number going – didn't she?"

To which I shrugged in vague agreement and Rebecca continued *"We heard her talk like that to you, right from the start."*

"Maybe you never saw—my—expression…" I smiled *"I—used—to find it amusing. I suppose that I'm not too horribly vulnerable, sensitive, or susceptible – so I don't necessarily take subjective rebukes terribly seriously. Subjective opinions are not really worth a great deal. Anyhow… I never felt she—meant—anything by her rebukes – well… not until the 3rd year got underway"* my smile was now absent *"… and, I suppose, I might have said something—earlier—but… y'know… I don't like to be critical. I knew that's how 'dette was from the start and, if it was alright then – why should I want to adjust her later?"*

"But…" Meryl commented *"… 'dette did want to adjust—you—didn't she?"*

"Yes… she did. Can't deny that, Meryl" I sighed *"and—in the end—that's why I've left."* PAUSE *"I suppose I—could—have pointed out the disparity between her desire to change me – and my acceptance of her."*

"I don't think it would have made any difference, though" Penelope sighed.

"No… I don't think it would've done. Your right… and—actually—I did point that out at one stage of the proceedings…" I laughed the slightest laugh. *"She told me that the disparity existed because there was nothing about her that needed to change – and that anyway, she was not open to changing. She was so comical about it however, that I didn't take her seriously."* PAUSE *"You know 'dette and her penchant for dramatic statements."*

"Yes… and she got away with a lot with the use of that" Rebecca argued *"but the disparity continued nonetheless…"*

"Yes… I suppose if I'd persisted with bringing it to her attention, she'd have to have dropped the 'I'm perfect' line."

"Knowing 'dette as I've done all these years…" Meryl mused *"I think… that would just've made her angry and led to a lot of nasty rows."*

"There would never have been rows though – because it takes two to have a row. It would have led to her shouting – and my making occasional replies, in a flat lifeless sort of way." PAUSE *"Y'know… 'dette used to get quite upset with me for not getting angry. She'd say that Buddhism wasn't good for me – or any Western person. Her father had told her that 'Buddhist passivity and acceptance' came from a culture where most people lived in poverty and died before they were forty."*

"Bloody self-satisfied bigot!" Rebecca almost shouted. *"But I'd be interested to hear what you said in reply."*

"Something to the effect that passivity and acceptance aren't ideas that can be used as simplistically as her father used them… I said that although I wasn't an expert… I'd studied quite seriously… and could only say that I had no reason to consider her father as having any more than a rudimentary understanding of Buddhism – especially as it's practised in the Nyingma lineage. He could know almost nothing of Tibetan Buddhism from the books currently available."

"Good for you" Penelope commented. *"So what did she say to that?"*

"She stated that my refusal to be angry was 'Buddhist' and dared me to deny it. Her father may not have read about my particular branch of Buddhism – but he had read widely and deeply." PAUSE *"Of course, I acknowledged that anger—was—regarded as a problem in Buddhism – but that my dislike of anger predated my becoming a Buddhist. I told her my father was an angry man – and that I'd always loathed it. I hated seeing my mother being subject to his anger."*

"What did she say to that?"

"She said that I always managed to find a loop hole to win an argument."

"She's impossible!" snorted Penelope.

"So am I" I laughed. *"I just replied that, that was what she always said to regain her ascendancy and that it didn't matter to me who won or lost – because for me it wasn't a battle or a competition."*

"That must have raised her hackles."

"Yes… she told me she didn't care either because anger was natural and healthy and if I wanted to be two-dimensional it was my own look out. She certainly wouldn't kowtow to my fanciful sensibilities."

"Yes…" opined Meryl *"… that would suit the way she sees things… So what was your take on anger being natural and healthy?"*

"I disagreed. I said anger's a learnt habit – and that, as such, it could be unlearned." PAUSE *"Of course that made me a repressed emotionless religious pedant."*

"Really! That's absurd—if anyone's repressed, it's 'dette—even though she can fly into a rage" Rebecca remonstrated with a swish of her hair. *"I mean – you're so repressed you'd wear a giraffe hide greatcoat with the tail still attached!"* At that the three ladies laughed.

"Yeah…" Rebecca nodded *"any attempt we ever made to give 'dette any home-truths—even in the gentlest way—led to her screeching at us like a scalded cat."*

"Yes… 'dette is—very—fragile under that cool cynical exterior" Penelope offered with a troubled expression. *"She's really quite frightened of life – which is probably not surprising. Having one's mother die when one's young – and then being quite cruelly jilted… That's enough to make anyone vulnerable and prickly. I think she must feel that she has to fight for her life or something."*

I told Penelope she was probably right and went off to town to buy the cheese for the evening's fondue.

The next day brought a somewhat cataclysmic revelation.

I came to understand from Penelope, Meryl, and Rebecca that I could have found a romantic partner in any one of them. 'dette had been wrong in her suspicions of me – but entirely correct in respect of Penelope, Meryl, and Rebecca. That was a revelation that surprised me more than anything had ever surprised me in my life before. It was like something from Shakespeare's *The Tempest* – believable only on stage.

They'd arranged it. Each would give space to each other, to find me alone for a *forlorn-hope* [2] *tête à tête*. Each coronary colloquy concluded in exactly the way each of them had anticipated. This gave rise to an anguish far beyond the end of my relationship with Lindie Dale or Alice. Quite apart from the assertion I'd made to "dette, I couldn't have taken up with one lady, whilst rejecting the other two. They knew it. I knew it. They knew that I knew it. The ladies, however, were committed to the *forlorn hope* – and despite everything, they felt it imperative to charge the ramparts of Heartbreak Hotel. The words of Düd'jom Rinpoche were there for me – as they always were *'With each life-circumstance: whatever is enacted, stare directly into the enactment – with all the senses.'*

It had been the bargain from hell. I'd assured 'dette that I had no intentions in that direction – a few days before. And there it was— entirely possible—but nothing could be done about it. It was hard to fathom how I'd lived in a house for almost three years with three ladies who would have liked me as a romantic partner – while I'd languished, by a default, in a doomed relationship. I should have left 'dette – but I was unwilling to put her at emotional risk before culmination of the degree course.

---

2   The forlorn hope was a contingent of infantry leading an assault where the death toll would be high. It was composed of volunteers and led by a junior officer with hopes of advancement. If the volunteers survived, they would benefit by promotion. The term derives from the Dutch 'verloren hoop' – *lost heap*. In the 1700s, it was used to refer to the first wave of soldiers attacking a breach in defences during a siege in which most would be killed or wounded. Some however, would survive long enough to seize a foothold that could be reinforced by a second wave.

A person needed to be unassailed by emotional turmoil at such a time. 'dette could come across as having the strength and invulnerability of an armoured battleship – but although she appeared titanic there were icebergs. 'dette was actually more susceptible than most. I could be jilted on the eve of amounting an exhibition – and simply plough my way through. I'd ploughed on before... but 'dette had no such experience – and no fundamental fortitude.

I'd had reasons enough to leave 'dette in the second year... but it had only become intolerable in the third year – and by then, I'd decided to simply see it out to the external assessments of Degree Shows. And now I'd parted from her – she wasn't as upset as I feared. On the other hand, I was far more upset than I'd anticipated – but for entirely different reasons.

I could have lived with the three ladies in perpetuity. 'dette had made it possible for me to live under the illusion that Penelope, Meryl, and Rebecca were simply extremely good friends – by making me romantically unavailable. Now that 'dette and I had separated – her words hung over me like Dorje Bernakchen's cleaver. She'd accused me of leaving her for one of her three friends. I'd denied it about as vehemently as anything of which one was innocent can ever be denied. It was a double-bind, in which I had no choice other but to lose everything.

'dette was possibly more perceptive than I was – and evidently intuited existential human facts that I'd missed. Was it Penelope, Rebecca, and Meryl's enthusiasm to pose for me as subjects for my *Speaking With Ravens* paintings? I'd thought that was simply their enthusiasm for my paintings. Maybe I was *that* naïve. Maybe I made too little of their removal of clothing to model for an oil painting in which they'd be morphed with ravens. They'd liked my *Speaking with Ravens* paintings so much that they each wanted to be painted in that mode. I'd seen nothing so unusual about that.

I'd sat naked for a painting of *Le Déjeuner sur l'herbe* [3] with two young ladies wearing Victorian dresses borrowed from Farnham Theatre. It had been an idea of a group of the Foundation Course ladies and they'd asked for a male volunteer. They'd wanted to paint a reversed gender version of the painting. Nothing amorous had come of that. We'd all taken it as normal at Art School. Well… maybe it was… but maybe they'd been thinking about me in a different light – and I was simply too naïve to have suspected anything other than Art.

Maybe I'd meet up with Penelope, Rebecca, or Meryl in the future – but they weren't going to remain single forever on the chance that I'd return from the Himalayas in search of one of them. There was nothing I could say before I left to give any indication of anything other than mystery. And even if I did meet up with one of them again – I'd have her parents to encounter. Their parents—I came to understand—made Mr Gascoigne look like a distinct social inferior. They told me this merely to explain that 'dette's father was a parvenu [4] – and thus she had no reason at all to lord it over me. Their parents were in the region of the upper middle class who rubbed shoulders with the aristocracy – but it failed to imbue them with the slightest degree of hauteur.

"It tends to be like that with the nouveau riche [5]" Penelope had commented. *"They're often insecure and need to establish as much social distance as they can from anyone they perceive as being of a lower class. The funny thing is that they tend to be more snobbish, the closer in social status they see other people as being – to the social bracket to which they want to belong, or pretend to belong."*

3   Le Déjeuner sur l'herbe *(Luncheon on the Lawn)* oil painting by Édouard Manet (1862–1863) depicts a naked lady with two fully dressed gentlemen in an arboreal setting. It was rejected by the Salon jury of 1863, but Édouard Manet exhibited it in the 1863 Salon des Refusés – where it caused notoriety and controversy. Le Déjeuner sur l'herbe now hangs in the Musée d'Orsay in Paris.
4   Parvenu — a person of humble origin having gained, influence or celebrity through newly acquired wealth.
5   *Nouveau riche* – those with recently acquired wealth, typically perceived as ostentatious and lacking in taste.

Suddenly I understood something *"Oh... I see now. She's in the jealous god realm."*

"The jealous good realm? What's that?" Penelope had asked with obvious fascination.

"It's one of six mind-states. It's a lot to go into – but basically, it's concerned with neurotic speed. The greater the neurotic speed the more hellish existence seems, and the slower – the more... heavenly. The Gods are all in the slowest cycle and so they're self-composed to the extent that they become seraphic or ethereal. They've made it to the top and nothing poses a threat to them. They have nothing left to achieve and they're free to languidly admire themselves or each other. They are relaxed enough to be kindly. The jealous gods however, are hard-wired rivals. They're obsessed with status and the higher levels of status they could attain. They have a corrosive kind of vanity."

"Where do human beings fit into the picture?"

"Well... the human realm is the one where realisation is possible – because there's a sense of humour."

Penelope had burst out laughing at that point – to which I had responded *"Exactly."*

Later, with this conversation emerging from memory, I said to Meryl *"You know... you have each been as good friends to me as Steve and Ron. I'm sadder to leave here than I can express. I could've stayed here in this house with you three forever – but life isn't like that... is it..."*

"No..." Meryl sighed, her eyes brimming *"I..."* then it was too much for her and she plunged her face into her hands and sobbed. That was too much for me – and I sat there weeping with her. Meryl, Rebecca, and Penelope had wanted a relationship with me. Each was in love with me – and, as soon as it was expressed, I found myself in love with each of them.

It was utterly impossible. Inexplicable. Incomprehensible. Unfathomable. Implausible. Inconceivable. The three ladies—one after another—drove a corkscrew into my pericardium. It twisted itself sans remorse – or rather, I twisted.

It was passing strange… It was—to be melodramatic—a harrowing scene from a Shakespearian tragedy.

> *'My story being done, she gave me for my pains a world of sighs. She swore, in faith 'twas strange, 'twas passing strange; 'twas pitiful; 'twas wondrous pitiful. She wish'd she had not heard it, yet she wish'd that heaven had made her such a man.'*
> Willian Shakespeare—Othello—Act I—scene iii

The days passed. I was rejected by the RCA, without being called for an interview. They viewed my portfolio and decided I wasn't interesting. How was *that* possible? Not that I'm the best thing since Botticelli – but I'd got a 1st class honours degree. Derek Crowe had practically written me a purple-prose eulogy of a reference. So, what went wrong? Were the other candidates—*that*—much better?

My mind turned back to how much I'd been enticed by the prospect of having Dorje Bernakchen destroy my life. I'd felt vaguely heroic in making that decision. I'd felt that this was the correct course for a serious practitioner to take. Was Dorje Bernakchen now making me responsible for that choice? Was Dorje Bernakchen responsible for the tragic revelation of the mutually unrequitable love of three ladies? Was Dorje Bernakchen responsible for my rejection by the RCA? No… that would be eternalist superstition. Then a more down to earth memory trickled into the forefront of my memory.

Just before the external assessors arrived Dick Taylor—the Head of Department—made his rounds of the degree show. He paused at my exhibition – and said *"Well—Victor—**Simmer**—son… you never quite—came to the—**boil**—as an Illustrator… did you."* How long had he planned that I wondered? Since my *'Dick Taylorship'* remark in the first term? Dick Taylor on the first day of term—having bored everyone rigid for an hour or so with his philosophy of Graphic Design—told us *'… of course… there is room for different points of view – this isn't a dictatorship'* and I'd blurted out *'Sounds more like a Dick Taylorship.'*

I was such a balefully bolshie fellow in those days. I hoped I'd grown out of it – but I hadn't. Dick Taylor had made a joke about my name so I'd flung it back at him with a big grin *"No Dick… but then, I've never aspired to be a codpiece couturier."* There'd been muffled guffaws from the tutors—as before—but, this time, Dick Taylor's slight smile remained. *"You know the wise saw?"* he paused for effect. I raised my eyebrows to indicate that I was not aware of which wise saw to which he referred. *"He who laughs last, laughs longest…*[6] *you would do well to remember it."*

Then—still with his *slight* smile—he moved on to the next display; as if nothing had happened. When considering that, I realised that my rejection by the RCA had a cause other than Dorje Bernakchen. All Dick Taylor had to have done was to have written a private letter to the RCA. Derek Crowe, after all, wasn't the head of Graphic Design. Derek was the head of Illustration – which was a subset of Graphic Design. Illustration *did* operate as an autonomous entity – but, alas, it wasn't.

I had no proof however – and the thought of mentioning the possibility to Derek seemed like something I would—not—want to do. It would put Derek in a horribly awkward position – and to what end? If Dick Taylor had described me as some sort of maverick, dissident, rebel, or insurgent – I was scuppered in any case. I had no need to take Derek down with me. Dick was not a wonderful human being – but in the first year I'd still been, impetuous, impulsive, and terminally naïve. *Nobody's fault but mine…*[7]

It occurred to me that I could still be fighting my father. I had peculiar 'authority issues' which applied to some authorities – yet not others. With Kyabjé Düd'jom Rinpoche my 'authority issues' were entirely absent – so maybe I didn't have 'authority issues' in the conventional sense.

6   15th Century proverb – also expressed as *'He who laughs last, laughs best'* or *'He who laughs last, laughs loudest.'*
7   'Nobody's Fault but Mine' is a song first recorded by Blues artist Blind Willie Johnson in 1927 as a solo performance – vocals and slide guitar.

Whether conventional or unconventional however, my need to stand my ground with petty tyrants was not always wise let alone circumspect. Maybe it was rarely wise – but standing my ground was somehow too seductive when a witty repost appeared in an instant. Telling Dick Taylor that *'I'd never aspired to be a codpiece couturier'* was evidently far funnier than his line about *'Simmerson never having come to the boil'*. Two of the Graphic Design lecturers had expressed their appreciation for it in private after that event. They even told me that Dick Taylor had thoroughly deserved my response. They deemed it unworthy for a man of his age and status to attempt to humiliate a student – especially one who had just been awarded a 1st Class Honours degree. They told me that my remark had caused great mirth in the department.

'Yes…' I thought *'that was not intelligent. It may have been wonderfully witty – but at what a cost…'*

I remembered the words of Düd'jom Rinpoche *'With each life-circumstance: whatever is enacted, stare directly into the enactment – with all the senses.'*

I decided that the real razor-edge of Dorje Bernakchen's blade had to be the nature of my own decisions. There was a decision that I now *had* to make. Was I to apply again to the RCA in a year's time? That had been Derek Crowe's suggestion. It was a good one. He was prepared to help me build other aspects to my portfolio. I could either take that good advice – or I could look for my reflection in the blade of that shining copper cleaver.

The idea had been to take an MA and possibly a PhD in order to have the best possibility of securing a position as an Art School lecturer. That would have fitted well with Kyabjé Düd'jom Rinpoche's idea of how I ought to organise my life. I'd explained to him that I would have long holidays—and the possibility of occasionally taking sabbatical years— especially if I could combine it with learning thangka painting and studies in Vajrayana iconography. I could continue with my practices as I had done on my BA at Bristol – and similarly as an Art School lecturer.

It had been the perfect plan.

At that time however, a new policy was gaining sway with Art schools – that of not taking lecturing applicants immediately on conclusion of their degree courses. It was beginning to be seen as preferable for applicants to have had experience as working artists, illustrators, or graphic designers. It was not a bad idea in some ways – but it was not useful for a person who had no interest in being a professional working artist. I was naturally interested in continuing to paint. I was naturally interested in the possibility of exhibiting my work – but only from the basis of being a lecturer on an Art School Foundation Course. How could I throw myself into the efforts required to become a working artist if my plan was to give it up to be a lecturer at some later point? With respect to the benefit it purported to give to Art Schools it was also somewhat problematic. The result would be that lecturing applicants would be likely to be those who had failed in the commercial world. They would no longer get people who wanted to be lecturers as their first choice. Derek Crowe saw the problem immediately – and considered the new policy to be short-sighted. For once Derek had no immediate answer other than to bite the bullet and do what was necessary – although he acknowledged it would seem a dispiriting option for me. I thanked Derek for his advice – and, then booked a one-way ticket for Amritsar[8] on Afghan Air. The cleaver of Dorje Bernakchen had self-effectuated.

It required an overdraft – but that was accommodated by my bank. I would work to pay it off and also raise enough to cover my time in the Himalayas. I left myself enough time to accomplish that – but just enough. I was to have taken a year out in any case; before going to the RCA – and laboured longer to raise healthy collateral for my sojourn in the Himalayas. If I'd done that, I could have secured a return flight to Delhi. I wanted however, to hit the road as quickly as could now be managed.

---

8   Amritsar (ਅੰਮ੍ਰਿਤਸਰ) is a city in the Punjab, North-western India. It is the home of the Sikh religion.

I felt the need to see Kyabjé Düd'jom Rinpoche as soon as possible; to sit in the Düd'jom Gompa; circumambulate the Great Chörten in Bodha; and then, go to see Düd'jom Rinpoche – just as I had done in 1971. I had missed Düd'jom Rinpoche for the three years of the Illustration degree – but the feeling of separation had become exponentially intense. Buying the airline ticket was the answer. As soon as I had my ticket – it was as if I'd left it all behind. I sang *"Well I'm going away with no word of farewell – I will leave not a trace left behind. I could've done much better—didn't mean to be unkind—y'know that was the last thing on my mind."* [9]

Goodbye Forever. The idea of the one-way ticket also included the fact that I'd have to come back overland. I wanted to challenge myself, with as much insecurity as I could arrange. Life circumstances were—*not*—going to have the whip-hand. I was quite capable of facilitating my own emptiness. It made me feel better to have my hands on the handlebars with my right hand on the throttle. The thought that I could reject the notion of running for cover—quite utterly—seemed a strong position. I felt it was nobler *to welcome the slings and arrows of outrageous misfortune* [10] and jeer *'Is that the best you can do?'* Then I laughed at myself for being absurdly melodramatic.

I'd travel to McLeod Ganj first—to see Ngakpa Yeshé Dorje and Jétsunma Khandro Ten'dzin Drölkar and get my bearings—then straight to Nepal and speak with Kyabjé Düd'jom Rinpoche. He would set me on track for whatever was needed.

I left Bristol feeling confident—in terms of my plans—but almost as emotionally shell-shocked as I had been when Steve and Ron died back in 1970.

9   Parody of 'The Last Thing on my Mind' by Tom Paxton *'Are you going away with no word of farewell / Will there be not a trace left behind? / Well, I could have loved you better, / Didn't mean to be unkind / You know that was the last thing on my mind.'*

10   Adaptation of the soliloquy of Hamlet from Hamlet by William Shakespeare *'Whether 'tis nobler in the mind to suffer the slings and arrows of outrageous fortune or to take arms against a sea of troubles…'*

My Art career lay in ruins – just as my musical career had lain in ruins; just as my romance with Lindie Dale had lain in ruins; and, just as my romance with Anelie and Alice lay in ruins before that. Penelope, Meryl, and Rebecca had not died – but the possibility of romance had been given and taken away on the same day. The line from Steve's funeral service came back to me *'The Lord giveth and the Lord taketh away.'* I knew it from the Bible study classes between the ages of 12 and 16 with the pedantic Mrs Pendrake.

> *'… naked came I out of my mother's womb, and naked shall I return thither: the Lord giveth, and the Lord taketh away; blessed be the name of the Lord.'* The Bible—Job 1:21

I was not exactly thrilled by the idea of blessing anyone—particularly a putative uncreated creator—for having taken away what had been taken away – from me and from countless millions of mothers. Was the Lord to be blessed for the Nazi holocaust and the pogroms[11] in Russia? Considering the horrors inflicted since the dawn of time – my own tragedies became so utterly insignificant that my life may as well have been a continuous jamboree. I acknowledged that – but I was still left with some-sort-of dull ache in the area of my sternum. I knew it was a petty indulgence – but the sensation remained nonetheless. It could be intensified by immoderate speculative delving – but *that* could easily be relinquished. I could sit and allow self-absorption dissipate – so I sat. Where there is no self-absorption there is no self-pity, no sadness, and no emotional pain. Emotional pain was a choice to a certain extent – and a ngakpa had to make congruent choices about it. If I couldn't see myself justifying it to Düd'jom Rinpoche – I had no business feeling it.

---

11 Pogrom: massacre or expulsion of an ethnic or religious group, particularly aimed at Jews. The Slavic term entered the English language to describe 19th / 20th-century attacks on Jews in Russia. Significant pogroms in Russia included the Odessa pogroms: Warsaw pogrom in 1881; Kishinev pogrom in 1903; Kiev Pogrom in 1905; and Białystok pogrom in 1906.

I went home to Farnham and sought employment at Boots[12] Warehouse in Aldershot. I worked all the overtime on offer and spent the rest of my time either helping my mother look after my father—practising the Tröma Nakmo drüpthab—or lying in the garden reading books on Vajrayana. I saw no one. I went nowhere.

My father had suffered a series of strokes – and was incapacitated. He'd had a feverish few years in which he continued to drive his car. How he survived is vaguely miraculous. I'd once gone into Guildford with him and he clipped the wing mirrors of a couple of cars. *"Dreadful the way people park these days!"* he'd said. *"Yes"* I replied *"quite disgraceful."* Back when I was 16, I'd agree with him just to keep the peace in the house. He'd backed down on his hair-cutting threat – and so I felt it right and proper not to challenge any of his Tory concepts. He was a *hang'em and flog'em man* and whenever he'd express such an idea I'd respond *"It's the only way."* – but later—when clipping wing mirrors—I was more concerned not to call him to question. I was glad, in the end, that I never questioned his driving abilities – because he never had an accident in which he harmed anyone. Soon he had another stroke and became incapable of driving, or even walking. I felt sorry for him. Our *embattled history* had evaporated years before, in any case. I'd ceased to have any resentment toward him since 1968. Once I'd been free to wear what clothes I liked—and grow my hair as long as I wished—the fierce old father I'd known for 16 years disappeared along with all traces of resentment. I was pragmatic about resentment. There was nothing to be gained from it. I had my freedom – so I'd lived that freedom. I didn't even need to forgive him. There was nothing to forgive – and now, my pity was genuine. I'd talk to him whilst he was awake. I read when he was asleep – and then, one day, he never woke up. His life was over.

---

12 *Boots* is a health, beauty and pharmacy retail chain in Britain. Ireland, Italy, Norway, the Netherlands, and Thailand. It is one of the largest retailers in Britain in terms of revenue and shops – with 2,500 shops across Britain ranging from local pharmacies to large health and beauty shops, primarily located in high streets and shopping complexes.

The funeral was brief. Few people came. Uncle Bert was there—Aunt Elsie having died some years previously—and sat in the car with me, my mother, Græham and Jill. My mother put my father's Major's cap on the coffin and said *"Now eet iss a military funeral. Eet iss vott Earnest vould have vonted."*

"Well…" Uncle Bert responded *"… semi-military… let's say."*

Now, I liked Uncle Bert… but what a time to be *vaguely quasi-factual*. No one commented. My mother seemed unaffected by the remark. She was always wise that way – and, she'd observed my upward roll of the eyes.

My mother was adamant about my not changing the plan to leave for the Himalayas. I tried. I failed. It seemed it was better to allow my mother to be the strong woman she was. She was aware I'd been disappointed in a variety of ways. I'd told her about it – but only because she'd asked. Now she seemed determined I shouldn't be disappointed again so soon. I had to get on with my life. She'd be fine. There'd be far less work for her now. *"Just write me letters Veector—but not more than vonce a veek or so—-just to let me know zat you are vell and happy."*

I left Boots Warehouse—my last pay-cheque in hand—with the words 'goodbye forever' unspoken – but singing in every molecule of my nervous, lymphatic, vascular, and musculoskeletal system.

I remembered the words of Düd'jom Rinpoche *'With each life-circumstance: whatever is enacted, stare directly into the enactment – with all the senses.'*

27

jumping jack flashman

Boots Warehouse. Continental shifts[1] and two hours overtime every day. That was now history. I'd worked ten hours a day for eight weeks. I was glad—beyond words—to have left Boots Warehouse. I found factory work the most inhumane of all job options. Labouring on roadworks—or building sites—was far easier; even though the toil was physically harder. I had needed to earn money, however – and as swiftly as possible. I wanted to be in the Himalayas by the Autumn, so I had to take any work that was going.

There were two weeks left before my flight to India. I somehow felt in need of a rest before setting out. Not the kind of rest one requires when exhausted – because although the work at Boots warehouse had been hard, I felt no weariness once it was concluded. The rest I felt I needed was simply *space*: space in which there was nothing that had to happen; *space* sans timetable, schedule, agenda, programme, or itinerary.

I practised the Tröma Nakmo drüpthab. I spent time with my mother. We watched television in the evenings. Not often – just old movies, when they happened to be screened. *Casablanca. The African Queen. Gone with the Wind.* We sat in the garden. We ate delicious *English* scones with fine *German* coffee. Normal is *whatever it is.* I remembered the words of Düd'jom Rinpoche '*With each life-circumstance: whatever is enacted, stare directly into the enactment – with all the senses.*'

I was no longer an Art student – and, although I occasionally drew parts of the apple tree, I came to wonder why. Merely habit? Maybe. Did I enjoy it? Yes. Did I draw merely because I felt morally impelled? Possibly… Was I even an artist anymore?

---

1   The continental shifts operated at Boots Warehouse were 4am to 12 noon; 12 noon to 8pm; and, 8pm to 4am – in a three-week cycle. Two hours overtime could be added to each shift.

Yes… but how was that *artist* going to create images beyond the sacred precincts of an Art School? There'd be thangka painting studies in the Himalayas – but that was an entirely different field of endeavour from Art as I knew it at *Art School*.

I'd not been a Bluesman for years. Occasionally I wondered about that – and about Kyabjé Düd'jom Rinpoche's advice always to sing *Hoochie Coochie Man* – the song I had sung at his request in 1971. *Hoochie Coochie Man* then, was the one song I sang – once a week without fail, in order to keep what I felt to be damtsig.[2] I was, however, not singing it to any audience. The song amused my mother – because she didn't even recognise the language as English. That made me smile – because Frank Berner had taught me well in terms of Black American Southern accent. I could still do that – although how I'd sound to a Black American audience was open to question. I still had a few harps – a B, A, and G. The G was my favourite as it was the lowest. Some people liked the higher pitched harps – but they were castrato[3] squeakers as far as I was concerned. I wished that the companies who made them offered lower-register harps. Would it hurt them to make a low F?[4] My mother liked to hear me play harp. She said that it was good for me to play and to remember my old friends. She always called them Stephen and Ronald. I was touched that my mother should remember Steve and Ron as musicians and that she regarded the Savage Cabbage Blues Band as having been an important part of my life. She told me that they would not have wanted me to give up playing the music we loved.

2   Damtsig *(dam tshig / samaya)* sacred word / commitment – the sacred pledges or commitments of Vajrayana practice. Samayas consist of maintaining harmonious relationship with the Lama and ones vajra siblings.
3   Castrato – classical male singing voice equivalent to that of a soprano. The voice is produced by castration of the singer before puberty. Castration before puberty prevents the larynx from being transformed by the physiological effects of puberty. The prepubescent vocal range is thus retained. Prepubescent castration for this purpose diminished greatly in the late 18th century and was made illegal in 1870. The modern equivalent—occurring without surgical intervention—is termed *counter tenor*.
4   No reference seems to be available vis-à-vis dates – but a lower range of harmonicas began to be made by the 21st Century.

She asked me if I ever missed being on stage. Well, yes, I did… I did when I thought about it – when I cast my mind back. It had always been magical, standing there, on a stage – or even simply at one end of a room in a pub. Somehow *there was never anyone there –* in terms of *what 'I' sensed myself to be.* That 'I' had been a member of the Savage Cabbage Blues Band – and, as a member, I was almost a cypher. Strangely I never saw 'singing' as being a skill – because I thought anyone could sing. Steve and Ron were the heroes—Jack was the drummer—and I was *merely there.* That could sound as if I was uninvolved, detached, distant, or indifferent – but that was distinctly not the case. It was simply that I had no sense of myself. I had no sense of being anyone. There was no sense of being important, prominent, or remarkable. That I was *in-the-public-eye* played no part in what I was doing there. I was simply occupying a space where I felt *absolutely* at home. Sometimes it felt as if I was someone in *a film that was being watched* – and that *all I was*, was light shining through celluloid. Now… the projector-light had ceased to shine. The switch had been thrown. The plug had been pulled. Only static celluloid remained in terms of the Bluesman I had been.

Generally—post Boots Warehouse—I seemed to be *no-thing…* a *presence on the brink of some-thing.* That *some-thing* was a locus I only understood intermittently. Did I see things in this way because of my Vajrayana studies? Was this something that arose naturally through practice? This amorphousness was not *what it once was.* Back in the Summer of 1970 with the loss of Lindie Dale—and the deaths of Ron and Steve—I'd been aware of being *a space that was intermittently defined by other factors* – but then it had not been joyous. I was not exactly 'joyous' at this point in time – but I was *somewhat* serene; now that I was no longer at Boots Warehouse. I had moments of monumental joy whenever it occurred to me that I would soon see Kyabjé Düd'jom Rinpoche again. I tried, however, not to fixate too much on the future. Devotion was one thing – but absconding from the present moment was not something that would have met with Düd'jom Rinpoche's approbation.

I had no doubts about my life as a ngakpa or even distantly, as a potential Lama – I'd embraced that in 1971. That was my life, whichever way I was to live it. My vague sense of apprehension was more concerned with what the *shape* of my life was going to be. It would have been easier if I'd been a thoroughgoing card-carrying-hippie – but I had a sense of responsibility. I didn't merely want to drift. I didn't want to end up as a pathetic free-loader. I concluded—every time I thought about it—that it was too early to tie myself up with such considerations. If I was serious – I would make something worthwhile of my functional life; whatever happened. I wasn't lazy – so I should take solace in that as a redeeming characteristic.

Packing was not a huge concern. I'd pick up extra robes in McLeod Ganj. I knew a good tailor. He'd get them ready in under a week. I only needed two of each article to travel. It seemed surreal… knowing that I was going to be away from Britain for six months – but then… life was generally surreal. I'd exchanged some letters with Penelope, Meryl, and Rebecca. I'd also written to 'dette – but 'dette hadn't answered. I had her telephone number – but decided that I'd respect her wish to sever all ties. I'd already sent a letter—and two cards—so it was unlikely they'd *all* been lost in the post. Maybe it was for the best. The one who leaves, has the psychological advantage – and friendships can only be established when the rejected partner has a new beau or belle.

One afternoon, I realised that I'd forgotten to obtain a bottle of Dr Collis Brown's Chlorodyne. [5] My father had recommended it as '… *a fine cure for Delhi-belly*…' It had stood me in good stead back in 1971 when I first went out to India.

5   Dr John Collis Browne's Chlorodyne was a famous British patent medicine. It was formulated in the 19th century by Dr John Collis Browne, a doctor in the British Indian Army as a treatment for cholera. Pharmacist John Thistlewood Davenport advertised it for pain relief as well as a treatment for diarrhœa, insomnia, neuralgia, and migraines. Its principal ingredients were a mixture of laudanum (alcohol solution of opium), tincture of cannabis, and chloroform.

My father had always feared that I'd become a drug-fiend – and so it amused me, many years later, to discover that my father had been my first and only pusher. DR COLLIS BROWN'S CHLORODYNE had an opiate content. I had no idea of this – but as I only resorted to it when I needed to calm the effects of amœbic dysentery, I never became aware of it as a mind-altering substance. If the truth were known, it wasn't just the DR COLLIS BROWN'S CHLORODYNE that prompted me to grab a bus into Farnham. I wanted to make a last visit – just for old time's sake. I was *nothing* if not sentimental.

I jumped a bus—took a seat—and sat watching the still-familiar landscape glide by. The bus rolled past the road where Timothy Fry had demonstrated his hauteur as a kamikaze warrior. That had been back in 1965. We were cycling down the hill toward Farnham after school. Timothy Fry told me that he was studying to be a kamikaze warrior. I didn't believe a word of it. He explained that it was a correspondence course – but that not everyone was selected. He'd been chosen out of a thousand applicants.

"So…" I asked *"How exactly do you train to be a suicide pilot by correspondence course?"*

"Simple" he replied. *"You write and explain your acts of bravery."*

"Such as…?" I asked.

"Such as this!" he yelled and swerved to the other side of the road to face the oncoming car. I immediately pulled over to the side of the road to create as much distance as I could between us. Timothy Fry then charged the on-coming car waving his bicycle pump round his head screaming *"Bonsai!"* [6] He'd mistaken Bonsai for *"Banzai"* [7] but I wasn't of a mind to argue the point.

6 Bonsai (盆栽) is a Japanese art form. It creates miniature trees grown in containers. A bonsai is created from a cutting, seedling. Bonsai can be created from almost any perennial tree and is cultivated to remain small through pot confinement, crown pruning, and tap-root pruning.
7 Banzai is a traditional Japanese exclamation meaning '10,000 years!' A Banzai charge is a last desperate military attack.

The car—hooting loudly— swerved over to my side of the road to avoid him and Timothy Fry made good his escape down Monkton Lane. The incident was never reported to the police – or if it was, he was never brought to book for it. The driver didn't stop to question me and so I cycled on wondering how long Timothy Fry was going to live.

Remembering the event made me laugh aloud. I could imagine the kamikaze trainer saying to his trainees *"Watch carefully lads – I'm only going to show you this once."* Passengers looked 'round at me. A middle-aged woman moved to another seat. The image of Timothy Fry—the kamikaze cyclist—screaming *"Stunted Ornamental Japanese Tree!"* had just erupted out of nowhere.

Timothy Fry had shaved since he was eight—by his own account —and by the stubble on his face, I could well believe it. I was thought unusual to have had a moustache at the age of 14 – but that was nothing on Timothy Fry. He even *had* to shave his nose. No word of a lie – I saw the bristles on his nose one day when he'd not shaved for a couple of days. He was a thin as a rake, smoked like a chimney, and suffered almost permanent bronchitis. That memory brought on a welter of other memories. Then— almost surprisingly—I found myself in Farnham. I obtained a bottle of DR COLLIS BROWN'S CHLORODYNE and—having stowed it in my shoulder bag—proceeded to walk down the river to Hatch Mill, the site of the Foundation course. There was no one there. That should have been obvious – so I sat looking at the building, wondering why I'd taken the trouble of walking there from the town.

I rose to my feet from the tree stump on which I'd sat. I wandered past the willow trees where I'd sat for the gender reversed painting of *Le déjeuner sur l'herbe*. I'd been the naked man having a picnic with two ladies dressed in Victorian apparel borrowed from Farnham Theatre. I still had the idea of being some sort of key-figure in the world of the Arts in those days. I'd been younger and somehow blessed—if I can use such a word—with an outrageous degree of naïveté.

Anything had been possible – but that was in 1970. Now it was 1975 – and it felt as if a century had passed. How could that bright young fellow have died? Well… everyone's *a bright-young-something-or-other* at Art School – but then you're eventually out in the world having to create your own meaning. Even if I'd been accepted by the RCA for an MA—even if I'd gone on to take a PhD—it would all have come to an end. Gradually the students around me would have become increasingly *something else…* something other than *students of the '60s.*

I felt *ever-so-slightly* desolate. A few too many losses had piled up. The incremental effect seemed to be weighing on me – but in ways that were not simple to calculate. I knew my father had to die at some point. I had known his time was nearing an end for a while.

I remembered the words of Düd'jom Rinpoche *'With each life-circumstance: whatever is enacted, stare directly into the enactment – with all the senses.'*

Although we'd got on fairly well since '68 we'd not had the degree of closeness that would allow a deep sense of grief – but grief was there nonetheless. I felt sorry for the way his life had gone and the way he'd never obtained what he wanted. Having become a major from entering the Army as a private soldier – he'd thought he could segue into the class of his fellow officers. That had not happened – partially because he was unwilling to toe the line. I had become very much like him in certain ways – and was glad I was able to admit it. Years before I would have said that I was nothing like my father in any respect – but I was wrong. It was good to be able to thank my father—if only in my own mind—for giving me the example of holding to principles and not being swayed by fashion.

The list of identifiers, indicators, and reference-points that pointed to 'me' were being nullified one-by-one leaving only… a *space* which observed *what it wasn't.*

Before I knew where I was – I was somewhere else. I was back in Farnham town and approaching Downing Street.

I found myself walking into *The Nostril Café*. It wasn't called *The Nostril Café*; that's just what the lads had called it – but what it was actually called, eludes me. It was made to look like a cave inside with badly constructed blue stalagmites and stalactites. This was always where we went to pass an hour with an indifferent cup of coffee. The coffee was better than most places – but still nowhere near German coffee.

There was a face I gradually recognised as I looked for a free table. Jack Hackman.

"Jack…?" I began *"Is that you…?"*

"Jumping Jack Flashman!" he grinned with unbridled glee. ***"Man****—of the Moment."*

"Flashman?"

"Yeah mate… changed me name, di'n' I! Long story though – 'less you're not up for it."

"I'm up for it, Jumping Jack" I replied with much more enthusiasm than I felt. *"Testify brother!"*

"Good f'you my man!" Then, theatrically *"I was born in a cross-fire hurricane!"* he laughed somewhat manically *"But… before I tell you the amazing tale… I s'pose you're not Farquhar Arbuthnot now, either."*

I shook my head.

"S'what monica [8] *d'you rejoice under these days, me ol' china?"* [9]

What a question. Who was I? *"On'y monica I ever know'd, Jack…"* I said in a Southern drawl *"wuz* **har**-*monica, y'know—Blues harp."* then back to my normal speaking voice, I continued *"… but… as to names… that's all a bit in the air."*

---

8   *Monica* means *name*. Various derivations exist but there seems to be no consensus as to its origin. One derivation is Cockney Rhyming slang: *Monica James* to rhyme with *name*.
9   *China*—as in china plate—is Cockney rhyming slang for *mate* – i.e. friend.

"So… whassat mean 'en?"

I took my seat, whilst speaking out the John Lennon line *"The dream is over—what can I say—the dream is over, yesterday / I was Vic Simmerson… but now he's gone."*

"Well 'e may be gone – but 'e still takes liberties with lyrics as much as 'e ever did."

"Yeah Jack…" I sighed *"still do… but — what I mean, is that I don't believe in a lot of things anymore. That was the purport of John Lennon's song—y'know—he sings 'I don't believe in Beatles' but he ends 'I just believe in me.'… Thing is Jack… I don't think I believe in 'me' either."*

"Bloody 'ell, that's a bit depressing – if yer don't mind me sayin'…?"

"No… not at all. I don't mind" I grinned. *"You see… it might sound depressing – but it's more… surreal… than anything. Life's just become mysterious and the future has no shape that I recognise."*

Jack shook his head in a mixture of amusement and faint derision and moved his hand in a way that I recognised as a prompt for me to continue.

"Oh right" I laughed. *"My name, I never said."*

"That's right" Jack laughed, turning his eyes heavenward *"Y'never said – so, out with it then."*

"It's still officially Vic… but I'm not 'The Man of the Moment' or anything like that. That's what I don't believe anymore – or maybe 'it' doesn't believe in me."

"Y'what?"

"Well… it seems I was a fictional character – and, reality got wise to it."

Jack was obviously not understanding a word I was saying and I found myself wishing I hadn't opened up a useless bag of sincere yet incoherent blatheration.

I was not usually so oblique in conversation – but the juxtaposition of life scenarios had created an ambience of heightened Surrealism… and I was vaguely dissimulating. I'd never dropped acid – but I imagined that this is how an acid trip might have felt. I'd been at Samŷe Ling in Scotland with Gyalwa Karmapa back in the Spring and it had been such a powerful experience that it felt as if I'd only left that environment yesterday – and now I was here in the Nostril Café with Jumping Jack Flashman trying to explain my life. Who was I to explain my life? I had no fixed idea what my life was – and only an attenuated sense of where it might be going.

"Victor Simmerson's what's on my passport and driving license… but… these days Vic's fading fast. Soon… he'll be gone for ever."

"So?" Jack asked with slight exasperation *"… 'oo's replacin' 'im?"*

"… Chögyam…" the name that seemed so normal at Samŷe Ling, suddenly sounded exotic and I couldn't decide whether I should have used it or not.

"Cobham…?" Jack responded with a look of incredulity *"like… errr, like the village up the road where Savage Cabbage played that time?"*

"No" I grinned. *"Good try Jack. It's Chögyam:* Cher—Gyam. *It's a Tibetan name. I got that name when I took robes out in Nepal in* 1971. *I took ordination in a Tibetan Buddhist non-celibate order – and… I'm just about to leave for the Himalayas again in a few days."*

"Jeeeee—sus mate!" Jacked chuckled. *"Bloody Nora… I mean – never took—you—f'r'n 'ari Krishna!"*

"No Jack…" I laughed *"nothing even—remotely—similar. No need to be alarmed, I'm not going to try to sell you an album by unknown musicians or anything: y'know—like they do—name-dropping George Harrison as if he played on the album."* PAUSE *"I suppose I shouldn't really have told you something like that out-of-the-blue – but… my life is a little strange at the moment… transitional. I'm half way between this and that – and it's hard to know what to say."*

"Sorry—yeah mate—I suppose I was a bit flip. You better tell me what it's all about" Jack replied, trying to look as if he was sincerely interested.

"I think I'd rather not bore you with the details, Jack. I completely understand your reaction… I've seen a lot of loony stuff connected with the East. I'm more-or-less the same as I ever was – so I'm not going to preach at you or tell you a bunch of stuff from the astral plane or anything. I've… just grown a bit tired of everything that I was… or rather – what I was trying to be."

"You're not saying…" Jacked interrupted my flow *"you wouldn't like to be back with—Savage Cabbage—again?"*

"Got me—there—Jack… you got me there…" I chuckled with mild melancholia *"Yes. I would. I—really—would. There've been many times when I'd have liked nothing better than to turn the clock back… to have Steve and Ron back… to be playing Blues again together – and… having the future stretching out like the goddamn miracle it could have been – or should have been. A Buddhist has to do something to make a living – and Savage Cabbage would have been ideal."* PAUSE *"I think… when I was on stage with Savage Cabbage – that I was doing something that I can do – perhaps better than an Art School lecturer."*

"So… Art School wasn't good?" Jack looked puzzled and made a movement with his head to betoken the need for further information; so, I gave it.

"I'm not saying I didn't enjoy Art School – it was brilliant. I wouldn't have missed it for the world… but… in terms of feeling 'This is me! I'm right where I belong!'… I think—that—was more me… back then… out there on stage with you lads, than most other places I've been, apart from the Himalayas, of course."

"Yeah… we were bloody great!" Jack hooted – ignoring my reference to the Himalayas. *"Gotta 'dmit 'aven'tcher! Bloody great!"*

"Yeah Jack…" I agreed *"we—were—great…"* What else could I say?

"Ron and Steve were great—and we… we were lucky to have played Blues with them." PAUSE *"Those may have been the best days of our lives you know…"* A sense of loss stole over me all over again – as if Ron and Steve had died five days ago rather than five years.

"Yeah… well…" Jack looked at me a little strangely *"I'm 'oping to 'ave some more-a-those days."*

"So… Jack Bruce just teamed up with Buddy Guy – and they've asked you to be their drummer?"

"Wouldn't say no to that!" Jack laughed *"But no: nothing like that."*

My mind was now full of Ron and Steve and the ancient past. Ron had been a rare musical prodigy who made most other guitarists dim in comparison. Steve—although he wasn't in Ron's league of unqualified genius—had been a world-class bassist. I waited— peering incredulously at Jack—for what wonders were going to tumble forth.

"To be honest… that time was a mixed thing for me." PAUSE *"Savage Cabbage was bloody brilliant – but… I had me poxy parents and sodding Cynth in the background. And, I—'ated—school. For Ron and Steve, school work was a doddle—they got straight 'A's in everythin' without bleedin' effort—and all you did was write bloody poetry and paint weird pictures."*

"Well… I did have History and Sociology in the first-year 6th."

"Yeah alright… but I was never any good at any of that. I was never interested in how many wives 'enry the bloody Eighth 'ad – so school was just endless memorisation of pointless bleedin' information."

"I can see that… I guess I was pretty free – I only had Art and English in the second-year 6th, so life was much better for me."

"Yeah… s'pose there was Lindie though. That couldn't've bin much fun – nearly being' lynched by her soddin' upper-class parents."

"… true enough Jack… It took me a while to get over that… quite a long while."

"I thought you said you 'ad a whale of a time at Art School?"

"I did… but… Lindie never really faded from view…"

"You never 'ad another girlfriend?" Jack almost squawked. *"Never gottcher leg-over?"* [10]

"I had other relationships, Jack – but none of them worked out. And… it wasn't because those ladies weren't Lindie. I only realised they weren't Lindie, when the relationships concluded. Then it just became obvious. No one ever matched up to Lindie in the end. I didn't start out judging them as to how much like Lindie they were—or I don't think I did—but by the end it always stared me in the face."

"So, it's Lindie or nothin'?" Jack asked with a look of incredulity.

"No Jack…" I chuckled mirthlessly. *"I'm not quite the incurable romantic you always made me out to be. I'm not looking to meet up with Lindie again – just someone—like—her. Even if I bumped into Lindie this afternoon she'd still have her middle upper-middle class parents. I've come to the conclusion that—sometimes—you have to leave the past in the past."*

"Yeah mate! Too bloody right! My parents c'n stay in the frigging past an' so c'n sodding Synthetic Cynthia!"

"Nice alliteration Jack."

"Yeah well… you should know. I know that's what you three always called 'er." PAUSE *"Synthetic Cynthia."* PAUSE *"Shoulda **listened**, shouldn' I."* PAUSE *"Shoulda bin more **determined**… y'know… like I was on that day when I went wild on me drums?"*

"Yeah Jack! Now—that—was a good session! You really showed us how far you'd come that day! That was the day after you quit Cynthia wasn't it?" Jack nodded. *"I mean, you didn't say so but we—all—knew. And we—all— felt glad for you"* I beamed.

"Yeah… knew that… knew, you all knew." PAUSE *"… but then… but then… Ron and Steve died di'n' they…"*

---

10 *Getting a leg over* British slang for sexual intercourse.

Jack wiped a tear from his eye *"and then… and then… I just—**lost**—me—fuckin'—nerve."* Jack looked round warily to see whether any of the staff had heard him swear. They threw people out of the Nostril for swearing. The odd 'bloody' was permissible – but 'the f-word' was strictly prohibited. *"I **lost** me nerve."*

"Don't blame you Jack… I wasn't in a good state after that – but… I had Art School ahead of me and you didn't."

"Yeah… and I had the f…" he held back on the word *"Midland Bank… Midland Bank! 'Midland' they called it – shoulda been Barclays,*[11] *'cause it was full of'em. Can you imagine it! Getting up—every—day to work for—eight—hours under the beady eye of Cynth's f… fat-gutted father!?"*

"Yeah… well… I can imagine. Sounds pretty ghastly."

*"Yeah and—**every**—day I just sat there dreamin' I was back with Savage Cabbage—livin' a real life—rather than… rather than… ekin' out me bloody days in a soddin' mortu'ry fulla rottin' robots. All they'd talk about was what-was-on-tele the night before or what new stupid thing they bought to stick in the garden."* Jack assumed a farcical expression: imitating an employee of Midland Bank *"Oh how—lovely! You have a lovely new gnome! We have a new gnome too – we've put it in the gazebo! What colour hat does your gnome have? Does it match the others? Does it contrast with the others in your pergola? And how are your potted aspidistras?"*

"Yeah…" I laughed. *"I think I'd rather hobo. I'd rather live under some viaduct than have that kind of job."* PAUSE *"It's the same for me… I got some glimpse of possibility with Savage Cabbage and… I must admit that it has haunted me periodically."*

"Yeah! We were at the f'—Glory Station—*just about to board* the gravy-train! For… life! For life, me old china! Money galore! Groupies galore! Maseratis! Lamborghinis! Ferraris! Fancy French friggin' Restaurants! Villa in the South-a-France! Swimmin' in the Med, man! And*—Everything Else!*"

---

11 *Barclays*—as in Barclays Bank—is Cockney rhyming slang for *wank* (masturbate). A Barclay was therefore a wanker.

"Well… not quite what I meant – but yeah… all that would've been there – although I'm not a big fan of the high life." PAUSE *"But… what interested me—mainly—apart from a reasonably decent car and house – was being creative. The money was nothing in itself—not that money's not useful—but… it was what it would've given me in terms of access to creative people…"*

"Like?" Jack enquired.

"Like Muddy Waters, Jack Bruce, John Lennon, Bob Dylan… Salvador Dalí even…"

"Being able to meet them?"

"Yes… but more than that – what I was wanting was to be able to get Bob Dylan on the telephone and say 'Hey Bob, I've been looking through my poetry and thought we could get together on a collaboration.' Then he'd reply 'Yeah come over and we'll throw it 'round. The stuff you sent me looked real interesting.' And then he'd make something great out of it and have Savage Cabbage as his backing band on one album – maybe with me joining him on the vocals."

"Bigger bloody dream than I ever 'ad!" Jack laughed. *"You always 'ad your sights set—very—high didn'tcher…"*

"Yeah… but why not? You have to set your sights somewhere—and Ron and Steve were world-class musicians—so it was all possible as far as I could see. You do remember that Ron played his first piano recital at the age of four or something."

"Yeah…" sighed Jack *"chance in a million playing with them. But— seriously—you wouldn't've gone for the groupies?"*

"No Jack…" I laughed. *"I'm kind of old fashioned like that. I just want a good relationship with a lady who'll be my best friend."*

"Oh yeah… I remember… you only 'ad eyes for Lindie. No int'rest in slipping one under the pussy-pelmet [12] *on tour."*

---

12 *Pussy pelmet* refers to a mini skirt. A pelmet is a narrow border of fabric or plywood, fitted across the top of window to conceal curtain fittings.

'Pussy pelmet'… That was such a bizarre idea. Jack's vocabulary was so alien from the way I regarded romance – so remote in terms of what ladies were in my vision of reality. For me, ladies— even before I came to see them as khandro[13]—were people with personalities. The fact that Jack could abstract them into sexual cyphers heightened my sense of distance from whatever the normal world appeared to be. Was this the normal world? Was Jack perfectly acceptable in the average flow of life? It was not that I was offended in particular. I was never 'political' about my views. I was simply bewildered – and in that bewilderment I realised I was a foreigner. I was no longer English and I was looking in from the outside as a culturally estranged spectator of a mindset so alien to my own that I often had no idea how to respond. I remembered the words of Düd'jom Rinpoche *'With each life-circumstance: whatever is enacted, stare directly into the enactment – with all the senses.'*

Jack was on a roll *"Me? I'd've been getting' me end away—every—town we played! Every bloody town, mate! Anyway – takes all kinds dunnit."*

"Yes…" I replied in a somewhat baffled tone. *"It takes all kinds. As the adage goes: Jumping Jack would eat no fat, and Vic would eat no lean – but, together both, they ate their fill and licked the platter clean."* [14]

Jack shook his head as if to say *'Where—do—you dig these things up?'*

---

13 *mKha' 'gro ma (dakini* डाकिनी) – literally 'sky goer' or poetically 'sky dancer'. The term applies to realised women – but also to all women. The Sanskrit word dakini is related to di-ya-te meaning 'to fly'. Khandros are often represented as consorts in yabyum coital union with yidams. The male equivalent is dPa'wo *(dPa' bo / daka)* hero or warrior. Khandros in various guises can be a human Lama, a yidam, or protector.

14 *Jack Sprat would eat no fat, his wife would eat no lean – but, together both, they ate their fill and licked the platter clean.* In the 16th Century, the name Jack Sprat pertained to short men. It is a mid-17th Century proverb which originated as a satire on King Charles I—a short man who was left 'lean' when parliament denied his taxation—so with Queen Henrietta Maria he was free to 'lick the platter clean' after he dissolved parliament.

Then after a pause *"S'pose you 'eard about me'n'Cynth getting cashed and bruted?"* [15]

"Cashed and bruted?"

"Married and divorced me old mate."

"Oh, right, I'm not quite as au fait with the slang as I was when I lived here. Heard you'd got married Jack… but not divorced. Sorry…"

"Nothin' to be sorry about mate – part from getting' married to that—steamin'—great—cow—in the first place. Jesus mate—that—was a bloody —nightmare! She was like something from a Greek tragedy – y'know one of those things with snakes coming out of its 'ead."

"Medusa?" [16] Jack looked confused so I elaborated *"A gorgon."*

"Oh yeah – she was a right gorgonzola! She must've been 17 stone [17] *at least! Sight of—'er—let alone the sound of her screaming—would give you a limp 'ampton* [18] *for eternity and the day after."*

"That, as—well—as turning you to stone eh? An impressive feat. An impressive weight – was she tall?" I asked in a vain attempt to respond in what would seem a friendly manner.

"Nah! Not much taller than me mate – so you can imagine the size of the cow."

15 *Cashed*—as in *Cash and Carry*—is Cockney rhyming slang for *married*. *Bruted*—as in *brute force*—is Cockney rhyming slang for *divorced* – although *bruted* could be 'Mockney' an invented form of Cockney that does not originate in the East End of London.

16 Medusa (Μέδ"ουσα) was a Gorgon. The three Gorgon sisters—Medusa, Stheno, and Euryale—were children of the sea gods Phorcys and Ceto – chthonic monsters. The sisters were winged and had snakes as hair. Medusa's hideous face was so terrible that the sight of it would turn any observer to stone.

17 There are 14 pounds in a stone, so 17 stone is 238 pounds or 108 kilos.

18 *Hampton*—as in *Hampton Wick*—is Cockney rhyming slang for *dick* i.e. penis.

"I'm trying not to imagine, Jack…" I replied in a haze of confusion – feeling as if I was hallucinating *"but seriously—I'm sorry—it sounds as if you had a rough time of it."*

*"**ROUGH**!?"* Jack almost screeched *"I should cocoa* [19] *… rough ain't the half of it—rough!?—too—bloody right mate, it was rough!"* Then he whispered *"Rough as sliding down a bleedin' scaffolding plank with no sodding underwear…"*

"So… why was it—exactly—that you got back with her after calling it off?"

"Yeah… I know—I know—I know…" PAUSE *"But… listen… when Ron and Steve died… well"* PAUSE *"Y'know how it was… I mean…"* Jack shook his head indicating that getting back with Cynthia was just too painful to explain. *"Anyway… I'm more-or-less out of me parents' life now – don't see'em now. In fact… I keep away from them completely – and that's how they want it too. But… back then… it was like bloody prison! They 'ad me by the short-n'curlies!"* [20] PAUSE *"so… I… I just gave in… y'know"* PAUSE *"I know… I shouldn've given in – but… well… it's what 'appened. No use cryin' over spilt milk ain't it?"*

I nodded sympathetically.

"So any'ow… once we were married it got even worse – if you can believe that. We 'ad to play bloody bridge with her pox-ridden parents—and—mine. We 'ad to talk about 'the weather', politics, and the sodding stock market. I had to 'ear about 'ow wonderful the toss-bag Tory party was—all—the time. Wankers… I mean—'struth—I like money as much as the next fella – but talking about investment shares for hours? I mean: Do—whatcher—**do** *to get it. Then spend it – and forget it!"*

"Good policy" I added – just for the sake of saying something supportive.

---

19 *Cocoa* is Cockney rhyming slang for *say so*.
20 *Short and curlies* i.e. pubic hair – British slang for testicles, 'balls': *They 'ad me by the short-n'curlies!*

"Yeah—'xactly—and I was 'xpected to 'ave comments on bloody banking when—far as I'm concerned—it's just a soddin' job. It pays the money that gets the decent car: end—of—bloody—story. It was bad enough workin' there —all—day long without havin' to—talk—about it—all—evenin'. There was no escape from the bank! Can you imagine it!? I mean can—you... f— imagine it!? Playin' cards with yer boss—and—being 'xpected to discuss the f —Financial Times!?"

I shook my head in dismay. The full horror was not lost on me. *"Blimey Jack... that sounds like something out of 'The Stepford Wives*[21]*..."*

Jack shook his head to indicate incomprehension.

"Oh, right—The Stepford Wives—it's a story about small-town-America; a place called Stepford where they turn all their wives into robots who... would probably be quite like Cynthia apart from being irredeemably pleasant and submissive."

"Yeah—well, 'pleasant and submissive' would've made it more bearable – but she was as boring as a bloody privet 'edge." PAUSE *"She was always leanin' on me to be more enthusiastic about me career so we'd be able to buy more gnomes than the bloody neighbour. Then Cynth—'er parents and mine—all rounded on me to get me hair cut – because of what they were thinkin' about it at the bank... so... I gave in on that one too – bloody riah zhoosher*[22] *job . So I was the bloody Stetson 'usband!"* PAUSE *"The barnet's* [23] *longer now – but it'll be twice the length next year"* he added, preening himself. *"It was a lot bloody shorter when I was still at the bank... looked like a blinkin' thrup'ney."* [24]

I thought Jack's hair was a distinct improvement on the mullet he used to have – but made no comment.

---

21 *The Stepford Wives* was a 1975 science-fiction film based on a novel—of the same name—by Ira Levin published in *1972.*
22 *Riah zhoosher* – Palarie slang for barber or hairdresser; 'riah' being 'hair' spelled backwards.
23 *Barnet*—as in *Barnet Fair*—is Cockney rhyming slang for *hair.*
24 *Thrup'ney*—as in *Thru'penny bit (three-penny piece:* pre-decimalised British currency)—is Cockney rhyming slang for *twit* or *tit* – i.e. idiot.

"I like those mutton-chop sideburns – they suit you really well."

"Yeah well… they were another cause of 'er screamin' at me! Cynth couldn't stand to see 'air on a bloke's face. Insane. I was her bloody pet project. She was going to turn me into 'Mister Middle Management' or something. But that's not the worst of it! Sex was non-existent! Jesus! *The very idea of a blow job would give 'er screaming hysterics! She'd scream at me for an hour and throw things at me—telling me I was a criminal pervert—and that it was all—your—fault!"*

"How d'you mean Jack…" I laughed. *"I'd gone down on you once too often – and got you addicted…?"*

That made Jack splutter with laughter. That had been my intention, of course, because Jack looked as if he was re-living some kind of nightmare. I was glad that I could approximate a response that was linguistically congruent with Jack's view of reality.

"Nah mate… I made the mistake of tellin' 'er 'bout you and that nympho Swiss au pair when you was fourteen… 'course she said she'd've reported it to the police. So, anything she thought was disgusting 'ad to be something 'eard from you" he cackled. *"She blamed—you—for—everythin'—'bout me, she di'n't like."*

"Good to be famous for something, Jack" I sighed. Ngakpa Chögyam the criminal pervert… That image of me was a long way from how I saw myself – but I was glad it amused Jack. A moment passed in which I wondered why Jack had described Anelie as a nymphomaniac. It'd been nothing I'd said. I was never given to prurient playground revelations. I decided it wasn't worth enquiring *"You were, enthusiastic… I suppose – about returning the favour?"*

"King-o'the-muff-divers,[25] *me! Ain't it! Yeah… no 'preciation fer a man's skill. Y'see… to 'er it was all disgustin'."*

---

25 *Muff-diver* — from Medieval Latin *muffula*—via Old French mofle 'thick glove, large mitten' and Middle French moufle 'mitten' – which in the 17th–18th centuries came to be associated with pubic hair, and from the 1690s one who performs cunnilingus.

Jack adopted a hoity-toity high-pitched voice *"Only heroin addicts and criminals do—that—kind of thing!"*

"Really… that is alarmingly Victorian, Jack. But, maybe, I've just lost all connection with the average mores… but whatever… that does sound somewhat inhibited for 1975."

"Yeah… really… tell me 'bout it… But that's not all! She got as fat as the proverbial pig! Jesus! Khyber [26] *the size-a-the bloody Northwest frontier. Lallies* [27] *like lard barrels. 'er willets* [28] *were nothing to write home about t'start with – but they just disappeared in 'er general dewlaps and bulbous rolls of hideous flab. Bloody* **dis**—*gusting! I thought she was pregnant at first! 'course… now I realise that was 'ardly likely with a lights-out-shag once a fortnight—if—I was lucky! And after being the good 'Semi-detached Suburban Mister Jones'* [29] *for weeks on end."* Jack adopted the hoity-toity high-pitched voice again *"Oh yes darling, let's buy another gnome! It would be so charming with the other eighty gnomes on the veranda – and the three 'undred in the logia. They look so gorgeous with their fuchsia smocks and violet hats. We could have a few more on the trellis couldn't we."*

I winced at the description. I had no massive sympathy for Cynthia – but felt ill-at-ease listening to the personal details of her physique. How could I tell Jack I found his description of Cynthia crude and demeaning? I couldn't be as disapproving as I felt – whilst still being friendly. He would *not* understand – so I kept my disapproval to myself. Thoughts of that nature apart: was I mistaken, or had Jack developed a decidedly full-on East-end London accent? Ron had adopted that—to the annoyance of his parents—but I could not recall Ron dropping as many Cockneyisms as Jack was trotting out.

26 *Khyber*—as in *Khyber Pass*—is Cockney rhyming slang for *arse* i.e. buttocks. The Khyber Pass was in the Northwest frontier of the British Empire – between Pakistan and Afghanistan.
27 *Lallies* – Palarie slang for *legs*.
28 *Willets* – Palarie slang for *breasts*.
29 Often misremembered as *Semi-Detached Suburban Mr Jones*, D'Abo's first big hit with Manfred Mann was *Semi-Detached Suburban Mr James*. It *was* nearly recorded as 'Mr Jones' but it occurred to Manfred Mann that it might be interpreted as a reference to Paul Jones, their previous vocalist.

From my memory of Jack Hackman in Savage Cabbage I recalled that he spoke a fairly average English – with possibly a slight West Country lilt… but Jumping Jack Flashman was now a born again Eastender. There was also a smattering of Palarie[30] in his speech—which he may have mistaken for Cockney—or perhaps it had just entered the general pattern of slang and was now indistinguishable. It had been popularised by the BBC radio comedy *Round the Horne* [31] back in the 1960s – and maybe it had just become part of the general patter.

"So…" I asked, to change the subject *"what made you leave in the end?"*

"The possibility of getting her pregnant scared me" he whispered *"absolutely shitless… I'd-a-bin stuck with 'er after that – and suicide would-a-bin the only way out. That was the—effin' end—of it as far as I was concerned. Never 'ad another Aylesbury.*[32] *Luckily, she didn't seem to notice. Long as she could stuff chocolates down 'er neck she was 'appy. Ett'em by the cartload, didn' she. I decided that I'd 'ave-t' leave – fast as possible. So I found another place to live – and, as soon as I did, I packed me bags."* PAUSE *"Took the Friday afternoon off work di'n' I…"* he grinned *"…y'know – complained 'bout severe gut ache and kept whizzin' off to the Kharzi.*[33] *Worked a charm mate. I wasn't going back any'ow 'cause I gotta job with a builder—right—started Monday. Electrician's mate, eh! Best thing I ever did —as it turns out—'cause I got me qualifications, di'n' I!*

30 Palarie *(Polari, Parlare, Parlary, Palare, Palari)* from Italian *parlare* to talk. Palarie is a mixture of Romance Italian and thieves' cant which incorporated both Cockney and Yiddish words in the 20th century. It is a type of British slang associated with gay culture, actors, circus and fairground performers, merchant navy sailors, and the demimonde. It originates in the 19th century but traces can be found as far back as the 16th century. Punch and Judy performers traditionally used conversational Palarie.
31 *Round the Horne* was a BBC Radio comedy (1965 to 1968) featuring Julian and Sandy *(played by Hugh Paddick and Kenneth Williams),* two camp homosexual characters in mainstream entertainment when homosexuality was illegal in Britain. They were not ridiculed – rather, the sketches pivoted on Kenneth Horne's ignorance of Palarie slang, and Kenneth Horne was thus the target of humour.
32 *Aylesbury—as in Aylesbury Duck—*Cockney rhyming slang for *fuck.*
33 *Kharzi—*Palarie slang—although now general London slang—*for toilet.*

*"Now I'm a self-employed electrician—***JJ Flashman***—Total 'ome Electrics. Nice little Bunsen too"* [34] Jack beamed.

I returned his grin—raised my eyebrows—and gave a nod of my head to indicate approval of his improved circumstances.

"Varda—the—Callards" [35] Jacked grinned, indicating his puce leather trousers. *"These don't come cheap, I c'n tell yer."*

"I'll wager they don't. As fine a set of strides [36] *as I ever did see, Jack."* Jack had now set me off into cant—I wasn't usually in the habit of calling trousers *strides*—but Jack's high density of slang was becoming infectious. *"Puce isn't a common colour these days – they suit you very well."*

"Whatcher mean 'puce'?" Jack retorted indignantly.

"Puce? Dark dusky purple, Jack. Isn't that how you'd describe them?"

Jack grinned sheepishly *"Oh, right – didn't know that's what puce meant."* Jack then laughed *"It's like talkin' to the Longer bloody Oxford Diction'ry,* [37] *talking t'you."*

"Sorry Jack… you're not the only one who's ever complained about that" I replied to put Jack at his ease. *"Glad your business is successful."*

"Yeah mate. I'll tell you 'bout that later. Any'ow… I'd worked it all out so it gave me the weekend to settle into the new lattie. [38] *No room to swing a cat of course – but I was free as a bird! Gotta much better place now. Any'ow back to the story of leaving Cynth. Everythin' was goin' to plan – but Cynth came 'ome early, di'n't she. Still don't know 'ow—***that***—'appened. I was packin' the car like – an' all-a-sudden there she was! Found me packin' me boxes onto the back seat."*

---

34 *Bunsen*—as in *Bunsen Burner*—is Cockney rhyming slang for *earner.*
35 *Varda* is Palarie slang for look or 'check out' / 'look at'. *Callards*—as in *Callard and Bowsers*—is Cockney rhyming slang for *trousers.* 'Callard and Bowsers' were a British toffee manufacturer.
36 *Strides* – Palarie slang for *trousers.*
37 There is no 'Longer Oxford Dictionary.'
38 *Lattie* – Palarie slang for *flat* or *apartment.*

"Blimey Jack" I gasped *"That… that must have been… well… dire…"*

"Yeah mate – as in, diarrhœa!" Jack whispered with a chuckle. *"Told 'er I was leaving, di'n' I. Said 'No 'ard feelings Cynth – but it ain't gonna work with us.'*

"What happened then?" I enquired.

"Went ape-shit, di'n't she! Screamed like a burnin' bloody banshee! Tried to break me boxes open – 'ad to threaten to whack her if she carried on. Wouldn't've done—obviously—but I 'ad to make her believe it. So—any'ow—I grabbed the steak-tenderiser – and made, like, to go for her with it."

Somehow, I found myself laughing. It's wasn't that I had no trace of sympathy for Cynthia – but the image of Jack wielding a meat tenderiser—somehow like Thor with his hammer Mjolnir—was comical. Jack laughed and looked highly gleeful. He was obviously happy that I found his tale amusing.

"Kept 'er distance – then, didn't she… but, it didn't stop 'er screaming. God it was awful! The neighbours started lookin' out of their nasty little mock-Tudor windows as well – but that turned out to be just as well 'cause it quietened 'er down."

"Glad you got out alive Jack… How did you settle up with the flat? That must have been difficult?"

"Nah mate! Piece-a-cake! Piece-a-bloody-cake! We only rented, see. It was in —'er—name any'ow: so I just did a runner. Out the—f'-door—never t'be —seen—again!" he chuckled gleefully. *"I knew 'er parents would top-up the Burton[39] for 'er – either that or take 'er 'ome again."*

"Lucky…"

"Yeah… I s'pose… only bit-a-luck in the bloody story." PAUSE *"So… any'ow – didn't give 'er me address did I."* PAUSE *"Still doesn't know where I live!"* he cackled delightedly. *"Nor do 'er Nazi parents—or mine—for that matter! Bugger 'em all."*

---

39 *Burton*—as in *Burton-on-Trent*—is Cockney rhyming slang for *rent.*

"You first, Jack" I grinned – glad again that I could respond in a way to which Jack could relate. He nearly choked on his coffee.

"That's the thing with you i'n'it!" Jack laughed. *"You come over all—mister 'oly man—and then you say somethin' like that: just when a fella's gotta mouthful-a-coffee!"*

As Jack laughed – I caught a glimpse of something. Nothing visual – merely the sense of the absurdity of myself as a tulku. Who was this incarnation of Aro Yeshé? How much of Aro Yeshé existed in this wild assortment of conditioned perceptions? My life looked nothing like those of the Lamas of whom I'd read. They were all absolutely consistent. They practised. They gained realisation. They taught. They performed wonders. I merely bumbled along— lurching from one fiasco to another—and here I was in the Nostril Café engaged in a conversation about the ludicrous breakup of a marriage that should never have taken place. I thought of Chögyam Trungpa Rinpoche and realised that I'd crashed into yet another joke shop. That being said… I had not been unkind to Jack. He obviously still had emotional pain concerning his life. I'd tried to enter his world as much as I could to be supportive to him. I'd done my best – as far as my best would stretch. I remembered the words of Düd'jom Rinpoche *'With each life-circumstance: whatever is enacted, stare directly into the enactment – with all the senses.'*

26

the shrink of the outfit

Jack, having laughed heartily, reclined in his seat at the Nostril Café. He extended his legs. He cradled his head in his hands for optimal comfort – and, stretched languidly. He looked up— dreamily—at the ceiling. A dim distant look in his eye. Then, almost wistful *"Me parents…"* he commenced. Then an emotional cough *"Well… may as well tell yer."* PAUSE *"Disowned me, di'n' they. Cut off without a f—penny."* This followed by a slightly manic cackle. *"Just like Wuthering bloody Heights!"* Then a decidedly manic cackle *"Phoned'em."* PAUSE *"D'know why?"* PAUSE *"I… 'spose I wanted to—try— to explain why I left Cynth – but… she'd got in there* first, *d'n't she! The f —cow! I mean they're—my—bloody parents – not 'ers! She put the story like as I tried to 'it her with an 'ammer. Can you believe that!? Can you f— believe that!? It was only a bloody wooden steak-tenderizer! An' I never 'it her with it! Never got nowhere near! Just waved it 'round – y'know, just to keep 'er from breaking me bloody boxes open."* PAUSE *"So… they did the 'You're no longer a son of ours!' number."*

"Blimey Jack… Wuthering Heights is the least of it… I'm sorry."

"No need to be sorry mate. I told 'em – told'em straight 'Suits me bloody fine! Go stick yer bleedin' 'eads up a bear's bum!' And—that—was it. I'm free of the whole friggin' lot of'em."

"I guess at least you won't be spending time out on the moor shouting 'Cathy'—or rather—'Cynthia come home'." [1]

"Not bloody likely" Jack laughed.

---

1   Quotation error: *Cathy Come Home* was a 1966 BBC television play by Jeremy Sandford.

"Still, Jack…" I sighed *"That makes the scene with my father look like Noddy and Big Ears in Toyland."* [2]

"Too right mate! But… being' disowned is one thing I can be—'appy—about!"

"Yeah… well…" I ran out of words.

"Yeah – to be honest, I 'ate 'em. I really do… I 'ate 'em!"

"Hate…?" I enquired, slightly shocked. I never *hated* my father – even in the worst moments. I had plenty of resentment at one time – but I'd never have called it *hatred*.

"Well… you know what they're like… they're not f—'uman!"

"So… you were raised by a toothless, bearded hag? Schooled with a strap right across your back?"

"Yeah but it's—all—right now, in fact, it's a gas! I'm Jumping Jack Flashman, it's a gas—gas—gas!" Jack cackled maniacally.

"I see you're as free with lyrics as I am Jack. It does have a value, doesn't it?"

"Yeah… see yer point. I love that song – because… '… I was—drowned —I was washed up and left for—dead. I fell—down—to my feet and I saw they—bled. I—frowned—at the crumbs of a crust of—bread; I was —crowned—with a spike right through my—head. But it's—all—right now, in fact, it's a gas! I'm Jumping Jack Flashman, it's a gas-gas-gas!' "

"Nice one Jack" I smiled. *"I can see you've made this your own."*

---

2   *Noddy* and *Big Ears* are characters created by Enid Blyton, published between 1949 and 1963. A television series based on the characters ran on British television from 1955 and continues to appear to the present day. Noddy is a little wooden boy who lives in his own house in Toyland. His friend Big Ears is a friendly gnome. Noddy is a self-employed taxi driver with a red and yellow taxi.

"I should cocoa! It's my *song."* PAUSE *"But as I was saying – me parents are bloody Anglo-Nazis! Yeah – that's what they are! Like Osborne bloody Mosby!*[3] *All I was to them was property! They'd've 'ad—you—in the gas-chamber fer starters mate! Hanging was too—good—for the likes of you. You should've 'eard'em talk about you! Nose like a kanga*[4] *they said – right front wheeler.*[5] *Bleedin' racist turds."* PAUSE *"Told'em: 'e's no bloomin' kanga – 'is mother's a shorty and 'is Dad's English. But would they listen? Nah…"*

"There you've lost me Jack. My mother's a shorty? She's five foot eight at least – but what's that got to do with me being Jewish."

"Bein' Jewish's down to yer schnozz."[6]

"Fair enough, Jack – my nose isn't exactly diminutive."

"… and Shorty's—short'n'stout, mate—Kraut. Dintcher know that?"

"No Jack—unlike you—I wasn't born within the sound of the Bow Bells."[7]

"Alright Cobham" Jack chuckled knowingly, with a shake of his head. *"You weren't born in Tibet either – but you probably know enough of the lingo."*

"Fair enough Jack – but don't judge me too severely for not understanding as much Cockney as you do. Remember that I've spent the last three years in Bristol."

3   Jack meant Oswald Mosley. Oswald Mosley, 6th Baronet of Ancoats (1896–1980) was a politician and founder of the British Union of Fascists. He was a Member of Parliament for Harrow, 1918–1924, and Smethwick, 1926–1931, as well as Chancellor of the Duchy of Lancaster in the Labour Government, 1929–1931. He resigned due to disagreement with the Government's unemployment policy – and formed a new political party which merged with the Blackshirts (British Union of Fascists) in 1932.
4   *Kanga*—as in *Kangaroo*—is Cockney rhyming slang for *Jew*.
5   *Front wheeler*—as in *front wheel skid*—is Cockney rhyming slang for *Yid* i.e. Jew.
6   *Schnozz* – contraction of schnozzle. A modification of Yiddish shnoitsl, diminutive of shnoits, or snout. Originally from German *Schnauze* meaning snout. This is one of a number of Yiddish words co-opted into Cockney.
7   *Bow Bells* are the bells of the church of St Mary-le-Bow, Cheapside, London. To be born within the sound of Bow Bells is the traditional definition of a Cockney. Jack Hackman was born and raised mainly in Wiltshire.

"Lucky you – I coulda done with three years of Bristols [8] *I'd 'ad to've found Cynth's with a bleedin' magnifyin' glass."*

"Doesn't sound as if it was too much fun for either of you, Jack" I sighed. There was no stopping him, so I changed the subject *"Still – I wish you'd've recorded that conversation with your parents… I think it would've made me laugh… however… can't say that I hate them… But also, I can't say I was sorry they banned me from your house – apart from the fact it made things awkward. It would've been good to have called on you, y'know."*

"You'd-a-called?"

"Sure Jack" I answered with a mild degree of vehemence. *"What d'you think?"*

"Never thought… never thought you liked me that much…"

I didn't quite know how to reply to that. *"… Jack… what d'you think I'm—sitting—here for? I know we're different—personality-wise—and that we didn't always see eye-to eye on, my… rubato… but you were my friend… and… I don't quite know how to put this… but… I was on—your—side about not getting your bass drum mic-ed, when Ron was getting heavy about it… and… I was on your side about a few things. I always liked the way you played heavy on the cymbals – and so did Steve."* PAUSE *"I know… you always thought I didn't deserve my place in the band… you know—the position you thought Ron and Steve gave me—but… I never felt bad about that – because, I tried to put myself in your position. I—could—see it from your side you know."*

Jack had developed a somewhat stony face as I was speaking—as if layers of latent resentment were stirring in his depths—but by the end his expression softened.

"Well" he partially snorted *"it was 'ard being with you three y'know. You were like sodding blood-brothers or something – the three bloody musketeers."*

---

8   *Bristols*—as in *Bristol Cities*—is Cockney rhyming slang for *titties* i.e. breasts.

"Yeah Jack... That's true – but I didn't set it up like that. I'd known Steve since I was eight, f'crying out loud. But the rest—with Ron—just happened – and... for my part, I wasn't trying to keep you—out—of the brotherhood. Beside which, there were four musketeers when D'Artagnan joined."

"Oh yeah – forgot about that..." Jack shrugged *"...you always were the literary buff."*

I ignored Jack's comment and continued *"You were our percussionist as far as I was concerned – and we were all in it for life."*

"Really?"

"Really, Jack" and it wasn't merely tact.

"Sorry..." Jack whispered. A slight blush affected his face and he looked away toward the door. Then he saw something or someone outside that made him blanch. He scooted flat and disappeared under the table. *"Bloody 'ell, Cynth's outside"* he hissed. *"Jesus mate, gettcher 'ead down."*

"She's never seen me Jack. She won't come in on my account. If she does... I'll think of something – don't worry. Anyway – she'll have to climb over me to get you."

"Cheers mate – just tell me when she's gone."

I moved my satchel across to where Jack had sat—and surreptitiously edged my Levi jacket over that end of the bench chair—so that no one could look under the table from the side. I heard a voice whisper *"Cheers mate."*

I looked out through the front window of the Nostril. There was a morbidly obese young woman looking through it with a scowl that would peel paint. I pulled my poetry notebook out of my bag. I removed my fountain pen from its leather container. I proceeded to read through some poetry-in-process, whilst keeping a discreet eye on the door. *"If it—is—her Jack... she... appears to be coming in. She's wearing a sort of pale pink trouser-suit."*

"Jesus Christ! That's 'er – she wears that kind of thing to work" Jack whispered. *"Just don't let on I'm here what—ever—yer do."*

"… do my best Jack" I whispered, scratching my nose to hide the fact that I was communicating to someone. I started making notes as Cynthia stumped toward our table. Fortunately, the set-up of the tables and benches—together with the subdued lighting—made Jack's presence undetectable unless Cynthia decided to get down on the floor. That was unlikely. The tightness of her trouser suit would have made her unbendable. I acted as if she was just another customer and tried to look suitably surprised when she addressed me.

"Is your name Ah-BUTH-*knot?"* she asked in a manner bereft of all courtesy. She meant Arbuthnot—as in Farquhar Arbuthnot—my band name in Savage Cabbage. Jack always used to address me as 'Mister Arbuthnot'.

"Pardon?" I replied with a look of confusion that was partially realistic.

"Do people call you A-BUTH-knot or something like that?"

"No…" I shook my head. *"I've been called a lot of things I wouldn't like to repeat…"* I smiled *"but no – nobody calls me that. Sorry…"* I concluded with a shrug *"can't help you."*

"Oh…" she replied rather curtly. *"You look like someone my ex-husband told me about once – he was in a rock group."*

"Thanks for the compliment… but sorry—can't help you there—I'm no one famous."

"They weren't famous!" she snapped.

"Sorry to hear it" I replied – and I was. I turned my face back to my notebook. I thought it would be a normal thing to do, if I was impersonating someone who'd been gruffly importuned. She continued to stand next to the table – and, in the end, I looked up and with the slightest of smiles said *"Never was in any Rock group."*

I was trying not to lie. Savage Cabbage was a Blues band. She continued to glower – and it occurred to me that—under normal circumstances—this would cause annoyance. I therefore looked up and said *"I don't mean this unkindly – but I would really rather you didn't stand there hovering over me like that. As I said, I can't help you – and now I really would like to get on with my writing without feeling—how should I say—crowded?"*

Cynthia glowered at me a little longer. I wondered what else I could say to dissemble. *"Alright then – but after this, I really must get on with my writing. What's your ex-husband called?"*

"John, John Hackman – but he called himself Jack."

"Sorry… don't know any John or Jack Hackman." It was true. I didn't. I knew *Jumping Jack Flashman*. That *was* his name now, so I was still being marginally honest – albeit in an entirely dishonest way. *"Why not ask a member of staff?"*

"Is anyone sitting there?" she asked with a peculiar look on her face.

"No. Or rather yes – I'm reserving the seat for a friend. He'll be appearing sometime soon – but now, if you don't mind going and sitting down somewhere —rather than looming over me—I'm in the middle of writing up ideas and I really need to get back to it. Sorry I could be of no use to you."

"Oh!" she said with a tight snap and turned abruptly to sit at another table. I felt an enormous relief. What if she'd wanted to sit 'til my friend appeared? She proceeded to keep a wary eye on me – positioning herself between my table and the toilet. I guessed she suspected that Jack was hiding in the toilet. She must have caught a glimpse of him before he scooted under the table – and all I could hope was that she'd eventually decide it had been some kind of hallucination.

This was about the most ridiculous situation I'd found myself in for a long time. I wondered how it would all end up – and whether I could describe such a scene to Düd'jom Rinpoche. I could not imagine how he might respond to hearing such an account.

491

There was no way that I would hide it from him. I would have to ask him whether I had acted appropriately or not. I remembered the words of Düd'jom Rinpoche *'With each life-circumstance: whatever is enacted, stare directly into the enactment – with all the senses.'*

A member of staff approached Cynthia and said *"You'll need to order something to eat or drink. You can't just sit here – the café's for paying customers."* Cynthia ordered a cup of coffee with cream. It arrived. I had her in my peripheral vision – and noted the three heaped spoons of sugar she shovelled into her coffee. She then sat sipping it with a seriously sullen expression. I continued making notes around the theme of poetry that I was writing.

> *Within the swollen ark of time, acrid tang of weak coffee: open distance between café windows and walls*
> *Dull pink envelope of arithmetically distended vision: trouser-suited gorgonzola – snapping sullen questions.*
> *A body, asking to be real, tight thumbs & swollen fingers—arch above chartered indices falling through heat*
> *Turbid tyrannical flubness. Point blank barrage: birdless-bird on wingless-wings of airless wordless verbiage.*
> *Blizzard of gizzard flapping blind – burst duvet-sunset of flying feathers, cross referencing in forever never.*
> *Boneless indicators of visual somnolence—flesh disappears—overawed by inviolable velvet of early evening.*
> *Night tunnelling toward night, through night—composed of night— sucking night—in the pink rip-tide*
> *Distance lies—whether travelling backwards or forwards—but spies on itself in order to inhale its carnival*
> *Attar of Roses eats the air—sears floor—already baked with hyacinth and ruddy after-images of violence*

"You Ah-BUTH-knot?! And when did you last see your father?" [9]
"He died two weeks ago. Please go away."

Not my finest work by any means – but with Cynthia, glowering at me like a bird of prey, writing poetry was not the totally absorbing pursuit it could be.

In the end however, Cynthia gave up her vigil. A man had exited the toilet. He didn't appear to be Jack, sideburns notwithstanding, and so she must have decided that her errand was fruitless. She and her pink trouser-suit stood up and proceeded to leave the Nostril. I continued crossing out words of poetry and replacing them with better words. I pretended to jot down notes. And all the while I tried to keep her retreating mass indirectly in sight. She paid for her coffee. She left – but hung around outside for some moments. She occasionally seemed to be leaving the vicinity of the café – but then she'd suddenly re-appear. I kept a running report to Jack under the table 'til she finally vanished. I caught sight of her a few minutes later *"She's... now crossing West Street – and... about to go into Woolworths* [10] *so... unless it's a ruse... I think you're safe."*

"Whew! That was close!" Jack sighed. *"Y'know... I live in—dread—of bumping into that—evil—mutant cow. She'd attack me in the f—street y'know! There'd be no 'olding 'er back – and that'd be really bad for business! I mean, if any of me customers got to see me lunatic ex-wife screamin' at me in the street, they'd run a mile!*

9   *'And When Did You Last See Your Father?'* is an 1878 oil painting by William Frederick Yeames (1835–1918) depicting the son of a Royalist being questioned by Parliamentarians in an imaginary Royalist household during the English Civil War. The painting is held at the Walker Art Gallery, Liverpool. Madame Tussauds has a life-size waxwork tableau of the scene, reproduced from the painting.
10 *Woolworths* was a chain store in Britain. Originally it was part of the American FW Woolworth Company. There were over 800 Woolworths in Britain prior to closure. Woolworths had its own Ladybird children's clothing range, amongst others. On 26th November 2008, trading of shares in Woolworths Group was suspended. In September 2019, it was announced that Woolworths would make a comeback to Britain in 2020.

"God – she's worse than one of those things in Doctor Who [11] *– y'know, the rabid squealin' bastards that eatcher-alive if y'fall into the radioactive swamp!"*

"I remember those things… Blimey Jack – if it's that bad… I mean—if she ever did attack you in the street—you could get a restraining order."

"A what?"

"A restraining order. [12] *It's something you can get from the court if you're beleaguered."*

"Be-what-ed?"

"Beleaguered – y'know hounded, hassled, hectored, or harangued."

"Right – so what then?"

"You just need to satisfy a judge that you're subject to harassment – so you'd need a witness. You'd see a solicitor about making the application – but someone would have to have seen her attacking you. I mean… I could speak up about how she came in here stalking you – but I've not seen anything worse than that, yet."

"Really… maybe it would be worth it… getting attacked, just for the once I mean."

---

11 *Doctor Who* is a science fiction programme produced by the BBC since 1963. It depicts the adventures of a Time Lord called 'the Doctor'. He explores the universe in a time-travel craft called the TARDIS (Time and Relative Dimension in Space). Its exterior appears as a blue British police box – a common sight in the 1960s. Accompanied by a number of companions, the Doctor combats a variety of menaces in helping people in need. A significant part of British popular culture, it gained a cult following.

12 A restraining order is a court order that requires someone to carry out, or to refrain from performing, certain acts. These orders emanate from a court's power to grant equitable remedies. A person who refuses to comply faces criminal or civil penalties and may have to pay damages. Breaches of restraining orders can be considered serious criminal offences which merit arrest and prison sentences. Restraining orders are most commonly issued in respect of domestic violence, harassment, stalking, or sexual assault. In the case of infringement, victims can request the police or courts to enforce the order.

494

"Well… she's over in Woolworth's, if you're up for it. I'll go with you if you like."

"Mmmm… well, maybe not today… I've got… well, there's this fierce bird I'm meetin' later and I don't want a black eye or nothing, if yer know what I mean."

"… can understand that Jack."

"Y'know, she accused me of ruinin' 'er life! Can you—b'lieve—it? Like now —she's—a di-vor-cee, or whatever, and it's damaged 'er chances of marriage. I told 'er—right out mate—that being a sexless, boring, obese, slob was the main thing that ruined her chances of marriage."

"That was… tactful of you, Jack" I grinned in a somewhat vague manner.

Jack burst out laughing *"Yeah mate… know whatcher mean—know whatcher mean—but! It did me* good *to say it!"* he cackled. *"You know… I can't always… summon up the nerve to stand up for m'self… and… well… she couldn' 'ave it—all—'er own way, could she – I mean, with screamin' abuse an' that. Y'know me… I've… well… I've always chickened out… but sometimes I–can—rise to the occasion y'know – like the Little Red Rooster!"*

"Yeah Jack—you can—and you could've won the Pullet Surprise [13] *for that one."* Jack missed my pun – but I had not wished to vaunt my wit at his expense. *"I remember how it was when you faced your parents down"* I continued *"over splitting up with Cynthia the first time. You were a hero."*

"Yeah… bloody hero alright… but that di'n't last long. Then… then they just all ganged-up on me di'n't they. They just bloody wore me down! They kept up the pressure—day—after sodding—day—'til I gave in." PAUSE *"Yeah—don't say it—I know… You'd've left 'ome – like over that military 'air-cut thing with yer father."*

---

13 Pulitzer Prize. Award for achievement in journalism, literature, and musical composition in America – established in 1917 by Joseph Pulitzer. Administered by Columbia University, prizes are awarded yearly in twenty-one categories.

"Wasn't thinking of mentioning it Jack. Wasn't in my mind. I'm the last person to judge anyone for decisions they feel forced to make. I've not always been as brave as I appeared to be back then…" PAUSE *"… all I'd say is that I—was—still in Farnham at the time you were being forced to marry Cynth – and… it's a shame you couldn't have called me up… y'know, for support or whatever. I could have found you a place to stay with someone at Art School."*

"Really? You'd-a-done that?"

"No question, Jack…" I answered in some astonishment. *"Why wouldn't I have wanted to help you out?"*

Jack looked a little embarrassed *"Right… well… yeah."* PAUSE *"Cheers mate—even though it's a bit late now—it's always good to 'ear."* Jack lay back in his seat again as he had done earlier. He stretched his legs and put his hands behind his head. He stared at the ceiling and a resentful look clouded his face again *"She was like something out of a bloody lunatic asylum for the obese, by the time I left! You should have seen her!"*

"I just did, Jack… if you remember…"

"Right… yeah, of course. What did she look like? I couldn't see her from where I was. She was the size of a bloody rigid dirigible when I left her: Marsh Mallow Zeppelin is what I used to call 'er."

"Well Jack… I've never been one to have a prejudice against size or anything – but I can't take issue with the fact that she's a… generous addition to the planet."

"Exactly a fat ugly sow the size of 'alf a dozen blue whales." Jack responded with some vehemence. I knew I should not have given him the encouragement of my concluding remark – so I said *"Blue whales are noble creatures Jack – I saw a documentary once…"* but Jack was on a roll and continued *"Y'know, I 'ad to wait—two years—for a bloody divorce because she contested it! I finally got it on two years separation. Anyhow, now it's over—gone—out the bleedin' window! Good riddance to bad rubbish I say!"*

"Well Jack… lucky escape, I'd say." PAUSE *"I hope you'll find someone pleasant, generous, and kind-hearted next time."*

"Too right mate! Some luscious bint with whacking great carpets [14] *who Gladstones* [15] *like a nym-pher-maniac rabbit!"*

Jack had not improved in terms of his view of women or sexuality and I tried my best not to look too appalled by his statement of intent.

"Good luck Jack – as I said… I hope you find someone pleasant, generous, and kind-hearted… and—y'know Jack—the most important thing – is that, whoever she is, she will be your friend. *Cynth was—never—your* friend. *That, was the main problem. I know you didn't respect her – but she didn't respect you either. And—that—is a recipe for disaster. I think both your families saw your marriage as some sort of business agreement. I don't think sexuality—let alone love—was part of the picture they had in mind."*

"Well that's true enough – it wasn't fun being married to the hippo from hell."

"Well maybe Jack… but if that hippopotamus had loved *you and been your* friend *– you might have found yourself having a different view. Y'know… people tend to say things about people being 'fat' or 'skinny' mainly when they have unpleasant personalities. D'you remember that girl Miranda Morton who used to get up and dance at the Queen's Oak? She was fairly Rubenesque* [16] *– and she was a real live wire. She was witty and good natured – and I'd have been interested in her if it hadn't been for Lindie… well, that and the fact that it was obvious to the rest of us that she gave you the glad eye more than once."*

"Did she now…" Jack smiled, obviously feeling pleased. *"Right… interestin'… never thought about it like that…"*

---

14 *Carpets*—as in *Carpets and Rugs*—is Cockney rhyming slang for *jugs* – i.e. breasts.

15 *Gladstone*—as in *Gladstone bag*—is Cockney rhyming slang for *shag* – i.e. to have sex.

16 *Rubenesque* applied to a woman of similar proportions to those painted by the Flemish painter Peter Paul Ruben: attractively plump; a woman who is alluring but not of the emaciated build presently vaunted as desirable by the media.

"It's worth remembering, Jack. Everyone looks like hell when they get old – and it's best to grow old with your best friend. So, when I said I hoped you'd find someone pleasant – that is what I meant."

"Right… see whatcher mean." Jack was lost in a reverie for some moments – but then suddenly *"Look—right—thanks for coverin' for me; I mean really. Couldn't-a-bin easy. But man—you—were as* cool *as the proverbial cucumber. Never—'eard—the like. Thought you Buddhists didn't tell porkies* [17] *though?"*

"We don't… and… I didn't tell any absolute flat-out porkies, Jack." PAUSE *"I suppose I obfuscated…"*

"Even though yer what?"

"Obfuscated… y'know: masked, disguised, veiled, obscured, concealed, confounded, camouflaged, masqueraded, put out a decoy, threw up a smoke screen, shook her off the scent, confused the trail…"

"You always did talk like you'd swallowed the dictionary" Jacked laughed. *"Anyhow… tell me how you didn't tell any porkies then?"*

"Well… I said I wasn't Farquhar Arbuthnot, because I'm not. I wasn't even Farquhar Arbuthnot at the time. You called me that – but Ron called me Frank. Steve called me Vic."

"Yeah… true enough…"

"Now I'm Chögyam – so, that much is also true."

"Alright."

"I know I said I didn't know any John or Jack Hackman – because I don't, not at this point in time at least. You're Jumping Jack Flashman now – so that's also true… in a manner of speaking."

"Right… and then – you said you was savin' the seat f'r-a-friend oo'd be—appearin'—soon! Yeah! I geddit! And then I 'ppeared, didn' I – just like you said. Very bloody clever, if I may say so. You'd make a great con-artist."

---

17 *Porkies*—as in *pork pies*—is Cockney rhyming slang for *lies*.

"… a great con-artist eh…" How had *this* happened? How had I started out simply trying to be friendly and non-judgemental – and ended up giving the impression that Buddhists could be confidence tricksters? *"… thing about the 'lying' Jack… is that I wasn't lying to gain anything for myself. I'm… not about to launch into a discussion of Buddhism or anything—s'don't get worried—but I wouldn't like to leave you with a false impression. Buddhism's primarily concerned with intention and motivation – and my purpose was to spare you the wrath of the pink-trouser-suited avenger – and… I'm glad I did. Y'know… that pink trouser-suit almost gave me brain damage as it was – but…"* I moved my head slowly from side to side, almost reeling from the memory of the vitriol I'd seen in Cynthia's face *"… she had more rage in her than… well I don't think I've ever seen that much contained rage before. I really do think she'd have made a horrible scene here… if nothing else."*

"Yeah… right… so you—see—what I mean." PAUSE *"Anyhow – enough of the homicidal harpy from Haslemere…"* [18]

"Nice alliteration, Jack" I threw in, to change the subject.

"Yeah… well, I used to like the way you did that – an'… it 'it me—sort of —that there was nothin' stoppin' me kissin' the Blarney Stone too! Goes down well in my line-a-work. Tell yer 'bout that later – but, tell us 'bout this In-ja thing? 'ow long yer goin' for?"

"Around… nine months or so."

"Bloody 'ell mate! What'll you do there all that time?"

"I'll study… and then… practise what I've studied." I was trying to make it simple.

"Right… well… that'll be… interesting, will it?"

"Yes… and there'll be painting as well—I'll be learning Tibetan iconographic painting—and, well, best not to bore you with the details."

"So… that'll get you good money at some point will it?"

---

18 Haslemere is a town in Surrey, England, close to the border with both Hampshire and West Sussex.

"Probably not… no."

"Then what the 'ell y'doin' it for?"

"The only answer to that Jack… is that I'm just doing it—because it's what I love to do—and then… I'll see what happens." How was I to make sense of Vajrayana for Jumping Jack Flashman?

"So – didn't you do well at Art School? Can't imagine—you—failin'."

"Nah mate!" I laughed, deciding to join Jack in his penchant for Cockney. *"Got me a Randolf."* [19]

"Friggin' Randolf eh… good f'you! Knew it! Di'n' I! Didn't think y'd getter an Attila or Desmond let alone a Douglas. [20] *But couldn'tcher get a good job with that?"*

"Maybe… but it's not what I want. Going to the Himalayas is…" What would Jack understand? *"… an adventure. I'll be staying in some fairly remote and ancient regions — places that are off the tourist map."*

"So… I s'pose you'll write a book about your escapades?"

"More than likely" I obfuscated.

"Sort-a-like… Lawrence of Arabia?"

"Sort of, Jack…" I chuckled *"… but without the camels."*

"Right… they have yaks there, don't they?"

"Yaks and dri – yeah Jack… The dri are the females."

---

19 *Randolf*—as in *Randolph Hearst*—is Cockney rhyming slang for *first* – i.e. first class honours degree.

20 *Desmond*—as in *Desmond Tutu*—is Cockney rhyming slang for a 2:2 – i.e. lower second-class degree. A 2:1 is an *Attila* – as in *Attila the Hun*. A 3rd is a *Douglas* – as in *Douglas Hurd*: Baron Hurd of Westwell, a Conservative politician. Douglas Hurd was born in 1930 in Marlborough, Wiltshire. His father Lord Anthony Hurd and grandfather Sir Percy Hurd were also Members of Parliament. His uncle, Sir Archibald Hurd, was a leading Fleet Street shipping correspondent, who was knighted in 1928.

"Yeah I think I married one-a-those." PAUSE *"Still, 'nougha—that—subject."*

"I meant to ask you about—your—name change Jack?"

"Yeah well… I didn't want anyone findin' me through me name, did I. Wanted to cut off—ev'ry—connection. My parents disowned me so what's bloody 'Hackman' to me? John sodding—Hackman—*is no more! It's Jack Flashman now, Jumping—Jack—Flashman.* Statuary Declaration of Name Change! *All it cost me was a Lady.*[21] *Got me own van now with—* **JJ FLASHMAN ESQUIRE**—*in that fierce em'rald green letterin' on dark-blue – y'know the way you did it for Savage Cabbage. Always liked that! 'ad real class, that!"*

"Good name Jack—like it—it's got style with that double J." PAUSE *"No connection with the Flashman character in Tom Brown's School I suppose?"*

"You 'it the proverbial nail right *on the 'ead Mister Arbuthnot—I mean Cobham—so, 'owjer say that?"*

"Chögyam. Chö as in church *but ending with a 'g' – and 'yam' as in* sweet potato. *But Cobham is fine with me."*

"Right… 'Cherg Yam'?" Jack tried. I smiled. Nodded approval.

"So then… got the name from 'Flashman at the Charge' [22] *… Playboy* [23] *serialised it – 'e's the same bloke as Tom Brown's School Days… but it's 'is later life as this adventurin' sojer."*

As I listened to Jack gleefully describe the dissolute, dissipated, debauched, unscrupulous, pusillanimous, anti-hero after whom he'd named himself. It all made sense to me.

---

21 *Lady*—as in *Lady Godiva*—is Cockney rhyming slang for a *fiver* – i.e. £5.
22 Sir Harry Paget Flashman VC KCB KCIE is a character created by George MacDonald Fraser. See glossary: *Flashman.*
23 *Playboy* is an American magazine featuring female nude photography along with journalism and fiction. It was founded in Chicago in 1953 by Hugh Hefner. It has published short stories by George MacDonald Fraser, Arthur C. Clarke, Ian Fleming, Vladimir Nabokov, Chuck Palahniuk, PG Wodehouse, and Margaret Atwood.

Jack was indeed a coward… but… there's something disarming about a coward who freely admits his cowardice. Jack wasn't trying to pretend he was a bold dreadnought kind of fellow who'd stand at the gates of hell and not back down. He'd run away from Cynthia. He was still on the run – even to the extent of having to hide under a table for 20 minutes.

"So… I feel a little bit like 'arry Flashman—not that I'd do the dirty on a friend—but… I just don't 'ave that bravery thing that people like you 'ave. Wouldn't catch me going to Inja. Not even France with their pissars."

"Pissoirs" I interjected – and immediately wished I hadn't. I had not enjoyed that aspect of Claudette – and now, here was I, being just as much of a supercilious know-it-all.

"Right… Pissoirs – *never was any good at French."*

"Nor was I Jack – but every other freak at Art School threw French around like you do with Cockney. Then all my girlfriends attended Grammar School – so I picked up a little Latin as well. It makes me sound more educated than I am – but with your flair for Cockney you could pick it up as easily as I did."

"Good idea… I'll look into it. That could come in 'andy. But, like I was sayin', I just don't seem to 'ave it in me to fight – like when… when runnin' away makes more sense. I knew Cynth'd turn into a bloody banshee brontosaurus 'bout my leaving 'er – so I just planned it so as I di'n't have-t'face 'er. Di'n't see why I should put me-self through it. Why get beaten up if you can avoid it? And what good would it've done any'ow?" PAUSE *"Yeah, y'don't have to say it… 'spose… I'm a Frankie…"* [24]

I wasn't sure how to answer that at first – but started speaking anyway *"Y'know… we're all Frankies in our own ways Jack… and, I guess, we all have different kinds of cowardice. I mean, I wouldn't have whipped under the table when I saw Cynthia – but then… that—was— pretty imaginative. But… no… I guess I wouldn't have done that.*

---

24 *Frankie*—as in *Frankie Howard*—is Cockney rhyming slang for a *coward*. Frankie Howard was a popular comedian in the 1960s.

"Not because I'm brave – but because I'd've been too cowardly to let you *see me do that… if you see what I mean."* Then I launched into poetry…

> *"… 'Then sware Lord Thomas Howard: '–'fore God I am no coward;*
> *But I cannot meet them here, for my ships are out of gear,*
> *And half my men are sick. I must fly, but follow quick.*
> *We are six ships of the line; can we fight with fifty three?'*
> *Then spake Sir Richard Grenville: 'I know you are no coward;*
> *You fly them for a moment to fight with them again.*
> *But I've ninety men and more who are lying sick ashore.*
> *I should count myself the coward if I left them, my Lord Howard,*
> *To those Inquisition dogs and the devildoms of Spain.'*

Sorry about the – Tennyson… I still remember it from 'O' Level English. I get carried away sometimes…" I trailed off.

Jack smiled. *"Yeah… apart from the bloody poetry…"* Jack laughed *"I see whatcher mean. Good of yer to see it that way."*

"Well Jack… I've never been the chest-beating kind y'know… I've never been one of those apes who need to make something out of their supposed bravery. I—will—stand my ground – but not to prove anything to anyone… it's just how I live. I stood my ground with my father because… well… because there was no way in hell I'd go on stage with a short-back-and-sides. It would've taken far more bravery to go on stage with short hair than to have faced my father down. It would have been easier to live under a hedge or whatever than have short hair."

"Yeah… I can see that. An' then… in the end… I 'ad to face Cynthia down anyway. I chickened out in the past mate – but then! The bloody chicken came 'ome to roast *di'n' 'e! And 'e 'ad the—*muscle—*of a 'lympic bloody ostrich!"*

"Quite" I grinned. *"That must have been… fowl."* Jack laughed at the pun – and I continued *"I mean—realistically—you didn't give in to her when she started breaking your boxes of stuff open, did you? And that must have taken ciooiuarge."*

503

"Yeah… see whatcher mean – true 'nough mate. It'd make a film in full technicolour – best seller novel!"

"Yeah" I grinned *"you could win the Pullet Surprise with that story."* I'd run the joke a second time before I realised it – and had to explain that 'Pullet Surprise' was a pun on 'Pulitzer Prize'. It worked well however – and had Jack in tears of laugher. When he recovered, he said *"Gonna use that one me self sometime!"*

"I hope you do. So, I don't think you—have—to think of yourself as cowardly, do you?" making an attempt to bolster his confidence. *"It obviously wasn't a good idea to let your parents and Cynthia dragoon you into marriage and take a job—under martial law—with you father-in-law at the Midland – but—maybe—that's the last time you'll—ever—have to do something like that. We all have to learn from life – and we can always learn. I'm always having to learn. I should have quit my last relationship a year before I did."*

Jack just stared at me and at first I thought I offended him by pontificating – but after a moment's reverie, he said *"Cheers mate… I think this Buddhism thing is turning you into a wise-man or something."*

"Wise-guy, more like" I laughed.

"No seriously… I remember that Ron used to call you the 'shrink of the outfit' because you always seemed to know what made people tick. Have you always been into Buddhism? I mean – were you even into it back then?"

"Since I was 14 Jack – or even 8, if you go back to the first picture-book of Tibet I ever saw – and…" I was interrupted…

"Jesus!" Jack suddenly exclaimed *"Is that the time! I'm meeting this really fierce bird at 6! I need to get back to the flat 'ave a shower – and change. Here's my card—take a butchers [25] at that!"*

"Impressive" I grinned.

---

25 *Butcher's*—as in *butcher's hook*—is Cockney rhyming slang for *look.*

"So, yeah, drop me a card from Yeti-land" he said standing up and donning his black velvet jacket *"like if they have cards up there in Shangri-La."*

"Certainly, Jack. Have fun" I grinned. *"I hope the 'fierce bird' will be a good friend to you."*

Jack turned and waved with a broad smile as he approached the door to the Nostril Café.

And there I was. And there was Jack's card. There were two of them: **JJ FLASHMAN ESQUIRE – TOTAL HOME ELECTRICAL WORK**; and, **JUMPING JACK FLASHMAN – SOUND, LIGHT, AND BEYOND**.

Then the door closed and he was gone. It was almost as if he'd never been there. It was as if I'd fallen asleep and dreamed the entire episode. I remembered the words of Düd'jom Rinpoche *'With each life-circumstance: whatever is enacted, stare directly into the enactment – with all the senses.'*

I sat for a while, simply sensing the ambience of the surroundings. How had all that happened? There was a moment in which I had no idea who I was. I found myself sitting there, simply aware of the colour of the café. There was no past or future. There were no names, places, or dates. Then I had a vivid visual impression of Kyabjé Düd'jom Rinpoche. The vision lasted for an undefinable period of time. I'd not looked at my watch – so I had no idea whether time has passed or not. It could have been an hour, a minute, or a second.

Then I had no idea whether it was a vision or a day dream. It was not that I saw Kyabjé Düd'jom Rinpoche in the Nostril Café – he was simply there in space. It was not a flash-back to the room where I used to speak with him in Bodha. It was more as if the Nostril Café had vanished and Kyabjé Düd'jom Rinpoche was the only visual subject in existence.

When the visual impression dissolved, the colours around me were more intense than they had been before. I was left feeling that Düd'jom Rinpoche knew what had taken place in the Nostril Café – and was not displeased. Did I detect laughter? I decided that was wishful thinking. Then I decided it was pointless coming to any conclusion. To be hypercritical to the point of nihilism was as bad as indulging in eternalist fantasy. I simply felt cheered by the strong impression of Düd'jom Rinpoche that had called itself into existence. It felt natural – and I felt cheered. Kyabjé Düd'jom Rinpoche had said he would always be with me – and he always was.

29

fields of the unknowable and inexpressible

And if you can fasten on that moment and expand through the afterglow,
you can reverse your mind in time and travel back to when: the earth was
formed; the sky was born; and the universe began.
Paul Kantner, Grace Slick, and David Freiberg—Your Mind Has Left Your
Body—Baron von Tollbooth & the Chrome Nun—May 1973

Goodbye forever. I never entered the Nostril Café again – and, at this point in time, I can't remember the actual name of the café. It may have been 'The Cave' or 'The Cavern'. Too much time has passed to recall. [1]

My meeting with Jack indicated that another epoch of life was over. I was glad however, that—although I'd been culturally foreign—Jack had seen some value in the Buddhist I'd become. His words *"I think this 'Buddhism thing' is turning you into a wise-man or something"* had been meaningful to me. I hadn't taken it as a compliment – but as an indication that I hadn't entirely failed in terms of living as a ngakpa in the West. That is what Kyabjé Düd'jom Rinpoche had encouraged – and I'd attempted to follow his advice to the best of my ability. I didn't feel I had done that well. Maybe however, in spite of the bizarre scene in the Nostril Café—with its degraded demeaning descriptions of Cynthia—something good had come out of it. Maybe I'd planted some seeds for Jack's better relationships with ladies – and for his developing confidence in his innate capacity for courage.

I was glad Jack had freed himself from a bad marriage. Having seen Cynthia—and exchanged a few words—I felt that Steve Bruce had described her accurately. I had asked him what she was like – and he'd replied *"Better not to know."* I felt sorry for her.

---

1   It is now the *Barista Lounge* 11 Downing Street, Farnham – but no mention can be found of any previous name.

Being obese, let alone morbidly obese, is a sad trap for a human being. I know. I put on weight from time to time. Somehow however, I always manage to reverse the situation, through self-control and exercise – but then, I have been lucky to have had recourse to vows. I know that if I make a vow – there is no possibility of breaking it. I am careful what vows I make – and never make vows that I cannot keep.

I conjectured that Cynthia must have been a sad frustrated person who ate for comfort. Maybe she had little else in life to give her joy. She must have known that Jack didn't love her – but then she didn't love Jack. Jack had merely been an acquisition. Cynthia had merely been a fall-back choice – because Jack had no self-confidence and felt his choices were limited. It had been a recipe for disaster from the outset – and their parents were not sufficiently intelligent or kindly to act differently. Both sets of parents wanted a business deal – because that is how they saw life. This much was clear to me without a psychology degree. I wished her well and hoped she'd be able to make a better life for herself. I wished Jack well. I had the sense that he *would* develop if he was able to remember my words in relation to finding a woman who would be his friend.

When Steve had told me, it was better not to know what Cynthia was like – I'd replied that I felt it would be useful to know to understand Jack better. So, Steve told me. *"She sulks."* Steve had nicknamed her 'the incredible sulk'. *"She's a hypochondriac, like Jack's mother. She finds Monty Python irritating – but enjoys Benny Hill.*[2] *As to her being attractive, Ron and I think Jack would have made a better-looking girl. Basically she's… a water buffalo who laughs like a hyena and prattles like a parrot."*

Of course, I'd asked Steve what he thought the attraction was as far as Jack was concerned. Steve had told me Jack saw himself as looking like a gnome.

2   Benny Hill—Alfred Hawthorne Hill (1924–1992)—was an English comedian whose television programme—The Benny Hill Show—was characterised by farce and juvenile double entendre.

Jack was short and concluded that his chances of romance were negligible. I remembered the poster I'd drawn for Savage Cabbage. Jack wasn't keen on the poster and had said *"That's bloody awful – you've made me look like a sodding gnome!"* Ron laughed and replied *"Perfect likeness then. Don't see what a canary* [3] *like you gotta to complain about."* Ron had no mercy on Jack.

Thinking back to the sad young woman I'd met in the Nostril Café, I couldn't help wondering what *her* story might have been. I guessed that Jack wasn't exactly Prince Charming. I also wondered about Jack's parents. Had they really disowned him? I assumed they had – because it would have been typical of them. I'd met Jack's parents once. They'd be no great loss to Jack. They'd probably adopt Cynthia as a pseudo-daughter… They'd probably felt morally righteous in disowning Jack – and maybe they felt it necessary in order to save face with Cynthia's parents. My father— for all his shortcomings—was a model of parental perfection in comparison with those sad cardboard cut-out examples of humanity. Then I felt sorry for them. What a miserable fate… to become constipated with status to such an extent.

And then, Jack… Jack had a *great* deal to learn in terms of relating to ladies – and relating to *himself* in relation to ladies. He would have had no help from his parents in this regard – and he'd not had Anelie Mandelbaum to educate him. It occurred to me that I'd had *adventitious covert coaching* – and was thus not exactly mainstream in how I related to women. I could therefore not feel too superior in terms of my view of Jack's attitudes. He'd not had any of my advantages in life. In addition to Anelie Mandelbaum, I'd had the example of the Trevelyans—the parents of Alice—and, the parents of Steve Bruce. In terms of girlfriends, Alice and Lindie had been my intellectual and educational superiors – so I had no sense of women as subordinate.

I hoped that maybe someone kind—*and suitably feisty*—could improve Jack. Sometimes that's all it takes.

---

3 *Canary*—as in *Canary Wharf*—is Cockney rhyming slang for *dwarf*.

A person has to have reasons to change – and maybe the right lady could provide those reasons for Jack.

I went home—watched Genghis Khan on television with my mother—and got to see a few camels. Time was ticking away. It was both exciting and vacuous. I'd arranged everything – and now events would take care of themselves.

I thought about my meeting with Jumping Jack Flashman off-and-on during the days leading up to my departure. Despite the fact that there were facets of Jack of which I was critical – his life seemed to contain something from which I could learn… *if* I could decipher it. In some ways Jack had landed on his feet. He'd been lucky – but he'd made that luck work. Some people squander their luck – but Jack had invested it and was reaping the dividends. He'd become an electrician's mate—more-or-less a fetch-and-carry menial—but he'd studied to become an electrician. Now he was *his own man with his own van* – and, more than that, he had interesting prospects. There was some sense of *social poetry* in Jack becoming an electrician. He'd returned to his roots. His *upper-working / lower middle-class* parents had *done a runner* from Wiltshire and cut themselves off from everyone they'd ever known. They'd re-established themselves in Surrey as *nouveaux middle aspiring to upper-middle class* – replete with all the painfully-silly pretentious affectations they imagined were 'upper-middle class'. That's why I'd been banned from their house. I was working-class and they wanted Jack—or John as he was to them—to have nothing to do with the lower echelons.

I'd talked about this with the ladies in Hotwells – and Penelope had an interesting observation to make *"The reason they disliked you so much was probably because you were so similar to them – from their perspective. They were pretending to be upper middle class – and they imagined you were engaged in the same pretence. The problem for them—from what you've explained of your encounters—was that you were far more skilled than they were in the pretence. You were far more cultured and had a far larger vocabulary.*

"That's why they told Jack you were pretentious and that you gave yourself airs. You just made them feel too uncomfortable. Imagine how they must have felt when a 16-year-old upstaged them at their own charade."

That had come as a complete surprise to me – but it made sense immediately. What made it even worse, I realised – was that I must have come across as utterly blasé in my affectations. And there was I having no idea at all that there was anything unusual about my conversational mien.

Steve Bruce's parents were a culturally-educated middle-class couple – but they had no problem with me. Ron Larkin's parents were upper-middle class and they had no problems with me either. Their take seemed to be that I was polite and well spoken. I was equipped with an unusually wide vocabulary – and I was culturally au fait with a broad range of the Arts. I had my father to thank for my vocabulary. He was a self-made man who'd become a major in the Army. He'd started out as a 14-year-old dock worker in Chatham, Kent. My mother was a highly cultured woman whose considerable family fortunes had crashed in the war due to her father's refusal to teach Nazi propaganda in the school of which he was the headmaster. Be that as it may, Jack's parents had tried to force him into the vector they'd taken – only to have him find a career that was more in line with their own despised origins.

Jack had hated grammar school. He hated academic study – but thrived as soon as he'd been taken on by an electrician. He'd then gone on to study electronics. He now knew about sound and lighting systems. He had his everyday work as an electrician – but he fixed amplifiers, re-wired guitars, and sometimes set up the electrics on stage for bands. He'd got back to the place he loved to be – whereas I'd failed. He told me how a band member had seen him eyeing up the drum kit and asked him if he was interested in drumming. He'd said that he used to be a drummer and the fellow had said *"Let's see what you can do then."* Jack sat himself at the drums and – shook, rattled, and rolled. He made his name doing that, as: *the sound and light man who was a real part of the scene.*

511

Jack had never gone back to drumming – but it had stood him in good stead and established his name as *the man to hire*. There was a perfection in that, which I admired. One burst on the drums hadn't inflated Jack with impossible dreams. He'd simply been able to perform for five minutes and let it go. That was impressive. It made sense of his life. He was a sound and light engineer who'd enhanced his reputation by once having been a drummer. He was happy with that – and I respected him for it. He knew what he wanted from life. He knew various people in different bands. He had plans. He was going to develop JUMPING JACK AMPLIFICATION. He planned to develop an amplifier that could compete with MARSHALL. He had ideas about making a better HUMBUCKER guitar pickup. He had ideas about effects pedals. He had endless ideas. He thought that it wasn't impossible that he might even end up as an *electrician to the gods*—those were his words —but he also said that he wouldn't be holding his breath. The words of the Who song went through my mind *'Happy Jack wasn't tall, but he was a man. He lived in the sand in the Isle of Man.'*

That made *me* happy. What made me even happier however, was when I realised that I had no envy. I was simply happy for Jack. I was happy he'd crawled out of the wreckage of a life that had been imposed on him. He had a good career – whatever his parents might think about it. It was a good profession – and one that would give him pride in himself. Maybe he'd develop some bravery. Maybe I'd hear of him one day in the MELODY MAKER – but then I no longer read that, or the NEW MUSICAL EXPRESS. I used to read it as a businessman would read the FINANCIAL TIMES – but those days were gone.

What was it about *me* though? I'd accepted that my dreams had evaporated – and I had no resentment that Jack's dream was going to fly. I had no belief in destiny – so there was nothing to be gained by speculating in that direction.

I kept forgetting about Jack – but then, when I was least expecting it, I found myself feeling that I had something to learn from that peculiar scenario in the Nostril Café.

Every time I looked at it, I came to the same conclusion. It meant nothing more than it was. It was sad in some ways and amusing in others. I told my mother about it and she also found it both sad and amusing.

"How can zay disown zair own son – venn zay force him to marry ziss girl? Vott kind of parents are zay? Your farzer vould never have done somesing like ziss."

"No, Mum, he wouldn't… He wouldn't have forced me to marry anyone. I met the Hackmans once and they were… not exactly cultured people… in fact… they were semi-literate. Not that I'm saying semi-literacy is a crime… but when you combine it with affectation, pretention, snobbery, pomposity and lack of humanity – it's not a pleasant picture."

It occurred to me that Jack—as a product of his upbringing—was actually quite a reasonable human being. He had possibilities. In the right circumstances – he could develop and evolve a broader sense of what it was to be human. Maybe I'd find myself pleasantly surprised on meeting him again in the future.

As this thought was passing through – I suddenly stopped short. Did—I—have possibilities? Would—I—be pleasantly surprised by what I'd become in the future? That was the key issue. I'd seen what was possible for Jack – but what was possible for Ngakpa Chögyam? Would my time in India and Nepal change me for the better as far as Kyabjé Düd'jom Rinpoche was concerned? Would I be able to take authentic advantage of what I received? I'd already had such wonderful opportunities with Düd'jom Rinpoche —and recently with the 16th Gyalwa Karmapa—but I still felt a little too much like a dilettante in my own apprehension of where I was.

It wasn't that I was just playing with the idea of living as a ngakpa: I *knew* I was serious – but was that *serious* enough for what Düd'jom Rinpoche had intimated? I was supposed to receive visionary teachings. How could a person like *me* achieve that? I was supposed to have found a sangyum – but had fallen at the first hurdle with my choice of a lady friend.

513

Although—having said that—I realised that it hadn't been a choice. I'd simply acquiesced. Claudette Gascoigne had made the running – and I did nothing to alter the outcome she had in mind. I realised that she could have been almost anyone sufficiently intelligent and witty. Be that as it may… I'd gained three years living with three wonderful friends – and that, was entirely due to 'dette. I hoped I would be able to find a way to explain it all to Düd'jom Rinpoche without his concluding that I was the most dismal drivelling dolt – and an utter waste of time and space.

Were the Blues band dreams *(that I'd claimed to be dead)* actually dead? Or had my dreams just bottomed out? Was I just like Jack in my own way – merely *doing a runner*?

How could I answer such a question? Who could assist me with such an inquiry? Lama Chime Yönten had advised David Bowie[4] to stay with Rock music rather than becoming a monk. Akong Rinpoche had advised Leonard Cohen to remain a musician rather than taking monastic vows – because he could always do that when he was older. That was one possibility—if the story I'd been told was true—but Akong Rinpoche made no comment of that sort to me. Gyalwa Karmapa made no such comment either. So, what was I doing bandying such nonsense around in my head? I remembered the words of Düd'jom Rinpoche '*With each life-circumstance: whatever is enacted, stare directly into the enactment – with all the senses.*'

After a few days of mental meanderings, I pondered the possibility that my conjecture might merely be the result of anxiety. Might I be as much of a coward as Jack? Was I just afraid of nine months in the Himalayas? No… I was looking forward to it with enormous eagerness – but simultaneously questioning my capacity to *be what I needed to be*. It was the possibility of failure.

---

4   See *Goodbye Forever*—Volume I—chapter 16—Lama Chime: the doors of perception—Aro Books WORLDWIDE—2020.

I thought about what I'd said to Jack in the Nostril Café. *'Being on stage with Savage Cabbage was more truly what I was than anything else that has ever happened.'*

That wasn't completely true, however. I'd said it for Jack. I could have told Jack that there was another area of my life where I'd felt like that – and, actually, far more so. Although we touched on Buddhism briefly before we parted – there was no way I could have explained my experience of Düd'jom Rinpoche or Gyalwa Karmapa.

Being in the presence of those Lamas – was always timeless. There was no sense of anything lacking – or of any kind of expectation. There was nowhere to go in those situations other than where I was. Even when I was not with my Lamas – I was simply going about my life as a practitioner. That was entirely understandable in the Tibetan communities in which I'd lived.

As soon as these notions percolated sufficiently, I realised that what I was experiencing was a waiting room – a departure lounge. I was simply experiencing the *bag chags* of my old life. Bag chags—usually called 'karmic traces'—are residual patterns, unconscious propensities, and tenuous dispositions. They are impressions, imprints, inclinations, latent predispositions. I could also call them velleities. A velleity is a *desire so slight* that one is not inclined to act on it. Well… maybe I'd not act on these velleities – but they could certainly obfuscate a clear and restful state of mind.

As soon as that was clear – what had seemed like an approximate abyss, suddenly felt natural. The anxiety on the high diving board at Aldershot Swimming Pool when I was young had always vanished as soon as I dived. So—sitting in my mother's garden—I found myself having dived. The *Three Terrible Oaths* of Dorje Tröllö came to mind.

> *Whatever happens – may it happen.*
> *Whichever way it goes – may it go that way.*
> *There is no purpose.*

Each purpose was simply *its own movement in time*. There was no *one purpose*. There was no God *working his purpose out*. I remembered the hymn we sang at school:

> *God is working His purpose out as year succeeds to year; / God is working his purpose out, and the time is drawing near; / Nearer and nearer draws the time, the time that shall surely be, / When the earth shall be filled with the glory of God – as the waters cover the sea.*

What was *that* supposed to mean? *'As the waters cover the sea'*? The water is the sea – and the sea is the water. I supposed it was merely poor composition: poor linguistic usage. There was no *God* and no *purpose being worked out* in any case. There is simply the infinite purity of the phenomenal world – and the natural efflorescence of empathetic-appreciation. Phenomena are self-creating. What lay ahead of me would be created moment-by-moment, according to my perceptions and their concomitant responses.

Jack's choice could not be my choice. There was no *Jack's choice* for me. I'd already made my choice. I'd made it back in 1971 when I went to Nepal and met Kyabjé Düd'jom Rinpoche. I'd made it before that. I'd made it when I began reading Buddhist books – and practising silent sitting meditation at the age of 14. I'd made it even before that – at the age of eight when I first set my eyes on those Tibetan photographic-journal books in my school library. I'd made it in my infancy – when welcoming the presence of Khyungchen Aro Lingma in my bedroom, as a dream of clarity, as a visionary experience.

The choice had merely taken time to unravel – and it had only continued to unravel because I never let up on it. It had been a thread as far back as I could remember. It had been a thread that had always made sense – both intellectually and emotionally. Blues had been a thread too. It went back almost as far – but it wasn't vast and pervasive as Vajrayana was vast and pervasive. It was also less particular. I didn't have to become a Vajrayana performer. I was already a ngakpa – and that was all I ever wanted to be. I'd already arrived at my destination.

Now all I had to do was *live in that destination.* Part of *living that destination*, was travelling to the Himalayas. It was having *no direction home.* The words of Bob Dylan. I pondered: *How did it feel? To be on my own? Like a complete unknown? With no direction home? Like a rolling stone?*

It felt fine. I'd moved into the abyss. That was my home.

The last day became hours and the hours became minutes and—as if I'd only just left Bristol—I was leaving Woodsfield Lane for the Himalayas. I left knowing that I'd never return as the person who set out. That was almost exhilarating. I smiled about Jack's asking me whether I'd write a book about my adventures – like Lawrence of Arabia. Writing an adventure book was *the last thing on my mind.* Apart from my mother and brother – I'd *leave not a trace left behind.*

I remembered the words of Düd'jom Rinpoche *'With each life-circumstance: whatever is enacted, stare directly into the enactment – with all the senses.'*

The adventure I'd have was not going to be crossing torrents on rickety bridges.

I wasn't going to be scaling icy heights in savage winds.

I'd not circumambulate Mount Kailash evading bandits.

I wasn't going to ride wild yaks on the Changthang or ride with Golok brigands.

I wouldn't be marrying a Bhutanese princess yogini and living in a mountain hermitage that clung to the side of its staggering heights – lost in attenuated shreds of cloud.

The list of *what wasn't likely* was extensive – but, I had no dreams of high adventure. I simply wanted to absorb as much Vajrayana as I could and plunge into the visionary mechanics of it.

As to what would happen in the Himalayas… the list was: sculpted in temporal-sands; written in water – on droplets of mist; burnt into fire – with the quill of transparence; recorded in wind – with the lens of nonconceptual silence; and, translated in space—*by space*—as… space…

Final evening before leaving Britain. Walked in the woods. I set out to see the trees. I'd always known and loved those trees. I found the old yew where I used to perch as a child – and where I'd meditated as a teenager. The yew was not as large as I remembered it – but the branches didn't feel as if they wouldn't welcome me. I found the comfortable spot where I used to sit and settled into it. Time passed. Hours passed without a sense of anything unusual. I hadn't intended to sit for more than a brief period – but darkness was not far off when I suddenly became aware that Aro Lingma had sparkled out of the dim. I'd realised that her presence had been there – *before my notice of her* became apparent to my concept consciousness. I did not know how that was possible. I remembered the same thing had often occurred when I was a young child. As with every other time I'd witnessed Aro Lingma, there'd been no words – but communication had occurred. I'd known unknowable inexpressible fields of noetic value. On this occasion however – I knew that I was on the brink of a pluripotential juncture. I was approaching the culmination of a vector whose inception was inseparable from my conception; inseparable from my empty continuum. The only recognisable coordinate in that unfathomably vast expanse was Kyabjé Düd'jom Rinpoche Jig'drèl Yeshé Dorje.

30

Düd'jom Rinpoche

England. I'd lived a colourful, vigorous life in that Green and Pleasant Land. It had sometimes even been replete with Hope and Glory – but now, that life was gone. Well, that's not quite true. The artistic heroics of the 1960s had been slipping away since my first Himalayan journey in 1971 – but the interconnective tendrils had made the 1960s seem more tangible, at times, than they were.

The palpable connection with my life in the 1960s had been based on secondary causes – and as soon as those causes were not present, it seemed like an historical novel. It wasn't Jane Austen. It wasn't Jack Kerouac's *On the Road*[1] or *Dharma Bums*[2] – but it may as well have been. Almost every Art student had read Jack Kerouac – and most of them, before 1972, had seemed like extras from Kerouacian movies. There was a version of me who could have ridden out of one of those novels – or out of the movie *Easy Rider*.[3]

As soon as I stepped out of the bus outside Nowrojee's Store[4] in McLeod Ganj, 1971 segued into 1975. It was as if I'd been in England for a year.

1 *On the Road* (1957) was based on the travels of Kerouac and his friends across the United States. It is considered a defining work of the post-war Beat generation. It is a roman à clef which highlights Jazz and Poetry in the lives of key figures such as: William Burroughs, Allen Ginsberg, and Neal Cassady. Jack Kerouac—as Sal Paradise—is the narrator.
2 *The Dharma Bums* (1958) is a series of semi-fictional events occurring some years after the events of *On the Road*. The character Japhy Ryder is based on the poet Gary Snyder, who introduced Jack Kerouac to Buddhism. The book had a significant influence on the Hippie culture of the 1960s and early 1970s.
3 *Easy Rider* (1969) is a landmark counterculture movie that explores societal issues during the late 1960s. Written and produced by Peter Fonda and Dennis Hopper, with Terry Southern. Peter Fonda and Dennis Hopper act the parts of two hippie bikers riding through the American Southwest and South on chopped motorcycles.
4 Nowrojee and Sons General Store is one of the oldest shops in Himachal Pradesh. It has maintained its original wooden structure. See glossary: *Nowrojee and Sons*.

Then the year telescoped into a month, a week, a day – and now… into no time at all. It was as if I had simply fallen asleep and dreamed the three years Illustration degree. Bristol Art School had been a period in which two characters coexisted: Ngakpa Chögyam experimenting with *what life was like* for a Nyingma Vajrayanist in British Art School culture; and, Vic Simmerson – the Art student who maintained Düd'jom gTér practices in private.

Vic Simmerson obtained a first-class Honours Degree – but somehow, failed to be accepted for a Master's Degree at the Royal College of Art.[5] It didn't really matter one way or another to the young man who had returned to the Himalayas – and who would be with Kyabjé Düd'jom Rinpoche Jig'drèl Yeshé Dorje in a matter of weeks. Little remained of Vic Simmerson that had not suffered a *sea change*.[6]

> '*Full fathom five thy father lies; Of his bones are coral made; Those are pearls that were his eyes; Nothing of him that doth fade, But doth suffer a sea-change, Into something rich and strange. Sea-nymphs hourly ring his knell: Ding-dong. Hark! now I hear them – Ding-dong, bell.*'
> William Shakespeare—The Tempest—Act I—Scene ii

It wasn't that I'd altered entirely. I could still be a whimsical wag… but that 1960s' surrealist adventurer had become a set of clothes – an appearance sometimes worn. I could still sing Blues. I could still paint and write poetry – yet these propensities were now the chamæleoid inflections of a *changeling*.[7] I'd once felt like a Mississippi changeling – the misplaced son of a sharecropper.

5 See Chapter 25. Also see *an odd boy*—Volume IV—Doc Togden—Aro Books WORLDWIDE—2018 – in which the events are described in greater detail.
6 *Sea change* – idiomatic expression denoting a significant change in perspective. The provenance is a song sung by the spirit, Ariel – to Ferdinand, a prince of Naples, after Ferdinand's father's apparent death by drowning.
7 A *changeling* is a being—in European folklore—the offspring of a troll or elf who has been secretly left in the place of a human child. Sometimes the term is used to refer to the child who has been taken to another realm. The theme of the exchanged child is common in mediæval literature and reflects concern over infants afflicted by unknown disorders or mental abnormality.

It was never a hard-wired fantasy – merely the personal poetry of existence. I'd looked at photographs of Son House – and felt an impossible ethnic affinity. Son House was a man who was more-or-less the same age as my father. In some way he'd become my father – and that illusion had fuelled my stage persona with the Savage Cabbage Blues Band. Then, after Ron and Steve died, it fuelled me as a solo Delta Blues nonentity on the Home Counties pub circuit.

Now I was living in the Western Himalayas feeling the same kind of impossible ethnic affinity with the gö kar chang lo wing of the Nyingma Tradition. The Tibetans were refugees – and in some ways I was also a refugee. It struck me more than once that I found it easier to identify with the disenfranchised, than with the English. Could it be because I was half German? I gave that thought some time – but couldn't say I'd ever felt anything other than English. I had no pull to go and live in Germany – no matter how much I preferred the food.[8]

I'd always been a hybrid. I was the son of a working-class English father and an upper middle-class German mother.

My mother's family had moved down quite severely in society due to her father's antipathy to Hitler. My father had moved up in the world. He'd taken advantage of a military education and become a major – albeit a 'war-time major'. He had never been accepted on equal terms by other officers – and that never ceased to rankle with him. A disastrous divorce settlement had pulled him down; not into penury – but into a need for thrift that never settled well with him. My mother's family were ruined by Hitler and the war – and so our family was a curious anomaly. I was a working-class lad with upper-middle German class table-manners.

At school I was neither a Mod nor a Rocker. I failed to identify with either. Motorcycle jackets and US Army parka-coats seemed equally attractive. That was apparently not comprehensible to either camp.

---

8 Food in Britain was not acclaimed for its high quality or variety at that time.

Even though I'd grown my hair and looked like a hippie – I never bought the entire package. I abjured drugs. I didn't adopt counterculture jargon. I starched and ironed my Levi's. I wore brogues. As an Art student I was a hybrid inasmuch as I found my own niche as a figurative Fine Artist on an Illustration degree. Now I was an Englishman in India – and feeling more at home than I'd felt for three years.

I wondered what it would be like to hitch a ride with Doctor Who and meet: Vic Simmerson—beau of Lindie Dale—in 1968; Farquhar Arbuthnot—vocalist and back-up bass player with Savage Cabbage—in 1969; Frank Schubert—solo Delta Blues player and Art student—in 1970; and, finally, the first version of Chögyam—fresh back from the Himalayas—in 1971. Four years seemed like 40 years – even without recourse to time travel. The Beatles song from the Revolver album ran through my mind

> *'She said "I know what it's like to be dead. I know what it is to be sad"*
> *And she's making me feel like I've never been born.'*
> Lennon-McCartney—The Beatles—She Said, She Said—Revolver—1966

… and yes, I knew what it was like to be dead. To a certain extent, I knew what it was to be sad. Not that I was *fundamentally* sad – but I sometimes had a certain sense of mourning for the versions of myself who had died. That sadness never lasted more than a moment or two – because I was *fundamentally* happy. I was basically a paradox – even to myself. In some way, happiness and sadness had a similar flavour – when they were not too intense. In this, I made no pretension to nondual realisation. It was more as if these emotions were non-exclusive – and equally to be valued. I was happy because I'd made what felt to be the right decision – and, I was ever so slightly sad for the same reason. My mourning for the friends I'd lost was not something I wished to transcend.

This was because it was tied in with the depths of my appreciation for Steve Bruce and Ron Larkin...[9] and also, to a lesser extent, for Lindie Dale whose parents had decreed that she was not to consort with me. That was back in 1968. Steve and Ron however, were my treasure as well as my triste – and they were always there in some way, as part of the atmosphere I inhabited. I might not think of them for weeks at a time – but they were always there. They were there in my mind when I arrived in India – but took their leave as the rickety bus chugged higher into the foothills of Himachal Pradesh.

I would first spend time with Ngakpa Yeshé Dorje and Khandro Ten'dzin Drölkar in Forsyth Bazaar and McLeod Ganj – before setting out for Nepal.

I had met Ngakpa Yeshé Dorje and Khandro Ten'dzin Drölkar first in 1971 – and that meeting created a number of causes, the effects of which were now playing out. Certain people can take a jaunt to the Himalayas and return – others never return. I was one of the ones who never returned. Not that I stayed in the Himalayas – but *they* stayed with me.

I'd tried to work out a compromise. I'd planned to become an Art School lecturer and keep returning to the Himalayas in the Winter and Spring breaks. I was even to have taken a sabbatical every once in a while. Then—when I retired—I could spend as much time as I wished immersed in Vajrayana Buddhism. It's astonishing how a 19-year-old can plan the rest of his life – as if it wasn't extremely rare for life-plans to run their course. The plan didn't cause me any problems however – in fact it was necessary in order to make the most of Art School whilst also being a serious Vajrayana practitioner. I remembered Mrs Pendrake's Bible class at Netherfield School. She'd been an appalling teacher – but the Bible references and quotations had remained with me.

9   See *an odd boy*—Volumes I and II—Doc Togden—Aro Books WORLDWIDE—2011 and 2012; and *Goodbye Forever*—Volume I—Ngakpa Chögyam—Aro Books WORLDWIDE—2020.

'No man can serve two masters: for either he will hate the one, and love the other; or else he will hold to the one, and despise the other. Ye cannot serve God and mammon both.' The Bible—Matthew 6:24

I didn't see Art as mammon. It wasn't a question of adoring one and despising the other – but the energy required to experience anything totally, necessitates the death of divided loyalties. Divided loyalties had always caused me problems in the world of the Arts. At Art School I'd been obdurately interdisciplinary – but you can't be interdisciplinary as a disciple. If you arrange a list of priorities for your life – something has to take first place. After the first place is taken – everything else is secondary, tertiary, and so on 'til it hardly registers.

I stayed in McLeod Ganj for a month before setting out for Nepal. I'd have left earlier – but Düd'jom Rinpoche wouldn't have been in Bodhanath at that time. I was sorry not to be able to head out earlier – but I'd have the advantage of cooler weather crossing North India. The luck was *not* with me however and the train journey was barbaric in terms of temperature and the 22-hour delay at Gorakpur. Sitting at Gorakpur station waiting for a train that was 22 hours late was somewhat taxing. I couldn't leave the station because—according to the station supervisor—the train could arrive any minute *"Very soon coming sir – very soon"* and he said that every few hours.

I survived on chai—Indian tea—which was fortunately of rather poor quality. I say 'fortunately' because I've never liked sugar in tea —or full cream milk—and the usual condensed milk used in chai made it nauseating to me. Condensed milk would have been expensive – so the chai-wallah[10] spared me that horror… and stinted on the milk into the bargain. The chai was brought around every so often by a young lad—the chai wallah—and I relished it.

---

10 *Wallah* is a Hindi word which mean 'the one who does it' or 'the one who has it'. Chai wallahs serve tea; attar wallah sell perfumes; a kulfi wallah make ice-cream; dhobi wallahs wash clothes; and, a punka wallah operate the manual fans to cool rooms.

To make masala chai you need equals parts of milk and water with sugar, cardamom, cinnamon, ground cloves, and ginger. The mixture is then brought to a boil and loose black tea is added. The chai is immediately taken off the heat, covered, and allowed to sit for approximately 10 minutes to allow the black tea to infuse into the chai. The chai is then strained and served. The chai-wallah served it in *once-fired earthenware* beakers – which you'd simply throw onto the railway tracks when you'd drunk the tea. Because the beakers were *once-fired earthenware* they'd dissolve in the first rain and turn back into clay. There was perfection to that idea. It somehow gave me great cheer: litter-free litter, how amazing. I was also cheered by the delight on the chai wallah's face when I hurled my beakers onto the tracks and purchased another. I did offer to let him refill my beaker – but he'd have none of it *"No sir this I cannot doing – always new must be having."*

The train finally came and took me to Raxaul Junction and from thence I caught a bus at Birgunj – the border town for crossing into Nepal. By the time I got through customs and immigration— and caught the bus for Kathmandu—I was heartily relieved to be out of India and heading for a higher altitude with cooler weather.

Having ridden a bus to Kathmandu before – I decided to ride the roof rack. That's not as risky or uncomfortable as it might seem. The roof rack is usually laden with rucksacks and bales of this— and—that, which means you can snuggle down into a position where you're padded on all sides. The major advantage of riding the roof rack is that you can jump clear should the bus plummet into a 1,000-foot gorge. It happened. I'd seen the wreckage several times as the bus took mountain-road corners at inadvisable speed. Sometimes there'd be an ominous clunk as one of the wheels skimmed a boulder on the road side – just on the edge of an abyss. I never had to make that leap – although if I had, the result would have resulted in fractures, at least. Fractures however, seemed better than certain death trapped inside the bus.

I arrived in Kathmandu a little chilled from the mountain passes – but otherwise relatively perky, once I'd stretched enough to remove the aches of the journey.

Freak Street, Kathmandu, was as it ever was. I found a cheap place to stay. It was never possible to go directly to Bodhanath. That would have been my preference – but there are worse things in the world than a night spent on Freak Street.[11]

It was good to arrive in Bodhanath and leave the tourist buzz of Kathmandu in the dusty distance. I was met by my friends Amji Pema Dorje and Yeshé Khandro—who spoke extremely good English—and they took me to the room they'd secured for me. I was to live in the same house where they conducted their surgery. They were both Tibetan doctors and made life extremely easy for me. I'd made friends with Yeshé Khandro through the 'Tibetan Friendship Group' run by a Cockney Kagyüd nun—Gétsulma Tsültrim Zangmo—who lived in Bromley Kent with her mother Gétsulma Wangchuk. They'd been ordained by Gyalwa Karmapa in '69 and had a wealth of information that they'd put at my disposal. I'd designed letterheads and stationery—amongst other things—for the 'Tibetan Friendship Group' when I'd been at Bristol Art School and had kept in contact ever since.

Early the next day I went to the Düd'jom Gompa to sit for an hour. I had decided to replicate what I had done before I first met Kyabjé Düd'jom Rinpoche in 1971. This time as I entered the Gompa there were far more smiles and 'tashi delegs'[12] greetings. I was surprised that anyone would know who I was, let alone remember me. I concluded that it was the robes they remembered rather than their occupant, as Injis ngakpas were not exactly thick on the ground. I never saw another in the Himalayas during the 20th Century.

11 *Freak Street* runs south from Basantapur Square. Its real name is Joch-ne but since the late 1960s it has been better known as Freak Street. In its prime, the street was irresistible to hippies both for its beauty and shambling shabbiness.
12 Tashi delegs *(bKra shis bDe legs)* means auspicious delightful goodness – a ubiquitous Tibetan greeting.

I ended up staying in the Düd'jom Gompa longer than expected – as I was offered refreshments and treated with great kindness and hospitality. It was taken for granted that I had come to see Kyabjé Düd'jom Rinpoche Jig'drèl Yeshé Dorje. I was asked—as always— about my family. Great sympathy was shown with regard to my father having died. This surprised me slightly because I had considered that 'death' is 'what was to be expected' – according to Buddhist contemplation. I was used to reciting the words *Kyé tsèd mi-tag 'chi-wa'i chö-çan yin: Everything that is born is impermanent and consequently dies.* It was part of the Düd'jom gTér Ngöndro that I had recited in 1971 and I knew the words by heart.[13] I had obviously been highly literal about it and was thus surprised by the kindness I was shown. According to the monks in the Düd'jom Gompa, it was natural that one should be sad about the death of a close relative.

I was not the only literalist however – there seemed to be a culture of emotional negation amongst Western Buddhists. '*Impermanence*' was their response to any mention of loss – and I began to understand that there was a degree of psychological disorder in that kind of flat emotionless response... because it was not apparent in Tibetans. Knowledge of impermanence and sadness were not entirely mutually exclusive. I would remember this. I would never fall into the trap of using impermanence as a means of withholding sympathy. It was not that I felt this trap was likely – but it was valuable to bear in mind. I should never become blasé in respect of my being immune to developing an *artificial Buddhist personality*. I had seen people I used to know at school who had adopted *caricature personalities*. Some had become stereotypical conservatives. Some had become stereotypical socialists. Some had become stereotypical average work-a-day normalists. Some had become stereotypical hippies with adopted West Coast American accents. I wondered how many had the temerity to simply evolve as individuals?

13 See glossary: *impermanence verse*.

I was dislodged from this reverie by being told that Kyabjé Düd'jom Rinpoche had been expecting me. He had mentioned my coming to see him several times over the past month or so. *"Inji ngakpa—Aro Tulku—soon coming."* This is what he had been reported to have said.

This information was slightly startling – or rather, it threw me into a peculiar state of mind in which I felt as if I were experiencing a lucid dream. I ran a check list through my thoughts just to see whether I could summon up information that would not usually be available in a dream: my flight details; my mothers' address; my school qualifications. It was all there—accessible to me—so I concluded that I was awake and experiencing the real world.

I finally took my leave and circumambulated the Great Chörten three times reciting the verses of establishing confidence in actuality and active empathetic appreciation[14] before arriving at Düd'jom Rinpoche's door. I did not need to knock. Word had already got to Kyabjé Düd'jom Rinpoche that I was there – and a smiling monk was already at the door waiting for my approach.

"Like first time!" Düd'jom Rinpoche laughed as soon as I entered the room. *"Gompa sitting – then 'khora making, before door knocking."* He hastened to inform me that he was laughing with pleasure. He asked me if I was taller than before. I had to reply that I did not think so – but I had not measured my height since I was in my early teens. *"Then maybe taller coming"* he smiled. *"Any way – there is much to teach. You must be every day coming."*

Düd'jom Rinpoche was most generous in allowing me to ask questions. I mentioned that I'd spent a little time with Gyalwa Karmapa and received empowerments from him. Düd'jom Rinpoche was delighted to hear it. I told him about my dream of Chögyam Trungpa Rinpoche – and Gyalwa Karmapa explaining Chögyam Trungpa Rinpoche being an incarnation of Drukpa Künlegs. Düd'jom Rinpoche agreed – and said *"Chögyam Trungpa Rinpoche also Speech Incarnation of DoKhyentsé Yeshé Dorje."*

14 See glossary: *refuge verse.*

Then he looked at me almost mischievously *"Oh yah… you also like Drukpa Künlegs becoming"* he laughed. *"I saying 'you must be in West living and Western culture as ngakpa living.' And this you are doing"* he smiled. *"This you are very well doing!"* then he laughed more than I had ever heard him laugh before. *"With La-lo'i chö* [15] *myönpas* [16] *is— too—funny"* he laughed – but then he sighed with concern. *"Staying in house of La-lo'i chö myönpas very strange difficulties coming – but mind nothing changing—only kind and natural—no problems for you coming… all perfect result."*

How was this possible? I knew immediately that Düd'jom Rinpoche was referring to the utterly bizarre travesty of the Latihan in Liverpool. So, I admitted that it had been difficult. I had tried to follow his advice with regard to living as a ngakpa in Western culture *as it was*. I pointed out that what I had experienced was not exactly common in Western culture – but neither was it that rare. Düd'jom Rinpoche asked me to explain what Latihan was supposed to be – so I gave as succinct a description as I could of how it was supposed to be and how it had been distorted into some sort of naked freak-out.[17] I also mentioned having taken Jan's advice. I'd left before the situation became too stupid – although… I could have left even earlier, if I'd taken the advice in a timelier fashion.

"Oh yah" he smiled *"wrathful wisdom khandro must be always listening."*

My eyes must have widened because Düd'jom Rinpoche laughed heartily – and said that he could see my life through the window of my eyes. He then presented me with a cameo of Jan as a bathykolpian khandro – a good meditator with a good heart. This both startled me and put me at my ease – because it seemed that my life was an open book to Düd'jom Rinpoche.

---

15 *kLa kLo'i chos* – Islam / Islamic.
16 *sMyon pa* – mad person.
17 The term *freak out* is used here according to its late 1960s meaning: a party where anything goes – usually with the aid of whatever drugs are available.

I then told him that having been in such situations had worried me with regard to what he would think of me, letting myself be involved with such a thing. Düd'jom Rinpoche shook his head however. He told me that it was better that I had not avoided that evening. It was good for me to experience such deranged scenes. It was good because it tested my practice. He emphasised that I was not a monk or a practitioner of Outer Tantra – and that it was important for me not to avoid such negative secondary causes. *"You Dzogchen practising – so all secondary causes must be experiencing. Never hiding. Always open and natural remaining. All things seeing exactly clearly – then every circumstance like shrine room becoming."*

Düd'jom Rinpoche asked me to give a little more detail in terms of how I ended up at a naked hippie Latihan – and, with some degree of trepidation I told as much of the picaresque saga as he wished to hear. The story caused him a great deal of mirth and several times the details either caused him to exclaim *"Yatsen!"* [18] or *"Kyé-ma…"* [19] By the end of my slightly awkward account, I felt as if I had not acted entirely like a 'thom yor. Düd'jom Rinpoche nodded – and explained that there had been many secondary causes… but that they seemed to have no effect on me. Nothing was elicited – or if it was elicited, I had been able to override it. I had not become angry nor had I surrendered to pressure to be other than I was. He pointed out that I had not created the situation – I had simply witnessed it. Amy and Atlas had planned the Latihan for that evening and it would have taken place whether I had been there or not. There would therefore be no repercussion for me. In fact, I had tried my best to put Kate Partridger on her guard. I had taken responsibility for her wellbeing and had done what I could to be supportive.

---

18 *ya mTshan* – marvel! Also: marvellous, wondrous, strange, amazing, astonishing, wonderful, surprising, miraculous, extraordinary, or unruly. Here Düd'jom Rinpoche probably meant it in the sense of 'unruly' vis-à-vis outlandish or bizarre views.

19 *kye ma* – alas. Exclamation of unpleasant surprise. Also surprise with compassion and sorrow. An exclamation of regret.

There was nothing to regret… and in any case it had all transpired through going to Samŷe Ling Tibetan Centre – so I had not sought out a situation such as the one I had described. There was no need for shame or remorse. It was, in fact, hilarious – and he had enjoyed hearing about it.

"I am thinking – this Latihan, for you, maybe 'khor-dé ru shan [20] *similar coming."*

Kyabjé Düd'jom Rinpoche explained that secular activity usually increased attraction, aversion, and indifference. This obscured the *nature of Mind.* It seeded further primary karmas that caused delusion rather than causes for realisation. 'khor-dé ru shan however, integrated ordinary events with awareness without changing or adapting. This was unique to Dzogchen – and was elucidated in the *Dra Thal'gyur* [21] the *Root Tantra of Unimpeded Sound.* *"In Sutrayana and Vajrayana – methods of wholesome beneficial activity finding. Then visualisation of yidams with mantra reciting. Then absorptions of kyè-rim and dzog-rim.* [22] *But nothing of this kind – not ordinary events with awareness integrating. This only in Dzogchen finding."* Although it was good for most people that they practised with effort—and considered karma—with Dzogchen it was preferable to remain even and unaffected by volatile circumstances. *"With Dzogchen, perception and response inseparable. This view in the other vehicles, impossible. This extremely important for all crucial points of Dzogchen understanding."*

Kyabjé Düd'jom Rinpoche explained that 'khor-dé ru shan eliminated the conditioned cyclic nature of perceptual phenomena incited by previous perceptions and the concomitant responses. It terminated attraction, aversion, and indifference in terms of seeding further causes of 'khorwa.

---

20 *'khor 'das ru shan*
21 *sGra thal 'gyur rTsa ba'i rGyud* – the Dra Thalgyur Root Tantra is one of the 17 Dzogchen tantras.
22 Kyè-rim *(bsKyed rim)* is the generation phase in which the yidam is external and the environment is built gradually. Dzog-rim *(rDzogs rim)* is the completion phase in which one arises as the yidam and the environment is spontaneous.

"This is marvellous method for precisely identifying nature 'khor-dé. This ordinary body, speech, and mind liberating."

Düd'jom Rinpoche explained that the Outer 'khor-dé ru shan is undertaken in the wilderness. It facilitates a drastic reorientation of perception by distinguishing the events of mind from the nature of Mind. The nature of the facilitation involves driving body, speech, and mind beyond habitual limitations. In the practices of Outer 'khor-dé ru shan, one had to *act out* both beatific and agonal scenarios from whatever paradisiacal and perditional images were available. Then, with the conviction that *'khor* and *dé* have the same taste, one acts like a madman: crouching and standing, running and leaping; laughing and crying; speaking and shouting; whispering and singing. Thus, one alternates between being restrained and excited. One takes this to the point of exhaustion – and then rests in a state of effortlessness and ease.

By alternating these unrestrained enactments with formless awareness, one discovers how dualistic derangement and its cessation open out into referenceless presence. *"Both from ka dag emerging – beyond existence and nonexistence."* Dualistic derangement and its cessation cannot be differentiated if one has presence of awareness in primordial space. As one is not deluded by the nature of perception but by fixation, nondual realisation occurs naturally. One simply needs to recognise that fixation is merely mind attempting to grasp at its own empty manifestations. Through the radical experiential improvisation of Outer 'khor-dé ru shan one emancipates inhibitions and realises a free dimension of being, based on the nature of Mind rather than its transient expressions.

"When body, speech, and mind 'expression capacity' exhausting then resting in nalwa.[23] In this way practising – realisation naturally radiant and vast like sky becoming. Reference points disappearing. All action spontaneous becoming. Mind – free from beginninglessness. No beginning. No end. Speech like melodious echo becoming. Body like garuda in space soaring – like lion fearless in mountains roaming." PAUSE

23 *rNal du ba* – lucid relaxation.

"Oh yah. Tomorrow we Inner 'khor-dé ru shan speaking."

Düd'jom Rinpoche sat in silence for some moments – and I simply sat in his presence. I never attempted to practice anything specific at these moments, unless Düd'jom Rinpoche indicated it – so there is no way of describing what occurred. I cannot say I found myself in the nondual state – but neither can I say that it was not. It was an experience I can only describe as Kyabjé Düd'jom Rinpoche Jig'drèl Yeshé Dorje.

31

Presence of Guru Rinpoche

A timeless interim. Düd'jom Rinpoche laughed *"Oh yah!"* then quietly *"then with naked khandros swimming…"* then seriously *"maybe like Drukpa Künlegs becoming."*

This was a jest. At least I thought it was a jest? I suddenly had second thoughts – because no one was laughing. I flickered hot and cold. This was the first time I had been admonished by Düd'jom Rinpoche. The sensation hit me like a sledge hammer. I must have looked vaguely stunned because Düd'jom Rinpoche looked at me with concern. *"Aro Yeshé speech-emanation of Drukpa Künlegs. Many emanations of Drukpa Künlegs. Chögyam Trungpa mind emanation of Drukpa Künlegs – this why both 'Chögyam name' having. Maybe both with naked khandros swimming."*

Then everyone laughed. Then I realised that I was not being admonished for what had occurred at Samŷe Ling and accompanying three young ladies for a naked dip in the River Esk. Düd'jom Rinpoche enquired as to how it came about—but with a most benignly amused expression—and so, I explained that 'skinny dipping' was fairly normal in the hippie milieu of the early 1970s.

"Oh yah—many khandros always—but you must only one Sangyum finding. This important." Then Düd'jom Rinpoche laughed *"Like Drukpa Künlegs not possible in your country manifesting."*

I explained that although many strange things had happened to me in terms of young ladies – it was not something that I deliberately sought. I really did *only* want one partner. I was not really the wild libidinous type and did not want my life to be that of a myön héruka.[1] My choice—if it were mine to make—would be for a fairly level sort of life.

---

1   Myön Héruka *(sMyon he ru ka)* mad yogi. Also translated as mad siddha, crazed saint, or divine madman *(after Keith Dowman).*

I saw my future as being a contentedly married ngakpa with a wife who was a dedicated Nyingma practitioner.

"Oh yah!" Düd'jom Rinpoche laughed. *"This I am—very—well knowing."*

It still caught me by surprise when Düd'jom Rinpoche jested with me. It is not as if it were a rare occurrence – but it *always* took me by surprise.

I'd explained to Düd'jom Rinpoche that I was not entirely pleased with the way I'd lived my life – the fact that I simply fell into one bizarre situation after another. My explanation was prompted by what I had thought to have been an admonition: *"Like Drukpa Künlegs not possible in your country manifesting"* but Düd'jom Rinpoche clearly had no concerns on those grounds.

"Life of Chögyam; body-speech-mind nature of Chögyam" Düd'jom Rinpoche smiled *"I am too well knowing. Seeing 'only-one-wife' wanting. Only one sangyum wishing. Aro Yeshé two Sangyums having – but sisters. This system in Tibet finding. Sisters marrying* [2] *in Tibet possible—brothers* [3] *also—but this system in your country not possible. So not necessary like Aro Yeshé manifesting in body. Maybe like Aro Yeshé in speech and mind becoming."* PAUSE *"Maybe also speech of Drukpa Künlegs manifesting – from Aro Yeshé."*

I told Düd'jom Rinpoche that I would be far more than content with one sangyum – it was more a problem of *ever* finding such a person.

---

2   Polygyny *(chung ma mang bsTen gyi lam srol / ཆུང་མ་མང་བསྟེན་གྱི་ལམ་སྲོལ་)* – a man having several wives to prevent family land from being split (see following footnote).

3   Polyandry *(chung ma mang bsTen gyi lam srol / ཆུང་མ་མང་བསྟེན་གྱི་ལམ་སྲོལ་)* – a woman having several husbands. In Tibet, those husbands were brothers. The children are all considered to be the sons of the eldest brother. The reason for polyandry is to prevent land being split. Tibetan farmers families needed sufficient land to support their families. Another reason for polyandry is that mountainous terrain makes land difficult to farm, requiring more physical strength.

"Oh yah" he laughed *"no difficulty. You, Sangyum finding – for you no problem"* PAUSE *"… maybe soon"* PAUSE *"… maybe five years—maybe nine years—but not more years passing. This I am clearly seeing. Chögyam, not worrying necessary."*

"Maybe it would be better if I found a Tibetan lady?"

"No" Kyabjé Düd'jom Rinpoche shook his head. *"Maybe good for Tibetan learning. Maybe good for simple and devotion to Guru Rinpoche. But not good for gTérma – or western people Vajrayana teaching."*

Kyabjé Düd'jom Rinpoche explained in some detail that to marry a Tibetan lady would have an effect on my style of presentation. It would mean that I would find informality more difficult – and it was essential that I was able to be informal with my students. It was also important that I was free to explore the Arts in a Western context – and to develop Vajrayana appearances according to my own aesthetics. A Tibetan lady would want to recreate Tibet in the West and it would be better if I were not influenced in that way. This surprised me – because I thought that a Tibetan wife would be ideal; especially in terms of keeping me on track with what was appropriate. Düd'jom Rinpoche shook his head at that idea and said that he trusted my sense of what was appropriate – and that he did not think I would inappropriately Westernise anything. He told me that Chögyam Trungpa Rinpoche had a simpler aesthetic – and there was no reason why I should not evolve something similar. I would however need to be independent of a Tibetan wife's possible influence in that respect. *"Vajrayana must in new soil of Inji Lands growing. Same Nyingma rain watering – so no obstacle."*

We then conversed in a delightful manner about my time at Samŷe ling, on the various occasions I was there. Düd'jom Rinpoche was most pleased to hear of my meeting with the 16th Gyalwa Karmapa and told me that they had indeed spoken about me together. In fact, the 16th Gyalwa Karmapa had known he might meet me in Britain. This suddenly brought everything into focus. It seemed as if I would have had meetings with him under any circumstances.

Apparently, my almost having been excluded from the empowerments had played little part in it. I did wonder however, why—if Gyalwa Karmapa had known I was there—he had not simply required my presence? Maybe Akong Rinpoche had not informed him that I was there – and then, of course, why should he wish to see me the moment I arrived? Maybe he wanted to see what people would make of me? Maybe there was no reason at all. I would probably never know. There were often questions that simply could not be asked – according to my own sense of propriety, politesse, and appropriate cultural etiquette, of course. I can't say that I ever studied Tibetan etiquette – but somehow, I learned the rules or imagined I'd learned the rules.

Düd'jom Rinpoche was intrigued by the nature of an Art School and what was possible in such an institution. He wanted to know about etching and mezzotint printing in great detail – and so I did my best to convey the intricacies of the Art as well as I could. My discourse was punctuated with an occasional *"Ya-tsan!"* from Düd'jom Rinpoche. I spoke for what seemed a little too long – but Düd'jom Rinpoche was clearly fascinated by the whole subject of Fine Art print making.

After a long and wonderful series of teachings and conversations I found myself circumambulating the Great Chörten. It had become a custom with me to perform 'khora three times before and after my appointments with Düd'jom Rinpoche. It would have seemed inappropriate to have merely walked there and back from my lodgings. Düd'jom Rinpoche seemed to know where I was on the 'khora and one of his attendants would always be there to meet me at the door with a degree of precision that was almost magical.

My visits to Düd'jom Rinpoche took a certain form shortly after our initial reunion. He would launch almost immediately into a teaching – during which I worked away feverishly writing down every word. Once the teaching section was completed however our time together would become delightfully conversational. The topic was usually something to do with my life and how I'd lived it since I left Nepal in 1971.

He enquired concerning Claudette Gascoigne and what had happened since our parting. I explained that she had not answered my letters and obviously had no wish to have any further contact with me. Düd'jom Rinpoche shook his head *"Life for her…"* he sighed *"… not happy coming."*

I asked whether it was my responsibility that Claudette's life was not happy – and he shook his head again *"Nothing Chögyam doing. All own circumstances making. This I am seeing. Father tran-nèd [4] having, then dying. Then alone living. Friends not having because she too angry always speaking."*

Düd'jom Rinpoche was more interested to know about Claudette's three friends – with whom I'd lived for almost three years: Penelope Cholmondeley, Rebecca Albemarle, and Meryl Stanhope. The fact that they were all romantically drawn to me – but that I had somehow failed to be aware of it, struck him as intriguing in a positive sense. Düd'jom Rinpoche thought it highly auspicious that I could have such good friendships with ladies. He said this was a good sign in terms of my finding the right Sangyum. He found the antagonism of Todd Whelcombe and Veranda Nugent of no great concern or interest – and said that he knew people like this in Tibet, people who were overly concerned with status.[5] My account of Jack Hackman hiding under the table at the Nostril Café to avoid his ex-wife caused him great mirth. It caused him such hilarity that he re-told the story to several other Lamas – who also found it hilarious. Suddenly Jack Hackman—Jumping Jack Flashman—was a person of notoriety in Bodha.

The next day Düd'jom Rinpoche returned to the subject of Jack *"Kyé ma…"* he sighed. *"All good now with under-table-hiding one. He one wife and son soon – but in later years maybe from accident dying possible.*

---

4   Tran-nèd *(sKran nad)* – cancer.
5   Chog-mèn *(mChog dMan)* – social status.

"Then all gone from precious Bèd-tsé Ya'mèd [6] *— then now Chögyam only remaining. Too sad."* Then the translator said *"Rinpoche is so sorry — he such sadness for you saying."* A brief moment of silence passed after which Düd'jom Rinpoche said *"I see two friends happy re-birth finding."* PAUSE *"Maybe music again finding."* PAUSE *"Maybe meeting again possible."* There followed a long pause in which Kyabjé Düd'jom Rinpoche stared into space *"But… nothing certain. Many different circumstances coming. Life always in Western countries unstable. Families in different places living and never seeing. Everything changing — too quickly changing."*

Somehow Düd'jom Rinpoche expressing such sympathy caused a great wave of sorrow to arise in me and I barely stopped myself bursting into tears. Then we sat in silence for some moments — and the wave of sadness crashed on the shores of an empty land. There was suddenly nothing left of sadness. There was memory that sparkled. Impressions of Savage Cabbage. Impressions of Ron Larkin and Steve Bruce at their peak — and Jack Hackman grinning behind his welter of cymbals. Then the images vanished leaving only the brilliance of the room and the greater brilliance of Düd'jom Rinpoche who suddenly gave voice to a series of comments.

Düd'jom Rinpoche told me that he did not know what form the accident might take[7] for Jack. It had only been a fleeting premonition — the accident might or might not occur. I asked what could be done to save him from this possible accident — or make it more unlikely that the accident would occur. He answered that I would probably never meet Jack again. I would not be able to find him without paying an investigator. He advised against this.

6 Bèd-tsé Ya'mèd *(bad tshe ya 'med)* – Kyabjé Düd'jom Rinpoche's translation of 'Savage Cabbage', with regard to the Savage Cabbage Blues Band of 1966–1970. See *an odd boy*—Volumes I and II—Doc Togden—Aro Books WORLDWIDE—2011 and 2012; and *Goodbye Forever*—Volume I—chapters 11 to 13—Aro Books WORLDWIDE—2020.
7 Jack Hackman died in a hang-gliding accident in 1990. He was married with one son, James Marshall Flashman who became a percussionist (Classical Orchestral Music genre).

There was nothing that I could do. Jack's life was entirely unlike mine. My life was almost uncharted—according to Düd'jom Rinpoche—and I could therefore go in many different directions depending upon the people I met on my travels. He had seen this quite clearly in terms of the way in which I had lived my life up until that point. The only factor that was fixed was Vajrayana and my relationship with him. There would be other powerful relationship with Lamas in the future – and one in particular. This was not, however, the time to speak of that.

Düd'jom Rinpoche had previously asked me about the Savage Cabbage Blues Band and I had explained as much he wished to know. He had asked about the name 'Savage Cabbage' which had led me into having to explain Surrealism as a Western Art form. This was not a simple matter because I realised that I had no clear explanation which could be translated into Tibetan. My best attempt was to explain Surrealism as an Art form that exposed the nature of illusion. I described one of the paintings of Rene Magritte *Le domaine d'Arnheim*.[8]

"Rene Magritte tries to show a new way of seeing the reality. In one painting there is an eagle-shaped mountain seen through a stone opening in a wall. There are two eggs on the stone sill. The idea for this came to Rene Magritte when he woke up and saw a bird in a cage. He then fell asleep again, and dreamt that the bird had been replaced by a large egg that filled the cage. Another version of this painting shows the same eagle-headed mountain with a glazed window where the glass is broken and lies in shards on the windowsill. Fragments of the image of the mountain are still on the shards of glass – as if what was seen through the window had permeated the glass."

Düd'jom Rinpoche listened patiently whilst I explained these paintings – and at the end he asked a few questions to clarify the intention of the artist. He concluded that Western secular Art was a religious investigation and one he respected. He told me that it was good that I investigated works such as this.

8   *The Domain of Arnheim* 1938. Oil on canvas.

"... so... with the name Bèd-tsé Ya'mèd. This is linking two ideas that normally have no connection with each other... although there—is—the connection of the 'word sounds'—Savage and Cabbage—which makes it seem as if the words belong together."

"Ya-tsan!" he laughed. *"Western Arts like Yeshé thab-kyi cho'trül* [9] *becoming!"*

The day ended and I returned to my lodgings to have dinner with Amji Pema Dorje and Yeshé Khandro. They were always delighted to see me and beamed at me – almost as if I was imbued with Düd'jom Rinpoche. That I had spent this time with a Lama who was the living presence of Guru Rinpoche amazed them as much as it amazed me – but I could never really understand why they thought any reflected glory emanated from my being his guest. They asked no questions. They regarded anything I would have heard as being entirely beyond them. I did volunteer a few things – such as our discussions of Art and Savage Cabbage. Amji Pema Dorje and Yeshé Khandro were clearly astonished that Düd'jom Rinpoche would discuss such subjects – and concluded that my deeds must be like the deeds of historical Lama prodigies. I assured them that my life was quite ordinary – but this was deemed impossible if it was of interest to Düd'jom Rinpoche. They could only understand this as humility on my part – and so I gave up on the idea of trying to insist that I was nothing special. It seemed that insisting I was not special was just another way of making oneself look special. The only way I could deny being special was to act naturally. I showed the photographs of my family and answered their questions in such a way as to detract from any idea of having exalted origins. I told them how my father had been a dock worker in Gillingham, [10] Kent—and how his parents had been farm-workers in Lancashire—but nothing I could say detracted from my being special in their eyes.

---

9   *ye shes thabs kyi cho 'phrul* – wisdom-magic of skilful means.
10 Gillingham Docks were an outgrowth of Chatham Dockyard located on the Medway River which was established in the 16th century and expanded into neighbouring Gillingham in the 20th century.

As far as I was concerned, this simply demonstrated the compassion, wisdom, and power of Düd'jom Rinpoche.

The next time I saw Düd'jom Rinpoche he continued his explanation of 'khor-dé ru shan.

"Inner 'khor-dé ru shan you – must be khams drug visualising."

This is the envisionment of the six nucleus locations on the central channel and the soles of the feet. Each locus relates with both 'dualistic inhibition' and 'nondual potentiality'. At each nucleus one envisions the associated seed-syllables.[11]

With Inner 'khor-dé ru shan that clarification of perceptual obscurations is the preparation for Secret 'khor-dé ru shan. This commences with vajra posture.[12] *"This like dorje looking."* Düd'jom Rinpoche asked his attendant Gyür'mèd to demonstrate.

This forces body and mind into a state of potentiating tension that exhausts conceptuality. This position is maintained until physical collapse ensues. Then one lies just as one has fallen and remains in nondual awareness. If namtogs arise—from which one feels separate—one repeats the process. Vajra posture engages the physical body in terms of adjusting the currents of psycho-physical energy in order to destroy the patterns of referentiality that condition perception.

The physical practices of Secret 'khor-dé ru shan are followed by practices of sound in which the Blue seed-syllable Hung is vocalised, visualised, and infinitely proliferated – until the *Hungs* fill existing space.

---

11 In descending order: forehead A; throat Su; heart Nri, navel Tri; perineum Pré; and the soles of the feet Du. One then envisions White, Red, and Blue light resounding from the seed mantras Om—A'a:—Hung. Perception shifts from identification with the physical body to sNang gSal, luminosity. As with the practice of Outer 'khor-dé ru shan, attention to the physical body is alternated with periods of movement and nondual awareness in stasis.

12 Dorje Kyil-trung *(rDo rJe sKyil dKrungs)* – vajra posture. See *Roaring Silence*—Ngakpa Chögyam and Khandro Déchen—Shambhala 2002—ISBN 1-57062-944-7—Ch 8—Exercise 8—pages 99 to 105.

The *Hungs* fill the body and finally implode in space. At the conclusion of each session of visualisation one assumes a supine position – in which one rests in spacious presence.

Subsequent to Secret 'khor-dé ru shan one arrives at the *most-secret* [13] or *ultimate* 'khor-dé ru shan. Here, one employs the seed-syllable A, in order to enter direct experience in terms of inherent potentiality[14] in which all perception is dissolved into the effulgence of light. This is the unified state of luminous awareness which is beyond the remit of time and space.

Düd'jom Rinpoche presented this in far more detail than given here—with aspects that must remain hidden—but at the end of the day I was reeling. I had been taken on a journey in which time and space were almost irrelevant coordinates. I was ravenous because we had not stopped for lunch – but I had noticed no hunger at all until that point. *"Now to Amji Pema Dorje and Yeshé Khandro must be going"* he laughed. *"Dinner eating necessary."*

It was strange that it seemed so normal to circumambulate the Great Chörten, at night, amongst a throng of Tibetans – all performing their evening 'khora. In the dark, it could have been any point during the past millennium. There was only the guttering of butter lamps here and there – and the murmur of different mantras and invocations. I began to sing Dorje Tsigdun. A few Tibetans on either side recognised what I was singing and joined me. Where else on the planet would this have been possible? The sense of being in home territory was palpable. I wasn't even in Nepal. I was at some point in a continuum that contacted directly with Guru Rinpoche and Yeshé Tsogyel.

The next day was a pivotal day. Düd'jom Rinpoche told me that it was time to spend a day in retreat. It should preferably be longer – but he knew that my time was limited; even with the extension of my visa for the ostensible purposes of trekking.

---

13 Literally 'most-secret'. Yang-sang *(yang gSang)* equates to ultimate or innermost.
14 Rang-tsal *(rang rTsal)*

"Today we must essential Vajrayana speaking necessary. Time too quickly passing – and important Chögyam essential words receiving." Düd'jom Rinpoche looked at me most intently for a moment, then gave me a broad smile. *"Not root of phenomena examining – root of* Mind *examining. When root of Mind finding – this,* everything *liberating. If root of Mind not finding – then success in nothing finding, nothing knowing, nothing knowledge having."*

When meditating on Mind, be relaxed and breathe naturally. Gaze into Space. Space is directly before your wide-open eyes. This is to look directly into the face of Küntuzangpo. Strongly invoke the Tsawa'i Lama as inseparable from Guru Rinpoche – and your Mind will merge with his.

Once settled, you may not remain long in clear awareness. Your mind may move or become restless – and then what is experienced will not be the nature of Mind but namthogs. Do not follow the namthogs – because following namthogs is what will plunge you back into dualism. So, break the chain of namthogs – and then you will see awareness. When you see awareness, you will know – because it is translucent, uninhibited, and elated. It is not circumscribed or delineated by predetermined characteristics. There is nothing of 'khorwa or 'dé-pa[15] which is not encompassed. It is beginninglessly what you are. It has never been lacking – but it lies beyond the reach of engagement, endeavour, and ingenuity.

Düd'jom Rinpoche laughed at this point and asked *"But what, you are asking, is rigpa recognising? Although you are experiencing – describing not possible. Like when Chögyam young and speech difficulty coming* [16] *– and in school explaining necessary. Now all—very well—explaining. Now, no speech problem coming."*

It is not possible to differentiate resting in awareness and the awareness that is experienced.

---

15 'khorwa *('khor ba / samsara / dualistic circling).* 'dé-pa *('das pa / nirvana / cessation)*
16 Kyabjé Düd'jom Rinpoche was referring to the bad stammer I had as a child – and which sometimes rendered me incapable of speech.

545

When resting naturally in illimitable awareness, the rapidity of namthogs loses momentum and they have no sovereignty. They evaporate in the spacious sky of awareness.

Düd'jom Rinpoche looked at me keenly *"This awareness now, you naturally having. This chö-ku. State of awareness I am Chögyam showing – then recognising. Then self-introduction possible coming."*

The appearances of 'khorwa and 'de-pa are merely the display of your own awareness. Rest in this awareness. Waves swell from the sea and sink back into the sea. Clouds emerge from the sky and disperse into the sky. Namthogs arise and dissolve into awareness. Be certain of this dissolution. Find the state that is utterly devoid of meditator and meditation.

"Some people—when I this saying, 'no need meditation' thinking—but this only 'first recognising' – this is not liberation coming. All lives from beginninglessness, fabricated delusion habits remaining—so meditation must familiar becoming—and primordial uncontrived nature resting."

Düd'jom Rinpoche emphasised that mediation had to become spontaneously, naturally, constant presence – and asked *"How nature of Mind remaining?"* and answered his own question. *"When namthogs coming – you must be allowing. You must not namthog enemies, thinking. When namthogs arising, then in namthogs relaxing. When namthogs not arising, then absence namthogs relaxing. Simply in absence resting."*

When substantial, elaborate conceptual patterns appear, it is easy to distinguish them – but when insignificant, intangible movements ensue, it is difficult to apprehend them immediately. This is the undercurrent of conceptual meandering,[17] so it is important to observe carefully. If you can be continuously present in meditation and post mediation, when walking, sitting, eating, drinking, and sleeping – that is the principal point.

17 *rNam rTog g.Yo sGyu*

If you meditate, you will gain conviction – but if you do not meditate with joy, you will not recognise the natural state. So, meditate with resilient joy – and signs *will* appear! Signs will appear that display your familiarity with *remaining in the natural state*. Then tight obsessive cohering will gradually loosen. Obsession with the eight worldly dharmas will lessen. Authentic devotion to the Lama and the Lama's instructions will mature. Anxious fixations will evaporate. Diamonds and broken glass will then appear equal.

"You have stable foundation of devotion and vows having. You strong, joyful endeavour having. You no strong mundane concerns leaving – so extraordinary qualities Dzogchen naturally attaining. This I am seeing. This advice my blood of heart – so close keeping, always."

I was to come to see Kyabjé Düd'jom Rinpoche every day whilst I was in Nepal – because there was much that he wished to convey. This was to be an important time. It was apparent to him that some change was about to occur. Something would transpire quite soon – and I would need his guidance and close supervision.

An astounding time opened in front of me like a view arcing the vast sweep of the Himalayas and out into unending Space.

appendix one
gTérma

gTérma *(gTer ma)* are religious treasures hidden by Guru Rinpoche and Yeshé Tsogyel within the elements and minds of their disciples to be revealed at appropriate times by gTértöns *(treasure revealers)*. gTérma were also later concealed by the gTértöns themselves.

The Aro gTér—which is a gTérma of Yeshé Tsogyel—was initially revealed by the female gTértön Khyungchen Aro Lingma who was identified by Kyabjé Düd'jom Rinpoche Jig'drèl Yeshé Dorje as having attained rainbow body[1] in 1923.

Many gTérma were collected and collated by Jamgön Kongtrül and Jamyang Khyentsé Wangpo in the Rinchen gTérdzöd.[2] These gTérma, together with the Kama,[3] are the two modes of teaching transmission of the Nyingma Tradition. gTérma are divided into three categories, according to the manner in which they were concealed and discovered: earth gTérma (ས་གཏེར་ / *sa gTer),* which employ physical objects; mind gTérma (དགོངས་གཏེར་ / *gong gTer),* discovered within the mind-stream of the gTértön; and pure vision (དག་སྣང་གཏེར་ *dag sNang gTer)* teachings. Pure vision gTérma are revelations that owe their origin to Buddhas other than Guru Rinpoche. The Aro gTér, for example, emanates form Yeshé Tsogyel – and the Thangtong Thugthig from Thangtong Gyalpo.

---

1 Ja'lü *(ja' lus / འཇའ་ལུས་ / nirvikalpa)*
2 Rinchen gTérdzöd (རིན་ཆེན་གཏེར་མཛོད་ / *rin chen gTer mDzod),* Jewel Treasury of gTérma. One of The Five Great Treasures of Jamgön Kongtrül the Great. It is a compilation drawn from all the gTérmas that had been discovered up to his time, including Chok'gyür Lingpa's gTérma. Concerned that these gTérma would be lost, he commenced the compilation in 1855 with Jamyang Khyentsé Wangpo and completed it in 1889.
3 Kama *(bKa' ma* བཀའ་མ) means 'words of Buddha'. In general, it refers to the teachings given by Shakyamuni Buddha – but also Buddhas such as Küntuzangpo, Dorje Sempa, and Garab Dorje; which have transmitted orally from Lama to disciple to the present. The Nyingma tradition speaks of the kama and gTérma as the two bodies of teaching.

With earth gTérma, emblematic script inscribed on yellow parchment initiates the gTérma in a gTértön's mind. In the discovery of mind gTérma, nothing external is involved. It is mainly seeing or hearing, or seeing in visions, that allows the discovery of mind gTérma. gTérma are often discovered in tripartite form: Lama, Dzogchen, and Thug-jé Chenpo (བླ་རྫོགས་ཐུགས་གསུམ་ / *la dzog thug sum*): the peaceful, joyous, and wrathful drüpthabs of the Lama, Dzogchen teaching, and practice; and drüpthab of Chenrézigs *(thugjé chenpo)*. Another tripartite form is: Ka'gyèd, Gongdü, and Phurba.

The Ka'gyèd (བཀའ་བརྒྱད་ *bKa' brGyad)* are the eight principal yidams who are manifestations of nonduality: body *(sKu)*, speech *(gSung)*, mind *(thugs)*, qualities *(yon tan)* and activity *(phrin las)*. Lama Gongdü (བླ་མ་དགོངས་འདུས་ / *bLa ma dGongs 'dus),* The Gathered Intention of the Lamas, is one of the most important teachings of Dzogchen. Dorje Phurba (རྡོ་རྗེ་ཕུར་པ་ / *rDo rJe phur pa* / *Vajrakila* / *Vajrakilaya)* is the yidam deity who embodies the nondual activity of all buddhas and whose practice is the most powerful for removing obstacles, destroying the forces hostile to compassion, and liberating the religious pollution of this age.

appendix two
commemoration of tenth days

On the tenth day of the 6ᵗʰ month, Guru Rinpoche is lotus-born as Guru Tso-kyé Dorje on Lake Nor-gyi Dzöd.

On the tenth day of the 12ᵗʰ month, King Indrabhuti of Ögyen invests him as the Prince of Ögyen with Prabhavati as his princess.

On the tenth day of the 1ˢᵗ month, Guru Rinpoche abdicates to practise Dorje Ka-jor in the Cool Grove Charnel Ground as Guru Shakya Seng-gé, and brings all the Mamos under his authority.

On the tenth day of the 2ⁿᵈ month, as Guru Loden Chog-sé, he displays the appearance of taking transmission from Ananda; studying with many scholars and siddhas; and mastering Sutrayana and Vajrayana.

On the tenth day of the 3ʳᵈ month, King Arashadhar of Zahor attempts to burn him alive – but, as Guru Chhi'mèd Pema Jung-né, he transforms the pyre into a lake, takes Princess Mandarava as his consort, and establishes Zahor as a Vajrayana Kingdom.

On the tenth day of the 4ᵗʰ month, the ministers of Ögyen seek to burn him and Mandarava alive, but as Guru Padma Vajra Töd-treng Tsal he transforms the pyre into a lake.

On the tenth day of the 5ᵗʰ month, as Guru Seng-gé Dradog, his pronouncement of reality causes a cognitive earthquake that demolishes the fallacious ground of Tirthika reasoning.

On the tenth day of the 7ᵗʰ month, the Tirthikas of Zangling attempt to fling him into the Ganges, but as Guru Khalding Tsal he performs a vajra dance in the sky and reverses the flow of the river.

On the tenth day of the 8th month, the Tirthikas attempt to poison him – but he is unharmed, and as Guru Nyima 'ö-Zér he transforms the poison into düd-tsi, whereupon he becomes majestic and dazzling in his radiance.

On the tenth day of the 9th month, he practises Dorje Phurba at Yang-lé-shöd in Nepal – and, as Guru Dorje Tötreng Tsal, oath-binds the transdimensional entities of the Himalayas, and accomplishes the siddhis of Yangdag Héruka.

On the tenth day of the 10th month, he arrives in Tibet as Guru Padmasambhava and subjugates the unruly transdimensional entities of Tibet; causes Samyé to be built, and ignites the flame of Vajrayana.

On the tenth day of the 11th month, he assumes a wrathful primordial chaos form as Guru Dorje Tröllö at Taktsang, Mön, and many other places. He oath-binds the Sa bDag Earth Lords of Tibet and Bhutan as guardians of his gTérma. He then conceals an unimaginable number of gTérma and unique objects and substances. He also gives predictions and advice for safeguarding the gTérma.

Glossary of Extended Footnotes

25 disciples

The 25 disciples of Guru Rinpoche *(Jé-wang Nyér-nga / rJe 'bangs nyer lNga)*: Kharchen Khandro Yeshé Tsogyel *(mKhar chen bZa' mKha' 'gro ye shes mTsho rGyal)*; King Trisong Détsen *(khri srong lDe'u bTsan);* Dri'mèd Shényèn *(dri 'med bShes gNyen / Vimalamitra);* Vairotsana *(bai ro tsa na);* Shu-bu Palgyi Seng-gé *(shud bu dPal gyi seng ge)*; Palgyi Yeshé *(dPal gyi ye shes)*; 'o-Drèn Palgyi Wangchuk *('o dran dPal gyi dBang phyug)*; Kharchen Palgyi Wangchuk *(khar chen dPal gyi dBang phyug)*; Lhalung Palgyi Dorje *(lha lung dPal gyi rDo rJe)*; Khyéchung Lotsa *(khye'u chung lo tsa)*; Nyag Yeshé Zhö-nu *(gNyags ye shes gZhon nu)*; Sokpo Lhapal *(sog po lha dPal)*; Ma Rinchen Chog *(rMa rin chen mChog)*; Nubchen Sang-gyé Yeshé *(gNub chen sangs rGyas ye shes)*; Langdro Könchog Jung-né *(lang gro dKon mChog 'byung gNas)*; Nub Namkha'i Nyingpo *(nub nam mKha'i sNying po)*; Yudra Nyingpo *(gYu sGra sNying po)*; Na nam Zhang Yeshé De *(sNa nam zhang ye shes sDe)*; Denma Tsémang *(lDan ma rTse mang)*; Nanam Dorje Düd'jom *(na nam rDo rJe bBud 'joms)*; Lasum Gyalwa Changchub *(la sum rGyal ba byang chub)*; Ngan-lam Gyalwa Chöyang *(ngan lam rGyal ba mChog dByangs)*; Dré Gyalwa'i Lödrö *('bre rgyal ba'i bLo gros)*; Kawa Paltsèg *(sKa ba dPal brTsegs)*; Ba Yeshé Yang *(sba ye shes dByangs)*; and, Nyang Ting'dzin Zangpo *(myang ting 'dzin bZang po)*.

Akong Rinpoche

Chö-je Akong Rinpoche *(Chos rJe A dKon rin po che)* (1939–2013) was an incarnate Lama of the Kagyüd School and—together with Chögyam Trungpa Rinpoche—founder of Samŷe Ling. His name was Karma Shédrüp Chö-kyi Nyima Thrin-lé Künkyab Palzangpo Sog-lé Nampar Gyalwa'i Dé. He was born near Riwo-ché in Kham, Eastern Tibet near Amdo.

In 1959—at age 20—he fled to India in a party, of which only 13 survived by the time they arrived in India. In 1963 a sponsor funded Akong Rinpoche and Chögyam Trungpa Rinpoche to learn English at Oxford University.

Ariosophy

– an esoteric system invented by Jörg Lanz von Liebenfels in Austria from 1890 to 1930. Ariosophy means 'wisdom concerning the Aryans' and was a word first coined by Lanz von Liebenfels in 1915, and he used it in the 1920s. The term 'Ariosophy' is used generically to describe the Aryan-esoteric theories of a subset of the Völkische Bewegung. The ideas of Lanz von Liebenfels—inspired by historical Germanic paganism and esoteric influences from Theosophy—was part of an occult revival in Austria and Germany in the late 19th and early 20th centuries.

Atisha

see *lojong*.

bodicitta

see *chang chub sem*.

Bön

bon. The nine vehicles of Bön: **1.** Cha-shen thegpa *(phyva gShen theg pa)* Vehicle of Prediction: rituals of prognostication, healing, exorcism, amulets, sortilege, and astrology. **2.** Nang-shen thegpa *(sNang shen theg pa)* Vehicle of the Visual Dimension: Conjuring the psychophysical dimension. **3.** 'trül-shen thegpa *('phrul gShen theg pa)* Vehicle of Apparitions: rites for the dispersal of adversarial emanations and transdimensional beings. **4.** srid shen thegpa *(srid gShen theg pa)* Vehicle of Life: funeral and death rituals.

5. Gé-nyèn thegpa *(dGe bsNyen theg pa)* Vehicle of Non-monastics: Phar-chin chu *(phar phyin bCu)* the ten paramitas. **6.** drabg srong thegpa *(drang srong theg pa)* Vehicle of monasticism – Sutrayana. **7.** A-kar thegpa *(A dKar theg pa)* Vehicle of Primordial Sound – Mahayoga. **8.** Yé-shen thegpa *(ye gShen theg pa)* Vehicle of Primordial Thaumaturge: Auyoga. **9.** La'mèd thegpa *(bLa med theg pa)* Vehicle of Unsurpassed Naturalness: Dzogchen.

Chekhawa Yeshé Dorje

see *lojong*.

Crowley, Aleister

(1875–1947) – an English occultist / black magician who founded the Thelema religion – having appointed himself as the prophet who would guide humanity into the Æon of Horus. He was born to a wealthy family and educated at Trinity College, Cambridge. In 1898 he joined the Hermetic Order of the Golden Dawn – and he was trained in ceremonial magic by Samuel Liddell MacGregor Mathers and Allan Bennett. He then studied Hindu necromantic practices in India. In Cairo, Egypt, he claimed to have been visited by a being called *Aiwass*, who gave him *The Book of the Law*, which he took as the basis of *Thelema* – which admonishes its followers to 'Do what thou wilt'. He gained notoriety during his life as a megalomaniac who was interpersonally manipulative, bisexual, and given to drug abuse.

dissolution

On falling asleep or dying the psycho-physical elements—earth, water, fire, air, and space—dissolve, sequentially disappearing into each other. There is no consciousness of it however, unless a person has practiced mi-lam *(rMi lam / svapnadarsana / dream yoga)*.

The experiences of dream body, bardo body, vision body are known a yi-lü *(yid lus)*. The Nyingma lineage has seven transmissions *(Ka'bab dun / bKa' babs bDun)*—streams of authentication and empowerment *(dampa'i jin-lab / dam pa'i byin rLabs)*—that may provoke visions. Transmission is an empathetic coalescence of mindstreams. Though the emergence of these seven modalities of transmission may occur in the waking state they may also arise in the dream state. One transmission type particularly emphasised is pure vision *(dag-nang / dag sNang)* and the perception of yidams.

Dopyera, John

(Ján Dopjera 1893–1988) was a Slovak-American inventor and maker of stringed instruments, including the resonator. His father, Jozef Dopyera, was a gifted musician who played and built his own violins. Under his father's guidance, John built his first violin as a boy in Dolná Krupá. In 1908, the Dopyeras emigrated from Slovakia to California. In the 1920s, John Dopyera founded a shop in LA where he made and repaired violins, banjos, and guitars. He also patented several improvements to the banjo. In 1925 George Beauchamp asked John Dopyera to make him a guitar loud enough to be heard over other instruments. Dopyera invented a guitar with three aluminium cones mounted beneath the bridge, an amplification scheme similar to speaker cones, which was three times louder than a normal acoustic guitar and had a vibrant metallic sound rich with overtones. It became known as the NATIONAL RESOPHONIC guitar. Joined by his brothers Rudy and Emil, they founded the NATIONAL STRING INSTRUMENT CORPORATION, later, they separated from NATIONAL and founded DOBRO – a play on 'Do' from Dopyera and 'bro' from brothers. The word means 'good' in Slovak – which fitted their slogan: 'DOBRO *means good in any language.'*

Dorje Legpa

rDo rJe legs pa / རྡོ་རྗེ་ལེགས་པ་ / *Vajrasadhu*. Nyingma protector. Originally Dorje Legpa belonged to the Tibetan pre-Buddhist Bön religion, where he was a transdimensional entity connected with speculation, gambling, trickery, chicanery, hazard, and jeopardy. Dorje Legpa had opposed Guru Rinpoche – but Guru Rinpoche subjugated him and made him damçan (dam can) an oath-bound protector. Dorje Legpa is important in the Nyingma Tradition and also in Kagyüd Schools. In the Nyingma he is considered as being closely associated with Dzogchen. With Mamo Ékajati and Raksha gZa Rahula – Dorje Legpa is one of the Ma-zar-dor-sum *(ma gZa rDo gSum)* the three major protectors of the Nyingma. Dorje Legpa is depicted iconographically riding a mountain goat with spirally entwined horns – or upon a Snow Lion.

Dorje Tsig Dün

The seven thunderbolt phrases of Padmasambhava. *Ögyen yul gyi nub chang tsam: / Pema ké-sar dong-po la: / Ya tsan chö-gi ngö-drüp nyé: / Pema Jung-né Shé-su drag: / Khordu khandro mang-pö khor: / Khyé kyi jé-su dag drüb kyi: / Chin gyi lob chir shè su sol: / Guru Pema Siddhi Hung:* In the Northwest of the land of Ögyen: / On the pistil of the stem of lotus: / Endowed with the most marvellous attainments: / Renowned as the 'Lotus Born': / Surrounded by kyil'khors of many khandros: / I am the one who follows your example: / May I realise your knowledge and be irradiated by your presence.

Dr Strangelove

Dr Strangelove, Or How I Learned to Stop Worrying and Love the Bomb is a 1964 film, starring Peter Sellers. It concerns Jack D Ripper, a psychotic US Air Force General, and his plan to launch a nuclear attack on the Soviet Union.

General Jack Ripper believes there is a Communist conspiracy against 'precious bodily fluids' via fluoridated water. He orders the 843rd Bomb Wing past its fail-safe points into Russia. Group Captain Lionel Mandrake—Peter Sellers—an RAF officer participating in an exchange programme with the US Air Force, suspects that all is not as it seems. Meanwhile it is discovered that the Russians have a 'doomsday machine' designed to destroy the Earth if a nuclear attack is detected. The US President—again Peter Sellers—asks war expert ex-Nazi Dr Strangelove—also Peter Sellers—to discuss the problem. They decide to cooperate with the Russians in shooting US planes down unless they can be recalled. Colonel 'Bat' Guano at first fails to recognise Mandrake's RAF uniform—believing him to be leading a mutiny of *deviated preverts* (sic)— but finally relents, adventitiously aiding Mandrake in giving the President the recall code. The last B-52 *The Leper Colony* however cannot be recalled (a Russian anti-aircraft missile having triggered the self-destruct system of the radio). Damaged by the missile hit, and leaking fuel, the aircraft cannot reach its intended target. The plane continues evading the combined efforts of both the US and the USSR. The B-52's bay doors jam – so the pilot, Major 'King' Kong, kicks the atomic bomb free and rides out into the sky waving his Western hat, rodeo-style. The doomsday device is detonated and Vera Lynn sings *'We'll meet again, don't know where don't know when – but I'm sure we'll meet again some sunny day.'*

Dri'mèd Shényèn

dri 'med bShes gNyen / ཏྲི་འམེད་བཤེས་གཉེན་ / *Vimalamitra* – an Indian Buddhist Master. His teachers were Sang-gyé Sangwa *(sangs rGyas gSang ba* / སངས་རྒྱས་གསང་བ་ / *Buddhaguhya); Yeshé mDo (ye shes mDo* / ཡེ་ཤེས་མདོ / *Jnanasutra)* and Shri Singha *(shri sing ha* / ཤྲི་སིང་ཧ).

Shri Singha was the successor of Jampal Shényèn *(jam dPal bShes gNyen /* འཇམ་དཔལ་བཤེས་གཉེན་ */ Manjushrimitra)* the Chinese disciple of Buddha Garab Dorje in the Dzogchen lineage of transmission. He vowed to take incarnation every 100 years – and these incarnations include Rig'dzin Jig'mèd Lingpa, Khenchen Ngakchung, Kyabjé Drüpwang Rinpoche and Kyabjé Yang-thang Rinpoche. According to Gyalwa Karmapa, Kyabjé Chatral Sang-gyé Dorje (1913–2016) received a teng-ar (mantra beads) from a man dressed as an Indian sadhu. He recognised the sadhu as Dri'mèd Shényèn. His attendants—highly curious—returned to where they had met the sadhu but he could not be found anywhere even far further afield – and no one had seen anyone of that description on that day.

Düd'jom Rinpoche Jig'drèl Yeshé Dorje

Kyabjé Düd'jom Rinpoche Jig'drèl Yeshé Dorje (1904–1987) was born in the 'hidden land' of Pemakö. He was the head of the Nyingma Tradition. His personal name was Jig'drèl Yeshé Dorje – and was given to him by the 15th Karmapa, Gyalwa Kha-kyab Dorje. His father was Kathok Tulku Norbu Ten'dzin, who was a famous tulku of Pemakö who trained at Kathok. His mother—Namgyal Drölma—was descended from Ratna Lingpa (see *Wisdom Eccentrics* by Ngakpa Chögyam, Aro Books Inc, 2011).

eight manifestations

Padmakara is the primary form of Guru Rinpoche. The 8 manifestations are: Pema Gyalpo *(pad ma rGyal po / Padma Kumara)* the Lotus Prince of Ögyen – shown looking like a young man; Pema Jung-né *(pad ma 'byung gNas / Padmasambhava)* The Lotus Born – shown in monastic robes over blue shirt and leggings, carrying a skull-bowl in his left hand and a khatvangha;

Shakya Seng-gé *(sha kya seng ge / Śākya Simha)* the Lion of the Shakyas, who learns the Tantric practices of the 84 mahasiddhas – shown as Shakyamuni Buddha; Nyima 'ö-Zer *(nyi ma 'od zer / Guru Sūrya Raśmi)*, Rays of the Sun – shown as a yogi holding a khatvangha and conjuring the rays of the sun with his finger; Ögyen Tso-kyé Dorje Chang *(O rGyan mTsho sKye rDo-rje 'chang / Oddiyana Saroruhavajra Vajradhara)* the Lake Born Vajra-holder – shown as dark blue in colour and in union with Mandarava; Seng-gé Dradog *(seng ge sGra sGrogs / Simhanada)* the Lion's Voice – shown in wrathful form, dark blue in colour and holding a vajra in his right hand and a scorpion and noose in the left; Lo-den Chog-srè *(bLo lDan mChog sred / Mativat Vararuci)* the Vajra Emperor – shown in imperial clothes holding a skull-drum and skull-bowl; and, Dorje Tröllö *(rDo rJe gro lod / Vajra Audarika)* Thunderbolt Belly of Fire – shown as a wrathful phurba master with a loose hanging stomach, holding a vajra in his right hand and a phurba in his left hand.

Finnegan's Wake

– by James Joyce—renowned for its experimental style—is known as the most difficult English language novel. Published in 1939—and written in Paris over a 17-year period—it was James Joyce's final work. The book is composed of idiosyncratic language – admixtures of English lexical items and neologistic multi-lingual puns. Its linguistic experimentation, literary allusions, free dream associations, stream-of-consciousness style, and lack of both plot and characterisations, leave *Finnegan's Wake* unread by the general public. James Joyce began working on *Finnegan's Wake* after the publication of *Ulysses* in 1922. Initial reaction to *Finnegan's Wake* was negative – but the work has since come to assume a preëminent place in English literature.

Anthony Burgess praised the book as *'a great comic vision, one of the few books of the world that can make us laugh aloud on nearly every page.'* Harold Bloom wrote *'… if aesthetic merit were ever again to centre the canon, Finnegan's Wake, would be as close as our chaos could come to the heights of Shakespeare and Dante.'* In 1998, the Modern Library ranked *Finnegan's Wake* 77th on its list of the 100 best English-language novels of the 20th Century.

Flashman

Sir Harry Paget Flashman VC KCB KCIE was created by George MacDonald Fraser (1925–2008), based on the character in *Tom Brown's Schooldays* by Thomas Hughes (1822–1896). In Thomas Hughes' book, Flashman is a notorious bully at Rugby School who persecutes Tom Brown, and is finally expelled for drunkenness. In the Flashman books, he is a Victorian soldier who goes through many of the 19th Century wars. He rises to a high rank in the British Army—acclaimed as a great soldier—while remaining by his own admission *'a scoundrel, a liar, a cheat, a thief, and coward'*. George Fraser's Flashman runs from danger, betrays and abandons acquaintances, beats his servants with gusto, fornicates indiscriminately, carries off illegitimate prizes, gambles with abandon, and drinks to excess. However—through luck and cunning—he usually ends up being seen as a hero.

Gendün Rinchen

Gendün Rinchen Rinpoche was born in a cave near Taktsang and was referred to playfully as Dragphugpa *(Cave Man)*. He received the empowerments for the Rinchen gTérdzöd; Dzogchen Nying-thig, Longchenpa's Dzödun at Sam-yé. After returning to Bhutan, he entered a three-year meditation retreat at Taksang Palphug hermitage, followed by a further three-year retreat when he was forty years old at Kunga Chöling in Paro.

He received the Six Yogas of Naropa, Mahamudra, and Dzogchen from Lopön Sônam Zangpo, a disciple of gTértön Shakya Shri. He wrote many commentaries on Vajrayana. In 1990 he was enthroned as the 69th Je Khenpo of Bhutan and travelled throughout the country giving teachings. At the age of 61 he resigned from the post of Je Khenpo and retired to meditate at Jangchub Ding in Yangchenphug. In 1997, he died sitting in meditation posture and his body remained sitting for eleven days during which time his body remained flexible and showed no signs of decay. His physical remains are now preserved in a gold and silver reliquary chörten in the Shabdrung Chapel of Tashi Chö Dzong, Thimphu.

Geshe Ngawang Dhargyey

(1921–1995) was a Gélug Lama from in Ya-chak, Tréhor in Kham who received numerous teachings and empowerments from Kyabjé Trijang Dorje Chang, and Lhatsün Dorje Chang, Gönsar Dorje Chang, Sherab Wangchuk, and Gyür'mèd Khensur Ögyen Tsé-tèn. He studied in Séra Je Monastery until 1959. In 1971 he was asked by the Dalai Lama to start a teaching programme for Western people at the newly constructed Library of Tibetan Works and Archives near Upper Dharamsala with his disciples, Sharpa Rinpoche and Kamlung Rinpoche as translators. He taught there extensively until 1984.

Himmler, Heinrich Luitpold

Himmler believed the mission of the SS to be 'acting as the vanguard in overcoming Christianity and restoring a Germanic way of living' in preparation for the conflict between humans and 'subhumans'. Himmler and the Nazi movement thus inaugurated an offensive against Jews, Gypsies, and Communists.

By linking de-Christianisation with 're-Germanisation', Himmler provided the SS with a singular purpose. He was vehemently opposed to Christian sexual morality and mercy. He viewed both as deleterious to his offensive against 'subhumans'. In 1937, Himmler stated: *'We live in an era of the ultimate conflict with Christianity. It is part of the mission of the SS to give the German people in the next half century the non-Christian ideological foundations on which to lead and shape their lives. This task does not consist solely in overcoming an ideological opponent but must be accompanied at every step by a positive impetus: in this case that means the reconstruction of the German heritage in the widest and most comprehensive sense.'*

impermanence verse

Verse from the Düd'jom gTér Ngöndro: ན་མོ༔ བསླུ་མེད་གཏན་གྱི་མགོན་ པོ་བླ་མ་མཁྱེན༔ *Namo lu'mèd ten gyi gön-po lama khyen* / Esteemed Lama: unfailingly constant protector དལ་འབྱོར་འདི་ནི་ཤིན་ཏུ་རྙེད་པར་དཀའ༔ *Dal'jor 'di-ni shin-tu nyèd-par ka* / This free and endowed birth is difficult to obtain. སྐྱེ་ཚད་མི་རྟག་འཆི་བའི་ཆོས་ཅན་ཡིན༔ *kyé tsèd mi-tag 'chi-wa'i chö-çan yin* / Everything that is born is impermanent and consequently dies. དགེ་སྡིག་ལས་ཀྱི་རྒྱུ་འབྲས་བསླུ་བ་མེད༔ *Gé-dig lé-kyi gyu-'dré lu-wa 'mèd* / Positivity and negativity are the inevitable result of perception and response. ཁམས་གསུམ་འཁོར་བ་སྡུག་བསྔལ་རྒྱ་མཚོའི་ངང༔ *kham sum 'khor-wa dug-ngal gya-mTso'i ngang* / The three realms of 'khorwa *(cyclic experience / samsara)* are an ocean of unsatisfactoriness. དྲན་ནས་བདག་བློ་ཆོས་ལ་འགྱུར་བར་ཤོག༔ *Dren-né dag-lo chö-la 'gyur-war shog* / Recognising this, my mind turns towards reality.

Lingtsang Gyalpo

Lingtsang Gyalpo Wangchen Ten'dzin Rinpoche *(gLing tshang rGyal po dBang chen bsTan 'dzin* / གླིང་ཚང་རྒྱལ་པོ་དབང་ཆེན་བསྟན་འཛིན་)— (1857–1942)—was the Lord of Lingtsang in Kham. He was a gTértön and Nyingma ngak'phang Lama.

He was also a profound phurba master, and a body incarnation of Ling Gésar – the great realised warrior and hero of Tibet. He revealed the long-life practice of Tsé-yum Tsendali *(Chandali – the female consort of 'od pags 'med – Amitayus – the Buddha of long life)*. He was famous for his kindness, gentleness, and for remarkable siddhis in the sphere of phurba. He had three sons and one daughter, Sémo Déchen Tso, who became the mother of Khandro Tséring Chödrön, one of the foremost ngakmas of modern times, and Ma-yum Tséring Wangmo. Lingtsang Gyalpo took parinirvana in Dzongri Lingtsang in 1942, and his Gyalpo title was passed to his son Phuntsok Gelek Rabten, who manifested thugdam on his death in Kalimpong. Phüntsog Gelek Rabten had five children, among whom two are still alive, a son, Sé Jig'mèd, living in Chengdu and a daughter Sémo Yeshé in Dehradun. Lingtsang Gyalpo was the uncle of 'a-Shül Pema Legden – the previous incarnation of gTértön Aro Yeshé.

lojong

The Slogans of Chekhawa Yeshé Dorje are a synthesis of *Lojong, (bLo sByong)* – a mind training practice based on the 11th century aphorisms of Atisha. The 59 slogans are antidotes to negative mental habits. Lojong was developed over a 300-year period between 900 and 1200. Atisha (982–1054), the Bengali teacher, is the originator of Lojong – which he based on his studies with the Sumatran teacher Dharmarakshita, author of the *Wheel of Sharp Weapons*. Atisha journeyed to Sumatra and studied with Dharmarakshita for 12 years. He then returned to teach in India, but at an advanced age accepted an invitation to teach in Tibet, where he stayed for the rest of his life. A story is told that Atisha heard that the inhabitants of Tibet were very pleasant and easy to get along with.

Instead of being delighted, he was concerned that he would not have enough negative emotion to work with in his mind training practice. So he brought along his irascible Bengali servant, who criticised him incessantly. Tibetan teachers make humorous comments that when Atisha arrived in Tibet, he realised there was no need after all – the Tibetans were ill-natured enough for anyone.

mahamudra

Tshan'mè chag-chen *(mTshan 'med phyag chen* / མཚན་མེད་ཕྱག་ཆེན་ / *formless mahamudra)*. Chag-chen is a contraction of chag-gya chen-po *(phyag rGya chen po* / ཕྱག་རྒྱ་ཆེན་པོ་) meaning great seal, symbol, or gesture. It is a multivalent term which refers to a state of beings as well as to a corpus of teachings which are the culmination of the gSar ma schools of Himalayan Buddhism. The Kagyüd lineage divides mahamudra into: Sutric mahamudra, Tantric mahamudra, and formless or essential mahamudra. Sutric mahamudra relies on Madhamaka; Tantric mahamudra relies on gTummo, rMi Lam, and 'ö-Sel, of the Six Yogas of Naropa; formless mahamudra relies upon the direct instruction of a Lama.

marriage of monks in Japan

Marriage of monks in Japan existed as early as the Heian period (794–1185). From the time of hijiri, or wandering mendicants such as Shinran (1173–1262) and Ippen (1239–1289), there are many examples of the marriage of monks – particularly during the Kamakura (1185–1333), Muromachi (1336–1570), and Edo periods (1600–1867). An edict issued in 1872 stated that monks should be free to eat meat, take wives, or not shave their heads as they chose. The issue of celibacy differs in each lineage of Japanese Buddhism.

When Hônen (1133–1212) was asked whether a religious person should be celibate or not, he answered "*If it is easier with a spouse, it is better to marry. What is important is only how one expresses one's faith in reciting the name of the Buddha.*"

Maugham, William Somerset

(1874–1965) was an English playwright and novelist. His father —Robert Ormond Maugham—was a lawyer attached to the British embassy in Paris. On the death of his parents he was sent to his uncle, Henry MacDonald Maugham, the Vicar of Whitstable, in Kent. Henry Maugham proved emotionally cold and harsh. Somerset Maugham attended The King's School, Canterbury, where he was teased for his poor English *(French having been his first language)* and his shortness of stature. These circumstances gave him the stammer which would remain throughout his life. Somerset Maugham's reaction to the unkindness with which he was treated was to develop a talent for brilliant sarcasm – an ability reflected in his literary characters. 1907 announced the success of his play *Lady Frederick* and by the following year, he had four plays being simultaneously performed in London.

mind training

see *lojong.*

Nebesky-Wojkowitz, René de

(1923–1959) – an Austrian ethnologist and Tibetologist. Born in Groß Hoschütz in Moravia he completed his secondary education in Leitmeritz and Prague, and devoted himself to the study of Central Asian ethnology and the Tibetan,and Mongolian languages at the universities of Berlin and Vienna. From 1949 to 1950 he studied in Italy under the direction of Giuseppe Tucci and Joseph Rock, as well as in London at the School of Oriental and African Studies.

From 1950 to 1953 he stayed researching in Kalimpong India. His long sojourn gave him access to many texts and allowed him to benefit from the Tibetan Lamas who sought refuge there.

ngakpa / ngakma

sNgags pa / mantrin (male) or *sNgags ma / mantrini* (female) – a non-celibate ordainee according to Vajrayana and the equivalent of monastic ordination in Sutrayana. They belong to the gö kar chang lo'i dé *(gos dKar lCang lo'i sDe)* the white skirted long-haired community or ngak'phang gyi gendün *(sNgags 'phang gyi dGe mDun)* the mantra-hurling community. Ngakpa *(sNgags pa)* robes are the clothing of the gö kar chang lo'i dé *(gos dKar lCang lo'i sDe)* the non-celibate wing of the Tibetan Buddhist Nyingma Tradition.

ngak'phang

see *ngakpa / ngakma.*

Noggin the Nog

– was a children's 'cult classic' television series (1959–1965), and illustrated books (1965–1977), by Oliver Postgate and Peter Firmin. Noggin is a simple, kind, unassuming King of the Nogs in the Viking era. Noggin—son of Knut and Grunhilda—has to find a queen when King Knut dies – or forfeit the crown to his uncle, Nogbad the Bad. Noggin marries Nooka the Inuit princess of the Nooks – and becomes the new king. Other characters include Thor Nogson, of the Royal Guard *(Noggin's closest friend)*, who presents himself as ferocious – but is really rather kind and gentle; Olaf the Lofty – an eccentric inventor; Nogbad the Bad, who never relinquishes his claim to the throne – but always fails through some mischance or his own ineptitude.

Nowrojee and Sons

The Nowrojee and Sons General Store—established by a Parsi business family in 1860—is one of the oldest shops in Himachal Pradesh. It has maintained its original wooden structure. Nauzer Nowrojee looked after the store-cum-residence set up by his great-grandfather for over 60 years. The shop once provided everyday goods for British officers and their families: bakery, toiletries, wine and spirits, arms and ammunition, Vinolia white rose soap, and Calvert's carbolic medical soap.

Ögyen Dro'dül Thrin-lé Künkyab

Kyabjé Trülku Ögyen Dro'dül Thrin-lé Künkyab—the 3rd incarnation of gTértön Drukdra Dorje—was born in 1999 in the paradisal black-necked crane region of the Phob-ji-kha valley in Wangdü Phodrang. His father is Wangchuk Rin'dzin Rinpoche and his mother, Jomo Sônam Yuden. He amazingly recognised himself as the incarnation of gTértön Drukdra Dorje – and was formally recognised and enthroned as the yangsrid at the age of four by the 70th Je Khenpo Jig'mèd Chödra. His birth was accompanied by prodigies. At the age of three, he repeatedly expressed the desire to visit Chhimphu Lhakhang in Paro. On visiting, he remembered a cave, went to see it, and revealed gTérma that he had placed there previously. He described the history of the Lhakhang and recognised the gTérma statue of Dorje Phagmo revealed by gTértön Drukdra Dorje. Everyone was astonished with his accurate description of many incidents from his previous life. He became a personal friend of Ngak'chang Rinpoche and Khandro Déchen in 2019 – and thus the premonition of the 16th Gyalwa Karmapa was fulfilled.

Padmakara

– *see* eight manifestations.

Padmasambhava

– *see* eight manifestations.

precepts

Labpa-nga *(bsLab pa lNga)* the five precepts. 1. Srog gÇod songwa *(srog gCod pa song ba)* not to murder. 2. Ma-jin par len pongwa *(ma byin par len sPong ba)* not to steal. 3. 'död-pé log-par gwempa pong wa *('dod pas log par gwem pa sPong ba)* not to be sexually promiscuous. 4. Dzun-du mra pongwa *(brDzun du dMra sPong ba)* not to be dishonest 5. Myö-par 'gyürwa'i dungwa pongwa *(myos par 'gyur ba'i bDung ba sPong ba)* not becoming intoxicated.

prophecy of gTértön Drukdra Dorje

He prophesied the unequalled advance of Bhutan under his reign. In this prophecy he wrote '*Dear son, listen once again, In the hidden valleys of the southern Bhutan where three valleys merge – there is a beautiful place called 'ö-ma'i trong. In that auspicious place, in the Female Wood Sheep Year, a male child of incomparable character will be born. He will ascend the Golden Throne at the age of twenty and convey Bhutan, unchallenged, to supreme success. Then the people will enjoy unrivalled harmony and prosperity.*' 'ö-ma'i trong *('o ma'i grong)* —Land of Milk—is the archaic name for Déchen Chöling. 'ö-ma'i trong is mostly phonetically spelt 'wongtrong'.

refuge verse

འདི་བཟུང་བྱང་ཆུབ་སྙིང་པོ་མ་ཐོབ་བར༔ *'di zung chang-chub nying-po ma-thob bar* / From now until I realisation, བླ་མ་དཀོན་མཆོག་གསུམ་ལ་སྐྱབས་སུ་མཆི༔ *Lama kön-chog sum-la kyab-su chi* / I establish confidence in actuality; Lama, Buddha, Dharma, and Sangha.

ད་ནས་བཟུང་སྟེ་འཁོར་བ་མ་སྟོང་བར༔ *da né zung té 'khorwa ma-tong bar* / From now until 'khorwa is emptied, མ་གྱུར་སེམས་ཅན་ཀུན་གྱི་ཕན་བདེ་བསྒྲུབ༔ *Ma 'gyür semçan kün gyi phen-dé dru* / I shall work for the benefit and wellbeing of my mothers, all sentient beings.

Rig'dzin Godemchen Ngödrub Gyaltsen

rig 'dzin rGod lDem chen dNgos grub rGyal mTshan) was born 1337 in Nyenyul (gNyan yul), to the east of Trazang mountain *(bKra bZang)*. His father was Lopön Düd'dül *(sLob dPon bDud 'dul)*, who belonged to the family of Namolung *(sNa mo lung)* whose ancestry went back to the Mongolian king named Gur-sér *(gur ser)*. His mother was named Jo-çam Sônam Khyé'drèn *(jo lCam bSod nams khye 'dren)*. Lopön Düd'dül was a ngakpa with expertise in the practice of Phurba. When Rig'dzin Godem was 11, three feathery growths appeared on the top of his head. Because these growths looked like the feathers of a vulture, he became famed throughout Tibet, as Godkyi Demtruchen *(rGod kyi lDem 'phru can)* – the one with vulture's feathers.

Sogyal Lakar

(1947–2019) also known as Sogyal Rinpoche. He was born in in Trehor, Kham. His mother and courtesan aunt claimed that Jamyang Khyentsé Chökyi Lodrö recognised him as the incarnation of gTértön Sogyal and supervised his education at Dzongsar. This claim has no other source. He claims to have studied Buddhism with several tutors – but actually attended a Catholic school in Kalimpong and later Delhi University. In 1971, he went to study comparative religion at Trinity College, Cambridge – but never completed his studies. He set himself up as a Lama in 1974 when establishing Ögyen Chöling for Düd'jom Rinpoche in a house in Kilburn, London.

Due to Sogyal Lakar's lack of knowledge and sexual philandering, Düd'jom Rinpoche instructed him to return East to study and complete retreats. Sogyal Lakar refused, broke his vows with Düd'jom Rinpoche, and appropriated Kyabjé Düd'jom Rinpoche's London and Paris centres – renaming them 'Rigpa' centres. Sogyal Lakar was exposed as a sexually abusive cult leader in 2017. The Dalai Lama—in a speech made in Ladakh in 2018—commented that Sogyal Lakar "… *now disgraced.*" Sogyal Lakar's overtures to visit Samŷe Ling were never accepted. His book *The Tibetan Book of Living and Dying* was never stocked in Samŷe Ling book shop – in deference to the view of the 16th Karmapa. I was not to meet Sogyal Laker until 1976. An account—restricted to my personal experience—is given in Volume III of *Goodbye Forever*.

seven Line Song

see Dorje Tsig Dün.

Shérab Palden Beru

(1911–2012) the artist and thangka painter at Samŷe Ling. He devoted himself to thangka painting and training Western students. His work can be seen in centres throughout the world – but his major works are at Samŷe Ling: *the Kagyüd Lineage holders; the Kagyu Lineage Refuge Tree; a depiction of the Lama'i Naljor of Mi-kyö Dorje, the 8th Karmapa; Padmasambhava; and, the Mahasiddhas and the Guardians of the Four Directions.* In his 90s, he no longer painted – but fulfilled a rôle as consultant and leading authority for thangka artists. He died on 29th November 2012 at Samŷe Ling. His body was left undisturbed in tugdam mediation *(thugs dam la bZhugs pa)* for three days after his death. See also: *chapter* 8.

Speaking with Ravens

See *an odd boy*—Volume IV—chapter 12—Bower Ashton –
Speaking With Ravens —Aro Books WORLDWIDE—2018.
The raven paintings—eventually called *Speaking with Ravens*—
are characterised by the gradual abrasion of partial layers of
over-painting *(in oil paint)* which occlude an Art School model
(whose image had been allowed to dry). The technique evolved from
an exploration that began at Farnham Art School. Sometimes
the overpainting was rubbed back with a cloth soaked in
turpentine – or scrubbed with a stiff bristled scrubbing brush.
The scrubbing brush would striate the paint and further over-
painting filled the striations. This would be left to dry and
subject to further abrasion. Layer-after-layer of oil paint
would be added and abraded – and the textures achieved by
this means became exceedingly intricate and convoluted. One
or more ravens would then be added from photographs taken
at Bristol Zoo. These ravens would then be subject to the
same over-painting and abrasion. Prints can be purchased
from Aro Books, Inc. in New York. Please see the Aro Books,
Inc. website (https://www.arobooks.org/) for details.

swastika

– *see* yungdrung.

térma (gTérma)

gter ma / གཏེར་མ་ / *revealed treasure* are hidden Vajrayana
teachings. These teachings were originally hidden by
Padmasambhava and Yeshé Tsogyel during the 8th century, for
discovery at auspicious times by Lamas known as gTértöns.
gTérma represent a tradition of continuous revelation in
Himalayan Buddhism.

gTérma may be a physical object such as texts or Vajrayana appurtenances buried in earth, rock, crystal, or trees; hidden in lakes or rivers; hidden in the sky; or concealed within the mind of a gTértön. If the teaching is a text, it is often written in khandro cypher – an encoded form of writing that only the gTértön can decipher.

Vajra Crown

dorje zha-nak *(rDo rJe zhwa nag)*. The Vajra Crown is an important symbol of the Karmapas – the heads of the Karma Kagyüd school of Tibetan Buddhism. In a former life as an accomplished yogi, the Karmapa attained realisation. At that time, 100,000 khandromas *(mKha' 'gro ma – dakinis)* manifested their hair as a crown, and gave it to him as the sign of his accomplishment. The 1st Karmapa—Dusum Khyenpa —was the incarnation of that yogi and his appearance was predicted by the historical Buddha Shakyamuni in the Samadhiraja Sutra: *'A yogi with the roar of a lion will appear and use his power to benefit countless beings.'* The Karmapas were the teachers of the Ming Emperors of China. When the 5th Karmapa—Dé-zhin Shegpa—met Emperor Yung Lo, the Emperor perceived the Karmapa to be wearing a black crown on his head. Emperor Yung Lo offered to have a physical replica made so that others could also see it and be inspired. A crown set with precious stones and surmounted by a large ruby was decreed by Emperor Yung Lo and the 5th Karmapa began the tradition of the Vajra Crown Ceremony which was performed by successive Karmapa incarnations up through the time of the 16th Karmapa, Rang-jung Rigpa'i Dorje.

Waugh, Arthur Evelyn St John

(1903–1966) was a novelist, biographer, journalist, and reviewer.

His best-known books include his early satires *Decline and Fall* (1928), and *A Handful of Dust* (1934), *Brideshead Revisited* (1945), and his WWII trilogy *Sword of Honour* (1952–61). He is recognised as one of the great 20th century prose stylists. He was educated at Lancing and Hertford College, Oxford, and worked briefly as a school teacher before becoming a writer. As a young man, he had fashionable and aristocratic friends, and developed a life-long taste for that society

Weekend

(1967) a black comedy film written and directed by Jean-Luc Godard. Roland and Corinne are a bourgeois couple – each having a secret lover and each conspiring to murder the other. They drive to Corinne's parents' country home to secure her inheritance from her dying father, resolving on murder if necessary. During their picaresque journey their car is wrecked – and they wander through vignettes involving figures from literature and history. Corinne and Roland arrive but her father is already dead. Her mother refuses to part with any money. They kill her and leave, only to be waylaid by hippies known as the 'Seine and Oise Liberation Front' who live by larceny and cannibalism. Killed during an attempt to escape, Roland is cooked and eaten.

Widecombe Fair

– is a Devonshire folk song collected by the Reverend Baring-Gould. Its chorus includes a long list of people: *Bill Brewer, Jan Stewer, Peter Gurney, et cetera…* ending with *Old Uncle Tom Cobley and all.* Whether Tom Cobley or the other characters ever existed is uncertain. Local historians have attempted to trace them around Dartmoor. The most cogent claim lies with the village of Spreyton, to the north of Dartmoor, as churchyard boasts the grave of a Tom Cobley whose demise is given as the 11th of January 1844.

This however is argued to be the grave of the nephew of the actual Tom Cobley, who died in 1794.

yungdrung

g.Yung drung. The swastika is a symbol of good luck and prosperity in Hinduism where it appears in marriage ceremonies. In Jainism, a swastika is the symbol for Suparshvanatha – the seventh of 24 Tirthankaras (spiritual teachers). In several major Indo-European religions, the swastika symbolises lightning bolts, representing Thor, Zeus, and Jupiter. The swastika is otherwise known as the fylfot, gammadion, tetraskelion, or cross cramponnée – a term in Anglo-Norman heraldry; French: croix gammée; Italian: croce uncinata. In Mongolian it is called Xac and mainly used in seals. In Chinese it is called wan-zì meaning 'all things symbol', and manji in Japanese and manja in Korean.